OXFORD RE

THE O

SPEL

DICTIONARY

THE OXFORD
SPELLING
DICTIONARY

Compiled by
R. E. ALLEN

Oxford New York
OXFORD UNIVERSITY PRESS

Oxford University Press, Walton Street, Oxford OX2 6DP

Oxford New York Toronto
Delhi Bombay Calcutta Madras Karachi
Petaling Jaya Singapore Hong Kong Tokyo
Nairobi Dar es Salaam Cape Town
Melbourne Auckland

and associated companies in
Berlin Ibadan

Oxford is a trade mark of Oxford University Press

First published 1986
First issued as an Oxford University Press paperback 1990
Reprinted 1991

British Library Cataloguing in Publication Data
[The Oxford minidictionary of spelling].
The Oxford spelling dictionary.
1. English language—Orthography and
spelling—Dictionaries
I. Allen, R. E. (Robert Edward)
428.1   PE1146
ISBN 0–19–282670–0

Library of Congress Cataloging in Publication Data
The Oxford spelling dictionary.
Paperback ed. published under title: Oxford
minidictionary of spelling.
1. Spellers. I. Allen, R. E.
PE1145.4.094 1986   423'.1   86–792
ISBN 0–19–282670–0

Printed in Great Britain by
Richard Clay Ltd.
Bungay, Suffolk

CONTENTS

PREFACE

THE *Oxford Spelling Dictionary* is intended primarily to be a
quick and easy source of information about the spelling and
inflexion of words. It concentrates on problems and omits the
straightforward: for example, there is no need to give the
spelling of *book* or the plural of *house* but there is widespread
doubt about such matters as the plural of *plus* (*pluses* or
plusses?) and of *quango* (*quangos* or *quangoes*?), about the past
of the verb *ski* (*skied* or *ski'd* or what?), and about the choice
between *dryer* and *drier* and scores of other alternative and
confusable words. The vocabulary treated is based on that of
the seventh edition of the *Concise Oxford Dictionary* with the
omission of archaic and literary words and other words limited
in currency. Words of one syllable have generally been omitted
unless they have a spelling difficulty (either in themselves or
in their inflexion). An important additional feature of the book
is its extensive coverage of compound items and proper names,
contributing to a vocabulary base that is richer than any other
book of the same size and scope.

Within this compass systematic advice is given on the
division of words when these, in print, fall at the end of a line.
Here the maximum amount of information is given on a word-
by-word basis and as little as possible is dependent on the
interpretation of rules, although a few very simple rules are
given in the introductory *Guide to the Use of the Dictionary* to
assist with routine forms and inflexions which (because they
are regular) are not listed in the main vocabulary.

The spellings and other recommendations are drawn from
the resources of the English Dictionaries Department of
Oxford University Press, and I am grateful for advice to
colleagues in this and other departments of the Press
(especially the Printing House). The work was done in
association with electronic databases being produced by Wang
Electronic Publishing, and I must thank in particular Mr
Andrew Rosenheim, its European Editorial Director, for
stimulating and rewarding co-operation. For work on word-
division I am indebted to the painstaking contribution of Mr

D. J. Edmonds, and to Mr H. E. Boyce who gave useful advice
in the early stages.

I must thank above all those who worked on the dictionary
with me: Della Thompson (who took on a large share of the
editorial responsibility especially at the proof stages), Andrew
Hodgson, and Alana Dickinson; also Mrs A. Whear, who
worked on keyboarding and on-screen revision of the
computerized text during the editorial stages; finally Mrs B.
Burge, Dr M. A. Cooper, Mrs D. S. Eagle, and Ms L. Jones who
contributed to the critical reading of the proofs.

R.E.A.

December 1984

GUIDE TO THE USE OF THE DICTIONARY

1. General

1.1 This dictionary is concerned with the spelling of words, and not with their sense and status (except where necessary to clarify a point of spelling), nor with their behaviour in context. Most of the entries consist simply of headwords (with inflexions if any: see 2 below), and the sense of a word is given only in order to identify the word, especially to distinguish words close in spelling or pronunciation (e.g. **complement** and **compliment**, and **stationary** and **stationery**). The symbol △ alerts the reader to the existence of confusable forms. Identifying comments are kept as short as possible since the intention is simply to ensure that the user knows which word is being referred to.

1.2 Formations in *-less*, *-ly*, and *-ness* and agent nouns in *-er* have generally been included only where there is modification of the stem or some other spelling difficulty. Similarly only a selection can be included of the many words in *in-*, *re-*, and *un-*, and readers should refer to the unprefixed forms in cases of difficulty.

1.3 In treating compounds special attention has been given to the area of confusion where hyphened words may become one-word forms (such as **racecourse** formerly spelt **race-course**) and less coverage has been given of longer hyphened compounds where the alternative is to spell as two spaced words (such as **laughing-gas**). Phrase-based compounds such as **like-minded** and **panic-stricken**, and straightforward combinations such as **lightning-conductor** and **orange-peel**, are generally not treated.

1.4 Spellings, where alternatives exist, are those recommended by the house style of Oxford University Press.

2. Inflexion

2.1 Irregular or difficult inflexion of words is given in brackets after the headword.

2.2 The comparative and superlative of adjectives and adverbs of one syllable formed by adding -er and -est to the stem are not normally given.

2.3 Forms in -able are given when there is a spelling difficulty as in **lovable** and **changeable**.

3. Word-division

3.1 This is given for all words and inflexions listed on the criteria given above. The main consideration in deciding word-division has been to facilitate recognition of the divided word and of its pronunciation without violating its overall structure and etymology. Pronunciation has not been regarded as an overriding factor, because the appearance of the printed word on the page also matters and many words when divided without adequate regard to their etymology look awkward or absurd, thereby drawing attention to the division when the aim is to make the division as natural and unobtrusive as possible.

3.2 Where there is a well-established tradition of dividing a certain word, this has been followed even when it is contrary to the other rules given here.

3.3 The preferred division (if any) of a word is marked by | ; less recommended division (mainly for work in narrower measures) is marked by ¦ . Wherever possible the preferred division should be followed. Words which carry no recommendation (especially words of four letters or less and words of one syllable) should not be divided, and those which carry only a secondary recommendation (especially words of six or five letters) should only be divided when division is unavoidable.

3.4 The recommended divisions are such that at least two letters are left at the end of the line and at least three letters are taken over to the next line. Certain suffixes (e.g. -able and -ory) are regarded as for the most part automatically detachable. In addition, exception may be made to the three-letter rule in narrow-measure work in the case of the following separable two-letter suffixes and word-endings:

-ad forming nouns as in **myriad** and **Olympiad**

-al forming nouns and adjectives as in **arrival** and **topical**

-an forming nouns and adjectives as in **Anglican** and **republican**

-en forming verbs as in **deepen** and **hearten** (except as at *-er* below)

-er forming agent nouns as in **farmer** and **pointer** (but not when the *e* affects the pronunciation of the preceding part, as in **charger** and **poker**)

-fy forming verbs as in **pacify** and **identify**

-ic forming nouns and adjectives as in **Arabic** and **poetic**

-or forming agent nouns as in **inventor** and **creditor**

3.5   In verbal inflexion where there is no modification of the stem the participial ending *-ing* may be taken over (as in **sending** and **carrying**).

3.6   The hyphen (-) is used in the word-list only to indicate a compound that is always hyphened, and not as an end-of-line mark.

3.7   In hyphened compounds and words with a hyphened prefix (such as **co-operate**) division should be at the hyphen. In narrow-measure work, the second element may be divided in accordance with the recommendation for it as a word as long as at least three letters are left at the end of the line.

3.8   Words of one syllable cannot be divided, nor can very short words such as **mica** and **very**.

3.9   Some words of more than one syllable cannot be divided because the resulting first half would be misleading (e.g. **beauty, sluicing**).

3.10   Letters pronounced as one syllable (e.g. the second half of **carriage**) cannot be divided.

3.11   Some short final syllables containing an indeterminate vowel-sound (especially in inflexion) cannot be taken over to stand on their own (e.g. *-ened* in **happened** and *-ored* in **doctored**).

ABBREVIATIONS AND SYMBOLS
USED IN THE DICTIONARY

STANDARD abbreviations (such as etc. and lb.) are not given. Some abbreviations appear in italics.

a.	adjective	derog.	derogatory
abbr.	abbreviation	dial.	dialect
acc.	according		
adv.	adverb	Eccl.	Ecclesiastical
Aeronaut.	Aeronautics	Ecol.	Ecology
Afr.	Africa(n)	Electr.	Electricity
allus.	allusively	Eng.	English
Amer.	American	esp.	especially
Anat.	Anatomy	Eur.	European
anc.	ancient	exc.	except
Angl.	Anglicized		
Ant.	Antiquity	f.	from
Archaeol.	Archaeology	fem.	feminine
Archit.	Architecture	Fr.	French
assoc.	association		
attrib.	attributive,	gen.	general
	used attributively	Geog.	Geography
Aus.	Austrian	Geol.	Geology
Austral.	Australian	Geom.	Geometry
		Ger.	German
		govt.	government
Bibl.	Biblical	Gr.	Greek
Biol.	Biology	Gram.	Grammar
Bot.	Botany		
Brit.	British	Heb.	Hebrew
		Her.	Heraldry
Chem.	Chemistry	hist.	historical
Chin.	Chinese		
collect.	collective	incl.	including
colloq.	colloquial	Ind.	Indian
Comm.	Communist	inhab.	inhabitant
Comp.	Computer(s)	int.	interjection
compar.	comparative	Ir.	Irish
conj.	conjunction	It.	Italian
		Jap.	Japanese
dept.	department	joc.	jocular

lang.	language	prep.	preposition
		pres.	present (tense)
masc.	masculine	pron.	pronounced
Math.	Mathematics	propr.	proprietary term (see below)
Mech.	Mechanics		
Med.	Medicine		
Meteorol.	Meteorology	RC	Roman Catholic
Mil.	Military	relig.	religious
mod.	modern	Relig.	Religion
mon.	monetary	Russ.	Russian
Mt(s).	Mountain(s)		
Mus.	Music	Sc.	Scottish
myth.	mythical	Scand.	Scandinavian
Myth.	Mythology	Sci.	Scientific, in science
		sing.	singular
n.	noun	sl.	slang
Naut.	Nautical	Sp.	Spanish
Norw.	Norwegian	superl.	superlative
NT	New Testament	syll.	syllable(s)
NZ	New Zealand	symb.	symbol
orig.	originally	techn.	in technical use
OT	Old Testament	Theol.	Theology
		Turk.	Turkish
Parl.	Parliament		
Path.	Pathology	US	American, in American use
Philos.	Philosophy		
Phonet.	Phonetics	usu.	usually
phr.	phrase		
pl.	plural	v.	verb
Polit.	Politics	var.	variant(s)
pop.	popular(ly)		
Port.	Portuguese	Zool.	Zoology
p.p.	past participle		
predic.	predicative, used predicatively	⚠	do not confuse (see 1.1)

PROPRIETARY STATUS

A

Aachen
aard|vark
aard|wolf (*pl.*
  aard|wolves)
Aar|gau
Aar|on
abac
ab|aca
aback
aba|cus (*pl.*
  aba|cuses)
Ab|ad|don
ab|aft
aban|don
aban|doned
aban|donee
aban|don|ment
abase (abas|ing)
abase|ment
abash
abask
abate (abat|ing)
abate|ment
ab|at|toir
ab|bacy (*pl.*
  ab|ba|cies)
Ab|basid
ab|ba|tial
abbé
Abbe
ab|bess
Abbe|vil|lian
ab|bey
ab|bot
ab|bre|vi|ate
  (ab|bre|vi|at|ing)
ab|bre|vi|ation
ab|bre|vi|at|ory
ab|dic|ate
  (ab|dic|at|ing)
ab|dica|tion
ab|do|men
ab|dom|inal
ab|dom|in|ally
ab|duct
ab|duc|tion
ab|ductor
abeam

abe|ce|dar|ian
à Becket
abed
abele
Ab|er|deen
Ab|er|do|nian
ab|er|rance
ab|er|rancy
ab|er|rant
ab|er|ra|tion
Ab|er|yst|wyth
abet (abet|ted,
  abet|ting)
abet|ment
abet|ter (*Law*
  abet|tor)
abey|ance
abey|ant
ab|hor
  (ab|horred,
  ab|hor|ring)
ab|hor|rence
ab|hor|rent
abid|ance
abide (abode *or*
  abided, abid|ing)
Abi|djan
abi|gail
abil|ity (*pl.*
  abil|it|ies)
ab ini|tio
abio|gen|esis
abio|genic
abio|gen|ically
abi|otic
ab|ject
ab|jec|tion
ab|jura|tion
ab|jure
  (ab|jur|ing)
ab|late
  (ab|lat|ing)
ab|la|tion
ab|lat|ive
ab|laut
ablaze
able (abler,
  ablest)

able-bodied
abloom
ablush
ab|lu|tion
ab|lu|tion|ary
ably
ab|neg|ate
  (ab|neg|at|ing)
ab|nega|tion
ab|neg|ator
ab|nor|mal
ab|nor|mal|ity (*pl.*
  ab|nor|mal|it|ies)
ab|nor|mally
ab|norm|ity (*pl.*
  ab|norm|it|ies)
aboard
abode
ab|ol|ish
ab|ol|ish|ment
ab|oli|tion
ab|oli|tion|ism
ab|oli|tion|ist
ab|om|asum (*pl.*
  ab|om|asa)
A-bomb
ab|om|in|able
ab|om|in|ably
ab|om|in|ate
  (ab|om|in|at|ing)
ab|om|ina|tion
ab|ori|ginal
  (Ab|ori|ginal
  with ref. to
  Australia)
ab|ori|gin|al|ity
ab|ori|gin|ally
ab|ori|gines *pl.*
  (Ab|ori|gines
  with ref. to
  Australia; for
  sing. use
  aboriginal)
abort
abor|ti|fa|cient
abor|tion
abor|tion|ist
abort|ive

abou|lia (loss of
  will-power)
aboulic
abound
about
about-face *v.*
about-turn *v.*
above
above-board
ab|ra|ca|dabra
ab|rade
  (ab|rad|ing)
Ab|ra|ham
ab|ra|sion
ab|ras|ive
ab|re|act
ab|re|ac|tion
ab|re|act|ive
abreast
abridge
  (abridging)
abridge|ment
abroach
abroad
ab|rog|ate
  (ab|rog|at|ing)
ab|roga|tion
ab|rupt
ab|rup|tion
Abruzzi
abs|cess
ab|scissa (*pl.*
  ab|scis|sas *or*
  ab|scis|sae)
ab|scis|sion
ab|scond
ab|sconder
ab|seil
ab|sence
ab|sent
ab|sentee
ab|sent|ee|ism
absent-minded
ab|sinth (plant)
ab|sinthe (liqueur)
ab|sit omen
ab|so|lute
ab|so|lutely

ab'so'lu|tion
ab'so|lut|ism
ab'so|lut|ist
ab|solve
 (ab|solv|ing)
ab|sorb
ab|sorb|ency
ab|sorb|ent
ab|sorb|ing
ab|sorp'tion
ab|sorpt|ive
ab|stain
ab|ste'mi|ous
ab|sten|tion
ab|ster|gent
ab|ster|sion
ab|sters|ive
ab|stin|ence
ab|stin|ency
ab|stin|ent
ab|stract
ab|strac'ted
ab|strac'tion
ab|strac'tion|ism
ab|strac'tion|ist
ab|stractor
ab|struse
ab'surd
ab'surd|ity (pl.
 ab'surd|it|ies)
Abu Dhabi
abund|ance
abund|ant
ab'use (as v.,
 ab'us|ing)
Abu Sim|bel
ab'us|ive
abut (abut'ted,
 abut'ting)
abut|ment
abysm
abys|mal
abys|mally
abyss
abyssal
aca'cia
aca|deme
aca|demic
aca|dem'ical
aca'dem'ic|ally
aca|demi|cian
aca|demi|cism
acad'em|ism

acad|emy (place of
 study, pl.
 acad|em|ies;
 Acad|emy with
 ref. to institution
 or to Plato)
Aca|dian (of Nova
 Scotia)
acan|thus
a cap|pella
ac'arid
acarp|ous
acata|lectic
Accadian use
 Akkadian
ac|cede
 (ac|ced'ing)
ac'cel'er|ando (pl.
 ac'cel'er|an'dos)
ac'cel'er|ate
 (ac'cel'er|at'ing)
ac'cel'era'tion
ac'cel'er|at|ive
ac'cel'er|ator
ac'cel'er|ometer
ac'cent
ac|centor (bird)
ac|cen'tual
ac'cen'tu|ate
 (ac'cen'tu|at'ing)
ac'cen'tu|ation
ac'cept
ac'cept|ab'il|ity
ac'cept|able
ac'cept|ably
ac'cept|ance
ac'cept|ant
ac'cepta|tion
ac'cepter (Law
 and Sci.
 ac|ceptor)
ac|cess
accessary use
 accessory
ac'cess|ib'il|ity
ac'cess|ible
ac'cess|ibly
ac'ces|sion
ac'cess|ory (pl.
 ac'cess|or'ies)
acciac'ca|tura
ac'ci|dence
ac'ci|dent
ac'ci|dental
ac'ci|dent|ally
ac'ci|die

ac|claim
ac|clama|tion
ac'clim'ata|tion
ac|clim|ate
 (ac'clim|at|ing)
ac'cli|ma'tion
ac'cli'mat|iza'tion
ac'cli'mat|ize
 (ac'cli'mat|iz|ing)
ac'cliv'it|ous
ac'cliv|ity (pl.
 ac'cliv|it|ies)
ac|col|ade
ac'com'mod|ate
 (ac'com'mod|
   at|ing)
ac'com|moda|tion
ac'com'pani|ment
ac'com'pan|ist
ac'com'pany
 (ac'com'pan|ies,
  ac'com'pan|ied,
  ac'com'pany|ing)
ac|com|plice
ac'com|plish
ac'com'plished
ac'com'plish|
          ment
ac'cord
ac'cord|ance
ac'cord|ant
ac'cord|ing
ac'cord|ingly
ac'cor|dion
ac'cor|di'on|ist
ac|cost
ac'couche|ment
ac'couch|eur
ac|count
ac'count|ab'il|ity
ac'count|able
ac'count|ably
ac'count|ancy
ac'count|ant
ac'count|ing
ac|coutred
ac'cou'tre|ment
Ac'cra
ac|credit
 (ac|cred'ited,
  ac|cred'it|ing)
ac'cred|ita'tion
ac|crete
 (ac|cret'ing)
ac|cre'tion
ac|crual

ac'crue
 (ac|cru|ing)
ac'cul'tur|ate
 (ac'cul'tur|at|
          ing)
ac'cul|tura|tion
ac'cul'tur'at|ive
ac'cu'mu|late
 (ac'cu'mu|
        lat|ing)
ac'cu'mu|la'tion
ac'cu'mu|lat|ive
ac'cu'mu|lator
ac'cur|acy
ac'cur|ate
ac'cur|ately
ac'cur'sed
ac|cusal
ac|cusa'tion
ac'cus'at|ival
ac'cus'at|ive
ac'cus'at|orial
ac'cus'at|ory
ac|cuse
 (ac|cus|ing)
ac|cuser
ac|cus|ingly
ac|cus|tom
ac|cus|tomed
Acel|dama (scene
 of slaughter)
aceph'al|ous
acerb
acerbic
acerb|ity
aces|cence
aces|cent
acet'al'de|hyde
acet|ate
acetic̦
acet|one
acet|ous
acetyl
acet'yl|chol|ine
acet'yl|ene
Achaean
Achae|menid
ache (ach|ing)
ach'ene
Acheu|lian
achiev|able
achieve
 (achiev|ing)
achieve|ment
achiever
Achil'les

Achil'les' heel
achrom|atic
achrom|at'ic|ally
achrom|ati|city
achro'mat|ism
achy
acid
acidic
acidi|fica|tion
acid|ify
 (acidi|fies,
 acidi|fied,
 acidi|fy'ing)
aci'di|meter
aci'di|metry
acid|ity
acid|osis (pl.
 acid|oses)
acid|ulate
 (acidu|lat'ing)
acid|ulous
acinus (pl. acini)
ack-ack
ackee
ack emma
ac'know|ledge
 (ac'know|
        ledging)
ac'know'ledge|
        ment
ac'linic
acme
acne
aco|lyte
Ac'on|cagua
acon|ite
acon|itic
acon'it|ine
acorn
aco'ty|ledon
aco'ty|led'on|ous
acous|tic
acous'tical
acous'tic|ally
acous'ti|cian
acous|tics
ac|quaint
ac|quaint|ance
ac|quain'ted
ac|quaint'ance|
        ship
ac|quest (Law)
ac'qui|esce
 (ac'qui|es|cing)
ac'qui|es|cence
ac'qui|es|cent

ac|quire
 (ac|quir'ing)
ac|quire|ment
ac|quisi|tion
ac|quis'it|ive
ac|quit
 (ac|quit'ted,
 ac'quit'ting)
ac'quit|tal (freeing
 from charge)
ac'quit|tance
 (payment of debt)
acre
acre|age
acred
ac'rid (acrider,
 ac'rid|est)
ac'rid|ine
ac'rid|ity
ac'ri|flav|ine
ac|ri|mo'ni|ous
ac'ri|mony
ac'ro|bat
ac'ro|batic
ac'ro|bat'ic|ally
ac'ro|bat|ics
ac'ro|gen
ac'ro|gen|ous
ac'ro|meg|aly
ac'ro|nycal
ac'ro|nyc'ally
ac'ro|nym
ac'ro|petal
ac'ro|pet'ally
ac'ro|pho'bia
ac'ro|polis
Ac'ro|polis (in
 Athens)
across
ac'ros|tic
ac'rylic
act'ing
ac|tinia (pl.
 ac|tiniae)
ac|tinic
ac'tin|ide
ac'tin|ism
ac'ti|nium
ac'tino|meter
ac'tino|morphic
ac'tino|my'cetes
ac|tion
ac'tion|able
ac'tion|ably
ac'tiv|ate
 (ac'tiv|at'ing)

ac'tiva|tion
ac'tiv|ator
act|ive
act|ively
act|iv|ism
act|iv|ist
ac'tiv|ity (pl.
 ac'tiv|it'ies)
ac'ton
actor
act|ress
Acts (of the
 Apostles)
ac|tual
ac'tu|al'ity (pl.
 ac'tu|al'it|ies)
ac'tu|ally
ac'tu|ar'ial
ac'tu|ary (pl.
 ac'tu|ar'ies)
ac'tu|ate
 (ac'tu|at'ing)
ac'tu|ation
ac'tu|ator
acu'ity
acu|leate
acu'men
acu'min|ate
acu|punc'ture
acushla
acute (acuter,
 acut|est)
acutely
acyl
ad (colloq., =
 advertisement)
adage
ada'gio (pl.
 ada'gios)
Adam
ad'am|ant
ad'am|ant|ine
Ad'am|ite
Adam's apple
ad'apt
ad'apt|ab'il|ity
ad'apt|able
ad'apt|ably
ad'apta|tion
ad'apter (person)
ad'apt|ive
ad'aptor (device)
ad'dax (antelope)
ad'ded
ad'den|dum (pl.
 ad|denda)

ad'der
ad'der's tongue
 (fern)
ad'dict
ad'dic'tion
ad'dict|ive
add|ing
Ad'dis Ababa
Ad'di|son
ad'di|tion
ad'di|tional
ad'di|tion|ally
ad'dit|ive
addle (ad'dling)
ad|dress
ad|dressed
ad|dressee
Ad'dresso|graph
 (propr.)
ad|duce
 (ad|duc|ing)
ad|duc|ible
ad|duct
ad|duc'tion
Adel|aide
Aden
Ad'en|auer
ad'en|ine
ad'en|oidal
ad'en|oids
ad'en|oma
ad'en|os|ine
adept
ad'equacy
ad|equate
à deux
ad'here
 (ad|her'ing)
ad'her|ence
ad'her|ent
ad|he'sion
ad|hes|ive
ad|hibit
ad'hibi|tion
ad hoc
ad hom|inem
adia|batic
adia|bat'ic|ally
adi|antum
adieu (pl. adieus)
ad in'fin|itum
adi'po|cere
ad'ip|ose
ad'ip'os|ity
adit
ad|ja'cency

ad|ja|cent
ad|ject|ival
ad|ject|iv|ally
ad|ject|ive
ad|join
ad|journ
ad|journ|ment
ad|judge
 (ad|judging)
ad|judge|ment
ad|ju|dic|ate
 (ad|ju|dic|at|ing)
ad|ju|dica|tion
ad|ju|dic|at|ive
ad|ju|dic|ator
ad|junct
ad|junct|ive
ad|jura|tion
ad|jure
 (ad|jur|ing)
ad|just
ad|just|able
ad|just|ment
ad|jut|age
ad|jut|ancy
ad|jut|ant
Adjutant-General
ad|juv|ant
Ad|ler
ad lib (as *v.*, ad
 libbed, ad
 lib|bing)
ad|man (*pl.*
 ad|men)
ad|meas|ure
 (ad|meas|ur|ing)
ad|meas|ure|ment
ad|min
ad|min|icle
ad|min|icu|lar
ad|min|is|ter
ad|min|is|trable
ad|min|is|trate
 (ad|min|is|
          trat|ing)
ad|min|is|tra|tion
ad|min|is|trat|ive
ad|min|is|trator
ad|min|is|trat|rix
ad|mir|able
ad|mir|ably
ad|miral
ad|mir|alty (*pl.*
 ad|mir|al|ties)
ad|mira|tion

ad|mire
 (ad|mir|ing)
ad|mirer
ad|miss|ib|il|ity
ad|miss|ible
ad|mis|sion
ad|miss|ive
ad|mit
 (ad|mit|ted,
 ad|mit|ting)
ad|mit|table
ad|mit|tance
ad|mit|tedly
ad|mix
ad|mix|ture
ad|mon|ish
ad|mon|ish|ment
ad|moni|tion
ad|mon|it|ory
ad nau|seam
ad|nom|inal
ado
adobe
ado|les|cence
ado|les|cent
Adonis
ad|opt
ad|op|tion
ad|opt|ive
ad|or|able
ad|or|ably
ad|ora|tion
ad|ore (ad|or|ing)
ad|orer
ad|orn
ad|orn|ment
ad|renal
ad|ren|alin
Adrian
adrift
adroit
ad|sorb
ad|sorb|ate
ad|sorb|ent
ad|sorp|tion
adu|late
 (adu|lat|ing)
ad|ula|tion
adu|lator
adu|lat|ory
Adul|lam|ite
ad|ult
adul|ter|ant
adul|ter|ate
 (adul|ter|at|ing)
adul|tera|tion

adul|ter|ator
adul|terer
adul|teress
adul|ter|ine
adul|ter|ous
adul|tery
adult|hood
ad|um|brate
 (ad|um|brat|ing)
ad|um|bra|tion
ad|um|brat|ive
ad|vance (as *v.*,
 ad|van|cing)
ad|vance|ment
ad|vant|age (as *v.*,
 ad|vant|aging)
ad|vant|age|ous
ad|vec|tion
ad|vect|ive
ad|vent
Ad|vent (of Christ;
 season)
Ad|vent|ism
Ad|vent|ist
ad|ven|ti|tious
ad|ven|ture (as *v.*,
 ad|ven|tur|ing)
ad|ven|turer
ad|ven|ture|some
ad|ven|turess
ad|ven|tur|ous
ad|verb
ad|ver|bial
ad|ver|bi|ally
ad|vers|ary (*pl.*
 ad|vers|ar|ies)
ad|vers|at|ive
ad|verse
ad|vers|ity (*pl.*
 ad|vers|it|ies)
ad|vert
ad|vert|ise
 (ad|vert|ising)
ad|vert|ise|ment
ad|vert|iser
ad|vice
ad|vis|ab|il|ity
ad|vis|able
ad|vis|ably
ad|vise
 (ad|vis|ing)
ad|visedly
ad|viser
ad|vis|ory
ad|vo|caat
ad|vo|cacy

ad|voc|ate (as *v.*,
 ad|voc|at|ing)
ad|voc|at|ory
adytum (*pl.*
 adyta)
adze
ae|dile
Ae|gean (Sea)
ae|gis
ae|gro|tat
Ae|neid
Ae|olic
ae|olo|tropy
aeon
ae|py|or|nis
aer|ate
 (aer|at|ing)
aera|tion
aer|ator
aer|ial
aeri|al|ity
aeri|ally
aerie *use* eyrie
aeri|form
aero|batics
aer|obe
aer|obic
aero|bio|lo|gist
aero|bio|logy
aero|drome
aero|dy|namic
aero|dy|nam|ics
aero|dy|nam|ic|
               ally
aero|foil
aero|lite
aero|lo|gist
aero|logy
aero|nautic
aero|naut|ical
aero|naut|ics
aero|nomy
aero|plane
aero|sol
aero|space
aer|ugin|ous
Aes|chy|lus
Aes|cu|la|pian
Ae|sop
aes|thete
aes|thetic
aes|thet|ic|ally
aes|theti|cism
aes|thet|ics
aes|tival

aes¦tiv¦ate
 (aes¦tiv¦at¦ing)
aes¦tiva¦tion
aether *use* ether
ae¦ti¦olo¦gical
aeti¦olo¦gic¦ally
ae¦ti¦ology
afar
af¦fa¦bil¦ity
af¦fable
af¦fably
af¦fair
affairé (busy)
af¦fect
af¦fecta¦tion
af¦fec¦ted
af¦fec¦tion
af¦fec¦tion¦ate
af¦fect¦ive
af¦fect¦iv¦ity
af¦fen¦pin¦scher
af¦fer¦ent
af¦fi¦ance
 (af¦fi¦an¦cing)
af¦fi¦da¦vit
af¦fili¦ate
 (af¦fili¦at¦ing)
af¦fili¦ation
af¦fined
af¦fin¦ity (*pl.*
 af¦fin¦it¦ies)
af¦firm
af¦firm¦able
af¦firma¦tion
af¦firm¦at¦ive
af¦firm¦at¦ory
af¦fix
af¦fix¦ture
af¦flatus
af¦flict
af¦flic¦tion
af¦flict¦ive
af¦flu¦ence
af¦flu¦ent
af¦flux
af¦force
 (af¦for¦cing)
af¦ford
af¦for¦est
af¦for¦esta¦tion
af¦franch¦ise
 (af¦franch¦ising)
af¦fray
af¦freight¦ment
af¦fric¦ate
af¦fright

af¦front
af¦fu¦sion
af¦ghan (blanket
 or shawl)
Af¦ghan (hound)
Af¦ghan¦is¦tan
afi¦cion¦ado (*pl.*
 afi¦cion¦ados)
afield
afire
aflame
af¦la¦toxin
afloat
afoot
afore
afore¦men¦tioned
afore¦said
afore¦thought
a for¦ti¦ori
afraid
afresh
Af¦rica
Af¦rican
Af¦ric¦an¦ism
Af¦ric¦an¦ist
Af¦ric¦an¦ize
 (Af¦ric¦an¦iz¦ing)
Af¦ri¦kaans
af¦rik¦ander
Af¦ri¦kaner
Afro
Afro-American
Afro-Asian
Afro-Indian
afr¦or¦mo¦sia
after
after¦birth
after-care
after-effect
af¦ter¦glow
af¦ter¦grass
af¦ter¦life
af¦ter¦light
af¦ter¦math
af¦ter¦most
af¦ter¦noon
af¦ter¦pains
af¦ters
af¦ter¦shave
after-taste
af¦ter¦thought
af¦ter¦wards
af¦ter¦word
aga (*pl.* agas)
again
against

Aga Khan
agama
agamic
agamo¦gen¦esis
agamo¦gen¦etic
agam¦ous
ag¦ap¦anthus
agape (love-feast;
 3 sylls.)
agape (gaping)
agar
ag¦aric
ag¦ate
agave
agaze
age (as *v.*, age¦ing)
aged (old; 2 sylls.)
age¦less
agency (*pl.*
 agen¦cies)
agenda (list of
 items, *pl.*
 agen¦das)
agent
agen¦tial
*agent
 pro¦vo¦ca¦teur*
ag¦giorna¦mento
ag¦glom¦er¦ate
 (ag¦glom¦er¦at¦
    ing)
ag¦glom¦era¦tion
ag¦glom¦er¦at¦ive
ag¦glu¦tin¦ate
 (ag¦glu¦tin¦at¦ing)
ag¦glu¦tina¦tion
ag¦glu¦tin¦at¦ive
ag¦glu¦tinin
ag¦grand¦ize
 (ag¦grand¦iz¦ing)
ag¦grand¦ize¦
    ment
ag¦grav¦ate
 (ag¦grav¦at¦ing)
ag¦grava¦tion
ag¦greg¦ate (as *v.*,
 ag¦greg¦at¦ing)
ag¦grega¦tion
ag¦greg¦at¦ive
ag¦gres¦sion
ag¦gress¦ive
ag¦gressor
ag¦grieve
 (ag¦griev¦ing)
ag¦gro
aghast

agile
agil¦ity
agin
agio (*pl.* agios)
agio¦tage
agist
agist¦ment
agit¦ate
 (agit¦at¦ing)
agita¦tion
agit¦ator
agit¦prop
ag¦let
agley
aglow
ag¦nail
ag¦nate
ag¦natic
ag¦na¦tion
ag¦no¦men
ag¦nostic
ag¦nos¦ti¦cism
Agnus Dei
ago
agog
ag¦onic
ag¦on¦istic
ag¦on¦ist¦ic¦ally
ag¦on¦ize
 (ag¦on¦iz¦ing)
ag¦ony (*pl.*
 ag¦on¦ies)
ago¦ra¦phobia
ago¦ra¦phobic
agouti (*pl.*
 agou¦tis)
agrapha
ag¦rar¦ian
agree (agreed,
 agree¦ing)
agree¦able
agree¦ably
agree¦ment
ag¦ri¦busi¦ness
ag¦ri¦cul¦tural
ag¦ri¦cul¦ture
ag¦ri¦cul¦tur¦ist
ag¦ri¦mony (*pl.*
 ag¦ri¦mon¦ies)
ag¦ro¦nomic
ag¦ro¦nom¦ical
ag¦ro¦nom¦ics
ag¦ro¦nom¦ist
ag¦ro¦no¦my
aground
ague

ahead
ahimsa (*pl.*
  ahim|sas)
ahis|toric
ahis|tor|ical
ahoy
ahull
Aida
aide
aide-de-camp (*pl.*
  aides-de-camp)
aide-mémoire (*pl.*
  aide-mémoires)
ai|kido
ail|eron
ail|ing
ail|ment
aim|less
air|borne
air-brick
air|brush
air|bus
air-conditioned
air-conditioner
air-conditioning
air-cooled
air|craft
aircraft-carrier
air|craft|man (*pl.*
  air|craft|men)
air|craft|wo|man
  (*pl.* air|craft|
          wo|men)
air|crew
air-cushion
Aire|dale
air|field
air|frame
air|glow
air|gun
air host|ess
air|ily
airi|ness
air-jacket
air|lift
air|line (of
  aircraft)
air line (pipe)
air|lock
air|mail
air|man (*pl.*
  air|men)
air|miss
air|port
air|screw
air|ship

air|sick
air|space
air|strip
air|tight
air|way
air|wo|man (*pl.*
  air|wo|men)
air|wor|thy
airy (air|ier,
  airi|est)
airy-fairy
aisle
aisled
ait (small isle in
  river)
aitch|bone
ajar
akimbo
akin
Ak|ka|dian
Ala|bama
ala|bas|ter
ala|bas|trine
à la carte
alac|rity
Alad|din
à la mode
Alan
alar
alarm
alarm clock
alarm|ism
alarm|ist
alar|ums (and
  excursions)
alas
Alaska (US State;
  baked confection)
al|ate
al|ba|core
Al|ba|nia
Al|ba|nian
al|bata
al|ba|tross
al|bedo (*pl.*
  al|bedos)
al|beit
Al|bert
Al|berta
al|bes|cent
Al|bi|gen|ses
Al|bi|gen|sian
al|bin|ism
al|bino (*pl.*
  al|bi|nos)
al|bin|otic

Al|bion
alb|ite
al|bum
al|bu|men (white
  of egg)
al|bu|min
  (protein)
al|bu|min|oid
al|bu|min|ous
al|bu|min|uria
Al|bu|quer|que
al|bur|num
al|caic
al|calde (Sp. etc.
  mayor)
al|chemic
al|chem|ical
al|chem|ist
al|chemy
al|cher|inga
Al|ci|bi|ades
al|co|hol
al|co|holic
al|co|hol|ism
al|cove
al|de|hyde
al|de|hydic
al|der
al|der|man (*pl.*
  al|der|men)
al|der|manic
Al|der|ney
Al|dis lamp
ald|rin
aleat|ory
alee
ale|gar
ale|house
al|em|bic
aleph
alert
aleuron
aleur|one
Al|ex|an|der
al|ex|an|ders
  (plant)
Al|ex|an|dra
Al|ex|an|dria
Al|ex|an|drian
al|ex|an|drine
  (verse)
al|ex|an|drite
al|exin
alex|ine
al|exi|pharmic
alfa

al|falfa
al|fresco
alga (usu. in *pl.*
  al|gae)
algal
al|ge|bra
al|geb|raic
al|geb|ra|ical
al|geb|ra|ic|ally
al|ge|bra|ist
Al|geria
al|gi|cide
algid
alg|id|ity
Al|giers
al|gin|ate
al|ginic
alg|oid
Al|gol (Comp.
  language)
al|go|lo|gical
al|go|lo|gist
al|go|logy
Al|gon|quian
al|go|rithm
al|go|rithmic
al|gua|zil
Al|ham|bra
Al|ham|bresque
alias
Ali Baba
alibi
ali|cyc|lic
al|id|ade
alien
alien|ab|il|ity
alien|able
alien|age
alien|ate
  (ali|en|at|ing)
ali|ena|tion
ali|form
Ali|ghieri (family
  name of Dante)
alight
align
align|ment
alike
ali|mental
ali|ment|ary
ali|menta|tion
ali|mony
A-line (skirt)
ali|phatic
ali|quot
Al|ison

alive
al¦iz¦arin
al¦ka¦hest
al¦kali (pl.
 al'ka¦lis)
al¦kal¦ify
 (al'kali¦fies,
 al'kali¦fied,
 al'kali¦fy'ing)
al'ka¦li¦meter
al'ka¦li¦metry
al'kal¦ine
al'ka¦lin¦ity
al'kal¦oid
al'kal¦osis (pl.
 al'kal¦oses)
al'kane
al'ka¦net
al'kene
al'kyd
al'kyl
alla breve
Al'lah
al'lan¦tois (pl.
 al'lan'to¦ides)
al'lay
all-clear
al'lega¦tion
al'lege (al¦leging)
al¦legedly
al'le¦gi¦ance
al'leg¦oric
al'leg¦or¦ical
al'leg¦or¦ic¦ally
al'leg¦or¦ist
al'leg¦or¦ize
 (al'leg¦or¦iz¦ing)
al'leg¦ory (pl.
 al'leg¦or¦ies)
al'leg¦retto (pl.
 al'leg¦ret'tos)
al'legro (pl.
 al'leg'ros)
al'lele
al'lelo¦morph
al'le¦luia
al'le¦mande
al'ler¦gen
al'ler¦genic
al'ler¦gic
al'lergy (pl.
 al'ler¦gies)
al'le¦vi¦ate
 (al'le¦vi¦at¦ing)
al'le¦vi¦ation
al'le¦vi¦at¦ive

al'le¦vi¦at'ory
al'ley
Al'leyn¦ian
alley-way
al'li¦aceous
al'li¦ance
al'li¦ga¦tor
al'lit¦er¦ate
 (al'lit¦er¦at¦ing)
al'lit¦era¦tion
al'lit¦er¦at¦ive
al'lium
Al'loa
al'loc¦able
al'loc¦ate
 (al'loc¦at¦ing)
al'loca¦tion
al'locu¦tion
al'lo¦dial
al'lo¦dium
al'lo¦gamy
al'lo¦morph
al'lo¦morphic
al'lo¦path
al'lo¦pathic
al'lo¦path¦ist
al'lo¦pathy
al'lo¦phone
al'lo¦phonic
al'lot (al¦lot¦ted,
 al'lot¦ting)
al'lot¦ment
al'lo¦trope
al'lo¦tropic
al'lo¦trop¦ical
al'lo¦tropy
al'lot¦tee
al'low
al'low¦ance
al'loy
all right
all-rounder
all¦seed
all¦spice
al'lude
 (al'lud¦ing)
al'lure (al¦lur¦ing)
al'lure¦ment
al'lu¦sion
al'lus¦ive
al'lu¦vial
al'lu¦vion
al'lu¦vium (pl.
 al'lu¦via)

ally (as v., al'lies,
 al'lied, al'ly¦ing;
 as n., pl. al'lies)
al'lyl
Alma Ma¦ter
al¦manac (but
 Oxford and
 Whitaker's
 Almanack)
al'mand¦ine
al'mighty
Al¦mighty (with
 ref. to God)
al'mirah
al'mond
al'moner
al'monry
al'most
alms
alms¦house
alms¦man (pl.
 alms¦men)
al'mu¦can¦tar
aloe
alo¦etic
aloft
alo'gical
alo'gic¦ally
alone
along
along¦shore
along¦side
aloof
alo¦pe'cia
aloud
al'paca
al'par¦gata
al'pen¦horn
al'pen¦stock
al'pha
al'pha¦bet
al'pha¦betic
al'pha¦bet¦ical
al'pha¦bet¦ic¦ally
al'pha¦bet¦ize
 (al'pha¦bet¦iz¦
 ing)
al'pha¦nu'meric
Alp'ine
Alp¦in¦ist
al'ready
alright use all
 right
Al'sace
Al'sa'tia
Al'sa'tian

al'sikc
also
al'tar
altar-piece
alt¦azi¦muth
Alte
 Pi'na¦ko¦thek
al'ter
al'tera¦tion
al'ter¦at¦ive
al'ter¦cate
 (al'ter¦cat¦ing)
al'ter¦ca¦tion
al' ter ego
al'tern¦ance
al'tern¦ant
al'tern¦ate (as v.,
 al'tern¦at¦ing)
al'tern¦ately
al'terna¦tion
al'tern¦at¦ive
al'tern¦ator
alt¦horn
al¦though
al'ti¦meter
al'ti¦tude
alto (pl. al'tos)
al'to¦gether
alto-relievo (pl.
 alto-relievos)
al'tri¦cial
al'tru¦ism
al'tru¦ist
al'tru¦istic
al'tru¦ist¦ic¦ally
alum
alu¦mina
alu¦mi'nium
alu¦min¦iza¦tion
alu¦min¦ize
 (alu¦min¦iz¦ing)
alum¦nus (pl.
 alumni)
al've¦olar
al've¦ol¦ate
al've¦olus (pl.
 al've¦oli)
al'ways
aly¦sum
ama¦da'vat
ama'dou
amah
am'al¦gam
am'al¦gam¦ate
 (am'al¦gam¦at¦
 ing)

am|al|gama|tion
am|anu|en|sis (pl.
 am|anu|en|ses)
am|ar|anth
am|ar|anth|ine
ama|ryl|lis
amass
ama|teur
ama|teur|ish
ama|teur|ism
Amati (violin etc.)
am|at|ive
am|at|ory
am|aur|osis (pl.
 am|aur|oses)
am|aze (amaz|ing)
amaze|ment
am|azon (strong
 woman)
Am|azon
 (legendary female
 warrior, river)
ama|zo|nian
am|ba|ges
am|bas|sador
am|bas|sad|orial
am|bas|sad|ress
am|batch
am|ber
am|ber|gris
am|bi|ance
 (details in work of
 art) △ ambience
am|bi|dex|ter|ity
am|bi|dex|trous
am|bi|ence
 (surroundings)
 △ *ambiance*
am|bi|ent
am|bi|gu|ity (pl.
 am|bi|gu|it|ies)
am|bigu|ous
am|bit
am|bi|tion
am|bi|tious
am|bi|val|ence
am|bi|val|ency
am|bi|val|ent
am|bi|ver|sion
am|bi|vert
amble (am|bling)
am|bler
am|bly|opia
am|bly|opic
ambo (pulpit; pl.
 am|bos)

am|boyna
am|bro|sia
am|bro|sial
ambry use
 aumbry
am|bu|lance
am|bu|lant
am|bu|lat|ory (as
 n., pl. am|bu|
 lat|or|ies)
am|bus|cade
am|bush
ameli|or|ate
 (ameli|or|at|ing)
ameli|ora|tion
ameli|or|at|ive
ameli|or|ator
amen
amen|ab|il|ity
amen|able
amen|ably
amend
amend|ment
amends
amen|ity (pl.
 amen|it|ies)
amen|or|rhoea
ament
amen|tia
amen|tum (catkin;
 pl. amenta)
amerce
 (amer|cing)
amerce|ment
amer|ci|able
Am|er|ica
Am|er|ican
Am|er|ic|ana
Am|er|ic|an|ism
Am|er|ic|an|ize
 (Am|er|ic|an|iz|
 ing)
am|eri|cium
Am|er|ind
Am|er|in|dian
ameth|yst
ameth|yst|ine
Am|haric
ami|ab|il|ity
ami|able
ami|ably
ami|anthus
am|ic|ab|il|ity
am|ic|able
am|ic|ably
am|ice

amid
amide
am|id|one
amid|ships
amidst
amine
amino acid
amir
amir|ate
amiss
am|ity
Am|man
am|meter
ammo
ammo|nia
am|mo|niac
am|mo|ni|acal
am|mo|ni|ated
am|mon|ite
am|mo|nium
am|mu|ni|tion
am|ne|sia
am|ne|siac
am|nesic
am|nesty (as n., pl.
 am|nes|ties; as v.,
 am|nes|ties,
 am|nestied)
am|nio|cen|tesis
 (pl. am|nio|
 cen|teses)
am|nion (pl.
 am|nia)
am|ni|otic
amoeba (pl.
 amoe|bas)
amoe|bean
amoebic
amoeb|oid
amok
among
amongst
Amon|til|lado (pl.
 Amon|til|la|dos)
amoral
amor|ally
am|or|ist
amor|oso (pl.
 amor|osos)
am|or|ous
amorph|ous
amort|iza|tion
amort|ize
 (amort|iz|ing)
amount
amour

amour|ette
amour propre
am|pel|op|sis
am|per|age
am|pere (*Electr.*)
Am|père (man)
am|per|sand
am|phet|amine
Am|phi|bia
am|phi|bian
am|phi|bi|ology
am|phi|bi|ous
am|phibo|logy
 (quibble; pl.
 am|phibo|logies)
am|phi|brach
am|phi|brachic
amph|ic|tyon
amph|ic|ty|onic
amph|ic|ty|ony
am|phi|gam|ous
am|phi|gouri
am|phi|mictic
am|phi|mixis (pl.
 am|phi|mixes)
am|phi|oxus
am|phi|pod
Am|phi|poda
 (order)
am|phis|baena
am|phi|theatre
Am|phi|tryon
am|phora (pl.
 am|phorae)
am|pho|ter|ic
ample (amp|ler,
 amp|lest)
amp|li|fica|tion
amp|li|fier
amp|lify
 (amp|li|fies,
 amp|li|fied,
 amp|li|fy|ing)
am|pli|tude
am|ply
am|poule
am|pulla (pl.
 am|pul|lae)
am|pu|tate
 (am|pu|tat|ing)
am|pu|ta|tion
am|pu|tee
Am|ster|dam
amu|let
Amund|sen
Amur

amuse (amus¦ing)
amuse¦ment
amus¦ive
amyl
amyl¦ase
amyl¦op¦sin
Amy¦tal (sedative;
 propr.)
ana¦bapt¦ism
ana¦bapt¦ist
ana¦bas
ana¦basis (*pl.*
 ana¦bases)
ana¦batic
ana¦bi¦osis (*pl.*
 ana¦bi¦oses)
ana¦bi¦otic
ana¦bolic
ana¦bol¦ism
ana¦branch
ana¦chronic
ana¦chron¦ism
ana¦chron¦istic
ana¦chron¦istic¦
 ally
an¦aco¦luthic
an¦aco¦lu¦thon (*pl.*
 an¦aco¦lu¦tha)
ana¦conda
Anac¦reon
ana¦cre¦ontic
ana¦cru¦sis (*pl.*
 ana¦cru¦ses)
ana¦drom¦ous
an¦ae¦mia
an¦aemic
an¦aer¦obe
an¦aer¦obic
an¦aes¦the¦sia
an¦aes¦thesi¦ology
an¦aes¦thetic
an¦aes¦thet¦ic¦ally
an¦aes¦thet¦ist
an¦aes¦thet¦iza¦
 tion
an¦aes¦thet¦ize
 (an¦aes¦thet¦iz¦
 ing)
ana¦glyph
ana¦glyphic
ana¦gno¦risis (*pl.*
 ana¦gno¦rises)
an¦agoge
an¦ago¦gic
an¦ago¦gical
ana¦gram

ana¦gram¦matic
anal
ana¦lecta
ana¦lects
ana¦leptic
an¦al¦gesia
an¦al¦gesic
anally
ana¦lo¦gic
ana¦lo¦gical
ana¦lo¦gic¦ally
ana¦lo¦gist
ana¦lo¦gize
 (ana¦lo¦giz¦ing)
ana¦log¦ous
ana¦logue
ana¦logy (*pl.*
 ana¦lo¦gies)
ana¦lys¦able
ana¦lys¦and
ana¦lyse
 (ana¦lys¦ing)
ana¦lyser
ana¦lysis (*pl.*
 ana¦lyses)
ana¦lyst
ana¦lytic
ana¦lyt¦ical
ana¦lyt¦ic¦ally
ana¦mnesis (*pl.*
 ana¦mneses)
ana¦morphic
ana¦mor¦phosis
 (*pl.* ana¦mor¦
 phoses)
ana¦nas
an¦an¦drous
ana¦paest
ana¦paestic
ana¦phora
ana¦phoric
an¦aph¦ro¦dis¦iac
ana¦phyl¦actic
ana¦phyl¦axis (*pl.*
 ana¦phyl¦axes)
ana¦ptyctic
ana¦ptyxis (*pl.*
 ana¦ptyxes)
an¦arch
an¦archic
an¦arch¦ical
an¦arch¦ic¦ally
an¦arch¦ism
an¦arch¦ist
an¦arch¦istic
an¦ar¦chy

ana¦stig¦mat
ana¦stig¦matic
ana¦stom¦ose
 (ana¦stom¦os¦ing)
ana¦stom¦osis (*pl.*
 ana¦stom¦oses)
ana¦stro¦phe
ana¦thema
ana¦them¦at¦ize
 (ana¦them¦at¦iz¦
 ing)
ana¦tom¦ical
ana¦tom¦ic¦ally
ana¦tom¦ist
ana¦tom¦ize
 (ana¦tom¦iz¦ing)
ana¦tomy (*pl.*
 ana¦tom¦ies)
anatta *use*
 annatto
an¦bury (*pl.*
 an¦bur¦ies)
an¦cestor
an¦ces¦tral
an¦ces¦trally
an¦ces¦tress
an¦ces¦try (*pl.*
 an¦ces¦tries)
an¦chor
an¦chor¦age
an¦chor¦ess
an¦chor¦etic
an¦chor¦ite
 (hermit)
an¦chor¦man (*pl.*
 an¦chor¦men)
an¦cho¦veta
an¦chovy (*pl.*
 an¦cho¦vies)
an¦chusa (plant)
anchylose *use*
 ankylose
an¦cien régime
 (*pl.* an¦ciens
 régimes)
an¦cient
an¦cil¦lary
ancon
Anda¦lu¦sia
An¦da¦man
an¦dante
an¦dan¦tino (*pl.*
 an¦dan¦ti¦nos)
And¦er¦sen, H. C.
An¦des

An¦dhra
 Pra¦desh
and¦iron
An¦dorra
An¦drew
an¦droe¦cium (*pl.*
 an¦droe¦cia)
an¦dro¦gen
an¦dro¦genic
andro¦gyne
an¦dro¦gyn¦ous
an¦dro¦gyny
an¦droid
an¦ec¦dot¦age
an¦ec¦dotal
an¦ec¦dot¦ally
an¦ec¦dote
an¦ec¦dotic
an¦echoic
an¦emo¦graph
an¦emo¦graphic
an¦emo¦meter
an¦emo¦met¦ric
an¦emo¦metry
anemone
an¦emo¦phil¦ous
anent
an¦er¦oid
an¦eurin
an¦eur¦ysm
an¦eur¦ys¦mal
anew
an¦frac¦tu¦os¦ity
an¦gary
an¦gel
An¦gela
an¦gelic
an¦gel¦ica (plant)
an¦gel¦ical
an¦gel¦ic¦ally
An¦gel¦ico
an¦gelus
an¦ger
An¦gevin
an¦gina
an¦gio¦sperm
angle (as *v.*,
 ang¦ling)
ang¦ler
Angles (tribe)
An¦gle¦sey
An¦glian
An¦glican
An¦glic¦an¦ism
an¦glice (in
 English; 3 sylls.)

An'gli|cism
An'gli|cize
  (An'gli|ciz|ing)
Ang'list
Ang'list|ics
Anglo-American
Anglo-Catholic
Ang'lo|cent'ric
Anglo-French
Anglo-Irish
Anglo-Latin
Ang'lo|mania
Anglo-Norman
Ang'lo|phile
Ang'lo|pho'bia
ang'lo|phone
Anglo-Saxon
An'gola
an'gora (fabric)
an'gos|tura
An'gos|tura
  (Bitters; *propr.*)
An'gou|mois
an'grily
angry (angr'ier,
  angri|est)
ång|ström
an'guine
an'guish
an'gu|lar
an'gu|lar|ity
an'hed'ral
an'hyd'ride
an'hyd'rite
an'hyd'rous
an|iconic
ani'cut
an'ile
an'il|ine
an'il|ity
an'ima
an'im|ad'ver|sion
an'im|ad'vert
an'imal
an'im|al|cule
an'im|al|ism
an'im|al|ity
an'im|al|iza|tion
an'im|al|ize
  (an'im|al|iz|ing)
an'im|ate (as *v.*,
  an'im|at|ing)
an'ima|tion
an'im|ator
an'imé (resin)
an'im|ism

an'im|ist
an'im|istic
an'im|os|ity (*pl.*
  an'im|os|it|ies)
an'imus
an'ion
an|ionic
an'ise
ani|seed
an'is|ette
an|iso|tropic
an|iso|tropy
An'jou
An'kara
ankh (anc. Egypt)
ankle
ank|let
an'kyl|ose
  (an'kyl|os|ing)
an'kyl|osis (*pl.*
  an'kyl|oses)
Anna Ka'ren|ina
an'nal
an'nal|ist
an'nal|istic
an'nal|istic|ally
an'nals
An'na|purna
an'nates (*RC Ch.*)
an'natto (dye)
an'neal
an'nect|ent
an'nelid
an'nel|idan
an'nex *v.*
an'nexa|tion
an'nexe *n.*
annicut *use*
  anicut
an'ni'hil|ate
  (an'ni'hil|at|ing)
an'ni'hila|tion
an'ni'hil|ator
an'ni|vers|ary (*pl.*
  an'ni|vers|ar|ies)
Anno Dom'ini
an'not|ate
  (an'not|at|ing)
an'nota|tion
an'not|ator
an'nounce
  (an'noun|cing)
an'nounce|ment
an'noun|cer
an'noy
an'noy|ance

an'nual
an'nu|ally
an'nu|it'ant
an'nu|ity (*pl.*
  an'nu|it|ies)
an'nul (an|nulled,
  an'nul|ling)
an'nu|lar
an'nu|late
an'nu|let
an'nul|ment
an'nu|lus (*pl.*
  an|nuli)
an'nun'ci|ate
  (an'nun'ci|at|ing)
an'nun'ci|ation
An'nun'ci|ation
  (feast)
an'nun'ci|ator
anoa (wild ox)
an'odal
an'ode
an'odic
an'od|ize
  (an'od|iz|ing)
ano|dyne
ano'esis (*pl.*
  ano'eses)
ano|etic
anoint
an'om|al|istic
an'om|al|ous
an'om|al|ure
  (rodent)
an'om|aly (*pl.*
  an'om|al|ies)
anomic
anomy
anon (soon)
an'ona|ceous
an'onym
an'onym|ity
an'onym|ous
an'oph|eles
  (mosquito)
an'orak
an|or'ectic
an|or'exia
  (ner'vosa)
an|or'exic
an|os'mia
an|os'mic
an|other
Anou|ilh
an'ovu|lant
an'ox|ae'mia

an|oxia
an|oxic
an|schluss (union)
an'ser|ine
an'swer
an'swer|ab'il|ity
an'swer|able
ant|acid
ant|ag'on|ism
ant|ag'on|ist
ant|ag'on|istic
ant|ag'on|ist'ic|
      ally
ant|ag'on|ize
  (ant|ag'on|iz|ing)
Ant|arc'tic
Ant|arc'tica
ante (stake; as *v.*,
  an'tes, an'ted,
  ante|ing)
ant-eater
ante|cedence
ante|cedent
ante|cham'ber
ante|chapel
ante|date (as *v.*,
  ante|dat'ing)
ante|di'lu|vian
ante|lope (*pl.*
  same *or*
  ante|lopes)
ante-mortem *a.*
ante|mund'ane
ante|natal
an'tenna (*pl.*
  an|ten'nae)
an'ten|nal
an'ten|nary
ante|nup'tial
ante|pen'dium
  (*pl.* ante|pen|dia)
ante|pen'ult
ante|pen|ul'tim|
      ate
ante-post (of
  racing bets)
ante|pran'dial
an|terior
an'teri|or'ity
ante-room
an'the'lion (*pl.*
  an'the|lia)
an'thel|mintic (*or*
  an'thel|minthic)
an'them

an|the|mion (*pl.*
  an|the|mia)
an|ther
an|theral
an|ther|id|ium (*pl.*
  an|ther|idia)
ant|hill
an|tho|lo|gize
  (an|tho|lo|giz|
          ing)
an|tho|lo|gist
an|tho|logy (*pl.*
  an|tho|lo|gies)
An|thony
an|tho|zoan
an|thra|cene
an|thra|cite
an|thra|citic
an|thrax
an|thro|po|
        cen|tric
an|thro|po|
        cen|trism
an|thro|po|genic
an|thro|po|geny
an|thro|po|
        graphy
an|throp|oid
an|thro|po|
        lo|gical
an|thro|po|
        lo|gically
an|thro|po|lo|gist
an|thro|po|logy
an|thro|po|
        met|ric
an|thro|po|metry
an|thro|po|
        morphic
an|thro|po|
        morph|ism
an|thro|po|
        morph|ize
  (an|thro|po|
        morph|iz|ing)
an|thro|po|
        morph|ous
an|thro|po|phag|
          ous
an|thro|po|phagy
anti (*pl.* antis)
anti-aircraft *a.*
an|tiar (Javan
  tree)
an|ti|bi|osis (*pl.*
  an|ti|bi|oses)

an|ti|bi|otic
an|ti|body (*pl.*
  an|ti|bod|ies)
an|tic
an|ti|cath|ode
An|ti|christ
an|ti|chris|tian
an|ti|cip|ate
  (an|ti|cip|at|ing)
an|ti|cipa|tion
an|ti|cip|at|ive
an|ti|cip|ator
an|ti|cip|at|ory
anti|cler|ical
an|ti|cli|mactic
an|ti|cli|mact|ic|
          ally
anti|climax
an|ti|clinal
an|ti|cline
an|ti|clock|wise
an|ti|co|agu|lant
an|ti|con|vuls|ant
an|ti|cyc|lone
an|ti|cyc|lonic
an|ti|dotal
an|ti|dote
an|ti|freeze
an|ti|gen
an|ti|genic
anti-gravity
An|tigua
anti-hero
  (*pl.* anti-heroes)
an|ti|his|tam|ine
an|ti|knock
An|til|les
an|ti|log
an|ti|log|ar|ithm
an|ti|logy (*pl.*
  an|ti|lo|gies)
an|ti|ma|cas|sar
an|ti|masque
an|ti|mat|ter
an|ti|mon|arch|
          ical
an|ti|mo|nial
an|ti|monic
an|ti|mo|ni|ous
an|ti|mony
  (silvery-white
  element)
  △ antinomy
an|ti|node
an|ti|no|mian

an|ti|nomy
  (contradiction in a
  law) △ antimony
anti-novel
an|ti|par|ticle
an|ti|pasto (*pl.*
  an|ti|pasti)
an|ti|path|etic
an|ti|path|et|ical
an|ti|path|et|ic|
          ally
an|ti|pathic
an|ti|pathy (*pl.*
  an|ti|path|ies)
anti-personnel
  (bomb etc.)
an|ti|per|spir|ant
an|ti|phlo|gistic
an|ti|phon
an|ti|phonal
an|ti|phon|ally
an|ti|phon|ary (*pl.*
  an|ti|phon|ar|ies)
an|ti|phony (*pl.*
  an|ti|phon|ies)
an|ti|podal
an|ti|pode
an|ti|po|dean
an|ti|podes
an|ti|pole
an|ti|pope
an|ti|pro|ton
an|ti|pyr|etic
an|ti|quar|ian
an|ti|quary (*pl.*
  an|ti|quar|ies)
an|ti|quated
an|tique (as *v.*,
  an|tiqued,
  an|tiquing)
an|tiquity (*pl.*
  an|tiquit|ies)
an|tir|rhinum
an|ti|sab|bat|
          ar|ian
An|ti|sana
an|ti|scor|bu|tic
an|ti|scrip|tural
anti-Semite
anti-Semitic
anti-Semitism
an|ti|sep|sis
an|ti|sep|tic
an|ti|sep|tic|ally
an|ti|serum (*pl.*
  an|ti|sera)

an|ti|so|cial
an|ti|so|ci|ally
an|ti|static
an|ti|stat|ic|ally
an|ti|strophe
an|ti|strophic
an|ti|the|ism
an|ti|the|ist
an|ti|thesis (*pl.*
  an|ti|theses)
an|ti|thetic
an|ti|thet|ical
an|ti|thet|ic|ally
an|ti|toxic
an|ti|toxin
an|ti|trade
an|ti|trin|it|ar|ian
an|ti|type
an|ti|typ|ical
an|ti|ven|ene (*or*
  an|ti|venin)
an|ti|vi|vi|
        sec|tion|ism
an|ti|vi|vi|
        sec|tion|ist
ant|ler
antlered
ant|ono|ma|sia
Ant|ony and
  Cleo|patra
ant|onym
ant|onym|ous
an|tral
An|trim
an|trum (*pl.*
  an|tra)
Ant|werp
anus
an|vil
an|xi|ety (*pl.*
  an|xi|et|ies)
anxious
any
any|body
any|how
any|one
any|place
any|thing
any|way
any|where
any|wise
An|zac
aor|ist
aor|istic
aorta
aor|tic

aou|dad
à ou|trance
apace
apache (ruffian; 2
  sylls.)
Apa|che (Red Ind.;
  3 sylls.)
ap|an|age
apart
apart|heid
apart|ment
apa|thetic
apa|thet|ic|ally
ap|athy
ap|at|ite
ape (as v., ap|ing)
apeak
ape|like
ape-man
  (pl. ape-men)
Ap|en|nines
aperi|ent
aperi|odic
aper|itif
aper|ture
apery (pl.
  aper|ies)
apet|al|ous
apex (pl. apexes
  or api|ces)
ap|fel|stru|del
aph|aer|esis (pl.
  aph|aer|eses)
apha|sia
aphasic
aph|elion (pl.
  aph|elia)
aph|esis (pl.
  aph|eses)
aph|etic
aphid
aphis (pl.
  aphi|des)
aphonia
aphony
aph|or|ism
aph|or|ist
aph|or|istic
aph|or|ist|ic|ally
aph|or|ize
  (aph|or|iz|ing)
aph|ro|dis|iac
aphyl|lous
Apia
apian
api|ar|ist

api|ary (pl.
  api|ar|ies)
ap|ical
ap|ic|ally
api|cul|tural
api|cul|ture
api|cul|tur|ist
apiece
apish
ap|lanat
ap|lan|atic
apla|sia
aplastic
aplenty
aplomb
apnoea
apo|ca|lypse
  (revelation)
Apo|ca|lypse (NT
  book)
apo|ca|lyp|tic
apo|ca|lyp|tical
apo|ca|lyp|tic|ally
apo|carp|ous
apo|chro|mat
apo|chro|matic
apo|cope
apo|crine
Apo|cry|pha
apo|cryphal
apo|cryph|ally
apodal
apo|dictic
apo|dict|ic|ally
apo|dosis (pl.
  apo|doses)
apo|gean
apo|gee
apo|laustic
apol|it|ical
apol|it|ic|ally
Apol|lin|aire
Apol|lin|aris
Apol|lin|arius
Apollo (pl.
  Apol|los)
Apol|lo|nian
Apol|lyon
apo|lo|getic
apo|lo|get|ic|ally
apo|lo|get|ics
apo|lo|gia
apo|lo|gist
apo|lo|gize
  (apo|lo|giz|ing)
apo|logue

apo|logy (pl.
  apo|lo|gies)
apo|lune
apo|mictic
apo|mixis (pl.
  apo|mixes)
apo|phatic
apoph|thegm
apoph|theg|matic
apoph|
  theg|mat|ic|ally
apo|plectic
apo|plect|ic|ally
apo|plexy (pl.
  apo|plex|ies)
apo|sem|atic
apo|sio|pesis (pl.
  apo|sio|peses)
apos|tasy (pl.
  apos|tas|ies)
apos|tate
apo|stat|ical
apos|tat|ize
  (apos|tat|iz|ing)
a pos|teri|ori
apostle (gen.
  senses)
Apostle (one of 12)
Apostles' Creed
apos|tol|ate
apo|stolic
apo|stol|ical
apo|stol|ic|ally
apo|strophe
apo|strophic
apo|stroph|ize
  (apo|stroph|iz|
    ing)
apo|thec|ary (pl.
  apo|thec|ar|ies)
apo|them (Geom.)
apo|the|osis (pl.
  apo|the|oses)
apo|theo|size
  (apo|theo|siz|ing)
apo|tro|paic
ap|pal (ap|palled,
  ap|pal|ling)
Ap|pa|lach|ian
  (Mts.)
Ap|pa|loosa
appanage use
  apanage
ap|parat (Comm.
  party machine)

ap|par|at|chik (pl.
  ap|par|at|chiks
  or ap|par|at|
    chiki)
ap|par|atus
ap|par|atus
  criti|cus
ap|parel
ap|par|elled
ap|par|ent
ap|pari|tion
ap|par|itor
ap|peal (as v.,
  ap|pealed,
  ap|peal|ing)
ap|pear
ap|pear|ance
ap|pease
  (ap|peas|ing)
ap|pease|ment
ap|pel|lant
ap|pel|late
ap|pel|la|tion
ap|pel|lat|ive
ap|pend
ap|pend|age
ap|pend|ant
ap|pen|dic|
    ec|tomy
  (pl. ap|pen|dic|
      ec|tom|ies;
  also ap|pend|
      ec|tomy,
  pl. ap|pend|
      ec|tom|ies)
ap|pen|di|citis
ap|pendix (pl.
  ap|pen|di|ces)
Ap|pen|zell
ap|per|ceive
  (ap|per|ceiv|ing)
ap|per|cep|tion
ap|per|cept|ive
ap|per|tain
ap|pet|ence
ap|pet|ency
ap|pet|ent
ap|pet|ite
ap|pet|it|ive
ap|pet|izer
ap|pet|iz|ing
ap|plaud
ap|plause
apple
Appleby
ap|ple|cart

ap'pli|ance
ap'plic|ab'il|ity
ap'plic|able
ap'plic|ably
ap'plic|ant
ap'plica|tion
ap'plic|ator
ap'pli|qué (as v.,
 ap'pli|qués,
 ap'pli|quéd,
 ap'pli|qué|ing)
ap'ply (ap'plies,
 ap'plied,
 ap'ply|ing)
ap'pog|gia|tura
ap'point
ap'pointee
ap'point|ive
ap'point|ment
ap'port
ap'por|tion
ap'por|tion|ment
ap'pos|ite
ap'posi|tion
ap'posi|tional
ap'prais|able
ap'praisal
ap'praise
 (ap'prais|ing)
ap'praise|ment
ap'praiser
ap'prais|ive
ap'pre|ciable
ap'pre|ciably
ap'preci|ate
 (ap'pre'ci|at|ing)
ap'pre'ci|ation
ap'pre'ci|at|ive
ap'pre'ci|at|ory
ap'pre|hend
ap'pre|hens|ib'il|
 ity
ap'pre|hens|ible
ap'pre|hen|sion
ap'pre|hen|sive
ap'pren|tice (as v.,
 ap'pren|ti'cing)
ap'pren'tice|ship
ap'prise
 (ap'pris|ing)
ap'pro
ap'proach
ap'proach|ab'il|
 ity
ap'proach|able

ap'prob|ate
 (ap'prob|at'ing)
ap'proba|tion
ap'prob|at|ive
ap'prob|at'ory
ap'pro'pri|ate (as
 v., ap'pro'pri|
 at'ing)
ap'pro'pri|ation
ap'pro'pri|at|ive
ap'pro'pri|ator
ap'proval
ap'prove
 (ap'prov'ing)
ap'prox'im|ate (as
 v., ap'prox'im|
 at'ing)
ap'prox'ima|tion
ap'prox'im|at|ive
ap'pur'ten|ance
ap'pur'ten|ant
après-ski
ap'ri|cot
Ap'ril
Ap'ril Fool's Day
a pri'ori
apri'or|ism
ap'ron
apron|ful (*pl.*
 apron|fuls)
apron-strings
apro|pos
apse
ap'sidal
ap'sis (*pl.*
 ap|sides)
ap'ter|ous
ap'teryx
ap'ti|tude
Apu'lia
aqua
aqua|cul'ture
aqua for'tis
aqua|lung
aqua|mar'ine
aqua|naut
aqua|plane (as v.,
 aqua|plan'ing)
aqua re'gia
aqua|relle
Aquar|ian
aquar|ist
aquar|ium (*pl.*
 aquar|iums)
Aquar|ius
aquatic

aqua|tint
aqua|vit
aqua vi'tae
aque|duct
aque|ous
aqui|fer
aqui|le'gia (plant)
aquil|ine
Aquinas
Aqui|taine
Arab
ar'ab|esque
Ara|bian
ar'abic (numerals)
Ar'abic
ar'abis (plant)
Ar'ab|ism
Ar'ab|ist
ar'able
Ar'aby
arach|nid
arach|noid
Ara'gon
arak *use* arrack
Aral (Sea)
Ar'ald|ite (epoxy
 resin; *propr.*)
Ara|maic
Aran (in Ireland)
ara|paima
ara|ponga
Ara'rat
ar'au|caria
ar'bal|est
ar'biter
ar'bit|rage
ar'bit|ra'geur
ar'bit|ral
ar'bit|ra|ment
ar'bit|rar|ily
ar'bit|rari|ness
ar'bit|rary
ar'bit|rate
 (ar'bit|rat'ing)
ar'bit|ra|tion
ar'bit|rator
ar'bit|ress
ar'bor (axle,
 spindle)
△ arbour
ar'bora|ceous
ar'bor|eal
ar'bor|eous
ar'bor|es|cence
ar'bor|es|cent

ar'bor|etum (*pl.*
 ar'bor|eta)
ar'bori|cul'tural
ar'bori|cul'ture
ar'bori|cul'tur|ist
ar'bor|iza|tion
arbor vi'tae
 (conifer)
ar'bour (bower)
△ arbor
ar'bu|tus
arc (*Electr.*; as v.,
 arced, arc|ing)
ar'cade
ar'caded
Ar'ca|dian
Ar'cady
ar'cane
ar'canum (*pl.*
 ar'cana)
Arc de Tri|omphe
Ar'chaean
archae|olo'gical
archae|olo'gic|
 ally
archae|olo'gist
archae|ology
archaeo|pteryx
ar'chaic
archa'ic|ally
archa|ism
archa|ist
archa|istic
archa|ist|ic|ally
archa|ize
 (archa|iz|ing)
arch|an'gel
Arch|an'gel
 (Arkhangel'sk, in
 USSR)
arch|an'gelic
arch|bishop
arch|bish'op|ric
arch|deacon
arch|deac'onry
 (*pl.* arch|deac'on|
 ries)
arch|di'ocesan
arch|di'ocese
arch|ducal
arch|duch'ess
arch|duchy (*pl.*
 arch|duch'ies)
arch|duke
arche|go'nium
 (*pl.* arche|go'nia)

arch-enemy (*pl.*
 arch-enemies)
archer
Archer (sign of
 Zodiac)
arch|ery
arche|typal
arche|typ|ally
arche|type
arche|typ|ical
archi|di|ac|onal
archi|di|ac|on|ate
archi|epis|copal
ar|chil
archi|man|drite
Archi|me|dean
Archi|me|des
archi|pe|lago (*pl.*
 archi|pe|la|gos)
archi|tect
archi|tec|tonic
archi|tec|ton|ics
archi|tec|tural
archi|tec|tur|ally
archi|tec|ture
archi|trave
arch|ive
arch|iv|ist
archi|volt
arch|way
arc|tic (very cold)
Arc|tic
ar|cu|ate
ar|dency
ar|dent
ar|dour
ar|du|ous
area
areal
areca
areg (*pl.* of
 erg=dunes)
arena
ar|en|aceous
aren't
are|ola (*pl.*
 are|olae)
are|olar
ar|ête (ridge)
ar|gala (bird)
ar|gali (sheep)
ar|gent
ar|gen|ti|fer|ous
Ar|gen|tina
ar|gen|tine (of
 silver)

Ar|gen|tine (of
 Argentina)
Ar|gen|tin|ian
ar|gil
ar|gil|la|ceous
Arg|ive
Argo
ar|gol
ar|gon
ar|go|naut
 (sea-animal)
Ar|go|nauts
 (Jason's heroes)
Ar|gos
ar|gosy (*pl.*
 ar|gos|ies)
ar|got
ar|gu|able
ar|gu|ably
ar|gue (ar|gu|ing)
ar|guer
ar|gufy
 (ar|gu|fied,
 ar|gu|fy|ing)
ar|gu|ment
ar|gu|men|ta|tion
ar|gu|ment|at|ive
Ar|gus
ar|gute
argy-bargy (as *v.*,
 argy-bargies,
 argy-bargied,
 argy-bargying)
aria
Ar|ian
Ari|an|ism
arid
arid|ity
ar|iel (gazelle)
Ar|ies
aright
aril
arise (arose,
 arisen, aris|ing)
aris|ings
ar|is|to|cracy (*pl.*
 ar|is|to|cra|cies)
ar|is|to|crat
ar|is|to|cratic
ar|is|to|crat|ic|
 ally
Ar|is|to|phanes
Ar|is|to|telian
Ar|is|totle
ar|ith|metic *a.*
arith|metic *n.*

ar|ith|met|ical
ar|ith|met|ic|ally
ar|ith|meti|cian
Arius
Ari|zona
Ar|kan|sas
ar|mada
ar|ma|dillo (*pl.*
 ar|ma|dil|los)
Ar|ma|ged|don
Ar|magh
ar|ma|ment
ar|ma|men|
 tarium
 (*pl.* ar|ma|men|
 taria)
ar|ma|ture
arm|chair
Ar|menia
Ar|me|nian
arm|ful (*pl.*
 arm|fuls)
arm|hole
Ar|mi|nian
Ar|mi|nius
ar|mis|tice
arm|let
ar|mor|ial
ar|mor|ist
ar|mory (heraldry)
ar|mour
ar|moured
ar|mourer
armour-plate
ar|moury (*pl.*
 ar|mour|ies)
arm|pit
army (*pl.* arm|ies)
ar|nica
aroma
aro|matic
aro|mat|ic|ally
around
arousal
arouse
 (arous|ing)
ar|peg|gio (*pl.*
 ar|peg|gios)
arquebus *use*
 harquebus
ar|rack
ar|raign
ar|raign|ment
Arran (in
 Scotland)

ar|range
 (ar|ran|ging)
ar|range|ment
ar|rant
ar|ras
ar|ray
ar|rear
ar|rear|age
ar|rears
ar|rest
ar|rest|able
ar|resta|tion
ar|rester
ar|rest|ment
arrière-pensée
 (*pl.* *arrière-*
 pensées)
ar|ris
ar|rival
ar|rive
 (ar|riv|ing)
ar|riv|isme
ar|riv|iste
ar|rog|ance
ar|rog|ancy
ar|rog|ant
ar|rog|ate
 (ar|rog|at|ing)
ar|roga|tion
ar|ron|disse|ment
ar|row
arrow-grass
ar|row|head
ar|row|root
ar|senal
ar|senic
ar|sen|ical
ar|seni|ous
ars|ine
ar|sis (*pl.* ar|ses)
ar|son
ar|son|ist
ars|phen|am|ine
arte|fact
ar|ter|ial
ar|teri|al|iza|tion
ar|teri|al|ize
 (ar|teri|al|iz|ing)
ar|terio|scler|osis
 (*pl.* ar|terio|scler|
 oses)
ar|terio|scler|otic
ar|ter|itis
ar|tery (*pl.*
 ar|ter|ies)
ar|te|sian

art-form
art|ful
art|fully
arth|ritic
arth|ritis
arth|ro|pod
Ar|thur
Ar|thur|ian
ar|ti|choke
art|icle
art|icled
ar|ticu|lacy
ar|tic|ular
ar|ticu|late (as v.,
 ar|ticu|lat|ing)
ar|ticu|la|tion
ar|ticu|lat|ory
artifact use
 artefact
ar|ti|fice
ar|ti|fi|cer
ar|ti|fi|cial
ar|ti|fi|ci|al|ity
ar|ti|fi|cial|ize
 (ar|ti|fi|cial|iz|
    ing)
ar|ti|fi|cially
ar|til|ler|ist
ar|til|lery (pl.
 ar|til|ler|ies)
ar|til|lery|man (pl.
 ar|til|lery|men)
ar|tisan
ar|tis|an|ate
art|ist
ar|tiste
art|istic
art|ist|ic|ally
art|istry
art|less
art nou|veau
Ar|tois
art|work
arty (art|ier,
 ar|ti|est)
arum
Ar|un|achal
 Pra|desh
Aryan
aryl
asa|foe|tida
as|bes|tos
as|bes|tos|ine
as|bes|tosis
as|carid
as|cend

as|cend|ancy (pl.
 as|cend|an|cies)
as|cend|ant
as|cender
as|cen|sion
As|cen|sion (feast)
as|cent
as|cer|tain
as|cer|tain|ment
as|cesis (pl.
 as|ceses)
as|cetic
as|cet|ic|ally
as|cet|icism
as|cid|ian
as|ci|tes
As|cle|piad
as|cor|bic
ascrib|able
ascribe
 (ascrib|ing)
ascrip|tion
as|dic
ase|ity
asep|sis
aseptic
asex|ual
asexu|al|ity
asexu|ally
ashamed
ash-bin
ash|en
Ashes (cricket
 trophy)
ash|et
Ash|ken|azi (pl.
 Ash|ken|azim)
Ash|ken|azic
Ash|kha|bad
ash|lar
Ash|molean
 (Museum)
ashore
ash|pan
ash-plant
ash|ram
ash|tray
ashy (ash|ier,
 ashi|est)
Asia
Asian
Asi|atic
aside
as|in|ine
as|in|in|ity
askance

askesis use
 ascesis
askew
aslant
asleep
aso|cial
aso|ci|ally
as|par|agus
as|pect
as|pect|ual
as|pen
as|per|gil|lum
as|per|ity
as|perse
 (as|pers|ing)
as|per|sion
as|per|sor|ium (pl.
 as|per|soria)
as|phalt
as|phaltic
as|pho|del
as|phyxia
as|phyxi|ant
as|phyxi|ate
 (as|phyxi|at|ing)
as|phyxi|ation
as|pic
as|pi|dis|tra
as|pir|ant
as|pir|ate (as v.,
 as|pir|at|ing)
as|pira|tion
as|pir|ator
as|pire
 (as|pir|ing)
as|pirin
asquint
As|sad
as|sai
as|sail
as|sail|able
as|sail|ant
As|sam
as|sas|sin
as|sas|sin|ate
 (as|sas|sin|at|ing)
as|sas|sina|tion
as|sas|sin|ator
as|sault
as|saulter
as|sault|ive
as|say
as|say|able
as|se|gai
as|sem|blage

as|semble
 (as|sem|bling)
as|sem|bly (pl.
 as|sem|blies)
as|sem|bly|man
 (pl.
 as|sem|bly|men)
as|sent
as|senter (one who
 assents)
as|sen|tient
as|sentor (in
 election)
as|sert
as|ser|tion
as|sert|ive
as|sertor
as|sess
as|sess|able
as|sess|ment
as|ses|sor
as|ses|sor|ial
as|set
as|sev|er|ate
 (as|sev|er|at|ing)
as|sev|cra|tion
as|sib|il|ate
 (as|sib|il|at|ing)
as|sib|ila|tion
as|si|du|ity
as|sidu|ous
as|sign
as|sign|able
as|sig|na|tion
as|signee
as|sign|ment
as|signor
as|sim|il|able
as|sim|il|ate
 (as|sim|il|at|ing)
as|sim|ila|tion
as|sim|il|at|ive
as|sim|il|ator
as|sim|il|at|ory
as|sist
as|sist|ance
as|sist|ant
as|size
as|so|ci|ab|il|ity
as|so|ci|able
as|so|ci|ate (as v.,
 as|so|ci|at|ing)
as|so|ci|ate|ship
as|so|ci|ation
as|so|ci|ational
as|so|ci|at|ive

as|so|ci|ator
as|so|ci|at|ory
as|son|ance
as|son|ant
as|son|ate
 (as|son|at|ing)
as|sort
as|sort|at|ive
as|sor|ted
as|sort|ment
as|suage
 (as|sua|ging)
as|suage|ment
as|sum|able
as|sume
 (as|sum|ing)
as|sump|tion
As|sump|tion
 (feast)
as|sumpt|ive
as|sur|ance
as|sure
 (as|sur|ing)
as|suredly
As|syria
As|syr|ian
astable
astatic
astat|ine
as|ter
as|ter|isk
as|ter|ism
astern
as|ter|oid
as|ter|oidal
as|the|nia
as|thenic
asthma
asth|matic
asth|mat|ic|ally
astig|matic
astig|mat|ism
as|tilbe
astir
Asti spu|mante
as|ton|ish
as|ton|ished
as|ton|ish|ment
astound
astoun|ded
astraddle
as|tra|gal
as|trag|alus
as|tra|khan
as|tral
astray

astride
astrin|gency (pl.
 astrin|gen|cies)
astrin|gent
as|tro|bot|any
as|tro|dome
as|tro|hatch
as|tro|labe
as|tro|lo|ger
as|tro|lo|gic
as|tro|lo|gical
as|tro|lo|gic|ally
as|tro|logy
as|tro|naut
as|tro|naut|ical
as|tro|naut|ics
as|tro|nomer
as|tro|nom|ical
as|tro|nom|ic|ally
as|tro|nomy (pl.
 as|tro|nom|ies)
as|tro|phys|ical
as|tro|phys|icist
as|tro|phys|ics
As|tur|ias
as|tute
Asun|ción
asun|der
asy|lum
asym|met|ric
asym|met|rical
asym|met|ric|ally
asym|metry (pl.
 asym|met|ries)
asymp|tote
asymp|totic
asymp|tot|ic|ally
asyn|chron|ous
asyn|detic
asyn|deton (pl.
 asyn|deta)
Atabrine use
 Atebrin
at|ar|ac|tic
at|ar|axia
at|ar|axic
at|ar|axy
Ata|turk
at|av|ism
at|av|istic
ataxia
ataxic
ataxy
At|eb|rin (propr.)
atel|ier

Athana|sian
Athan|as|ius
athe|ism
athe|ist
athe|istic
athem|atic
Athe|nian
Ath|ens
ath|ero|scler|osis
 (pl. ath|ero|scler|
  oses)
ath|ero|scler|otic
athirst
ath|lete
ath|lete's foot
ath|letic
ath|let|ic|ally
ath|let|icism
ath|let|ics
athwart
At|lan|tean
at|lan|tes
At|lantic
at|lan|to|saurus
at|las
At|las (Titan)
at|mo|sphere
at|mo|spheric
at|mo|spher|ic|
 ally
at|mo|spher|ics
atoll
atom
atomic
atom|ic|ally
at|om|ism
at|om|ist
at|om|istic
atom|ist|ic|ally
at|om|iza|tion
at|om|ize
 (at|om|iz|ing)
at|om|izer
atonal
aton|al|ity
aton|ally
atone (aton|ing)
atone|ment
atonic
atony
at|ra|bili|ous
at|rium (pl. at|ria
 or at|ri|ums)
at|ro|cious
at|ro|city (pl.
 at|ro|cit|ies)

at|rophy (as v.,
 at|ro|phies,
 at|ro|phied,
 at|ro|phy|ing)
at|rop|ine
at|tach
at|tach|able
at|taché
at|tach|ment
at|tack
at|tacker
at|tain
at|tain|ab|il|ity
at|tain|able
at|tain|der
at|tain|ment
at|taint
at|tar
at|tempt
at|tempt|able
at|tend
at|tend|ance
at|tend|ant
at|tender
at|ten|tion
at|tent|ive
at|tenu|ate (as v.,
 at|tenu|at|ing)
at|tenu|ation
at|tenu|ator
at|test
at|testa|tion
at|testor
at|tic (top storey)
At|tic (of Attica)
At|tica
at|ti|cism
at|tire (at|tir|ing)
at|ti|tude
at|ti|tu|dinal
at|ti|tu|din|ize
 (at|ti|tu|din|iz|
  ing)
Att|lee
at|tor|ney
Attorney-General
at|tract
at|tract|able
at|tract|ant
at|trac|tion
at|tract|ive
at|trib|ut|able
at|tri|bute n.
at|trib|ute v.
 (at|trib|ut|ing)
at|tri|bu|tion

at'trib|ut'ive
at'tri|tion
at'tune
  (at'tun|ing)
atyp|ical
atyp'ic|ally
au|*bade*
au|*berge*
au'ber|gine
au'brie|tia
au'burn
Auck|land
auc|tion
auc'tion|eer
au'da|cious
au'da|city
Au'den
aud|ib'il|ity
aud|ible
aud|ibly
au'di|ence
aud|ile
au'dio
au'di|olo'gist
au'di|ol|ogy
au'di|ometer
au'dio|phile
audio-visual
audit (as *v.*,
  au'dited,
  au'dit|ing)
au'di|tion
aud'it|ive
aud|itor
aud'it|or'ial
aud'it|or'ium (*pl.*
  aud'it|or'iums)
aud'it|ory
Aud'rey
au fait
au fond
Au|gean
au|ger (tool)
aug|ite
aug|ment
aug|men'ta|tion
aug|ment'at|ive
au gra'tin
au|gur (portend)
au|gural
au|gury (*pl.*
  au'gur|ies)
au|gust
Au'gust (month)
Au|gustan
Au'gust|ine

Au|gust'in|ian
auk
auld lang syne
aulic
aum'bry (*pl.*
  aum|bries)
au nat|urel
Au'nis
aunt
aunty (*pl.*
  aunt'ies)
au pair
aura
aural
aur|ally
au're|ate
au're|ola
au'reo|my'cin
au re'voir
auric
aur|icle
au'ri|cula
au'ri|cu'lar
au'ri|culate
au'ri|fer|ous
Au'rig'na|cian
aur|ist
aur'ochs
au|rora (*pl.*
  au|roras *or*
  au|rorae)
au|rora aus'tralis
au|rora bo're|alis
au|roral
aus'cul|ta'tion
aus'cul'tat|ory
aus|pice
aus|pi'ces
aus'pi|cious
Aus'sie
Aus'ten, Jane
aus|tere
  (aus|terer,
  aus|terest)
aus'ter|ity (*pl.*
  aus'ter|it'ies)
Aus'tin
aus|tral
Aus'tra|la'sian
Aus'tra'lia
Aus'tra'lian
Aus'tra'lo|
          pith'ec|ine
Aus'tra'lo|
          pith'ecus
Aus|tria

aut|archic
aut'arch|ical
aut'|archy
  (absolute
  sovereignty; *pl.*
  aut'arch'ies)
aut|arkic
aut'ark|ical
aut'ark|ist
aut'arky
  (self-sufficiency)
au'then|tic
au'then'tic|ally
au'then'tic|ate
  (au'then'tic|
                at'ing)
au'then'tica|tion
au'then'tic|ator
au'then'ti|city
au'thor
au'thor|ess
au'thor|ial
au'thor'it|ar'ian
au'thor'it|at'ive
au'thor|ity (*pl.*
  au'thor|it'ies)
au'thor|iza'tion
au'thor|ize
  (au'thor|iz'ing)
au'thor|ship
aut|ism
aut|istic
auto (*pl.* autos)
auto|bahn
auto|bio|grapher
auto|bio|graphic
auto|bio|graph|
                ical
auto|bio|graphy
  (*pl.* auto|bio|
            graph'ies)
auto|car
auto|ceph'al|ous
au'toch|thon
au'toch|thon|ous
auto|clave
auto|code
auto|cracy (*pl.*
  auto|cra'cies)
auto|crat
auto|cratic
auto|crat'ic|ally
auto|cross
Auto|cue (*propr.*)
auto-da-fé (*pl.*
  autos-da-fé)

auto|di'dact
auto|di'dactic
auto-erotic
auto-eroticism
auto-erotism
auto|gamy
auto|gen|ous
auto|giro (*pl.*
  auto|giros)
auto|graft
auto|graph
auto|graphic
auto|graphy
autogyro *use*
  autogiro
auto|harp
auto-immune
auto-immunity
auto-intoxication
auto|lysis
auto|lytic
auto|mate
  (auto|mat'ing)
auto|matic
auto|mat'ic|ally
auto|ma'ti|city
auto|ma'tion
auto|mat|ism
auto|mat|ize
  (auto|mat'iz|ing)
au'to|maton (*pl.*
  au'to|mat'ons,
  collect.
  au'to|mata)
auto|mo'bile
auto|mot'ive
auto|nomic
auto|nom|ist
auto|nom|ous
auto|nomy
auto|pi'lot
auto|pista
aut|opsy (*pl.*
  aut|op'sies)
auto|ra'dio|graph
auto|ra'dio|
          graphic
auto|ra'dio|
          graphy
auto|route
auto|strada (*pl.*
  auto|strade)
auto-suggestion
auto|telic
auto|tomy
auto|toxic

auto|toxin
auto|trophic
auto|type
au|tumn
au|tum|nal
Au|vergne
aux|an|ometer
aux|ili|ary (as n.,
  pl. aux|ili|ar|ies)
auxin
avadavat use
  amadavat
avail
avail|ab|il|ity
avail|able
avail|ably
ava|lanche (as v.,
  ava|lanch|ing)
avant-garde
avant-gardism
avant-gardist
av|ar|ice
av|ari|cious
avast
av|atar
ave (farewell)
Ave (prayer)
avenge
  (aven|ging)
aven|ger
avens (plant)
aven|tur|ine
av|enue
aver (averred,
  aver|ring)
av|er|age (as v.,
  av|er|aging)

aver|ment
averse
aver|sion
avert
Avesta
Avestan
Avestic
avian
avi|ary (pl.
  avi|ar|ies)
avi|ate
  (avi|at|ing)
avi|ation
avi|ator
avi|at|rix
avid
avid|ity
avi|fauna
avi|on|ics
avit|amin|osis (pl.
  avit|amin|oses)
aviz|an|dum (Sc.
  Law)
avo|cado (pl.
  avo|ca|dos)
avoca|tion
avo|cet
Avo|gadro
Avo|gadro's law
avoid
avoid|able
avoid|ance
avoir|du|pois
Avon
avow
avow|able
avowal

avowedly
avul|sion
avun|cu|lar
await
awake (awoke,
  awoken,
  awak|ing)
awaken
award
aware
awash
away
awe (as v., aw|ing)
aweigh
awe|some
awe|stricken
awe|struck
aw|ful
aw|fully
awhile
awk|ward
awn|ing
awry
axe (as v., ax|ing)
axel (movement in
  skating) △ axil,
  axle
ax|ial
axi|al|ity
axi|ally
axil (angle
  between leaf and
  stem etc.) △ axel,
  axle
ax|illa (armpit; pl.
  ax|il|lae)
ax|il|lary

axio|lo|gical
axi|olo|gist
axi|ology
ax|iom
ax|io|matic
ax|io|mat|ic|ally
axis (pl. axes)
Axis (Ger. alliance
  1939)
axle (spindle)
  △ axel, axil
Ax|min|ster
  (carpet)
axo|lotl
axon
ay (yes, pl. ayes)
ayah
aya|tol|lah
aye-aye (lemur)
Ayles|bury
Ayr
Ayr|shire
aza|lea
azeo|trope
azeo|tro|pic
Azer|bai|jan
Azil|ian
azi|muth
azi|muthal
azoic
Azores
Azov, Sea of
Az|tec
azure
azy|gous

B

Baal (*pl.* Ba¦alim)
baa-lamb
Ba¦al¦ism
baas¦skap
baba
Bab¦bage
bab¦bitt (alloy)
Bab¦bitt
 (complacent
 business man)
Bab¦bittry
babble
 (bab¦bling)
bab¦bler
ba¦bel (scene of
 confusion)
Ba¦bel (tower)
Babi
ba¦bi¦roussa
Bab¦ism
Bab¦ist
ba¦boon
ba¦bushka
baby (as *n.*, *pl.*
 ba¦bies; as *v.*,
 ba¦bies, ba¦bied,
 ba¦by¦ing)
ba¦by¦hood
ba¦by¦ish
Ba¦by¦lon
Ba¦by¦lon¦ian
baby-sit
 (baby-sat,
 baby-sitting)
baby-sitter
bac¦ca¦laur¦eate
bac¦carat
bac¦cate
Bac¦chanal
Bac¦chan¦a¦lia
Bac¦chan¦a¦lian
Bac¦chant (*pl.*
 Bac¦chants *or*
 Bac¦chan¦tes)
Bac¦chante
Bac¦chantic
Bac¦chic
baccy
Bach

bach¦elor
bach¦el¦or¦hood
ba¦cil¦lary
ba¦cil¦li¦form
ba¦cil¦lus (*pl.*
 ba¦cilli)
back (*superl.*
 back¦most)
back¦ache
back-bench
back-bencher
back¦bite
 (back¦bit,
 back¦bit¦ing)
back¦biter
back¦board
back-boiler
back¦bone
back¦chat
back¦cloth
back¦comb
back-cross
back¦date
 (back¦dat¦ing)
back¦drop
backer
back-fill
back¦fire
 (back¦fir¦ing)
back-formation
back¦gam¦mon
back¦ground
back¦hand
back¦han¦ded
back¦hander
back¦ing
back¦lash
back¦less
back¦list
back¦log
back¦marker
back¦most
back¦pack
back-pedal
 (back-pedalled,
 back-pedalling)
back¦rest
Backs (at
 Cambridge)

back-scattering
back¦scratcher
back-seat *a.*
backsheesh *use*
 baksheesh
back¦side
back¦sight
back¦slap¦ping
back¦slide
 (back¦slid¦ing)
back¦slider
back¦space
 (back¦spa¦cing)
back¦stage
back¦stay
back¦stitch
back¦stroke
back¦track
back-up *n.* & *a.*
back¦ward *a.*
back¦warda¦tion
back¦wards *a.* &
 adv.
back¦wash
back¦water
back¦woods
back¦woods¦man
 (*pl.* back¦woods¦
 men)
back¦yard
ba¦con
Ba¦con
 (philosopher)
Ba¦co¦nian
bac¦teria (*pl.* of
 bacterium)
bac¦terial
bac¦teri¦cide
bac¦terio¦lo¦gical
bac¦teri¦olo¦gist
bac¦teri¦ology
bac¦teri¦olysis (*pl.*
 bac¦teri¦olyses)
bac¦teri¦olytic
bac¦terio¦phage
bac¦terio¦stasis
 (*pl.* bac¦terio¦
 stases)
bac¦terio¦static

bac¦terium (*pl.*
 bac¦teria)
bad (worse,
 worst)
bad¦dish
baddy (*pl.*
 bad¦dies)
bade (*past* of bid)
Baden
badge
badger
bad¦in¦age
bad¦min¦ton
bad-mouth *v.*
Bae¦deker
Baf¦fin (Bay,
 Island)
baffle (baf¦fling)
baffle-board
baf¦fle¦ment
baffle-plate
baf¦fler
bag (as *v.*, bagged,
 bag¦ging)
ba¦garre
ba¦gasse
ba¦ga¦telle
ba¦gel
bag¦ful (*pl.*
 bag¦fuls)
bag¦gage
bag¦gi¦ness
baggy (bag¦gier,
 bag¦gi¦est)
Bagh¦dad
bag¦man (*pl.*
 bag¦men)
bagnio (*pl.*
 bagnios)
bag¦pipe (as *v.*,
 bag¦pip¦ing)
bag¦piper
ba¦guette
bag¦wash
bag-wig
Ba¦ha'i
Ba¦ha'ism
Ba¦ha'ist
Ba¦ha'ite
Ba¦ha¦mas

Ba¦ha¦mian
Baha Ul¦lah
Bah¦rain
baign¦oire
Bai¦kal, Lake
bail (security for
  prisoner, cross-
  piece over stumps
  in cricket, outer
  line of fortifica-
  tions, to deliver
  goods in trust, to
  scoop water out of,
  to secure release
  on bail) △ bale
bail¦able
bailee (one to
  whom goods are
  entrusted)
bailey (outer wall
  of castle)
Bailey (bridge)
bailie (*Sc.*, =
  alderman)
bail¦iff
bai¦li¦wick
bail¦ment
bailor (one who
  entrusts goods to a
  bailee)
bails¦man (*pl.*
  bails¦men)
bain-marie (*pl.*
  bains-marie)
Bai¦ram
Baird
Bai¦riki
bairn
bait (enticement,
  to torment) ·
  △ bate
baize
bajra
bake (bak¦ing)
bake¦house
bake¦lite
baker
bakery (*pl.*
  baker¦ies)
Bake¦well
baking-powder
baking-soda
bak¦lava
bak¦sheesh
Bala, Lake
Ba¦la¦clava

ba¦la¦laika
bal¦ance (as *v.*,
  bal¦an¦cing)
balance-wheel
balas
Bal¦brig¦gan
bal¦cony (*pl.*
  bal¦con¦ies)
bal¦da¦chin
bal¦der¦dash
bald-faced
bald¦head
bald-headed
bald¦ing
bald¦money
bald¦pate
bale (package,
  destruction, woe,
  to make into a
  package; as *v.*,
  bal¦ing) △ bail
Ba¦le¦aric
  (Islands)
ba¦leen
bale¦ful
bale¦fully
Bali
Ba¦li¦nese
balk *v.* △ baulk
Bal¦kan
Bal¦kan¦ize
  (Bal¦kan¦iz¦ing)
Bal¦kans
Bal¦khash, Lake
balky (balk¦ier,
  balk¦iest)
bal¦lad
bal¦lade
bal¦lad¦eer
ballad-monger
bal¦ladry (*pl.*
  bal¦ladries)
bal¦last
ball-bearing
ball¦boy
ball¦cock
bal¦ler¦ina
bal¦let
bal¦letic
bal¦leto¦mane
bal¦leto¦mania
ball-flower
bal¦lista (*pl.*
  bal¦listae)
bal¦listic
bal¦list¦ics

bal¦locks (*sl.*)
bal¦lon d'es¦sai
  (*pl.* *bal¦lons*
  d'es¦sai)
bal¦lonet
bal¦loon
bal¦loon¦ist
bal¦lot (as *v.*,
  bal¦loted,
  bal¦lot¦ing)
ballot-box
ballot-paper
ball¦park
ball-pen
ball-point
ball¦room
bally
bal¦ly¦hoo
bal¦ly¦rag
  (bal¦ly¦ragged,
  bal¦ly¦rag¦ging)
balm-cricket
balm¦ily
balmi¦ness
bal¦moral (flat
  cap)
Bal¦moral (in
  Scotland)
balmy (balm¦ier,
  balmi¦est)
bal¦neary
bal¦ne¦ology
baloney *use*
  boloney
balsa
bal¦sam
bal¦samic
bal¦sami¦fer¦ous
balsa-wood
Bal¦tic
bal¦ti¦more (bird)
bal¦us¦ter
bal¦us¦trade
Bal¦zac
Ba¦mako
bam¦bino (*pl.*
  bam¦bini)
bam¦boo
bam¦boozle
  (bam¦booz¦ling)
bam¦boozle¦ment
ban (as *v.*,
  banned,
  ban¦ning)
banal

ban¦al¦ity (*pl.*
  ba¦nal¦it¦ies)
ban¦ally
ba¦nana
ban¦ausic
Ban¦bury
banc (*Law*)
band¦age (as *v.*,
  band¦aging)
ban¦danna
ban¦deau (*pl.*
  ban¦deaux)
ban¦ded
ban¦der¦ole
ban¦di¦coot
ban¦dit (*pl.*
  ban¦dits *or*
  ban¦ditti)
ban¦ditry
band¦mas¦ter
ban¦do¦leer
band-saw
bands¦man (*pl.*
  bands¦men)
band¦stand
band¦wagon
band¦width
bandy (as *v.*,
  ban¦dies,
  ban¦died; as *a.*,
  ban¦dier,
  ban¦di¦est)
bandy-legged
bane
bane¦berry (*pl.*
  bane¦ber¦ries)
bane¦ful
bane¦fully
Banff
banger
Bang¦kok
Ban¦gla¦desh
bangle
bang¦tail
Ban¦gui
ban¦ian
ban¦ish
ban¦ish¦ment
ban¦is¦ter
banjo (*pl.* ban¦jos)
ban¦jo¦ist
Ban¦jul
bank¦able
bank-book
banker
banket

bank|ing
bank|note
bank|roll
bank|rupt
bank|ruptcy (*pl.*
 bank|rupt|cies)
bank|sia
ban|ner
bannister *use*
 banister
ban|nock
Ban|nock|burn
banns
ban|quet (as *v.*,
 ban|queted,
 ban|quet|ing)
ban|quette
ban|shee
ban|tam
ban|tam|weight
ban|ter
bant|ling
Bantu (*pl.*
 Ban|tus, *collect.*
 Bantu)
Ban|tu|stan
banyan *use*
 banian
ban|zai
bao|bab
bap|tism
bap|tis|mal
bapt|ist (one who
 baptizes)
Bapt|ist
 (denomination)
bap|tist|ery (*pl.*
 bap|tist|er|ies)
bap|tize
 (bap|tiz|ing)
bar (as *v.*, barred,
 bar|ring)
ba|ra|thea
Bar|ba|dian
Bar|ba|dos
Bar|bara
bar|bar|ian
bar|baric
bar|bar|ic|ally
bar|bar|ism
bar|bar|ity (*pl.*
 bar|bar|it|ies)
bar|bar|iza|tion
bar|bar|ize
 (bar|bar|iz|ing)
bar|bar|ous

Bar|bary
bar|be|cue (as *v.*,
 bar|be|cued,
 bar|be|cu|ing)
bar|bel (fish)
bar|bell (weights)
barber
bar|berry (*pl.*
 bar|ber|ries)
barbet (tropical
 bird)
barb|ette (gun
 platform)
bar|bi|can
bar|bit|one
bar|bit|ur|ate
bar|bit|uric
bar|bola
barb|ule
bar|car|ole
Bar|ce|lona
bardic
bard|ol|atry
bare (as *v.*, bared,
 bar|ing; as *a.*,
 barer, barest)
bare|back
bare|faced
bare|foot
bare|footed
ba|rège
bare|headed
barely
Bar|ents (Sea)
bar|gain
barge (as *v.*,
 barged,
 bar|ging)
barge-board
bar|gee
Bar|gello
barge|man (*pl.*
 barge|men)
barge-pole
ba|rilla
ba|ri|tone
bar|ium
barker
bar|ley
barley-mow
barley-water
bar-line
bar|maid
bar|man (*pl.*
 bar|men)
Bar|me|cide

bar mitz|vah
barmy (bar|mier,
 bar|mi|est)
Barn|aby Rudge
barn|acle
barn-door
bar|ney
barn-owl
Barns|ley
barn|storm
barn|stormer
barn|yard
ba|ro|graph
ba|ro|meter
ba|ro|met|ric
ba|ro|met|rical
ba|ro|met|ric|ally
ba|ro|metry
baron
bar|on|age
bar|on|ess
bar|onet
bar|on|et|age
bar|on|etcy (*pl.*
 bar|on|et|cies)
ba|ro|nial
bar|ony (*pl.*
 bar|on|ies)
ba|roque
barque
bar|quen|tine
bar|rack
barrack-room
bar|racks
bar|ra|couta (fish
 of S. Pacific etc.)
bar|ra|cuda (W.
 Indian fish)
bar|rage
bar|ra|mundi
bar|rator
bar|rat|rous
bar|ratry
barre
bar|rel (as *v.*,
 bar|relled,
 bar|rel|ling)
barrel-organ
bar|ren
 (bar|rener,
 bar|ren|est)
bar|ren|wort
bar|ret (small cap)
bar|rette (clip etc.
 for hair)

bar|ri|cade (as *v.*,
 bar|ri|cad|ing)
bar|rier
bar|ring
bar|rio (*pl.*
 bar|rios)
bar|ris|ter
bar|row
Barrow-in-
 Furness
Barry
Bar|sac
bar|tender
bar|ter
bar|tizan
Bar|tok
Bart's
ba|ryon
ba|ry|onic
ba|ry|sphere
baryta
bary|tes
barytic
ba|ry|tone
basal
bas|alt
ba|saltic
bas|cule
base (as *a.*, baser,
 basest; as *v.*,
 bas|ing)
base|ball
base|born
base|less
base|line
base|load
base|man (*pl.*
 base|men)
base|ment
ba|ses (*pl.* of base
 and basis)
bash|ful
bash|fully
bashi-bazouk
ba|sic
Ba|sic (Comp.
 language)
ba|sic|ally
ba|si|city (*pl.*
 ba|si|cit|ies)
ba|sid|ium (*pl.*
 ba|sidia)
basil
bas|ilar
ba|sil|ica
ba|sil|ican

Ba¦si¦li¦cata
ba¦si¦lisk
ba¦sin
bas¦inet
 (headpiece)
△ bassinet
ba¦sin¦ful (*pl.*
 ba¦sin¦fuls)
ba¦si¦petal
ba¦si¦pet¦ally
ba¦sis (*pl.* ba¦ses)
Bas¦ker¦ville
bas¦ket
bas¦ket¦ball
bas¦ket¦ful (*pl.*
 bas¦ket¦fuls)
bas¦ketry
bas¦ket¦work
Basle
basnet *use*
 basinet
basque (bodice)
Basque
bas-relief
bass (fish; *pl.* bass
 or basses)
bas¦set
basset-horn
basset-hound
bas¦sinet (cradle,
 pram) △ basinet
bass¦ist
basso (*pl.* bas¦sos
 or bassi)
bas¦soon
bas¦soon¦ist
bass¦wood
bas¦taard (*S. Afr.*,
 person of mixed
 race)
bas¦tard
bas¦tard¦iza¦tion
bas¦tard¦ize
 (bas¦tard¦iz¦ing)
bas¦tardy
baste (bast¦ing)
bas¦tille
Bas¦tille (in Paris)
bas¦ti¦nado (*pl.*
 bas¦ti¦nados)
bas¦tion
bat (as *v.*, bat¦ted,
 bat¦ting)
ba¦tata
Ba¦ta¦via
Ba¦ta¦vian

bate (to restrain,
 sl. rage; as *v.*,
 bat¦ing) △ bait
bat¦eau (*pl.*
 bat¦eaux)
ba¦te¦leur
Bates¦ian
Bath
bathe (bath¦ing)
bather
bath¦etic
batho¦lith
ba¦tho¦meter
Bath¦onian
bathos
bath¦otic
bath¦robe
bath¦room
bath-tub
bathy¦scaphe
bathy¦sphere
batik
ba¦tiste
bat¦man (*pl.*
 bat¦men)
baton
bat¦ra¦chian
bats¦man (*pl.*
 bats¦men)
bats¦man¦ship
bat¦tal¦ion
bat¦tels
bat¦ten
bat¦ter
battered
battering-ram
bat¦tery (*pl.*
 bat¦ter¦ies)
battle (as *v.*,
 bat¦tling)
bat¦tle¦axe
battle-cry (*pl.*
 battle-cries)
bat¦tle¦dore
bat¦tle¦dress
bat¦tle¦field
bat¦tle¦ground
bat¦tle¦ment
bat¦tle¦mented
bat¦tle¦ship
bat¦tue
batty (bat¦tier,
 bat¦ti¦est)
bat¦wing
bat¦wo¦man (*pl.*
 bat¦wo¦men)

bauble
Bau¦de¦laire
Bau¦haus
baulk (of timber;
 in billiards)
△ balk
baux¦ite
baux¦itic
Ba¦varia
bawd¦ily
bawdi¦ness
bawdy (baw¦dier,
 baw¦di¦est)
bawdy-house
bay¦ad¦ère
Bay¦ard
bay¦berry (*pl.*
 bay¦ber¦ries)
bay-leaf
 (*pl.* bay-leaves)
bay¦onet (as *v.*,
 bay¦on¦eted,
 bay¦on¦et¦ing)
Bay¦reuth
ba¦zaar
ba¦zooka
bdel¦lium
beach (shore)
△ beech
beach-ball
beach¦comber
beach-head
beach-la-mar
beacon
bead¦ily
beadi¦ness
bead¦ing
beadle
beads¦man (*pl.*
 beads¦men)
beady (bead¦ier,
 beadi¦est)
beagle
beag¦ling
beaker
be-all
beamer
beamy (beam¦ier,
 beam¦iest)
bean¦feast
beanie
beano (*pl.*
 beanos)
bean¦pole
bean¦stalk

bear (bore, borne
 or born)
bear¦able
bear¦ably
bear¦ded
bearer
bear¦gar¦den
bear¦ing
bear¦leader
Béarn
Béarn¦aise
bear's-breech
bear's-ear
bear's-foot
bear¦skin
beastings *use*
 beestings
beast¦li¦ness
beastly
 (beast¦lier,
 beast¦li¦est)
beat (as *v.*, beat,
 beaten)
beater
be¦atif¦ic
be¦atif¦ic¦ally
be¦ati¦fica¦tion
be¦atify
 (be¦ati¦fies,
 be¦ati¦fied,
 be¦ati¦fy¦ing)
beat¦ing
be¦ati¦tude
beat¦nik
beau (*pl.* beaux)
Beau¦fort scale
beau ideal
Beau¦jo¦lais
Beau¦maris
beau monde
Beaune (wine)
beaut (*sl.*)
beau¦te¦ous
beau¦ti¦cian
beau¦ti¦fi¦ca¦tion
beau¦tif¦ier
beau¦ti¦ful
beau¦ti¦fully
beau¦tify
 (beau¦ti¦fies,
 beau¦ti¦fied,
 beau¦ti¦fy¦ing)
beauty (*pl.*
 beau¦ties)
beaux arts
beaux yeux

bea'ver (*pl.*
  bea'ver *or*
  bea'vers)
Bea'ver|board
be'bop
be'bop|per
be'calm
be'cause
bec'ca|fico (*pl.*
  bec'ca|fi'cos)
béch|amel
becket
Beck|ett, S.
beckon
be'cloud
be'come
  (be'came,
  be'come,
  be'com|ing)
bec|querel (unit)
Bec|querel (man)
bed (as *v.*,
  bed'ded,
  bed'ding)
be'dabble
  (be'dab|bling)
be'daub
be'dazzle
  (be'daz'zling)
be'daz'zle|ment
bed|bug
bed|cham'ber
bed|clothes
bed|dable
bed'der
bed'ding
Bede
be'deck
bed|eguar
be|devil
  (be'dev'illed,
  be'dev'il|ling)
be'dev'il|ment
be'dew
bed|fast
bed|fel|low
Bed|ford
Bed'ford|shire
be'dim
  (be'dimmed,
  be'dim|ming)
be'dizen
bed|jacket
bed|lam
Bed'ling|ton
bed|maker

bed|ouin (*pl.*
  same)
bed|pan
bed|plate
bed|post
be|draggle
  (be'drag|gling)
bed-rest
bed'rid|den
bed|rock
bed|room
bed|side
bed-sit
bed-sitter
bed-sitting-room
bed|sock
bed|sore
bed|spread
bed|stead
bed|straw
bed|table
bed|time
Beeb (*colloq.*)
beech (tree)
  △ beach
beech-fern
beech|mast
beech|wood
beef (in sense
  'complaint', *pl.*
  beefs; in sense
  'ox', *pl.* beeves)
beef|bur'ger
beef|cake
beef|eater
beefi|ness
beef|steak
beefy (beef|ier,
  beef|iest)
bee|hive
bee-line
Be'el|ze'bub
beeper
beer|house
beer-mat
beery
beest|ings (milk)
bees|wax
bees|wing
Beet|hoven
beetle (as *v.*,
  beet|ling)
beet|root
beezer
be'fall (be'fell,
  be'fallen)

be'fit (be'fit'ted,
  be'fit|ting)
be'fog (be'fogged,
  be'fog|ging)
be'fool
be'fore
be'fore|hand
be'foul
be'friend
be'fuddle
  (be'fud|dling)
beg (begged,
  beg|ging)
be'gad
be'get (be'got *or*
  be'gat,
  be'got|ten,
  be'get|ting)
be'get|ter
beg'gar
beg'gar|li|ness
beg'garly
beg|gary
be'gin (be'gan,
  be'gun,
  be'gin|ning)
be'gin|ner
be'gin|ning
be'gird (be'girt)
be'gone
be|go'nia
be'gorra
be'grime
  (be'grim|ing)
be'grudge
  (be'grudg|ing)
be'guile
  (be'guil|ing)
be'guile|ment
be'guine
be'gun (*p.p.* of
  begin)
be'half
be'have
  (be'hav|ing)
be'ha'vi|our
be'ha'vi|oural
be'ha'vi|our|ism
be'ha'vi|our|ist
be'ha'vi|our|istic
be'head
be'head|ing
be'he'moth
be'hest
be'hind
be'hind|hand

be'hold (be'held)
be|holden
be'hoof
be'hove
  (be'hov'ing)
beige
beigel *use* bagel
Bei|jing (Peking)
be'ing
Bei|rut
be'jew'elled
bel (= 10 decibels)
be|la'bour
be|lated
be'lay
bel canto
belcher
be|lea'guer
bel es'prit (*pl.*
  beaux es'prits)
Bel|fast
bel'fry (*pl.*
  bel|fries)
Bel|gian
Bel'gic
Bel|gium
Bel|grade
Bel'gra|via
Bel'gra|vian
Be|lial
be'lie (be'ly|ing)
be'lief
be'liev|able
be|lieve
  (be'liev|ing)
be|liever
Be'li|sha (beacon)
be|little
  (be'lit|tling)
be'little|ment
Be'lize
bel'la|donna
bell|boy
belle
belle époque
belles-lettres
bel|let'rism
bel|let'rist
bel|let'ristic
bel|li|cose
bel|li|cos|ity
bel'li|ger'ence
bel'li|ger'ency
bel'li|ger'ent
bell-jar

bell|man (*pl.*
  bell|men)
bel|low
bel|lows
bell-pull
bell-push
bell-wether
belly (as *n.*, *pl.*
  bel|lies; as *v.*,
  bel|lies, bel|lied,
  bel|ly|ing)
belly|ache (as *v.*,
  belly|ach|ing)
belly-button
belly-dance
belly-flop (as *v.*,
  belly-flopped,
  belly-flopping)
belly|ful (*pl.*
  belly|fuls)
Bel|mo|pan
be|long
be|long|ings
Be|lo|rus|sia
Be|lo|rus|sian
be|loved
be|low
bel paese (cheese)
Bel|tane
be|luga
bel|ve|dere
be|mire
  (be|mir|ing)
be|moan
be|muse
  (be|mus|ing)
bencher
bench-mark
bench-warrant
bend (bent)
bender
bendy (bend|ier,
  bend|iest)
be|neath
be|ne|di|cite
  (blessing, grace)
Be|ne|di|cite
  (canticle from
  Apocrypha)
be|ne|dick
Bene|dict|ine
  (monk or nun;
  liqueur, *propr.*)
be|ne|dic|tion
be|ne|dict|ory

Be|ne|dic|tus
  (canticle, part of
  Mass)
be|ne|fac|tion
be|ne|factor
be|ne|fact|ress
be|ne|fic
be|ne|fice
be|ne|ficed
be|ne|fi|cence
be|ne|fi|cent
be|ne|fi|cial
be|ne|fi|cially
be|ne|fi|ciary (*pl.*
  be|ne|fi|ciar|ies)
be|ne|fi|cia|tion
be|ne|fit (as *v.*,
  bene|fited,
  bene|fit|ing)
Be|ne|lux
be|ne|vol|ence
be|ne|vol|ent
Ben|gal
Ben|gali
be|nighted
be|nign
be|nig|nancy
be|nig|nant
be|nig|nity
Be|nin
ben|ison
ben|ja|min
  (benzoin)
Ben|ja|min
  (youngest child)
ben|net
Ben Nevis
benni (sesame)
Ben|tham
Ben|tham|ism
Ben|tham|ite
ben|thic
ben|thos
ben|ton|ite
bent|wood
be|numb
Benz
Ben|ze|drine
  (amphetamine,
  propr.)
ben|zene
  (substance
  obtained from
  coal-tar)
ben|zen|oid

ben|zine (spirit
  obtained from
  petroleum)
ben|zoic
ben|zoin (resin of
  Jap. tree)
ben|zol (crude
  benzene)
Beo|wulf
be|queath
be|quest
be|rate
  (be|rat|ing)
Ber|ber
ber|beris
ber|ceuse
be|reave
  (be|reaved *or*
  be|reft,
  be|reav|ing)
be|reaved
  (deprived by death
  of a relation)
be|reave|ment
be|reft (robbed)
beret
ber|ga|masque
ber|ga|mot
Ber|gen
berg|schrund
ber|gylt (fish)
beri|beri
Ber|ing
  (Sea/Strait)
berk (*sl.*, fool)
Berke|leian
Berke|ley
ber|ke|lium
Berk|shire
ber|lin (carriage)
Ber|lin
Ber|liner
Ber|lioz
Ber|muda
Ber|mu|das
Ber|mu|dian
Ber|nar|dine
Berne
berry (as *n.*, *pl.*
  ber|ries; as *v.*,
  ber|ries,
  ber|ried,
  ber|ry|ing)
ber|serk
ber|tha
beryl

be|ryl|lium
be|seech
  (be|seeched *or*
  be|sought)
be|set (be|set,
  be|set|ting)
be|set|ment
be|side
be|sides
be|siege
  (be|sieging)
be|sieger
be|slaver
be|slob|ber
be|smear
be|smirch
be|som
be|sot (be|sot|ted,
  be|sot|ting)
be|spangle
  (be|spang|ling)
be|spat|ter
be|speak
  (be|spoke,
  be|spoken)
be|spec|tacled
be|sprinkle
  (be|sprink|ling)
Bes|semer
  (process)
bes|tial
bes|ti|al|ity
bes|ti|al|ize
  (bes|ti|al|iz|ing)
bes|ti|ally
bes|ti|ary (*pl.*
  bes|ti|ar|ies)
be|stir
  (be|stirred,
  be|stir|ring)
be|stow
be|stowal
be|stow|ment
be|strew (*p.p.*
  be|strewed *or*
  be|strewn)
be|stride
  (be|strode,
  be|strid|den,
  be|strid|ing)
bet (as *v.*, bet *or*
  bet|ted, bet|ting)
beta
be|take (be|took,
  be|taken,
  be|tak|ing)

be|ta|tron
betel-nut
bête noire (*pl.*
　bêtes noires)
bethel
beth|esda
be|think
　(be|thought)
Beth|le|hem
be|tide
be|times
bêt|ise
Betje|man
be|token
bet|ony (*pl.*
　bet|on|ies)
be|tray
be|trayal
be|troth
be|trothal
bet|ter (*compar.* of
　good; one who
　bets)
bet|ter|ment
bet|ting
bettor (one who
　bets) *use* better
be|tween
be|twixt
bevel (bev|elled,
　bev|el|ling)
bev|er|age
Bev|er|ley
bevy (*pl.* bev|ies)
be|wail
be|ware
be|wil|der
be|wildered
be|wil|der|ment
be|witch
bey (Turk.
　governor)
bey|lic
bey|ond
bez|ant
bezel
be|zique
be|zoar
be|zo|nian
Bhagavad-gita
Bhu|tan
bi|an|nual
　(half-yearly)
　△ biennial
bi|an|nu|ally

bias (as *v.*,
　bi|ased,
　bi|as|ing)
bi|ath|lon
bi|axial
bib-cock
bibe|lot
Bible
bib|lical
bib|lic|ally
bib|lio|grapher
bib|lio|graphic
bib|lio|graph|ical
bib|lio|graph|ic|
　　　ally
bib|lio|graph|ize
　(bib|lio|graph|iz|
　　　ing)
bib|lio|graphy (*pl.*
　bib|lio|graph|ies)
bib|lio|mancy
bib|lio|mania
bib|lio|maniac
bib|lio|phile
bib|lio|philic
bib|lio|phily
bib|lio|pole
bib|lio|poly
bibu|lous
bi|cam|eral
bi|carb
bi|car|bon|ate
bi|cen|ten|ary (*pl.*
　bi|cen|ten|ar|ies)
bi|cen|ten|nial
bi|ceph|al|ous
bi|ceps
bicker
bi|con|cave
bi|con|vex
bi|cuspid
bi|cycle (as *v.*,
　bi|cyc|ling)
bi|cyc|list
bid (as *v.*, bid *or*
　bade, bid *or*
　bid|den,
　bid|ding)
bid|dab|il|ity
bid|dable
bid|der
bid|ding
biddy (*pl.*
　bid|dies)
bide (bid|ing)
bi|det

bid|on|ville
Bie|der|meier
bi|en|nial
　(two-yearly)
　△ biannual
bi|en|ni|ally
bi|en|nium (*pl.*
　bi|en|ni|ums)
bier (frame for
　coffin)
biffin
bifid
bi|focal
bi|foc|als
bi|furc|ate
　(bi|furc|at|ing)
bi|furca|tion
big (big|ger,
　big|gest)
bi|gam|ist
bi|gam|ous
bi|gamy
big-head
big-hearted
big|horn
bight
bigot
big|oted
big|otry
big|wig
Bi|har
Bi|hari
bi|jou (*pl.* bi|joux)
bike (as *v.*,
　bik|ing)
biker
bi|kini
bi|lat|eral
bi|lat|er|al|ism
bi|lat|er|ally
bil|berry (*pl.*
　bil|ber|ries)
Bil|dungs|roman
bile-duct
bilge (as *v.*,
　bil|ging)
bil|har|zia
bil|har|ziasis
bili|ary
bi|lin|gual
bi|lin|gual|ism
bi|li|ous
bil|la|bong
bill|board

bil|let (as *v.*,
　bil|leted,
　bil|let|ing)
billet-doux (*pl.*
　billets-doux)
bill|head
bill|hook
bil|liards
bill|ing
Bil|lings|gate (in
　London)
bil|lion
bil|li|onth
bil|lon (alloy)
bil|low
bil|lowy
billy (*pl.* bil|lies)
bil|ly|can
billy-goat
billy-o
bi|lob|ate
bi|lobed
bi|manal
bi|man|ous
bim|bashi
bimbo (*pl.*
　bim|bos)
bi|met|al|lic
bi|met|al|lism
bi|met|al|list
bi|monthly (as *n.*,
　pl. bi|month|lies)
bin|ary (as *n.*, *pl.*
　bin|ar|ies)
bin|ate
bin|aural
bind (bound)
binder
bind|ery (*pl.*
　bind|er|ies)
bind|ing
bind|weed
Binet
Binet-Simon
bingo (*pl.* bin|gos)
bin|nacle
bin|ocu|lar
bi|no|mial (of two
　terms in algebra)
bi|nom|inal (of
　two names)
bio|chem|ical
bio|chem|ist
bio|chem|istry
bio|coen|o|logy

bio|coen|osis (*pl.*
 bio|coen|oses)
bio|coen|otic
bio|de|grad|ab|il|
                ity
bio|de|grad|able
bio|de|grada|tion
bio|feed|back
bio|gen|esis
bio|gen|etic
bio|genic
bio|grapher
bio|graphic
bio|graph|ical
bio|graphy (*pl.*
 bio|graph|ies)
bio|lo|gical
bio|lo|gic|ally
bio|lo|gist
bio|logy
bio|lu|min|
        es|cence
bio|lu|min|es|cent
bio|mass
bio|ma|themat|ics
bio|met|ric
bio|met|rical
bio|met|ri|cian
bio|met|rics
bio|metry
bio|morph
bio|morphic
bi|onic
bi|on|ics
bi|onom|ics
bio|phys|ical
bio|physi|cist
bio|phys|ics
bi|opsy (*pl.*
 bi|ops|ies)
bio|rhythm
bio|scope
bio|sphere
bio|syn|thesis (*pl.*
 bio|syn|theses)
bi|ota
bi|otic
bi|otin
bi|par|tisan
bi|part|ite
bi|ped
bi|pedal
bi|pin|nate
bi|plane
bi|po|lar
birchen

birch|wood
bird-bath
bird|brain
bird|brained
bird|cage
birdie
bird|lime
bird|seed
bird's-eye (plant)
bird's-foot (plant)
bird-song
bird-strike
bird-table
bird-watch
bi|refrin|gence
bi|refrin|gent
bi|reme
bi|retta
Bir|ken|head
Bir|ming|ham
Biro (*propr.*; *pl.*
 Biros)
birth|day
birth|mark
birth|place
birth|right
bis|cuit
bi|sect
bi|sec|tion
bi|sec|tor
bi|sex|ual
bi|sexu|al|ity
bishop
bish|op|ric
bisk *use* bisque
Bis|marck
bis|muth
bi|son (*pl.* same)
bisque
Bis|sau
bis|sex|tile
bi|stable
bis|tort
bis|toury (*pl.*
 bis|tour|ies)
bis|tre (pigment)
bis|tro
 (restaurant; *pl.*
 bis|tros)
bi|sul|phate
bit (as *v.*, bit|ted,
 bit|ting)
bitch|ily
bitchi|ness
bitchy (bitch|ier,
 bitchi|est)

bite (bit, bit|ten,
 bit|ing)
bit|ter
bit|ter|ling
bit|tern
bit|ters
bitter-sweet
bitts (*Naut.*)
bitty (bit|tier,
 bit|ti|est)
bitu|men
bi|tu|min|iza|tion
bi|tu|min|ize
 (bi|tu|min|iz|ing)
bi|tu|min|ous
bi|va|lency
bi|va|lent
bi|valve
biv|ouac (as *v.*,
 biv|ou|acked,
 biv|ou|ack|ing)
bivvy (*pl.*
 biv|vies)
bi-weekly (as *n.*,
 pl. bi-weeklies)
bi-yearly
bi|zarre
bi|zar|rerie
Bi|zet
blab (blabbed,
 blab|bing)
blab|ber
black|amoor
black|ball *v.*
black|berry (*pl.*
 black|ber|ries)
black|ber|ry|ing
black|bird
black|board
black|boy (tree)
black|buck
Black|burn
black|cap (bird)
black|cock
black|cur|rant
blacken
black|fish
black|fly (*pl.*
 black|flies)
black|guard
black|guardly
black|head
black|ing
black|ish
black|jack
black|lead

black|leg (as *v.*,
 black|legged,
 black|leg|ging)
black|list
black|mail
black|mailer
black-out *n.*
Black|pool
black|shirt
black|smith
black|spot
black|thorn
Black|wood
blad|der
bladed
blae|berry (*pl.*
 blae|ber|ries)
blag (as *v.*,
 blagged,
 blag|ging)
bla|*gueur*
blame (blam|ing)
blame|able
blame|ful
blame|fully
blame|less
blame|wor|thi|
              ness
blame|wor|thy
blanc|mange
blanco (as *v.*,
 blan|coes)
bland|ish
bland|ish|ment
blan|ket (as *v.*,
 blan|keted,
 blan|ket|ing)
blank|ety
blanky
blan|*quette*
blare (blar|ing)
blar|ney
blasé
blas|pheme
 (blas|phem|ing)
blas|phemer
blas|phem|ous
blas|phemy (*pl.*
 blas|phem|ies)
blas|ted
blaster
blast-furnace
blast-hole
blast-off *n.*
blas|tula (*pl.*
 blas|tu|lae)

bla|tancy
bla|tant
blather
blaze (as v.,
 blaz|ing)
blazer
blazon
blaz|on|ment
blaz|onry
bleacher
bleary (blear|ier,
 bleari|est)
bleary-eyed
bleat
bleed (bled)
bleeder
bleed|ing
blem|ish
blende (zinc
 sulphide)
blender
Blen|heim
blenny (pl.
 blen|nies)
bleph|ar|itis
bles|bok
bless (blessed or
 blest)
blessed
bles|sed|ness
bless|ing
blether use
 blather
blew|its
blighter
Blighty (=
 England)
bli|mey
blimp|ery
blimp|ish
blinder
blind|fold
blind|ing
blind-man's buff
blind-stitch
blind|worm
blinker
blink|ing
blip (as v.,
 blipped,
 blip|ping)
bliss|ful
bliss|fully
blis|ter
blith|er|ing
blithe|some

blitz|krieg
bliz|zard
bloated
bloater
bloc (grouping)
block
block|ade (as v.,
 block|ad|ing)
block|board
block-buster
block|head
block|house
Blok, A.
blond
blonde (woman)
blood-bath
blood-brother
blood-curdling
blood-donor
blood|hound
blood|ily
bloodi|ness
blood|less
blood-letting
blood-lust
blood-money
blood-poisoning
blood|shed
blood|shot
blood-stained
blood|stock
blood|stone
blood|stream
blood|sucker
blood|thirsty
blood-vessel
blood|worm
blood-wort
bloody (as a.,
 blood|ier,
 bloodi|est; as v.,
 blood|ies,
 blood|ied,
 bloody|ing)
bloody-minded
bloomer
bloomers
bloom|ing
Blooms|bury
blos|som
blos|somy
blot (as v.,
 blot|ted,
 blot|ting)

blotchy
 (blotch|ier,
 blotchi|est)
blot|ter
blotting-paper
blotto
blouse (as v.,
 blous|ing)
blouson
blow (blew,
 blown)
blow-dry
 (blow-dries,
 blow-dried)
blower
blow-fish
blow|fly (pl.
 blow|flies)
blow-hole
blow|lamp
blow-out n.
blow|pipe
blow|torch
blow-up n.
blowy (blow|ier,
 blowi|est)
blowzy
 (blowz|ier,
 blowzi|est)
blub (blubbed,
 blub|bing)
blub|ber
bludgeon
blue (as v., blues,
 blued, blue|ing)
Blue|beard
blue|bell
blue|berry (pl.
 blue|ber|ries)
blue-bird
blue|bottle
blue-collar attrib.
blue-eyed
blue|fish
blue-pencil
 (censor v.,
 blue-pencilled,
 blue-pencilling)
blue|print
blues
blue|stock|ing
blue|stone
blue|throat
blu|ish
blun|der
blun|der|buss

blunge
 (blun|ging)
blun|ger
blur (as v.,
 blurred,
 blur|ring)
blusher
blush|ful
blus|ter
blus|tery
boa
boarder
boarding-house
boarding-school
board|room
boast|ful
boast|fully
boatel use botel
boater
boat|ful (pl.
 boat|fuls)
boat-house
boat|load
boat|man (pl.
 boat|men)
boat|swain
boat-train
boat-yard
bob (as v.,
 bobbed,
 bob|bing)
bob|bin
bob|binet
bob|bish
bobble
bobby (pl.
 bob|bies)
bob|cat
bo|bo|link
bob-sled
bob-sleigh
bob|stay
bob|tail
boc|age
bode (bod|ing)
bode|ful
bo|dega
bode|ment
bodge (bodging)
Bod|hi|sat|tva
bod|ice
bodi|less
bod|ily
bod|kin
Bod|leian
 (Library)

Bod|ley
Bod|min
Bo|doni
body (as *n.*, *pl.*
 bod|ies; as *v.*,
 bod|ies, bod|ied)
body-blow
body|guard
body|line
body|work
Boe|otian
Boer
bof|fin
Bo|fors (gun)
bog (as *v.*, bogged,
 bog|ging)
bo|gey (*Golf*)
boggle
 (bog|gling)
boggy (bog|gier,
 bog|gi|est)
bo|gie (wheeled
 undercarriage)
bogle
Bo|gotá
bo|gus
bogy (evil spirit;
 pl. bo|gies)
bo|gy|man (*pl.*
 bo|gy|men)
bo|hea
Bo|he|mia
Bo|he|mian
bo|hemi|an|ism
Bohr, N.
boiler
boiler-plate
boil|ing
boiling-point
bois|ter|ous
bo|las
bole (trunk of tree,
 clay)
bol|ection
bol|ero (*pl.*
 bol|eros)
bol|ide
Bo|livia
boll (seed-vessel)
bol|lard
bollocks *use*
 ballocks
bol|ogna (sausage)
Bol|ogna
Bo|lognese
bo|lo|meter

bo|lo|met|ric
bo|lo|metry
bo|lo|ney
Bol|shevik
Bol|shev|ism
Bol|shev|ist
Bol|shie
bol|ster
bolter
bolt-hole
Bol|ton
bolus
bom|bard
bom|bard|ier
bom|bard|ment
bom|bardon
bom|bast
bom|bastic
bom|bast|ic|ally
Bom|bay
bom|baz|ine
bomb-disposal
bomber
bomb|shell
bomb-sight
bomb-site
bona fide
bona fi|des
bon|anza
bon-bon
bond|age
bon|ded
bonds|man (*pl.*
 bonds|men)
bond|stone
bone (as *v.*,
 bon|ing)
bone-dry
bone|head
bone|headed
bone|less
bone-meal
bone-oil
boner
bone-setter
bone-shaker
Bo|nete
bone-yard
bon|fire
bongo (drum; *pl.*
 bon|gos)
bongo (antelope;
 pl. same *or*
 bon|gos)
bon|homie
bon|hom|ous

Bo|ni|face
boni|ness
bon|ism
bon|ist
bo|nito (fish; *pl.*
 bo|ni|tos)
bonk|ers
bon mot (*pl.* bons
 mots*)
Bonn
bonne bouche (*pl.*
 bonnes bouches*)
bon|net
bon|neted
bon|nily
bon|ni|ness
bonny (bon|nier,
 bon|ni|est)
bon|sai
bo|nus
bon viv|ant (one
 fond of good food)
bon viv|eur (one
 who lives well)
bon voyage
bony (bo|nier,
 bo|ni|est)
bon|zer
boo|book
booby (*pl.*
 boo|bies)
boo|by|hatch
booby-trap (*v.*,
 booby-trapped,
 booby-trapping)
boodle
boogie-woogie
book|binder
book|bind|ing
book|case
book-ends
bookie
book|ing
booking-office
book|ish
book|keeper
book|keep|ing
book|let
book|maker
book|mak|ing
book|man (*pl.*
 book|men)
book|mark
book|marker
book-plate
book-post

book-rest
book|sel|ler
book|shop
book|stall
book|store
book-trough
book|work
book|worm
Boo|lean (algebra)
boomer
boom|er|ang
boom|slang
boor|ish
booster
boot|black
booted
bootee
boot-faced
boot|jack
boot|lace
Bootle
boot|leg (as *v.*,
 boot|legged,
 boot|leg|ging)
boot|leg|ger
boot|less
boot|licker
boot|straps
boot-tree
booty (plunder)
booze (as *v.*,
 booz|ing)
boozer
boozy (booz|ier,
 boozi|est)
bop|per
bora
bor|acic
bor|age
borak
bor|ate
borax
bor|azon
bor|bo|ryg|mic
bor|bo|ryg|mus
 (*pl.*
 bor|bo|rygmi)
Bor|deaux
bor|del
bor|dello (*pl.*
 bor|del|los)
bor|der
bor|der|eau (*pl.*
 bor|der|eaux)
bor|derer
bor|der|land

bor|der|line
Bor|ders (Sc. region)
bord|ure
bore (as v., bor|ing)
bor|eal
bore|dom
bore|hole
borer
Bor|ghese (Gallery)
boric
born (with ref. to birth)
borne (carried; of birth with mother's name)
borné
Bor|neo
Born|holm (disease)
Bo|ro|din
boro|fluor|ide
boron
bo|ro|nia
boro|si|lic|ate
bor|ough
bor|row
Bor|stal
bortsch
bor|zoi
bosc|age
Bosch
bos'n
Bos|nia
bosom
bos|omy
bo|son
bossa nova
boss-eyed
boss-shot
bossy (bos|sier, bos|si|est)
Bos|ton
Bos|well
Bos|wel|lian
bot (worm)
bo|tanic
bo|tan|ical
bot|an|ist
bot|an|ize (bot|an|iz|ing)
bot|any
Bot|any (wool)

bo|targo (pl. bo|tar|goes)
bo|tel
bot-fly (pl. bot-flies)
bother
both|era|tion
both|er|some
bo-tree
Bot|swana
bott (worm) use bot
bott-fly use bot-fly
Bot|ti|celli
bottle (as v., bot|tling)
bottle-neck
bot|tom
bot|tom|less
bot|tom|most
bot|tomry (as v., bot|tom|ries, bot|tom|ried)
botu|lism
bouclé
Bou|dicca
bou|doir
bouf|fant
bou|gain|vil|laea
bou|gie
bouil|la|baisse
bouil|lon
boul|der
boule (inlay) use buhl
boule (Fr. bowls)
Boule (Gr. council)
bou|le|vard
Boulez
Bou|logne
bounce (as v., boun|cing)
boun|cer
bouncy (boun|cier, boun|ci|est)
bound|ary (pl. bound|ar|ies)
bounden
bounder
bound|less
boun|teous
boun|ti|ful
boun|ti|fully
bounty (pl. boun|ties)

bou|quet
bou|quet garni
bou|quetin
bour|bon (whisky)
Bour|bon (US reactionary)
Bour|bon|nais
bour|don
bour|geois
bour|geoisie
bourn (stream, limit)
Bourne|mouth
bour|rée
bourse (money-market)
bou|stro|phe|don
bou|tique
bou|ton|nière
bou|zouki
bo|vine
bov|ver (sl.)
bowd|ler|ism
bowd|ler|iza|tion
bowd|ler|ize (bowd|ler|iz|ing)
bowel
bower
bower-bird
bow|ery (as n., pl. bow|er|ies)
bow|fin
bow-head
bowie
bow-legged
bow-legs
bowler
bowler hat
bowl|ful (pl. bowl|fuls)
bow|line
bowl|ing
bowling-alley
bowling-crease
bowling-green
bow|man (pl. bow|men)
bow|shot
bow|sprit
bow|string (as v., bow|stringed or bow|strung)
bow-tie
bow-window
bow|yer
box|calf

box|car
boxer
box|ful (pl. box|fuls)
box-haul
box|ing
Box|ing Day
box-kite
box-office
box-pleat
box-room
box-spring
box|wood
boxy (box|ier, boxi|est)
boyar
boy|cott
boy-friend
boy|hood
boy|ish
Boyle
boyo (pl. boyos)
boy|sen|berry (pl. boy|sen|ber|ries)
Bra|bant
brace (as v., bra|cing)
brace|let
bracer
bra|chial
bra|chi|ate (bra|chi|at|ing)
bra|chi|ation
bra|chi|ator
bra|chio|pod
bra|chio|saurus
bra|chis|to|chrone
bra|chy|ceph|alic
bra|chy|ceph|al|ous
bra|chy|logy (pl. bra|chy|lo|gies)
bracken
bracket (as v., brack|eted, brack|et|ing)
brack|ish
brad|awl
Brad|ford
Brad|shaw
brady|car|dia
brady|seism
brae (Sc., hillside) △ bray

brag (as v.,
 bragged,
 brag|ging)
brag|gart
brahma (fowl)
Brahma (Hindu
 god)
brah|ma|putra
 (fowl)
Brah|ma|putra
 (river)
brah|min
brah|minic
brah|min|ical
brah|min|ism
brail (to haul up)
Braille (writing for
 the blind)
brain-child (pl.
 brain-children)
brain|less
brain|power
brain|storm
brain|wash
brain|wash|ing
brain|wave
brain|work
brainy (brain|ier,
 braini|est)
braise (to cook,
 brais|ing)
 ⚠ braze
brake (as v.,
 brak|ing)
brake-block
brake-drum
brake|less
brake|man (pl.
 brake|men)
brake-shoe
brakes|man (pl.
 brakes|men)
brake-van
bramble
bram|bling
brambly
Bram|ley (apple)
bran|chia
bran|chiae
bran|chial
bran|chi|ate
branch|let
branchy
bran|dish
brand|ling
brand-new

brandy (pl.
 bran|dies)
brandy-snap
brank-ursine
 (acanthus)
bran-tub
Brase|nose
Bra|silia
brass|age
bras|sard
bras|serie
bras|sica
bras|sie (golf-club)
bras|si|ère
brass|ily
brassi|ness
brass|ware
brassy (brass|ier,
 brassi|est)
Bra|ti|slava
brat|tice
bra|vado (pl.
 bra|va|does)
brave (as v.,
 brav|ing; as a.,
 braver, bravest)
bravery
bravo (cry of
 approval; pl.
 bra|vos)
bravo (desperado;
 pl. bra|voes)
bra|vura
braw|ni|ness
brawny
 (braw|nier,
 braw|ni|est)
bray (cry of
 donkey, etc.)
 ⚠ brae
braze (to solder;
 braz|ing)
 ⚠ braise
brazen
bra|zier
braz|iery
Bra|zil
Bra|zil|ian
Brazil-nut
Brazil-wood
Braz|za|ville
breach (of law etc.,
 breaking)
 ⚠ breech
bread-bin
bread|board

bread|crumb
bread-fruit
bread|line
breadth|ways
breadth|wise
bread-winner
break (as v.,
 broke, broken)
break|able
break|age
break|away n. &
 a.
break|down n.
breaker
break|fast
break-in n.
breaking-point
break|neck
break-out n.
break|through n.
break|up n.
break|wa|ter
bream (fish; pl.
 same)
breast|bone
breast-feed
 (breast-fed)
breast-feeding
breast|plate
breast-stroke
breast|sum|mer
breast|work
breath|alyse
 (breath|alys|ing)
breath|alyser
breathe
 (breath|ing)
breather
breath|ily
breathi|ness
breath|less
breath-taking
breathy
 (breath|ier,
 breathi|est)
brec|cia
brec|ci|ate
 (brec|ci|at|ing)
Breck|nock
breech (part of
 gun; buttocks)
 ⚠ breech
breech birth
breech-block
breeches
breeches-buoy

breech-loading
breed (as v., bred)
breed|ing
breeze (as v.,
 breez|ing)
breeze-block
breeze|less
breeze|way
breez|ily
breezi|ness
breezy (breez|ier,
 breezi|est)
Bremen
brems|strahl|ung
Bren gun
brent-goose (pl.
 brent-geese)
Breton
brevet (as v.,
 brev|eted,
 brev|et|ing)
bre|vi|ary (pl.
 bre|vi|ar|ies)
brev|ity
brewer
brew|ery (pl.
 brew|er|ies)
brew|ster
Brian
Bri|ard
briar use brier
brib|able
bribe (as v.,
 brib|ing)
bribery
bric-à-brac
brick|bat
brickie
brick|layer
brick|lay|ing
brick-red
brick|work
brick|yard
bri|dal
bri|dally
bride|groom
brides|maid
bridge (as v.,
 bridging)
bridge|head
Bridge|town
bridge|work
bridle (as v.,
 brid|ling)
bridle-path
bridle-way

bri|doon
Brie (cheese)
brief|case
brief|less
brier
brier-rose
bri|ery
bri|gade (as v.,
  bri|gad|ing)
bri|gad|ier
brigadier-general
bri|ga|low
brig|and
brig|and|age
brig|an|dine
brig|and|ish
brig|and|ism
brig|andry
brig|an|tine (ship)
brighten
bright|ish
Brighton
Bright's disease
bright|work
bril|liance
bril|liancy
bril|liant
bril|liant|ine
brim (as v.,
  brimmed,
  brim|ming)
brim-full
brim|less
brim|stone
brim|stony
brindle
brindled
brine (as v.,
  brin|ing)
bring (brought)
brin|jal
brink|man|ship
briny
brio
bri|oche
bri|quette
Bris|bane
brisken
bris|ket
bris|ling (fish)
bristle (as v.,
  brist|ling)
bristle|tail (insect)
bristle|worm
bristly
Bris|tol

Brit|ain
Bri|tan|nia
Bri|tan|nic
Briti|cism
Brit|ish
Brit|isher
Briton
Brit|tany
Brit|ten
brittle
brit|tlely
britzka (open
  carriage)
broach (to pierce,
  to raise subject, a
  spit) △ brooch
broad|cast (as v.,
  broad|cast or
  broad|cas|ted,
  broad|cast)
broad|cloth
broaden
broad-leaved
broad|loom
broad|minded
Broad|moor
broad|sheet
broad|side
broad|sword
broad|tail
broad|way (broad
  road)
Broad|way (New
  York theatre life)
broad|ways
broad|wise
Brob|ding|nag
Brob|ding|na|
            gian
bro|cade (as v.,
  bro|cad|ing)
broc|coli
broch (tower)
bro|chette
bro|chure
brock (badger)
brocket
bro|derie
  ang|laise
brogue
broiler
broken-down
broken-hearted
broken-winded
broker
broker|age

brok|ing
brolly (pl.
  brol|lies)
brom|ate
bro|me|lia (plant)
bro|me|liad
bro|mic
brom|ide
brom|ine
brom|ism
bron|chia
bron|chial
bron|chi|ole
bron|chitic
bron|chitis
bron|cho|cele
bron|cho|scope
bron|chus (pl.
  bron|chi)
bronco (pl.
  bron|cos)
Brontë
bron|to|saurus
bronze (as v.,
  bronz|ing)
bronzy
brooch
  (ornamental
  fastening)
  △ broach
brooder
broodi|ness
broody
  (brood|ier,
  broodi|est)
brook|lime
brook|weed
broom|rape
broom|stick
brothel
brother (pl.
  broth|ers, in
  relig. senses also
  breth|ren)
broth|er|hood
brother-in-law
  (pl. brothers-in-
            law)
broth|er|li|ness
broth|erly
brow|beat
  (brow|beat,
  brow|beaten)
Brown|ian
brownie (goblin)

Brownie (junior
  Guide)
brown|ing
brown|ish
browse (as v.,
  brows|ing)
browser
bru|cel|losis
Bruck|ner
Brue|gel (Pieter
  the elder)
Brue|ghel (Pieter
  the younger, Jan)
Bruin (bear)
bruise (as v.,
  bruis|ing)
bruiser
brumby (pl.
  brum|bies)
Brum|ma|gem
Brum|mie
bru|mous
Bru|nei
Bru|nel
bru|net (masc.)
bru|nette (fem.)
Bruns|wick
brush|fire
brush|less
brush-off n.
brush-up n.
brush|wood
brush|work
brushy
brusque
brus|querie
Brus|sels
brut
bru|tal
bru|tal|ism
bru|tal|ity (pl.
  bru|tal|it|ies)
bru|tal|iza|tion
bru|tal|ize
  (bru|tal|iz|ing)
bru|tally
bru|tish
bry|olo|gist
bry|ology
bry|ony
bryo|phyte
bryo|zoan
bryo|zo|ology
Bry|thonic
bu|bal

bubble (as v.,
 bub|bling)
bubbly
 (bub|blier,
 bub|bli|est)
bubo (pl. bu¦boes)
bu|bonic
bu|bono|cele
buc¦cal
buc|can|eer
buc|can|eer|ish
buc|cin|ator
Bu¦cha|rest
Buch¦man|ism
Buch¦man|ite
buck|bean
buck|board
bucket (as v.,
 buck|eted,
 buck¦et|ing)
buck¦et|ful (pl.
 buck¦et|fuls)
bucket-shop
buck|eye
buck-horn
buck-hound
Buck¦ing¦ham|
        shire
buckle (as v.,
 buck|ling)
buck|ler
buck|ram
buck|shee
buck|shot
buck|skin
buck|thorn
buck-tooth
buck|wheat
bu|colic
bu¦col¦ic|ally
bud (as v.,
 bud¦ded,
 bud|ding)
Bu¦da|pest
Bud¦dha
Bud|dhism
Bud|dhist
Bud|dhistic
Bud¦dhist|ical
bud|dleia
buddy (as n., pl.
 bud¦dies; as v.,
 bud¦dies,
 bud¦died,
 bud¦dy|ing)
budge (budging)

budger|igar
budget (as v.,
 budgeted,
 budget|ing)
budget|ary
budgie
Bue¦nos Ai¦res
buf¦falo (pl.
 buf¦fa|loes)
buf¦fer
buf¦fet (as v.,
 buf¦feted,
 buf¦fet|ing)
buf¦fle|head
buffo (as n., pl.
 buf¦fos)
buf¦foon
buf¦foon|ery
buf¦foon|ish
bug (as v.,
 bugged,
 bug|ging)
bug|bear
bug¦ger
bugger-all
bug¦gery
Bug¦gins's turn
buggy (pl.
 bug|gies)
bugle (as v.,
 bu¦gling)
bugle-horn
bu¦gler
bu|gloss (plant)
buhl (inlay)
build (built)
builder
build|ing
buildup n.
built-in
built-up
Bu¦jum|bura
bulb|ous
bul¦bul (bird)
Bul¦gar
Bul¦garia
Bul¦gar|ian
bulge (as v.,
 bul¦ging)
bulgy (bul|gier,
 bul¦gi|est)
bu|li¦mia
bulk|head
bulk|ily
bulki|ness

bulky (bulk|ier,
 bul¦ki|est)
bul|lace
bul|late
bull|dog
bull|doze
 (bull|doz¦ing)
bull|dozer
bul¦let
bul|letin
bullet-proof
bull|fight
bull|fighter
bull|fight¦ing
bull|finch
bull|frog
bull|head
bull-headed
bul|lion
bull|ish
bul|lock
bull|ring
bull's-eye
bull|shit
bull-terrier
bull|trout
bully (as n., pl.
 bul|lies; as v.,
 bul|lies, bul|lied,
 bul¦ly|ing)
bully-boy
bul|rush
bul|wark
bum (as v.,
 bummed,
 bum|ming)
bumble (as v.,
 bum|bling)
bumble-bee
bum¦ble|dom
bumble-puppy
bumf
bum|malo (fish; pl.
 same)
bum|maree
bump-ball
bumper
bumph use bumf
bump|ily
bum¦pi|ness
bump|kin
bump|tious
bumpy
 (bum|pier,
 bum¦pi|est)
buna

bunchy
bunder
Bun¦des|tag
bundle (as v.,
 bund|ling)
bun¦do|bust
bun-fight
bun¦ga¦loid
bun¦ga|low
bung-hole
bungle (as v.,
 bun|gling)
bun|gler
bun¦ion
bunk-bed
bunker
bun¦kum
bunny (pl.
 bun|nies)
Bun¦sen
bun¦tal
bunt|ing
bunt|line
Buñ¦uel
bunya
buoy (float)
buoy|age
buoy|ancy (pl.
 buoy|an¦cies)
buoy|ant
bur (clinging
 seed-vessel or
 catkin) △ burr
burble
 (burb|ling)
bur¦bot
bur¦den
bur¦den|some
bur|dock
bur¦eau (pl.
 bur¦eaux)
bur¦eau|cracy (pl.
 bur¦eau|cra¦cies)
bur¦eau|crat
bur¦eau|cratic
bur¦eau|crat¦ic|
        ally
bur¦eau¦crat|ize
 (bur¦eau¦crat|iz¦
        ing)
bur|ette
bur¦gee
Bur¦gen|land
bur|geon
burger
bur¦gess

burgh (*Sc.*)
burghal
burgher
burg|lar
burg|lari|ous
burg|lary (*pl.*
 burg|lar|ies)
burgle (burg|ling)
bur|go|mas|ter
bur|gundy (*pl.*
 bur|gun|dies)
Bur|gundy
burial
burin
burka
burke (burk|ing)
Burke
bur|lap
bur|lesque (as *v.*,
 bur|lesquing)
bur|li|ness
burly (bur|lier,
 bur|li|est)
Burma
Bur|man
Burm|ese (as *n.*,
 pl. same)
burn (as *v.*,
 burned or burnt)
burner
bur|net
Burn|ham (scale)
burn|ing
burn|ish
Burn|ley
bur|nous
burr (rough edge,
 rough sounding of
 letter *r*, kind of
 limestone) △ bur
bur|ra|wang
bur|row
bursa (*pl.*
 bur|sae)
bursal
bur|sar
bur|sar|ial

bur|sar|ship
burs|ary (*pl.*
 burs|ar|ies)
burs|itis
burst (as *v.*, burst)
burst|proof
bur|ton
Bur|ton (upon
 Trent)
Bur|undi
bury (bur|ies,
 bur|ied,
 bury|ing)
Bury
Bury St
 Ed|munds
bus (as *v.*, bused,
 bus|ing)
bus|bar
busby (*pl.*
 bus|bies)
bush-baby (*pl.*
 bush-babies)
bush|buck
bushed
bushel
bush|el|ful (*pl.*
 bush|el|fuls)
bu|shido
bushi|ness
bush|ing
bush|man
 (*Austral.*; *pl.*
 bush|men)
Bush|man (*S.Afr.*;
 pl. Bush|men)
bush|mas|ter
bush|veld
bush-whacker
bushy (as *a.*,
 bush|ier,
 bushi|est; as *n.*,
 pl. bush|ies)
busily
busi|ness
busi|ness|like
busi|ness man

busker
bus|kin
bus|kined
busk|ing
bus|man (*pl.*
 bus|men)
bus-shelter
bus-stop
bus|tard
bus|tee
bus|ter
bustle (as *v.*,
 bust|ling)
bust-up *n.*
busty (bust|ier,
 busti|est)
busy (as *a.*,
 busier, busi|est;
 as *v.*, busies,
 busied, busy|ing)
busy|body (*pl.*
 busy|bod|ies)
but (as *v.*, but|ted,
 but|ting)
bu|ta|di|ene
bu|tane
but|cher
but|cherly
but|chery (*pl.*
 bu|tcher|ies)
but|ler
butt-end
but|ter
butter-bean
but|ter|bur (plant)
butter-cream
but|ter|cup
butter-fingers
but|ter|fly (*pl.*
 but|ter|flies)
but|teri|ness
but|ter|milk
but|ter|scotch
but|ter|wort
but|tery (as *n.*, *pl.*
 but|ter|ies)
but|tock

but|ton
but|ton|hole (as *v.*,
 but|ton|holing)
but|ton|hook
but|ton|less
but|tons
 (page-boy)
but|tress
butty (*pl.* but|ties)
bu|tyl
bu|tyr|ate
bu|tyric
buxom
buy (bought)
buz|zard
buzzer
buzz-word
bwana
by-blow
bye-bye
by-election
by|gone
by-lane
by-law
by|linc
by|name
by|pass
by|path
by-product
byre
by-road
By|ron
By|ronic
bys|sin|osis (*pl.*
 bys|sin|oses)
bys|sus
by|stander
by-street
byte
by|way
by|word
By|zan|tine
By|zan|tin|ism
By|zan|tin|ist
By|zan|tium

C

ca¦bal
ca¦bal¦lero (*pl.*
  ca¦bal¦leros)
cab¦a¦ret
cab¦bage
cab¦bagy
cab¦bala
cab¦bal¦ism
cab¦bal¦ist
cab¦bal¦istic
cabby (*pl.*
  cab¦bies)
ca¦ber
cabin
cab¦inet
Cab¦inet (*Polit.*)
cable (as *v.*,
  ca¦bling)
cable-car
ca¦ble¦gram
ca¦ble¦way
cab¦man (*pl.*
  cab¦men)
ca¦bo¦chon
ca¦boodle
ca¦boose
cab¦ot¦age
ca¦botin (*fem.*
  ca¦bot¦ine)
cab¦ri¦ole
cab¦ri¦olet
ca'¦canny (*pl.*
  ca'¦can¦nies)
ca¦cao (*pl.*
  ca¦caos)
cach¦alot
cache (as *v.*,
  cach¦ing)
cach¦ectic
cachet
cach¦exia
cach¦exy (*pl.*
  cach¦ex¦ies)
cach¦in¦nate
  (cach¦in¦nat¦ing)
cach¦in¦na¦tion
cach¦in¦nat¦ory
ca¦cho¦long
cachou

ca¦chu¦cha
ca¦cique
ca¦ciquism
cack-handed
cackle (cack¦ling)
ca¦co¦de¦mon
caco¦dyl
ca¦co¦dylic
caco¦epy (*pl.*
  caco¦ep¦ies)
ca¦co¦grapher
ca¦co¦graphic
ca¦co¦graph¦ical
ca¦co¦graphy
ca¦co¦logy (*pl.*
  ca¦co¦lo¦gies)
ca¦co¦mistle
ca¦co¦phon¦ous
ca¦co¦phony (*pl.*
  ca¦co¦phon¦ies)
cac¦ta¦ceous
cactal
cact¦oid
cac¦tus (*pl.* cacti)
ca¦cu¦minal
ca¦das¦tral
ca¦da¦ver
ca¦da¦veric
ca¦da¦ver¦ous
cad¦die (in golf; as
  v., cad¦died,
  cad¦dy¦ing)
cad¦dis
cad¦dish
caddy (tea-box, *pl.*
  cad¦dies)
ca¦dence
ca¦denced
ca¦dency
ca¦den¦tial
ca¦denza
ca¦det
ca¦det¦ship
cadge (cadging)
cadger
Cad¦mean
cad¦mium
cadre
ca¦du¦city

ca¦du¦cous
caecal
cae¦cil¦ian
caecitis
caecum (*pl.*
  caeca)
Caer¦nar¦fon
Caer¦philly
Cae¦sar
Cae¦sar¦ean
cae¦si¦ous
cae¦sium
caes¦ura
caes¦ural
ca¦fard
café
caf¦et¦eria
caf¦feine
caf¦tan
cage (as *v.*,
  caging)
cage-bird
cagey (ca¦gier,
  ca¦gi¦est)
ca¦gey¦ness
ca¦gily
ca¦goule
ca¦hoots
Cai¦no¦zoic
ca¦ique
cairn
cairn¦gorm
Cairo
cais¦son
ca¦jole (ca¦jol¦ing)
ca¦jole¦ment
ca¦jolery
cake (as *v.*,
  cak¦ing)
cake¦walk
Cala¦bar
cala¦bash
ca¦la¦brese
Ca¦lab¦ria
ca¦la¦man¦der
cala¦mary (*pl.*
  cala¦mar¦ies)
cal¦amine
cala¦mint

ca¦lam¦it¦ous
ca¦lam¦ity (*pl.*
  ca¦lam¦it¦ies)
ca¦lan¦dria
ca¦lash
cal¦ca¦neum (*pl.*
  cal¦ca¦nea)
cal¦care¦ous
cal¦ce¦olaria
cal¦ce¦ol¦ate
cal¦ces (*pl.* of calx)
cal¦ci¦fer¦ous
cal¦cific
cal¦ci¦fica¦tion
cal¦cify
  (cal¦ci¦fies,
  cal¦ci¦fied,
  cal¦ci¦fy¦ing)
cal¦cina¦tion
cal¦cine
  (cal¦cin¦ing)
cal¦cite
cal¦cium
calc-sinter
calc¦spar
calc-tuff
cal¦cul¦able
cal¦cu¦late
  (cal¦cu¦lat¦ing)
cal¦cu¦la¦tion
cal¦cu¦lat¦ive
cal¦cu¦lator
cal¦cu¦lous (*Med.*)
cal¦cu¦lus (*Med.*,
  pl. cal¦culi)
cal¦cu¦lus (*Math.*,
  pl. cal¦cu¦luses)
Cal¦cutta
cal¦dera
Ca¦le¦do¦nian
ca¦le¦fa¦cient
ca¦le¦fact¦ory (*pl.*
  ca¦le¦fact¦or¦ies)
cal¦en¦dar
  (almanac)
△ calender,
  colander

cal¦en|der (press)
△ calendar,
  colander
ca¦lend|ric
ca¦lend|rical
cal|ends
ca¦len|dula
cal¦en|ture
calf (pl. calves)
calf|ish
calf|skin
Cali|ban
cal¦ib|rate
  (cal¦ib|rat¦ing)
cal¦ib¦ration
cal¦ib¦rator
cal|ibre
ca¦li¦ces (pl. of
  calix)
ca|liche
cal|icle
cal|ico (pl.
  cal|icoes)
Ca¦li¦for¦nia
ca¦li¦for|nium
cali|pash
cali|pee
ca¦liph
ca¦liph|ate
ca¦lix (pl.
  ca¦li¦ces)
calla (plant)
Cal|laghan
call-box
call-boy
call-girl
cal¦li|grapher
cal¦li|graphic
cal¦li|graph|ist
cal¦li|graphy
call|ing
cal¦li|per
cal¦li|pygian
cal¦li|pyg¦ous
cal¦lis|thenic
cal¦lop
cal¦los|ity (pl.
  cal¦los|it¦ies)
cal|lous
cal|low
cal|luna
call-up n.
cal¦lus
calm¦at|ive
ca¦lo|mel
Calor (gas; propr.)

cal|oric
cal|orie
cal¦or|ific
cal¦ori|meter
ca¦lori|met¦ric
ca¦lori|metry
ca|lotte
calque
cal|trop
calu|met
ca¦lum¦ni|ate
  (ca¦lum¦ni|at¦ing)
ca¦lum¦ni|ation
ca¦lum¦ni|ator
ca¦lum¦ni|at¦ory
ca¦lum¦ni|ous
cal|umny (as n.,
  pl. cal¦um|nies;
  as v., cal¦um|nies,
  cal¦um|nied,
  cal¦um|ny|ing)
cal|va¦dos
Cal|vary
calve (calv|ing)
calves (pl. of calf)
Cal¦vin
Cal¦vin|ism
Cal¦vin|ist
Cal¦vin¦ist|ical
Cal¦vin|ize
  (Cal¦vin|iz|ing)
calx (pl. cal¦ces)
ca|lypso (pl.
  ca¦lyp|sos)
ca¦lyx (Bot. and
  Biol.; pl.
  ca|ly¦ces)
ca¦ma¦ra|derie
ca¦ma|rilla
ca¦ma|ron
cam¦ber
Cam¦ber|well
camb|ist
cam|bium
Cam¦bo|dia
Cam¦bo|dian
Cam|brian
cam|bric
Cam|bridge
Cam¦bridge|shire
camel
camel-back
cam¦el|eer
ca¦mel|lia

cam|elry (pl.
  cam¦el|ries)
camel's-hair (or
  camel-hair)
Cam¦em|bert
ca¦meo (pl.
  cam¦eos)
cam|era
cam¦era|man (pl.
  cam¦era|men)
cam¦er|lingo (pl.
  cam¦er|lingos)
Cam¦er|oon
cam¦i|knick¦ers
cam|ion
Cam|oens
camo|mile
cam¦ou|flage (as
  v., cam¦ou|
    fla¦ging)
cam|paign
cam|paigner
Cam|pa¦nia
cam|pa|nile
cam¦pano|lo¦ger
cam¦pano|lo¦gical
cam¦pano|lo¦gist
cam¦pano|logy
cam|pan|ula
cam|panu|late
camp-bed
camper
cam|phor
cam|phor|ate
  (cam¦phor|
    at¦ing)
cam|phoric
cam|pion
cam|pus
campy (cam|pier,
  cam¦pi|est)
cam|shaft
Camus
cam|wood
can (as v., 'put in
  can'; canned,
  can|ning)
can ('be able';
  could)
Ca¦naan
Can|ada
Ca|na|dian
ca|naille
ca¦nal
Ca¦na|letto
can¦al|iza|tion

can¦al|ize
  (can¦al|iz|ing)
can¦apé
ca¦nard
Ca|nar|ies
ca|nary (pl.
  ca¦nar|ies)
ca|nasta
  (card-game)
ca¦nas|ter
  (tobacco)
Can|berra
can|can
can|cel
  (can|celled,
  can¦cel|ling)
can¦cel|late (Biol.)
can¦cel|lated
  (Biol.)
can¦cel|la|tion
can¦cel|lous
can|cer
Can|cer (sign of
  Zodiac)
can|cer|ous
can|croid
can|dela
can¦de|lab|rum
  (pl. can¦de|labra)
can¦des|cence
can¦des|cent
can¦did
can¦did|acy (pl.
  can¦did|acies)
can¦did|ate
can¦di|da|ture
Can|dide
candle (as v.,
  cand|ling)
candle-light
Can¦dle|mas
can¦dle|stick
can¦dle|wick
Can|dolle
cand|our
candy (as n., pl.
  can|dies; as v.,
  can|dies,
  can|died,
  can¦dy|ing)
candy-floss
candy-stripe
candy|tuft
cane (as v.,
  can¦ing)
cane-sugar

can|ine
can|is|ter
can|ker
can|ker|ous
canna
can|na|bis
canned
can|nel
can|nel|loni n.pl.
can|nel|ure
can|ner
can|nery (pl.
 can|ner|ies)
Cannes
can|ni|bal
can|ni|bal|ism
can|nib|al|istic
can|ni|bal|ize
 (can|ni|bal|iz|
  ing)
can|ni|kin
can|nily
can|ni|ness
can|non
can|non|ade (as
 v.,
 can|non|ad|ing)
cannon-ball
cannon-fodder
can|not
can|nula (pl.
 can|nulae or
 can|nulas)
can|nu|late
 (can|nu|lat|ing)
canny (can|nier,
 can|ni|est)
ca|noe (as v.,
 ca|noed,
 ca|noe|ing)
ca|noe|ist
canon (fem.
 ca|non|ess)
ca|nonic
ca|non|ical
ca|non|ic|ally
ca|non|ic|ate
ca|non|icity
can|on|ist
can|on|iza|tion
can|on|ize
 (can|on|iz|ing)
can|onry
ca|noodle
 (ca|nood|ling)
can-opener

Ca|no|pic
can|opy (as n., pl.
 can|op|ies; as v.,
 can|op|ied,
 can|opy|ing)
ca|nor|ous
can't
can|ta|bile
Can|ta|bri|gian
can|tal (cheese)
can|ta|loup
can|tan|ker|ous
can|tata
Can|tate
can|ta|trice
can|teen
can|ter
can|ter|bury
 (stand; pl.
 can|ter|bur|ies)
Can|ter|bury
can|tha|rides
can|thus (pl.
 canthi)
cant|icle
can|ti|lena
can|ti|lever
can|til|late
 (can|til|lat|ing)
can|til|la|tion
cantle
canto (pl. can|tos)
can|ton
Can|ton
can|tonal
Can|ton|ese
can|ton|ment
can|tor
Can|tor
can|tor|ial
can|toris
cant|rail
can|vas (cloth)
can|vass (solicit
 votes)
can|vasser
can|yon
caout|chouc
cap (as v., capped,
 cap|ping)
cap|ab|il|ity (pl.
 cap|ab|il|it|ies)
cap|able
cap|ably
ca|pa|cious
ca|pa|cit|ance

ca|pa|cit|ate
 (ca|pa|cit|at|ing)
ca|pa|cit|at|ive
ca|pa|cit|ive
ca|pa|citor
ca|pa|city (pl.
 ca|pa|cit|ies)
ca|par|ison
cape
Cape (of Good
 Hope)
cape|lin
cape|skin
Cape Verde
cap|ful (pl.
 cap|fuls)
cap|ias (Law)
ca|pil|lar|ity
ca|pil|lary (pl.
 ca|pil|lar|ies)
cap|ital
cap|it|al|ism
cap|it|al|ist
ca|pit|al|istic
ca|pit|al|ist|ic|ally
cap|it|al|iza|tion
cap|it|al|ize
 (cap|it|al|iz|ing)
cap|it|ally
cap|ita|tion
Cap|itol
Ca|pi|tol|ine
 (Museum)
ca|pit|ular
ca|pit|ulary (pl.
 cap|it|ular|ies)
ca|pit|ulate
 (ca|pit|ulat|ing)
ca|pit|ula|tion
ca|pit|ulum (pl.
 ca|pit|ula)
capo (pl. ca|pos)
ca|pon
ca|pon|ier
ca|pon|ize
 (ca|pon|iz|ing)
ca|pot (ca|pot|ted,
 ca|pot|ting)
ca|pote
cap|pucci|no (pl.
 cap|pucci|nos)
Capri
cap|ric (Chem.)

ca|pric|cio (pl.
 ca|pric|cios)
ca|price
ca|pri|cious
Cap|ri|corn (or
 Cap|ri|cornus)
cap|rine
cap|ri|ole
 (cap|ri|oled,
 cap|ri|ol|ing)
cap|roic (Chem.)
Cap|sian
cap|sicum
capsid
cap|sizal
cap|size
 (cap|siz|ing)
cap|stan
cap|stone
cap|su|lar
cap|sule
cap|sul|ize
 (cap|sul|iz|ing)
cap|tain
cap|taincy (pl.
 cap|tain|cies)
captain-general
cap|tain|ship
cap|tion
cap|tious
cap|tiv|ate
 (cap|tiv|at|ing)
cap|tiva|tion
cap|tive
cap|tiv|ity
captor
cap|ture (as v.,
 cap|tur|ing)
ca|pu|chin (of
 monkey or pigeon)
Ca|pu|chin
 (Franciscan)
ca|ra|bin|eer
ca|ra|bin|iere
 (It. soldier, pl.
 ca|ra|bin|ieri)
ca|ra|cal (lynx)
Ca|ra|cas
ca|ra|cole
 (ca|ra|col|ing)
ca|rafe
cara|mel
cara|mel|ize
 (cara|mel|iz|ing)
cara|pace
carat

Ca'ra|vag'gio
cara|van
 (cara'vanned,
 cara'van|ning)
ca'ra'van|serai
cara|vel
ca'ra|way
car'ba|mate
carb|ide
car|bine
car'bo|hyd'rate
car|bolic
car|bon
car'bona|ceous
car'bon|ade
car'bon'ado (pl.
 car'bon|ados)
car'bon|ate (as v.,
 car'bon|at'ing)
car|bonic
car'bon|if'er|ous
Car'bon|if'er|ous
 (Geol.)
car'bon|iza|tion
car'bon|ize
 (car'bon|iz|ing)
Car'bor|un'dum
 (propr.)
carb|oxyl
carb|oxylic
car|boy
car|buncle
car'bun|cu'lar
car|bura|tion
car|buret
 (car'bur|et|ted,
 car'bur'et|ting)
car'bur|et'tor
car'ca|jou
car|cass
car'ci|no|gen
carci|no|genic
car'ci|no|gen|ic
 ally
car'cin|oma (pl.
 car'cin|omata)
car'da|mom
car'dan
card|board
card-game
car|diac
Car|diff
car'di|gan
Car'di|gan
car|dinal
car'din'al|ate

car'din|ally
car'din'al|ship
card-index
car'dio|gram
car'dio|graph
car'dio|grapher
car'dio|graphy
car'di|ology
cardio-vascular
car|doon
card-sharp
card-sharper
card-table
care (as v.,
 car'ing)
ca'reen
ca'reen|age
ca'reer
ca'reer|ist
care|free
care|ful
care|fully
care|less
caress
care|taker
caret (omission
 mark)
care|worn
car'fax
cargo (pl.
 car|goes)
Carib
Ca'rib|bean
ca'ri|bou (pl.
 same)
ca'ri|ca|tural
ca'ri|ca|ture (as v.,
 ca'ri|ca|tur'ing)
ca'ri|ca|tur'ist
car|ies
ca'ril|lon
ca'rina (Biol.)
ca|rinal
car'in|ate
Car'in|thia
ca'ri|oca
cario|genic
ca'ri|ous
Car|ley (raft)
car|line
Car|lisle
car|load
Car|low
car|man (pl.
 car|men)
Car'mar|then

Car'mel|ite
car'min'at|ive
car|mine
Car|naby Street
carn|age
car|nal
car'nal|ity
car'nal|ize
 (car'nal|iz|ing)
car|nally
car'nas|sial
car'na|tion
car|nauba
car|net
car'ni|val
Car'ni|vora
car'ni|vore
car'ni|vor|ous
carny (as v.,
 car|nies,
 car|nied,
 car'ny|ing)
carob
carol (as v.,
 ca'rolled,
 car'ol|ling)
Carol
Ca'ro|lean
Caro|lina
Car'ol|ine
Ca'ro|lin|gian
car'ot|ene
ca'rot'en|oid
ca|rotid
ca|rouse (as v.,
 ca'rous|ing)
ca'rou|sel
carpal a. (Anat.)
car-park
Car'pa|thian
 (Mts.)
car'pel n. (Bot.)
car'pel|lary
car|pen'ter
car'pen|try
car'pet (as v.,
 car|peted,
 car'pet|ing)
carpet-bag
carpet-bagger
car'pho|logy
 (delirious
 fumbling)
car'po|logy (study
 of fruits)
car|port

carpus (pl. carpi)
car|rack
car'ra|geen
Car'ran|tuo'hill
car|rel
car|riage
car'riage|way
Car|rick (on
 Shannon)
car|rick bend
 (Naut.)
car|rier
carrier-bag
car'ri|ole
car|rion
car'ron|ade
car|rot
car|roty
carry (as v.,
 car|ries,
 car|ried,
 car'ry|ing; as n.,
 pl. car|ries)
carry-all n.
carrying-on (pl.
 carryings-on)
carry-on n.
car|sick
cart|age
carte blanche
car|tel
car'tel|iza|tion
car'tel|ize
 (car'tel|iz|ing)
carter
Car'tes|ian
Car'tes|ian|ism
cart|ful (pl.
 cart|fuls)
Car'tha|gin|ian
cart-horse
Car'thu'sian
car'til|age
car'ti|la|gin|oid
car'ti|la|gin|ous
cart-load
car'to|gram
car'to|grapher
car'to|graphic
car'to|graph|ical
car'to|graph|
 ically
car'to|graphy
car'to|mancy
car'ton
car|toon

car|toon|ist
car|touche
cart|ridge
car|tu|lary (*pl.*
 car|tu|lar|ies)
cart-wheel
cart-wright
car|uncle
carve (carv|ing)
carver
carve-up *n.*
ca|ry|atid
ca|ry|op|sis (*pl.*
 ca|ry|op|ses)
Ca|sa|blanca
Ca|sa|nova
casbah *use*
 kasbah
cas|cade (as *v.*,
 cas|cad|ing)
cas|cara
case (as *v.*,
 cas|ing)
case-book
case-bound
case-harden
ca|sein
case-law
case|mate
case|ment
ca|se|ous
case-study (*pl.*
 case-studies)
case|work
case|worker
cash-book
cashew
cashew-nut
cash|ier
cash|mere
cas|ing
ca|sino (*pl.*
 ca|si|nos)
cas|ket
Cas|lon
Cas|pian (Sea)
Cas|san|dra
cas|sata
cas|sa|tion
 (annulment)
Cas|sa|tion (Court
 of)
cas|sava
cas|ser|ole (as *v.*,
 cas|ser|ol|ing)
cas|sette

cas|sia
cas|sis
cas|sit|er|ite
cas|sock
cas|socked
cas|sou|let
cas|so|wary (*pl.*
 cas|so|war|ies)
cast (as *v.*, cast)
Cas|ta|lian
cas|ta|net
cast|away
caste
caste|ism
cas|tel|lan
cas|tel|lated
cas|tel|la|tion
Castelnuovo-
   Tedesco
caster (one who
 casts) △ castor
cas|tig|ate
 (cas|tig|at|ing)
cas|tiga|tion
cas|tig|ator
cas|tig|at|ory
Cas|tile
Cas|til|ian
cast iron *n.*
cast-iron *a.*
Castle|bar
castle (as *v.*,
 cast|ling)
Castle|reagh
cast-net
castor (perforated
 jar; wheel; oil;
 substance; hat)
 △ caster
cas|trate
 (cas|trat|ing)
cas|tra|tion
cas|trat|ive
cas|trato (*pl.*
 cas|trati)
Cas|tries
Cas|tro
Cas|tro|ism
cas|ual
casu|ally
casu|alty (*pl.*
 casu|al|ties)
ca|su|ar|ina
ca|su|ist
ca|su|istic
ca|su|ist|ical
ca|su|istry

casus belli
cat (*Naut.*; as *v.*,
 cat|ted, cat|ting)
cata|bolic
cata|bol|ic|ally
cata|bol|ism
cata|chre|sis (*pl.*
 cata|chre|ses)
cata|chrestic
cata|chrest|ical
cata|clasis (*pl.*
 cata|clases)
cata|clasm
cata|clastic
cata|clysm
cata|clys|mal
cata|clys|mic
cata|comb
cata|drom|ous
cata|falque
Ca|ta|lan
cata|lase
cata|lectic
cata|lepsy (*pl.*
 cata|lep|sies)
cata|leptic
cata|logue (as *v.*,
 cata|logued,
 cata|loguing)
cata|loguer
Ca|ta|lo|nia
ca|talpa
cata|lyse
 (cata|lys|ing)
cata|lysis (*pl.*
 cata|lyses)
cata|lyst
cata|lytic
cata|ma|ran
cata|mite
cat|amoun|tain
cat|ananche
cat-and-dog
cata|plectic
cata|plexy (*pl.*
 cata|plex|ies)
cata|pult
cat|ar|act
ca|tarrh
ca|tar|rhal
ca|tar|rhine
cata|strophe
cata|strophic
cata|stroph|ic|
           ally
cata|stroph|ism

cata|stroph|ist
cata|to|nia
cata|tonic
ca|tawba
cat|bird
cat|boat
cat|call
catch (as *v.*,
 caught)
catch-all
catcher
catch|fly (*pl.*
 catch|flies)
catch|ing
catch|ment
catch|penny (*pl.*
 catch|pen|nies)
catch-phrase
catch-points
catch-pole
catch-22
catch-weight
catch|word
catchy (catch|ier,
 catch|iest)
cat-door
cat|ech|etic
cat|ech|et|ical
cat|ech|et|ic|ally
cat|ech|ism
cat|ech|is|mal
cat|ech|ist
cat|ech|ize
 (cat|ech|iz|ing)
cat|ech|izer
cat|echu
cat|echu|men
cat|egor|ial
cat|egor|ical
cat|egor|ic|ally
cat|egor|ize
 (cat|egor|izing)
cat|egory (*pl.*
 cat|egor|ies)
ca|tena (*pl.*
 ca|tenae)
ca|ten|ary (*pl.*
 ca|ten|ar|ies)
cat|en|ate
 (cat|en|at|ing)
cat|ena|tion
ca|ter
cat|eran
caterer
cat|er|pil|lar
 (larva)

Cat|er|pil|lar
(vehicle; *propr.*)
cat|er|waul
cat|fish
cat|gut
Cathar (*pl.*
Cath|ars *or*
Cath|ari)
Cath|ar|ism
Cath|ar|ist
cath|ar|sis (*pl.*
cath|ar|ses)
cath|artic
Ca|thay
cat|head
cath|ec|tic
ca|thed|ral
Cath|er|ine
Cath|er|ine wheel
cath|eter
cath|et|er|ize
(cath|et|er|iz|ing)
ca|the|to|meter
cath|exis (*pl.*
cath|exes)
cath|odal
cath|ode
cathode-ray tube
cath|odic
cath|olic
(universal etc.)
Cath|olic (in relig.
senses)
cath|ol|ic|ally
cath|oli|cism
cath|oli|city
cath|oli|cize
(cath|oli|ciz|ing)
cath|ol|icon
cat-ice
Ca|ti|lin|ar|ian
Cati|line
cat|ion
cat|ionic
cat|kin
cat-lap
cat|lick
cat|like
cat|mint
cat|nap (as *v.*,
cat|napped,
cat|nap|ping)
cat|nip
cat-o'-nine-tails
cat|opt|ric
cat's-cradle

cat's-eye (precious
stone)
Cat's-eye (on road;
propr.)
cat's-foot
cat's-meat
cat's-paw
cat's-tail
cat|suit
cat|tery (*pl.*
cat|ter|ies)
cat|tily
cat|ti|ness
cat|tish
cattle
cattle-cake
cattle-grid
cat|tleya
catty (cat|tier,
cat|ti|est)
Ca|tul|lus
cat|walk
Cau|ca|sian
Cau|casus
cau|cus
caudal
caud|ally
caud|ate
cau|dillo (*pl.*
cau|dil|los)
caul
caul|dron
cau|li|flower
caulk
caulker
causal
caus|al|ity
caus|ally
causa|tion
caus|at|ive
cause (caus|ing)
cause cé|lèbre (*pl.*
causes cé|lèbres)
causer
caus|erie
cause|way
caus|tic
caus|tic|ally
caus|ti|city
caus|ti|cize
(caus|ti|ciz|ing)
caut|er|iza|tion
caut|er|ize
(caut|er|iz|ing)
caut|ery (*pl.*
caut|er|ies)

cau|tion
cau|tion|ary
cau|tious
Ca|vafy
ca|val|cade
ca|va|lier
Ca|va|lier (*hist.*)
cav|alry (*pl.*
cav|al|ries)
cav|al|ry|man (*pl.*
cav|al|ry|men)
Cavan
ca|va|tina
cave (as *v.*,
cav|ing)
cav|eat
cav|eat emptor
cave|man (*pl.*
cave|men)
cav|en|dish
caver
cav|ern
cav|erned
cav|ern|ous
cav|es|son
ca|vetto (*pl.*
ca|vetti)
cavi|are
cavil (cav|illed,
cav|il|ling)
cav|il|ler
ca|vit|a|tion
cav|ity (*pl.*
cav|it|ies)
ca|vort
cavy (*pl.* ca|vies)
cay|enne
cay|man
(alligator)
Cay|man (Islands)
ce|an|othus
cease (ceas|ing)
cease-fire
cease|less
ce|city
ce|dar
ce|darn
cede (ced|ing)
ce|dilla
Cee|fax (*propr.*)
cei|lidh
ceil|ing
ce|la|don
cel|an|dine
Cel|ebes
ce|leb|rant

cel|eb|rate
(cel|eb|rat|ing)
cel|eb|ra|tion
cel|eb|rator
cel|eb|rat|ory
ce|leb|rity (*pl.*
ce|leb|rities)
ce|leriac
ce|ler|ity
cel|ery
cel|esta
cel|este
ce|les|tial
ce|les|ti|ally
cel|ib|acy
cel|ib|ate
cel|lar
cel|lar|age
cel|larer
cel|laret
cell|ist
cello (*pl.* cel|los)
Cel|lo|phane
(wrapping; *propr.*)
cel|lu|lar
cel|lu|lar|ity
cel|lu|late
cel|lu|la|tion
cel|lule
cel|lu|litis
cel|lu|loid
cel|lu|lose (as *v.*,
cel|lu|los|ing)
cel|lu|losic
cel|lu|lous
Cel|sius
celt (*Archaeol.*)
Celt (people)
Celtic
Cel|ti|cism
cem|balo (*pl.*
cem|ba|los)
ce|ment
ce|menta|tion
cement-mixer
cem|et|ery (*pl.*
cem|et|er|ies)
ceno|taph
ce|note
cense (cens|ing)
cen|ser (vessel)
cen|sor (of films
etc.)
cen|sor|ial
cen|sori|ally
cen|sori|ous

cen|sor|ship
cen|sur|able
cen|sure (as *v.*,
 cen|sur|ing)
cen|sus
cent (US coin)
cen|tal
cen|taur
cen|taury (plant;
 pl. cen|taur|ies)
cen|ten|ar|ian
cen|ten|ary (*pl.*
 cen|ten|ar|ies)
cent|en|nial
cen|tes|imal
cen|tes|im|ally
cen|ti|grade
cen|ti|gram
cen|ti|litre
cent|ime
cen|ti|metre
cen|ti|pede
cento (*pl.* cen|tos)
Cento (Central
 Treaty
 Organization)
cent|ral
Cent|ral (Sc.
 region)
Cent|ra|lia
cent|ral|ism
cent|ral|ist
cent|ral|ity
cent|ral|iza|tion
cent|ral|ize
 (cent|ral|iz|ing)
cent|rally
centre (as *v.*,
 cent|ring)
centre|board
centre-fold
centre-forward
centre-half
centre|most
centre-piece
cent|ric
cent|rical
cent|ri|city
cen|tri|fu|gal
cent|ri|fu|gally
cent|ri|fu|ga|tion
cent|ri|fuge (as *v.*,
 cent|ri|fu|ging)
cent|ri|petal
cent|ri|pet|ally
cent|rism

cent|rist
cent|uple (as *v.*,
 cent|up|ling)
cen|tur|ion
cen|tury (*pl.*
 cen|tur|ies)
cep (mushroom)
ceph|alic
ceph|alo|pod
ce|ph|alo|thorax
ce|pheid
ce|ramic
cer|am|ist
ce|ras|tes
ce|rast|ium
Cer|berus
cer|eal
ce|re|bel|lar
ce|re|bel|lum (*pl.*
 ce|re|bella)
ce|reb|ral
ce|reb|rally
cer|eb|rate
 (cer|eb|rat|ing)
ce|reb|ra|tion
cerebro-spinal
cerebro-vascular
cer|eb|rum (*pl.*
 ce|rebra)
cere|cloth
cere|ments
ce|re|mo|nial
ce|re|mo|ni|al|ism
ce|re|mo|ni|al|ist
ce|re|mo|ni|ally
ce|re|mo|ni|ous
ce|re|mony (*pl.*
 ce|re|mon|ies)
cer|esin
ce|rise
cerium
cer|met
cero|graphy
cero|plastic
cer|tain
cer|tainty (*pl.*
 cer|tain|ties)
cer|ti|fi|able
cer|ti|fi|ably
cer|ti|fic|ate (as *v.*,
 cer|ti|fic|at|ing)
cer|ti|fica|tion
cer|tify
 (cer|ti|fies,
 cer|ti|fied,
 cer|ti|fy|ing)

cer|*ti*|*or*|*ari*
cer|ti|tude
ce|ru|lean
ce|ru|men
cer|use
Cer|van|tes
cer|velat
cer|vical
cer|vine
cer|vix (*pl.*
 cer|vi|ces)
ces|sa|tion
cesser
ces|sion
ces|sion|ary (*pl.*
 ces|sion|ar|ies)
cess|pit
cess|pool
cest|ode
cest|oid
ce|ta|cean
ce|ta|ceous
cet|ane
cet|er|ach
ce|*teris par*|*ibus*
Cey|lon
Cey|lon|ese
Céz|anne
Chab|lis
cha-cha
 (*or* cha-cha-cha)
cha|conne
chae|to|gnath
chae|to|pod
chafe (as *v.*,
 chaf|ing)
chafer
chaff
chaf|fer
chaf|ferer
chaf|finch
chaff|iness
chaffy
chafing-dish
Chag|all
Cha|gas' (*or*
 Cha|gas's)
dis|ease
chag|rin
chain-gang
chain-gear
chain|less
chain-mail
chain-saw
chain-smoker
chain-stitch

chair|lady (*pl.*
 chair|la|dies)
chair-lift
chair|man (*pl.*
 chair|men)
chair|man|ship
chair|per|son
chair|woman (*pl.*
 chair|women)
chaise
chaise longue (*pl.*
 chaises longues)
cha|laza (*pl.*
 cha|lazae)
chal|ced|ony (*pl.*
 chal|ced|on|ies)
chal|cent|eric
chal|cent|er|ous
chal|co|lithic
chal|co|pyr|ite
Chal|dean
Chal|dee
chal|dron
cha|let
Cha|li|apin
chal|ice (goblet)
chalki|ness
chalk-stone
chalky (chalk|ier,
 chalki|est)
chal|lenge (as *v.*,
 chal|len|ging)
chal|lenge|able
chal|len|ger
chal|lis (cloth)
cha|lyb|eate
cham|ae|phyte
cham|ber
cham|ber|lain
cham|ber|maid
chamber-pot
Cham|ber|tin
cham|bray
chambré
cha|meleon
cha|mele|onic
cham|fer
cham|ois
cham|pagne
 (wine)
Cham|pagne
cham|paign (open
 country)
cham|per|tous
cham|perty (*pl.*
 cham|per|ties)

cham|pion
cham'pi|on|ship
champ|levé
Champs-Élysées
chance (as *v.*,
  chan'cing)
chan|cel
chan'cel|lery (*pl.*
  chan'cel|ler'ies)
chan'cel|lor
chan'cery (*pl.*
  chan'cer|ies)
chan'cily
chan'ci|ness
chan|cre
chan|croid
chancy (chancier,
  chanci|est)
chan|de'lier
Chan'di|garh
chand|ler
chand|lery
change (as *v.*,
  chan'ging)
change|ab'il|ity
change|able
change|ably
change|ful
change|less
change|ling
change-over *n.*
chan|nel (as *v.*,
  chan'nelled,
  chan'nel|ling)
Cha'nnel (English
  Channel)
chan'nel|ize
  (chan'nel|iz|ing)
chanter
chan'ter|elle
chant|euse
chan'ti|cleer
Chan|tilly
chantry (*pl.*
  chant|ries)
chaos
cha|otic
cha'ot'ic|ally
chap (as *v.*,
  chapped,
  chap|ping)
cha'par|ral
cha|patti (*pl.*
  cha|pat'tis)
chap-book
chapel
chap'elry (*pl.*
  chap'el|ries)

chap|eron
chap|er'on|age
chap|lain
chap|laincy (*pl.*
  chap'lain|cies)
chap|let
chap|ter
char (as *v.*,
  charred,
  char|ring)
cha'ra|banc
char|ac'ter
char'ac'ter|istic
char'ac'ter|ist|
      ic'ally
char'ac'ter|iza|
      tion
char'ac'ter|ize
  (char'ac'ter|iz|
      ing)
char'ac'ter|less
char'ac'ter'o|logy
cha'rade
charas
char|coal
charge (as *v.*,
  char'ging)
charge|able
chargé d'affaires
  (*pl.* chargés
  d'affaires)
char'ger
char'ily
chari|ness
cha|riot
cha'ri'ot|eer
cha'risma (*pl.*
  cha'ris|mata)
cha'ris|matic
cha'ris|mat'ic|ally
char'it|able
char'it|ably
char'ity (*pl.*
  char'it|ies)
cha'ri|vari
char|lady (*pl.*
  char|la'dies)
char|latan
char|lat'an|ism
char|lat'anry
Charles
Charles's Wain
Charles|ton
char|lie
char|lock
char|lotte

char|lotte russe
charmer
charm|euse
charm|ing
charm|less
charnel-house
Char'ol|lais
Charon
char|poy
char'ter
Chart|ism
Chart|ist
char|treuse
char|wo'man (*pl.*
  char|wo'men)
chary (charier,
  chari|est)
Cha'ryb|dis
chase (as *v.*,
  chas|ing)
chaser
chasm
chasse (liqueur)
chassé (step)
chas|sis
chaste
chasten
chas|tise
  (chas|tising)
chas|tise|ment
chast|ity
chas|uble
chat (as *v.*,
  chat'ted,
  chat|ting)
chat|eau (*pl.*
  chat|eaux)
chat|tel
chat|ter
chat'ter|box
chat|tily
chat'ti|ness
chatty (chat'tier,
  chat'ti|est)
Chau|cer
Chau|cer'ian
chaud-froid
chauf|feur (*fem.*
  chauf|feuse)
chaul|moo'gra
chau'vin|ism
chau'vin|ist
chau'vin|istic
chau'vin|ist'ic|
      ally
cheapen

chcap|ish
cheap|jack
checker
check'er|berry
  (*pl.* check'er|
      ber'ries)
check'er|man (*pl.*
  check'er|men)
check-in *n.*
check-list
check|mate (as *v.*,
  check|mat|ing)
check-out *n.*
check-point
check|room
check-up *n.*
check|weigh|man
  (*pl.* check|weigh|
      men)
Ched|dar
cheek-bone
cheek|ily
chee'ki|ness
cheeky
  (chee'kier,
  chee'ki|est)
cheer|ful
cheer|fully
cheer|ily
cheeri|ness
cheer|ing
cheerio
cheer-leader
cheer|less
cheerly
cheery (cheer|ier,
  cheeri|est)
cheese (as *v.*,
  chees|ing)
cheese|board
cheese|bur'ger
cheese|cake
cheese|cloth
cheese-head
cheesi|ness
cheese-mite
cheese|mon'ger
cheese-paring
cheese|wood
cheesy (cheesier,
  cheesi|est)
chee|tah
chef
chef-d'œuvre (*pl.*
  chefs-d'œuvre)
Chek|hov

chela ('novice', *pl.*
  che|las; 'claw', *pl.*
  che|lae)
che|late (as *v.*,
  che|lat|ing)
che|la|tion
Chel|lean
Chelms|ford
Chel|sea
Chel|ten|ham
Chel|to|nian
chem|ical
chem|ic|ally
chemi|lu|min|
        es|cence
chemi|lu|min|
        es|cent
chemin de fer
che|mise
chemi|sorp|tion
chem|ist
chem|istry
chemo|syn|thesis
chemo|ther|apy
che|nille
che|ong|sam
cheque
cheque-book
chequer
Che|quers
Cher|en|kov
  ra|di|ation
cher|ish
cher|no|zem
Che|ro|kee
che|root
cherry (*pl.*
  cher|ries)
cherry-wood
cher|son|ese
chert
cherub (*pl.*
  cher|ubs, *Heb. pl.*
  cher|ubim)
cher|ubic
cher|vil (herb)
Chesh|ire
chess|board
ches|sel
chess-man (*pl.*
  chess-men)
Ches|ter
ches|ter|field
chest|ily
chesti|ness
chest|nut

chesty (ches|tier,
  ches|ti|est)
chet|nik
cheval-glass
che|va|lier
che|vet
chev|iot (wool)
Chev|iot (sheep)
chev|ron
chev|ro|tain
chewi|ness
chewing-gum
chewy (chew|ier,
  chewi|est)
Cheyne-Stokes
chez
chi (Gr. letter)
Chi|ang Kai-shek
Chi|anti
chiaro|scuro (*pl.*
  chiaro|scuros)
chi|as|mus
chi|astic
chi|bouk
chic (chic-er,
  chic-est)
Chi|cago
chi|cane (as *v.*,
  chi|can|ing)
chi|canery
Chi|ches|ter
chi|chi
chicken
chicken-feed
chicken-pox
chicken-wire
chick|ling
chick-pea
chick|weed
chicle
chic|ory
chide (chid|ing;
  past chided or
  chid; *p.p.* chided
  or chid|den)
chief|dom
chief|tain
chiff-chaff
chif|fon
chif|fon|ier
chig|ger
chi|gnon
chi|goe
chi|hua|hua
chil|blain

child (*pl.*
  chil|dren)
child|bed
child|birth
child|hood
child|ish
child|less
child|like
child-minder
child-proof
chil|dren (*pl.* of
  child)
Chile
Chi|lean
chil|iad
chili|asm
chili|ast
chi|li|astic
chilli (*pl.* chil|lies)
chil|li|ness
chill|some
chilly (chil|lier,
  chil|liest)
Chil|tern
  Hun|dreds
Chim|bor|azo
chime (as *v.*,
  chim|ing)
chi|mera
  (monster)
chi|mere (robe)
chi|mer|ical
chim|ney
chimney-breast
chimney-piece
chimney-pot
chimney-stack
chimney-sweep
chim|pan|zee
china
China
chi|na|graph
Chi|na|man (*pl.*
  Chi|na|men)
Chi|na|town
chi|na|ware
chin|cher|in|chee
chin|chilla
chin-chin
Chin|dit
chine (as *v.*,
  chin|ing)
chiné (mottled)
Chi|nese (as *n.*, *pl.*
  same)
chin|less

chi|nois|erie
chi|nook
chintz
chintzi|ness
chintzy
  (chintz|ier,
  chintz|iest)
chin-wag (as *v.*,
  chin-wagged,
  chin-wagging)
chi|ono|doxa
chip (as *v.*,
  chipped,
  chip|ping)
chip|board
chip|munk
chi|po|lata
Chip|pen|dale
chip|pi|ness
chip|ping
chippy (as *n.*, *pl.*
  chip|pies)
chiral
chir|al|ity
chi-rho
chiro|graphy
chiro|mancy
chi|ro|pod|ist
chi|ro|pody
chiro|practic
chiro|practor
chir|op|teran
chir|opter|ous
chirp|ily
chirpi|ness
chirpy (chir|pier,
  chir|pi|est)
chirr
chir|rup (as *v.*,
  chir|ruped,
  chir|rup|ing)
chisel (as *v.*,
  chis|elled,
  chis|el|ling)
chis|el|ler
chi-square
chi|tal
chit-chat (as *v.*,
  chit-chatted,
  chit-chatting)
chi|tin
chi|tin|ous
chiton
chit|ter|lings
chiv|al|ric
chiv|al|rous

chiv|alry
chiv (chivved,
  chiv|ving)
chivvy (chiv|vies,
  chiv|vied,
  chiv|vy|ing)
chla|my|do|
     mo|nas
chloral
chlor|am|pheni|
     col
chlor|ate
chlor|ella
chloric
chlor|ide
chlor|in|ate
  (chlor|in|at|ing)
chlor|ina|tion
chlor|ine
chlor|ite
chlo|ro|form
Chloro|my|cetin
  (propr.)
chloro|phyll
chloro|plast
chlor|osis (pl.
  chlor|oses)
chlor|otic
chlor|ous
chlor|pro|maz|ine
choc-ice
chock-a-block
chocker
chock-full
choc|olate
chocolate-box
Choc|taw
choir
choir|boy
choir|mas|ter
choke (as v.,
  chok|ing)
choke|berry (pl.
  choke|ber|ries)
choke-damp
choker
chok|ily
choki|ness
choko (pl.
  chokos)
choky (as a.,
  chok|ier,
  choki|est)
chol|an|gi|
     ography

chole|cys|to|
     graphy
chol|era
chol|er|aic
chol|eric
cho|ler|ic|ally
cho|les|terol
choli (bodice)
cho|li|amb
cho|li|ambic
cho|line
chon|drite
choose (chose,
  chosen,
  choos|ing)
chooser
choos|ily
choosi|ness
choosy
  (choos|ier,
  choosi|est)
chop (as v.,
  chopped,
  chop|ping)
chop-chop
Chopin
chop|per
chop|pily
choppi|ness
choppy
  (chop|pier,
  chop|pi|est)
chop|stick
chop-suey
choral a.
chor|ale n.
chor|ally
chord (Mus. etc.)
  △ cord
chordal
chord|ate
cho|rea
cho|reo|graph
cho|reo|grapher
cho|reo|graphic
cho|reo|graph|ic|
     ally
cho|reo|graphy
cho|ri|am|bic
cho|ri|am|bus (pl.
  cho|ri|ambi)
choric
chor|ion
chor|is|ter
cho|ro|grapher
cho|ro|graphic

cho|ro|graph|ic|
     ally
cho|ro|graphy
chor|oid
choro|lo|gical
choro|lo|gic|ally
choro|lo|gist
choro|logy
chortle (as v.,
  chort|ling)
chorus
chorus-girl
chorus-master
chou (pl. choux)
chou|croute
chough (crow)
chow-chow
chow mein
chre|mat|istic
chres|to|mathy
  (pl. chres|to|
     math|ies)
chrism (oil)
chrisom (robe)
Christ
Christ|adel|phian
chris|ten
Chris|ten|dom
Christ|hood
Chris|tian
Chris|ti|ania
Chris|ti|an|ity
Chris|tie
Chris|tine
Christ|like
Christ|mas
Christ|massy
Christmas-tide
Christ|olatry
Christo|logy
Christo|phany
Chris|to|pher
Christy
chroma
chro|mate
chro|matic
chro|mat|ic|ally
chro|ma|ti|city
chro|matin
chro|mat|ism
chro|ma|to|gram
chro|ma|to|graph
chro|ma|to|
     graphic
chro|ma|to|
     graph|ic|ally

chro|ma|to|
     graphy
chro|mat|op|sia
chrome
chrome-nickel
chro|mic
chro|min|ance
chro|mite
chro|mium
chromium-plate
  (as v.,
  chromium-
  plating)
chro|mo|li|tho|
     graph
chro|mo|li|tho|
     grapher
chro|mo|li|tho|
     graphy
chro|mo|somal
chro|mo|some
chro|mo|sphere
chro|mo|spheric
chronic
chron|ic|ally
chron|icity
chron|icle (as v.,
  chron|icling)
chron|ic|ler
Chron|icles (OT
  book)
chro|no|gram
chro|no|gram|
     matic
chro|no|graph
chro|no|graphic
chro|no|lo|ger
chro|no|lo|gical
chro|no|lo|gic|
     ally
chro|no|lo|gist
chro|no|lo|giza|
     tion
chro|no|lo|gize
  (chro|no|lo|giz|
     ing)
chro|no|logy (pl.
  chro|no|lo|gies)
chro|no|meter
chro|no|met|ric
chro|no|met|rical
chro|no|met|ric|
     ally
chro|no|metry
chro|no|scope

chrys|alis (pl.
chrys|al|ides)
chrys|anth
chrys|an|themum
chrys|ele|phant|
ine
chryso|beryl
chryso|lite
chryso|prase
chthonic
chub (fish; pl.
same)
Chubb (lock;
propr.)
chub|bi|ness
chubby
(chub|bier,
chub|bi|est)
chucker-out
chuckle (as v.,
chuck|ling)
chuffed
chug (as v.,
chugged,
chug|ging)
chu|kar (Ind.
partridge)
chuk|ker (in polo)
chum (as v.,
chummed,
chum|ming)
chum|mily
chum|mi|ness
chummy
(chum|mier,
chum|mi|est)
chunk|ily
chun|ki|ness
chunky
(chun|kier,
chun|ki|est)
chun|ter
chupatty use
chapatti
church-goer
church-going
Church|ill
Church|il|lian
chur|chi|ness
church|man (pl.
church|men)
church|man|ship
church|war|den
church|wo|man
(pl. church|
wo|men)

church|yard
churchy
(church|ier,
churchi|est)
chu|ringa (pl.
chu|rin|gas)
churl
churl|ish
churn
churr
Chur|ri|guer|
esque
chute
chut|ney
chutz|pah
chyle
chyme
chypre
ciao
ci|bor|ium (pl.
ci|boria)
ci|cada (pl.
ci|ca|das or Biol.
ci|ca|dae)
ci|ca|trice (scar)
ci|ca|tri|cial
ci|ca|trix (in
surgery 'scar', pl.
ci|ca|trices)
ci|ca|triza|tion
ci|ca|trize
(ci|ca|triz|ing)
ci|cely (plant)
Ci|cero
ci|cer|one (pl.
ci|cer|oni)
Ci|cero|nian
cich|lid (fish)
cider
cider-press
ci-devant
ci|gar
ci|gar|ette
ci|gar|illo (pl.
ci|gar|il|los)
ciggy (pl. cig|gies)
cil|iary
cili|ate
cili|ated
cili|ation
cil|ice
cil|ium (pl. cilia)
cim|ba|lom
Cim|mer|ian
cinch
cin|chona

cin|chon|ine
cinc|ture (as v.,
cinc|tur|ing)
cin|der
Cin|der|ella
cin|dery
cine
ci|ne|aste
cin|ema
cinema-goer
cine|matic
cine|mat|ic|ally
cine|ma|to|graph
cine|ma|to|
grapher
cine|ma|to|
graphic
cine|ma|to|
graph|ic|ally
cine|ma|to|
graphy
cin|er|aria
cin|er|arium
cin|er|ary
cin|er|eous
cin|gu|lum (pl.
cin|gula)
cin|na|bar
cin|na|mon
cinque
cin|que|cent|ist
cin|que|cento
cinque|foil
Cinque Ports
Cin|zano (propr.;
pl. Cin|zanos)
ci|pher
cip|olin (marble)
circa (about)
cir|ca|dian
Cir|cas|sian
Cir|cean
cir|cin|ate
cir|citer (about)
circle (as v.,
circ|ling)
circ|let
cir|cuit
circuit-breaker
cir|cu|it|ous
cir|cuitry
cir|cu|lar
cir|cu|lar|ity
cir|cu|lar|ize
(cir|cu|lar|iz|ing)

cir|cu|late
(cir|cu|lat|ing)
cir|cu|la|tion
cir|cu|lat|ive
cir|cu|lator
cir|cu|lat|ory
cir|cum|am|bi|
ency
cir|cum|am|bi|ent
cir|cum|circle
cir|cum|cise
(cir|cum|cis|ing)
cir|cum|cis|ion
cir|cum|fer|ence
cir|cum|fer|en|tial
cir|cum|fer|en|
tially
cir|cum|flex
cir|cum|flu|ence
cir|cum|flu|ent
cir|cum|fuse
(cir|cum|fus|ing)
cir|cum|ja|cent
cir|cum|lit|toral
cir|cum|lo|cu|tion
cir|cum|lo|cu|tory
cir|cum|lunar
cir|cum|nav|ig|
ate
(cir|cum|nav|ig|
at|ing)
cir|cum|nav|iga|
tion
cir|cum|nav|ig|
ator
cir|cum|ocu|lar
cir|cum|po|lar
cir|cum|scribe
(cir|cum|
scrib|ing)
cir|cum|scrip|tion
cir|cum|so|lar
cir|cum|spect
cir|cum|spec|tion
cir|cum|stance
cir|cum|stanced
cir|cum|stan|tial
cir|cum|stan|tial|
ity
cir|cum|stan|
tially
cir|cum|ter|res|
trial
cir|cum|val|late
(cir|cum|val|lat|
ing)

cir|cum|vent
cir|cum|ven|tion
cir|cum|vo|lu|tion
cir|cus
ciré
cirque
cir|rho|sis (*pl.*
 cir|rho|ses)
cir|ri|ped
cir|rose
cir|rous
cir|rus (*pl.* cirri)
cis|alp|ine
cis|at|lan|tic
cisco (*pl.* cis|coes)
cis|lu|nar
cis|pad|ane
cis|pont|ine
cist
Cis|ter|cian
cis|tern
cis|tus
cit|adel
ci|ta|tion
cite (cit|ing)
cit|ies (*pl.* of city)
citify (citi|fies,
 citi|fied,
 citi|fy|ing)
cit|izen
cit|izen|hood
cit|izen's ar|rest
cit|izens' band
cit|izen|ship
ci|ti|zenry
Citlal|te|petl
cit|ole
cit|rate
cit|ric
cit|rine
cit|ron
cit|ron|ella
cit|rous
cit|rus
cit|tern
city (*pl.* cit|ies)
City (*the* City, part
 of London)
ci|ty|scape
city-state
ci|ty|ward
cit|y|wards
civet
civic
civ|ic|ally
civil

ci|vil|ian
ci|vil|ity (*pl.*
 ci|vil|it|ies)
ci|vil|iz|able
ci|vil|iza|tion
civ|il|ize
 (civ|il|iz|ing)
civ|il|ized
civ|illy
Civil Service
civ|vies
Civvy Street
clad (clad|ded,
 clad|ding)
clade
cla|dis|tics
clad|ode
claim|able
claim|ant
clair|voy|ance
clair|voy|ant
clam (as *v.*,
 clammed,
 clam|ming)
clam|ant
clam|ber
clam|mily
clam|mi|ness
clammy
 (clam|mier,
 clam|mi|est)
clam|or|ous
clam|our
clamp-down *n.*
clan|des|tine
clanger
clan|gor|ous
clang|our
clan|nish
clan|ship
clans|man (*pl.*
 clans|men)
clap (clapped,
 clap|ping)
clap|per
clapper-board
clap|trap
claque
claqueur
cla|ra|bella
clar|ence
Clar|en|ceux
claret
cla|ri|fica|tion

cla|rify
 (cla|ri|fies,
 cla|ri|fied,
 cla|ri|fy|ing)
cla|ri|net
cla|ri|net|tist
clar|ion
clar|ity
clar|kia (plant)
clary (*pl.* clar|ies)
clasper
clasp-knife (*pl.*
 clasp-knives)
class|able
clas|sic
clas|sical
clas|sic|ally
clas|si|cism
clas|si|cist
clas|si|fi|able
clas|si|fica|tion
clas|si|fic|at|ory
clas|si|fier
clas|sify
 (clas|si|fies,
 clas|si|fied,
 clas|si|fy|ing)
clas|sily
clas|si|ness
class|less
class-mate
class-room
classy (clas|sier,
 clas|si|est)
clastic
clath|rate
clat|ter
clau|di|ca|tion
clausal
claus|ally
clause
claus|tral
claus|tro|pho|bia
claus|tro|pho|bic
claus|tro|pho|bic|
       ally
clav|ate
cla|vi|cem|balo
 (*pl.* cla|vi|
    cem|ba|los)
clavi|chord
clav|icle
cla|vic|ular
cla|vier
clavi|form
claw-back *n.*

claw-hammer
clayey
clay|more
clean-cut
cleaner
clean|lily
clean|li|ness
clean-living
cleanly
 (clean|lier,
 clean|li|est)
cleanse
 (cleans|ing)
clean-shaven
clean|skin
clean-up *n.*
clear|ance
clear-cut
clear-headed
clear|ing
clearing-house
clear-sighted
clear-thinking
clear|way
cleat
clcav|ablc
cleav|age
cleave ('split',
 clove *or* cleft *or*
 cleaved; cloven
 or cleft *or*
 cleaved;
 cleav|ing)
cleave ('stick fast',
 cleaved *or* clave;
 cleaved;
 cleav|ing)
cleaver
cleis|to|gamic
cleis|to|gam|ic|
        ally
cle|ma|tis
clem|ency
clem|ent
clem|en|tine
clep|sydra
clere|story (*pl.*
 clere|stor|ies)
clergy
cler|gy|man (*pl.*
 cler|gy|men)
cleric
cler|ical
cler|ic|al|ism
cler|ic|al|ity
cler|ic|ally

cleri|hew
cler|isy (*pl.*
 cler|is|ies)
clerk
clerk|ship
Cleve|land
clever (clev|erer,
 clev|er|est)
clevis
clew (*Naut.*)
 ⚠ clue
cli|an|thus
cli|ché
cli|chéd
clicker
cli|ent
cli|en|tele
cliff-hanger
cliff-hanging
cliffiness
cliffy (clif|fier,
 clif|fi|est)
cli|mac|teric
cli|mac|tic
cli|mac|tic|ally
cli|mate
cli|matic
cli|ma|to|lo|gical
cli|ma|to|logy
cli|max
climb
climb-down *n.*
climber
clinch
clincher
cline
cling (clung)
clinic
clin|ical
clin|ic|ally
cli|ni|cian
clinker
clinker-built
clink|stone
cli|no|meter
clio|met|rics
clip (as *v.*,
 clipped,
 clip|ping)
clip|board
clip-clop
 (clip-clopped,
 clip-clopping)
clip-joint
clip-on *a.*
clip|per

clip|pie
clique
cliquish
cliquism
cliquy
clit|oral
clit|oris
clo|aca (*pl.*
 clo|acae)
clo|acal
cloak|room
clob|ber
cloche
clock|wise
clock|work
clod|dish
clod|hop|per
clod-hopping
clod|poll
clog (as *v.*,
 clogged,
 clog|ging)
clog-dance
cloggy (clog|gier,
 clog|gi|est)
clois|onné
clois|ter
clois|tral
clo|nal
clone (as *v.*,
 clon|ing)
clonic
Clon|mel
clo|nus
close (as *v.*,
 clos|ing; as *a.*,
 closer, clos|est)
closed-circuit
closet
clos|eted
close-up *n.*
clos|ure
clot (clot|ted,
 clot|ting)
clothe (clothed *or*
 formal etc. clad;
 cloth|ing)
clothes-line
clo|thier
cloth|ing
cloud|berry (*pl.*
 cloud|ber|ries)
cloud|burst
cloud-cuckoo-
 land
cloud|ily

cloudi|ness
cloud-land
cloud|less
cloud|let
cloud|scape
cloudy (cloud|ier,
 cloudi|est)
clough (ravine)
clove, cloven *see*
 cleave
clover
clown|ery
clown|ish
club (as *v.*,
 clubbed,
 club|bing)
club|bable
club-foot (*pl.*
 club-feet)
club|house
club|land
club-man (*pl.*
 club-men)
cluck|ily
clucki|ness
clucky (cluck|ier,
 cluck|iest)
clue (piece of
 evidence etc.)
 ⚠ clew
clued
clue|less
Clum|ber
clum|sily
clum|si|ness
clumsy
 (clum|sier,
 clum|si|est)
Clu|niac
Cluny
clus|ter
clut|ter
Clwyd
Clyde
Clydes|dale
cly|peal
cly|pe|ate
clyp|eus (*pl.*
 clypei)
Cnut
co|acer|vate
co|acer|va|tion
coach-house
coach|man (*pl.*
 coach|men)
coach|wood

coach|work
co|ad|ju|tor
co|agu|lable
co|agu|lant
co|agu|late
 (co|agu|lat|ing)
co|agu|la|tion
co|agu|lator
co|agu|lat|ory
co|agu|lum (*pl.*
 co|agula)
co|aita
coal-bed
coal-black
coal-dust
coaler
co|alesce
 (co|ales|cing)
co|ales|cence
co|ales|cent
coal-face
coal|field
coal-hole
coal-house
co|ali|tion
co|ali|tion|ist
coal|man (*pl.*
 coal|men)
coal-mine
coal|mouse (*pl.*
 coal|mice)
coal-tit
coam|ing
coarse (coarser,
 coars|est)
coar|sen
coastal
coaster
coast|guard
coast|line
coast|wise
coatee
co|ati
co|ati|mundi
coat|ing
coat|less
coat-tails
co-author
co|axial
co|axi|ally
co|balt
co|baltic
co|balt|ous
cob|ber
cobble (as *v.*,
 cob|bling)

cob|bler
cobble-stone
Cob|den|ism
co-bel|li|ger|ence
co-bel|li|ger|ency
co-bel|li|ger|ent
coble
 (fishing-boat)
cob-nut
Co|bol (Comp.
 language)
co|bra
cob|web
cob|webbed
cob|webby
coca
Coca-Cola (*propr.*)
co|caine
co|cain|ism
coc|cal
coc|ci|di|osis (*pl.*
 coc|ci|di|oses)
coc|coid
coc|cus (*pl.* cocci)
coc|cy|geal
coc|cyx (*pl.*
 coc|cy|ges)
cochin
coch|in|eal
coch|lea (*pl.*
 coch|leae)
cock|ade
cock|aded
cock-a-doodle-
 doo
cock-a-hoop
Cock|aigne
cock-a-leekie
cocka|lorum
cock-and-bull
 story
cocka|tiel
cocka|too
cocka|trice
cock|boat
cock|chafer
cock-crow
cocker
Cocker
cock|erel
cock-eyed
cock-fight
cock-fighting
cock-horse
cock|ily
cocki|ness

cockle (as *v.*,
 cock|ling)
cockle-shell
cock-loft
cock|ney
cock|pit
cock|roach
cocks|comb
cocks|foot
cock-shy
cock|sure
cock|tail
cock-up *n.*
cocky (cock|ier,
 cocki|est)
coco (tree, *pl.*
 co|cos)
co|coa (powder)
coco-de-mer
co|co|nut
co|coon
co|coon|ery
co|cotte
Coc|teau
cod (as *v.*,
 cod|ded,
 cod|ding)
coda
cod-bank
coddle
 (cod|dling)
cod|dler
code (as *v.*,
 cod|ing)
code-book
cod|eine
code-name
code-number
coder
co|dex (*pl.*
 co|di|ces)
cod|fish
codger
co|di|cil
co|di|cil|lary
co|di|fica|tion
co|di|fier
co|dify (co|di|fies,
 co|di|fied,
 co|di|fy|ing)
cod|ling (small
 cod, apple)
cod-liver
co|don
cod|piece
co-driver
cods|wal|lop

coed
co|edu|ca|tion
co|edu|ca|tional
co|edu|ca|tion|
          ally
co|ef|fi|cient
coel|ac|anth
coel|en|ter|ate
coel|iac
coelom (*pl.*
 coel|oms *or*
 coel|omata)
coe|lom|ate
coe|lo|stat
coen|ob|ite
coen|ob|itic
coen|ob|it|ical
co|equal
co|equal|ity
co|equally
co|erce
 (co|er|cing)
co|er|cible
co|er|cion
co|er|cive
co|es|sen|tial
co|eta|ne|ous
co|eter|nal
co|eter|nally
co|eval
co|ev|al|ity
co|ev|ally
co|ex|ist
co|ex|ist|ence
co|ex|ist|ent
co|ex|tens|ive
cof|fee
coffee-break
coffee-pot
cof|fer
coffer-dam
cof|fin
coffle
co|gency
co|gent
cogged
co|git|able
co|git|ate
 (co|git|at|ing)
co|gita|tion
co|git|at|ive
co|gito
cognac
cog|nate
cog|natic
cog|ni|tion

cog|ni|tional
cog|nit|ive
cog|niz|able
cog|niz|ably
cog|niz|ance
cog|niz|ant
cog|nize
 (cog|niz|ing)
cog|no|men
co|gnos|cente (*pl.*
 cog|nos|centi)
cog|no|vit
cog-wheel
co|habit
 (co|hab|ited,
 co|hab|it|ing)
co|hab|ita|tion
co|here
 (co|her|ing)
co|her|ence
co|her|ency
co|her|ent
co|herer
co|he|sion
co|hes|ive
Cohn, F.J.
coho (*pl.* cohos)
co|hort
coif
coif|feur
coif|feuse
coif|fure
coign
coin|age
coin-box
co|in|cide
 (co|in|cid|ing)
co|in|cid|ence
co|in|cid|ent
co|in|cid|ental
co|in|cid|ent|ally
coiner
coin-op
Coin|treau
 (liqueur; *propr.*)
coir
co|ital
co|ition
co|itus
coke (as *v.*,
 cok|ing)
Coke (drink;
 propr.)
col (*Geog.* and
 Meteorol.)
cola

col|an|der
(strainer)
△ calendar,
calender
co-lati|tude
col|can|non (Irish
dish)
col|chic|ine
col|chicum (plant)
cold-blooded
cold-hearted
cold|ish
cold-work
cole (cabbage)
co|le|op|ter|ist
co|le|op|ter|ous
(of beetles)
co|le|opt|ile
Co|ler|idge
cole-seed
cole|slaw
co|leus (plant)
co|ley
colic
col|icky
Colin
col|itis
col|lab|or|ate (col|
lab|or|at|ing)
col|lab|ora|tion
col|lab|or|at|ive
col|lab|or|ator
col|lage
col|la|gen
(protein)
col|lagist
col|lapse (as v.,
col|laps|ing)
col|laps|ible
col|lar
collar-bone
col|lar|ette
col|late
(col|lat|ing)
col|lat|eral
col|lat|er|al|ity
col|lat|er|ally
col|la|tion
col|lator
col|league
col|lect
col|lect|able
col|lec|ta|nea (*pl.*)
col|lect|ible
col|lec|tion
col|lect|ive

col|lect|iv|ism
col|lect|iv|ist
col|lec|tiv|ity
col|lector
col|leen
col|lege
col|leger
col|legial
col|legi|al|ity
col|legian
col|legi|ate
col|len|chyma
Colles frac|ture
col|let
col|lide
(col|lid|ing)
col|lie
col|lier
col|li|ery (*pl.*
col|lier|ies)
col|lig|ate
(col|lig|at|ing)
col|liga|tion
col|lim|ate
(col|lim|at|ing)
col|lima|tion
col|lim|ator
col|lin|ear
col|lin|ear|ity
Col|lins (drink)
col|li|sion
col|li|sional
col|loc|ate
(col|loc|at|ing)
col|loca|tion
col|loc|utor
col|lo|dion
col|logue
(col|loguing)
col|loid
col|loidal
col|lop
col|lo|quial
col|lo|qui|al|ism
col|lo|qui|ally
col|loquium (*pl.*
col|loquia)
col|lo|quy (*pl.*
col|lo|quies)
col|lo|type
col|lude
(col|lud|ing)
col|lu|sion
col|lus|ive
col|lyrium (*pl.*
col|lyria)

col|ly|wobbles
co|lo|bus
co|lo|cynth
co|logne
Col|ogne
Co|lom|bia
Col|ombo
co|lon
col|onel
col|on|elcy
co|lo|nial
co|lo|ni|al|ism
co|lo|ni|al|ist
co|lo|ni|ally
co|lonic
col|on|ist
col|on|iza|tion
col|on|ize
(col|on|iz|ing)
col|on|izer
col|on|nade
col|on|naded
col|ony (*pl.*
col|on|ies)
colo|phon
(endpiece)
co|lo|phony
(rosin)
Col|or|ado
col|ora|tion
col|ora|tura
col|or|ific
col|ori|meter
col|ori|met|ric
col|ori|metry
co|los|sal
co|los|sally
Co|los|seum
co|los|sus (*pl.*
co|lossi)
co|los|tomy (*pl.*
co|los|tom|ies)
co|los|trum
co|lo|tomy (*pl.*
co|lo|tom|ies)
col|our
col|our|able
col|our|ant
colour-blind
col|our|ful
col|our|fully
col|our|ist
col|our|less
colour-sergeant
col|oury
col|por|teur

col|po|scope
col|po|tomy (*pl.*
col|po|tom|ies)
Colt (gun; *propr.*)
colt|ish
colts|foot
col|ub|rine
col|um|barium
(*pl.* col|um|baria)
Co|lum|bia
col|um|bine
(plant)
Col|um|bine
(Harlequin's
partner)
co|lumb|ite (ore)
co|lum|bium
Col|um|bus
col|umn
co|lum|nar
co|lure (*Astron.*)
colza (rape plant)
colza-oil
coma (*Bot.*,
hair-tuft; *Astron.*,
part of comet; *pl.*
co|mae)
coma (*Med.*; *pl.*
co|mas)
co|ma|tose
comb
com|bat
(com|bated,
com|bat|ing)
com|bat|ant
com|bat|ive
combe *use* coomb
comber
com|bina|tion
com|bin|at|ive
com|bin|at|or|ial
com|bine (as v.,
com|bin|ing)
comb|ing
combo (esp. in
jazz; *pl.* com|bos)
com|bust
com|bust|ib|il|ity
com|bust|ible
com|bust|ibly
com|bus|tion
come (came,
come, com|ing)
come-at-able
come-back *n.*

Com|econ
 (economic assoc.)
co|median
com|edic
co|medi|enne
com'ed|ist
come-down *n.*
com'edy (*pl.*
 com'ed|ies)
come'li|ness
comely
 (come|lier,
 come'li|est)
come-on *n.*
comer
com'est|ible
comet
come-uppance
com|fort
com'fort|able
com'fort|ably
com|forter
com|frey
comfy (com|fier,
 com'fi|est)
comic
com|ical
com'ic|ally
com'ic'al|ity
Com|in'tern
 (communist
 assoc.)
co'mi|tadji
com|ity
comma
com|mand
com|mand|ant
com|man|deer
com|mander
com|mand|ment
com|mando
com'media
 dell'arte
comme il faut
com|mem'or|ate
 (com|mem'or|
 at'ing)
com|mem'ora|
 tion
com|mem'ora|tive
com|mem'ora|tor
com|mence
 (com|men'cing)
com|mence|ment
com|mend
com'mend|able

com'mend|ably
com|menda|tion
com|mend'at|ory
com|mensal
com'mens'al|ism
com|men'sur|
 ab'il|ity
com|men'sur|able
com|men'sur|ably
com|men'sur|ate
com|ment
com'ment|ary (*pl.*
 com'ment|ar'ies)
com'ment|ate
 (com'ment'at|
 ing)
com'ment|ator
com|merce
com|mer'cial
com|mer'cial|ism
com|mer'cial|ize
 (com|mer'cial|iz|
 ing)
com|mer'cially
com|mère (female
 compère)
Com|mie (*sl.*,
 Communist)
com|mina'tion
com|min'at|ory
com|min'ute
 (com|min'ut|ing)
com|minu'tion
com'mis
com|mis'er|ate
 (com|mis'er|
 at'ing)
com|mis'era|tion
com|mis'era|tive
com'mis'sar
com'mis'sarial
com'mis'sariat
com'mis'sary (*pl.*
 com'mis'sar'ies)
com'mis'sion
com|mis'sion|aire
 (attendant)
com'mis'sioner
 (one who
 commissions)
Com'mis|sioner
 (official)
com'mis'sural
com'mis'sure

com|mit
 (com|mit'ted,
 com|mit'ting)
com|mit'ment
com|mit'table
com|mit'tal
com|mit'tee
com|mode
com|modi|ous
com|mod|ity (*pl.*
 com|mod'it'ies)
com'mo|dore
com'mon
 (com'moner,
 com'mon|est)
com'mon|able
com'mon|age
com'mon'al|ity
com'mon|alty
com'moner
common-law *a.*
com'mon|ness
com'mon|place *n.*
 & *a.*
common-room
com'mon sense
common-sense *a.*
com'mon|
 sen'sical
Com|mons (*Parl.*)
com'mon|wealth
com|mo'tion
com|munal
com'mun'al|ism
com'mun'al|istic
com'mun'al|ist'ic|
 ally
com'mun'al|ize
 (com'mun'al|iz|
 ing)
com'mun|ally
com'mun|ard
com|mune (as *v.*,
 com'mun|ing)
com|mun'ic|ab'il|
 ity
com|mun'ic|able
com|mun'ic|ably
com|mun'ic|ant
com|mun'ic|ate
 (com|mun'ic|at|
 ing)
com|mun'ica'tion
com|mun'ic'at|ive
com|mun'ic|ator

com|mu'nion
 (sharing)
Com|mu'nion
 (Eucharist)
com|mu'ni'qué
com|mun|ism
 (system of society)
Com'mun|ism
 (polit. party)
com'mun|ist
 (supporter of
 social system)
Com'mun|ist
 (member of party)
com'mun|istic
com'mun|ist'ic|
 ally
com|mu'nit|arian
com|mun|ity (*pl.*
 com|mu|nit|ies)
com'mun|iza'tion
com'mun|ize
 (com'mun|iz|ing)
com'mut|ab'il|ity
com'mut|able
com'mut|ate
 (com'mut|at|ing)
com|muta'tion
com'mut'at|ive
com'mut|ator
com|mute
 (com'mut|ing)
com|muter
Com|oro (Islands)
co'mose
com|pact
com|pac'tion
com|pactor
com|pa'ges
com|pan'ion
com|pan'ion|able
com|pan'ion|ably
com|pan'ion|ate
companion-way
com|pany (*pl.*
 com|pan'ies)
com'par|ab'il|ity
com'par|able
com'par|ably
com|par'at|ist
com|par'at|ive
com|par'ator
com|pare
 (com|par'ing)
com|par|ison
com|part|ment

com|part|mental
com|part|ment|al|
      ize
(com|part|
  ment|al|iz|ing)
com|part|men|ted
com|pass (*pl.*
 com|passes)
com|pas|sion
com|pas|sion|ate
com|pat|ib|il|ity
com|pat|ible
com|pat|ibly
com|pat|riot
com|pat|ri|otic
com|peer
com|pel
 (com|pelled,
 com|pel|ling)
com|pen|di|ous
com|pen|dium (*pl.*
 com|pen|dia)
com|pens|ate
 (com|pens|at|ing)
com|pensa|tion
com|pensa|tional
com|pens|at|ive
com|pen|sator
com|pens|at|ory
compère (as *v.*,
 com|pèred,
 com|pèr|ing)
com|pete
 (com|pet|ing)
com|pet|ence
com|pet|ency
com|pet|ent
com|peti|tion
com|pet|it|ive
com|pet|itor
com|pila|tion
com|pile
 (com|pil|ing)
com|piler
com|pla|cence
 (self-satisfaction)
 △ complaisance
com|pla|cency
com|pla|cent
 (self-satisfied)
 △ complaisant
com|plain
com|plain|ant
com|plaint

com|plais|ance
 (acquiescence)
 △ complacence
com|plais|ant
 (acquiescent)
 △ complacent
com|ple|ment
 (that which
 completes)
 △ compliment
com|ple|mental
com|ple|ment|ary
 (completing) △
 complimentary
com|plete
 (com|plet|ing)
com|ple|tion
com|plex
com|plex|ion
com|plex|ity (*pl.*
 com|plex|it|ies)
com|pli|ance
com|pli|ancy
com|pli|ant
com|plic|acy
com|plic|ate
 (com|plic|at|ing)
com|plica|tion
com|pli|city
com|pli|ment
 (expression of
 praise)
 △ complement
com|pli|ment|ary
 (expressing
 praise) △
 complementary
com|pline
com|ply
 (com|plies,
 com|plied,
 com|ply|ing)
compo
com|pon|ent
com|pose
 (com|pos|ing)
com|poser
com|pos|ite
com|posi|tion
com|posi|tional
com|pos|itor
com|pos men|tis
com|pos|sible
com|post
com|pos|ure

com|pote
com|pound
com|pra|dor
com|pre|hend
com|pre|hens|
       ib|il|ity
com|pre|hens|ible
com|pre|hens|ibly
com|pre|hen|sion
com|pre|hens|ive
com|press
com|press|ible
com|pres|sion
com|press|ive
com|press|or
com|pris|able
com|prise
 (com|pris|ing)
com|prom|ise
 (as *v.*,
 com|prom|ising)
compte rendu (*pl.*
 comptes rendus)
Comp|tom|eter
 (*propr.*)
comp|trol|ler
com|pul|sion
com|puls|ive
com|puls|or|ily
com|puls|ori|ness
com|puls|ory
com|punc|tion
com|punc|tious
com|pur|ga|tion
com|pur|gator
com|pur|gat|ory
com|put|able
com|put|ably
com|pu|ta|tion
com|pute
 (com|put|ing)
com|puter
com|pu|ter|iza|
        tion
com|pu|ter|ize
 (com|puter|
      iz|ing)
com|rade
Comt|ism
 (positivism)
Comt|ist
 (positivist)
con (as *v.*, conned,
 con|ning)
con|acre

Con|akry
con amore
co|na|tion
con|at|ive
con brio
con|cat|en|ate
 (con|cat|en|
      at|ing)
con|cat|ena|tion
con|cave
con|cav|ity (*pl.*
 con|cav|it|ies)
con|ceal
con|ceal|ment
con|cede
 (con|ced|ing)
con|ceit
con|ceiv|ab|il|ity
con|ceiv|able
con|ceiv|ably
con|ceive
 (con|ceiv|ing)
con|cel|eb|rant
con|cel|eb|rate
 (con|cel|eb|
      rat|ing)
con|cel|eb|ra|tion
con|cen|trate
 (con|cen|trat|ing)
con|cen|tra|tion
con|cen|trat|ive
con|cen|trator
con|centre
 (con|cent|ring)
con|cent|ric
con|cent|ric|ally
con|cent|ri|city
con|cept
con|cep|tion
con|cep|tional
con|cep|tion|ally
con|cept|ive
con|cep|tual
con|cep|tu|al|ism
con|cep|tu|al|ist
con|cep|tu|al|ize
 (con|cep|tu|al|iz|
        ing)
con|cep|tu|ally
con|cern
con|cern|ment
con|cert
con|cer|ted
con|cer|tina (as *v.*,
 con|cer|tinaed,
 con|cer|ti|na|ing)

con|cer|tino (*pl.*
  con|cer|ti|nos)
con|certo (*pl.*
  con|cer|tos)
con|certo grosso
  (*pl.* con|certi
  grossi)
con|ces|sion
con|ces|sion|aire
con|ces|sion|ary
con|cess|ive
conch (*pl.* conchs)
con|cha (*pl.*
  conchae)
conch|oidal
concho|lo|gical
concho|lo|gic|ally
concho|lo|gist
concho|logy
con|chy (*sl., pl.*
  conch|ies)
con|ci|erge
con|cil|iar
con|ci|li|ate
  (con|ci|li|at|ing)
con|ci|li|ation
con|ci|li|at|ive
con|ci|li|ator
con|ci|li|at|ory
con|cin|nity
con|cise
con|cision
con|clave
con|clude
  (con|clud|ing)
con|clu|sion
con|clus|ive
con|coct
con|coc|tion
con|coctor
con|com|it|ance
con|com|it|ancy
con|com|it|ant
con|cord
con|cord|ance
con|cord|ant
con|cordat
con|course
con|cres|cence
con|cres|cent
con|crete (as *v.*,
  con|cret|ing)
con|cre|tion
con|cret|iza|tion
con|cret|ize
  (con|cret|iz|ing)

con|cu|bin|age
con|cu|bin|ary
con|cu|bine
con|cu|pis|cence
con|cu|pis|cent
con|cur
  (con|curred,
  con|cur|ring)
con|cur|rence
con|cur|rent
con|cuss
con|cus|sion
con|demn
con|dem|nable
con|dem|na|tion
con|dem|nat|ory
con|dens|able
con|dens|ate
con|densa|tion
con|dense
  (con|dens|ing)
con|denser
con|dens|ery (*pl.*
  con|dens|er|ies)
con|des|cend
con|des|cen|sion
con|dign
con|di|ment
con|di|tion
con|di|tional
con|di|tion|al|ity
con|di|tion|ally
con|di|tioner
con|do|lat|ory
con|dole
  (con|dol|ing)
con|dol|ence
con|dom
con|do|min|ium
  (*pl.* con|do|mini|
    ums)
con|dona|tion
con|done
  (con|don|ing)
con|dor
con|dot|ti|ere (*pl.*
  con|dot|ti|eri)
con|duce
  (con|du|cing)
con|du|cive
con|duct
con|duct|ance
con|duct|ible
con|duc|tion
con|duct|ive

con|duct|iv|ity (*pl.*
  con|duct|iv|it|ies)
con|ductor
con|duc|tress
con|duit
con|dyle
con|dyl|oid
cone (as *v.*,
  con|ing)
Co|ney (Island)
con|fabu|late
  (con|fabu|lat|ing)
con|fabu|la|tion
con|fabu|lat|ory
con|fec|tion
con|fec|tion|ary *a.*
con|fec|tioner
con|fec|tion|ery *n.*
  (*pl.* con|fec|tion|
    er|ies)
con|fed|er|acy (*pl.*
  con|fed|er|acies)
Con|fed|er|acy
  (*US hist.*)
con|fed|er|ate (as
  v., con|fed|er|
    at|ing)
Con|fed|er|ate
  (*US hist.*)
con|fed|era|tion
con|fer
  (con|fer|ring)
con|feree
con|fer|ence
con|fer|en|tial
con|fer|ment
con|fer|rable
con|fess
con|fess|ant
con|fes|sion
con|fes|sional
con|fessor
con|fetti
con|fid|ant (*masc.*)
con|fid|ante (*fem.*)
con|fide
  (con|fid|ing)
con|fid|ence
con|fid|ent
con|fid|en|tial
con|fid|en|ti|al|ity
  (*pl.* con|
    fid|en|ti|al|it|ies)
con|fid|en|tially
con|fig|ura|tion
con|fig|ura|tional

con|fine
  (con|fin|ing)
con|fine|ment
con|firm
con|firma|tion
con|firm|at|ive
con|firm|at|ory
con|fis|cable
con|fis|cate
  (con|fis|cat|ing)
con|fis|ca|tion
con|fis|cator
con|flag|ra|tion
con|flate
  (con|flat|ing)
con|fla|tion
con|flict
con|flic|tion
con|flu|ence
con|flu|ent
con|flux (*pl.*
  con|fluxes)
con|form
con|form|ab|il|ity
con|form|able
con|form|ably
con|formal
con|form|ally
con|form|ance
con|forma|tion
con|former
con|form|ism
con|form|ist
con|form|ity
con|found
con|foun|ded
con|fra|tern|ity
  (*pl.* con|fra|tern|
    it|ies)
con|frère
con|front
con|fronta|tion
Con|fu|cian
Con|fu|cian|ism
Con|fu|cius
con|fus|able
con|fuse
  (con|fus|ing)
con|fu|sion
con|fu|ta|tion
con|fute
  (con|fut|ing)
conga (as *v.*,
  congaed,
  con|ga|ing)

congé
con|geal
con|geal|able
con|geal|ment
con|gela|tion
con|gener
con|gen'eric
con|gen'er|ous
con|gen|ial
con|geni'al|ity
con|geni|ally
con|gen'ital
con|gen'it|ally
con'ger (eel)
con'ger|ies
con|gest
con|ges'tion
con|gest|ive
con|glom'er|ate
 (as *v.*, con|
  glom'er|at'ing)
con|glom'era|tion
Congo
Con'gol|ese
con'gou
con|gratu|lant
con|gratu|late
 (con|gratu|
  lat'ing)
con|gratu|la'tion
con|gratu|lat|ive
con|gratu|lator
con|gratu|lat'ory
con|greg|ant
con|greg|ate
 (con|greg|at'ing)
con|grega|tion
con|grega|tional
Con|grega|tional
 (special sense)
Con|grega|
  tion'al|ism
Con|grega|
  tion'al|ist
con|gress
 (meeting)
Con|gress (State
 body or party)
con|gres|sional
Con'gress|man
 (*pl.*
 Con'gress|men)
Con'gress|
   wo'man
 (*pl.* Con'gress|
   wo'men)

con|gru'ence
con|gru'ency (*pl.*
 con|gru'en'cies)
con|gru'ent
con|gru'ity (*pl.*
 con|gru|it'ies)
con|gru'ous
conic
con|ical
con'ic|ally
co'nid|ium (*pl.*
 co|nidia)
con|ifer
con|ifer|ous
coni|form
coni|ine
con|jec'tur|able
con|jec'tur|ably
con|jec'tural
con|jec'tur'ally
con|jec'ture (as *v.*,
 con|jec'tur'ing)
con|join
con|joint
con|jugal
con'jug|ally
con'jug|ate
 (con'jug|at'ing)
con|juga'tion
con|juga|tional
con|junct
con|junc'tion
con|junc'tional
con|junc'tion|ally
con|junc'tiva
con|junc'tival
con|junct|ive
con|junc'tiv|itis
con|junc'ture
con|jura'tion
con|jure
 (con|jur|ing)
con|juror
conker
con moto
con|nate
con|nat'ural
con|nat'ur|ally
con|nect
con|nect|able
con|necter
 (person)
con|nect|ible
Con|nec't|icut
con|nec'tion
con|nect|ive

con|nector (thing)
conning-tower
con|niv'ance
con|nive
 (con|niv'ing)
con|nois|seur
con|no'ta'tion
con|not'at|ive
con|note
 (con|not'ing)
con|nu'bial
con|nu'bi'al|ity
con|nu'bi|ally
con|oid
con|quer
con|queror
con|quest
con|quis'ta|dor
 (*pl.* con|quis'ta|
            dores)
Con|rad
con-rod
con|san'guin|
            eous
con|san'guin|ity
con|science
con|scien'tious
con|scious
con|scribe
 (con|scrib'ing)
con|script
con|scrip'tion
con|sec'rate
 (con|sec'rat|ing)
con|sec'ra'tion
con|sec'rator
con|sec'rat'ory
con|secu'tion
con|sec'ut|ive
con|sen'sual
con|sen'su'ally
con|sensus
con|sent
con|sent'an|eous
con|sen'tient
con|sequence
con|sequent
con|sequen'tial
con|sequen'ti'al|
                ity
con|sequen'tially
con|ser'vancy (*pl.*
 con|ser'van'cies)
con|ser'va'tion
con|ser'va'tion|ist
con|ser'vat|ism

con|ser'vat|ive
Con|ser'vat|ive
 (*Polit.*)
con|ser'va|toire
con|ser'vator
con|
   ser'vat|or'ium
con|ser'vat|ory
 (*pl.* con|ser'vat|
            or'ies)
con|serve (as *v.*,
 con|serv'ing)
con|sider
con|sid'er|able
con|sid'er|ably
con|sid'er|ate
con|sid'era'tion
con|sign
con|signee
con|sign|ment
con|signor
con|sist
con|sist|ence
con|sist|ency (*pl.*
 con|sist|en|cies)
con|sist|ent
con|sist|or|ial
con|sist|ory
con|so'ci|ate
 (con|so'ci|at'ing)
con|so'ci|ation
con|sol'able
con|sola'tion
con|sol'at|ory
con|sole (as *v.*,
 con|sol'ing)
con|soler
con|sol'id|ate
 (con|sol'id|
            at'ing)
con|sol'ida'tion
con|sol'id|ator
con|sol'id|at'ory
con|sols
con|sommé
con|son|ance
con|son|ant
con|son|antal
con|sort
con|sor'tium (*pl.*
 con|sor'tia)
con|spe'cific
con|spectus
con|spicu|ous
con|spir|acy (*pl.*
 con|spir|acies)

con|spir|ator
con|spir|at|or|ial
con|spir|at|ori|
       ally
con|spire
 (con|spir|ing)
con|stable
con|stabu|lary
 (pl. con|stabu|
      lar|ies)
con|stancy
con|stant
con|stantan
con|stata|tion
con|stel|late
 (con|stel|lat|ing)
con|stel|la|tion
con|stern|ate
 (con|stern|at|ing)
con|sterna|tion
con|stip|ate
 (con|stip|at|ing)
con|stipa|tion
con|stitu|ency (pl.
 con|stitu|en|cies)
con|stitu|ent
con|sti|tute
 (con|sti|tut|ing)
con|sti|tu|tion
con|sti|tu|tional
con|sti|tu|tion|al|
      ism
con|sti|tu|tion|al|
      ist
con|sti|tu|tion|al|
      ity
con|sti|tu|tion|al|
      ize
 (con|sti|tu|
   tion|al|iz|ing)
con|sti|tu|tion|
      ally
con|stitu|tive
con|sti|tutor
con|strain
con|straint
con|strict
con|stric|tion
con|strict|ive
con|strictor
con|strual
con|struct
con|struc|tion
con|struc|tional
con|struc|tion|
      ism

con|struct|ive
con|struct|iv|ism
con|struct|iv|ist
con|structor
con|strue
 (con|stru|ing)
con|sub|stan|tial
con|sub|stan|ti|al|
      ity
con|sub|stan|ti|
      ate
 (con|sub|stan|ti|
     at|ing)
con|sub|stan|ti|
      ation
con|su|et|ude
con|su|etud|in|
      ary
con|sul
con|su|lar
con|sul|ate
con|sult
con|sult|ancy (pl.
 con|sult|an|cies)
con|sult|ant
con|sul|ta|tion
con|sult|at|ive
con|sum|able
con|sume
 (con|sum|ing)
con|sumer
con|sumer|ism
con|sumer|ist
con|sum|mate (as
 v., con|sum|
      mat|ing)
con|sum|ma|tion
con|sum|mat|ive
con|sum|mator
con|sump|tion
con|sump|tive
con|tact
con|ta|gion
con|ta|gious
con|tain
con|tain|able
con|tainer
con|tain|er|ize
 (con|tain|er|iz|
      ing)
con|tain|ment
con|tam|in|ant
con|tam|in|ate
 (con|tam|in|
     at|ing)
con|tam|ina|tion

con|tango (pl.
 con|tan|gos)
con|tem|plate
 (con|tem|
      plat|ing)
con|tem|pla|tion
con|tem|plat|ive
con|tem|pla|tor
con|tem|por|an|
      eity
con|tem|por|an|
      eous
con|tem|por|ary
 (pl. con|tem|por|
      ar|ies)
con|tem|por|ize
 (con|tem|por|iz|
      ing)
con|tempt
con|tempt|ib|il|ity
con|tempt|ible
con|tempt|ibly
con|temp|tu|ous
con|tend
con|tender
con|tent
con|tented
con|ten|tion
con|ten|tious
con|tent|ment
con|ter|min|ous
con|tessa
con|test
con|test|able
con|test|ant
con|testa|tion
con|text
con|tex|tual
con|tex|tu|ally
con|ti|gu|ity
con|tigu|ous
con|tin|ence
con|tin|ent
Con|tin|ent (Eur.
 mainland)
con|tin|ental
Con|tin|ental
 (Eur.)
con|tin|ent|ally
con|tin|gency (pl.
 con|tin|gen|cies)
con|tin|gent
con|tinu|able
con|tinual
con|tinu|ally
con|tinu|ance

con|tinu|ant
con|tinua|tion
con|tinu|at|ive
con|tinu|ator
con|tinue
 (con|tinu|ing)
con|tinu|ity (pl.
 con|tinu|it|ies)
con|tinuo (pl.
 con|tinuos)
con|tinu|ous
con|tinuum (pl.
 con|tinua)
con|tort
con|tor|tion
con|tor|tion|ist
con|tour
con|tra
con|tra|band
con|tra|band|ist
con|tra|bass
con|tra|cep|tion
con|tra|cept|ive
con|tract
con|tract|able
con|tract|ible (in
 sense of
 restricting or
 shortening)
con|tract|ile
con|tract|il|ity
con|trac|tion
con|tract|ive
con|tractor
con|trac|tual
con|trac|tu|ally
con|tra|dict
con|tra|dict|able
con|tra|dic|tion
con|tra|dic|tious
con|tra|dictor
con|tra|dict|or|ily
con|tra|dict|ori|
      ness
con|tra|dict|ory
con|tra|
 dis|tinc|tion
con|tra|dis|tin|
      guish
con|trail
contra-indication
con|tralto (pl.
 con|tral|tos)
con|tra|posi|tion
con|tra|pos|it|ive

con|trap|tion
con|tra|puntal
con|tra|punt|ally
con|tra|punt|ist
con|tra|ri|ety (*pl.*
 con|tra|ri|et|ies)
con|trar|ily
con|trari|ness
con|trari|wise
con|trary (as *n.*,
 pl. con|tra|ries)
con|trast
con|trast|ive
con|trasty
con|tra|vene
 (con|tra|ven|ing)
con|tra|ven|tion
con|tre|temps
con|trib|ute
 (con|trib|ut|ing)
con|tri|bu|tion
con|trib|utor
con|trib|ut|ory
con|trite
con|tri|tion
con|triv|able
con|triv|ance
con|trive
 (con|triv|ing)
con|triver
con|trol (as *v.*,
 con|trolled,
 con|trol|ling)
con|trol|lable
con|trol|lably
con|trol|ler
con|tro|ver|sial
con|tro|ver|sial|
 ism
con|tro|ver|sial|
 ist
con|tro|ver|sially
con|tro|versy (*pl.*
 con|tro|ver|sies)
con|tro|vert
con|tro|vert|ible
con|tu|ma|cious
con|tu|macy
con|tu|me|li|ous
con|tumely
con|tuse
 (con|tus|ing)
con|tu|sion
con|un|drum
con|ur|ba|tion
con|ure

con|valesce
 (con|val|es|cing)
con|val|es|cence
con|val|es|cent
con|vec|tion
con|vec|tional
con|vect|ive
con|vector
con|ven|ances
con|vene
 (con|ven|ing)
con|vener
con|veni|ence
con|veni|ent
con|vent
con|ven|ticle
con|ven|tion
con|ven|tional
con|ven|tion|al|
 ism
con|ven|tion|al|ist
con|ven|tion|
 al|ity
 (*pl.* con|ven|tion|
 al|it|ies)
con|ven|tion|al|
 ize
 (con|ven|tion|al|
 iz|ing)
con|ven|tion|ally
con|ven|tual
con|verge
 (con|ver|ging)
con|ver|gence
con|ver|gency
con|ver|gent
con|vers|ance
con|vers|ancy
con|vers|ant
con|ver|sa|tion
con|ver|sa|tional
con|ver|sa|tion|al|
 ist
con|ver|sa|tion|
 ally
con|ver|sa|tion|ist
con|verse (as *v.*,
 con|vers|ing)
con|ver|sion
con|vert
con|verter
con|vert|ib|il|ity
con|vert|ible
con|vert|ibly
con|vex
con|vex|ity

con|vey
con|vey|ance
con|vey|an|cer
con|vey|an|cing
con|veyer (person)
con|veyor (thing)
con|vict
con|vic|tion
con|vict|ive
con|vince
 (con|vin|cing)
con|vince|ment
con|vin|cible
con|vin|cibly
con|viv|ial
con|vi|vi|al|ity
con|viv|ially
con|voca|tion
con|voca|tional
con|voke
 (con|vok|ing)
con|vo|luted
con|vo|lu|tion
con|volve
 (con|volv|ing)
con|vol|vu|lus
con|voy
con|vuls|ant
con|vulse
 (con|vul|sing)
con|vul|sion
con|vuls|ive
cony (*pl.* co|nies)
cook|book
cooker
cook|ery
cook|house
cookie
cook|ing
coo|la|bah
cool|ant
cooler
coolie
cooling-off
coolly
coomb (valley)
co-op
cooper
co-operant
co-operate
 (co-operating)
co-operation
co-operative
co-operator
co-opt
co-optation

co-option
co-optive
co-ordinate (as *v.*,
 co-ordinating)
co|ord|in|ate
 (*Math.*)
co-ordination
co-ordinative
co-ordinator
cop (as *v.*, copped,
 cop|ping)
co|paiba
co|pal
co|part|ner
cope (cop|ing)
co|peck
Cop|en|hagen
cope|pod
coper
Co|per|nican
Co|per|ni|cus
cope-stone
copier
co-pilot
coping-stone
co|pi|ous
co|pita
co|pla|nar
co|planar|ity
co|poly|mer
cop-out *n.*
cop|per
cop|peras
cop|per|head
cop|per|plate
cop|pery
cop|pice (as *v.*,
 cop|picing)
copra
co-precipitation
cop|rol|ite
cop|ro|logy
cop|ro|phag|ous
cop|ro|philia
cop|ro|phi|liac
cop|rosma
copse (as *v.*,
 cops|ing)
copsy
Coptic
cop|ula
cop|ular
cop|ulate
 (cop|ulat|ing)
cop|ula|tion
copu|lat|ive

cop|ulat|ory
copy (as *n.*, *pl.*
  cop|ies; as *v.*,
  cop|ies, cop|ied,
  copy|ing)
copy-book
copy-cat
copy-editor
copy|hold
copy|holder
copy|right
copy-typist
copy-writer
coq au vin
coquetry
coquette (as *v.*,
  coquet|ting)
coquet|tish
co|quito
cor|acle
cor|ac|oid
coral
cor|al|line
cor|al|lite
cor|al|loid
cor ang|lais (*pl.*
  cors ang|lais)
cor|bel (as *v.*,
  cor|belled,
  cor|bel|ling)
cor|bie
corbie-steps
cord (twine etc.,
  vocal membrane)
  △ chord
cord|age
cord|ate
cor|del|ier
cor|dial
cor|di|al|ity
cor|di|ally
cor|dil|lera
cord|ite
cor|don
cor|don bleu
cor|do|van
cor|du|roy
cord|wood
core (as *v.*,
  cor|ing)
co|rella
co|re|op|sis (*pl.*
  co|re|op|ses)
corer

co-respondent (in
  divorce)
  △ correspondent
corf (*pl.* corves)
Corfu
corgi (*pl.* cor|gis)
co|ri|aceous
  (leathery)
co|ri|an|der
Cor|inth
Co|rin|thian
cor|ium
cork|age
corker
cork|screw
cork|wood
corky (cor|kier,
  cor|ki|est)
cor|mor|ant
corn|brash
corn-cob
corn|crake
cor|nea
cor|neal (of
  cornea)
Cor|neille
cor|nel (plant)
cor|ne|lian
corn|eous (horny)
cor|ner
corner-stone
cor|ner|ways
cor|ner|wise
cor|net
cor|netcy
cor|net|tist
cor|netto (*pl.*
  cor|netti)
corn|field
corn|flakes
corn|flour
  (thickening agent)
corn|flower
  (plant)
cor|nice
cor|niced *a.*
cor|niche
Corn|ish
corn|starch
corn|stone
cor|nu|co|pia
cor|nu|co|pian
Corn|wall
corny (cor|nier,
  cor|ni|est)
co|rolla

co|rol|lary (*pl.*
  co|rol|lar|ies)
co|rona (halo; *pl.*
  co|ro|nae)
co|rona (cigar; *pl.*
  co|ro|nas)
co|ro|nach (dirge)
co|ro|na|graph
cor|onal
cor|on|ary (*pl.*
  cor|on|ar|ies)
cor|ona|tion
cor|oner
cor|onet
Corot
co|rozo (*pl.*
  co|ro|zos)
cor|pora (*pl.* of
  corpus)
cor|poral
cor|por|al|ity
cor|por|ally
cor|por|ate
cor|pora|tion
cor|por|at|ism
cor|por|at|ive
cor|por|at|iv|ism
cor|por|eal
cor|por|eal|ity
cor|por|eally
cor|por|eity
cor|po|sant
corps (*sing.* and
  pl.; body of troops
  etc.)
corps de ballet
corps dip|lo|
          ma|tique
corpse
cor|pu|lence
cor|pu|lency
cor|pu|lent
cor|pus (*pl.*
  cor|pora)
Cor|pus Christi
  (feast)
cor|pus de|licti
cor|pus lu|teum
  (*pl.* cor|pora
  lu|tea)
cor|puscle
cor|pus|cu|lar
cor|ral (as *v.*
  cor|ralled,
  cor|ral|ling)
cor|ra|sion (*Geol.*)

cor|rect
cor|rec|tion
cor|rec|ti|tude
cor|rect|ive
cor|rector
Cor|reg|gio
cor|rel|ate
  (cor|rel|at|ing)
cor|rela|tion
cor|rel|at|ive
cor|rel|at|iv|ity
cor|res|pond
cor|res|pond|ence
cor|res|pond|ent
  (letter-writer)
  △ co-respondent
cor|rida
cor|ridor
cor|rie
cor|ri|gendum (*pl.*
  cor|ri|genda)
cor|rigible
cor|rob|or|ant
cor|rob|or|ate
  (cor|rob|or|
          at|ing)
cor|rob|ora|tion
cor|rob|or|at|ive
cor|rob|or|ator
cor|rob|or|at|ory
cor|rob|oree
cor|rode
  (cor|rod|ing)
cor|ro|sion
cor|ros|ive
cor|rug|ate
  (cor|rug|at|ing)
cor|ruga|tion
cor|rug|ator
cor|rupt
cor|rupt|ible
cor|rup|tion
cor|rupt|ive
cor|sac
cors|age
cor|sair
corse|lette
cor|set
cor|seti|ère
cor|setry
Cor|sica
Cor|sican
cors|let
cor|tège

Cor¦tes (Sp.
 legislative
 assembly)
Cor¦tés (man)
cor¦tex (*pl.*
 cor¦ti¦ces)
Corti (organ of)
cor¦tical
cor¦tic¦ate
cor¦ti¦co¦trophic
cor¦ti¦co¦trophin
cor¦ti¦co¦tropic
cor¦ti¦co¦tropin
cor¦tis¦one
co¦run¦dum
co¦rus¦cate
 (co¦rus¦cat¦ing)
co¦rus¦ca¦tion
cor¦vée
corves (*pl.* of corf)
cor¦vette
cor¦vina
cor¦vine
cory¦bantic
cor¦ymb
cor¦ymb¦ose
cory¦phaeus (*pl.*
 cory¦phaei)
cory¦phée
co¦ryza
co¦sec¦ant
co¦seis¦mal
co¦set
cosher
Così fan tutte
co¦sies (*pl.* of cosy)
co-signatory (*pl.*
 co-signatories)
co¦sily
co¦sine
co¦si¦ness
cos¦mea
cos¦metic
cos¦met¦ic¦ally
cos¦met¦ician
cos¦meto¦logy
cos¦mic
cos¦mical
cos¦mic¦ally
cos¦mo¦gonic
cos¦mo¦gon¦ical
cos¦mog¦ony
cos¦mo¦grapher
cos¦mo¦graphic
cos¦mo¦graph¦ical

cos¦mo¦graphy
cos¦mo¦log¦ical
cos¦mo¦lo¦gist
cos¦mo¦logy
cos¦mo¦naut
cos¦mo¦polis
cos¦mo¦pol¦itan
cos¦mo¦pol¦it¦an¦
                ism
cos¦mo¦pol¦ite
cos¦mos
Cos¦sack
cos¦set (cos¦seted,
 cos¦set¦ing)
cost (as *v.*, cost)
costal
co-star (as *v.*
 co-starred,
 co-starring)
cost¦ard
Costa Rica
cost¦ate
cost-effective
coster
cost¦er¦mon¦ger
cost¦ive
cost¦li¦ness
costly (cost¦lier,
 cost¦li¦est)
cost¦mary (plant)
cos¦tume (as *v.*,
 cos¦tum¦ing)
cos¦tu¦mier
cosy (as *a.*,
 co¦sier, co¦si¦est;
 as *n.*, *pl.* co¦sies;
 as *v.*, co¦sies,
 co¦sied,
 co¦sy¦ing)
cot (as *v.*, cot¦ted,
 cot¦ting)
co¦tan¦gent
cot-death
cote (for doves)
Côte d'Az¦ure
co¦terie
co¦term¦in¦ous
co-tidal
co¦til¦lion
co¦ton¦eas¦ter
Co¦to¦paxi
Cots¦wold
cotta
cot¦tage
cot¦tager
cot¦tagey

cot¦tar
cot¦ton
cot¦ton¦tail
cot¦ton¦wood
cot¦tony
coty¦le¦don
coty¦le¦don¦ous
cou¦cal
couch¦ant
couch¦ette
coudé
Coué
Coué¦ism
cou¦gar
cough
couldn't
cou¦lée
cou¦lisse
coul¦oir
cou¦lomb
cou¦lo¦met¦ric
cou¦lo¦metry
coul¦ter
cou¦ma¦rin
cou¦ma¦rone
coun¦cil
 (assembly)
coun¦cil¦lor
 (member of
 council)
coun¦sel (as *n.*,
 consultation; as *v.*,
 coun¦selled,
 coun¦sel¦ling)
coun¦sel¦lor
 (adviser)
count¦down *n.*
coun¦ten¦ance (as
 v., coun¦ten¦
                an¦cing)
coun¦ter
coun¦ter¦act
coun¦ter¦ac¦tion
coun¦ter¦act¦ive
counter-attack
coun¦ter¦bal¦ance
 (as *v.*, coun¦ter¦
                bal¦an¦cing)
coun¦ter¦blast
coun¦ter¦change
 (coun¦ter¦
                chan¦ging)
coun¦ter¦charge
 (as *v.*, coun¦ter¦
                char¦ging)
coun¦ter¦check

counter-claim
counter-
                clockwise
counter-
                espionage
coun¦ter¦feit
coun¦ter¦feiter
coun¦ter¦foil
counter-
                intelligence
coun¦ter¦mand
coun¦ter¦march
coun¦ter¦
                meas¦ure
coun¦ter¦mine (as
 v., coun¦ter¦
                min¦ing)
coun¦ter¦move
counter-offensive
coun¦ter¦pane
coun¦ter¦part
coun¦ter¦point
coun¦ter¦poise (as
 v., coun¦ter¦
                pois¦ing)
counter-
                productive
counter-
                reformation
Counter-
                Reformation
 (*hist.*)
counter-
                revolution
coun¦ter¦scarp
coun¦ter¦shaft
coun¦ter¦sign
coun¦ter¦sig¦na¦
                ture
coun¦ter¦sink
 (coun¦ter¦sunk)
coun¦ter¦stroke
counter-tenor
coun¦ter¦vail
coun¦ter¦value
coun¦ter¦weight
count¦ess
counting-house
count¦less
coun¦tri¦fied
coun¦try (*pl.*
 coun¦tries)
coun¦try¦man (*pl.*
 coun¦try¦men)
coun¦try¦side
country-wide

coun|try|wo|man
(*pl.* coun|try|
  wo|men)
county (*pl.*
 coun|ties)
coup (notable
move)
coup de grâce
coup d'état
coup d'œil
coupe (dish)
coupé (car)
couple (as *v.*,
 coup|ling)
coup|ler
coup|let
cou|pon
cour|age
cour|age|ous
cour|ante
cour|gette
cour|ier
cour|lan
course (as *v.*,
 cours|ing)
courser
court
court-card
cour|te|ous
cour|tesan
cour|tesy (*pl.*
 cour|tes|ies)
court-house
court|ier
court|li|ness
courtly
court mar|tial *n.*
 (*pl.* courts
 mar|tial)
court-martial *v.*
 (court-
  martialled,
 court-
  martial|ling)
court|ship
court|yard
cous|cous
cousin
cousin-german
couth
cou|ture
cou|tur|ier (*masc.*)
cou|turi|ère (*fem.*)
couv|ade
cou|vert
cou|ver|ture

co|va|lence
co|va|lency (*pl.*
 co|va|len|cies)
co|va|lent
cove (as *v.*,
 cov|ing)
coven
cov|en|ant
cov|en|anter (one
 who covenants)
Cov|en|anter (*Sc.*
 hist.)
cov|en|antor
 (*Law*)
Cov|en|try
cover
cov|er|age
cov|er|all
cov|er|let
cov|ert
cov|er|ture
cover-up *n.*
covet (coveted,
 cov|et|ing)
cov|et|ous
covey
covin (*Law*)
cow|age
cow|ard
cow|ard|ice
cow|bane
cow|bell
cow|berry (*pl.*
 cow|ber|ries)
cow|boy
cower
cow-grass
cow|herd
cow|hide
cow|itch
cowl
cow-lick
cow|man (*pl.*
 cow|men)
co-worker
cow-parsley
cow-pat
cow|pox
cow|rie
cow|shed
cow|slip
coxa (*pl.* coxae)
coxal
cox|comb
cox|swain
coy|ote

coypu
cozen
coz|en|age
crab-apple
crab|bily
crab|bi|ness
crabby
 (crab|bier,
 crab|bi|est)
crab (as *v.*,
 crab|bed,
 crab|bing)
crab|wise
crack-down *n.*
cracker
cracker|jack
crackle (as *v.*,
 crack|ling)
crackly
crack|nel
crack|pot
cracks|man (*pl.*
 cracks|men)
crack-up *n.*
cracky
Cra|cow
cradle (as *v.*,
 cra|dling)
craft|ily
crafti|ness
crafts|man (*pl.*
 crafts|men)
crafts|man|ship
crafty (craft|ier,
 crafti|est)
craggy (crag|gier,
 crag|gi|est)
crags|man (*pl.*
 crags|men)
cram (crammed,
 cram|ming)
crambo (*pl.*
 cram|boes)
cram|mer
cramp-iron
cram|pon
cran|age
cran|berry (*pl.*
 cran|ber|ries)
crane (as *v.*,
 cran|ing)
crane-fly (*pl.*
 crane-flies)
crane's-bill
cra|nial
cra|ni|ate

cra|ni|olo|gical
cra|ni|olo|gist
cra|ni|ology
cra|ni|ometry
cra|nium (*pl.*
 cra|nia)
crank|case
crank|ily
cranki|ness
crank|pin
crank|shaft
cranky
 (crank|ier,
 cranki|est)
cran|nied
cran|nog
cranny (*pl.*
 cran|nies)
crap (as *v.*,
 crapped,
 crap|ping)
crape (as *v.*,
 crap|ing)
crappy
 (crap|pier,
 crap|pi|est)
crapu|lence
crapu|lent
crapu|lous
crapy
craque|lure
crash-dive (as *v.*,
 crash-diving)
crash-helmet
crash-land
crasis (*pl.* crases)
crass
cras|sit|ude
crate (as *v.*,
 crat|ing)
crater
cra|vat
cra|vat|ted
crave (crav|ing)
craven
craw|fish (*pl.*
 same)
crawler
cray|fish (*pl.*
 same)
crayon
craze (as *v.*,
 craz|ing)
cra|zily
cra|zi|ness

crazy (cra|zier,
  cra|zi|est)
creak (noise)
  ⚠ creek
creaky (creak|ier,
  creaki|est)
creamer
cream|ery (pl.
  cream|er|ies)
creamy
  (cream|ier,
  creami|est)
crease (creas|ing)
cre|at|able
cre|ate
  (cre|at|ing)
cre|at|ine
cre|ation
cre|at|ive
cre|at|iv|ity
cre|ator (one who
  creates)
Cre|ator (God)
crea|ture
crèche
credal
cre|dence
cre|den|tial
cre|denza
cred|ib|il|ity
cred|ible
cred|ibly
credit (as v.,
  cred|ited,
  cred|it|ing)
cred|it|able
cred|it|ably
cred|itor
credo (pl. cre|dos)
cre|du|lity
credu|lous
creedal
creek (river)
  ⚠ creak
creep (crept)
creeper
creepy (creep|ier,
  creepi|est)
creepy-crawly
  (pl. creepy-
    crawlies)
cre|mate
  (cre|mat|ing)
cre|ma|tion
crem|at|or|ium
  (pl. crem|at|oria)

crem|at|ory
crème de menthe
cren|ate
cren|ated
cren|ation
crena|ture
crenel
cren|el|late
  (cren|el|lat|ing)
cre|nel|la|tion
Cre|ole
cre|ol|ize
  (cre|ol|iz|ing)
creo|sote (as v.,
  creo|sot|ing)
crêpe
crêpe de Chine
crêpe Su|zette
crep|it|ant
crep|it|ate
  (crep|it|at|ing)
crep|ita|tion
crep|itus
cre|pus|cu|lar
cres|cendo (pl.
  cres|cen|dos)
cres|cent
cre|sol
crest|fal|len
cre|ta|ceous
Cre|ta|ceous
  (Geol.)
Cretan
Crete
cretic
cretin
cret|in|ism
cret|in|ous
cre|tonne
cre|vasse
crev|ice
crewel
crew|man (pl.
  crew|men)
crib (as v.,
  cribbed,
  crib|bing)
crib|bage
cribo (pl. cri|bos)
crib|ri|form
cricket
crick|eter
cric|oid
cri de cœur (pl.
  cris de cœur)
crier

cri|key
crime-sheet
crime-writer
crim|inal
cri|min|al|istic
cri|min|al|ity
crim|in|ally
crim|in|ate
  (crim|in|at|ing)
cri|mina|tion
crim|in|at|ive
crim|in|at|ory
crim|ino|lo|gical
crim|ino|lo|gist
crim|ino|logy
crimpy
crim|son
cringe (crin|ging)
cringle
crinkle (as v.,
  crink|ling)
crinkly
  (crink|lier,
  crink|li|est)
crin|oid
crin|oidal
crin|ol|ine
cri|ollo (pl.
  cri|ol|los)
cripes
cripple (as v.,
  crip|pling)
cri|sis (pl. cri|ses)
crisp|ate
crisp|bread
crispy (cris|pier,
  cris|pi|est)
criss-cross
crista (pl. cris|tae)
crist|ate
cris|to|bal|ite
cri|ter|ial
cri|terion (pl.
  cri|teria)
critic
crit|ical
crit|ic|al|ity
crit|ic|ally
crit|ic|as|ter
cri|ti|cism
cri|ti|cize
  (cri|ti|ciz|ing)
cri|tique
croaker
croak|ily

croaky
  (croak|ier,
  croaki|est)
Croat
Cro|atia
Cro|atian
cro|ceate
cro|chet (as v.,
  cro|cheted,
  cro|chet|ing)
cro|cid|ol|ite
crock|ery
crocket
Crock|ford
cro|co|dile
cro|co|dil|ian
cro|cus
Croe|sus
crofter
crois|sant
Cro-Magnon
crom|bec
crom|lech
crony (pl.
  cro|nies)
crooked
  (crookeder,
  crook|ed|est)
crook|ery
Crookes
crooner
crop (as v.,
  cropped,
  crop|ping)
crop|per
cro|quet (game)
cro|quette (roll or
  ball of food etc.)
crore
cro|sier
cross|bar
cross-beam
cross-bench
cross-bencher
cross|bill
cross-bones
cross|bow
cross-breed (as v.,
  cross-bred)
cross-Channel
cross-check
cross-country
cross-current
cross-cut
crosse (*Lacrosse*)

cross-
   examination
cross-examine
  (cross-
    examining)
cross-eyed
cross-fertilize
  (cross-fertilizing)
cross-fire
cross-grain
cross-hatch
cross-legged
cross-link
cross-linkage
cross-over *n. & a.*
cross-patch
cross-piece
cross-ply
cross-pollinate
  (cross-
    pollinating)
cross-pollination
cross-question
cross-reference
  (as *v.*, cross-
   referencing)
crossroad
cross-section
cross-stitch
cross-talk
cross-trees
cross-voting
cross|ways
cross-wind
cross-wire
cross|wise
cross|word
crot|chet
crot|chet|eer
crot|chety
cro|ton
croup
crou|pier
croupy
croû|ton
crow (as *v.*, *past*
  crowed *or* crew)
crow|bar
crow|berry (*pl.*
  crow|ber|ries)
crow|foot (plant)
Crown Derby
crow's-feet
crow's-nest
cru|ces (*pl.* of
  crux)

cru|cial
cru|cially
cru|cian
cru|ci|ate
cru|cible
cru|ci|fer|ous
cru|ci|fix
cru|ci|fix|ion
cru|ci|form
cru|cify
  (cru|ci|fies,
  cru|ci|fied,
  cru|ci|fy|ing)
cru|dity (*pl.*
  cru|dit|ies)
cruel (cruel|ler,
  cruel|lest)
cruelly
cruelty (*pl.*
  cruel|ties)
cruet
cruise (as *v.*,
  cruis|ing)
cruiser
cruis|er|weight
cruise|way
crumble (as *v.*,
  crum|bling)
crum|bly
  (crum|blier,
  crum|bli|est)
crumby
  (crumb|ier,
  crumbi|est)
crum|mi|ness
crummy
  (crum|mier,
  crum|mi|est)
crum|pet
crumple
  (crump|ling)
crunchy
  (crunch|ier,
  crunchi|est)
crup|per
crural
cru|sade (as *v.*,
  cru|sad|ing)
cru|sader
crus|ta|cean
crus|ta|ce|ology
crus|ta|ceous
crust|ily
crus|ti|ness
crusty (crus|tier,
  crus|ti|est)

crux (*pl.* cru|ces)
cru|zeiro
  (cru|zeiros)
cry (cries, cried,
  cry|ing)
cry-baby
  (*pl.* cry-babies)
cryo|bio|logy
cryo|gen
cryo|genic
cryo|lite
cryo|pump
cryo|stat
cryo|sur|gery
crypt
crypt|ana|lysis
crypt|ana|lyst
crypt|ana|lyt|ical
cryptic
crypt|ic|ally
cryp|to|gam
cryp|to|gamic
cryp|to|gam|ous
cryp|to|gram
cryp|to|grapher
cryp|to|graphic
cryp|to|graphy
cryp|to|meria
cryp|to|zoic
crys|tal
crys|tal|line
crys|tal|lin|ity
crys|tal|lite
crys|tal|liza|tion
crys|tal|lize
  (crys|tal|liz|ing)
crys|tal|lo|
         grapher
crys|tal|lo|
         graphic
crys|tal|lo|graphy
crys|tal|loid
cten|oid
cteno|phore
cub (as *v.*,
  cubbed,
  cub|bing)
Cuba
Cu|ban
cubby-hole
cube (as *v.*,
  cu|bing)
cu|beb
cu|bic
cu|bical (cube-
  shaped)

cu|bic|ally
cu|bicle (small
  room)
cu|bi|form
cu|bism
cu|bist
cu|bit
cu|bital
cu|boid
cu|boidal
cuck|old
cuck|oldry
cuckoo
cuckoo-pint
cuckoo-spit
cu|cum|ber
cu|cur|bit
cu|cur|bit|aceous
cud|bear
cuddle
  (cud|dling)
cud|dly
  (cud|dlier,
  cud|dli|est)
cud|gel (as *v.*,
  cud|gelled,
  cud|gel|ling)
cud|weed
cue (as *v.*, cued,
  cue|ing)
cue|ist
cuesta
cuff-link
Cufic *use* Kufic
cui bono?
cuir|ass
cuir|ass|ier
cuis|ine
cul-de-sac (*pl.*
  culs-de-sac)
cu|lin|ary
cul|let
Cul|lo|den
cul|mi|fer|ous
cul|min|ant
cul|min|ate
  (cul|min|at|ing)
cul|mina|tion
cu|lottes
culp|ab|il|ity
culp|able
culp|ably
cul|prit
cultic
cult|ism
cult|ist

cul'ti|var
cul'tiv|ate
  (cul'tiv|at|ing)
cul'tiva|tion
cul'tiv|ator
cul|tural
cul'tur|ally
cul|ture
  (cul|tur'ing)
cul|vert
cum'ber
Cum'ber|land
cum'ber|some
Cum|bria
Cum|brian
cum|brous
cumin
cum'mer|bund
cumquat *use*
  kumquat
cu'mu|late
  (cu'mu|lat|ing)
cu'mu|lat|ive
cu'mul|ous *a.*
cu|mulus (*pl.*
  cu'muli)
cu|ne'ate
cu'nei|form
cun'ni|lin'gus
cun|ning
  (cun|ninger,
  cun'ning|est)
cup (as *v.*,
  cupped,
  cup|ping)
Cu'par
cup|bearer
cup|board
cup-cake
cu|pel (as *v.*,
  cu|pelled,
  cu'pel|ling)
cu'pel|la'tion
cup|ful (*pl.*
  cup|fuls)
Cu'pid
cu'pid|ity
cu|pola
cuppa
cupr'am|mo'nium
cup|reous
cup|ric
cup'ri|fer'ous
cupro-nickel
cup|rous
cu|pule

cur'able
cura|çao (*pl.*
  cura|çaos)
cur'acy
cur'are
cur'ar|ine
cur'ar|ize
  (cur'ar|iz|ing)
cur'as|sow
cur'ate
cur'at|ive
cur'ator
cur'at|orial
curb (restrain)
  △ kerb
cur|cuma
curdle (curd|ling)
curdy
cure (as *v.*,
  cur|ing)
cure-all
cur'et|tage
cur'ette (as *v.*,
  cur'et|ting)
cur|few
Curia (papal court)
Curial
curie (unit)
Curie (person)
curio (*pl.* curios)
curi|os'ity (*pl.*
  curi|os|it'ies)
curi|ous
curium
curler
cur|lew
cur'li|cue
cur'li|ness
curl|ing
curly (curl|ier,
  curl|iest)
cur'mud'geon
cur'mud'geonly
cur'rant (dried
  fruit)
cur'rency (*pl.*
  cur|ren'cies)
cur|rent (present;
  tide; electricity)
cur'ric|ular
cur'ric|ulum (*pl.*
  cur'ric|ula)
cur'ric|ulum
  vitae (*pl.*
  cur'ric|ula vitae)
cur'rier

cur'rish
curry (as *n.*, *pl.*
  cur'ries; as *v.*,
  cur'ries,
  cur'ried,
  cur'ry|ing)
curry-comb
curse (as *v.*,
  cursed or curst,
  curs|ing)
curs|ive
cursor
curs'or|ial
curs'or|ily
curs'ori|ness
curs|ory
cur'tail
cur'tail|ment
cur|tain
cur|tana
cur'til|age
Cur'tis
curtsy (as *n.*, *pl.*
  curt'sies; as *v.*,
  curt'sies,
  curt'sied,
  curt'sy|ing)
cur'va|ceous
cur'va|ture
curve (as *v.*,
  cur|ving)
cur'vet (as *v.*,
  cur'vet|ted,
  cur'vet|ting)
cur'vi|lin'ear
curvy (cur|vier,
  cur'vi|est)
cus'cus
cu|sec
cush|ion
cush|iony
Cush|itic
cushy (cush|ier,
  cushi|est)
cusp|ate
cusped
cusp'idal
cusp'id|ate
cus|sed
cus'tard
cus|to'dial
cus|to'dian
cus|tody
cus'tom
cus'tom|ar'ily
cus'tom|ari|ness

cus'tom|ary
custom-built
cus|tomer
cus'tom|ize
  (cus'tom|iz|ing)
custom-made
Cus|toms (Govt.
  dept.)
cut (as *v.*, cut,
  cut|ting)
cu'ta|ne'ous
cut|away
cut-back *n.*
cute (cuter,
  cutest)
cut|icle
cu'tic|ular
cu'tis
cut|lass
cut|ler
cut|lery
cut|let
cut-line *n.*
cut-off *n.*
cut-out *n.*
cut-price *a.*
cut-rate *a.*
cut|ter
cut|throat
cuttle
cuttle-bone
cuttle|fish
cutty (*pl.* cut|ties)
cut|water
cut|worm
cu'vée
cu|vette
Cu|vier
Cwm|bran
cyan
cy'an|am'ide
cy|an'ic
cy'an|ide
cy'ano|co'bal|
         amin
cy'ano|gen
cy'an|osis (*pl.*
  cy'an|oses)
cy'ber|na'tion
cy'ber|netic
cy'ber|net'ics
cycad
Cyc'la'des
Cyc|ladic
cyc'la'mate
cyc'la'men

cycle (as *v.*,
  cyc|ling)
cycle-track
cyc|lic
cyc|lical
cyc|lic|ally
cyc|list
cyclo-cross
cyc|lo|graph
cyc|loid
cyc|loidal
cyc|lo|meter
cyc|lone
cyc|lonic
cyc|lo|pae|dia
cyc|lo|paedic
cyc|lo|pa|raf|fin
Cyc|lo|pean
cyc|lops (copepod;
  pl. same *or*
  cyc|lo|pes)

Cyc|lops (one-eyed
  giant; *pl.*
  Cyc|lo|pes)
cyc|lo|rama
cyc|lo|stome
cyc|lo|style (as *v.*,
  cyc|lo|styl|ing)
cyc|lo|thy|mia
cyc|lo|thymic
cy|clo|tron
cyg|net
cy|lin|der
cy|lin|drical
cy|lin|dric|ally
cyma
cym|bal (*Mus.*)
cym|bal|ist
cym|balo (*pl.*
  cym|ba|los)
cym|bid|ium
cym|bi|form
cyme (*Bot.*)

cym|ose
Cym|ric (Welsh)
Cymru (Wales)
cyng|han|edd
cynic
cyn|ical
cyn|ic|ally
cyn|icism
cyno|ceph|alus
  (*pl.* cyno|
           ceph|ali)
cy|no|glos|sum
cy|nos|ure
cy pres (*Law*)
cy|press
Cyp|rian (of
  Cyprus)
cyp|rin|oid (like
  carp)
Cyp|riot (native or
  language)
cyp|ri|pe|dium

Cy|prus
cyp|sela (achene
  with calyx; *pl.*
  cyp|selae)
Cy|rene
Cy|re|naic
Cyr|il|lic
cystic
cyst|itis
cys|to|scope
cys|to|tomy (*pl.*
  cys|to|tom|ies)
cy|tid|ine
cyto|logy
cy|to|plasm
cy|to|sine
Czech
Czecho|slo|vak
Czecho|slo|va|kia
Czecho|
    slo|va|kian

D

dab (as v.,
 dabbed,
 dab|bing)
dabble
 (dab|bling)
dab|bler
dab|chick
da capo
da'cha
dachs|hund
da'coit
dac'tyl
dac|tylic
Dada
Da'da|ism
Da'da|ist
daddy (pl.
 dad|dies)
daddy-long-legs
dado (pl. da'dos)
Dadra
Dae'da|lian
Daed|alus
dae'mon (in Gr.
 myth.)
daf'fo|dil
dag'ger
dago (pl. da'gos)
Da|guerre
da'guerre|otype
da'ha|bee'yah
dah'lia
Dáil Éire|ann
daily (as n., pl.
 dai'lies)
dai'mon
dai|monic
dain'tily
dain'ti|ness
dainty (as n., pl.
 dain'ties; as a.,
 dain'tier,
 dain'ti|est)
dai|quiri
dairy (pl. dair'ies)
dairy|ing
dairy|man (pl.
 dairy|men)
dais

daisy (pl. dais'ies)
daisy-chain
Da'kar
Da'kota
Da'lai Lama
dales|man (pl.
 dales|men)
Dali
dal'li|ance
dal|lier
dally (dal'lies,
 dal|lied,
 dal'ly|ing)
Dal|ma'tian
dal|matic
dal segno
dal'ton|ism
Dal'ton|ize
 (Dal'ton|iz|ing)
dam (as n., barrier
 etc.; as v.,
 dammed,
 dam|ming)
⚠ damn
dam|age (as v.,
 dam|aging)
dam'age|able
Daman
dam'as|cene (as
 v.,
 dam'as'cen|ing)
Da'mas|cus
dam'ask
dame (woman)
Dame (title)
dam'mar
dam'mit
damn (condemn
 etc.) ⚠ dam
damn|able
damn|ably
dam'na|tion
dam'nat|ory
damned|est
dam'ni|fica|tion
dam'nify (Law;
 dam'ni|fies,
 dam'ni|fied,
 dam'ni|fy|ing)

damn|ing
dam'num (Law)
Damo|cles
dampen
damper
damp-proof
dam'sel
dam'son
dance (as v.,
 dan'cing)
dance-hall
dan'cer
dan'cetty
dan|delion
dan'der
dan'dify
 (dan'di|fies,
 dan'di|fied,
 dan'di|fy|ing)
dandle
 (dand|ling)
dan|druff
dandy (as n., pl.
 dan|dies)
dandy-brush
dan'dy|ish
Dane
Dane|geld
Dane|law
Danes'-blood
dane|weed
dane|wort
dan'ger
dan'ger|ous
dangle
 (dang|ling)
Dan'iel
Dan'iel Der|onda
Dan'ish
danse ma|cabre
 (pl. danses
 ma|cabres)
danseur
danseuse
Dante
Dan|tean
Dant|esque
dan'tho'nia
Dan|ube

dap (dapped,
 dap|ping)
daphne
dap'per
dapple (as v.,
 dap|pling)
dapple-grey
Darby and Joan
dare (as v.,
 dar'ing)
dare|devil
daren't
Dar es Sa'laam
dari|ole
darken
darkle (dark|ling)
dark-room
darky (pl.
 dark'ies)
dar|ling
Dar'ling|ton
dar'nel
dar|shan
dart|board
darter
Dart|moor
dartre
dart|rous
Dar'win
Dar'win|ian
Dar'win|ism
Dar'win|ist
dash|board
da'shiki
das'sie
dast|ard
dast|ardly
dasy|ure
data (pl. of datum)
data|bank
data|base
data-processing
 (attrib.)
date (as v.,
 dat'ing)
date|less
date-line
date-palm
date-stamp

da'ti|val
da'ti|vally
dat'ive
da'tum (*pl.* data)
da'tura
daub (smear)
daube (stew)
dauber
daub|ster
dauby
daugh|ter
daughter-in-law
  (*pl.* daughters-in-
                 law)
Daum'ier
daunt
daunt|less
dauphin
Dau|phiné
da'ven|port
Da'vid
Da'vid
  Cop'per|field
Da'vis (apparatus)
davit
Davy Jones's
  locker
Davy lamp
dawdle (as *v.*,
  dawd|ling)
day-bed
day-boy
day|break
day-dream
day-girl
day|light
day-return
day-room
day-school
day|time
day|work
daze (as *v.*,
  daz'ing)
dazzle (as *v.*,
  daz|zling)
D-Day
dea'con
dea'con|ate
dea'con|ess
de|ac'tiv|ate
  (de|ac'tiv|at'ing)
de|ac'tiva|tion
de|ac'tiv|ator
dead-beat
deaden
dead-end *a.*

dead-eye
dead|head
dead|light
dead|line
dead'li|ness
dead|lock
deadly (dead|lier,
  dead'li|est)
dead-on
dead|stock
de-aerate
  (de-aerating)
de-aeration
deaf-aid
deafen
deal (as *v.*, dealt,
  dealing) △ dele
dealer
de|am'bul|la'tion
de|am'bu|lat'ory
dean (head of
  faculty etc.)
  △ dene
dean'ery (*pl.*
  dean|er'ies)
dearie
dearth
deasil (clockwise)
  △ diesel
death
death|bed
death-blow
death-knell
death'li|ness
death-mask
death-rattle
death-roll
death-toll
death-trap
death-warrant
death-watch
  beetle
death-wish
dé|bâcle
debag
  (de|bagged,
  de'bag|ging)
debar (de|barred,
  de|bar|ring)
de'bark
de|barka|tion
de'base
  (de|bas'ing)
de|base|ment
de|bat'able
de|bat'ably

de'bate (as *v.*,
  de|bat'ing)
de|bater
de|bauch
de|bauch'ee
de|baucher
de|bauch|ery
de'beak
de'ben|ture
de|bil'it|ate
  (de'bil'it|at'ing)
de'bil|ity (*pl.*
  de|bil|it'ies)
debit (deb|ited,
  deb'it|ing)
de'bon|air
Deb|orah
de|bouch
de|bouch|ment
Deb|rett (Peerage)
de|brief
deb'ris
debtor
de'bug
  (de|bugged,
  de|bug|ging)
de'bunk
de'bus
  (de|busses,
  de|bussed,
  de|bus|sing)
De|bussy
dé'but
dé'but|ante
dec|adal
dec'ade
dec'ad|ence
dec'ad|ent
dec'ad|ent|ism
dec|adic
de|caf'fein|ate
  (de|caf'fein|
            at'ing)
deca|gon
deca|gonal
deca|gyn'ous
deca|hed'ral
deca|hed'ron (*pl.*
  deca|hedra)
de|cal'ci|fica'tion
de|cal'cify
  (de|cal'ci|fies,
  de|cal'ci|fied,
  de|cal'ci|fy|ing)
deca|litre

Deca|logue
Dec|am'eron
de'camp
de'canal
dec|and'rous
de'cani
de'cant
de'canter
de|cap'it|ate
  (de|cap'it|at'ing)
de|cap'ita|tion
deca|pod
de|car'bon|iza|
              tion
de|car'bon|ize
  (de|car'bon|iz|
            ing)
deca|style
de|casu'al|iza|
              tion
de|casu'al|ize
  (de|casu'al|iz|
            ing)
deca|syl'labic
deca|syl'lable
dec|ath'lete
dec|ath'lon
de'cay
de'cease
  (de|ceas'ing)
de'ceit
de'ceit|ful
de'ceit|fully
de'ceiv|able
de|ceive
  (de'ceiv|ing)
de|ceiver
de|cel'er|ate
  (de|cel'er|at'ing)
de|cel'era'tion
de|cel'er|ator
de|cel'ero|meter
De|cem|ber
de|cency (*pl.*
  de'cen|cies)
decen|nial
decen|ni'ally
decen|nium (*pl.*
  decen|nia)
de'cent
de|cen'tral|iza|
              tion
de|cen'tral|ize
  (de|cen'tral|iz|
            ing)
de'cep|tion

de|cept|ive
de|ce|reb|rate
deci|bel
de|cid|able
de|cide
 (de|cid|ing)
de|cidedly
de|cider
de|cidu|ous
deci|gram
deci|litre
decimal
decim|al|iza|tion
decim|al|ize
 (decim|al|iz|ing)
decim|ally
decim|ate
 (decim|at|ing)
decima|tion
deci|metre
de|cipher
de|cision
de|cisive
deck-chair
deck-hand
deckle
de|claim
de|clama|tion
de|clam|at|ory
de|clar|ant
de|clara|tion
de|clar|at|ive
de|clar|at|ory
de|clare
 (de|clar|ing)
de|clarer
dé|classé (fem.
 dé|clas|sée)
de|clas|si|fica|
   tion
de|clas|sify
 (de|clas|si|fies,
 de|clas|si|fied,
 de|clas|si|fy|ing)
de|clen|sion
de|clin|able
de|clina|tion
de|clina|tional
de|cline (as v.,
 de|clin|ing)
de|clino|meter
de|cliv|it|ous
de|cliv|ity (pl.
 de|cliv|it|ies)
de|clutch
de|coct

de|coc|tion
de|cod|able
de|code
 (de|cod|ing)
de|coder
de|coke (as v.,
 de|cok|ing)
de|col|late
 (de|col|lat|ing)
de|col|la|tion
dé|col|let|age
dé|col|leté (fem.
 dé|col|letée)
de|col|on|iza|tion
de|col|or|iza|tion
de|col|or|ize
 (de|col|or|iz|ing)
de|com|pos|able
de|com|pose
 (de|com|pos|ing)
de|com|pos|ite
de|com|posi|tion
de|com|pound
de|com|press
de|com|pres|sion
de|com|pres|sor
de|con|gest|ant
de|con|sec|rate
 (de|con|sec|rat|
   ing)
de|con|sec|ra|tion
de|con|tam|in|ate
 (de|con|
   tam|in|at|ing)
de|con|tam|ina|
   tion
de|con|trol
 (de|con|trolled,
 de|con|trol|ling)
dé|cor
dec|or|ate
 (dec|or|at|ing)
dec|ora|tion
dec|or|at|ive
dec|or|ator
dec|or|ous
de|cor|tic|ate
 (de|cor|tic|at|ing)
de|cor|tica|tion
de|corum
dé|coup|age
de|couple
 (de|coup|ling)
de|coy
de|crease (as v.,
 de|creas|ing)

de|cree (de|creed,
 de|cree|ing)
de|cree nisi (Law)
decre|ment
de|crepit
de|crep|it|ate
 (de|crep|it|at|ing)
de|crep|ita|tion
de|crep|it|ude
de|cres|cendo (pl.
 de|cres|cen|dos)
de|cres|cent
de|cretal
de|crier
de|crim|in|al|iza|
   tion
de|crim|in|al|ize
 (de|crim|in|al|iz|
   ing)
de|cry (de|cries,
 de|cried,
 de|cry|ing)
de|crypt
de|cryp|tion
decu|man
de|cum|bent
dec|uple (as v.,
 decu|pling)
decu|plet
de|cus|sate (as v.,
 de|cus|sat|ing)
de|cus|sa|tion
de|dans
ded|ic|ate
 (ded|ic|at|ing)
ded|ic|ated
ded|ic|atee
ded|ica|tion
ded|ic|at|ive
ded|ic|ator
ded|ic|at|ory
de|duce
 (de|du|cing)
de|du|cible
de|duct
de|duct|ible
de|duc|tion
de|duct|ive
deed-box
deed poll
deem v.
de-emphasize
 (de-emphasizing)
deem|ster
deepen

deep-freeze (as v.,
 deep-froze,
 deep-frozen,
 deep-freezing)
deep-fried
deep|ing
deep-laid
deep-rooted
deep-seated
deer|skin
deer|stalker
de-escalate
 (de-escalating)
de-escalation
de|face
 (de|fa|cing)
de|face|able
de|face|ment
de facto
de|falc|ate
 (de|falc|at|ing)
de|falca|tion
de|falc|ator
de|fama|tion
de|fam|at|ory
de|fame
 (de|fam|ing)
de|fat (de|fat|ted,
 de|fat|ting)
de|fault
de|faulter
de|feas|ance
de|feas|ib|il|ity
de|feas|ible
de|feas|ibly
de|feat
de|feat|ism
de|feat|ist
de|fec|ate
 (de|fec|at|ing)
de|feca|tion
de|fec|ator
de|fect
de|fec|tion
de|fect|ive
de|fector
de|fence
de|fence|less
de|fend
de|fend|ant
de|fender
de|fen|es|trate
 (de|fen|es|
   trat|ing)
de|fen|es|tra|tion
de|fens|ib|il|ity

de|fens|ible
de|fens|ibly
de|fens|ive
de|fer (de|ferred,
 de|fer|ring)
de|fer|ence
de|fer|en|tial
de|fer|en|tially
de|fer|ment
de|fer|rable
de|fer|ral
de|fi|ance
de|fi|ant
de|fi|ciency (*pl.*
 de|fi|cien|cies)
de|fi|cient
de|fi|cit
de|fier
de|fil|ade (as *v.*,
 de|fil|ad|ing)
de|file (as *v.*,
 de|fil|ing)
de|file|ment
de|fin|able
de|fin|ably
de|fine
 (de|fin|ing)
def|in|ite
def|ini|tion
de|fin|it|ive
de|flag|rate
 (de|flag|rat|ing)
de|flag|ra|tion
de|flag|rator
de|flate
 (de|flat|ing)
de|fla|tion
de|fla|tion|ary
de|fla|tion|ist
de|flect
de|flector
de|flex|ion
de|flora|tion
de|flower
de|fo|cus
 (de|focused,
 de|fo|cus|ing)
De|foe
de|fo|li|ant
de|fo|li|ate
 (de|fo|li|at|ing)
de|fo|li|ation
de|for|est
de|for|esta|tion
de|form
de|forma|tion

de|forma|tional
de|form|ity (*pl.*
 de|form|it|ies)
de|fraud
de|fray
de|fray|able
de|frayal
de|frock
de|frost
de|funct
de|fuse
 (de|fus|ing)
defy (de|fies,
 de|fied,
 de|fy|ing)
dé|gagé (*fem.*
 dé|ga|gée)
de|gas (de|gasses,
 de|gassed,
 de|gass|ing)
De|gas
de Gaulle
de|gauss
de|gen|er|acy
de|gen|er|ate (as
 v., de|gen|er|
 at|ing)
de|gen|era|tion
de|grad|able
de|grada|tion
de|grad|at|ive
de|grade
 (de|grad|ing)
de|grease
 (de|greas|ing)
de|gree
de|gres|sive
dé|grin|go|lade
de haut en bas
de|hisce
 (de|his|cing)
de|his|cence
de|his|cent
de|hu|man|iza|
 tion
de|hu|man|ize
 (de|hu|man|iz|
 ing)
de|hyd|rate
 (de|hyd|rat|ing)
de|hyd|ra|tion
de-ice (de-icing)
dei|cide
deictic
dei|fica|tion
dei|form

deify (dei|fies,
 dei|fied,
 dei|fy|ing)
deign
Dei gra|tia
de|ion|iza|tion
de|ion|ize
 (de|ion|iz|ing)
deip|no|soph|ist
de|ism
de|ist
de|istic
de|ist|ical
de|ity (*pl.*
 de|it|ies)
De|ity (God,
 Creator)
déjà vu
de|ject
de|jec|tion
de jure
dekko (*pl.*
 dek|kos)
De|la|croix
de|laine
de la Mare
De|la|roche
Dela|ware
de|lay
del cre|dere
dele (delete;
 deled, del|ing)
△ deal
de|lect|able
de|lect|ably
de|lecta|tion
del|eg|acy (*pl.*
 del|eg|acies)
del|eg|ate (as *v.*,
 del|eg|at|ing)
del|ega|tion
de|lete (de|let|ing)
de|le|teri|ous
de|le|tion
delft|ware
Delhi
de|lib|er|ate (as *v.*,
 de|lib|er|at|ing)
de|lib|era|tion
de|lib|er|at|ive
del|ic|acy (*pl.*
 del|ic|acies)
del|ic|ate
de|li|ca|tes|sen
de|li|cious
de|light

de|light|ful
de|light|fully
De|li|lah
de|limit
 (de|lim|ited,
 de|lim|it|ing)
de|lim|it|ate
 (de|lim|it|at|ing)
de|lim|ita|tion
de|lin|eate
 (de|lin|eat|ing)
de|lin|eation
de|lin|eator
de|lin|quency (*pl.*
 de|lin|quen|cies)
de|lin|quent
de|li|quesce
 (de|li|ques|cing)
de|li|ques|cence
de|li|ques|cent
de|li|ri|ous
de|li|rium
de|li|rium
 tre|mens
de|liver
de|liv|er|ance
de|liv|ery (*pl.*
 de|liv|er|ies)
de|louse
 (de|lous|ing)
Del|phi
Del|phian
Del|phic
del|phi|nium
del|phin|oid
delta
del|taic
del|ti|olo|gist
del|ti|ology
delt|oid
de|lude
 (de|lud|ing)
de|luge (as *v.*,
 de|lu|ging)
de|lu|sion
de|lu|sional
de|lus|ive
de|lus|ory
de|lustre
 (de|lust|ring)
de luxe
delve (delv|ing)
de|mag|net|iza|
 tion

de|mag'net|ize (de|mag'net|iz| ing)
dem|agogic
dem|agogue
dem|agoguery
dem|agogy
de|mand
de|mand|ant
de|mant|oid
de|marc|ate (de|marc'at|ing)
de|marca'tion
dé'marche
de|ma'teri|al|iza| tion
de|ma'teri|al|ize (de|ma'teri|al|iz| ing)
Dem|av'end
de|mean
de|mean|our
de|ment
de|men'ted
dé'menti (official denial)
de|men|tia
de|men|tia prae'cox
dem|er'ara (sugar)
Dem|er'ara (in Guyana)
de|merit
de|mer'it|ori|ous
de|mer'sal
de|mesne
demi|god (*fem.* demi|god'dess)
demi|john
de|mil'it'ar|iza| tion
de|mil'it'ar|ize (de|mil'it'ar|iz| ing)
demi-mondaine
demi-monde
de|min'er|al|iza| tion
de|min'er|al|ize (de|min'er|al|iz| ing)
demi-pension
de|mise (as *v.*, de|mis'ing)
demi|semi|quaver

de|mis'sion
de|mist
de|mister
demi|tasse
de|mit (de|mit'ted, de|mit'ting)
demi|urge
demi|ur'gic
demi-vierge
demo (*pl.* demos)
de|mob (as *v.*, de|mobbed, de|mob'bing)
de|mo'bil'iza|tion
de|mo'bil|ize (de|mo'bil|iz|ing)
demo|cracy (*pl.* demo|cra'cies)
demo|crat
Demo|crat (supporter of US party)
demo|cratic
Demo|cratic (of US polit. party)
demo|crat'ic|ally
demo|crat|ism
demo|crat|iza| tion
demo|crat|ize (demo'crat|iz| ing)
de|modu'la|tion
demo|grapher
demo|graphic
demo|graph|ical
demo|graph'ic| ally
demo|graphy
de|mois'elle
de|mol|ish
de|moli|tion
de|mon (evil spirit)
de|mon'et|iza|tion
de|mon'et|ize (de|mon'et|iz|ing)
de|mo|niac
de|moni|acal
de|moni|ac'ally
de|monic
de|mon|ism
de|mon|ize (de|mon|iz|ing)
de|mono|latry

de|mono|logy
dem'on|strab|il| ity
dem'on|strable
dem'on|strably
dem'on|strate (dem'on| strat'ing)
de|mon|stra'tion
de|mon|strat|ive
de|mon|strator
de|mor'al|iza'tion
de|mor'al|ize (de|mor'al|iz|ing)
De'mos|thenes
de'mote (de|mot'ing)
dem|otic
de|mo'tion
de|mount
de|mul|cent
de|mur (as *v.*, de|murred, de|mur|ring)
de|mure (de|murer, de|murest)
de|mur|rable
de|mur|rage
de|mur|rant
de|mur|rer
demy (paper size)
de|mys'ti|fica'tion
de|mys'tify (de|mys'ti|fies, de|mys'ti|fied, de|mys'ti|fy|ing)
de|mytho|lo'gize (de|mytho| lo'giz'ing)
den|arius (*pl.* den|arii)
den|ary
de|na'tional|iza| tion
de|na'tion|al|ize (de|na'tion|al|iz| ing)
de|natur'al|iza| tion
de|natur'al|ize (de|natur'al|iz| ing)
de|na'tur|ant
de|na'tura|tion

de|na'ture (de|na'tur|ing)
de|na'zi|fica|tion
de|na'zify (de|na'zi|fies, de|na'zi|fied, de|na'zi|fy|ing)
dend|rite
dend|ritic
dend|rit|ic|ally
den'dro|chrono| lo'gist
den'dro|chrono| logy
dend|roid
dend|ro|lo'gist
dend|ro|logy
dene (sand-hill; vale) △ dean
dene-hole
dengue
deni|able
de|nial
den|ier
den|ig'rate (den|ig'rat|ing)
den|ig|ra'tion
den|ig|rator
den|ig|rat'ory
denim
Den|ise
de|nit'ri|fica'tion
de|nit'rify (de|nit'ri|fies, de|nit'ri|fied, de|nit'ri|fy|ing)
den|izen
Den|mark
de|nom'in|ate (de|nom|in|at| ing)
de|nom|ina'tion
de|nom|ina'tional
de|nom|in|at|ive
de|nom|in|ator
de|no'ta'tion
de|not'at|ive
de|note (de|not'ing)
de|noue|ment
de|nounce (de|noun'cing)
de nou'veau
de novo
dense (denser, dens|est)

dens|ito|meter
dens|ity (*pl.*
 dens|it|ies)
dental (of teeth)
den|ta|lium (*pl.*
 den|ta|lia)
dent|al|ize
 (dent|al|iz|ing)
dent|ate
dent|icle
dent|ic|ulate
den|ti|frice
dentil (*Archit.*)
den|ti|lin|gual
dent|ine
dent|ist
dent|istry
den|ti|tion
den|ture
de|nuc|lear|iza|
 tion
de|nuc|lear|ize
 (de|nuc|lear|iz|
 ing)
de|nuda|tion
de|nud|at|ive
de|nude
 (de|nud|ing)
de|nu|mer|ab|il|
 ity
de|nu|mer|able
de|nun|ci|ation
de|nun|ci|at|ive
de|nun|ci|ator
de|nun|ci|at|ory
deny (de|nies,
 de|nied,
 deny|ing)
deoch an doris
de|odar
de|odor|ant
de|odor|iza|tion
de|odor|ize
 (de|odor|iz|ing)
Deo gra|tias
de|ontic
de|onto|lo|gical
de|onto|lo|gist
de|onto|logy
Deo vo|lente
de-oxygenate (de-
 oxygenating)
de-oxygenation
de|oxy|ribo|
 nucleic
 (acid)

de|part
de|par|ted
de|part|ment
de|part|mental
de|part|ment|al|
 ize
 (de|part|ment|al|
 iz|ing)
de|part|ment|ally
de|par|ture
de|pas|tur|age
de|pas|ture
 (de|pas|tur|ing)
de|pend
de|pend|ab|il|ity
de|pend|able
de|pend|ably
de|pend|ant *n.*
de|pend|ence
de|pend|ency (*pl.*
 de|pend|en|cies)
de|pend|ent *a.*
de|per|son|al|iza|
 tion
de|per|son|al|ize
 (de|per|son|al|iz|
 ing)
de|pict
de|pic|tion
de|pict|ive
de|pil|ate
 (de|pil|at|ing)
de|pila|tion
de|pil|at|ory (*pl.*
 de|pil|at|or|ies)
de|plane
 (de|plan|ing)
de|plete
 (de|plet|ing)
de|ple|tion
de|plor|able
de|plor|ably
de|plore
 (de|plor|ing)
de|ploy
de|ploy|ment
de|plume
 (de|plum|ing)
de|pol|ar|iza|tion
de|pol|ar|ize
 (de|pol|ar|iz|ing)
de|pol|iti|ciza|tion
de|pol|iti|cize (de|
 pol|iti|ciz|ing)
de|poly|mer|iza|
 tion

de|poly|mer|ize
 (de|poly|mer|iz|
 ing)
de|pon|ent
de|popu|la|tion
de|popu|late
 (de|popu|lat|ing)
de|port
de|porta|tion
de|portee
de|port|ment
de|pose
 (de|pos|ing)
de|posit (as *v.*,
 de|pos|ited,
 de|pos|it|ing)
de|pos|it|ary
 (person; *pl.*
 de|pos|it|ar|ies)
de|pos|ition
de|pos|itor
de|pos|it|ory
 (storehouse; *pl.*
 de|pos|it|or|ies)
de|prava|tion
de|prave
 (de|prav|ing)
de|prav|ity (*pl.*
 de|prav|it|ies)
de|prec|ate
 (disapprove of;
 de|prec|at|ing)
de|pre|ca|tion
de|prec|ator
de|prec|at|ory
de|pre|ci|ate
 (lower in value,
 belittle; de|pre|ci|
 at|ing)
de|pre|ci|ation
de|pre|ci|at|ory
de|preda|tion
de|pred|ator
de|press
de|press|ant
de|press|ible
de|pres|sion
de|press|ive
de|pressor
 (muscle)
de|pres|sur|iza|
 tion
de|pres|sur|ize
 (de|pres|sur|iz|
 ing)

de|prival
de|priva|tion
de|prive
 (de|priv|ing)
depth
de|pur|ate
 (de|pur|at|ing)
de|pura|tion
de|pur|at|ive
de|pur|ator
de|pu|ta|tion
de|pute (as *v.*,
 de|put|ing)
depu|tize
 (depu|tiz|ing)
dep|uty (*pl.*
 dep|uties)
de|rail
de|rail|ment
de|range
 (de|ran|ging)
de|range|ment
de|rate
 (de|rat|ing)
de|ra|tion
derby (low-heeled
 shoe; *pl.* der|bies)
Derby (place,
 horse-race; *pl.*
 Der|bies)
Der|by|shire
de|re|gis|ter
de|re|gis|tra|tion
de règle
der|el|ict
de|rel|ic|tion
de|re|quis|ition
de|res|trict
de|res|tric|tion
de|ride
 (de|rid|ing)
de rigueur
de|ri|sion
de|ris|ive
de|ris|ory
de|riv|able
de|riva|tion
de|riva|tional
de|riv|at|ive
de|rive
 (de|riv|ing)
dermal
der|ma|titis
der|ma|to|lo|gical
der|ma|to|logist
der|ma|to|logy

dermic
dermis
der|og|ate
  (der|og|at|ing)
de|roga|tion
de|rog|at|or|ily
de|rog|at|ory
der|rick
der|rin|ger
der|ris
derv (fuel oil)
der|vish
Der|went Wa|ter
de|sal|in|ate
  (de|sal|in|at|ing)
de|sal|ina|tion
de|salt
de|scale
  (de|scal|ing)
des|cant
Des|cartes
des|cend
des|cend|ant
des|cender
des|cend|ible
des|cent
de|scrib|able
de|scribe
  (de|scrib|ing)
de|scrip|tion
de|script|ive
de|scriptor
des|cry (des|cries,
  des|cried,
  des|cry|ing)
de|sec|rate
  (de|sec|rat|ing)
de|sec|ra|tion
de|sec|rator
de|seg|reg|ate
  (de|seg|reg|
      at|ing)
de|seg|rega|tion
de|sens|it|iza|tion
de|sens|it|ize
  (de|sens|it|iz|ing)
de|sert
  (recompense;
  abandon)
des|ert (barren
  region) △ dessert
de|serter
de|ser|tion
de|serve
  (de|ser|ving)
de-sex

de|sexu|al|ize (de|
  sexu|al|iz|ing)
dés|ha|billé
de|sic|cant
de|sic|cate
  (de|sic|cat|ing)
de|sic|ca|tion
de|sic|cat|ive
de|sic|cator
de|sid|er|at|ive
de|sid|er|atum (*pl.*
  de|sid|er|ata)
de|sign
des|ig|nate (as *v.*,
  des|ig|nat|ing)
des|ig|na|tion
de|sign|edly
de|signer
de|sign|ing
de|sir|ab|il|ity
de|sir|able
de|sir|ably
de|sire (as *v.*,
  de|sir|ing)
de|sir|ous
de|sist
desk-bound
des|man (*pl.*
  des|mans)
des|ol|ate (as *v.*,
  des|ol|at|ing)
des|ola|tion
des|ol|ator
de|sorb
de|sorb|ent
de|sorp|tion
des|pair
despatch *use*
  dispatch
des|per|ado (*pl.*
  des|per|adoes)
des|per|ate
des|pera|tion
de|spic|able
de|spic|ably
des|pise
  (des|pis|ing)
des|pite
des|pite|ful
de|spoil
de|spo|li|ation
des|pond
des|pond|ency
des|pond|ent
des|pot
des|potic

des|pot|ic|ally
des|pot|ism
de|squam|ate
  (de|squam|
      at|ing)
de|squama|tion
de|squam|at|ive
de|squam|at|ory
des|sert (sweet
  course) △ desert
des|sert|spoon
des|tina|tion
des|tine
  (des|tin|ing)
des|tiny (*pl.*
  des|tin|ies)
des|ti|tute
des|ti|tu|tion
des|troy
des|troy|able
des|troyer
de|struct|ib|il|ity
de|struct|ible
de|struc|tion
de|struct|ive
de|structor
de|suet|ude
des|ul|tor|ily
des|ul|tori|ness
des|ul|tory
de|tach
de|tach|able
de|tach|ment
de|tail
de|tain
de|tainee
de|tainer
de|tect
de|tect|able
de|tect|ably
de|tec|tion
de|tect|ive
de|tector
de|tent (a
  mechanical catch)
dé|tente (cessation
  of strained
  relationships
  between States)
de|ten|tion
dé|tenu (*fem.*
  dé|tenue)
de|ter (de|terred,
  de|ter|ring)
de|ter|gent

de|teri|or|ate
  (de|teri|or|at|ing)
de|teri|ora|tion
de|teri|or|at|ive
de|ter|ment
de|ter|min|able
de|ter|min|acy
de|ter|min|ant
de|ter|min|ate
de|ter|mina|tion
de|ter|min|at|ive
de|ter|mine
  (de|ter|min|ing)
de|ter|min|ism
de|ter|min|ist
de|ter|min|istic
de|ter|rence
de|ter|rent
de|test
de|test|able
de|test|ably
de|testa|tion
de|throne
  (de|thron|ing)
det|inue (*Law*)
det|on|ate
  (det|on|at|ing)
det|ona|tion
det|on|at|ive
det|on|ator
de|tour
de|tox|ic|ate
  (de|tox|ic|at|ing)
de|tox|ica|tion
de|toxi|fica|tion
de|tox|ify
  (de|toxi|fies,
  de|toxi|fied,
  de|toxi|fy|ing)
de|tract
de|trac|tion
de|tract|ive
de|tractor
de|train
de|train|ment
de|trib|al|iza|tion
de|trib|al|ize
  (de|trib|al|iz|ing)
det|ri|ment
det|ri|mental
det|ri|ment|ally
de|trital
de|trited
de|tri|tion
de|tritus
De|troit

de trop
de|tumes|cence
deuce
deus ex mach'ina
deu'ter|ag'on|ist
deu'ter|ate
 (deu'ter|at'ing)
deu'tera|tion
deu'ter|ium
Deutero-Isaiah
deu'teron
Deu'tero|nomic
Deu'tero|nom'ical
Deu'tero|nom|ist
Deu'tero|nomy
Deutsch|mark
deut|zia
de|valu|ation
de|value
 (de|val'ued,
 de|valu'ing)
De'va'na|gari
dev'ast|ate
 (dev'ast|at'ing)
dev'asta|tion
dev'ast|ator
de|velop
 (de|veloped,
 de|vel'op|ing)
de|vel'op|able
de|vel'oper
de|vel'op|ment
de|vel'op|mental
de|vel'op|ment|
 ally
de|vi|ance
de|vi|ancy
de|vi|ant
de|vi|ate (as *v.*,
 de|vi|at'ing)
de|vi|ation
de|vi|ational
de|vi|ation|ism
de|vi|ation|ist
de|vi|ator
de|vice
devil (as *v.*,
 dev'illed,
 dev'il|ling)
dev'il|dom
devil-fish
dev'il|ish
dev'il|ism
devil-may-care
dev'il|ment

dev'ilry (*pl.*
 dev'il|ries)
devils-on-
        horseback
de|vi|ous
de|vis'able
de|vise
 (de|vis'ing)
de|visee
de|viser (one who
 devises)
△ divisor
de|visor (*Law*)
△ divisor
de|vi'tal|iza|tion
de|vi'tal|ize
 (de|vi'tal|iz'ing)
de|vit'ri|fica|tion
de|vit'rify
 (de|vit'ri|fies,
 de|vit'ri|fied,
 de|vit'ri|fy'ing)
de|void
de|vol'ute
 (de|vol'ut|ing)
de|volu|tion
de|volu|tion|ary
de|volu|tion|ist
de|volve
 (de|vol'ving)
Devon
Dev'on|ian
Dev'on|shire
de|vote
 (de|vot'ing)
de|votee
de|vote|ment
de|vo|tion
de|vo|tional
de|vour
de|vout
de|wan
dewar
dew|berry (*pl.*
 dew|ber'ries)
Dewey (library
 system)
dew'ily
dewi|ness
dew'lap
Dews|bury
dewy
dex'ter
dex'ter|ity
dex'tral
dex'tral|ity

dex'trally
dex|tran
dex|trin
dex'tro|ro'tat'ory
dex'trorse
dex'trose
dex'trous
Dhaka
dhal
dharma
Dhau'la|giri
dhobi
dhoti
dhow
dia|betes
dia|betic
di'ab|lerie
dia|bolic
dia|bol|ical
dia|bol'ic|ally
di'ab|ol|ism
di'ab|ol|ist
di'ab|ol|ize
 (di'ab|ol|iz|ing)
di|abolo (*pl.*
 di|abo|los)
dia|chronic
dia|chron'ic|ally
dia|chron|ism
dia|chron|istic
dia|chron|ous
dia|chrony
di'ac|onal
di'ac|on|ate
dia|critic
dia|crit|ical
di|adelph|ous
dia|dem
di|aer|esis (*pl.*
 di|aer|eses)
Di'ag|hilev
dia|gnose
 (dia|gnos'ing)
dia|gnosis (*pl.*
 dia|gnoses)
dia|gnostic
dia|gnost'ic|ally
dia|gnos'ti|cian
dia|gnos'tics
di|ag|onal
di|ag'on|ally
dia|gram (as *v.*,
 dia|grammed,
 dia|gram|ming)
dia|gram|matic

dia|gram|mat|ize
 (dia|gram|mat|iz|
                ing)
dia|grid
dial (as *v.*,
 di|alled,
 di|al|ling)
dia|lect
dia|lectal
dia|lec'tic
dia|lect|ical
dia|lect'ic|ally
dia|lec'ti|cian
dia|lecto|lo'gist
dia|lecto|logy
dia|lo'gic
dia|lo'gist
dia|logue
dia|lyse
 (dia|lys|ing)
dia|lysis (*pl.*
 dia|lyses)
dia|lytic
dia|mag'netic
dia|mag'net|ism
di'amanté
di'aman'ti|fer|ous
di'amant|ine
dia|meter
dia|met'ral
dia|met'rical
dia|met'ric|ally
dia|mond
dia|mondi|fer|ous
Di|ana
di|and'rous
di|anthus
dia|pason
dia|pause
di|aper
dia|phan|ous
dia|phor|etic
dia|phragm
dia|phrag'matic
dia|pos'it|ive
di|archal
di|archic
di|archy
di|ar|ist
di|ar|istic
di|ar|ize
 (di|ar|iz|ing)
dia|rrhoea
dia|rrhoeal
dia|rrhoeic

di¦ary (*pl.*
  di¦ar¦ies)
dia¦scope
Dia¦spora
dia¦stase
dia¦stasic
dia¦static
dia¦stole
dia¦stolic
dia¦tes¦saron
dia¦therm¦ancy
dia¦therm¦an¦ous
dia¦thermic
dia¦thermy
dia¦thesis (*pl.*
  dia¦theses)
di¦atom
di¦at¦oma¦ceous
di¦at¦omic
di¦at¦om¦ite
dia¦tonic
dia¦tribe
di¦azo
dib (dibbed,
  dib¦bing)
di¦basic
dib¦ber
dibble (as *v.*,
  dib¦bling)
dice (as *v.*, di¦cing)
dicey (di¦cier,
  di¦ci¦est)
di¦cho¦tom¦ize
  (di¦cho¦tom¦iz
        ing)
di¦cho¦tom¦ous
di¦cho¦tomy (*pl.*
  di¦cho¦tom¦ies)
di¦chroic
di¦chro¦ism
di¦chro¦matic
di¦chro¦mat¦ism
dick¦ens (*colloq.*)
Dick¦ens
Dick¦ens¦ian
dicker
dicky (as *n.*, *pl.*
  dick¦ies; as *a.*,
  dick¦ier,
  dicki¦est)
dicky-bird
di¦cot
di¦co¦ty¦le¦don
di¦co¦ty¦le¦don¦
        ous
di¦crotic

dicta (*pl.* of
  dictum)
Dic¦ta¦phone
  (*propr.*)
dic¦tate
  (dic¦tat¦ing)
dic¦ta¦tion
dic¦tator
dic¦tat¦or¦ial
dic¦tat¦ori¦ally
dic¦tion
dic¦tion¦ary (*pl.*
  dic¦tion¦ar¦ies)
Dic¦to¦graph
  (*propr.*)
dictum (*pl.* dicta)
did¦ache
di¦dactic
di¦dact¦ic¦ally
di¦dac¦ti¦cism
di¦dap¦per
diddle (did¦dling)
did¦dler
Di¦derot
didgeri¦doo
di¦di¦coi
didn't
di¦dy¦mium
die (as *n.*, *pl.* dice;
  as *v.*, died,
  dy¦ing) △ dye
die-away *a.*
die-hard *n.*
diel¦drin
di¦elec¦tric
di¦ene
diesel
diesel-electric
dies¦el¦ize
  (dies¦el¦iz¦ing)
dies non (*Law*)
die-stamping
diet
di¦et¦ary (as *n.*, *pl.*
  di¦et¦ar¦ies)
di¦et¦etic
di¦et¦et¦ic¦ally
di¦et¦et¦ics
di¦eti¦tian
dif¦fer
dif¦fer¦ence
dif¦fer¦ent
dif¦fer¦en¦tia (*pl.*
  dif¦fer¦en¦tiae)
dif¦fer¦en¦tial
dif¦fer¦en¦ti¦ally

dif¦fer¦en¦ti¦ate
  (dif¦fer¦en¦ti¦at¦
        ing)
dif¦fer¦en¦ti¦ation
dif¦fi¦cult
dif¦fi¦culty (*pl.*
  dif¦fi¦cult¦ies)
dif¦fid¦ent
dif¦fid¦ence
dif¦fract
dif¦frac¦tion
dif¦fract¦ive
dif¦fracto¦meter
dif¦fuse (as *v.*,
  dif¦fus¦ing)
dif¦fus¦ible
dif¦fusion
dif¦fu¦sion¦ist
dif¦fus¦ive
dig (as *v.*, dug,
  dig¦ging)
di¦gam¦ist
di¦gamma
di¦gam¦ous
di¦gamy (*pl.*
  di¦gam¦ies)
di¦gast¦ric
di¦gest
di¦gest¦ib¦il¦ity
di¦gest¦ible
di¦ges¦tion
di¦gest¦ive
dig¦ger
dig¦ging
di¦git
di¦gital
di¦gi¦talin
di¦gi¦talis
di¦git¦al¦ize
  (di¦git¦al¦iz¦ing)
di¦git¦ally
di¦git¦ate
di¦gita¦tion
di¦giti¦grade
di¦git¦ize
  (di¦git¦iz¦ing)
dig¦nify
  (dig¦ni¦fies,
  dig¦ni¦fied,
  dig¦ni¦fy¦ing)
dig¦nit¦ary (*pl.*
  dig¦nit¦ar¦ies)
dig¦nity (*pl.*
  dig¦nit¦ies)
di¦graph
di¦gress

di¦gres¦sion
di¦gress¦ive
di¦hed¦ral
di¦hyd¦ric
dike
dik¦tat
di¦lap¦id¦ated
di¦lap¦ida¦tion
di¦lat¦able
di¦lata¦tion
di¦late (di¦lat¦ing)
di¦la¦tion
di¦lator
dil¦at¦or¦ily
dil¦at¦ori¦ness
dil¦at¦ory
dildo (*pl.* dil¦dos)
di¦lemma
di¦let¦tante (*pl.*
  di¦let¦tanti *or*
  di¦let¦tan¦tes)
di¦let¦tant¦ish
di¦let¦tant¦ism
di¦li¦gence
di¦li¦gent
dilly-dally
  (dilly-dallies,
  dilly-dallied,
  dilly-dallying)
dilu¦ent
di¦lute (di¦lut¦ing)
di¦lutee
di¦lu¦tion
di¦lu¦vial
di¦lu¦vi¦al¦ist
di¦lu¦vium (*pl.*
  di¦lu¦via)
dim (as *a.*,
  dim¦mer,
  dim¦mest; as *v.*,
  dimmed,
  dim¦ming)
dime
di¦men¦sion
di¦men¦sional
dimer
di¦meric
di¦mer¦ous
di¦meter
di¦midi¦ate
di¦min¦ish
di¦minu¦endo (*pl.*
  di¦minu¦en¦dos)
di¦mi¦nu¦tion
di¦min¦ut¦ival
di¦min¦ut¦ive

di|mis|sory
dim|ity
dimly
dim|mer
dim|mish
di|morphic
di|morph|ism
di|morph|ous
dimple (as *v.*,
 dim|pling)
dim|ply
 (dim|plier,
 dim|pli|est)
dim-wit
dim-witted
din (as *v.*, dinned,
 din|ning)
di|nar
dine (din|ing)
diner
diner-out
din|ette
dinghy (small
 boat; *pl.*
 dingh|ies)
△ dingy
din|gily
din|gi|ness
dingle
dingo (*pl.*
 din|goes)
din|gus
Ding|wall
dingy (dull;
 din|gier,
 din|gi|est)
△ dinghy
dining-car
dining-hall
dining-room
dining-table
dinky (din|kier,
 din|ki|est)
din|ner
dinner-dance
dinner-jacket
dinner-service
dinner-set
dinner-table
din|or|nis
di|no|saur
di|no|saur|ian
di|no|there
dio|cesan
dio|cese
di|ode

di|oecious
Dio|genes
Di|onys|iac
Di|onys|ian
Di|onysus
Dio|phant|ine
di|optre
di|op|tric
di|or|ama
di|or|amic
di|or|ite
di|or|itic
Dio|scor|ides
di|ox|ide
dip (as *v.*, dipped,
 dip|ping)
di|pept|ide
diph|theria
diph|ther|ial
diph|theric
diph|ther|itic
diph|ther|oid
diph|thong
diph|thongal
diph|thong|ize
 (diph|thong|iz
 ing)
dip|lo|coc|cus
 (*pl.*dip|lo|cocci)
dip|lo|docus
dip|loid
dip|loidy
dip|loma
dip|lo|macy
dip|lo|ma'd (*or*
 dip|lo|maed)
dip|lo|mat
dip|lo|mate
dip|lo|matic
dip|lo|mat|ic|ally
dip|lo|mat|ist
dip|lo|mat|ize
 (dip|lo|mat|iz
 ing)
di|polar
di|pole
dip|per
dipso (*pl.* dip|sos)
dip|so|ma|nia
dip|so|ma|niac
dip-stick
dip-switch
dip|teral
dip|teran
dip|ter|ous
dip|tych

dir|ect
dir|ec|tion
dir|ec|tional
dir|ec|tion|ally
dir|ect|ive
Dir|ect|oire
 (imitation of style
 of French
 Directory)
dir|ector
dir|ect|or|ate
director-general
dir|ect|ory (*pl.*
 dir|ect|or|ies)
Dir|ect|ory (*hist.*)
dir|ect|ress
dir|ect|rix (*pl.*
 dir|ect|rices)
dirge
dir|ham
di|ri|gible
di|ri|ment
dirndl
dirt|ily
dirti|ness
dirt-track
dirty (as *a.*,
 dir|tier, dir|ti|est;
 as *v.*, dirt|ies,
 dirt|ied,
 dir|ty|ing)
dis|ab|il|ity (*pl.*
 dis|ab|il|it|ies)
dis|able
 (dis|ab|ling)
dis|able|ment
dis|ab|use
 (dis|ab|us|ing)
dis|ac|cord
dis|ad|vant|age
 (as *v.*, dis|
 ad|vanta|ging)
dis|ad|vant|age|
 ous
dis|af|fec|ted
dis|af|fec|tion
dis|af|fili|ate
 (dis|af|fili|at|ing)
dis|af|fili|ation
dis|af|firm
dis|af|firma|tion
dis|af|for|est
dis|af|for|esta|
 tion

dis|ag|ree
 (dis|ag|reed,
 dis|ag|ree|ing)
dis|ag|ree|able
dis|ag|ree|ably
dis|ag|ree|ment
dis|al|low
dis|am|bigu|ate
 (dis|am|bigu|
 at|ing)
dis|am|bigu|ation
dis|amen|ity (*pl.*
 dis|amen|it|ies)
dis|an|nul
 (dis|an|nulled,
 dis|an|nul|ling)
dis|an|nul|ment
dis|ap|pear
dis|ap|pear|ance
dis|ap|point
dis|ap|point|ment
dis|ap|proba|tion
dis|ap|prob|at|ive
dis|ap|prob|at|
 ory
dis|ap|proval
dis|ap|prove
 (dis|ap|prov|ing)
dis|arm
dis|arma|ment
dis|ar|range
 (dis|ar|ran|ging)
dis|ar|range|ment
dis|ar|ray
dis|ar|ticu|late
 (dis|ar|ticu|
 lat|ing)
dis|ar|ticu|la|tion
dis|as|semble
 (dis|as|sem|
 bling)
dis|as|sem|bly
dis|as|so|ci|ate
 (dis|as|so|ci|
 at|ing)
dis|as|so|ci|ation
dis|as|ter
dis|ast|rous
dis|avow
dis|avowal
dis|band
dis|band|ment
dis|bar
 (dis|barred,
 dis|bar|ring)
dis|bar|ment

dis|be|lief
dis|be|lieve
 (dis|be|liev|ing)
dis|be|liever
dis|bench
dis|bound
dis|bud
 (dis|bud|ded,
 dis|bud|ding)
dis|bur|den
dis|bursal
dis|burse
 (dis|burs|ing)
disc (gen.)
dis|calced
dis|card
dis|carn|ate
dis|cern
dis|cern|ible
dis|cern|ing
dis|charge (as v.,
 dis|char|ging)
dis|ciple
dis|cip|lin|able
dis|cip|linal
dis|cip|lin|ar|ian
dis|cip|lin|ary
dis|cip|line (as v.,
 dis|cip|lin|ing)
dis|cipu|lar
dis|claim
dis|claimer
dis|close
 (dis|clos|ing)
dis|clos|ure
disco (pl. dis|cos)
dis|co|bolus (pl.
 dis|co|boli)
dis|co|grapher
dis|co|graphy (pl.
 dis|co|graph|ies)
dis|coid
dis|col|ora|tion
dis|col|our
dis|comfit (thwart;
 dis|com|fited,
 dis|com|fit|ing)
dis|com|fit|ure
dis|com|fort
dis|com|mode
 (dis|
    com|mod|ing)
dis|com|modi|ous
dis|com|pose
 (dis|com|pos|ing)
dis|com|pos|ure

dis|con|cert
dis|con|cer|tion
dis|con|firm
dis|con|firma|tion
dis|con|nect
dis|con|nec|tion
dis|con|sol|ate
dis|con|tent
dis|con|tent|ment
dis|con|tinu|ance
dis|con|tinue
 (dis|con|tinu|ing)
dis|con|tinu|ity
 (pl. dis|con|tinu|
    it|ies)
dis|con|tinu|ous
dis|cord
dis|cord|ance
dis|cord|ancy (pl.
 dis|cord|an|cies)
dis|cord|ant
dis|co|thèque
dis|count
dis|count|able
dis|coun|ten|ance
 (dis|coun|ten|
    an|cing)
dis|cour|age
 (dis|cour|aging)
dis|cour|age|ment
dis|course (as v.,
 dis|cours|ing)
dis|cour|teous
dis|cour|tesy (pl.
 dis|cour|tes|ies)
dis|cover
dis|cov|er|able
dis|cov|erer
dis|cov|ery (pl.
 dis|cov|er|ies)
dis|credit
 (dis|cred|ited,
 dis|cred|it|ing)
dis|cred|it|able
dis|cred|it|ably
dis|creet (prudent)
dis|crep|ancy (pl.
 dis|crep|an|cies)
dis|crep|ant
dis|crete
 (separate)
dis|cre|tion
dis|cre|tion|ary
dis|crim|in|ate
 (dis|crim|in|
    at|ing)

dis|crim|ina|tion
dis|crim|in|at|ive
dis|crim|in|ator
dis|crim|in|at|ory
dis|crown
dis|curs|ive
dis|cus (disc)
dis|cuss (to
 debate)
dis|cuss|ant
dis|cus|sion
dis|dain
dis|dain|ful
dis|dain|fully
dis|ease
dis|eased a.
dis|econ|omy (pl.
 dis|econ|om|ies)
dis|em|bark
dis|em|barka|tion
dis|em|bar|rass
dis|em|bar|rass|
    ment
dis|em|bodi|ment
dis|embody
 (dis|em|bod|ies,
 dis|em|bod|ied,
 dis|em|body|ing)
dis|em|bogue
 (dis|em|bogued,
 dis|em|boguing)
dis|em|bowel (dis|
 em|bowelled,
 dis|
  em|bowel|ling)
dis|em|bowel|
    ment
dis|em|broil
dis|en|chant
dis|en|chant|ment
dis|en|cum|ber
dis|en|dow
dis|en|dow|ment
dis|en|gage
 (dis|en|ga|ging)
dis|en|gage|ment
dis|en|tail
dis|en|tangle
 (dis|en|tang|ling)
dis|en|tangle|
    ment
dis|en|thral
 (dis|en|thralled,
 dis|en|thral|ling)
dis|en|title
 (dis|en|titling)

dis|en|tomb
dis|equi|lib|rium
dis|es|tab|lish
dis|eur (fem.
 dis|euse)
dis|fa|vour
dis|fig|ure
 (dis|fig|ur|ing)
dis|fig|ure|ment
dis|for|est
dis|fran|chise
 (dis|fran|chising)
dis|fran|chise|
    ment
dis|gorge
 (dis|gor|ging)
dis|grace (as v.,
 dis|gra|cing)
dis|grace|ful
dis|grace|fully
dis|gruntled
dis|gruntle|ment
dis|guise (as v.,
 dis|guis|ing)
dis|gust
dis|gust|ful
dis|gust|ing
dis|ha|bille
dis|har|mo|ni|ous
dis|har|mon|ize
 (dis|har|mon|iz|
    ing)
dis|har|mony (pl.
 dis|har|mon|ies)
dish|cloth
dish|hear|ten
dish|ev|elled
dish|ev|el|ment
dish|ful (pl.
 dish|fuls)
dis|hon|est
dis|hon|esty
dis|hon|our
dis|hon|our|able
dis|hon|our|ably
dish|washer
dishy (dish|ier,
 dishi|est)
dis|il|lu|sion
dis|il|lu|sion|ment
dis|in|cent|ive
dis|in|clina|tion
dis|in|cline
 (dis|in|clin|ing)

dis|in|cor|por|ate
(dis|in|cor|por|
at|ing)
dis|in|fect
dis|in|fect|ant
dis|in|fec|tion
dis|in|fest
dis|in|festa|tion
dis|in|fla|tion
dis|in|fla|tion|ary
dis|in|forma|tion
dis|in|genu|ous
dis|in|herit
(dis|in|her|ited,
dis|in|her|it|ing)
dis|in|her|it|ance
dis|in|teg|rate
(dis|in|teg|
rat|ing)
dis|in|teg|ra|tion
dis|in|teg|rator
dis|in|ter
(dis|in|terred,
dis|in|ter|ring)
dis|in|ter|est
dis|in|ter|es|ted
dis|in|ter|ment
dis|in|vest|ment
dis jecta mem|bra
dis|join
dis|joint
dis|junc|tion
dis|junct|ive
disk (*Comp.*)
dis|lik|able
dis|like (as *v.*,
dis|lik|ing)
dis|lo|cate
(dis|lo|cat|ing)
dis|loca|tion
dis|lodge
(dis|lodging)
dis|lodge|ment
dis|loyal
dis|loy|al|ist
dis|loy|ally
dis|loy|alty (*pl.*
dis|loy|al|ties)
dis|mal
dis|mally
dis|mantle
(dis|mant|ling)
dis|mast
dis|may
dis|mem|ber

dis|mem|ber|
ment
dis|miss
dis|missal
dis|miss|ible
dis|mis|sion
dis|miss|ive
dis|mount
Dis|ney
Dis|ney|esque
dis|obedi|ence
dis|obedi|ent
dis|obey
dis|ob|lige
(dis|ob|li|ging)
dis|order
dis|or|der|li|ness
dis|or|derly
dis|or|gan|iza|
tion
dis|or|gan|ize
(dis|or|gan|iz|
ing)
dis|ori|ent
dis|ori|ent|ate
(dis|ori|ent|
at|ing)
dis|ori|enta|tion
dis|own
dis|owner
dis|par|age
(dis|par|aging)
dis|par|age|ment
dis|par|ate
dis|par|ity (*pl.*
dis|par|it|ies)
dis|pas|sion|ate
dis|patch
dis|pel
(dis|pelled,
dis|pel|ling)
dis|pens|able
dis|pens|ary (*pl.*
dis|pens|ar|ies)
dis|pensa|tion
dis|pens|at|ory
dis|pense
(dis|pens|ing)
dis|penser
dis|persal
dis|pers|ant
dis|perse
(dis|pers|ing)
dis|per|sion
dis|pers|ive

dis|pirit
(dis|pir|ited,
dis|pir|it|ing)
dis|place
(dis|pla|cing)
dis|place|ment
dis|play
dis|please
(dis|pleas|ing)
dis|pleas|ure (as
v., dis|pleas|ur|
ing)
dis|port
dis|pos|ab|il|ity
dis|pos|able
dis|posal
dis|pose
(dis|pos|ing)
dis|posi|tion
dis|pos|sess
dis|pos|ses|sion
dis|praise (as *v.*,
dis|prais|ing)
dis|proof
dis|pro|por|tion
dis|pro|por|tion|
ate
dis|prove
(dis|prov|ing)
dis|put|able
dis|put|ably
dis|put|ant
dis|pu|ta|tion
dis|pu|ta|tious
dis|pute (as *v.*,
dis|put|ing)
dis|quali|fica|tion
dis|qual|ify
(dis|quali|fies,
dis|quali|fied,
dis|quali|fy|ing)
dis|quiet (as *v.*,
dis|quieted,
dis|quiet|ing)
dis|quiet|ude
dis|quisi|tion
dis|quisi|tional
Dis|raeli
dis|reg|ard
dis|reg|ard|ful
dis|reg|ard|fully
dis|re|mem|ber
dis|repair
dis|rep|ut|able
dis|rep|ut|ably
dis|rep|ute

dis|res|pect
dis|res|pect|ful
dis|res|pect|fully
dis|robe
(dis|rob|ing)
dis|rupt
dis|rup|tion
dis|rupt|ive
dis|sat|is|fac|tion
dis|sat|isfy
(dis|sat|is|fies,
dis|sat|is|fied,
dis|sat|is|fy|ing)
dis|sect
dis|sec|tion
dis|sector
dis|seise
(dis|seis|ing)
dis|seisin
dis|semble
(dis|sem|bling)
dis|sem|bler
dis|sem|in|ate
(dis|sem|in|
at|ing)
dis|sem|ina|tion
dis|sem|in|ator
dis|sen|sion
dis|sent
dis|sentient
dis|ser|ta|tion
dis|serve
(dis|ser|ving)
dis|ser|vice
dis|sever
dis|sev|er|ance
dis|sev|er|ment
dis|sid|ence
dis|sid|ent
dis|sim|ilar
dis|sim|il|arity (*pl.*
dis|sim|il|ar|
it|ies)
dis|sim|il|ate
(dis|sim|il|at|ing)
dis|sim|ila|tion
dis|sim|il|at|ory
dis|sim|il|it|ude
dis|simu|late
(dis|simu|lat|ing)
dis|simu|la|tion
dis|simu|lator
dis|sip|ate
(dis|sip|at|ing)
dis|sip|ated
dis|sipa|tion

dis|sip|at|ive
dis|so|ci|ate
 (dis|so|ci|at|ing)
dis|so|ci|ation
dis|so|ci|at|ive
dis|sol|ub|il|ity
dis|sol|uble
dis|sol|ubly
dis|sol|ute
dis|solu|tion
dis|solv|able
dis|solve
 (dis|sol|ving)
dis|solv|ent
dis|son|ance
dis|son|ant
dis|suade
 (dis|suad|ing)
dis|sua|sion
dis|suas|ive
dis|sym|met|rical
dis|sym|metry (*pl.*
 dis|sym|met|ries)
dis|taff
distal
dist|ally
dis|tance (as *v.*,
 dis|tan|cing)
dis|tant
dis|taste
dis|taste|ful
dis|taste|fully
dis|tem|per
dis|tend
dis|tens|ib|il|ity
dis|tens|ible
dis|ten|sion
dis|tich
dis|til (dis|tilled,
 dis|til|ling)
dis|til|late
dis|til|la|tion
dis|til|lat|ory
dis|til|ler
dis|til|lery (*pl.*
 dis|til|ler|ies)
dis|tinct
dis|tinc|tion
dis|tinct|ive
dis|tin|gué (*fem.*
 dis|tin|guée)
dis|tin|guish
dis|tin|guish|able
dis|tin|guish|ably
dis|tort
dis|tor|tion

dis|tor|tional
dis|tract
dis|trac|tion
dis|train
dis|trainee
dis|trainer
dis|train|ment
dis|trainor
dis|traint
dis|trait (*fem.*
 dis|traite)
dis|traught
dis|tress
dis|tressed
dis|tress|ful
dis|tress|fully
dis|trib|ut|able
dis|tribu|tary (*pl.*
 dis|tribu|tar|ies)
dis|trib|ute
 (dis|trib|ut|ing)
dis|tri|bu|tion
dis|tri|bu|tional
dis|tribu|tive
dis|trib|utor
dis|trict
dis|trin|gas (*Law*)
dis|trust
dis|trust|ful
dis|trust|fully
dis|turb
dis|turb|ance
di|sulph|ide
dis|union
dis|unite
 (dis|unit|ing)
dis|unity (*pl.*
 dis|unit|ies)
dis|use (as *v.*,
 dis|us|ing)
disyl|labic
disyl|lable
ditch
ditch-water
di|theism
di|theist
dither
dith|ery
di|thy|ramb
di|thy|rambic
dit|tany (*pl.*
 dit|tan|ies)
ditto (*pl.* dit|tos)
dit|to|graphic
dit|to|graphy (*pl.*
 dit|to|graph|ies)

ditty (*pl.* dit|ties)
Diu (Ind. island)
di|ur|esis (*pl.*
 di|ur|eses)
di|ur|etic
di|urnal
di|urn|ally
diva
di|val|ent
di|van
di|var|ic|ate
 (di|var|ic|at|ing)
di|var|ica|tion
dive (as *v.*,
 div|ing)
dive-bomb
diver
di|verge
 (di|ver|ging)
di|ver|gence
di|ver|gency (*pl.*
 di|ver|gen|cies)
di|ver|gent
di|verse
di|ver|si|fi|able
di|ver|si|fica|tion
di|ver|sify
 (di|ver|si|fies,
 di|ver|si|fied,
 di|ver|si|fy|ing)
di|ver|sion
di|ver|sion|ary
di|ver|sion|ist
di|vers|ity (*pl.*
 di|vers|it|ies)
di|vert
di|ver|ticu|litis
di|ver|ticu|losis
di|ver|tic|ulum
 (*pl.* di|ver|tic|ula)
di|ver|ti|mento
 (*pl.* di|ver|ti|
          menti)
di|ver|tisse|ment
Dives
di|vest
di|vest|it|ure
di|vest|ment
di|vide (as *v.*,
 di|vid|ing)
di|vi|dend
di|vider
divi-divi
Di|vina
 Com|media
div|ina|tion

div|in|at|ory
di|vine (as *a.*,
 di|viner,
 di|vinest; as *v.*,
 di|vin|ing)
di|viner *n.*
diving-board
divining-rod
di|vin|ity (*pl.*
 di|vin|it|ies)
div|in|ize
 (div|in|iz|ing)
di|vis|ib|il|ity
di|vis|ible
di|vi|sion
di|vi|sional
di|vis|ive
di|visor
△ deviser,
devisor
di|vorce (as *v.*,
 di|vor|cing)
di|vor|cee (*also*
 di|vorcé *masc.*,
 di|vor|cée *fem.*)
divot
di|vul|ga|tion
di|vulge
 (di|vul|ging)
di|vulge|ment
di|vul|gence
divvy (as *n.*, *pl.*
 div|vies; as *v.*,
 div|vies,
 div|vied,
 divvy|ing)
Di|wali
dixie (*pl.* dix|ies)
Dixie (US states)
Dixie|land
diz|zily
diz|zi|ness
dizzy (as *a.*,
 diz|zier,
 diz|zi|est; as *v.*,
 diz|zies, diz|zied,
 diz|zy|ing)
D-layer
Dnie|per
Dnies|ter
do (does, did,
 done, do|ing)
do|able
dob|bin
Do|ber|mann
 pinscher

Do|cetic
Do|cet|ism
Do|cet|ist
do|cile
do|cil|ity
dock|age
docker
docket (as v.,
 dock|eted,
 dock|et|ing)
dock|land
dock|yard
doc|tor
doc|toral
doc|tor|ate
doc|tor|ial
doc|trin|aire
doc|trin|air|ism
doc|trinal
doc|trin|ally
doc|trine
doc|trin|ism
doc|trin|ist
docu|ment
docu|mental
docu|ment|al|ist
docu|ment|ary
 (pl. docu|ment|
 ar|ies)
docu|menta|tion
dod|der
dod|derer
dod|dery
doddle
do|deca|gon
do|deca|hed|ron
 (pl. do|deca|
 hedra)
do|deca|phonic
do|deca|syl|lable
dodge (as v.,
 dodging)
dodgem
dodger
dodgy (dodgier,
 dodgi|est)
dodo (pl. do|dos)
doer
doesn't
doe|skin
doff
dog (as v., dogged,
 dog|ging)
do|gate (office of
 doge)

dog|berry (pl.
 dog|ber|ries)
dog-biscuit
dog|cart
dog-collar
doge
dog-eared
dog|fight
dog|fish
dog|ged a.
dog|ger (Dutch
 boat; dingo-
 hunter)
Dog|ger (Geol.)
dog|gerel
dog|gie n.
dog|gi|ness
dog|gish
doggo
dog|gone
doggy a.
 (dog|gier,
 dog|gi|est)
dog|house
dog-leg
dogma
dog|matic
dog|mat|ic|ally
dog|mat|ism
dog|mat|ist
dog|mat|ize
 (dog|mat|iz|ing)
do-gooder
dog-paddle
 (dog-paddling)
dog|rose
dogs|body (pl.
 dogs|bod|ies)
dog-violet
dog|wood
doh (Mus.)
Doha
doily (pl. doil|ies)
do-it-yourself
dojo (pl. do|jos)
dolce far niente
dolce vita
dol|drums
dole (as v.,
 dol|ing)
dole|ful
dole|fully
dol|er|ite
Dol|gel|lau
do|li|cho|
 ceph|alic

do|li|cho|ceph|al|
 ous
do|lina
dol|lar
dol|lop (as v.,
 dol|loped,
 dol|lop|ing)
dolly (as n., pl.
 dol|lies; as v.,
 dol|lies, dol|lied,
 dolly|ing)
dolly-bird
dol|man (robe)
dol|men (tomb)
do|lo|mite
do|lo|mitic
dol|or|ous
dol|phin
dol|phin|ar|ium
 (pl. dol|phin|ar|
 iums)
dolt|ish
do|main (estate)
do|maine
 (vineyard)
do|man|ial
Dom|bey and Son
dome (as v.,
 dom|ing)
Domes|day Book
do|mestic
do|mest|ic|able
do|mest|ic|ally
do|mest|ic|ate
 (do|mest|ic|
 at|ing)
do|mest|ica|tion
do|mest|icity
domic
dom|ical
domi|cile (as v.,
 domi|cil|ing)
domi|cili|ary
dom|in|ance
dom|in|ant
dom|in|ate
 (dom|in|at|ing)
dom|ina|tion
dom|in|eer
Do|min|ica
dom|in|ical (of
 Sunday)
Do|min|ican (of St
 Dominic or order
 of friars)

dom|inie
 (schoolmaster)
do|min|ion
dom|ino (pl.
 dom|in|oes)
dom|in|oed
domy
don (as v.,
 donned,
 don|ning)
Don|ald
do|nate
 (do|nat|ing)
do|na|tion
don|at|ive
Don|cas|ter
donee
Don|egal
donga
Don Gio|vanni
Do|ni|zetti
don|jon
Don Juan
don|key
donkey-work
donna (It., Sp., or
 Port. lady)
Donna (title)
Donne, J.
don|née (basic
 fact)
don|nish
Don|ny|brook
 (scene of uproar)
donor
Don Quix|ote
don't
doo|dah
doodle (as v.,
 dood|ling)
doodle-bug
dood|ler
dooms|day
doom|watch
door|bell
door|knob
door|man (pl.
 door|men)
door|mat
door|nail
door|post
door|step
door|stop
door-to-door
door|way
dopa

dop|ant
dope (as v.,
  dop|ing)
dopey
dop|pel|gänger
Dop|per
Dop|pler (effect)
dor|ado (pl.
  dor|ados)
Dor|ches|ter
Dor|een
Dor|ian
Doric
Dork|ing
dorm|ancy
dorm|ant
dormer
dorm|it|ory (pl.
  dorm|it|or|ies)
dor|mouse (pl.
  dor|mice)
dormy
Dor|noch
Do|ro|thy
dorp
dor|sal
dor|sally
Dor|set
Dort|mund
dory (pl. dor|ies;
  also (John) Dory,
  pl. Dor|ies; fish)
dos|age
dose (as v.,
  dos|ing)
dosi|meter
do|si|met|ric
do|si|metry
dos|sal
dosser
doss-house
dos|sier
Dos|to|ev|sky
dot (as v., dot|ted,
  dott|ing)
dot|age
dot|ard
dote (dot|ing)
dot|terel
dot|ti|ness
dottle
dotty (dot|tier,
  dot|ti|est)
Douai (in France)
dou|ane
Douay (Bible)

double (as v.,
  doub|ling)
double-barrelled
double-bass
double-breasted
double-check
double-cross
double-dealing
double-decker
double-declutch
double-edged
double en|tendre
double-jointed
double-park
double-quick
doub|let
double-talk
double|ton
doub|loon
doub|lure (book-
  cover lining)
doubly
doubt
doubt|ful
doubt|fully
doubt|less
douce
douche (as v.,
  douch|ing)
dough
dough|nut
dought|ily
doughti|ness
doughty
  (dought|ier,
  doughti|est)
doughy
Doug|las
doum-palm
dour
Douro (river)
dour|ou|couli
douse (drench;
  doused,
  dous|ing)
△ dowse
dove-coloured
dove|cot
dove|kie
Do|ver
dove|tail
dow|ager
dow|dily
dow|di|ness
dowdy (dow|dier,
  dow|di|est)

dowel (as v.,
  dowelled,
  dow|el|ling)
dower
Dow-Jones
  (Index)
dow|las
down-and-out
down|beat
down|cast
downer
down|fall
down|grade
  (down|grad|ing)
down|hill
down|ily
downi|ness
Down|ing Street
down-market
Down|pat|rick
down|pipe
down|pour
down|right
Down's
  syn|drome
down|stairs
down|stream
down|throw
down-to-earth
down|town
down|trodden
down|ward
down|warp
down|wind
downy (dow|nier,
  dow|ni|est)
dowry (pl.
  dow|ries)
dowse (use
  divining-rod;
  dows|ing)
△ douse
dowser
dowsing-rod
doxo|grapher
doxo|graphic
doxo|graphy
doxo|logy (pl.
  doxo|lo|gies)
doxy (pl. dox|ies)
doyen (fem.
  doy|enne)
D'Oyly Carte
doze (doz|ing)
dozen

dozy (do|zier,
  do|zi|est)
drabble
  (drab|bling)
drachm
drachma (pl.
  drach|mas)
dra|cone
  (container)
Dra|con|ian
Drac|ula
draff (dregs)
draft (sketch,
  conscript, draw
  off) △ draught
draftee
drafter
drafts|man (one
  who drafts; pl.
  drafts|men)
  △ draughtsman
drag (as v.,
  dragged,
  drag|ging)
dra|gée
draggle
  (drag|gling)
drag-net
drago|man (pl.
  drago|mans)
dragon
drag|onet
dragon-fly (pl.
  dragon-flies)
dra|goon
drag|ster
drail
drain
drain|age
drainer
draining-board
drain-pipe
drake
dram (small drink)
drama
dra|matic
dra|mat|ic|ally
dra|matis
  per|sonae
dram|at|ist
dram|at|iza|tion
dram|at|ize
  (dram|at|iz|ing)
dram|at|urge
dram|at|ur|gic
dram|at|ur|gical

dram|at|urgy
Dram|buie
 (liqueur; *propr.*)
drape (as *v.*,
 drap|ing)
draper
drapery (*pl.*
 draper|ies)
dras|tic
dras|tic|ally
drat (drat|ted,
 drat|ting)
draught (air-
 current, drink,
 traction, etc.)
 △ draft
draught-board
draught|horse
draugh|ti|ness
draughts (*pl.*,
 game)
draughts|man
 (one who makes
 drawings, plans,
 etc.; *pl.*
 draughts|men)
 △ draftsman
draughty
 (draugh|tier,
 draugh|ti|est)
Dra|vid|ian
draw (as *v.*, drew,
 drawn)
draw|back
draw|bridge
drawee
drawer
drawer|ful (*pl.*
 drawer|fuls)
draw|ing
drawing-board
drawing-pin
drawing-room
drawl
draw-string
dray (cart) △ drey
dray-horse
dray|man (*pl.*
 dray|men)
dread
dread|ful
dread|fully
dread|nought
dream (dreamed
 or dreamt,
 dream|ing)

dream-boat
dream|ily
dreami|ness
dreamy
 (dream|ier,
 dreami|est)
drear|ily
dreari|ness
dreary (drear|ier,
 dreari|est)
dredge
 (dredging)
dredger
dreggy
*Drei|grosch|en|
 oper*
Dreiser
drench
Dren|the
Dres|den
dress|age
dresser
dressi|ness
dress|ing
dressing-gown
dressing-room
dressing-table
dress|maker
dress|making
dress-shirt
dressy (dress|ier,
 dressi|est)
drey (squirrel's
 nest) △ dray
drib
dribble
 (drib|bling)
dribbly
drib|let
drier (as *n.*; as *a.*,
 compar. of dry)
driest (*superl.* of
 dry)
drift|age
drifter
drift-net
drift-wood
drily
drink (drank,
 drunk)
drink|able
drinker
drinking-water
drip (as *v.*,
 dripped,
 drip|ping)

drip-dry
 (drip-dries,
 drip-dried,
 drip-drying)
drip-feed
drip|ping
drippy (drip|pier,
 drip|pi|est)
driv|able
drive (as *v.*, drove,
 driven, driv|ing)
drive-in *a.* & *n.*
drivel (drivelled,
 driv|el|ling)
driv|el|ler
drive-on *a.*
driver
drive|way
driving-licence
driving-range
drizzle (as *v.*,
 drizz|ling)
drizzly
drogue
droit
droll
droll|ery
drolly
drom|ed|ary (*pl.*
 drom|ed|ar|ies)
drone (as *v.*,
 dron|ing)
drongo (*pl.*
 dron|gos)
droopy
 (droop|ier,
 droopi|est)
drop (as *v.*,
 dropped,
 drop|ping)
drop-head
drop-kick
drop-leaf
drop|let
drop-out *n.*
drop|per
drop|ping
drop-shot
drop|sical
dropsy
droshky (*pl.*
 drosh|kies)
droso|phila
drossy (dross|ier,
 dros|si|est)
drought

droughty
drove (as *v.*,
 drov|ing)
drover
drown
drowse
 (drows|ing)
drows|ily
drow|si|ness
drowsy
 (drow|sier,
 drow|si|est)
drub (drubbed,
 drub|bing)
drudge (as *v.*,
 drudging)
drudgery (*pl.*
 drudger|ies)
drug (as *v.*,
 drugged,
 drug|ging)
drug|get
drug|gist
druggy
 (drug|gier,
 drug|gi|est)
drug|store
Druid (*fem.*
 Dru|id|ess)
Dru|idic
Drui|id|ical
Dru|id|ism
drum (as *v.*,
 drummed,
 drum|ming)
drum|beat
drum|lin
drum|lin|oid
drum|mer
drum|stick
drunk|ard
drunken
drunk|en|ness
drup|aceous
drupe (type of
 fruit)
drupel
drupe|let
druse (cavity)
Druse (Muslim
 sect)
dry (as *a.*, drier,
 driest; as *v.*,
 dries, dried,
 dry|ing)
dryad

dry-clean
dry-cleaner
Dry|den
dryer (as *n.*, *use*
 drier)
dry|ish
dry|ness
dry|stone
dual *a.* (of two)
 △ duel
du|al|ism
du|al|ist
du|al|istic
du|al|ity
du|al|ize
 (du|al|iz|ing)
du|ally
dual-purpose
dub (as *v.*,
 dubbed,
 dub|bing)
dub|bin (as *v.*,
 dub|bined,
 dub|bin|ing)
du|bi|ety
du|bi|ous
du|bita|tion
du|bit|at|ive
Dub|lin
Dub|liner
du|cal
ducat
duch|ess
duch|esse
duchy (*pl.*
 duch|ies)
duck|bill
duck-billed
 platy|pus
duck-board
ducking-stool
duck|ling
duck|weed
ducky
duct
duct|ile
duct|il|ity
dudgeon
Dud|ley
duel (as *v.*,
 duelled,
 du|el|ling)
 △ dual
du|el|list
du|ende
du|enna
duet

du|et|tist
Dufay
duff (as *v.*, duffed,
 duff|ing)
duffer
duffle
duffle-coat
du|gong
dug-out
duiker
duke|dom
Dukhobor
 (member of Russ.
 relig. sect)
dul|cet
dul|ci|fica|tion
dul|cify
 (dul|ci|fies,
 dul|ci|fied,
 dul|ci|fy|ing)
dul|ci|mer
dul|ci|tone
du|lia
dull|ard
dully (in a dull
 manner)
dulse
duly (rightly, in
 due course)
Du|mas
Du|maur|ier
dumb
Dum|bar|ton
dumb-bell
dumb|found
dum|dum (bullet)
Dum|fries
dummy (as *n.*, *pl.*
 dum|mies; as *v.*,
 dum|mies,
 dum|mied,
 dum|my|ing)
dumper
dump|ily
dumpi|ness
dump|ling
dumpy
 (dum|pier,
 dum|pi|est)
dun (as *v.*,
 dunned,
 dun|ning)
dunce
Dun|dalk
Dun|dee
dun|der|head

dun|gar|ees *n. pl.*
dung-beetle
dun|geon
dung|hill
Dun|kirk
Dun Laoghaire
dun|lin
dunn|age
dunno
dun|nock
dunny (*pl.*
 dun|nies)
duo (*pl.* duos)
duo|decimal
duo|decim|ally
duo|decimo (*pl.*
 duo|deci|mos)
duo|denal
duo|den|ary
duo|den|itis
duo|denum
duo|logue
duomo (*pl.*
 duo|mos)
duo|tone
dup|able
dupe (as *v.*,
 dup|ing)
dupery
du|pion
duple
du|plex
du|plic|ate (as *v.*,
 du|plic|at|ing)
du|plica|tion
du|plic|ator
du|pli|cit|ous
du|pli|city (*pl.*
 du|pli|ci|ties)
duppy (*pl.*
 dup|pies)
dur|ab|il|ity
dur|able
dur|ably
Dur|alu|min
 (alloy; *propr.*)
dura ma|ter
dur|amen
dura|tion
dur|at|ive
dur|bar
durch|kom|pon|
          iert
Dürer
dur|ess
Dur|ham

dur|ian
dur|ing
dur|mast
durra
durum
durzi
dusk|ily
duski|ness
dusky (dus|kier,
 dus|ki|est)
Düs|sel|dorf
dust-bath
dust|bin
dust-cart
duster
dust|ily
dusti|ness
dusting-powder
dust-jacket
dust|man (*pl.*
 dust|men)
dust|pan
dust-sheet
dust-trap
dust-up
dusty (dus|tier,
 dus|ti|est)
Dutch
Dutch|man (*pl.*
 Dutch|men)
Dutch|wo|man
 (*pl.* Dutch|
      wo|men)
du|teous
du|ti|able
du|ti|ful
du|ti|fully
duty (*pl.* du|ties)
duty-bound
duty-free
duty-paid
Du|val|ier
du|vet
Dvořák
dwale
dwarf (*pl.* dwarfs)
dwarf|ish
dwarf|ism
dwell (dwelt)
dweller
dwell|ing
dwindle
 (dwind|ling)
dyad
dy|adic
Dyak

dyb|buk (*pl.*
 dyb|buk**im** *or*
 dyb|buks)
dye (colour; as *v.*,
 dyed, dye|ing)
 △ die
dyer
dye|stuff
Dyfed
dy|ing
dyke *use* dike
dy|namic
dy|nam|ical
dy|nam|ic|ally
dy|nam|icist

dy|namics
dy|nam|ism
dy|nam|ist
dy|nam|ite (as *v.*,
 dy|nam|it|ing)
dy|namo (*pl.*
 dy|na|mos)
dy|namo|meter
dyn|ast
dyn|astic
dyn|ast|ic|ally
dyn|asty (*pl.*
 dyn|ast|ies)
dy|na|tron
dyne (unit)

dys|en|teric
dys|en|tery
dys|func|tion
dys|func|tional
dys|genic
dys|graphia
dys|lexia
dys|lexic
dys|lo|gistic
dys|lo|gist|ic|ally
dys|men|or|rhoea
Dy|son
dys|pep|sia
dys|peptic
dys|phem|ism

dys|phoria
dys|phoric
dys|pla|sia
dys|plastic
dys|pnoea
dys|pnoeic
dys|pro|sium
dys|to|pia
dys|trophy
dys|uria
dzho (*pl.* dzhos *or*
 dzho)
dzig|ge|tai

E

eager
eagle
eag|let
ear|ache
ear-drum
ear|ful (*pl.*
 ear|fuls)
ear|ing (*Naut.*)
earl|dom
earli|ness
early (earl|ier,
 earli|est)
ear|mark
ear-muff
earn|est
earn|ings
ear|phone
ear-piece
ear-plug
ear-ring
ear|shot
earthed
earthen
earth|en|ware
earthi|ness
earth|li|ness
earth|ling
earthly
earth-nut
earth|quake
earth|ward
earth|wards
earth|work
earth|worm
earthy (earth|ier,
 earthi|est)
ear|wig (as *v.*,
 ear|wigged,
 ear|wig|ging)
ease (as *v.*,
 eas|ing)
easel
ease|ment
eas|ily
easi|ness
east|about
east|bound
East|bourne
East-Ender

Easter
east|erly (as *n.*, *pl.*
 east|er|lies)
east|ern
east|erner
east|ern|most
East|er|tide
east|ing (*Naut.*
 etc.)
east-north-east
east-south-east
east|ward
east|wards
easy (eas|ier,
 easi|est)
easy|going
eat (ate, eaten)
eat|able
eater
eat|ery (*pl.*
 eat|er|ies)
eating-house
eau-de-Cologne
eau suc|rée (water
 and sugar)
eaves
eaves|drop
 (eaves|dropped,
 eaves|drop|ping)
eaves|drop|per
E-boat
eb|on|ite
eb|ony
Ebro
ebul|li|ence
ebul|li|ency
ebul|li|ent
ebul|li|tion
ecad
écarté
Ecce Homo
ec|cent|ric
ec|cent|ric|ally
ec|cent|ri|city (*pl.*
 ec|cent|ri|cit|ies)
Eccles cake
ec|cle|sia
Ec|cle|si|as|tes
ec|cle|si|astic

ec|cle|si|ast|ical
ec|cle|si|ast|ic|
            ally
ec|cle|si|asti|cism
Ec|cle|si|ast|icus
ec|cle|si|olo|gical
ec|cle|si|ology
ec|crine
ec|dysis (*pl.*
 ec|dyses)
ech|elon
ech|everia
ech|idna
ech|in|ite
ech|ino|derm
ech|in|oid
ech|inus
echo (as *n.*, *pl.*
 ech|oes; as *v.*,
 ech|oed,
 echo|ing)
echo|gram
echo|graph
echoic
echo|ic|ally
echo|ism
echo|la|lia
echt
éclair
ec|lamp|sia
ec|lamptic
éclat
ec|lectic
ec|lect|ic|ally
ec|lect|icism
ec|lipse (as *v.*,
 ec|lips|ing)
ec|liptic
ec|lipt|ic|ally
ec|logue
ec|lo|sion
eco|cli|mate
eco|lo|gical
eco|lo|gist
eco|logy
eco|no|met|ric
eco|no|met|rical
eco|no|met|ric|
            ally

eco|no|met|ri|cian
eco|no|met|rics
eco|nomic
eco|nom|ical
eco|nom|ic|ally
eco|nom|ics
eco|nom|ist
eco|nom|iza|tion
eco|nom|ize
 (eco|nom|iz|ing)
eco|nom|izer
eco|nomy (*pl.*
 eco|nom|ies)
eco|sphere
écos|saise
eco|sys|tem
ecru
ec|stas|ize
 (ec|stas|iz|ing)
ec|stasy (*pl.*
 ec|stas|ies)
ec|static
ec|stat|ic|ally
ec|to|blast
ec|to|derm
ec|to|gen|esis
ec|to|gen|etic
ec|to|gen|et|ic|
            ally
ec|to|genic
ec|to|gen|ic|ally
ec|to|gen|ous
ec|to|morph
ec|to|morphic
ec|topic
ec|to|plasm
ec|to|zoon
Ecua|dor
ecu|men|ical
ecu|men|ic|al|ism
ecu|men|ic|ally
ecu|men|icity
ecu|men|ism
ec|zema
ec|ze|mat|ous
Edam
ed|aphic
Edda (poems)
Ed|ding|ton

eddy (as *n.*, *pl.*
 ed|dies; as *v.*,
 ed|dies, ed|died,
 ed|dy|ing)
edel|weiss
Eden
edent|ate
edge (as *v.*,
 edging)
edge|ways
edge|wise
edgily
edgi|ness
edgy (edgier,
 edgi|est)
edh (letter)
ed|ib|il|ity
ed|ible
edict
edictal
edi|fica|tion
edi|fice
edify (edi|fies,
 edi|fied,
 edi|fy|ing)
Ed|in|burgh
Edi|son
edit (ed|ited,
 ed|it|ing)
edi|tion
edi|tio prin|ceps
 (*pl.* *edi|ti|ones*
 prin|cipes)
ed|itor
ed|it|ori|al
ed|it|ori|al|ist
ed|it|ori|al|ize
 (ed|it|ori|al|iz|
  ing)
ed|it|ori|ally
ed|it|or|ship
ed|it|ress
edu|cab|il|ity
edu|cable
edu|cate
 (edu|cat|ing)
edu|ca|tion
edu|ca|tional
edu|ca|tion|ally
edu|ca|tion|ist
edu|cat|ive
edu|cator
educe (edu|cing)
edu|cible
educ|tion

edul|cor|ate
 (edul|cor|at|ing)
edul|cora|tion
Ed|ward
Ed|ward|ian
eel|worm
eely
eerie (eer|ier,
 eeri|est)
eer|ily
eeri|ness
ef|face (ef|fa|cing)
ef|face|able
ef|face|ment
ef|fect
ef|fect|ive
ef|fector
ef|fec|tual
ef|fec|tu|ally
ef|fec|tu|ate
 (ef|fec|tu|at|ing)
ef|fec|tu|ation
ef|fem|in|acy
ef|fem|in|ate
ef|fendi
ef|fer|ent
ef|fer|vesce
 (ef|fer|ves|cing)
ef|fer|ves|cence
ef|fer|ves|cent
ef|fete
ef|fi|ca|cious
ef|fi|cacy
ef|fi|ci|ency
ef|fi|ci|ent
ef|figy (*pl.*
 ef|fi|gies)
ef|flor|esce
 (ef|flor|es|cing)
ef|flor|es|cence
ef|flor|es|cent
ef|flu|ence
ef|flu|ent
ef|flu|vium (*pl.*
 ef|flu|via)
ef|flux
ef|flux|ion
ef|fort
ef|fort|ful
ef|fort|less
ef|front|ery
ef|ful|gence
ef|ful|gent
ef|fuse (as *v.*,
 ef|fus|ing)
ef|fu|sion

ef|fus|ive
egal|it|ar|ian
egal|it|ar|ian|ism
Egeria
egg-cup
egger (moth)
egg-flip
egg|head
eggi|ness
egg-nog
egg-plant
egg|shell
egg-spoon
egg-white
eggy (eg|gier,
 eg|gi|est)
eg|lan|tine
ego (*pl.* egos)
ego|cent|ric
ego|cent|ric|ally
ego|cent|ri|city
ego|ism
ego|ist
ego|istic
ego|ist|ical
ego|ist|ic|ally
ego|ma|nia
ego|ma|niac
egot|ism
egot|ist
egot|istic
egot|ist|ical
egot|ist|ic|ally
egot|ize
 (egot|iz|ing)
ego-trip
egre|gious
egress
egres|sion
eg|ret
Egypt
Egyp|tian
Egypto|lo|gist
Egypto|logy
Ehr|lich
ei|der
ei|der|down
 (quilt)
eider-down (down
 of eider)
ei|detic
ei|dolon (*pl.*
 ei|dol|ons *or*
 ei|dola)
Eifel (Mts.)
Eif|fel (Tower)

ei|gen|fre|quency
ei|gen|value
eight|een
eight|eenmo
eight|eenth
eighth
eigh|ti|eth
eight|some
eighty (*pl.*
 eight|ies)
eighty|fold
ein|korn
Ein|stein
ein|stein|ium
ei|ren|icon
Eis|en|hower
ei|stedd|fod (*pl.*
 ei|stedd|fods)
ei|ther
ejacu|late
 (ejacu|lat|ing)
ejacu|la|tion
ejacu|lat|ory
eject
ejec|tion
eject|ive
eject|ment
ejector
eke (ek|ing)
ekka
elab|or|ate (as *v.*,
 elab|or|at|ing)
elab|ora|tion
elab|or|at|ive
eland
elapse (elap|sing)
elas|mo|branch
elas|mo|saurus
elastic
elast|ic|ally
elast|ic|ated
elasti|city
elasti|cize
 (elasti|ciz|ing)
elasto|mer
elasto|meric
elate (elat|ing)
elated
elater (beetle)
ela|tion
E-layer
Elbe
el|bow
elbow-grease
elbow-room
El|brus

El|burz
elder (earlier-
 born)
el|der (tree)
el|der|berry (pl.
 el|der|berries)
eld|er|li|ness
eld|erly
eld|er|ship
eld|est
el|dor|ado (pl.
 el|dor|ados)
Ele|atic
ele|cam|pane
elect
elec|tion
elec|tion|eer
elect|ive
elector
elect|oral
elect|or|ate
elect|or|ship
Elec|tra
elec|tret
elec|tric
elec|trical
elec|tric|ally
elec|tri|cian
elec|tri|city
elec|tri|fica|tion
elec|trify
 (elec|tri|fies,
 elec|tri|fied,
 elec|tri|fy|ing)
elec|tro (pl.
 elec|tros)
elec|tro|bio|logy
elec|tro|car|dio|
 gram
elec|tro|car|dio|
 graph
elec|tro|car|dio|
 graphy
elec|tro|chem|ical
elec|tro|
 chem|istry
elec|tro|cute
 (elec|tro|cut|ing)
elec|tro|cu|tion
elec|trode
elec|tro|dyn|amic
elec|tro|
 en|ceph|alo|gram
elec|tro|en|ceph|
 alo|graph

elec|tro|en|ceph|
 alo|graphy
elec|tro|lier
elec|tro|lyse
 (elec|tro|lys|ing)
elec|tro|lysis (pl.
 elec|tro|lyses)
elec|tro|lyte
elec|tro|lytic
elec|tro|mag|net
elec|tro|mag|netic
elec|tro|
 mag|net|ic|ally
elec|tro|
 mag|net|ism
elec|tro|
 mech|an|ical
elec|tro|meter
elec|tro|met|ric
elec|tro|mot|ive
elec|tron
elec|tro|neg|at|ive
elec|tronic
elec|tron|ic|ally
elec|tron|ics
electron-volt
elec|tro|phonic
elec|tro|phor|esis
 (pl. elec|tro|
 phor|eses)
elec|tro|phor|etic
elec|tro|phorus
elec|tro|plate
 (elec|tro|plat|ing)
elec|tro|plexy
elec|tro|posit|ive
elec|tro|scope
electro-shock
elec|tro|static
elec|tro|tech|no|
 logy
elec|tro|
 ther|ap|ist
elec|tro|ther|apy
elec|tro|thermal
elec|tro|type
 (elec|tro|typ|ing)
elec|tro|va|lence
elec|tro|va|lency
elec|tro|va|lent
elec|trum
elec|tu|ary (pl.
 elec|tu|ar|ies)
ele|emo|syn|ary
el|eg|ance
el|eg|ant

ele|giac
ele|gist
ele|gize
 (ele|giz|ing)
elegy (pl. ele|gies)
ele|ment
ele|mental
ele|ment|al|ism
ele|ment|ar|ily
ele|ment|ari|ness
ele|ment|ary
el|emi
el|en|chus (pl.
 el|en|chi)
el|enc|tic
ele|phant
ele|phanti|asis
ele|phant|ine
ele|phant|oid
Eleu|sin|ian
el|ev|ate
 (el|ev|at|ing)
el|eva|tion
el|eva|tional
el|ev|ator
el|ev|at|ory
el|even
eleven-plus
el|ev|enses
el|ev|enth
el|evon
 (Aeronaut.)
elf (pl. elves)
elfin
elf|ish
El|gar
El|gin
eli|cit (eli|cited,
 eli|cit|ing)
elide (elid|ing)
eli|gib|il|ity
eli|gible
eli|gibly
elim|in|able
elim|in|ate
 (elim|in|at|ing)
elim|ina|tion
elim|in|ator
Eliot
eli|sion
élite
élit|ism
élit|ist
elixir
Eliza|beth
Eliza|bethan

elk (pl. elks or elk)
elk-hound
El|les|mere
 (Island)
El|lice (Islands)
el|lipse
el|lip|sis (pl.
 el|lip|ses)
el|lips|oid
el|lips|oidal
el|liptic
el|lipt|ical
el|lipt|ic|ally
el|lipti|city
elm|wood
elocu|tion
elocu|tion|ary
elocu|tion|ist
Elo|hist
elong|ate
 (elong|at|ing)
elonga|tion
elope (elop|ing)
elope|ment
elo|quence
elo|quent
El Sal|va|dor
El|san (propr.)
else|where
elu|ate
elu|cid|ate
 (elu|cid|at|ing)
elu|cida|tion
elu|cid|at|ive
elu|cid|ator
elu|cid|at|ory
elude (elud|ing)
elu|ent
elu|sion
elu|sive
elu|sory
elute (elut|ing)
elu|tion
elutri|ate
 (elut|ri|at|ing)
elut|ri|ation
elver
elves (pl. of elf)
elv|ish
Elys|ian
Elys|ium
Elytis
elyt|ron (pl.
 elytra)
ema|ci|ate
 (ema|ci|at|ing)

ema|ci|ation
em|an|ate
 (em|an|at|ing)
em|ana|tion
em|an|at|ive
eman|cip|ate
 (eman|cip|at|ing)
eman|cipa|tion
eman|cip|ator
eman|cip|at|ory
emas|cu|late (as
 v., emas|cu|
        lat|ing)
emas|cu|la|tion
emas|cu|lat|ory
em|balm
em|balm|ment
em|bank
em|bank|ment
em|bargo (*pl.*
 em|bar|goes)
em|bark
em|barka|tion
em|bar|rass
em|bar|rass|ing
em|bar|rass|ment
em|bassy (*pl.*
 em|bass|ies)
em|battle
 (em|batt|ling)
em|bay
em|bay|ment
em|bed
 (em|bed|ded,
  em|bed|ding)
em|bel|lish
em|bel|lish|ment
em|ber
ember-goose (*pl.*
 ember-geese)
em|bezzle
 (em|bezz|ling)
em|bez|zle|ment
em|bit|ter
em|bit|ter|ment
em|bla|zon
em|bla|zon|ment
em|bla|zonry
em|blem
em|blem|atic
em|blem|at|ical
em|blem|at|ize
 (em|blem|at|iz|
        ing)
em|ble|ment
em|bodi|ment

em|body
 (em|bod|ies,
 em|bod|ied,
 em|body|ing)
em|bolden
em|bol|ism
em|bol|ismic
em|bolus (*pl.*
 em|boli)
em|boss
em|boss|ment
em|bouch|ure
em|bower
em|brace
 (em|bra|cing)
em|brace|able
em|brace|ment
em|branch|ment
em|brangle
 (em|brang|ling)
em|brangle|ment
em|bras|ure
em|brittle
 (em|brit|tling)
em|brit|tle|ment
em|broca|tion
em|broider
em|broid|erer
em|broid|ery
em|broil
em|broil|ment
em|brown
em|bryo (*pl.*
 em|bryos)
em|bryo|gen|esis
em|bry|ology
em|bry|onic
em|bus
 (em|bussed,
 em|bus|sing)
emend
emenda|tion
emend|ator
emend|at|ory
em|er|ald
em|er|ald|ine
emerge
 (emer|ging)
emer|gence
emer|gency (*pl.*
 emer|gen|cies)
emer|gent
emer|itus
emer|sion
em|ery
emery-board

emery-cloth
emery-paper
emery-wheel
em|etic
emig|rant
emig|rate
 (emig|rat|ing)
emig|ra|tion
emig|rat|ory
émi|gré
Emilia-Romagna
em|in|ence
ém|in|ence grise
em|in|ent
emir
emir|ate
emis|sary (*pl.*
 emis|sar|ies)
emis|sion
emis|sive
emis|siv|ity
emit (emit|ted,
 emit|ting)
emit|ter
Emma
Em|men|tal
em|mer
emol|li|ent
emolu|ment
emote (emot|ing)
emo|tion
emo|tional
emo|tion|al|ism
emo|tion|al|ist
emo|tion|al|ity
emo|tion|al|ize
 (emo|tion|al|iz|
        ing)
emo|tion|ally
emo|tive
emo|tiv|ity
em|panel
 (em|pan|elled,
 em|pan|el|ling)
em|path|etic
em|pathic
em|path|ist
em|path|ize
 (em|path|iz|ing)
em|pathy
em|pen|nage
em|peror
em|phasis (*pl.*
 em|phases)
em|phas|ize
 (em|phas|iz|ing)

em|phatic
em|phat|ic|ally
em|phys|ema
em|pire
em|piric
em|pir|ical
em|pir|ic|ally
em|piri|cism
em|piri|cist
em|place|ment
em|plane
 (em|plan|ing)
em|ploy
em|ploy|able
em|ployee
em|ployer
em|ploy|ment
em|por|ium (*pl.*
 em|poria)
em|power
emp|ress
emp|tily
empti|ness
empty (as *a.*,
 emp|tier,
 emp|ti|est; as *v.*,
 emp|ties,
 emp|tied,
 emp|ty|ing)
empty-handed
empty-headed
em|purple
 (em|purp|ling)
em|py|ema
em|pyr|eal
em|pyr|ean
emu
emu|late
 (emu|lat|ing)
emu|la|tion
emu|lat|ive
emu|lator
emu|lous
emul|si|fi|able
emul|si|fica|tion
emul|si|fier
emul|sify
 (emul|si|fies,
 emul|si|fied,
 emul|si|fy|ing)
emul|sion
emuls|ive
en|able
 (en|ab|ling)
en|act
en|ac|tion

en|act|ive
en|act|ment
en|act|ory
en|amel (as v.,
  en|am|elled,
  en|am|el|ling|
en|am|our
en|an|thema
en|an|tio|morph
en|an|tio|morph|
            ous
en|arth|rosis (pl.
  en|arth|roses)
en bloc
en|cae|nia
en|cage
  (en|ca|ging)
en|camp
en|camp|ment
en|cap|sul|ate
  (en|cap|sul|
            at|ing)
en|cap|sula|tion
en|case
  (en|cas|ing)
en|case|ment
en|cash
en|cash|able
en|cash|ment
en|caustic
en|ceinte
en|ceph|alic
en|ceph|al|itis
en|ceph|alo|gram
en|ceph|alo|
            graph
en|chain
en|chain|ment
en|chant
en|chanter
en|chant|ment
en|chant|ress
en|chase
  (en|chas|ing)
en|chil|ada
en|chir|idion
en|ci|pher
en|circle
  (en|circ|ling)
en|cir|cle|ment
en|clasp
en|clave
en|clitic
en|clit|ic|ally
en|close
  (en|clos|ing)

en|clos|ure
en|code
  (en|cod|ing)
en|coder
en|comi|ast
en|comi|astic
en|co|mium (pl.
  en|co|mi|ums)
en|com|pass
en|com|pass|ment
en|core (as v.,
  en|cor|ing)
en|coun|ter
en|cour|age
  (en|cour|aging)
en|cour|age|ment
en|crin|ite
en|croach
en|croach|ment
en|crust
encrustation *use*
  incrustation
en|crust|ment
en|cum|ber
en|cum|ber|ment
en|cum|brance
en|cyc|lic
en|cyc|lical
en|cyc|lo|pae|dia
en|cyc|lo|paedic
en|cyc|lo|paed|ist
en|cyst
en|cysta|tion
en|cyst|ment
en|dan|ger
en|dan|ger|ment
en|dear
en|dear|ment
en|deav|our
en|demic
en|dem|ic|ally
en|dem|icity
en|dem|ism
en|dermic
end-game
end|ing
en|dive
end|less
end-man
  (pl. end-men)
end|most
end-note
en|do|card|itis
en|do|car|dium
en|do|carp
en|do|crine

en|do|derm
en|do|gam|ous
en|do|gamy
en|do|gen
en|do|gen|ous
en|do|lymph
en|do|met|ritis
en|do|met|rium
en|do|morph
en|do|pa|ra|site
en|do|plasm
en|dorse
  (en|dors|ing)
en|dorse|ment
en|dorser
en|do|scope
en|do|skel|eton
en|do|sperm
en|do|spore
en|do|the|lium
en|do|thermic
en|dow
en|dow|ment
end|paper
end-play
end-point
end-product
en|due (en|dued,
  en|du|ing)
en|dur|able
en|dur|ance
en|dure
  (en|dur|ing)
end|ways
end|wise
en|ema (pl.
  en|emas)
en|emy (pl.
  en|em|ies)
en|er|getic
en|er|get|ic|ally
en|er|gize
  (en|er|giz|ing)
en|er|gu|men
en|ergy (pl.
  en|er|gies)
en|er|vate
  (en|er|vat|ing)
en|erva|tion
en|fant ter|rible
en|feeble
  (en|feeb|ling)
en|fee|ble|ment
en|feoff
en|feoff|ment
en|fet|ter

en|fil|ade (as v.,
  en|fil|ad|ing)
en|fold
en|force
  (en|for|cing)
en|force|able
en|force|ably
en|force|ment
en|franch|ise
  (en|franch|ising)
en|franch|ise|
            ment
en|gage
  (en|ga|ging)
en|gage|ment
en|gar|land
En|gels
en|gen|der
en|gine (as v.,
  en|gin|ing)
engine-driver
en|gin|eer
en|gin|eer|ing
en|gin|ery
en|gird
en|girdle
  (en|gird|ling)
Eng|land
Eng|lish
en|gorge
  (en|gor|ging)
en|gorge|ment
en|graft
en|grail
en|grain
en|gram
en|gram|matic
en|grave
  (en|grav|ing)
en|graver
en|gross
en|gross|ment
en|gulf
en|gulf|ment
en|hance
  (en|han|cing)
en|hance|ment
en|har|monic
en|har|mon|ic|
            ally
en|igma
en|ig|matic
en|ig|mat|ical
en|ig|mat|ic|ally
en|ig|mat|ize
  (en|ig|mat|iz|ing)

en|jamb|ment
en|join
en|joy
en|joy|able
en|joy|ably
en|joy|ment
en|kindle
 (en|kind|ling)
en|lace
 (en|la|cing)
en|lace|ment
en|large
 (en|lar|ging)
en|large|able
en|large|ment
en|lar|ger
en|lighten
en|light|en|ment
En|light|en|ment
 (*hist.*)
en|list
en|list|ment
en|liven
en|liven|ment
en masse
en|mesh
en|mesh|ment
en|mity (*pl.*
 en|mit|ies)
en|nead
En|nis
En|nis|kil|len
en|noble
 (en|nob|ling)
en|no|ble|ment
en|nui
enorm|ity (*pl.*
 enorm|it|ies)
enorm|ous
en|osis
enough
enounce
 (enoun|cing)
enounce|ment
en|quire (ask;
 en|quir|ing) See
 also **inquire**
en|quiry (*pl.*
 en|quir|ies) See
 also **inquiry**
en|rage
 (en|ra|ging)
en|rap|ture
 (en|rap|tur|ing)
en|rich
en|rich|ment

en|robe
 (en|rob|ing)
en|rol (en|rolled,
 en|rol|ling)
en|rol|ment
en route
en|sconce
 (en|scon|cing)
en|semble
en|shrine
 (en|shrin|ing)
en|shrine|ment
en|shroud
en|si|form
en|sign
en|signcy
en|sil|age (as *v.*,
 en|sil|aging)
en|sile (en|sil|ing)
en|slave
 (en|slav|ing)
en|slave|ment
en|snare
 (en|snar|ing)
en|sue (en|sued,
 en|su|ing)
en suite
en|sure
 (make sure;
 en|sur|ing)
 △ **insure**
en|swathe
 (en|swath|ing)
en|swathe|ment
en|tab|la|ture
en|ta|ble|ment
en|tail
en|tail|ment
en|tangle
 (en|tang|ling)
en|tan|gle|ment
en|tasis
en|tel|echy
en|tente
en|tente
 cor|di|ale
en|ter
en|ter|able
en|teric
en|ter|itis
en|tero|stomy (*pl.*
 en|tero|stom|ies)
en|tero|tomy (*pl.*
 en|tero|tom|ies)
en|tero|virus
en|ter|prise

en|ter|pris|ing
en|ter|tain
en|ter|tainer
en|ter|tain|ing
en|ter|tain|ment
en|thalpy
en|thral
 (en|thralled,
 en|thral|ling)
en|thral|ment
en|throne
 (en|thron|ing)
en|throne|ment
en|thron|iza|tion
en|thuse
 (en|thus|ing)
en|thu|si|asm
en|thu|si|ast
en|thu|si|astic
en|thu|si|ast|ic|
 ally
en|thym|eme
en|tice (en|ti|cing)
en|tice|ment
en|tire
en|tirely
en|tir|ety (*pl.*
 en|tir|eties)
en|ti|tat|ive
en|title
 (en|ti|tling)
en|ti|tle|ment
en|tity (*pl.*
 en|tit|ies)
en|tomb
en|tomb|ment
en|tomic
en|to|mo|lo|gical
en|to|mo|lo|gist
en|to|mo|logy
en|to|mo|phag|
 ous
en|to|mo|phil|ous
en|to|pa|ra|site
en|to|phyte
en|tour|age
entr'|acte
en|trails
en|train
en|train|ment
en|tram|mel
 (en|tram|melled,
 en|tram|mel|ling)
en|trance *n.*

en|trance *v.*
 (throw into trance;
 en|tran|cing)
en|trance|ment
ent|rant
en|trap
 (en|trapped,
 en|trap|ping)
en|trap|ment
en|treat
en|treaty (*pl.*
 en|treat|ies)
en|tre|côte
en|trée
en|trench
en|trench|ment
en|tre|pôt
en|tre|pren|eur
en|tre|pren|eur|
 ial
en|tre|pren|eur|
 ship
en|tre|sol
en|tropy
en|trust
entry (*pl.* ent|ries)
en|twine
 (en|twin|ing)
enuc|leate
 (enuc|leat|ing)
enuc|le|ation
enu|mer|able
enu|mer|ate
 (enu|mer|at|ing)
enu|mera|tion
enu|mer|at|ive
enu|mer|ator
enun|ci|ate
 (enun|ci|at|ing)
enun|ci|ation
enun|ci|at|ive
enun|ci|ator
enure
en|ur|esis
en|ur|etic
en|velop (*v.*,
 en|veloped,
 en|vel|op|ing)
en|vel|ope *n.*
en|velop|ment
en|venom
en|vi|able
en|vi|ably
en|vi|ous
en|viron
en|vir|on|ment

en|vir|on|mental
en|vir|on|ment|al
            ist
en|vir|ons
en|vis|age
 (en|vis|aging)
en|vis|age|ment
en|vi|sion
en|voy
envy (as *v*.,
 en|vies, en|vied,
 envy|ing)
enweave *use*
 inweave
en|wind
 (en|wound)
en|wrap
 (en|wrapped,
 en|wrap|ping)
en|wreathe
 (en|wreath|ing)
en|zo|otic
en|zym|atic
en|zyme
en|zymic
en|zymo|logy
Eo|cene
eo|lith
eo|lithic
eon *use* aeon
eosin
eos|ino|phil
ep|act
ep|arch
ep|ar|chy (*pl.*
 ep|arch|ies)
epaul|ette
épée
épée|ist
epeiro|gen|esis
epeiro|geny
ep|en|thesis (*pl.*
 ep|en|theses)
ep|en|thetic
epergne
ep|exe|gesis (*pl.*
 ep|exe|geses)
ep|exe|get|ical
eph|ebe
eph|edra
eph|ed|rine
eph|em|era
 (insect, *pl.*
 eph|em|eras; *see*
 ephemeron)
eph|em|eral

eph|em|er|al|ity
eph|em|er|ally
eph|em|eris (*pl.*
 eph|em|er|ides)
eph|em|eron
 (insect, *pl.*
 eph|em|er|ons;
 printed item, *pl.*
 eph|em|era)
ephod
ephor
eph|or|ate
eph|or|ship
epi|blast
epic
ep|ical
ep|ic|ally
epi|carp
epi|ce|dian
epi|ce|dium (*pl.*
 epi|ce|dia)
epi|cene
epi|centre
epi|clesis (*pl.*
 epi|cleses)
epi|con|tin|ental
epi|cotyl
epi|cure
epi|cur|ean (of
 pleasure)
Epi|cur|ean (*hist.*)
epi|cur|ism
Epi|curus
epi|cycle
epi|cyc|lic
epi|cyc|loid
epi|cyc|loidal
epi|deictic
epi|demic
epi|dem|ical
epi|dem|ic|ally
epi|demi|ology
epi|dermal
epi|dermic
epi|dermis
epi|derm|oid
epi|dia|scope
epi|di|dy|mis
epi|dural
epi|fauna
epi|gast|ric
epi|gast|rium
epi|geal
epi|gene
epi|glot|tal
epi|glot|tic

epi|glot|tis
epi|gone (*pl.*
 epi|gones)
epi|gram
epi|gram|matic
epi|gram|mat|ic|
          ally
epi|gram|mat|ist
epi|graph
epi|graphic
epi|graph|ist
epi|graphy
epil|ate
 (epil|at|ing)
epila|tion
epi|lepsy
epi|leptic
epi|lim|nion (*pl.*
 epi|lim|nia)
epi|lo|gist
epi|logue
epi|mer
epi|meric
epi|mer|ism
epi|mer|ize
 (epi|mer|iz|ing)
epi|nasty
epi|neph|rine
epi|phanic
epi|phany (*pl.*
 epi|phan|ies)
Epi|phany (of
 Christ)
epi|phen|om|enon
 (*pl.* epi|phen|om|
         ena)
epi|physis (*pl.*
 epi|physes)
epi|phytal
epi|phyte
epi|phytic
Epirot
epis|cop|acy (*pl.*
 epis|cop|acies)
epis|copal
epis|co|pa|lian
epis|co|pa|li|an|
         ism
epis|co|pal|ism
epis|co|pally
epis|cop|ate
epi|scope
epi|sem|atic
epis|ode
epis|odic
epis|od|ic|ally

epi|staxis
epi|stemic
epi|stem|ic|ally
epi|stemo|lo|gical
epi|stemo|lo|gic|
          ally
epi|stemo|lo|gist
epi|stemo|logy
epistle
epis|tol|ary
epis|toler
epi|strophe
epi|style
epi|taph
epi|taxial
epi|taxy
epi|tha|la|mial
epi|tha|lamic
epi|tha|la|mium
 (*pl.*
 epi|tha|la|mia)
epi|the|lial
epi|the|lium (*pl.*
 epi|the|lia)
epi|thet
epi|thetic
epi|thet|ical
epi|tome
epi|tom|ist
epi|tom|ize
 (epi|tom|iz|ing)
epi|zoon (*pl.*
 epi|zoa)
epi|zo|otic
epoch
epochal
ep|ode
ep|onym
ep|onym|ous
ep|opee
epos
ep|ox|ide
epoxy (*pl.*
 ep|ox|ies)
ep|si|lon
Ep|som
epyl|lion (*pl.*
 epyl|lia)
equ|ab|il|ity
equ|able
equ|ably
equal (as *v*.,
 equalled,
 equal|ling)
equal|it|ar|ian
equal|ity

equal|iza|tion
equal|ize
 (equal|iz|ing)
equal|izer
equally
equan|im|ity
equan|im|ous
equat|able
equat|ably
equate
 (equat|ing)
equa|tion
equa|tional
equator
equat|or|ial
Equat|or|ial
 Guinea
equat|ori|ally
equerry (pl.
 equer|ries)
eques|trian (as n.,
 fem. eques|tri|
 enne)
eques|tri|an|ism
equi|an|gu|lar
equi|dist|ant
equi|lat|eral
equi|lib|rate
 (equi|lib|rat|ing)
equi|lib|ra|tion
equi|lib|rist
equi|lib|rium (pl.
 equi|lib|ria)
equine
equi|noc|tial
equi|nox
equip (equipped,
 equip|ping)
equip|age
equi|par|ti|tion
equip|ment
equi|poise (as v.,
 equi|pois|ing)
equi|pol|lence
equi|pol|lency
equi|pol|lent
equi|pon|der|ant
equi|pon|der|ate
 (equi|pon|der|
 at|ing)
equi|po|ten|tial
equit|able
equit|ably
equita|tion
equity (pl.
 equit|ies)

equi|val|ence
equi|val|ency
equi|val|ent
equi|vocal
equi|voc|al|ity
equi|voc|ally
equi|voc|ate
 (equi|voc|at|ing)
equi|voca|tion
equi|voque
era
erad|ic|able
erad|ic|ate
 (erad|ic|at|ing)
erad|ica|tion
erad|ic|ator
eras|able
erase (eras|ing)
eraser
Eras|mus
eras|ure
er|bium
Ere|bus
erect
erect|ile
erec|tion
erector
er|em|ite
er|em|itic
er|em|it|ical
ereth|ism
ergo
er|go|nomic
er|go|nom|ic|ally
er|go|nom|ics
er|go|nom|ist
er|go|sterol
er|got (fungus)
er|got|ism
er|ica
Erie, Lake (in US
 & Canada)
erig|eron
Erin
Erinys (pl.
 Erinyes)
eristic
Er|lang
erl-king
er|mine
er|mined
erne (eagle)
Ernie
erode (erod|ing)
erod|ible
ero|gen|ous

Eros
ero|sion
ero|sive
erotic
erot|ica n. pl.
erot|ic|ally
eroti|cism (erotic
 character)
erot|ism (sexual
 desire)
eroto|genic
eroto|gen|ous
eroto|logy
eroto|ma|nia
er|rancy
er|rand
er|rant
er|rantry (pl.
 er|rant|ries)
er|ratic
er|rat|ic|ally
er|ratum (pl.
 er|rata)
er|ro|ne|ous
error
er|satz
Erse
erst|while
eru|bes|cent
eruc|ta|tion
eru|dite
eru|di|tion
erupt
erup|tion
erupt|ive
erupt|iv|ity
eryngo (pl.
 eryn|gos)
ery|sip|elas
eryth|ema
eryth|emal
eryth|ro|blast
eryth|ro|cyte
es|ca|drille
es|cal|ade
es|cal|ate
 (es|cal|at|ing)
es|cala|tion
es|cal|ator
es|cal|lo|nia
es|cal|lop (Her.)
es|cal|ope (of
 meat)
es|cap|able
es|cap|ade

es|cape (as v.,
 es|cap|ing)
es|capee
es|cape|ment
es|cap|ism
es|cap|ist
es|capo|lo|gist
es|capo|logy
es|car|got
es|carp
es|carp|ment
eschato|lo|gical
eschato|lo|gist
eschato|logy
es|chew
es|chewal
esch|scholt|zia
es|cort
es|cribe
 (es|crib|ing)
es|crit|oire
es|crow
es|cudo (pl.
 es|cu|dos)
es|cu|lent
es|cut|cheon
es|ker
Es|kimo (pl.
 Eski|mos)
eso|teric
eso|ter|ical
eso|ter|ic|ally
eso|teri|cism
eso|teri|cist
es|pa|drille
es|pal|ier
es|parto (pl.
 es|par|tos)
es|pe|cial
es|pe|cially
Es|per|anto
es|pial
es|pi|on|age
es|plan|ade
es|pousal
es|pouse
 (es|pous|ing)
es|presso (pl.
 es|pressos)
es|prit de corps
espy (es|pies,
 es|pied,
 es|py|ing)
es|quire
es|say
es|say|ist

Es|sen
es|sence
Es|sene
es|sen|tial
es|sen|ti|al|ity
es|sen|tially
Es|sex
es|tab|lish
es|tab|lish|ment
es|tate
es|teem
es|ter
es|ter|ify
 (es|teri|fies,
 es|teri|fied,
 es|teri|fy|ing)
es|tim|able
es|tim|ate (as v.,
 es|tim|at|ing)
es|tima|tion
es|tim|at|ive
es|tim|ator
es|tival use
 aestival
Es|tonia
Es|to|nian
es|top (es|topped,
 es|top|ping)
es|top|page
es|top|pel
est|overs
es|trade
es|trange
 (es|tran|ging)
es|trange|ment
es|treat
Es|tre|ma|dura
es|tu|ar|ine
es|tu|ary (pl.
 es|tu|ar|ies)
esuri|ence
esuri|ency
esuri|ent
eta (Gr. letter)
et|aerio (pl.
 et|aerios)
et|alon
et cet|era
et|cet|eras n. pl.
etch|ant
etcher
etch|ing
eternal
etern|al|ize
 (etern|al|iz|ing)
etern|ally

etern|ity (pl.
 etern|it|ies)
etern|ize
 (etern|iz|ing)
Et|es|ian
eth|ane
eth|anol
ether
eth|er|eal
eth|er|eal|ity
eth|er|eal|ize
 (eth|er|eal|iz|ing)
eth|er|eally
eth|eric
eth|er|iza|tion
eth|er|ize
 (eth|er|iz|ing)
ethic
eth|ical
eth|ic|al|ity
eth|ic|ally
ethi|cize
 (ethi|ciz|ing)
eth|ics
Ethi|opia
Ethi|op|ian
Ethi|opic
eth|moid
eth|moidal
eth|narch
eth|nar|chy (pl.
 eth|narch|ies)
eth|nic
eth|nical
eth|nic|ally
eth|ni|city
eth|no|cen|tric
eth|no|cen|tric|
 ally
eth|no|cen|tri|city
eth|no|cen|trism
eth|no|grapher
eth|no|graphic
eth|no|graph|ical
eth|no|graph|ic|
 ally
eth|no|graphy
eth|no|lo|gic
eth|no|lo|gical
eth|no|lo|gic|ally
eth|no|lo|gist
eth|no|logy
etho|lo|gical
etho|lo|gic|ally
etho|lo|gist
etho|logy

ethos
ethyl
ethyl|ene
ethyl|enic
eti|ol|ate
 (eti|ol|at|ing)
eti|ola|tion
eti|quette
Etna
Eton
Eton|ian
ét|rier
Et|ruria
Et|rus|can
ét|ude
étui
ety|mo|lo|gic
ety|mo|lo|gical
ety|mo|lo|gic|ally
ety|mo|lo|gist
ety|mo|lo|gize
 (ety|mo|lo|giz|
  ing)
ety|mo|logy (pl.
 ety|mo|lo|gies)
ety|mon (pl.
 etyma)
eu|ca|lyptus
eu|charis (plant)
Eu|char|ist
Eu|char|istic
Eu|char|ist|ical
eu|chre (as v.,
 eu|chring)
Euc|lid
Euc|lid|ean
eu|de|monic
eu|de|mon|ism
eu|de|mon|ist
eu|de|mon|istic
eu|dio|meter
eu|dio|met|ric
eu|dio|met|rical
eu|dio|metry
Eu|gene On|egin
eu|genic
eu|gen|ic|ally
eu|gen|ics
eu|gen|ist
eu|hem|er|ism
Euler
eu|lo|gist
eu|lo|gistic
eu|lo|gium (pl.
 eu|lo|gi|ums)

eu|lo|gize
 (eu|lo|giz|ing)
eu|logy (pl.
 eu|lo|gies)
Eu|men|ides n. pl.
eu|nuch
eu|nuch|oid
eu|onymus
eu|peptic
eu|phem|ism
 (mild word)
△ euphuism
eu|phem|istic
eu|phem|ize
 (eu|phem|iz|ing)
eu|phonic
eu|pho|ni|ous
eu|pho|nium
eu|phon|ize
 (eu|phon|iz|ing)
eu|phony (pl.
 eu|phon|ies)
eu|phor|bia
eu|phoria
eu|phori|ant
eu|phoric
eu|phor|ic|ally
eu|phrasy (pl.
 eu|phras|ies)
Eu|phra|tes
eu|phu|ism (florid
 style)
△ euphemism
eu|phu|ist
eu|phu|istic
Eur|asian
Eur|atom
eur|eka
eu|rhythmic
Euri|pides
euro (pl. euros)
Euro|
 com|mu|nism
Euro|crat
Euro|dol|lar
Eur|ope
Euro|pean
Euro|pean|ism
Euro|pean|iza|
  tion
Euro|pean|ize
 (Euro|pean|iz|
  ing)
euro|pium
Euro|vis|ion
Eus|ta|chian

eu|stasy
eu|static
eu|tectic
eu|tha|nasia
eu|trophic
eu|trophy
evacu|ant
evacu|ate
 (evacu|at|ing)
evacu|ation
evacuee
evad|able
evade (evad|ing)
eva|gin|ate
 (eva|gin|at|ing)
eva|gina|tion
evalu|ate
 (evalu|at|ing)
evalu|ation
evalu|at|ive
evan|esce
 (evan|es|cing)
evan|es|cence
evan|es|cent
evan|gel|ical
evan|gel|ic|ally
evan|gel|ism
evan|gel|ist
evan|gel|istic
evan|gel|iza|tion
evan|gel|ize
 (evan|gel|iz|ing)
evap|or|able
evap|or|ate
 (evap|or|at|ing)
evap|ora|tion
evap|or|at|ive
evap|or|ator
eva|sion
evas|ive
evec|tion
even (as a.,
 evener, even|est)
even|ing
even|song
event
event|ful
even|tide
even|tual
even|tu|ality (pl.
 even|tu|alit|ies)
even|tu|ally
even|tu|ate
 (even|tu|at|ing)
ever
Ev|er|est

ever|green
ever|last|ing
ever|sion
evert
every
every|body
every|day
Every|man (man
 in the street)
every|one
every|thing
every|way
every|where
evict
evic|tion
evictor
evid|ence (as v.,
 evid|en|cing)
evid|ent
evid|en|tial
evid|en|tially
evid|en|tiary
evil
evilly
evince (evin|cing)
evin|cive
evis|cer|ate
 (evis|cer|at|ing)
evis|cera|tion
evoca|tion
evoc|at|ive
evoc|at|ory
evoke (evok|ing)
evol|ute (as v.,
 evol|ut|ing)
evolu|tion
evolu|tional
evolu|tion|ary
evolu|tion|ism
evolu|tion|ist
evolu|tion|istic
evol|ut|ive
evolve (evol|ving)
evolve|ment
evul|sion
ev|zone
ewe (sheep)
ewer
ex|acer|bate
 (ex|acer|bat|ing)
ex|acer|ba|tion
ex|act
ex|act|able
ex|ac|tion
ex|ac|ti|tude
ex|actor

ex|ag|ger|ate
 (ex|ag|ger|at|ing)
ex|ag|gera|tion
ex|ag|ger|at|ive
ex|ag|ger|ator
ex|alt
ex|al|ta|tion
exam
ex|am|ina|tion
ex|am|ine
 (ex|am|in|ing)
ex|am|inee
ex|am|iner
ex|ample
ex|an|im|ate
ex|an|thema
ex|arch
ex|arch|ate
ex|as|per|ate
 (ex|as|per|at|ing)
ex|as|pera|tion
ex cath|edra
ex|cav|ate
 (ex|cav|at|ing)
ex|cava|tion
ex|cav|ator
ex|ceed
ex|ceed|ingly
ex|cel (ex|celled,
 ex|cel|ling)
ex|cel|lence
ex|cel|lency (pl.
 ex|cel|len|cies)
ex|cel|lent
ex|cel|sior
ex|cen|tric (Math.)
ex|cept
ex|cep|tion
ex|cep|tion|able
ex|cep|tional
ex|cep|tion|al|ity
ex|cep|tion|ally
ex|cerpt
ex|cerpt|ible
ex|cerp|tion
ex|cess
ex|cess|ive
ex|change (as v.,
 ex|chan|ging)
ex|change|able
ex|chequer
ex|cis|able
ex|cise (as v.,
 ex|cis|ing)
ex|cision
ex|cit|ab|il|ity

ex|cit|able
ex|cit|ably
ex|cit|ant
ex|cita|tion
ex|cit|at|ive
ex|cit|at|ory
ex|cite (ex|cit|ing)
ex|cite|ment
ex|cit|ing
ex|citon
ex|claim
ex|clama|tion
ex|clam|at|ory
ex|clave
ex|clos|ure
ex|clude
 (ex|clud|ing)
ex|clu|sion
ex|clu|sion|ary
ex|clus|ive
ex|clus|iv|ity
ex|cog|it|able
ex|co|git|ate
 (ex|co|git|at|ing)
ex|co|gita|tion
ex|co|git|at|ive
ex|com|mu|nic|
          ate
 (ex|com|mu|nic|
         at|ing)
ex|com|mu|nica|
          tion
ex-convict
ex|cori|ate
 (ex|cori|at|ing)
ex|cori|ation
ex|cre|ment
ex|cres|cence
ex|cres|cent
ex|cres|cen|tial
ex|creta n. pl.
ex|crete
 (ex|cret|ing)
ex|cre|tion
ex|cret|ive
ex|cret|ory
ex|cru|ci|ate
 (ex|cru|ci|at|ing)
ex|cru|ci|ation
ex|culp|ate
 (ex|culp|at|ing)
ex|culpa|tion
ex|culp|at|ory
ex|cur|sion
ex|curs|ive
ex|cursus

ex|cus|able
ex|cus|ably
ex|cus|at|ory
ex|cuse (as v.,
ex|cus|ing)
ex-directory
ex|eat
ex|ec|rable
ex|ec|rate
(ex|ec|rat|ing)
ex|ec|ra|tion
ex|ec|rat|ive
ex|ec|rat|ory
ex|ecu|tant
ex|ecute
(ex|ecut|ing)
exe|cu|tion
exe|cu|tion|ary
exe|cu|tioner
ex|ec|ut|ive
ex|ecutor (of plan
etc.)
ex|ec|utor (of a
will)
ex|ec|ut|or|ial
ex|ec|ut|rix
ex|egesis (pl.
ex|egeses)
ex|egete
ex|egetic
ex|eget|ical
ex|eget|ist
ex|em|plar
ex|em|plar|ily
ex|em|plary
ex|em|pli|fica|tion
ex|em|plify
(ex|em|pli|fies,
ex|em|pli|fied,
ex|em|pli|fy|ing)
ex|em|plum (pl.
ex|em|pla)
ex|empt
ex|emp|tion
ex|equa|tur
ex|equies
ex|er|cise (as v.,
ex|er|cis|ing)
ex|ergual
ex|ergue
ex|ert
ex|er|tion
exes n. pl.
Ex|eter
ex|fo|li|ate
(ex|fo|li|at|ing)

ex|fo|li|ation
ex gratia
ex|hala|tion
ex|hale
(ex|hal|ing)
ex|haust
ex|haust|ib|il|ity
ex|haust|ible
ex|haus|tion
ex|haust|ive
exhaust-pipe
ex|hibit (as v.,
ex|hib|ited,
ex|hib|it|ing)
ex|hibi|tion
ex|hi|bi|tioner
ex|hibi|tion|ism
ex|hibi|tion|ist
ex|hibi|tion|istic
ex|hib|itor
ex|hib|it|ory
ex|hil|ar|ant
ex|hi|lar|ate
(ex|hil|ar|at|ing)
ex|hil|ara|tion
ex|hil|ar|at|ive
ex|hort
ex|horta|tion
ex|hort|at|ive
ex|hort|at|ory
ex|hu|ma|tion
ex|hume
(ex|hum|ing)
exi|gence
exi|gency (pl.
exi|gen|cies)
exi|gent
exi|gible
exi|gu|ity
ex|igu|ous
ex|ile (as v.,
ex|il|ing)
ex|ilic
ex|ist
ex|ist|ence
ex|ist|ent
ex|ist|en|tial
ex|ist|en|tial|ism
ex|ist|en|tial|ist
ex|ist|en|tially
exit (as v., ex|ited,
ex|it|ing)
ex-libris (pl. same)
exo|bio|logy
exo|crine
exo|derm

ex|odus
Ex|odus (OT book)
ex of|fi|cio
exo|gam|ous
exo|gamy
exo|gen
exo|gen|ous
exon
ex|on|er|ate
(ex|on|er|at|ing)
ex|on|era|tion
ex|on|er|at|ive
ex|oph|thalmic
exo|plasm
ex|or|bit|ance
ex|or|bit|ant
ex|or|cism
ex|or|cist
ex|or|ciza|tion
ex|or|cize
(ex|or|cizing)
ex|or|dium
exo|skel|eton
exo|sphere
exo|teric
exo|ter|ical
exo|ter|ic|ally
exo|teri|cism
exo|thermal
exo|thermic
ex|otic
ex|ot|ica
ex|pand
ex|pand|able
ex|panse
ex|pans|ib|il|ity
ex|pans|ible
ex|pans|ile
ex|pan|sion
ex|pan|sion|ary
ex|pan|sion|ism
ex|pan|sion|ist
ex|pans|ive
ex|pans|iv|ity
ex parte (Law)
ex|pa|ti|ate
(ex|pa|ti|at|ing)
ex|pa|ti|ation
ex|pa|ti|at|ory
ex|pat|ri|ate
(ex|pat|ri|at|ing)
ex|pat|ri|ation
ex|pect
ex|pect|ancy (pl.
ex|pect|an|cies)
ex|pect|ant

ex|pecta|tion
ex|pect|or|ant
ex|pect|or|ate
(ex|pect|or|
at|ing)
ex|pect|ora|tion
ex|pe|di|ence
ex|pe|di|ency
ex|pe|di|ent
ex|ped|ite
(ex|ped|it|ing)
ex|pedi|tion
ex|pedi|tion|ary
ex|pedi|tion|ist
ex|pedi|tious
ex|pel (ex|pelled,
ex|pel|ling)
ex|pellee
ex|pel|lent
ex|pend
ex|pend|able
ex|pend|it|ure
ex|pense
ex|pens|ive
ex|peri|ence (as v.,
ex|peri|en|cing)
ex|peri|ence|able
ex|peri|enced
ex|peri|en|tial
ex|peri|en|ti|ally
ex|peri|ment
ex|peri|mental
ex|peri|ment|al|
ize
(ex|peri|ment|al|
iz|ing)
ex|peri|ment|ally
ex|peri|menta|
tion
ex|pert
ex|pert|ise n.
ex|pert|ize v.
(ex|pert|iz|ing)
ex|pi|able
ex|pi|ate
(ex|pi|at|ing)
ex|pi|ation
ex|pi|ator
ex|pi|at|ory
ex|pira|tion
ex|pir|at|ory
ex|pire
(ex|pir|ing)
ex|piry
ex|plain
ex|plain|able

ex|plana|tion
ex|plan|at|or|ily
ex|plan|at|ory
ex|plant
ex|planta|tion
ex|plet|ive
ex|plic|able
ex|plic|ate
 (ex|plic|at|ing)
ex|plica|tion
ex|plic|at|ive
ex|plic|at|ory
ex|pli|cit
ex|plode
 (ex|plod|ing)
ex|ploit
ex|ploita|tion
ex|ploit|at|ive
ex|ploit|ive
ex|plora|tion
ex|plor|at|ive
ex|plor|at|ory
ex|plore
 (ex|plor|ing)
ex|plorer
ex|plo|sion
ex|plos|ive
ex|po|nent
ex|po|nen|tial
ex|po|nen|ti|ally
ex|port
ex|porta|tion
ex|pose
 (ex|pos|ing)
ex|posé
ex|posi|tion
ex|pos|it|ive
ex|pos|itor
ex|pos|it|ory
ex|pos|tu|late
 (ex|pos|tu|
    lat|ing)
ex|pos|tu|la|tion
ex|pos|tu|lat|ory
ex|pos|ure
ex|pound
ex|press
ex|press|ible
ex|pres|sion
ex|pres|sional
ex|pres|sion|ism
ex|pres|sion|ist
ex|pres|sion|istic
ex|pres|sion|
    ist|ic|ally
ex|press|ive

ex|press|iv|ity
expresso use
 espresso
ex|press|way
ex|propri|ate
 (ex|pro|pri|
    at|ing)
ex|pro|pri|ation
ex|pul|sion
ex|pul|sive
ex|punc|tion
ex|punge
 (ex|pun|ging)
ex|purg|ate
 (ex|purg|at|ing)
ex|purga|tion
ex|purg|ator
ex|purg|at|or|ial
ex|purg|at|ory
ex|quis|ite
ex|san|guin|ate
 (ex|san|guin|
    at|ing)
ex|scind
ex|sert
ex-service
ex-serviceman
 (pl.
 ex-servicemen)
ex|sic|cate
 (ex|sic|cat|ing)
ex|tant
ex|tem|por|an|
    eous
ex|tem|por|ary
ex|tem|pore
ex|tem|por|iza|
    tion
ex|tem|por|ize
 (ex|tem|por|iz|
    ing)
ex|tend
ex|tend|ib|il|ity
ex|tend|ible
ex|tens|ib|il|ity
ex|tens|ible
ex|tens|ile
ex|ten|sion
ex|ten|sional
ex|tens|ive
ex|tenso|meter
ex|tensor
ex|tent
ex|tenu|ate
 (ex|tenu|at|ing)
ex|tenu|ation

ex|tenu|at|ory
ex|ter|ior
ex|teri|or|ity
ex|teri|or|ize
 (ex|teri|or|iz|ing)
ex|term|in|ate (ex|
    term|in|at|ing)
ex|term|ina|tion
ex|term|in|ator
ex|term|in|at|ory
ex|ternal
ex|tern|al|ity (pl.
 ex|tern|al|it|ies)
ex|tern|al|ize
 (ex|tern|al|iz|ing)
ex|tern|ally
ex|tero|cept|ive
ex|ter|ri|tor|ial
ex|ter|ri|tori|al|ity
ex|tinct
ex|tinc|tion
ex|tinct|ive
ex|tin|guish
ex|ting|uisher
ex|tirp|ate
 (ex|tirp|at|ing)
ex|tirpa|tion
ex|tirp|ator
ex|tol (ex|tolled,
 ex|tol|ling)
ex|tort
ex|tor|tion
ex|tor|tion|ate
ex|tort|ive
ex|tra
ex|tra|cra|nial
ex|tract
ex|tract|able
ex|trac|tion
ex|tract|ive
ex|tractor
extra-curricular
ex|tra|dit|able
ex|tra|dite
 (ex|tra|dit|ing)
ex|tra|di|tion
ex|tra|dos
ex|tra|ga|lactic
extra-illustrate
ex|tra|ju|di|cial
extra-marital
ex|tra|mund|ane
ex|tra|mural
ex|trane|ous
ex|tra|ord|in|
    ar|ily

ex|tra|ord|in|ary
ex|tra|phys|ical
ex|tra|pol|ate
 (ex|tra|pol|
    at|ing)
ex|tra|pola|tion
extra-sensory
ex|tra|ter|res|trial
ex|tra|ter|rit|or|
    ial
ex|tra|ter|rit|
    or|ial|ity
ex|tra|vag|ance
ex|tra|vag|ancy
 (pl. ex|tra|vag|
    an|cies)
ex|tra|vag|ant
ex|tra|vag|anza
ex|tra|vas|ate
 (ex|tra|vas|
    at|ing)
ex|tra|vasa|tion
extra-vehicular
extravert use
 extrovert
ex|tremal
ex|treme
ex|trem|ism
ex|trem|ist
ex|trem|ity (pl.
 ex|trem|it|ies)
ex|tremum (pl.
 ex|trema or
 ex|trem|ums)
ex|tric|able
ex|tric|ate
 (ex|tric|at|ing)
ex|trica|tion
ex|trinsic
ex|trins|ic|ally
ex|tro|ver|sion
ex|tro|vert
ex|trude
 (ex|trud|ing)
ex|trus|ile
ex|tru|sion
ex|trus|ive
ex|uber|ance
ex|uber|ant
ex|uber|ate
 (ex|uber|at|ing)
ex|ud|ate
ex|uda|tion
ex|ud|at|ive
ex|ude (ex|ud|ing)
ex|ult

ex¦ult¦ancy
ex¦ult¦ant
ex¦ulta¦tion
ex¦urb
ex|urban
ex|urb¦an¦ite
ex|urbia
ex|uviae *n. pl.*
ex|uvial
ex|uvi¦ate
 (ex|uvi¦at¦ing)
ex|uvi¦ation

ex voto (offering)
eyas (young hawk)
eye (as *v.*, eyed,
 eye¦ing)
eye|ball
eye|bath
eye|black
eye|bright
eye|brow
eye¦ful (*pl.*
 eye|fuls)
eye|glass

eye|hole
eye|lash
eye|less
eye|let
eye-level
eye|lid
eye-opener
eye|piece
eye-rhyme
eye-shade
eye-shadow
eye|shot

eye|sight
eye|sore
eye-tooth
 (*pl.* eye-teeth)
eye|wash
eye|water
eye|wit¦ness
eyot *use* ait
eyra
Eyre, Lake (in
 Australia)
eyrie

F

Fa|bian
Fa|bi|an|ism
Fa|bi|an|ist
fable (as v.,
  fa|bling)
fa|bler
fab|liau (pl.
  fab|li|aux)
fab|ric
fab|ric|ate
  (fab|ric|at|ing)
fab|rica|tion
fab|ric|ator
fab|ulist
fabu|los|ity
fab|ulous
fa|çade
face (as v., fa|cing)
face-cloth
face-cream
face|less
face-lift
face-off
fa|cer
fa|cet
fa|ceted
fa|cetiae n. pl.
fa|cetious
fa|cia
fa|cial
fa|cially
fa|cies (pl. same)
fa|cile
fa|cil|it|ate
  (fa|cil|it|at|ing)
fa|cil|ita|tion
fa|cil|ity (pl.
  fa|cil|it|ies)
fa|cing
fac|sim|ile
fac|tice
fac|tion
fac|tional
fac|tious (of
  factions)
fac|ti|tious
  (artificial)
fac|tit|ive
fac|tor

fac|tor|age
fac|tor|ial
fac|tor|iza|tion
fac|tor|ize
  (fac|tor|iz|ing)
fact|ory (pl.
  fact|or|ies)
fac|totum (pl.
  fac|totums)
fac|tual
fac|tu|al|ism
fac|tu|al|ist
fac|tu|al|ity
fac|tu|ally
factum (pl.
  fac|tums or
  facta)
fac|ture
fac|ula (pl.
  fac|ulae)
fac|ular
fac|ulous
fac|ul|tat|ive
fac|ulty (pl.
  fac|ul|ties)
fad|dish
fad|dism
fad|dist
faddy (fad|dier,
  fad|di|est)
fade (fad|ing)
faecal
fae|ces n. pl.
Faer|oes
Faero|ese
fag (as v., fagged,
  fag|ging)
fag-end
fag|got
fag|goty
Fa|gin
fah (Mus.)
Fahr|en|heit
fai|ence
fail|ing
fail|ure
fai|néant

faint (lose
  consciousness;
  dim, pale) △ feint
fair|ground
fair|ing
Fair Isle (jersey
  etc.)
fair|water
fair|way
fairy (pl. fair|ies)
fairy|land
fairy-tale
fait ac|com|pli
faith|ful
faith|fully
faith|less
fake (as v.,
  fak|ing)
fakery
fakir
Fa|lange
Fa|lan|gism
Fa|lan|gist
fal|bala
falc|ate
fal|ci|form
fal|con
fal|conry
fal|deral
fald|stool
Fa|ler|nian
Falk|land
  (Islands)
fall (fell, fallen)
Falla
fal|la|cious
fal|lacy (pl.
  fal|la|cies)
fall|ib|il|ity
fall|ible
fall|ibly
Fal|lo|pian
fall-out n.
fal|low
false|hood
fal|setto (pl.
  fal|set|tos)
false|work
fals|ies n. pl.

falsi|fica|tion
fals|ify (fals|ifies,
  fals|ified,
  fals|ify|ing)
fals|ity
Fal|staff
fal|ter
fame
famed
fa|mil|ial
fa|mil|iar
fa|mili|ar|ity (pl.
  fa|mili|ar|it|ies)
fa|mili|ar|iza|tion
fa|mili|ar|ize
  (fa|mili|ar|iz|ing)
fam|ily (pl.
  fam|il|ies)
fam|ine
fam|ish
fam|ous
famu|lus (pl.
  fam|uli)
fan (as v., fanned,
  fan|ning)
fan|atic
fan|at|ical
fan|at|ic|ally
fan|at|icism
fan|at|icize
  (fan|at|iciz|ing)
fan|cier
fan|ci|ful
fan|ci|fully
fancy (as v.,
  fan|cies,
  fan|cied,
  fancy|ing; as n.,
  pl. fan|cies; as a.,
  fan|cier,
  fan|ci|est)
fan|dangle
fan|dango (pl.
  fan|dan|goes)
fan|fare
fan|far|on|ade
fan|light
fan|ner

fanny (pl.
 fan'nies)
fan|tail
fan|tasia
fan'tas|ist
fan'tas|ize
 (fan'tas|iz|ing)
fant|ast
fant|astic
fant'ast|ical
fant'ast|ic|al|ity
fant'ast|ic|ally
fant'ast|ic|ate
 (fant'ast|ic|
            at|ing)
fant'ast|ica|tion
fant'ast|icism
fant|asy (as n., pl.
 fant'as|ies; as v.,
 fant'as|ies,
 fant'as|ied,
 fant'asy|ing)
Fanti
fan'tod
fan|zine
faquir use fakir
far (fur|ther,
 fur|thest)
farad
fa'ra|day (unit)
Fa'ra|day (man)
fa|radic
far'an|dole
far-away a.
far|cical
far'cic|al|ity
far'cic|ally
farcy
far'ded
fare (as v., far'ing)
fare|well
far-fetched
far-flung
fa'rina
far'in|aceous
farmer
farm-hand
farm|house
farm|stead
farm|yard
faro
far-off
fa|rouche
far-out
far'ra'gin|ous

far|rago (pl.
 far|ra'gos)
far-reaching
far|rier
far'ri|ery
far|row
far|ruca
far-seeing
Farsi
far-sighted
farther use
 further
farthest use
 furthest
farth|ing
far'thin|gale
fart|lek
fas'ces n. pl.
fas'cia
fas'ci|ate
fas'ci|ated
fas|cia|tion
fas|cicle
fas|cicled
fas|cic|ular
fas'cic|ul|ate
fas|cic|ula|tion
fas|cic|ule
fas|cic|ulus (pl.
 fas'cic|uli)
fas|cin|ate
 (fas|cin|at'ing)
fas|cina|tion
fas|cin|ator
fas|cine
Fas|cism
Fas|cist
Fas|cistic
fash|ion
fash'ion|able
fash'ion|ably
fast|back
fasten
fast|ener
fast'en|ing
fas|ti|di|ous
fas'ti'gi|ate
fast|ness
fat (as a., fat'ter,
 fat'test; as v.,
 fat'ted, fat|ting)
fa'tal
fa'tal|ism
fa'tal|ist
fa'tal|istic

fat'al|ity (pl.
 fat'al|it'ies)
fa|tally
fate (as v., fat'ing)
fate|ful
fate|fully
fat-head
father
fath'er|hood
father-in-law (pl.
 fathers-in-law)
fath'er|land
fath'er|li|ness
fath'erly
fathom
Fatho|meter
 (echo-sounder;
 propr.)
fa'ti|dical
fa|tigue (as v.,
 fa|tigued,
 fa|tiguing)
Fat'iha (or
 Fat|ihah)
Fat|imid
Fat'im|ite
Fatso (pl.
 Fat'soes)
fat|stock
fat'ten
fat'ti|ness
fat|tish
fatty (as a.,
 fat|tier, fat'ti|est;
 as n., pl. fat|ties)
fa|tu|ity
fat|uous
fau'ces n. pl.
fau'cet
Faulk|ner
fault|finder
fault|find'ing
fault|ily
faulti|ness
faulty (faul|tier,
 faul'ti|est)
faun (deity)
 △ fawn
fauna (pl. faunas)
faunal
faun|ist
faun|istic
faun'ist|ical
Fauré
Faust
faute de mieux

fauv|ism
fauv|ist
faux pas (pl. same)
fa'vour
fa'vour|able
fa'vour|ably
fa'vour|ite
fa'vour|it|ism
fawn (deer, brown;
 behave servilely)
 △ faun
faze (fazed,
 faz'ing)
fealty
fear|ful
fear|fully
fear|less
fear|some
feas|ib'il|ity
feas|ible
feas|ibly
feat (act)
feather
feath'eri|ness
feather|weight
feath|ery
fea|ture (as v.,
 fea|tur'ing)
feb'ri|fugal
feb'ri|fuge
feb|rile
feb'ril|ity
Feb'ru|ary (pl.
 Feb'ru|ar|ies)
feck|less
fecu|lence
fecu|lent
fec'und
fec'und|ate
 (fec'und|at|ing)
fec'unda|tion
fe'cund|ity
fed'ay|een n. pl.
fed|eral
fed'eral|ism
fed'eral|ist
fed'er'al|ize
 (fed'er'al|iz|ing)
fed'er|ally
fed'er|ate
 (fed'er|at'ing)
fed'era|tion
fed'era|tion|ist
fed'er|at'ive
fe'dora
fee (as v., fee'd)

feeble (feeb|ler,
 feeb|lest)
feeble-minded
feebly
feed (fed)
feed|back
feed|stock
feel (felt)
feeler
feign
feijoa
feint (sham attack;
 pretend; of ruled
 lines) △ faint
feis (*hist.*; *pl.*
 feis|eanna)
fe|la|fel
feld|scher
feld|spar
feld|spathic
feld|spath|oid
fe|li|cific
fe|licit|ate
 (fe|licit|at|ing)
fe|licita|tion
fe|licit|ous
fe|licity
fe|line
fe|lin|ity
fel|lah (*pl.*
 fel|la|hin)
fel|late
 (fel|lat|ing)
fel|la|tio
fell|monger
fel|loe (wheel rim)
fel|low
fel|low|ship
felon
fe|loni|ous
fel|onry
fel|ony (*pl.*
 fel|on|ies)
felspar *use*
 feldspar
felt-tipped
fe|lucca
fel|wort
fe|male
feme (*Law*)
fem|inal
fem|in|al|ity
fem|in|eity
fem|in|ine
fem|in|in|ity
fem|in|ism

fem|in|ist
fem|in|ity
fem|in|iza|tion
fem|in|ize
 (fem|in|iz|ing)
femme fatale (*pl.*
 femmes fa|tales)
fem|oral
fem|to|metre
fe|mur (*pl.*
 fem|ora)
fence (as *v.*,
 fen|cing)
fen|cing
fender
fen|es|tella
fen|es|tra (*pl.*
 fen|es|trae)
fen|es|trate
fen|es|trated
fen|es|tra|tion
fen-fire
Fe|nian
Fe|ni|an|ism
fenks *n. pl.*
fen|man (*pl.*
 fen|men)
fen|nec
fen|nel
Fen|no|scan|dia
fenny
fenu|greek
feoff *use* fief
feral
fer de lance
 (snake)
fe|re|tory (*pl.*
 fe|re|tor|ies)
fer|ial
Fer|man|agh
fer|mata (*pl.*
 fer|matas)
fer|ment
fer|ment|able
fer|menta|tion
fer|ment|at|ive
fermi
fer|mion
fer|mium
fern|ery (*pl.*
 fern|er|ies)
ferny
fe|ro|cious
fe|ro|city
fer|rate
ferrel *use* ferrule

fer|ret (fer|reted,
 fer|ret|ing)
fer|rety
fer|ri|age
fer|ric
fer|ri|mag|netic
Ferris
fer|rite
fer|ritic
fer|ro|con|crete
fer|ro|el|ec|tric
fer|ro|mag|netic
fer|rous
fer|ru|gin|ous
fer|rule (metal
 cap) △ ferule
ferry (as *n.*, *pl.*
 fer|ries; as *v.*,
 fer|ried,
 fer|ry|ing)
fer|tile
fer|til|ity
fert|il|iza|tion
fert|il|ize
 (fert|il|iz|ing)
fert|il|izer
fer|ula
fer|ule (cane; as *v.*,
 fer|uled,
 fer|ul|ing)
 △ ferrule
fer|vency
fer|vent
fer|vid
fer|vour
Fes|cen|nine
fes|cue
fess (on shield)
festal
fest|ally
fes|ter
fest|ival
fest|ive
fest|iv|ity (*pl.*
 fest|iv|it|ies)
fes|toon
fes|toon|ery
Fest|schrift (*pl.*
 Fest|schriften)
fetch|ing
fête (as *v.*, fêt|ing)
fetid
fet|ish
fet|ish|ism
fet|ish|ist
fet|ish|istic

fet|lock
fetor (stench)
fet|ter (shackle)
fet|ter|lock
fettle (as *v.*,
 fet|tling)
fet|tler
fetus *use* foetus
feud
feudal
feud|al|ism
feud|al|ist
feud|al|istic
feud|al|ity
feud|al|iza|tion
feud|al|ize
 (feud|al|iz|ing)
feud|ally
feud|at|ory (as *n.*,
 pl. feud|at|or|ies)
feud|ist
fever
fever|few
fe|ver|ish
fe|ver|ous
fez (*pl.* fezzes)
fezzed
fi|acre
fi|ancé (*fem.*
 fi|an|cée)
fianch|etto (*pl.*
 fianch|et|toes)
fi|asco (*pl.*
 fi|as|cos)
fiat
fib (as *v.*, fibbed,
 fib|bing)
fib|ber
Fi|bo|nacci
fibre
fibre|board
fibred
fibre|glass
fib|ri|form
fib|ril
fib|ril|lar
fib|ril|lary
fib|ril|late
 (fib|ril|lat|ing)
fib|ril|la|tion
fib|rin
fib|rino|gen
fib|rin|oid
fibro (*pl.* fib|ros)
fibro-cement
fib|roid

fib|roin
fib|roma
fib|rosis (*pl.*
 fib|roses)
fib|ro|sitic
fib|ro|sitis
fib|rotic
fib|rous
fib|ster
fib|ula (*pl.*
 fib|ulae)
fib|ular
fiche (*pl.* same)
Fichte
fi|chu
fickle
fickly
fic|tile
fic|tion
fic|tional
fic|tion|al|iza|tion
fic|tion|al|ize
 (fic|tion|al|iz|ing)
fic|tion|eer
fic|tion|ist
fic|ti|tious
fict|ive
fiddle (as *v.*,
 fid|dling)
fiddle-de-dee
fiddle-faddle
 (as *v.*, fiddle-
 faddling)
fid|dler
fiddle|stick
fid|dling
fiddly (fid|dlier,
 fid|dli|est)
fi|de|ism
fi|de|ist
fi|de|istic
fi|del|ity
fid|get (as *v.*,
 fid|geted,
 fid|get|ing)
fid|geti|ness
fid|gety
fi|du|cial
fi|du|cially
fi|du|ciary (*pl.*
 fi|du|ciar|ies)
fief (*hist.*)
fief|dom
field
field-day
fielder

field|fare
field-glasses
Field|ing
field-mouse (*pl.*
 field-mice)
fields|man (*pl.*
 fields|men)
field|stone
field|work
field-worker
fiend
fiend|ish
fierce (fier|cer,
 fier|cest)
fi|eri fa|cias (*Law*)
fier|ily
fier|iness
fiery (fier|ier,
 fieri|est)
fi|esta
fife (as *v.*, fif|ing)
fifer
fife-rail
fif|teen
fif|teenth
fifth-columnist
fifthly
fif|tieth
fifty (*pl.* fif|ties)
fifty-fifty
fig (as *v.*, figged,
 fig|ging)
fight (as *v.*,
 fought)
fighter
fig-leaf
 (*pl.* fig-leaves)
fig|ment
fig|ural
fig|ura|tion
fig|ur|at|ive
fig|ure (as *v.*,
 fig|ur|ing)
figure-head
fig|ur|ine
fig|wort
Fiji
fila|ment
fila|ment|ary
fila|men|ted
fila|ment|ous
fil|aria (*pl.*
 fil|ariae)
fil|arial
fil|ari|asis
fila|ture

fil|bert
filch
file (as *v.*, fil|ing)
filet (net, lace;
 meat)
fi|lial
fi|li|ally
fi|li|ation
fili|beg
fili|bus|ter
fili|gree
fili|greed
fil|ing
Fi|li|pino (*pl.*
 Fi|li|pi|nos, *fem.*
 Fi|li|pina)
filler
fil|let (fil|leted,
 fil|let|ing)
fill|ing
filling-station
fil|lip (as *v.*,
 fil|liped,
 fil|lip|ing)
fil|lis
fil|lis|ter
fill-up *n.*
filly (*pl.* fil|lies)
film-goer
filmic
filmi|ness
filmo|graphy
film|set|ting
film-strip
filmy (film|ier,
 filmi|est)
fi|lo|selle
fil|ter
fil|ter|able
filter-bed
filter-paper
filter-tip
filth|ily
filthi|ness
filthy (filth|ier,
 filthi|est)
fil|trate (as *v.*,
 fil|trat|ing)
fil|tra|tion
fim|bri|ate
fim|bri|ated
fin (as *v.*, finned,
 finn|ing)
fin|able
fin|agle
 (fin|ag|ling)

fi|nal
fi|nale
fi|nal|ism
fi|nal|ist
fi|nal|istic
fi|nal|ity (*pl.*
 fi|nal|it|ies)
fi|nal|iza|tion
fi|nal|ize
 (fi|nal|iz|ing)
fi|nally
fin|ance (as *v.*,
 fin|an|cing)
fin|an|cial
fin|an|ci|ally
fin|an|cier
find (found)
find|able
finder
fin de siècle
find|ing
fine (as *v.*, fin|ing;
 as *a.*, finer,
 finest)
fine-drawn
finery (*pl.*
 finer|ies)
fines herbes
fine-spun
fin|esse (as *v.*,
 fin|ess|ing)
fine-tooth comb
fin|ger
finger-board
finger-bowl
fingered
fin|ger|ing
fin|ger|less
fin|ger|ling
finger-mark
finger-nail
finger-paint
finger-plate
finger-post
fin|ger|print
finger-stall
fin|ger|tip
fin|ial
fin|ical
fin|ic|al|ity
fin|ic|ally
fin|ick|ing
finicky
finis
fin|ish
fin|isher

fi¦nite
fi¦nit¦ism
fi¦nit¦ist
Fin¦land
fin¦nan
Fin¦ne¦gans Wake
fin¦ner
fin¦nesko (*pl.*
 same)
Finnic
Finn¦ish
Finno-Ugrian
Finno-Ugric
finny
fino (*pl.* fi¦nos)
Fi¦ona
fiord
fi¦ori¦tura
fipple
fir (tree) △ **fur**
fire (as *v.*, fir¦ing)
fire¦arm
fire¦back
fire-ball
fire-bird
fire-blast
fire-bomb
fire-box
fire¦brand
fire-break
fire-brick
fire-bug
fire-clay
fire¦cracker
fire¦crest
fire¦damp
fire¦dog
fire-drill
fire-eater
fire-engine
fire-escape
fire-fighter
fire¦fly (*pl.*
 fire¦flies)
fire-guard
fire-hose
fire¦house
fire-irons
fire¦light
fire-lighter
fire¦lock
fire¦man (*pl.*
 fire¦men)
fire¦place
fire-plug
fire¦proof

fire-screen
fire-ship
fire¦side
fire-storm
fire-trap
fire¦wood
fire¦work
fir¦ing
firing-line
firing-squad
fir¦kin
firma¦ment
firma¦mental
fir¦man
firry
first-born
first-class *a.* &
 adv.
first-foot
first-fruit
first¦hand *a.* &
 adv.
first¦ling
firstly
first-rate
fiscal
fisc¦al¦ity
fisc¦ally
fisher
fish¦er¦man (*pl.*
 fish¦er¦men)
fish¦ery (*pl.*
 fish¦er¦ies)
fish-eye
fish-farm
fish-hook
fish¦ily
fishi¦ness
fishing-rod
fish¦mon¦ger
fish-net
fish-plate
fish-pond
fish-tail
fish¦wife (*pl.*
 fish¦wives)
fishy (fish¦ier,
 fishi¦est)
fis¦sile
fis¦sil¦ity
fis¦sion
fis¦sion¦able
fis¦si¦par¦ity
fis¦si¦par¦ous
fis¦sure (as *v.*,
 fis¦sur¦ing)

fist¦ful (*pl.*
 fist¦fuls)
fisti¦cuffs
fis¦tula
fis¦tu¦lar
fis¦tu¦lous
fit (as *a.*, fit¦ter,
 fit¦test; as *v.*,
 fit¦ted, fit¦ting)
fit¦chew
fit¦ful
fit¦fully
fit¦ment
fit¦ter
fit¦ting
fit-up *n.*
Fitz¦ger¦ald, Scott
five¦fold
fiver
five-stones
fix¦ate (fix¦at¦ing)
fixa¦tion
fix¦at¦ive
fix¦edly
fix¦ed¦ness
fixer
fix¦ity
fix¦ture
fizz
fizzle (as *v.*,
 fizz¦ling)
fizzy (fiz¦zier,
 fiz¦zi¦est)
fjord *use* fiord
flab¦ber¦gast
flab¦bi¦ness
flabby (flab¦bier,
 flab¦bi¦est)
flac¦cid
flac¦cid¦ity
flag (as *v.*,
 flagged,
 flag¦ging)
flag-boat
fla¦gel¦lant
fla¦gel¦lar
fla¦gel¦late (as *v.*,
 fla¦gel¦lat¦ing)
fla¦gel¦la¦tion
fla¦gel¦lator
fla¦gel¦lat¦ory
fla¦gel¦li¦form
fla¦gel¦lum (*pl.*
 fla¦gella)
fla¦geolet
fla¦gi¦tious

flag-list
flag¦man (*pl.*
 flag¦men)
flag-officer
flagon
flag-pole
flag¦rancy
flag-rank
flag¦rant
flag¦ship
flag¦staff
flag¦stone
flail
flak
flake (as *v.*,
 flak¦ing)
flaky (fla¦kier,
 fla¦ki¦est)
flambé
flam¦beau (*pl.*
 flam¦beaus)
flam¦boy¦ance
flam¦boy¦ancy
flam¦boy¦ant
flame (as *v.*,
 flam¦ing)
fla¦men
fla¦menco (*pl.*
 fla¦men¦cos)
flame-proof
flame-thrower
flame-tree
flam¦ing
fla¦mingo (*pl.*
 fla¦min¦gos)
flam¦mab¦il¦ity
flam¦mable
flamy (fla¦mier,
 fla¦mi¦est)
flanch
Flan¦ders
flange (as *v.*,
 flan¦ging)
flanker
flannel (as *v.*,
 flan¦nelled,
 flan¦nel¦ling)
flan¦nel¦board
flan¦nel¦ette
flan¦nel¦graph
flan¦nelled
flan¦nelly
flap (as *v.*,
 flapped,
 flap¦ping)
flap¦doodle

flap|jack
flap'per
flappy (flap|pier,
 flap'pi|est)
flare (as v.,
 flar|ing)
flare-path
flare-up n.
flash|back
flash-board
flasher
flash-flood
flash-gun
flash|ily
flashi|ness
flash|ing
flash-lamp
flash|light
flash-over n.
flash|point
flashy (flash|ier,
 flashi|est)
flat (as a., flat|ter,
 flat'test; as v.,
 flat'ted, flat|ting)
flat-fish
flat|foot (pl.
 flat|feet)
flat-footed
flat-iron
flat|let
flat|ten
flat'ter
flat|tery
flat|tie
flat|tish
flatu|lence
flatu|lency
flatu|lent
flatus
flat|ware
flat|worm
Flau|bert
flaunty
flaut|ist
fla'ves|cent
flav|ine
fla|vo|pro'tein
fla'vor|ous
fla|vour
fla'vour|ful
fla'vour|less
fla'vour|some
flaw|less
flaxen
F-layer

flea-bag
flea|bane
flea-bite
flea-pit
flèche (Archit.)
flecker
Fled'er|maus
fledge (fledging)
fledge|ling
fleece (as v.,
 flee'cing)
fleecy (flee|cier,
 flee'ci|est)
flee (fled)
fleet|ing
Flem|ing
Flem|ish
flesher
fleshi|ness
flesh|ings
flesh'li|ness
fleshly
flesh-pots
fleshy (flesh|ier,
 fleshi|est)
Flet|ton
fleur-de-lis (pl.
 fleurs-de-lis)
fleuret
fleuron
fleury
flex|ib|il|ity
flex|ible
flex|ibly
flex|ion
flex'ional
flexi|time
flexor
flexu|os'ity
flex|uous
flex|ural
flex|ure
flib'ber'ti|gib'bet
flicker
flick-knife (pl.
 flick-knives)
*Flie'gende
 Hol|länder*
flier use flyer
flight-deck
flight|ily
flighti|ness
flight|less
flight-test
flighty (fligh'tier,
 fligh'ti|est)

flim|flam (as v.,
 flim|flammed,
 flim|flam|ming)
flim|flam'mery
flim'sily
flim'si|ness
flimsy (as n., pl.
 flim|sies; as a.,
 flim|sier,
 flim'si|est)
flind'ers
fling (as v., flung)
flint|ily
flinti|ness
flint|lock
flinty (flint|ier,
 flinti|est)
flip (as v., flipped,
 flip|ping)
flip-flop (as v.,
 flip-flopped,
 flip-flopping)
flip|pancy
flip|pant
flip|per
flip|ping
flirt
flir'ta|tion
flir'ta|tious
flirty (flir|tier,
 flir'ti|est)
flit (as v., flit'ted,
 flit|ting)
flitch
flit'ter
flix|weed
float|age
floatation use
 flotation
floater
float|ing
floc'cu|late
 (floc'cu|lat|ing)
floc'cu'la|tion
floc|cule
floc'cu|lence
floc'cu|lent
floc'cu|lus (pl.
 floc|culi)
floc|cus (pl. flocci)
flocky (flock|ier,
 flocki|est)
flog (flogged,
 flog|ging)
flood
flood|gate

flood|light
 (flood|lit)
flood-tide
floor-board
floor|ing
floor|less
floozie
flop (as v.,
 flopped,
 flop|ping)
floppy (flop|pier,
 flop'pi|est)
flora
floral
flor|ally
flor|eat
Flor|ence
Flor'en|tine
flor'es|cence
floret
flori|ate
 (flori|at|ing)
flo'ri|bunda
flo'ri|cul'tural
flo'ri|cul'ture
flo'ri|cul'tur|ist
florid
Flor|ida
Flo'rid|ian
flor|id|ity
flo'ri|fer'ous
flori|le'gium (pl.
 flori|legia)
florin
flor|ist
flor|istic
flor|ist|ic|ally
flor|ist|ics
flor|istry
flo'ruit
flos'cu|lar
flos'cu|lous
flossy (flos|sier,
 flos'si|est)
flo'ta|tion
flo|tilla
flot|sam
flounce (as v.,
 floun|cing)
floun|der
flour (grain, meal)
 △ flower
flour|ish
floury
flout

flower (plant)
△ flour
flowered
floweret
floweri|ness
flower|ing
flower|pot
flower-show
flowery
flow|ing
flow-sheet
flow|stone
flu (influenza)
△ flue
fluc'tu|ate
(fluc'tu|at|ing)
fluc'tu|ation
flue (smoke-duct
etc.) △ flu
flu|ence
flu|ency
flu|ent
fluffy (fluf|fier,
fluf'fi|est)
flu'gel|horn
fluid
flu|idic
flu'id|ics
flu'id|ify
(flu'idi|fies,
flu'idi|fied,
flu'idi|fy|ing)
flu'id|ity
flu'id|iza|tion
flu'id|ize
(flu'id|iz|ing)
fluke (as v.,
fluk'ing)
fluky (flu|kier,
flu'ki|est)
flume (as v.,
flum'ing)
flum|mery (pl.
flum'mer|ies)
flum|mox
flun|key
fluo|boric
fluor|esce
(fluor|es|cing)
fluor|es'cence
fluor|es'cent
flu'or|id|ate
(flu'or|id|at'ing)
fluor'ida|tion
flu'or|ide
flu'or|id|iza|tion

flu'or|in|ate
(flu'or|in|at'ing)
flu'or|ina|tion
flu|or'ine
flu|or'ite
flu'oro|car'bon
flu|oro|form
flu'oro|scope
flu'or|osis
flu'or|spar
flurry (as n., pl.
flur|ries; as v.,
flur|ries,
flur|ried,
flur'ry|ing)
flus'ter
flute (as v.,
flut'ing)
flut'ing
flut|ter
fluty (flu|tier,
flu'ti|est)
flu|vial
flu'vi|at|ile
fluvio-glacial
flu'vio|meter
flux|ion
flux|ional
flux'ion|ary
fly (as n., pl. flies,
but flys in sense
'carriage'; as v.,
flies, flew, flown,
fly|ing)
fly-away a.
fly-blown
fly-by n.
fly-by-night n. &
a.
fly|catcher
flyer
fly-half
(pl. fly-halves)
fly|ing
fly|leaf (pl.
fly|leaves)
fly|over n.
fly-past n.
fly|sheet
flyt'ing
fly|way
fly|weight
fly|wheel
f-number
foamy (foam|ier,
foami|est)

fob (as v., fobbed,
fob|bing)
focal
fo'cal|iza|tion
fo'cal|ize
(fo'cal|iz|ing)
fo'c's'le use
forecastle
fo'cus (as n., pl.
fo|cuses, Sci.
foci; as v.,
fo'cused,
fo'cus|ing)
fod'der
foe|man (pl.
foe|men)
foetal
foet|icide
foetus
fog (as v., fogged,
fog|ging)
fog-bank
fogey use fogy
fog|gily
fog'gi|ness
foggy (fog|gier,
fog'gi|est)
fog-horn
fog-lamp
fogy (pl. fo|gies)
föhn (wind)
foible
Foix
fold|away a.
fold|boat
folder
fold-out n.
fold-up a.
fo'li|aceous
fo'li|age
fo'liar
fo'li|ate (as v.,
foli|at'ing)
foli|ation
fo'lic
fo'lio (as n., pl.
fo'lios)
fo'li|ole
folk|lore
folk|loric
folk|lor'ist
folk-song
folksy
folk-tale
folk|weave
folky

foll|icle
fol'lic|ular
fol'lic|ulate
fol'lic|ulated
fol|low
fol|lower
fol|low|ing
follow-on n. & a.
follow-up n.
folly (pl. fol|lies)
fo'ment
fo'men'ta|tion
fond|ant
fondle (fond|ling)
fon'due
Fon'taine|bleau
fontal
fon'tan|elle
food|stuff
fool|ery (pl.
fool|er'ies)
fool|har'di|ness
fool|hardy
fool|ish
fool|proof
fools|cap
foot (pl. feet)
foot|age
foot|ball
foot|baller
foot|board
foot-brake
foot-bridge
footed
footer
foot|fall
foot|hill
foot|hold
foot|ing
footle (foot|ling)
foot|less
foot|lights
foot|ling
foot|loose
foot|man (pl.
foot|men)
foot|mark
foot|note
foot|path
foot|plate
foot|print
foot|sie
foot-slog (as v.,
foot-slogged,
foot-slogging)
foot|sore

foot|stalk
foot|step
foot|stool
foot|sure
foot|wear
foot|work
fop|pery (*pl.*
 fop|per|ies)
fop|pish
for|age (as *v.*,
 for|aging)
For|aker
fo|ra|men (*pl.*
 fo|ra|mina)
fo|ra|min|ate
fo|ra|min|if|er|ous
foray
for|bear (abstain;
 for|bore,
 for|borne)
 △ forebear
for|bear|ance
for|bid (for|bade,
 for|bid|den,
 for|bid|ding)
for|bid|den
for|bid|ding
for|bye
force (as *v.*,
 forced, for|cing)
force-feed
 (force-fed)
force|ful
force|fully
force-land
force ma|jeure
force|meat
for|ceps
force-pump
for|cible
for|cibly
for|cip|ate
fore|arm
fore|bear
 (ancestor)
 △ forbear
fore|bode
 (fore|bod|ing)
fore|bod|ing
fore|cast (as *v.*,
 forecast)
fore|castle
fore|close
 (fore|clos|ing)
fore|clos|ure
fore|con|scious

fore|court
for|edge (*Binding*)
fore|doom
fore-edge
fore|father
fore|feel
 (fore|felt)
fore|fin|ger
fore|foot (*pl.*
 fore|feet)
fore|front
forego (to go
 before; fore|goes,
 fore|went,
 fore|gone)
 △ forgo
fore|ground
fore|hand
fore|head
fore|hock
fore|hold
for|eign
for|eigner
fore|judge
 (fore|judging)
fore|know
 (fore|knew,
 fore|known)
fore|know|ledge
fore|land
fore|leg
fore|lock
fore|man (*pl.*
 fore|men)
fore|mast
fore|most
fore|name
for|ensic
for|ens|ic|ally
fore|or|dain
fore|or|dina|tion
fore|peak
fore|play
fore|run
 (fore|ran,
 fore|run,
 fore|run|ning)
fore|run|ner
fore|sail
fore|see
 (fore|saw,
 fore|seen)
fore|see|able
fore|shadow
fore-sheets
fore|shore

fore|shorten
fore|show
 (fore|shown)
fore|sight
fore|skin
for|est
fore|stall
fore|stal|ment
fore|stay
for|ester
for|estry
fore|taste (as *v.*,
 fore|tas|ted,
 fore|tast|ing)
fore|tell
 (fore|told)
fore|thought
fore|to|ken
fore|top
fore-topmast
fore-topsail
for ever (for
 always)
for|ever
 (continually)
fore|warn
fore|wo|man (*pl.*
 fore|wo|men)
fore|word
fore|yard
For|far
for|feit
for|feit|ure
for|gather
forge (as *v.*,
 for|ging)
for|ger
for|gery (*pl.*
 for|ger|ies)
for|get (for|got,
 for|got|ten,
 for|get|ting)
for|get|ful
for|get|fully
forget-me-not
for|get|table
for|giv|able
for|give (for|gave,
 for|given,
 for|giv|ing)
for|give|ness
forgo (to abstain
 from; for|goes,
 for|went,
 for|gone)
 △ forego

for|int
fork-lift (truck)
for|lorn
formal
form|al|de|hyde
form|alin
form|al|ism
form|al|ist
form|al|istic
form|al|ity (*pl.*
 form|al|it|ies)
form|al|iza|tion
form|al|ize
 (form|al|iz|ing)
form|ally
form|ant
for|mat (as *v.*,
 for|mat|ted,
 for|mat|ting)
form|ate
forma|tion
forma|tional
form|at|ive
forme (*Printing*)
for|mer
for|merly
formic
For|mica (*propr.*)
for|mica|tion
for|mid|able
for|mid|ably
form|less
for|mula (*pl.*
 for|mu|las, *Sci.*
 for|mu|lae)
for|mu|laic
for|mu|lar|ize
 (for|mu|lar|iz|
  ing)
for|mu|lary (*pl.*
 for|mu|lar|ies)
for|mu|late
 (for|mu|lat|ing)
for|mu|la|tion
for|mu|lism
for|mu|list
for|mu|lize
 (for|mu|liz|ing)
form|work
for|nic|ate
 (for|nic|at|ing)
for|nica|tion
for|ni|cator
for|rader

for|sake
(for|sook,
for|saken,
for|sak|ing)
for|sooth
For|ster
for|swear
(for|swore,
for|sworn)
For|syte Saga
for|sythia
forte (strong point;
2 sylls.)
forth|com|ing
forth|right
forth|with
for|ti|eth
for|ti|fi|able
for|ti|fica|tion
for|tify (for|ti|fies,
for|ti|fied,
for|ti|fy|ing)
for|tis|simo (*pl.*
for|tis|si|mos)
for|ti|tude
fort|night
fort|nightly (as *n.,*
pl. fort|night|lies)
For|tran (Comp.
language)
fort|ress
for|tu|it|ism
for|tu|it|ist
for|tu|it|ous
for|tu|ity (*pl.*
for|tu|it|ies)
for|tu|nate
for|tu|nately
for|tune
forty (as *n., pl.*
for|ties)
forty|fold
forum
for|ward
for|warder
for|wards
fossa (*Anat.; pl.*
fos|sae)
fosse (ditch)
fos|sick
fos|sil
fos|sil|if'er|ous
fos|sil|iza|tion
fos|sil|ize
(fos|sil|iz|ing)
fos|sor|ial

fos|ter
fos|ter|age
foster-brother
foster-child (*pl.*
foster-children)
foster-daughter
foster-father
fos|ter|ling
foster-mother
foster-parent
foster-sister
foster-son
Fou|cault
fou|gasse
foul (dirty etc.)
△ fowl
foul|ard
foully
foul-up *n.*
fou|mart
founda|tion
founda|tioner
founder
found|ling
found|ress
foundry (*pl.*
found|ries)
foun|tain
fountain-head
fourch|ette
Four|drin|ier
Four|ier
Four|ier|ism
four|pence
four|penny
four-poster
four|score
four|some
four-square
four|teen
four|teenth
fourthly
fo|vea (*pl.* fo|veae)
fo|veal
fo|ve|ate
fo|ve|ola (*pl.*
fo|ve|olae)
fo|ve|ol|ate
fowl (bird etc.)
△ foul
fox|glove
fox|hole
fox|hound
fox-hunt
fox-hunter
fox-hunting

foxi|ness
fox-mark
fox|tail
fox-terrier
fox|trot (as *v.,*
fox|trot|ted,
fox|trot|ting)
foxy (fox|ier,
foxi|est)
foyer
frab|jous
fra|cas (*pl.* same)
frac|tion
frac|tional
frac|tion|ally
frac|tion|ary
frac|tion|ate
(frac|tion|at|ing)
frac|tiona|tion
frac|tion|ize
(frac|tion|iz|ing)
frac|tious
frac|ture
(frac|tur|ing)
fraen|ulum (*pl.*
fraen|ula)
fraenum (*pl.*
fraena)
fra|gile
fra|gil|ity
frag|ment
frag|ment|ar|ily
frag|ment|ary
frag|menta|tion
frag|ment|ize
(frag|ment|iz|ing)
fra|grance
fra|grant
frailty (*pl.*
frail|ties)
Frak|tur
fram|boe|sia
frame (as *v.,*
fram|ing)
frame-saw
frame-up *n.*
frame|work
France
Fran|ces (*fem.*)
Franche-Comté
franch|ise (as *v.,*
franch|ising)
Fran|cis (*masc.*)
Fran|cis|can
fran|cium
Franck, César

Franco-German
fran|co|lin
Fran|co|ma|nia
Fran|co|phile
Fran|co|phobe
Fran|co|pho|bia
fran|co|phone
fran|gible
fran|gi|pane
(almond cream or
paste)
fran|gi|pani
(perfume, tree)
frang|lais
Frank|en|stein
frank|furter
frank|in|cense
Frank|ish
Frank|lin
fran|tic
fran|tic|ally
frap (frapped,
frap|ping)
frappé
frat (as *v.,*
frat|ted,
frat|ting)
fra|ternal
fra|tern|ally
fra|tern|ity (*pl.*
fra|tern|it|ies)
frat|ern|iza|tion
frat|ern|ize
(frat|ern|iz|ing)
frat|ri|cidal
frat|ri|cide
fraudu|lence
fraudu|lent
Frau (*pl.* Frauen)
Fräu|lein (*pl.*
same)
Fraun|hofer
frax|in|ella
frazzle (as *v.,*
frazz|ling)
freak
freaki|ness
freak|ish
freaky (freak|ier,
freaki|est)
freckle (as *v.,*
freck|ling)
freckly
Fred|er|ick

free (as *a.*, freer,
freest; as *v.*,
freed)
free|board
free|boot
free|booter
freed|man
(emancipated
slave; *pl.*
freed|men)
△ freeman
free|dom
free-for-all
free-hand *a.*
free-handed
free|hold
free|holder
free-lance (as *v.*,
free-lancing)
free-liver
free-loader
free|man (one
having freedom of
city; *pl.* free|men)
△ freedman
free|mar'tin
Free|ma'son
Free|ma'sonry
free-range *a.*
free|sia
free-spoken
free-standing
free-stone
free-style
Free|town
free|way
free-wheel *v.*
freeze (as *v.*, froze,
frozen, freez|ing)
freeze-dry
(freeze-dries,
freeze-dried,
freeze-drying)
freezer
freeze-up *n.*
freezing-point
Frei|burg (in W.
Germany)
freight|age
freighter
freight|liner
Frei|schütz
Frenchi|fica|tion

French|ify
(French|ifies,
French|ified,
French|ify'ing)
French|man (*pl.*
French|men)
French|wo'man
(*pl.*
French|wo'men)
Frenchy (*pl.*
French|ies)
fren|etic
fren'et|ic|ally
frenum *use*
fraenum
frenzy (as *n.*, *pl.*
fren'zies; as *v.*,
fren|zies,
fren|zied,
fren'zy|ing)
fre|quency (*pl.*
fre'quen|cies)
fre|quent
fre'quenta'tion
fre'quent'at|ive
fresco (*pl.*
fres'cos)
freshen
fresher
freshet
fresh|man (*pl.*
fresh|men)
fresh|wa'ter *a.*
fret (as *v.*, fret|ted,
fret|ting)
fret|ful
fret|fully
fret|saw
fret|work
Freud
Freud|ian
fri|ab'il|ity
fri|able
friar
fri|arly
fri|ary (*pl.*
fri'ar|ies)
fribble (as *v.*,
frib|bling)
Fri|bourg (in
Switzerland)
fric'an|deau (as
n., *pl.*
fric'an|deaux)
fric'as|see (as *v.*,
fric'as|seed)

fric'at|ive
fric'tion
fric|tional
Fri'day
fridge
friend
frien'ded
friend|less
friend'li|ness
friendly
(friend|lier,
friend'li|est)
friend|ship
frier *use* fryer
Fries
Frie|sian (breed of
cattle) △ Frisian
Fries|land
frieze
frig|ate
fright
frighten
fright|ful
fright|fully
fri'gid
fri|gid'ity
frill|ery (*pl.*
frill|er'ies)
fril'li|ness
frill|ing
frilly (as *a.*,
fril|lier, fril'li|est;
as *n.*, *pl.* fril|lies)
fringe (as *v.*,
frin'ging)
fringy
frip|pery (as *n.*, *pl.*
frip|per'ies)
frip|pet
Fris|bee (*propr.*)
Fris|ian (of
Friesland)
△ Friesian
frisket
frisky (fris|kier,
fris'ki|est)
fris|son
frit (as *v.*, frit|ted,
frit|ting)
frit-fly
(*pl.* frit-flies)
fri'til|lary (*pl.*
fri'til|lar'ies)
frit|ter
Friuli-Venezia
Giulia

frivol (friv|olled,
friv'ol|ling)
fri'vol|ity (*pl.*
fri'vol|it'ies)
friv'ol|ous
frizz
frizzle (as *v.*,
frizz|ling)
frizzly
frizzy (friz|zier,
friz'zi|est)
frock-coat
froe (tool) △ frow
Froe|bel
Froe'bel|ian
Froe'bel|ism
frog|ging
froggy
frog|man (*pl.*
frog|men)
frog-march *n.* & *v.*
frog-spawn
frolic (as *v.*,
frol|icked,
frol|ick|ing)
frol'ic|some
frond|age
frond|eur
frond|ose
front|age
front|ager
frontal
front|ally
front-bencher
fron|tier
fron'tiers|man (*pl.*
fron'tiers|men)
fron'tis|piece
front|let
fronto|gen'esis
fron'to|gen'etic
fronton
front|ward
front|wards
frost-bite
frost-bitten
frost|ily
frosti|ness
frost|ing
frosty (fros|tier,
fros'ti|est)
frothy (*pl.*
froth|ier,
frothi|est)
frot|tage
frou-frou

frow
(Dutchwoman;
housewife) △ froe
frowsti|ness
frowsty
(frows|tier,
frows'ti|est)
frow'zi|ness
frowzy (frow|zier,
frow'zi|est)
fruc'ti|fer'ous
fruc'ti|fica|tion
fruct|ify
(fructi|fies,
fructi|fied,
fructi|fy'ing)
fruct|ose
fruc'tu|ous
fru'gal
fru'gal|ity
fru'gally
fru'gi|vor'ous
fruit
fruit|age
fruit'ar|ian
fruit-cake
fruiter
fruit|erer
fruit|ful
fruit|fully
fruit|ily
fruiti|ness
fru|ition
fruit|less
fruit|let
fruity (fruit|ier,
fruiti|est)
fru|menty
frump|ish
frumpy
(frum|pier,
frum'pi|est)
frus|trate
(frus'trat|ing)
frus'tra|tion
frust|ule
frustum (pl.
frusta)
fru'tes|cent
fru'tex (pl.
fru|tices)
fru'tic|ose
fry (as v., fries,
fried, fry|ing; as
n., pl. fries)
fryer

frying-pan
fry-up n.
fubsy
fuch|sia
fuchs|ine
fucker
fuck|ing
fuc|oid
fu'cus (pl. fuci)
fuddle (as v.,
fud|dling)
fuddy-duddy (pl.
fuddy-duddies)
fudge (as v.,
fudging)
fuel (as v., fuelled,
fuel|ling)
fug (as v., fugged,
fug|ging)
fu'ga|cious
fu'gac|ity
fu'gal
fu'gally
fuggy (fug|gier,
fig'gi|est)
fu'git|ive
fugle (fug|ling)
fugle|man (pl.
fugle|men)
fugue (as v.,
fugued, fuguing)
fuguist
führer (despot)
Führer (of Hitler)
Fu'ji|yama
ful|crum (pl.
ful'cra)
ful'fil (ful|filled,
ful'fil|ling)
ful'fil|ment
ful|gent
ful'gura|tion
ful'gur|ite
fu'li|gin|ous
fuller
full-grown
full-length a.
full|ness
full-scale a.
full-time a.
fully
ful'mar
ful'min|ant
ful'min|ate (as v.,
ful'min|at'ing)
ful'mina|tion

ful'min|at'ory
fulness use
fullness
ful|some
ful'ves|cent
ful|vous
fu'mar|ole
fu'mar|olic
fumble (as v.,
fum|bling)
fume (as v.,
fum|ing)
fu'mig|ant
fu'mig|ate
(fu'mig|at'ing)
fu'miga|tion
fu'mig|ator
fu'mit|ory (pl.
fu'mit|or'ies)
fumy (fu|mier,
fu'mi|est)
Fu'na|futi
fun'am'bu|list
func'tion
func'tional
func'tion|al'ism
func'tion|al'ist
func'tion|ally
func'tion|ary (pl.
func'tion|ar'ies)
func'tion|ate
(func'tion|at'ing)
fun'da|ment
fun'da|mental
fun'da'ment|al|
ism
fun'da'ment|al'ist
fun'da'ment|al'ity
fun'da'ment|ally
fundus (pl. fundi)
fun|eb'rial
fu'neral
fu'ner|ary
fu'ner|eal
fu'ner|eally
fun-fair
fungal
fun'gible
fun'gi|cidal
fun'gi|cide
fun'gi|form
fun'gi|static
fun'gi|vor'ous
fung|oid
fung|ous a.

fungus n. (pl.
fungi)
fu'nicu|lar
fun'kia
funki|ness
funky (fun|kier,
fun'ki|est)
fun'nel (as v.,
fun|nelled,
fun'nel|ling)
fun|nily
fun'ni|ment
fun'ni|ness
fun'ni|os'ity (pl.
fun'ni|os'it|ies)
funny (as n., pl.
fun|nies)
funny-bone
fur (animal hair;
as v., furred,
fur|ring) △ fir
fur|below
fur|bish
furc|ate (as v.,
furc|at'ing)
furca|tion
fur'fur|aceous
furi|ous
furl
fur|long
fur|lough
fur|nace (as v.,
fur|nacing)
fur|nish
fur|nisher
fur|nish|ing
fur|ni|ture
fur|ore
fur|rier
fur'ri|ery
fur|row
fur|rowy
furry (fur|rier,
fur'ri|est)
fur|ther
fur'ther|ance
fur'ther|more
fur'ther|most
fur|thest
furt|ive
fur|uncle
fur'un'cular
fur'un'cul|osis
fur'un'cul|ous
fury (pl. fur'ies)

Fury (Gr. goddess;
　　pl. **Fur¦ies**)
furze
furzy
fusc|ous
fuse (as *v.*, **fus¦ing**)
fuse-box
fusee
fusel (oil)
fu¦sel¦age
fus¦ib¦il¦ity
fus¦ible
fu¦si¦form

fusil (musket)
fu¦sil¦ier
fu¦sil¦lade (as *v.*,
　　fu¦sil¦lad¦ing)
fu|sion
fu|sion|ist
fuss|ily
fussi|ness
fuss|pot
fussy (**fus|sier**,
　　fus¦si|est)
fus|tan|ella
fus|tian

fustic
fust¦ig|ate
　　(**fust¦ig|at¦ing**)
fust|iga|tion
fust|ily
fusti|ness
fusty (**fus|tier**,
　　fus¦ti|est)
fu|thorc
fu¦tile
fu¦til¦it¦arian
fu¦til|ity
fut|tock

fu|ture
fu¦tur|ism
fu¦tur|ist
fu¦tur|istic
fu¦tur|ity
fu¦turo|lo¦gist
fu¦turo|logy
fuzz-ball
fuzz|ily
fuzzi|ness
fuzzy (**fuz|zier**,
　　fuz¦zi|est)
fyl|fot

G

gab¦ar¦dine
gabble (as *v.*,
 gab¦bling)
gab¦bro (*pl.*
 gab¦bros)
gab¦broid
gabby (gab¦bier,
 gab¦bi¦est)
ga¦belle
ga¦bion
ga¦bi¦on¦ade
gable
gabled
gab¦let
Ga¦bon
Gab¦or¦one
gad (as *v.*,
 gad¦ded,
 gad¦ding)
gad¦about
Ga¦daffi
Gad¦ar¦ene
gad¦fly (*pl.*
 gad¦flies)
gadget
gadgetry
gadgety
Gad¦helic
gad¦oid
gad¦ol¦in¦ite
gado¦lin¦ium
gad¦roon
gad¦wall
Gael
Gael¦dom
Gaelic
Gael¦tacht
gaff (in fishing or
 sailing)
gaffe (blunder)
gaf¦fer
gag (as *v.*, gagged,
 gag¦ging)
gaga
gage (pledge,
 greengage)
△ gauge
gaggle (as *v.*,
 gag¦gling)

gag-man
 (*pl.* gag-men)
gag¦ster
gai¦ety (*pl.*
 gai¦et¦ies)
gail¦lar¦dia
gaily
gain¦ful
gain¦fully
gain¦say
 (gain¦said)
Gains¦bor¦ough
gaiter
gaitered
Gait¦skell
gala
ga¦lac¦ta¦gogue
ga¦lac¦tic
ga¦lago (*pl.*
 ga¦la¦gos)
Gala¦had
gal¦an¦tine
Ga¦la¦pa¦gos
 (Islands)
gal¦axy (*pl.*
 gal¦ax¦ies)
gal¦banum
galea
gal¦eate
gal¦eated
ga¦lena
ga¦lenic
ga¦len¦ical
Ga¦li¦cia
Ga¦li¦lean
ga¦li¦lee (porch
 etc.)
Ga¦li¦leo
ga¦li¦ma¦tias
gal¦in¦gale
gali¦pot (resin)
 △ gallipot
Galla
gal¦lant
gal¦lantry (*pl.*
 gal¦lant¦ries)
gall-bladder
gal¦leon

gal¦lery (as *n.*, *pl.*
 gal¦ler¦ies; as *v.*,
 gal¦ler¦ies,
 gal¦ler¦ied,
 gal¦lery¦ing)
gal¦ley
gall-fly
 (*pl.* gall-flies)
gal¦li¦ambic
gal¦li¦ard
gal¦lic (acid)
Gal¦lic (Gaulish,
 French)
Gal¦lican
gal¦lice (in French;
 3 sylls.)
Gal¦li¦cism
Gal¦li¦cize
 (Gal¦li¦ciz¦ing)
gal¦li¦gas¦kins
gal¦li¦maufry (*pl.*
 gal¦li¦mauf¦ries)
gal¦lina¦ceous
gall¦ing
gal¦lin¦ule
gal¦liot
gal¦li¦pot (small
 pot) △ galipot
gal¦lium
gal¦li¦vant
gal¦li¦wasp
gall-mite
gall¦nut
Gal¦lo¦mania
Gal¦lo¦man¦iac
gal¦lon
gal¦lon¦age
gal¦loon
gal¦lop (horse's
 pace; as *v.*,
 gal¦loped,
 gal¦lop¦ing)
 △ galop
Gal¦lo¦phile
Gal¦lo¦phobe
Gal¦lo¦pho¦bia
Gallo-Roman
gal¦lo¦way (horse)
Gal¦lo¦way

gal¦lows
gall¦stone
Gal¦lup
gall-wasp
ga¦loot
galop (dance; as *v.*,
 galoped,
 gal¦op¦ing)
 △ gallop
ga¦lore
ga¦losh
ga¦lumph
gal¦vanic
gal¦van¦ic¦ally
gal¦van¦ism
gal¦van¦ist
gal¦van¦iza¦tion
gal¦van¦ize
 (gal¦van¦iz¦ing)
gal¦vano¦meter
galvo (*pl.* gal¦vos)
Gal¦way
gamba
gam¦bade
gam¦bado (*pl.*
 gam¦ba¦dos)
Gam¦bia, The
gam¦bier
gam¦bit
gamble (as *v.*,
 gamb¦ling)
gam¦bler
gam¦boge
gam¦bol (as *v.*,
 gam¦bolled,
 gam¦bol¦ling)
gam¦brel
game (as *a.*,
 gamer, gamest;
 as *v.*, gam¦ing)
game¦cock
game¦fowl
game¦keeper
gam¦elan
games¦man (*pl.*
 games¦men)
games¦man¦ship
game¦some
game¦ster

gam|et|an|gium
(pl.
gam|et|an|gia)
gam|ete
gam|etic
gam|eto|phyte
gam|eto|phytic
gam|ily
gamin (masc.)
gam|ine (fem.)
gami|ness
gam|ing
gamma
gam|ma|dion
gam|mon
gammy
gamut
gamy (gam|ier,
gami|est)
gan|der
Gan|dhi
Gan|ges
gangle
(gang|ling)
gan|gli|form
gang|ling
gan|glion (pl.
gan|glia)
gan|gli|on|ated
gan|gli|onic
gan|gly
(gan|glier,
gan|gli|est)
gang|plank
gan|grene (as v.,
gan|gren|ing)
gan|gren|ous
gang|ster
gangue
gang|way
gan|is|ter
ganja
gan|net
gan|oid
gantry (pl.
gant|ries)
gaol
gaol|bird
gaol|break
gaoler
gape (as v.,
gap|ing)
gaper
gape|worm
gapped

gappy (gap|pier,
gap|pi|est)
gar|age (as v.,
gar|aging)
garb|age
garble (garb|ling)
gar|board
gar|çon
gar|den
gar|dener
gar|denia
gare|fowl
gar|fish (pl. same)
gar|ganey
gar|gan|tuan
gar|get
gargle (as v.,
garg|ling)
gar|goyle
ga|ri|baldi (biscuit
etc.)
Ga|ri|baldi
gar|ish
gar|land
gar|lic
gar|licky
gar|ment
gar|ner
gar|net
gar|nish
gar|nishee (as v.,
gar|nish|eed)
gar|nish|ment
gar|ni|ture
gar|pike
gar|ret
gar|ret|eer
gar|rison
gar|rotte (as v.,
gar|rot|ted,
gar|rott|ing)
gar|ru|lity
gar|rul|ous
gar|rya
gar|ter
ga|ruda
gas (as v., gassed,
gass|ing)
gas|bag
Gas|con
gas|con|ade
Gas|cony
gas|eous
gas|holder
gasi|fica|tion

gas|ify (gasi|fies,
gasi|fied,
gasify|ing)
Gas|kell
gas|ket
gas|kin
gas|light
gas|man (pl.
gas|men)
gasol|ine
gaso|meter
gasper
gas|per|eau (pl.
gas|per|eaus)
gasser
gassy (gas|sier,
gas|si|est)
gast|haus
gast|rec|tomy (pl.
gast|rec|tom|ies)
gast|ric
gast|ritis
gastro-enteritis
gast|ro|nome
gast|ro|nomic
gast|ro|nomy
gast|ro|pod
gast|ro|pod|ous
gast|ro|scope
gast|rula (pl.
gast|rulae)
gas|works
gate (as v.,
gat|ing)
gât|eau (pl.
gât|eaus)
gate|crash
gate|crasher
gate|fold
gate|house
gate|keeper
gate|leg
gate|legged
gate|man (pl.
gate|men)
gate|post
Gates|head
gate|way
gather
gath|er|ing
Gat|ling
gauche
gaucherie
gau|cho (pl.
gau|chos)
gaud|ily

gaudi|ness
gaudy (as n., pl.
gaud|ies; as a.,
gaud|ier,
gaudi|est)
gauge (measure;
as v., gauging)
△ gage
gauge|able
gauger
Gau|gin
Gaul
gau|leiter
Gaull|ish
Gaull|ism
Gaull|ist
Gaull|oise (propr.)
gaul|theria
gaunt|let
gauss (pl. same)
gauze
gauzy
gavel (as v.,
gav|elled,
gav|el|ling)
ga|votte
gawk|ily
gawki|ness
gawky (gaw|kier,
gaw|ki|est)
Gay-Lussac
ga|zania
ga|zebo (pl.
ga|zebos)
gaze (as v.,
gaz|ing)
gaz|elle
gaz|ette (as v.,
gaz|ett|ing)
gaz|ett|eer
gaz|pa|cho (pl.
gaz|pa|chos)
ga|zump
Gdansk
gear|box
gear|ing
gear-lever
gear|wheel
gecko (pl. geckos)
gee-gee
geezer
Ge|henna
Geiger counter
Gei|kie

gei'sha (*pl.*
 gel'shas *or*
 gei'sha)
Geiss|ler
gel (as *v.*, gelled,
 gel|ling)
gel'at|ine
ge'lat'in|ize
 (ge'la'tin|iz|ing)
ge'lat'in|ous
ge'la|tion
Gel'der|land
geld|ing
gelid
gel'ig|nite
gelly (*sl.*,
 gelignite)
gem (as *v.*,
 gemmed,
 gem|ming)
Ge'mara
Ge'mayel
gem'in|ate (as *v.*,
 gem'in|at|ing)
gem'ina|tion
Gem'in|ean
Gem'ini
gemma (*pl.*
 gemmae)
gem'ma|tion
gem'mi'fer'ous
gem'mi|par'ous
gem'mo|lo'gist
gem'mo|logy
gem|mule
gen (as *v.*, genned,
 gen|ning)
gen|darme
gen'darm|erie
gen'der
gene (*Biol.*)
 △ jean
genea|lo'gical
genea|lo'gic|ally
genea|lo'gist
genea|lo'gize
 (genea|lo'giz|ing)
genea|logy (*pl.*
 genea|lo'gies)
gen'era (*pl.* of
 genus)
gen|eral
gen'er'al|is'simo
 (*pl.* gen'er'al|
 is'si'mos)
gen'er'al|ist

gen'er'al|ity (*pl.*
 gen'er'al|it'ies)
gen'er'al|iza|tion
gen'er'al|ize
 (gen'er'al|iz|ing)
gen'er|ally
gen'er|ate
 (gen'er|at'ing)
gen'era|tion
gen'era|tional
gen'er'at|ive
gen'er|ator
gen|eric
gen'er'ic|ally
gen'er'os|ity (*pl.*
 gen'er'os'it|ies)
gen'er|ous
gen|esis (*pl.*
 gen|eses)
Gen|esis (OT book)
genet (civet-cat)
 △ jennet
gen|etic
gen'et'ic|ally
gen'eti|cist
gen'et|ics
ge'neva (gin)
Ge'neva
Gen|ghis Khan
gen|ial
geni|al'ity (*pl.*
 geni|al'it|ies)
geni|al|ize
 (geni|al|iz|ing)
geni|ally
genic
genie (*pl.* genii)
gen|ista
gen|ital
gen'it|alia
gen'it|als
gen'it|ival
gen'it|iv|ally
gen'it|ive
genito-urinary
genius (*pl.*
 geni|uses)
ge'ni|zah
Genoa
geno|cidal
geno|cide
Ge'no|ese
geno|type
geno|typic
genre
gens (*pl.* gen|tes)

gen|teel
gen'teel|ism
gen|teelly
gen|tian
gen|tile
gen'ti|li'tial
gen'til|ity
gentle (as *a.*,
 gent|ler,
 gent|lest; as *v.*,
 gentled,
 gent|ling)
gen'tle|folk
gen'tle|man (*pl.*
 gen'tle|men)
gentleman-at-
                arms
 (*pl.* gentlemen-
                at-arms)
gen'tle|manly
gen'tle|people
gen'tle|wo'man
 (*pl.* gen'tle|
                wo'men)
gently
gen|too
gentry *n. pl.*
genu|flect
genu|flector
genu|flect'ory
genu|flex'ion
genu|ine
genus (*pl.*
 gen'era)
geo|bot'any
geo|cent'ric
geo|chem'ical
geo|chem'ist
geo|chem'istry
geo|chro'no|
                lo'gical
geo|chro'no|logy
ge'ode
geo|desic
geo|des|ist
geo|desy
geo|detic
ge'odic
Geof|frey
geo|grapher
geo|graphic
geo|graph'ical
geo|graph'ic|ally
geo|graphy (*pl.*
 geo|graph'ies)
ge'oid

geo|lo'gic
geo|lo'gical
geo|lo'gic|ally
geo|lo'gist
geo|lo'gize
 (geo|lo'giz|ing)
geo|logy
geo|mag'netic
geo|mag'net|ism
geo|mancy
geo|mantic
geo|meter
geo|met'ric
geo|met'rical
geo|met'ric|ally
geo|met'ri|cian
geo|met'rize
 (geo|met'riz|ing)
geo|metry (*pl.*
 geo|met'ries)
geo|mor'pho'
                lo'gical
geo|mor'pho'lo'
                gist
geo|mor'pho'logy
gco|phone
geo|phys'ical
geo|physi|cist
geo|phys'ics
geo|pol'it'ical
geo|pol'it|ics
Geor|die
George
George|town
geor|gette
Geor'gia
Geor|gian
geo|sphere
geo|sta'tion|ary
geo|strophic
geo|thermal
geo|tropic
geo|trop'ism
Ger'ald
ge'ra|nium
ger|bera
ger'bil
ge're|nuk
ge'ri|at'ric
ge'ri|at'ri|cian
ge'ri|at'rics
ge'ri|at'rist
ger'man (of
 relationship)
Ger'man
ger'man|der

ger|mane
ger|manic (*Chem.*)
Ger|manic
Ger|man|ic|ism
Ger|man|ism
Ger|man|ist
ger|man|ium
ger|man|ous
Ger|many
germ-cell
ger|men
ger|mi|cidal
ger|mi|cide
ger|minal
ger|min|ally
germ|in|ant
ger|min|ate
 (ger|min|at|ing)
ger|mina|tion
ger|min|at|ive
ger|min|ator
ger|mon
germy (germ|ier,
 germi|est)
ge|ron|to|cracy
 (*pl.* ge|ron|to|
  cra|cies)
ge|ron|to|lo|gical
ge|ron|to|lo|gist
ge|ron|to|logy
ger|ry|man|der
ger|und
ger|und|ial
ger|und|ival
ger|und|ive
gesso (*pl.*
 ges|soes)
ges|ta|gen
ges|ta|genic
Ges|talt
Ge|stalt|ism
Ge|stalt|ist
Ge|stapo
gest|ate
 (gest|at|ing)
gesta|tion
gest|at|or|ial
ges|ticu|late
 (ges|ticu|lat|ing)
ges|ticu|la|tion
ges|ticu|lat|ive
ges|ticu|lator
ges|ticu|lat|ory
ges|tural
ges|ture (as *v.*,
 ges|tur|ing)

get (got, get|ting)
geta
get-at-able
get-away *n.*
get|table
get|ter
get-together *n.*
get-up *n.*
geum
gew|gaw
gey|ser
Ghana
Ghan|aian
gharry (*pl.*
 ghar|ries)
ghast|lily
ghast|li|ness
ghastly
 (ghast|lier,
 ghast|li|est)
ghat
Ghazi
ghee
ghe|rao (*pl.*
 ghe|raos)
gher|kin
ghetto (*pl.*
 ghet|tos)
Ghib|el|line
Ghib|el|lin|ism
ghost
ghost|li|ness
ghostly
 (ghost|lier,
 ghost|li|est)
ghost-word
ghoul
ghoul|ish
gi|ant
giant|ess
giant|ism
gia|our (non-
 Muslim)
Gia|our (by Byron)
gib|ber
gib|ber|el|lin
gib|ber|ish
gib|bet
gib|bon
gib|bos|ity
gib|bous
gibe (to sneer;
 gib|ing) △ gybe
gib|lets
Gib|ral|tar
gid|dily

gid|di|ness
giddy (as *a.*,
 gid|dier,
 gid|di|est; as *v.*,
 gid|dies,
 gid|died,
 gid|dy|ing)
Gide
Gid|eon
gif|ted
gift-horse
gift-wrap
 (gift-wrapped,
 gift-wrapping)
gig (as *v.*, gigged,
 gig|ging)
gi|gant|esque
gi|gantic
gi|gant|ic|ally
gi|gant|ism
giggle (as *v.*,
 gig|gling)
gig|gly (gig|glier,
 gig|gli|est)
gig|olo (*pl.*
 gig|olos)
gigot
Gila
gil|bert (unit)
Gil|bert (Islands)
Gil|bert|ian
gild (to cover with
 gold) △ guild
gil|gai
gill (organ in fish;
 unit; measure)
gil|la|roo
Gil|lian
gil|lie
gil|lion
gil|ly|flower
gilt-edged
gilt|wood
gim|bals
gim|crack
gim|let
gim|mick
gim|mickry
gim|micky
gimp (*sl.*, courage)
gin (as *v.*, ginned,
 gin|ning)
gin|ger
gin|ger|ade
ginger-ale
ginger-beer

gin|ger|bread
gin|gerly
ginger-nut
gin|gery
ging|ham
gin|gili
gin|gival
gin|giv|itis
gin|gly|mus (*pl.*
 gin|glymi)
ginkgo (*pl.*
 gink|gos)
gin|seng
Gio|conda
Giotto
gippy (*pl.*
 gip|pies)
gipsy *use* gypsy
gir|affe
gir|an|dole
gi|ra|sol
girder
girdle (as *v.*,
 gird|ling)
girl-friend
girl|hood
girlie
girl|ish
giro (credit
 transfer; *pl.* giros)
 △ gyro
girth
git|tern
give (gave, given,
 giv|ing)
give|able
give-away *n.*
giver
Giza
giz|zard
gla|bella (*pl.*
 gla|bellae)
glab|rous
glacé
gla|cial
gla|ci|ally
gla|ci|ated
gla|ci|ation
gla|cier
gla|ci|olo|gical
gla|ci|olo|gist
gla|ci|ology
gla|cis (*pl.* same)
glad (glad|der,
 glad|dest)
glad|den

glad-hand *v.*
gla'di|ator
gla'di|at'or|ial
gla'di|olus (*pl.*
  gla'di|oli)
glad|some
Glad|stone
Gla'go|litic
glair (white of egg)
glair|eous
glairy
Gla|mor'gan
glam'or|iza|tion
gla'mor|ize
  (gla'mor|iz|ing)
glam'or|ous
glam|our
glance (as *v.*,
  glan'cing)
glan'der|ous
glan|ders
glandu|lar
gland|ule
glans (*pl.*
  glan'des)
glare (as *v.*,
  glar'ing)
Glarus
glary
Glas|gow
glass|ful (*pl.*
  glass|fuls)
glass-gall
glass|house
glass|ily
glass|ine
glassi|ness
glass-paper
glass|ware
glass|wort
glassy (glass|ier,
  glas'si|est)
Glas|we'gian
Glau|ber
glauc|oma
glauc|omat|ous
glauc|ous
glaze (as *v.*,
  glaz'ing)
glaz|ier
glaz|iery
glaz'ing
glazy
gleamy
glee|ful
glee|fully

glee|man (*pl.*
  glee|men)
glee|some
glen|garry (*pl.*
  glen|gar'ries)
glen|oid
Glen|rothes
glia
glial
glide (as *v.*,
  glid'ing)
glider
glim|mer
glim|mer|ing
glimpse (as *v.*,
  glimps|ing)
gliss|ade (as *v.*,
  gliss|ad'ing)
glis|sando (*pl.*
  glis|sandi)
glissé
glis|ten
glit|ter
gloam|ing
global
glob|ally
globe (as *v.*,
  glob'ing)
globe-fish
globe-flower
globe-trotter
globe-trotting
glo'bi|ger'ina
glob|oid
glob|ose
globu|lar
globu|lar|ity
glob|ule
globu|lin
glock'en|spiel
glom'er|ate
glom'er|ular
glom'er|ule
glom'er|ulus (*pl.*
  glom'er|uli)
gloom|ily
gloomi|ness
gloomy
  (gloom|ier,
  gloom|iest)
gloria (aureole)
Gloria (liturgy)
glori|fica|tion
glor|ify (glori|fies,
  glori|fied,
  glori|fy'ing)

glori|ole
glori|ous
glory (as *n.*, *pl.*
  glor|ies; as *v.*,
  glor|ies, glor|ied,
  glory|ing)
glossal
gloss|ar'ial
gloss|ar'ist
gloss|ary (*pl.*
  gloss|ar'ies)
gloss|ator
gloss|eme
gloss|ily
glossi|ness
gloss|itis
glos'so|grapher
glos'so|lalia
glosso-laryngeal
glos'so|logy
glossy (as *a.*,
  glos'sier,
  glos'si|est; as *n.*,
  pl. glos|sies)
glot|tal
glot'tal|ize
  (glot'tal|iz|ing)
glot|tic
glot|tis
Glou'ces|ter
Glou'ces|ter|shire
glove (as *v.*,
  glov|ing)
glove|less
glover
glower
glow-worm
glox|inia
gloze (gloz'ing)
glu'ca|gon
Gluck
gluc|ose
gluc|os|ide
glue (as *v.*, glued,
  glu|ing)
gluey (glu|ier,
  glui|est)
glu|ma|ceous
glum|ose
glut (as *v.*,
  glut|ted,
  glut|ting)
glu'tam|ate
glu|tamic
glu|teal
glu'ten

glu|teus (*pl.*
  glu|tei)
glu|tin|ous
glut|ton
glut|ton|ous
glut|tony
gly'cer|ide
gly'cer|ine
gly|cerol
gly|cine
gly'co|gen
gly'co|gen'esis
gly'co|genic
glycol
glyc|ollic
gly'co|lysis (*pl.*
  gly'co|lyses)
gly'co|pro'tein
gly'cos|ide
glyc'os|uria
glyc'os|uric
Glynde|bourne
glyphic
glyptal
glyptic
glypto|don
glypto|graphy
gnarled
gnarly
gnat
gnathic
gnaw (bite)
gneiss
gneissic
gneiss|oid
gneiss|ose
gnoc|chi
gnome
gnomic
gnom'ic|ally
gnom|ish
gnomon
gnom|onic
gnosis (*pl.* gnoses)
gnos|tic (of
  knowledge)
Gnos|tic (heretic)
Gnos'ti|cism
gnos'ti|cize
  (gnos'ti|ciz|ing)
gnu
go (as *v.*, goes,
  went, gone; as *n.*,
  pl. goes)
Goa
go-ahead *a.* & *n.*

goalie
goal|keeper
goal-kick
goal|less
goal-line
goal-mouth
go|anna
goatee
goat|herd
goat|ish
goat|ling
goat's-beard
goat|skin
goat|sucker
goaty
gob (as v.,
 gobbed,
 gob|bing)
go|bang
gob|bet
gobble
 (gob|bling)
gobble|de|gook
gob|bler
gobby (pl.
 gob|bies)
Gob|elin
gobe|mouche
go-between n.
gob|let
gob|lin
gob-stopper
goby (pl. go|bies)
go-by n.
god|child (pl.
 god|chil|dren)
god-damn
god-damned
god-daughter
god|dess
go|det
go|de|tia
god|father
God-fearing
God-forsaken
god|head
god|less
god|li|ness
godly
God|man
god|mother
go|down
god|par|ent
god|send
god|son
God|speed

god|wit
God|wot|tery
Goeb|bels
goer
Goer|ing
Goethe
Goe|thian
gof|fer (to crimp,
 crimping iron)
 △ gopher
go-getter
goggle (as v.,
 gog|gling)
goggle-box
goggle-eyed
gog|let
go-go
Go|gol
Goi|del
Goi|delic
go|ing
going-over (pl.
 goings-over)
goings-on
goitre
goit|rous
go-kart
Gol|conda
gold|crest
gold-dust
golden
gold-field
gold|finch
gold|fish
goldi|locks
gold-mine
gold-plate v.
 (gold-plated,
 gold-plating)
gold-rush
gold|smith
golem
golf-bag
golf club
 (premises,
 association)
golf-club
 (implement)
golf-course
golfer
golf-links
Golgi
Go|li|ath
gol|li|wog

gol|lop (as v.,
 gol|loped,
 gol|lop|ing)
golly (as n., pl.
 gol|lies)
gom|been
gonad
gon|adal
gon|ado|trophic
gon|ado|tropic
gon|dola
gon|do|lier
goner
gon|fa|lon
gon|fa|lon|ier
gon|gor|ism
goni|ometer
go|ni|ometric
go|ni|omet|rical
goni|ometry
gonna (sl.)
go|no|coc|cus (pl.
 go|no|cocci)
go|nor|rhoea
go|nor|rhoeal
Gon|zalez
good (bet|ter,
 best)
good|bye
good-for-nothing
good|li|ness
goodly
good|ness
good|wife (pl.
 good|wives)
good|will
goody (pl.
 goodies)
goody-goody (as
 n., pl. goody-
 goodies)
gooey (goo|ier,
 gooi|est)
goof|ball
go-off n.
goofy (goof|ier,
 goofi|est)
googly (pl.
 goog|lies)
goos|an|der
goose (as n., pl.
 geese, in tailoring
 gooses; as v.,
 goos|ing)
goose|berry (pl.
 goose|ber|ries)

goose-flesh
goose-foot (pl.
 goose-foots)
goose|gog
goose-grass
goose|herd
goose-pimples
go|pher (tree,
 wood, burrowing
 animal) △ goffer
gopher-wood
goral
Gor|ba|chov
gor|bli|mey
gor|cock
Gor|dian
Gor|don
gore (as v.,
 gor|ing)
gorge (as v.,
 gor|ging)
gor|geous
gor|get
Gor|gio (pl.
 Gor|gios)
gor|gon
gor|go|nia
gor|go|nian
gor|gon|ize
 (gor|gon|iz|ing)
Gor|gon|zola
gor|illa
gor|ily
gor|mand|ize (to
 eat greedily;
 gor|mand|iz|ing)
 △ gourmandise
gor|mand|izer
gorm|less
Gor|sedd
gorsy (gor|sier,
 gor|si|est)
gory (gor|ier,
 gori|est)
gos|hawk
gos|ling
go-slow n.
gos|pel
gos|pel|ler
gos|samer
gos|samered
gos|sam|ery
gos|sip (as v.,
 gos|siped,
 gos|sip|ing)
gossip-monger

gos|sipy
gos|soon
Gotham
Goth|am|ite
Gothic
Goth|ic|ally
Gothi|cism
Got|land
gotta (*sl.*)
Göt|ter|däm|mer|
    ung
gou|ache
Gouda
gouge (as *v.*,
 gou|ging)
gou|lash
gou|rami
gourd
gour|mand
 (glutton)
gour|mand|ise
 (gluttony)
 △ gormandize
gour|mand|ism
gour|met (epicure)
gout-fly
 (*pl.* gout-flies)
gout|weed
gouty
gov|ern
gov|ern|able
gov|ern|ance
gov|ern|ess
gov|ern|essy
gov|ern|ment
gov|ern|mental
gov|ernor
gov|ern|or|ate
Governor-
    General
gowan
gowk
gowns|man (*pl.*
 gowns|men)
goy (*pl.* goyim)
Graaf
Graaf|ian
grab (as *v.*,
 grabbed,
 grab|bing)
grab|ber
grabble
 (grab|bling)
grabby
 (grab|bier,
 grab|bi|est)

graben (*Geol.; pl.*
 same or grabens)
grace (as *v.*,
 gra|cing)
grace|ful
grace|fully
grace|less
grace-note
gra|cile
gra|cil|ity
graci|os|ity
gra|cious
grackle
grad|ate
 (grad|at|ing)
grada|tion
grada|tional
grade (as *v.*,
 grad|ing)
Grad|grind
gra|di|ent
gra|dine
grad|ual
gradu|ally
gradu|and
gradu|ate (as *v.*,
 gradu|at|ing)
gradu|ation
gradu|ator
gradus
Grae|cism
Grae|cize
 (Grae|ciz|ing)
Grae|co|mania
Grae|co|man|iac
Grae|co|phile
Graeco-Roman
graf|fito (*pl.*
 graf|fiti)
Gra|ham
Grail
Grain|ger
graini|ness
grainy (grain|ier,
 graini|est)
gral|lat|or|ial
gral|loch
gram
Gram (method)
grama
gram-atom
gram-equivalent
gram-force
gra|min|aceous
gra|mi|ni|vor|ous

gram|ma|logue
gram|mar
gram|mar|ian
gram|mat|ical
gram|mat|ic|ally
gram|mat|icize
 (gram|mat|iciz|
    ing)
gramme *use* gram
gram-molecule
Gram-negative
gramo|phone
gramo|phonic
Gram|pian
Gram-positive
gram|pus
gra|na|dilla
gran|ary (*pl.*
 gran|ar|ies)
gran|dad
gran|dam
grand|aunt
grand|child (*pl.*
 grand|chil|dren)
grand-daddy (*pl.*
 grand-daddies)
grand|daugh|ter
gran|dee
grand|eur
grand|father
Grand Guignol
gran|di|flora
gran|di|loquence
gran|di|loquent
gran|di|ose
gran|di|os|ity
Gran|dis|on|ian
grandma
grand|mama
grand|mother
grand|nephew
grand|niece
grandpa
grand|papa
grand|par|ent
Grand Prix (*pl.*
 Grands Prix)
grand siècle
grand|sire
grand|son
grand|stand
grand|uncle
gran|ger|ism
gran|ger|ite
gran|ger|iza|tion

gran|ger|ize
 (gran|ger|iz|ing)
gra|ni|fer|ous
grani|form
gran|ita (*pl.*
 gran|itae)
gran|ite
granite-ware
gran|itic
gran|it|oid
grani|vor|ous
granny (*pl.*
 gran|nies)
grano|lithic
grant-aided
grantee
granter (one who
 grants)
Granth
grant-in-aid (*pl.*
 grants-in-aid)
grantor (*Law*)
gran tur|ismo
 (*pl. gran*
 tur|is|mos)
granu|lar
granu|lar|ity
granu|late
 (granu|lat|ing)
granu|la|tion
granu|lator
gran|ule
gran|ulo|cyte
gra|nu|lo|cytic
gra|nu|lo|metric
grape|fruit (*pl.*
 same)
gra|pery
grape-shot
grape-vine
graph|em|atic
graph|eme
graph|emic
graphic
graph|ical
graph|ic|ally
graph|ics
graph|ite
graph|itic
graph|it|ize
 (graph|it|iz|ing)
grapho|lo|gical
grapho|lo|gist
grapho|logy
graphy (*pl.*
 graph|ies)

grap|nel
grappa
grapple (as v.,
 grap|pling)
grappling-hook
grappling-iron
grap|to|lite
grasp|ing
grass-cloth
grass|hop|per
grass|land
grass-wrack
grassy (grass|ier,
 grassi|est)
grate (as v.,
 grat|ing)
grate|ful
grate|fully
grater
grat|ic|ule
grati|fica|tion
grat|ify
 (grati|fies,
 grati|fied,
 grati|fy|ing)
gra|tin (Cookery)
grat|ing
gra|tis
grat|it|ude
gra|tu|it|ous
gra|tu|ity (pl.
 gra|tu|it|ies)
gratu|lat|ory
gra|va|men
grave (as v.,
 graved, graven
 (except in sense
 'clean'), grav|ing)
grave-clothes
grave-digger
gravel (as v.,
 grav|elled,
 grav|el|ling)
gravel-blind
grav|elly
graver
Graves (wine; pl.
 same)
Graves' dis|ease
grave|stone
Gra|vet|tian
grave|yard
gravid
gra|vi|meter
gra|vi|metric
gra|vi|metry

grav|itas
grav|it|ate
 (grav|it|at|ing)
grav|ita|tion
grav|ita|tional
grav|ity (pl.
 grav|it|ies)
grav|ure
gravy (pl.
 gra|vies)
gravy-boat
gray (unit) △ grey
gray|ling
graze (as v.,
 graz|ing)
gra|zier
gra|zi|ery (pl.
 gra|zi|er|ies)
graz|ing
grease (as v.,
 greas|ing)
grease-paint
grease-proof
greaser
greas|ily
greasi|ness
greasy (greas|ier,
 greasi|est)
great|coat
greatly
greave (armour)
grebe (bird)
Gre|cian
Greco, El
Greece
greed|ily
greedi|ness
greedy (greed|ier,
 greedi|est)
gree|gree
green|ery (pl.
 green|er|ies)
green|finch
green|fly (pl.
 green|flies)
green|gage
green|gro|cer
green|gro|cery
 (pl. green|
 gro|cer|ies)
green|head
green|heart
green|horn
green|house
greening
green|ish

green|keeper
Green|land
Green|lander
green|let
green-room
green|sand
green|shank
green|sick
green|sick|ness
green-stick a.
green|stone
green|stuff
green|sward
green|weed
Green|wich
green|wood
greeny
green|yard
greet|ing
gref|fier
greg|ari|ous
Greg|or|ian
Greg|ory
grem|ial
grem|lin
Gre|nada
gren|ade
gre|na|dier
grenadilla use
 granadilla
gren|ad|ine
Gresham
gres|sor|ial
Gretna Green
grey (colour)
 △ gray
grey-back
grey|beard
grey-hen
grey|hound
grey|ish
grey|lag
grey|stone
grey|wacke
grid|ded
griddle (as v.,
 grid|dling)
gride (as v.,
 grid|ing)
grid|iron
grief
Grieg
griev|ance
grieve (griev|ing)
griev|ous

grif|fin (fabulous
 creature)
grif|fon (vulture;
 dog)
grill (on cooker)
grill|age
grille (grating)
grilse
grim (grim|mer,
 grim|mest)
grim|ace (as v.,
 grim|acing)
Gri|maldi
gri|mal|kin
grime (as v.,
 grim|ing)
Grimm
Grimsby
grimy (grim|ier,
 grimi|est)
grin (as v.,
 grinned,
 grin|ning)
grind (as v.,
 ground)
grinder
grind|stone
gringo (pl.
 grin|gos)
grip (as v.,
 gripped,
 grip|ping)
gripe (as v.,
 grip|ing)
gripe-water
grippe (influenza)
gris|aille
gri|seo|ful|vin
gris|ette
gris|kin
gris|li|ness
grisly (terrible)
 △ grizzly
grison
Gris|ons
gris|sini (pl.)
gristle
gristly (of gristle)
grit (as v., grit|ted,
 grit|ting)
grit|stone
gritty (grit|tier,
 grit|ti|est)
grizzle (grizz|ling)
grizzled

grizzly (grey-
  haired, bear; as *n.*,
  pl. grizz|lies)
  △ grisly
Gro|bian
gro|cer
gro|cery (*pl.*
  gro|cer|ies)
grog (as *v.*,
  grogged,
  grog|ging)
grog-blossom
grog|gily
grog|gi|ness
groggy
  (grog|gier,
  grog|gi|est)
grog|ram
groin (*Anat.* &
  Archit.) △ groyne
grom|well
Gron|in|gen
grooms|man (*pl.*
  grooms|men)
groove (as *v.*,
  groov|ing)
groov|ily
groovi|ness
groovy
  (groov|ier,
  groovi|est)
grope (grop|ing)
gros|beak
gro|schen
gros|grain
gross (*pl.* same)
grot|esque
grot|esquerie
grot|toed
grotto (*pl.*
  grot|toes)
grotty (grot|tier,
  grot|ti|est)
grouchy
  (grouch|ier,
  grouchi|est)
ground|age
ground-ash
ground-bait
grounder
ground|hog
ground|less
ground|ling
ground-note
ground-nut
ground-pine

ground-plan
ground-rent
ground|sel
ground|sheet
grounds|man (*pl.*
  grounds|men)
ground|work
grouper
groupie
group|ing
grouse (as *v.*,
  grous|ing)
grovel (grovelled,
  grov|el|ling)
grovy
grow (grew,
  grown)
grower
growler
grown-up
groyne
  (breakwater; as *v.*,
  groyn|ing)
  △ groin
grub (as *v.*,
  grub|bing)
grub-axe
grub|ber
grub|bily
grubbi|ness
grubby
  (grub|bier,
  grub|bi|est)
grub-screw
grudge (as *v.*,
  grudging)
gruel (as *v.*,
  gruelled,
  gru|el|ling)
grue|some
grumble (as *v.*,
  grumb|ling)
grum|met
grum|ous
grump|ily
grumpi|ness
grump|ish
grumpy
  (grum|pier,
  grum|pi|est)
Grundy
Grundy|ism
grun|ion
grunter
gruntled
Gruy|ère (cheese)

Gruy|ères (place)
gryphon *use*
  griffin
grys|bok
G-string
G-suit
guach|aro (*pl.*
  guach|aros)
Guad|al|qui|vir
guaiac
guai|acum
guan (bird)
guana (iguana,
  goanna)
gua|naco (*pl.*
  gua|na|cos)
guan|ine
guano (manure; as
  n., *pl.* gua|nos)
guar|ani (mon.
  unit)
Guar|ani (S.
  Amer. people)
guar|an|tee
  (assurance; as *v.*,
  guar|an|teed)
guar|antor
guar|anty
  (undertaking of
  liability; *pl.*
  guar|ant|ies)
guard|ant
guarded
guardee
guard|house
guard|ian
guardi|an|ship
guard|room
guards|man (*pl.*
  guards|men)
Guar|ner|ius
Gua|te|mala
guava
guay|ule
gub|bins
gudgeon
guelder rose
Guelph
Guelphic
Guelph|ism
gue|non
guern|sey (thick
  sweater)
Guern|sey
  (Channel Island,
  cow)

guer|rilla
guess|tim|ate
guess|work
guest-house
guest-night
guest-room
Gue|vara
guf|faw
Gug|gen|heim
  (Museum)
guggle (as *v.*,
  gug|gling)
guichet
guid|able
guid|ance
guide (as *v.*,
  guid|ing)
guide|book
guide-dog
guide-line
Guider
guide|way
guidon
Gui|enne
Guignol
Guign|ol|esque
guild (association)
  △ gild
guilder
Guild|ford
Guild|hall (in
  London)
Guild-hall (town
  hall)
guile|ful
guile|less
guil|le|mot
guil|loche
Guil|lotin
guil|lot|ine (as *v.*,
  guil|lot|in|ing)
guilt|ily
guilti|ness
guilt|less
guilty (guilt|ier,
  guilti|est)
guinea (money)
Guinea (in W.
  Africa)
Guinea-Bissau
guinea-corn
guinea-fowl
guinea-hen
guinea-pig
gui|pure
guise

gui|tar (as v.,
  gui|tarred,
  gui|tar|ring)
gui|tar|ist
Gu|ja|rat
Gu|ja|rati
gul|den
gulf-weed
gull|ery (pl.
  gull|er|ies)
gul|let
gull|ib|il|ity
gull|ible
gull|ibly
gull-wing a.
gully (as n., pl.
  gul|lies; as v.,
  gul|lies, gul|lied,
  gul|ly|ing)
gully-hole
gulpy
gum (as v.,
  gummed,
  gum|ming)
gum|boil
gum|boot
gumma
gum|mat|ous
gum|mily
gum|mi|ness
gummy (as a.,
  gum|mier,
  gum|mi|est; as n.,
  pl. gum|mies)
gump|tion
gum-shield
gum-tree
gun (as v.,
  gunned,
  gun|ning)
gun|boat
gun-fight
gun|fire
gung-ho
gun-lock
gun|man (pl.
  gun|men)
gun-metal
gun|nel (fish)
  △ gunwale
gun|ner

gun|nera
gun|nery
gunny
gun|point
gun|pow|der
gun|power
gun|room
gun-runner
gun-running
gun|ship
gun|shot
gun-shy
gun-site
gun-slinger
gun|smith
gun-stock
gun|ter
Gunter's chain
gun|wale (of ship)
  △ gunnel
gun|yah
guppy (pl.
  gup|pies)
gur|gita|tion
gurgle (as v.,
  gurg|ling)
gur|jun
Gurkha
gurn|ard
guru (pl. gurus)
gusher
gush|ing
gushy
gus|set
gus|seted
gusta|tion
gust|at|ive
gust|at|ory
gust|ily
gusti|ness
gusto (pl.
  gust|oes)
gusty (gus|tier,
  gus|ti|est)
gut (as v., gut|ted,
  gut|ting)
gut|less
gut-rot
gut|ser
guts|ily
gutsi|ness

gutsy (gut|sier,
  gut|si|est)
gutta-percha
gut|tate
gutter
gut|ter|ing
gut|ter|snipe
guttle (gut|tling)
gut|tural
gut|tur|al|ism
gut|tur|al|ize
  (gut|tur|al|iz|ing)
gut|tur|ally
Guy|ana
guzzle (guz|zling)
Gwent
Gwyn|edd
gwyn|iad
gybe (in sailing;
  gyb|ing) △ gibe
gym|khana
gym|nas|ial
gym|nas|ium
gym|nast
gym|nastic
gym|nast|ic|ally
gym|nast|ics
gym|no|soph|ist
gym|no|sophy
gym|no|sperm
gym|no|
      sperm|ous
gym-slip
gym|tunic
gyn|ae|ceum
  (women's
  apartments)
  △ gynoecium
gyn|ae|co|cracy
  (pl. gyn|ae|co|
      cra|cies)
gyn|ae|co|lo|gical
gyn|ae|co|log|ic|
      ally
gyn|ae|co|lo|gist
gyn|ae|co|logy
gyn|ae|co|mastia
gyn|and|ro|
      morph
gyn|an|dro|
      morphic

gyn|an|dro|
      morph|ism
gyn|and|rous
gyno|base
gyno|cracy (pl.
  gyno|cra|cies)
gyn|oe|cium
  (female organ of
  flower; pl.
  gyn|oe|cia)
  △ gynaeceum
gyno|pho|bia
gyp (as v.,
  gypped,
  gyp|ping)
gyppy use gippy
gyps|eous
gypsi|fer|ous
gypso|phila
gypsum
gypsy (pl.
  gyp|sies)
gypsy|fied
gypsy|ish
gyrate (as v.,
  gyr|at|ing)
gyra|tion
gyr|at|ory
gyre (as v.,
  gyr|ing)
gyr|fal|con
gyri (pl. of gyrus)
gyro (gyroscope,
  gyro-compass; pl.
  gyros) △ giro
gyro-compass
gyro|graph
gyro|mag|netic
gyro-pilot
gyro|plane
gyro|scope
gyro|scopic
gyro-stabilizer
gyrus (pl. gyri)
gyt|tja
gyve (as v.,
  gyv|ing)

H

haar
Hab|ak|kuk
hab|an|era
hab|eas cor|pus
hab|er|dasher
hab|er|dash|ery
 (*pl.* hab|er|
    dash|er|ies)
hab|er|geon
hab|ile
ha|bili|ments
ha|bil|it|ate
 (ha|bil|it|at|ing)
ha|bil|ita|tion
habit
hab|it|ab|il|ity
hab|it|able
hab|it|ably
hab|it|ant
hab|itat
hab|ita|tion
ha|bit|ual
ha|bitu|ally
ha|bitu|ate
 (ha|bitu|at|ing)
ha|bitu|ation
hab|it|ude
ha|bi|tué
ha|bu|tai
hach|ures
ha|ci|enda
hack|berry (*pl.*
 hack|ber|ries)
hack|ery (*pl.*
 hack|er|ies)
hack|ing
hackle (as *v.*,
 hack|ling)
hackly
hack|ma|tack
hack|ney
hack-saw
had|die
Had|ding|ton
had|dock (*pl.*
 same)
hade (as *v.*,
 had|ing)
Hades

Had|ith
hadj (pilgrimage)
hadji (pilgrim)
hadn't
had|ron
had|ronic
haec|ce|ity
haem
haemal
haem|atic
haem|atin
haem|at|ite
hae|ma|to|cele
haem|ato|crit
haem|ato|lo|gist
haem|ato|logy
haem|at|oma
haem|at|uria
hae|mo|cy|anin
hae|mo|globin
hae|mo|lysis (*pl.*
 hae|mo|lyses)
hae|mo|lytic
hae|mo|philia
hae|mo|phil|iac
hae|mo|philic
haem|or|rhage (as
 v., haem|or|
    rhaging)
haem|or|rhoid
hae|mo|stasis (*pl.*
 hae|mo|stases)
hae|mo|static
haer|emai
hafiz (Muslim)
Hafiz (poet)
haf|nium
hag|fish
Hag|ga|dah
Haggai
hag|gard
hag|gis
hag|gish
haggle (as *v.*,
 hag|gling)
ha|gio|cracy (*pl.*
 ha|gio|cra|cies)
Ha|gio|grapha (in
 OT)

ha|gio|grapher
ha|gio|graphic
ha|gio|graphy
ha|gio|later
ha|gio|latry
ha|gi|olo|gist
ha|gi|ology
ha|gio|scopic
hag|rid|den
Hague, The
ha ha (laughter)
ha-ha (sunk fence)
haik (Arab
 garment)
haiku (*pl.* same)
Haile Sel|as|sie
hail|stone
hail|storm
haily
Hain|aut
hair|breadth
hair|brush
hair|cloth
hair|cut
hair-do
 (*pl.* hair-dos)
hair|dresser
hair|dress|ing
hair-grip
hair|ily
hairi|ness
hair|less
hair-line
hair-piece
hair|pin
hair|spring
hair-style
hairy (hair|ier,
 hairi|est)
Haiti
hak|en|kreuz
 (swastika)
hakim
Hakka
Ha|la|chah
halal
hala|tion
hal|berd
hal|berd|ier

hal|cyon
hale (as *v.*, 'drag',
 hal|ing)
half (*pl.* halves)
half-back
half-breed
half-brother
half-caste
half-crown
half-dozen
half-hour
half-light
half-mast
half|penny (*pl.*
 half|pen|nies for
 coins, half|pence
 for sum)
half|penny|worth
half-price
half-sister
half-term
half-time
half-way
half-wit
half-witted
half-yearly
hal|ibut (*pl.* same)
hal|ide
hali|eutic
Ha|li|fax
hali|otis
hal|ite
hal|it|osis (*pl.*
 hal|it|oses)
Hal|ler
Hal|ley
halliard *use*
 halyard
hall|mark
hallo (as *n.*, *pl.*
 hal|los)
hal|loo
hal|low
Hal|low|e'en
Hal|low|mas
hall-stand
Hall|statt
hal|lu|cin|ant

hal¦lu¦cin¦ate
 (hal¦lu¦cin¦at¦ing)
hal¦lu¦cina¦tion
hal¦lu¦cin¦at¦ory
hal¦lu¦cin¦ogen
hal¦lu¦cin¦ogenic
hal¦lux (*pl.*
 hal¦lu¦ces)
hall¦way
halm *use* haulm
halma
halo (*pl.* ha¦loes)
hal¦ogen
ha¦lo¦gena¦tion
hal¦ter
hal¦teres
halve (halv¦ing)
hal¦yard
ham (as *v.*,
 hammed,
 ham¦ming)
ha¦ma¦dryad
ha¦ma¦melis
Ham¦burg
Ham¦burger (food)
Ham¦burger (of
 Hamburg)
ham-fisted
Ham¦il¦ton
Ham¦ite
Ham¦itic
ham¦let (village)
Ham¦let (by
 Shakespeare)
ham¦mam
ham¦mer
ham¦mer¦less
ham¦mer¦man (*pl.*
 ham¦mer¦men)
ham¦mock
Ham¦mond
 (organ)
hammy
 (ham¦mier,
 ham¦mi¦est)
ham¦per
Hamp¦shire
Hamp¦ton Court
ham¦ster
ham¦string
 (ham¦stringed *or*
 ham¦strung)
ham¦ulus (*pl.*
 ham¦uli)
hand¦bag
hand¦ball

hand¦bell
hand¦bill
hand¦book
hand¦brake
hand¦cart
hand¦clap
hand¦clap¦ping
hand¦craft
hand¦cuff
handed
hand¦ed¦ness
Han¦del
hand¦ful (*pl.*
 hand¦fuls)
hand¦glass
hand¦grip
hand¦guard
hand-gun
hand¦hold
han¦di¦cap (as *v.*,
 han¦di¦capped,
 han¦di¦cap¦ping)
han¦di¦cap¦per
han¦di¦craft
hand¦ily
handi¦ness
handi¦work
hand¦ker¦chief
 (*pl.*
 hand¦ker¦chiefs)
handle (as *v.*,
 hand¦ling)
handle¦bar
hand¦ler
hand¦less
hand¦line
hand¦list
hand¦made
hand¦maid
hand-me-down
hand-off *n.*
hand-out *n.*
hand¦rail
hand¦saw
hand¦sel (as *v.*,
 hand¦selled,
 hand¦sel¦ling)
hand¦set
hand¦shake
hand¦some
 (hand¦somer,
 hand¦som¦est)
hand¦spike
hand¦spring
hand¦stand
hand¦writ¦ing

hand¦writ¦ten
handy (han¦dier,
 han¦di¦est)
handy¦man (*pl.*
 handy¦men)
hang (hung, but
 hanged of capital
 punishment)
hangar (shed)
hangar¦age
hang¦dog
hanger (in senses
 of *v.*)
hanger-on
hang-glider
hang¦ing
hang¦man (*pl.*
 hang¦men)
hang¦nail
hang-out *n.*
hang¦over *n.*
hang-up *n.*
hanker
hanky (*pl.*
 han¦kies)
hanky-panky
Han¦ni¦bal
Ha¦noi
Han¦over
Han¦over¦ian
Han¦sard
Hanse
Han¦se¦atic
*Hän¦sel und
 Gretel*
han¦som
Ha¦nuk¦kah
ha¦nu¦man
 (langur)
Ha¦nu¦man (myth.
 creature)
*hapax
 leg¦om¦enon* (*pl.*
 *hapax
 leg¦om¦ena*)
hap¦haz¦ard
hap¦less
hap¦lo¦graphy
hap¦loid
hap¦lo¦logy
hap¦pen
hap¦pen¦ing
hap¦pen¦stance
happi (Jap. coat)
hap¦pily
hap¦pi¦ness

happy (hap¦pier,
 hap¦pi¦est)
happy-go-lucky
haptic
hara-kiri
har¦angue (as *v.*,
 har¦angued,
 har¦anguing)
Har¦are
har¦ass
har¦ass¦ment
har¦bin¦ger
har¦bour
har¦bour¦age
har¦bour¦less
harbour-master
hard¦back
hard¦bake
hard¦bit¦ten
hard¦board
hard-core *attrib.*
harden
hard-head
har¦di¦hood
hard¦ily
hardi¦ness
hard¦ish
hard-liner
hardly
hard¦shell *a.*
hard¦ship
hard¦standing
hard-top
hard¦ware
hard-wearing
hard¦wood
hard-working
hardy (har¦dier,
 har¦di¦est)
hare (as *v.*,
 har¦ing)
hare¦bell
hare-brained
hare¦lip
harem
hare's-ear
hare's-foot
hare¦wood
hari¦cot
hari¦jan
harken *use*
 hearken
har¦le¦quin
Har¦le¦quin (in
 pantomine)
har¦le¦quin¦ade

Har|ley Street
har|lot
har|lotry
har|mat|tan
harm|ful
harm|fully
harm|less
har|monic
har|mon|ica
har|mon|ic|ally
har|mon|ics
har|mo|ni|ous
har|mon|ist
har|mon|istic
har|mo|nium
har|mon|iza|tion
har|mon|ize
  (har|mon|iz|ing)
har|mony (*pl.*
  har|mon|ies)
har|ness
Har|old
harper
harp|ist
har|poon
har|pooner
harp|si|chord
harpy (*pl.*
  harpies)
har|que|bus
har|que|bus|ier
har|ri|dan
har|rier
Har|ris
Har|ro|vian
har|row (tool)
Har|row (place)
harry (har|ries,
  har|ried,
  har|ry|ing)
harshen
har|tal
har|te|beest
Hartle|pool
harts|horn
hart's-tongue
harum-scarum
ha|ru|spex (*pl.*
  ha|ru|spi|ces)
har|vest
har|ves|ter
har|vest|man (*pl.*
  har|vest|men)
Ha|ry|ana
has-been
Hash|em|ite

hash|ish
Hasid (*pl.*
  Has|idim)
Has|idic
has|let
hasn't
hassle (as *v.*,
  hass|ling)
has|sock
hast|ate
hasten
hast|ily
hasti|ness
Hast|ings
hasty (hast|ier,
  hasti|est)
hat (as *v.*, hat|ted,
  hat|ting)
hat|able
hat|band
hatch|back
hatch|ery (*pl.*
  hatch|er|ies)
hatchet
hatch|ling
hatch|ment
hatch|way
hate (as *v.*,
  hat|ing)
hate|ful
hate|fully
hat|ful (*pl.*
  hat|fuls)
hatha (yoga)
hat|less
hat-peg
hat-pin
hat|red
hat|ter
hau|berk
haught|ily
haughti|ness
haughty
  (haught|ier,
  haughti|est)
haul|age
hauler (in senses
  of *v.*)
haul|ier (with ref.
  to transport)
haulm
haulyard *use*
  halyard
Hausa
haus|frau
haute cou|ture

haute cuis|ine
haut|eur
Hav|ana
have (has, had,
  hav|ing)
have|lock
haven
have-not *n.*
haven't
haver
hav|er|sack
hav|er|sine
hav|il|dar
hav|ing
havoc (as *v.*,
  hav|ocked,
  hav|ock|ing)
Ha|waii
Ha|wai|ian
haw|finch
hawk|bit
hawker
hawk|ish
hawk|like
hawk's-bill
hawk|weed
haw|ser
haw|thorn
hay|box
hay|cock
Haydn
hay|field
hay-fork
hay|maker
hay|mak|ing
hay-mow
hay|rick
hay|seed
hay|stack
hay|ward
hay|wire
hazard
haz|ard|ous
haze (as *v.*,
  haz|ing)
hazel
hazel-nut
haz|ily
hazi|ness
Haz|litt
hazy (haz|ier,
  hazi|est)
H-bomb
head|ache
head|achy
head|age

head|band
head|board
head|bor|ough
head-cloth
head-dress
headed
header
head|fast
head|gear
head|ily
headi|ness
head|ing
head|lamp
head|land
head|less
head|light
head|line
head|liner
head|lock
head|long
head|man (*pl.*
  head|men)
head|master
head|mistress
head|most
head-note
head-on
head|phone
head|piece
head|quar|ters
head-rest
head|room
head-sail
head|scarf (*pl.*
  head|scarves)
head-set
head|ship
heads|man (*pl.*
  heads|men)
head|spring
head|square
head|stall
head|stock
head|stone
head|strong
head|ward
head-water
head|way
head|word
heady (head|ier,
  headi|est)
heal (cure etc.)
  △ heel, hele
health|ful
health|fully
health|ily

healthi|ness
healthy
 (health|ier,
 healthi|est)
hear (heard)
hear|able
hear|ing
hearken
hear|say
hearse
heart|ache
heart|beat
heart-break
heart-breaking
heart-broken
heart|burn
 (pyrosis)
heart-burn
 (jealousy)
hearten
heart|felt
hearth|rug
hearth|stone
heart|ily
hearti|ness
heart|land
heart|less
heart's-ease
heart|sick
heart|sore
heart-strings
heart-throb
heart-whole
heart|wood
hearty (heart|ier,
 hearti|est)
heatedly
heater
heath-bell
heathen
hea'then|dom
hea'then|ish
hea'then|ism
hea'then|ize
 (hea'then|iz|ing)
hea'thenry
heather
heath|ery
Heath Rob|in|son
heat-proof
heat-stroke
heat|wave
heave (as v.,
 heaved or Naut.
 hove, heav|ing)
heaven

heav'en|li|ness
heav|enly
heaven-sent
heaver
heav|ily
heavi|ness
Heavi|side (layer)
heavy (as n., pl.
 heavies; as a.,
 heav|ier,
 heavi|est)
heavy-handed
heavy-hearted
heavy|ish
heavy|weight
heb'domad
heb'dom|adal
Heb|raic
Heb'ra|ism
Heb'ra|ist
Heb'ra|istic
Heb'ra|ize
 (Heb'ra|iz|ing)
Heb'rew
Heb'rid|ean
Heb'ri'des
he'ca|tomb
heck'el|phone
heckle (as v.,
 heck|ling)
heck|ler
hec|tare
hec|tic
hec'tic|ally
hec'to|gram
hec'to|graph
hec'to|litre
hec'to|metre
hec'tor
Hedda Gab'ler
heddle
hedge (as v.,
 hedging)
hedge|hog
hedge-hop
 (hedge-hopped,
 hedge-hopping)
hedger
hedge|row
he|donic
hedonics
he'don|ism
he'don|ist
he'don|istic
heebie-jeebies
heed|ful

heed|less
hee-haw
heel (part of foot)
 △ heal, hele
heel|ball
heel|less
heel|tap
heft|ily
hef'ti|ness
hefty (hef'tier,
 hef'ti|est)
He'gel
He'gel|ian
he'ge|monic
he'ge|mony (pl.
 he'ge|mon'ies)
heg'ira
Hei'deg|ger
heifer
heigh-ho
heighten
Heine
hein|ous
heir|dom
heir|ess
heir|less
heir|loom
heir|ship
Heis'en|berg
hei-tiki
Hekla
HeLa (cells)
Hel'den|tenor
hele (plant,
 hel'ing) △ heal,
 heel
Helen
he'li|acal
he'li|anthus
hel|ical
hel'ic|ally
he'li|chrysum
hel'ic|oid
hel|icon (saxhorn)
Hel|icon (source of
 inspiration)
He'li'co|nian
heli|cop'ter
he'lio|cent'ric
he'lio|gram
he'lio|graph
he'li|ography
he'lio|gravure
he'lio|lithic
he'lio|meter

he'li|osis (pl.
 he'li|oses)
he'lio|stat
he'lio|ther'apy
he'lio|trope
he'lio|tropic
he'lio|tropism
he'lio|type
heli|port
he'lium
he'lix (pl.
 he'li'ces)
Hel|ladic
hell-bent
hel'le|bore
hel'le|bor|ine
Hel|lene
Hel|lenic
Hel'len|ism
Hel'len|ist
Hel'len|istic
Hel'len|ize
 (Hel'len|iz|ing)
hell-fire
hell-hole
hell-hound
hell|ish
hello (as n., pl.
 hel'los)
hel'met
hel|meted
hel|minth
hel'min'thi|asis
hel|minthic
hel|minth|oid
hel'mintho|lo'gist
hel'mintho|logy
helms|man (pl.
 helms|men)
helot (serf)
Helot (hist.)
hel'ot|ism
hel|otry
help|ful
help|fully
help|ing
help|less
help|mate
help|meet
Hel|sinki
helter-skelter
Hel've'tian
hem (as v.,
 hemmed,
 hem|ming)

hema-, hemo-
(*prefix* meaning
'blood') *use*
haema-, haemo-
he-man
(*pl.* **he-men**)
hem¦ero|cal'lis
hemi|an¦op¦ia
hemi|an¦op¦sia
hemi|cycle
hemi|demi|semi|
      qua¦ver
hemi|hedral
Hem¦ing|way
hemi|ple¦gia
hemi|ple¦gic
hemi|pter¦ous
hemi|sphere
hemi|spheric
hemi|spher¦ical
hemi|stich
hem-line
hem|lock
hempen
hem-stitch
hen|bane
hence|forth
hence|for¦ward
hench|man (*pl.*
  hench|men)
hen-coop
hen|de¦ca|gon
hen|de¦ca|
     syl¦labic
hen|de¦ca|
     syl¦lable
hen|dia¦dys
hen|equen
hen-house
henna
hennaed
heno|the¦ism
hen-party (*pl.*
  hen-parties)
hen|peck
henry (unit; *pl.*
  hen¦ries)
Henry (name)
he¦or¦to|lo¦gist
he¦or¦to|logy
hep|arin
hep¦ar¦in|ize
  (**hep¦ar¦in|iz|ing**)
hep|atic
hep¦at|ica
hep¦at|itis

hep¦ato|meg¦aly
Hepple|white
hep¦ta|chord
heptad
hep¦ta|glot
hep¦ta|gon
hep¦ta|gonal
hep¦ta|hed¦ron
  (*pl.* **hep¦ta|hedra**)
hep¦ta|mer¦ous
hep¦ta|meter
hept|ane
hept|archic
hept|arch¦ical
hept|archy (*pl.*
  hept|arch¦ies)
hep¦ta|syl¦labic
Hep¦ta|teuch
hep¦ta|val¦ent
her|ald
her|aldic
her|ald|ist
her|aldry
herb|aceous
herb|age
herbal
herb¦al|ist
herb|ar¦ium (*pl.*
  herb|aria)
herbi|cidal
herbi|cide
herbi|fer¦ous
herbi|vore
herbi|vor¦ous
herb|less
herby
Her¦ce|go¦vina
Her¦cu|la¦neum
Her¦cu|lean
Her¦cu¦les
Her¦cyn|ian
herds|man (*pl.*
  herds|men)
Herd|wick
here|about
here|abouts
here|after
hereby
her¦ed¦it|able
her¦ed¦ita|ment
her¦ed¦it¦ar|ily
her¦ed¦it¦ari|ness
her¦ed¦it¦ary
her¦ed¦ity
Here|ford
herein

here¦in|af¦ter
here¦in|be¦fore
hereof
her¦esi|arch
her¦esi|ology
her¦esy (*pl.*
  her¦es|ies)
her|etic
her¦et|ical
her¦et|ic¦ally
hereto
here¦to|fore
here¦un|der
here|upon
here|with
heriot
her¦it|able
her¦it|ably
her¦it|age
her|itor
herm|aph¦rod|ite
herm|aph¦rod|itic
herm|aph¦rod|it|
     ism
her¦men|eutic
her¦men|eutics
Hermes
her|metic
her¦met|ic¦ally
her¦met|ism
her¦mit
her¦mit|age
Her¦mit|age (art
  gallery)
her¦nia
her|nial
her¦ni|ary
her¦ni|ated
hero (*pl.* **her¦oes**)
Her¦od|otus
heroic
hero¦ic|ally
heroi-comic
hero|ics
heroin (drug)
hero|ine (female
  hero)
hero|ism
hero|ize
  (**hero|iz|ing**)
heron
her¦onry (*pl.*
  her¦on|ries)

hero-worship (as
  v., **hero-**
     worshipped,
  hero-
     worshipping)
her¦pes
her¦petic
her¦peto|lo¦gist
her¦peto|logy
Herr (*pl.* **Herren**)
Her¦ren|volk
  (master race)
her¦ring
Herrn|huter
her|self
Hert|ford
Hert|ford|shire
hertz (*pl.* same)
Hertz|ian
hes¦it|ance
hes¦it|ancy (*pl.*
  hes¦it|an¦cies)
hes¦it|ant
hes¦it|ate
  (**hes¦it|at|ing**)
hes¦ita|tion
hes¦it|at¦ive
Hes¦per|ian
Hes¦per|ides
hes¦per|idium (*pl.*
  hes¦per|idia)
Hes|perus
Hesse
hes|sian (coarse
  cloth)
Hes|sian (of
  Hesse)
het|aera (*pl.*
  het|aerae)
het|aer|ism
het¦ero|
     chro¦matic
het¦ero|clite
het¦ero|cyc¦lic
het¦ero|dox
het¦ero|doxy (*pl.*
  het¦ero|dox¦ies)
het¦ero|dyne (as
  v., **het¦ero|**
     dyn¦ing)
het¦ero|gam¦ous
het¦ero|gamy
het¦ero|gen¦eity
het¦ero|gen|eous
het¦ero|gen¦esis
het¦ero|gen¦etic

het¦ero¦geny
het¦ero¦gony
het¦ero¦graft
het¦ero¦log¦ous
het¦ero¦mer¦ous
het¦ero¦morphic
het¦ero¦
    morph¦ism
het¦ero¦nom¦ous
het¦ero¦nomy
het¦ero¦pathic
het¦ero¦phony
het¦ero¦phyl¦lous
het¦ero¦plastic
het¦ero¦ploid
het¦ero¦polar
het¦ero¦sexual
het¦ero¦sexu¦al¦ity
het¦er¦osis (*pl.*
  het¦er¦oses)
het¦ero¦taxy
het¦ero¦
    trans¦plant
het¦ero¦trophic
het¦ero¦zy¦gote
het¦ero¦zy¦gotic
het¦ero¦zyg¦ous
het¦man
heuch¦era
heur¦istic
he¦vea
hew (hewn)
hewer
hexa¦chord
hexad
hexa¦decimal
hexa¦gon
hexa¦gonal
hexa¦gram
hexa¦hed¦ral
hexa¦hed¦ron (*pl.*
  hexa¦hedra)
hex¦am¦er¦ous
hexa¦meter
hexa¦met¦ric
hexa¦met¦rist
hex¦ane
hexa¦pla
hexa¦pod
hexa¦pody (*pl.*
  hexa¦pod¦ies)
hexa¦style
hexa¦syl¦labic
Hexa¦teuch
hexa¦val¦ent
hex¦ode

hex¦ose
hey (dance) *use*
  hay
hey¦day
Hey¦er¦dahl
hi¦atus
Hia¦watha
hi¦bern¦ate
  (hi¦bern¦at¦ing)
hi¦berna¦tion
Hi¦bern¦ian
Hi¦bern¦icism
hi¦bis¦cus
hic¦cup (as *v.*,
  hic¦cuped,
  hic¦cuping)
hic¦cupy
hickey
hick¦ory (*pl.*
  hick¦or¦ies)
hi¦dalgo (*pl.*
  hi¦dal¦gos)
hide (as *v.*, hid,
  hid¦den, hid¦ing)
hide-and-seek
hide¦away
hide¦bound
hid¦eous
hide-out
hid¦ing
hiding-place
hid¦rosis (*pl.*
  hid¦roses)
hid¦rotic
hidy-hole
hier¦arch
hier¦archic
hier¦arch¦ical
hier¦arch¦ic¦ally
hier¦arch¦ism
hier¦archy (*pl.*
  hier¦arch¦ies)
hier¦atic
hiero¦cracy (*pl.*
  hiero¦cra¦cies)
hiero¦glyph
hiero¦glyphic
hiero¦gram
hiero¦graph
hiero¦latry
hiero¦logy
hiero¦phant
hiero¦phantic
hi-fi
higgle (hig¦gling)

higgledy-
    piggledy
high¦ball
high-born
high¦boy
high¦brow
high-class *a.*
high-falutin
high-flown
high-flyer
high-flying
high-grade
high-handed
high¦land (high
  land)
High¦land (Sc.
  region)
high¦lander
High¦lands (Sc.
  mts.)
high-level *a.*
high¦light
highly
highly-strung
high-minded
high¦ness
high-rise
high-speed *a.*
high¦tail
high-tech
high-up *n.*
high¦way
high¦way¦man (*pl.*
  high¦way¦men)
hi¦jack
hike (as *v.*,
  hik¦ing)
hiker
hil¦ari¦ous
hil¦ar¦ity
Hil¦ary
hill-billy
  (*pl.* hill-billies)
hill-fort
hill-man
  (*pl.* hill-men)
hil¦lock
hill¦side
hill¦top
hilly (hil¦lier,
  hil¦li¦est)
hi¦lum (*pl.* hila)
Hi¦machal
  Pra¦desh
Hi¦ma¦layan
Hi¦ma¦layas

hi¦ma¦tion
him¦self
Hi¦na¦yana
Hin¦de¦mith
hinder
Hindi
hind¦most
hind¦quar¦ters
hind¦rance
hind¦sight
Hindu
Hin¦du¦ism
Hin¦du¦ize
  (Hin¦du¦iz¦ing)
Hin¦du¦stan
Hin¦du¦stani
hinge (as *v.*,
  hin¦ging)
hinny (*pl.*
  hin¦nies)
hin¦ter¦land
hip-bath
hip-bone
hip-flask
hip-joint
hip¦pe¦ast¦rum
hip¦pie (person)
  △ hippy
hippo (*pl.* hip¦pos)
hip¦po¦cam¦pus
  (*pl.*
  hip¦po¦campi)
hip¦po¦cen¦taur
hip¦po¦cras
Hip¦po¦cra¦tes
Hip¦po¦cratic
hip¦po¦crene
hip¦po¦drome
hip¦po¦griff
hip¦po¦phagy
hip¦po¦phile
hip¦po¦pho¦bia
hip¦po¦pot¦amus
  (*pl.* hip¦po¦
    pot¦amuses)
hippy (large-
  hipped) △ hippie
hip¦ster
hi¦ra¦gana
hir¦cine
hire (as *v.*, hir¦ing)
hire¦able
hire-car
hire¦ling
hire-purchase
H-iron

Hi|ro|shima
hir|sute
hir|sut|ism
His|panic
His|pan|icist
Hispanist
hispid
his|tam|ine
his|to|gen|esis
his|to|gen|etic
his|to|geny
his|to|gram
his|to|logy
his|to|lysis
his|to|patho|logy
his|tor|ian
his|tori|ated
his|toric
his|tor|ical
his|tor|ic|ally
his|tor|icism
his|tor|icist
his|tor|icity
his|tori|ographer
his|tori|ographic
his|tori|ography
his|tory (*pl.*
 his|tor|ies)
his|tri|onic
his|tri|on|ic|ally
his|tri|on|icism
his|tri|on|ism
hit (as *v.*, hit,
 hit|ting)
hitch-hike (as *v.*,
 hitch-hiking)
hither
hith|erto
Hit|ler
Hit|tite
hive (as *v.*,
 hiv|ing)
hoard (store)
 △ horde
hoard|ing
hoar-frost
hoarhound *use*
 horehound
hoar|ily
hoari|ness
hoarse (hoarser,
 hoars|est)
hoarsen
hoar|stone
hoary (hoar|ier,
 hoari|est)

hoat|zin
Hobbes
hob|bit
hob|bitry
hobble (as *v.*,
 hob|bling)
hobbl|ede|hoy
hobby (*pl.*
 hob|bies)
hobby-horse
hob|gob|lin
hob|nail
hob|nailed
hob-nob
 (hob-nobbed,
 hob-nobbing)
hobo (*pl.* ho|boes)
Hob|son's choice
Ho Chi Minh
hockey
hock|ey|ist
Hock|tide
ho|cus (ho|cusses,
 ho|cussed,
 ho|cus|sing)
hocus-pocus (as
 n., *pl.* hocus-
 pocusses; as *v.*,
 hocus-pocusses,
 hocus-pocussed,
 hocus-
 pocussing)
hod|den
hodgepodge *use*
 hotchpotch
Hodg|kin's
 disease
ho|di|ernal
hod|man (*pl.*
 hod|men)
hodo|graph
hodometer *use*
 odometer
hoe (as *v.*, hoed,
 hoe|ing)
hoe-down
hog (as *v.*, hogged,
 hog|ging)
ho|gan
Ho|garth
hog|gery (*pl.*
 hog|ger|ies)
hog|get
hog|gin
hog|gish
hog|like

hog|manay
hog's-back
hogs|head
hog-tie (hog-tied,
 hog-tying)
hog-wash
hog|weed
hoi pol|loi (the
 masses)
hoity-toity
hokey
hokey-cokey
 (dance)
hokey-pokey
 (ice-cream; hocus-
 pocus)
hokku (*pl.* same)
hokum
hol|arc|tic
Hol|bein
hold (as *v.*, held)
hold|all
Höl|der|lin
hold|fast
hold|ing
hold-up *n.*
hole (as *v.*,
 hol|ing)
holey (full of holes)
holi|day
holiday-maker
ho|lily
ho|li|ness
hol|ism
hol|istic
hol|ist|ic|ally
holla (as *v.*,
 hol|laed)
hol|land (linen)
Hol|land
hol|land|aise
Hol|lander
Hol|lands (gin)
hol|low (*pl.* hol|los)
hol|low
holly
hol|ly|hock
Hol|ly|wood
holm
Holmes|ian
hol|mium
holm-oak
holo|caust
Holo|caust (*hist.*)
Holo|cene
holo|gram

holo|graph
holo|graphic
holo|graphy
holo|hed|ral
holo|meta|bol|ous
holo|phote
holo|thur|ian
Hol|stein
hol|ster
holus-bolus
holy (as *a.*, ho|lier,
 ho|li|est; as *n.*, *pl.*
 hol|ies)
Holy|rood
ho|ly|stone (as *v.*,
 ho|ly|ston|ing)
hom|age
Hom|burg
home (as *v.*,
 hom|ing)
home|body (*pl.*
 home|bod|ies)
home-coming
home|land
home|less
home|like
home|li|ness
homely
home-made
homeopath etc.
 use homoeopath
 etc.
homer
Ho|meric
home|sick
home|spun
home|stead
home|ward
home|wards
home|work
homey *use* homy
hom|icidal
hom|icid|ally
hom|icide
ho|mi|letic
ho|mil|iary (*pl.*
 ho|mil|iar|ies)
hom|ily (*pl.*
 hom|il|ies)
hom|ing
hom|inid
hom|in|oid
hom|iny
homo (as *n.*, *pl.*
 homos)
ho|mo|cent|ric

homoeo|path
hom'oe|opathic
hom'oe|opath'ist
hom'oe|opathy
hom'oeo|stasis
  (*pl.* hom'oeo|
       stases)
homo-erotic
ho'mo|gam'ous
homo|gen|eity
homo|gen'eous (of
same kind)
ho'mo|gen'etic
homo|gen|iza'tion
homo|gen|ize
  (homo'gen|iz'ing)
homo'gen|izer
homo|gen'ous
  (having common
  descent)
ho'mo|geny
homo|graft
homo|graph
homoio|thermic
homoi|ous|ian
homo'log|ate
  (homo'log|at'ing)
homo'loga|tion
homo|lo'gical
homo|lo'gize
  (homo|lo'giz|ing)
homo'log|ous
homo|logue
homo|logy
homo|morph
homo|morphic
homo|morph|ism
homo|morph'ous
hom'on'om'ous
hom|onym
hom|onymic
hom'onym|ous
homo|ous|ian
homo|phone
homo|phonic
homo|phon'ous
homo|phony
homo|plas'tic
homo|polar
homo|pter'ous
Homo sa'pi|ens
homo|sexual
homo|sexu'al|ity
homo|sexu'ally
homo|trans'plant
homo|zy'gote

homo|zy'gous
hom'un|cule
hom'un|cu'lus (*pl.*
  hom'un|culi)
homy
Hon|duras
hone (as *v.*,
  hon'ing)
hon|est
hon|esty
honey
honey-bee
hon'ey|comb
hon'ey|dew
hon|eyed
hon'ey|moon
hon'ey|mooner
honey-pot
hon'ey|suckle
Hong Kong
Ho'ni|ara
Hon|iton
honky (*pl.*
  honk'ies)
honky-tonk
Ho'no|lulu
hon'or|and
hon'or|ar'ium
hon'or|ary
hon'or|ific
hon|our
hon'our|able
hon'our|ably
hooded
hoodie
hood|lum
hood|wink
hooey
hoof (*pl.* hoofs)
hoofer
hoo-ha
hookah
Hooke
hooker
hookey
hook|less
hook|let
hook-up *n.*
hook|worm
hoo'li|gan
hoo'li|gan|ism
hoop-la
hoo'poe
hooray *use*
hurray
hoose|gow

Hoo|sier
hoote|nanny (*pl.*
  hoote|nan'nies)
hooter
hoover *v.*
Hoover *n.* (*propr.*)
hop (as *v.*,
  hopped,
  hop|ping)
hope (as *v.*,
  hop'ing)
hope|ful
hope|fully
hope|less
hop|head
hop|lite
hop-o'-my-thumb
hop'per
hopple (as *v.*,
  hop|pling)
Hop'pus
hop|sack
hop|sack|ing
hop|scotch
Hor'ace
hor'ary
Ho'ra|tian
horde (crowd etc.)
  ⚠ hoard
hore|hound
ho'ri|zon
ho'ri|zontal
ho'ri'zont|ally
horme
hor|monal
hor|mone
horn|beam
horn|bill
horn|blende
horn|book
horner
hor'net
horni|ness
horn|ist
horn|less
horn|pipe
horn-rimmed
horn|stone
horn|wort
horny (hor|nier,
  hor'ni|est)
ho'ro|loger
ho'ro|lo'gical
ho'ro|lo'gist
ho'ro|logy
horo|scope

ho'ro|scopy
hor'rend|ous
hor|rent
hor|rible
hor|ribly
hor'rid
hor|rific
hor'rif'ic|ally
hor'ri|fica|tion
hor|rify
  (hor'ri|fies,
  hor'ri|fied,
  hor'ri|fy|ing)
hor'ror
horror-stricken
horror-struck
hors con|cours
hors de com'|bat
hors-d'œuvre (*pl.*
  hors-d'œuvres)
horse (as *v.*,
  hors|ing)
horse|back
horse|bean
horse-box
horse-brass
horse-chestnut
horse|flesh
horse-fly (*pl.*
  horse-flies)
horse|hair
horse|leech
horse|less
horse|man (*pl.*
  horse|men)
horse'man|ship
horse|play
horse|power (*pl.*
  same)
horse-race
horse-racing
horse-radish
horse|shoe
horse|whip (as *v.*,
  horse'whipped,
  horse'whip|ping)
horse|woman (*pl.*
  horse|women)
hors|ily
horsi|ness
horsy (hor|sier,
  hor'si|est)
horta|tion
hort|at'ive
hort|at'ory
hor|ten'sia

hor|ti|cul|tural
hor|ti|cul|ture
hor|ti|cul|tur|ist
hos|anna
hose (as v.,
 hos|ing)
hose-pipe
ho|sier
ho|si|ery
hos|pice
hos|pit|able
hos|pit|ably
hos|pital
hos|pit|al|ism
hos|pit|al|ity
hos|pit|al|iza|tion
hos|pit|al|ize
 (hos|pit|al|iz|ing)
hos|pit|al|ler
hosta
host|age
hos|tel
hos|telry (pl.
 hos|tel|ries)
host|ess
hos|tile
hos|til|ity (pl.
 hos|til|it|ies)
host|ler
hot (as a., hot|ter,
 hot|test; as v.,
 hot|ted, hot|ting)
hot|bed
hot-blooded
hotch|pot (Law)
hotch|potch
ho|tel
ho|tel|ier
hot|foot
hot|head
hot|house
hot|plate
hot|pot
hot-press
hot|spur
Hot|ten|tot
hot|tish
hour|glass
houri
hourly
house (as v.,
 hous|ing)
house-agent
house|boat
house|bote (Law)
house-bound

house|boy
house|breaker
house|break|ing
house-broken
house|carl
house|coat
house|craft
house-dog
house|ful (pl.
 house|fuls)
house|hold
house|holder
house|keep
 (house|kept)
house|keeper
house|keep|ing
house|leek
house|less
house|maid
house|man (pl.
 house|men)
house|mas|ter
house|mis|tress
house-proud
house-room
house-top
house-trained
house-warming
house|wife (pl.
 house|wives)
house|wifely
house|wifery
house|work
housey-housey
hous|ing
hovel
hover
hov|er|craft (pl.
 same)
hover-fly (pl.
 hover-flies)
hover-plane
hov|er|port
hov|er|train
How|ards End
how|beit
how|dah
how-do-you-do
 (awkward
 situation; pl.
 how-do-you-dos)
howdy (pl.
 how|dies)
how|ever
how|it|zer
howler

howl|ing
how|so|ever
hoya
hoy|den
Huas|ca|ran
hubble-bubble
hub|bub
hubby (pl.
 hub|bies)
hub-cap
hub|ris
hub|ristic
hucka|back
 (rough linen
 fabric)
huckle
huckle-back
 (humpback)
huckle|berry (pl.
 huckle|ber|ries)
*Huckle|berry
Finn*
huck|ster
huck|stery
Hud|ders|field
huddle (as v.,
 hud|dling)
Hu|di|brastic
Hud|son (Bay)
hue|less
huff|ily
huffi|ness
huff|ish
huffy (huf|fier,
 huf|fi|est)
hug (as v.,
 hugged,
 hug|ging)
hugger-mugger
Hugo
Hu|gue|not
hula
hulk|ing
hul|la|ba|loo
hullo (as n., pl.
 hul|los)
hum (as v.,
 hummed,
 hum|ming)
hu|man
hu|mane
hu|man|ism
hu|man|ist
hu|man|istic
hu|man|it|ar|ian

hu|man|ity (pl.
 hu|man|it|ies)
hu|man|iza|tion
hu|man|ize
 (hu|man|iz|ing)
hu|man|kind
hu|manly
Hum|ber|side
humble (as v.,
 hum|bling)
humble-bee
hum|bly
Hum|boldt
hum|bug (as v.,
 hum|bugged,
 hum|bug|ging)
hum|bug|gery
hum|dinger
hum|drum
hu|meral
hu|merus (pl.
 hu|meri)
humic
hu|mid
hu|midi|fier
hu|mid|ify
 (hu|midi|fies,
 hu|midi|fied,
 hu|midi|fy|ing)
hu|mid|ity (pl.
 hu|mid|it|ies)
hu|midor
hum|ify
 (humi|fies,
 humi|fied,
 humi|fy|ing)
hu|mi|li|ate
 (hu|mi|li|at|ing)
hu|mi|li|ation
hu|mil|ity (pl.
 hu|mil|it|ies)
hum|mel
humming-bird
hum|mock
hum|mocky
hum|oral
hu|mor|esque
hu|mor|ist
hu|mor|istic
hu|mor|ous
hu|mour
hu|mour|less
hu|mour|some
hum|ous a.
hump|back
hump|backed

humph
humpty (pl.
 hump|ties)
Humpty-Dumpty
humpy (as n., pl.
 hump|ies)
hu|mus n.
hunch|back
hunch|backed
hun|dred
hun|dred|fold
hun|dredth
hun|dred|weight
Hun|gar|ian
Hun|gary
hun|ger
hung-over
hun|grily
hun|gri|ness
hun|gry
 (hun|grier,
 hun|gri|est)
hunker
hunk|ers
hunky (pl.
 hunk|ies)
Hun|nish
hunter
hunt|ing
Hun|ting|don
Hun|ting|don|
 shire
hunt|ress
hunts|man (pl.
 hunts|men)
hurdle (as v.,
 hurd|ling)
hurd|ler
hurdy-gurdy (pl.
 hurdy-gurdies)
hur|ley
hurl|ing
hurly-burly
Huron, Lake
hur|rah
hur|ray
hur|ric|ane
hurry (as v.,
 hur|ries,
 hur|ried,
 hur|ry|ing)
hurt (as v., hurt)
hurt|ful
hurt|fully
hurtle (hurt|ling)
Hus|ain

hus|band
hus|bandry
hush|aby
husk|ily
huski|ness
husky (as a.,
 hust|ling)
hus|kier,
 hus|ki|est; as n.,
 pl. husk|ies)
hus|sar
Huss|ite
hussy (pl.
 huss|ies)
hust|ings
hustle (as v.,
 hust|ling)
hust|ler
hut (as v., hut|ted,
 hut|ting)
hut|ment
Hut|ter|ite
Hut|ton
Hux|ley
huzzy use hussy
Hwang-Ho
hwyl (fervour)
hy|acinth
hy|acinth|ine
Hy|ades
hyaena use hyena
hy|al|ine
hy|al|ite
hy|al|oid
hy|brid
hy|brid|ism
hy|brid|ity
hy|brid|iza|tion
hy|brid|ize
 (hy|brid|iz|ing)
hy|datid
hy|dati|di|form
hy|dra
hy|dran|gea
hy|drant
hy|drate (as v.,
 hy|drat|ing)
hy|dra|tion
hy|draulic
hy|draul|ic|ally
hy|dra|zine
hy|dric
hy|dride
hy|dri|odic
hy|dro (pl.
 hy|dros)
hy|dro|bromic

hy|dro|car|bon
hy|dro|cele
hy|dro|ceph|alus
hy|dro|chloric
hy|dro|chlor|ide
hy|dro|cy|anic
hy|dro|dyn|amic
hy|dro|elec|tric
hy|dro|
 elec|tri|city
hy|dro|fluoric
hy|dro|foil
hy|dro|gen
hy|dro|gen|ate
 (hy|dro|gen|
 at|ing)
hy|dro|gena|tion
hy|dro|gen|ous
hy|dro|grapher
hy|dro|graphic
hy|dro|graph|ical
hy|dro|graphy
hy|droid
hy|dro|logist
hy|dro|logy
hy|dro|lyse
 (hy|dro|lys|ing)
hy|dro|lysis
hy|dro|lytic
hy|dro|mag|netic
hy|dro|mania
hy|dro|
 mech|anics
hy|dro|mel
hy|dro|meter
hy|dro|met|ric
hy|dro|metry
hy|dro|pathic
hy|dro|path|ist
hy|dro|pathy
hy|dro|phane
hy|dro|philic
hy|dro|phobia
hy|dro|phobic
hy|dro|phone
hy|dro|phyte
hy|dropic
hy|dro|plane
hy|dro|
 pneu|matic
hy|dro|pon|ics
hy|dro|quin|one
hy|dro|sphere
hy|dro|static
hy|dro|stat|ical
hy|dro|stat|ic|ally

hy|dro|ther|apy
hy|dro|thermal
hy|dro|thorax
hy|dro|trop|ism
hyd|rous
hy|drox|ide
hy|droxyl
hy|dro|zoan
hy|ena
Hy|geia
hy|geian
hy|giene
hy|gienic
hy|gien|ic|ally
hy|gien|ist
hy|gro|logy
hy|gro|meter
hy|gro|metric
hy|gro|metry
hy|gro|phil|ous
hy|gro|phyte
hy|gro|phytic
hy|gro|scope
hy|gro|scopic
Hyk|sos
hylic
hy|lo|morph|ism
hy|lo|the|ism
hy|lo|zo|ism
hy|lo|zo|ist
hy|men
 (membrane)
Hy|men (god)
hy|menal (of
 hymen)
hy|men|eal (of
 marriage)
hy|men|ium (pl.
 hy|menia)
hy|men|op|teran
hy|men|
 op|ter|ous
hym|nal
hym|nary (pl.
 hym|nar|ies)
hymn-book
hym|nic
hym|nist
hym|nod|ist
hym|nody
hym|no|grapher
hym|no|logist
hym|no|logy
hy|oid
hy|os|cine
hy|os|cy|am|ine

hyp|aeth|ral
hyp|al|lage
hype (as v.,
 hyp|ing)
hy|per|act|ive
hy|per|aemia
hy|per|aemic
hy|per|aes|thesia
hy|per|aes|thetic
hy|per|baton
hy|per|bola
 (curve)
hy|per|bole
 (exaggeration)
hy|per|bolic (of
 hyperbola)
hy|per|bol|ical (of
 hyperbole)
hy|per|bol|ism
hy|per|bol|ist
hy|per|bol|oid
hy|per|bol|oidal
hy|per|bor|ean (of
 extreme north)
Hy|per|bor|ean
 (Gr. Myth.)
hy|per|cata|lectic
hy|per|con|scious
hy|per|crit|ical
hy|per|crit|ic|ally
hy|per|crit|icism
hy|per|du|lia
hy|per|focal
hy|per|gamy
hy|per|golic
hyp|er|icum
hy|per|mar|ket
hy|per|met|ric
hy|per|met|rical
hy|per|met|ropia
hy|per|met|ropic
hyp|eron

hy|per|opia
hy|per|opic
hy|per|phys|ical
hy|per|sens|it|ive
hy|per|sens|it|iv|
 ity
hy|per|sonic
hy|per|son|ic|ally
hy|per|sthene
hy|per|ten|sion
hy|per|tens|ive
hy|per|ther|mia
hy|per|trophic
hy|per|tro|phied
hy|per|trophy (pl.
 hy|per|tro|phies)
hy|pha (pl.
 hy|phae)
hy|phen
hy|phen|ate
 (hy|phen|at|ing)
hy|phena|tion
hyp|no|gen|esis
hyp|no|logy
hyp|no|pae|dia
hyp|no|sis (pl.
 hyp|no|ses)
hyp|no|ther|apy
hyp|notic
hyp|not|ic|ally
hyp|not|ism
hyp|not|ist
hyp|not|ize
 (hyp|not|iz|ing)
hypo (pl. hy|pos)
hy|po|blast
hy|po|caust
hy|po|chlor|ite
hy|po|chlor|ous
hy|po|chon|dria
hy|po|chon|driac
hy|po|cor|istic

hy|po|cotyl
hy|po|crisy (pl.
 hy|po|cris|ies)
hy|po|crite
hy|po|crit|ical
hy|po|cyc|loid
hy|po|cyc|loidal
hy|po|derma
hy|po|dermal
hy|po|dermic
hy|po|derm|ic|
 ally
hy|po|gast|ric
hy|po|gast|rium
 (pl.
 hy|po|gastria)
hy|po|geal
hy|po|gean
hy|po|gene (Geol.)
hy|po|geum (pl.
 hy|po|gea)
hyp|oid
hy|po|lim|nion
 (pl.
 hy|po|lim|nia)
hy|po|mania
hy|po|manic
hy|po|nasty
hy|po|phys|eal
hy|po|physis (pl.
 hy|po|physes)
hy|po|stasis (pl.
 hy|po|stases)
hy|po|stas|ize
 (hy|po|stas|iz|
 ing)
hy|po|static
hy|po|stat|ical
hy|po|stat|ic|ally
hy|po|stat|ize
 (hy|po|stat|iz|
 ing)

hy|po|style
hy|po|sulph|ite
hy|po|tactic
hy|po|taxis
hy|po|ten|sion
hy|po|tens|ive
hy|po|ten|use
hy|po|thal|amus
hy|po|thec
hy|po|thec|ary
hy|po|thec|ate
 (hy|po|thec|
 at|ing)
hy|po|theca|tion
hy|po|ther|mia
hy|po|thesis (pl.
 hy|po|theses)
hy|po|thes|ize
 (hy|po|thes|iz|
 ing)
hy|po|thet|ical
hy|po|thet|ic|ally
hyp|oxia
hyp|oxic
hyp|so|graphic
hyp|so|graph|ical
hyp|so|graphy
hyp|so|meter
hyp|so|met|ric
hyrax
hy|son
hys|sop
hys|ter|ec|tomy
 (pl. hys|ter|
 ec|tom|ies)
hys|ter|esis (pl.
 hys|ter|eses)
hys|teria
hys|teric
hys|ter|ical
hys|ter|ic|ally

I

iamb
iambic
iamb|ics
iam|bus (*pl.*
  iam|buses)
iat|ro|genic
Ibáñez
Iber|ian
ibex
ibid.
ib|idem (in the
  same place)
ibis
Ibiza
Ibo (*pl.* Ibos)
Ib|sen
ice (as *v.*, icing)
ice|berg
ice|box
ice-cap
ice-cream
ice-cube
Ice|land
Ice|lander
Ice|landic
ice-pack
ice-pick
Icha|bod
i ching
ich'neu|mon
ich'no|graphy
ichor
ich'or|ous
ich'thy|ographer
ich'thy|ography
ich'thy|oid
ich'thy|olatry
ich'thy|olite
ich'thy|olo'gical
ich'thy|olo'gist
ich'thy|ology
ich'thy|ophag'ous
ich'thy|ophagy
ich'thy|osaurus
  (*pl*. ich'thy|
    osauri)
ich'thy|osis (*pl.*
  ich'thy|oses)
ich'thy|otic

icicle
icily
ici|ness
icing
icon
iconic
icono|clasm
icono|clast
icono|clastic
icono|grapher
icono|graph'ical
icono|graphy (*pl.*
  icono|graph'ies)
icono|latry
icono|logy
icono|meter
icono|metry
icono|stasis (*pl.*
  icono|stases)
ico'sa|hed'ral
ico'sa|hed'ron (*pl.*
  ico'sa|hedra)
ico'si|do'de'ca|
              hed'ron
  (*pl.* ico'si|
    do'de'ca|hedra)
ic|teric
ic|terus
ic'tus
icy (icier, ici|est)
Idaho
idea
ideal
ideal|ism
ideal|ist
ideal|istic
ideal|ity
ideal|iza|tion
ideal|ize
  (ideal|iz|ing)
ideally
ideate (ideat|ing)
ideation
ideational
idée fixe
identic
ident|ical
ident'ic|ally
iden'ti|fi|able

iden'ti|fica|tion
identi|fy
  (iden'ti|fies,
  iden'ti|fied,
  iden'ti|fy|ing)
Iden'ti|kit (*propr.*)
iden|tity (*pl.*
  iden'tit|ies)
ideo|gram
ideo|graph
ideo|graphic
ideo|graph'ical
ideo|graphy
ideo|lo'gical
ideo|lo'gist
ideo|logue
ideo|logy (*pl.*
  ideo|lo'gies)
idi|ocy (*pl.*
  idi|ocies)
idio|lect
idiom
idio|matic
idio|mat'ic|ally
idio|pathic
idio|pathy (*pl.*
  idio|path'ies)
idio|syn'crasy (*pl.*
  idio|syn'cras|ies)
idio|syn'cratic
idiot
idi|otic
idi'ot'ic|ally
idle (as *v.*, id'ling;
  as *a.*, idler, idlest)
idler
idly
Ido
idol
id'ol|ater (*fem.*
  id'ol|at'ress)
id'ol|at'rous
id'ol|atry (*pl.*
  id'ol|at'ries)
id'ol|iza|tion
id'ol|ize
  (id'ol|iz|ing)
id'olum (*pl.* id'ola)
idyll

idyllic
idyll|ist
ig'loo
ig'ne|ous
ig'nit|able
ig'nite (ig'nit|ing)
ig'ni|tion
ig'nit|ron
ig|noble
ig|nobly
ig'no'mi'ni|ous
ig'no|miny (*pl.*
  ig'no|min|ies)
ig'nor|amus
ig'nor|ance
ig'nor|ant
ig'nore
  (ig'nor|ing)
iguana
igua'no|don
ik|ebana
Île de France
il'eal
il'eitis
il'eum (intestine;
  pl. ilea) △ ilium
il'eus
ilex
iliac
Iliad
Ili|amna
il'ium (bone; *pl.*
  ilia) △ ileum
il'la|tion
il'lat|ive
il'legal
il'leg'al|ity (*pl.*
  il'leg'al|it'ies)
il'leg|ally
il'legib|il'ity
il'legible
il'legibly
il'le'git|im'acy (*pl.*
  il'le'git|im|acies)
il'le'git|im|ate
il'le'git|ima|tion
il'le'git|im|ize
  (il'le'git|im|iz|
    ing)

ill-fated
il'lib|cral
il'lib'er|al|ity
il'li'ber|ally
il'li|cit
il'lim'it|ab'il'ity
il'lim'it|able
il'lim'it|ably
Il'li|nois
il'li'quid
il'liquid|ity
il'lit'er|acy
il'lit'er|ate
ill|ness
il|lo'gical
il'lo'gic|al|ity
il'lo'gic|ally
ill-timed
ill-treat
il'lu'min|ance
il'lu'min|ant
il'lu'min|ate
 (il'lu'min|at|ing)
il'lum|in|ati
il'lu'mina|tion
il'lu'min|at|ive
il'lu'min|ator
il'lu'min|ism
il'lu'min|ist
ill-use (as v.,
 ill-using)
il'lu|sion
il'lu|sional
il'lu'sion|ism
il'lu'sion|ist
il'lus|ive
il'lus|or'ily
il'lus|ori|ness
il'lus|ory
il'lus|trate
 (il'lus'trat|ing)
il'lus|tra'tion
il'lus|trat|ive
il'lus|trator
il'lus|tri|ous
Il'lyr|ian
il'men|ite
im'age (as v.,
 im'aging)
im'agery (pl.
 im'ager|ies)
ima'gin|able
ima'gin|ably
ima'ginal
ima'gin|ar'ily
ima'gin|ary

ima'gina|tion
ima'gin'at|ive
ima'gine
 (ima'gin|ing)
ima'gism
ima'gist
imago (insect, pl.
 ima'gines;
 mental picture, pl.
 ima'gos)
imam
im'am|ate
im'bal'ance
im'be'cile
im'be'cilic
im'be'cil|ity (pl.
 im'be'cil|it|ies)
imbed use embed
im'bibe
 (im'bib|ing)
im'bibi|tion
im'bric'ate (as v.,
 im'bric|at|ing)
im'brica|tion
im'bro|glio (pl.
 im'bro|glios)
im'brue
 (imbrued,
 im'bru|ing)
im'brute
 (im'brut|ing)
im'bue (im'bued,
 im'bu|ing)
im'ide
im'it|able
im'it|ate
 (im'it'at|ing)
im'ita|tion
im'it|at'ive
im'it|ator
im'macu'lacy
im'macu|late
im'man|ence
 (inherency)
△ imminence
im'man|ency
im'man'ent
 (inherent)
△ imminent
im'ma'ter|ial
im'ma'teri|al|ity
im'ma'ture
im'ma'tur|ity
im'meas'ur|ab'il|
 ity
im'meas'ur|able

im'meas'ur|ably
im'me'di|acy
im'me'di|ate
im'med'ic|able
im'med'ic|ably
im'me'mor|ial
im'me'mori|ally
im'mense
im'mens|ity (pl.
 im'mens|it|ies)
im'merse
 (im'mers|ing)
im'mer|sion
im'mig|rate
 (im'mig'rat|ing)
im'mig|rant
im'mig'ra|tion
im'mig'rat|ory
im'min|ence
 (impendency)
△ immanence
im'min|ent
 (impending)
△ immanent
im'mis'cib|il|ity
im'mis|cible
im'mis|cibly
im'mit'ig|able
im'mit'ig|ably
im'mix'ture
im'mob'ile
im'mob'il|ism
im'mob'il|ity
im'mob'il|iza|tion
im'mob'il|ize
 (im'mob'il|iz|ing)
im'mod'er|ate
im'mod'est
im'mod'esty
im'mol|ate
 (im'mol'at|ing)
im'mola|tion
im'moral
im'mor'al|ity
im'mor|ally
im'mor'tal
im'mor'tal|ity
im'mor'tal|ize
 (im'mor'tal|iz|
 ing)
im'mor'tally
im'mor'telle
im'mov'ab'il|ity
im'mov|able
im'mov|ably
im'mune

im'mun|ity
im'mun|iza|tion
im'mun|ize
 (im'mun|iz|ing)
im'muno|lo'gical
im'muno|lo'gist
im'muno|lo'gy
im'mure
 (im'mur|ing)
im'mure|ment
im'mut|ab'il|ity
im'mut|able
im'mut|ably
im'pact
im'pac'tion
im'pair
im'pair|ment
im'pala
im'pale
 (im'pal|ing)
im'palp|ab'il|ity
im'palp|able
im'palp|ably
im'pari|syl'labic
im'park
im'part
im'parta|tion
im'par'tial
im'par'ti|al'ity
im'par'ti|ally
im'part|ible
im'part|ment
im'pass|ab'il|ity
im'pass|able (not
 traversable)
△ impassible
im'pass|ably
im'passe
im'pass|ib'il|ity
im'pass|ible
 (impassive)
△ impassable
im'pass|ibly
im'pas|sion
im'pass|ive
im'pass|iv'ity
im'pasto (pl.
 im'pas|tos)
im'pa'tience
im'pa'tient
im'peach
im'peach|able
im'pec'cab'il|ity
im'pec|cable
im'pec|cably
im'pec|cancy

im¦pec¦cant
im¦pe¦cu¦ni¦ous
im¦ped¦ance
im¦pede
 (im¦ped¦ing)
im¦pedi¦ment
im¦pedi¦menta *n.*
 pl.
im¦pedi¦mental
im¦pel (im¦pelled,
 im¦pel¦ling)
im¦pel¦lent
im¦pel¦ler
im¦pend
im¦pend¦ence
im¦pend¦ency
im¦pend¦ent
im¦pend¦ing
im¦pen¦et¦rab¦
 il¦ity
im¦pen¦et¦rable
im¦pen¦et¦rably
im¦pen¦et¦rate
 (im¦pen¦et¦rat¦
 ing)
im¦pen¦it¦ence
im¦pen¦it¦ency
im¦pen¦it¦ent
im¦per¦at¦ival
im¦per¦at¦ive
im¦per¦ator
im¦per¦at¦or¦ial
im¦per¦cept¦ib¦il¦
 ity
im¦per¦cept¦ible
im¦per¦cept¦ibly
im¦per¦ci¦pi¦ence
im¦per¦ci¦pi¦ent
im¦per¦fect
im¦per¦fec¦tion
im¦per¦fect¦ive
im¦per¦for¦ate
im¦per¦ial
im¦peri¦al¦ism
im¦peri¦al¦ist
im¦peri¦al¦istic
im¦peri¦ally
im¦peril
 (im¦per¦illed,
 im¦per¦il¦ling)
im¦peri¦ous
im¦per¦ish¦able
im¦per¦ish¦ably
im¦per¦man¦ence
im¦per¦man¦ency
im¦per¦man¦ent

im¦per¦meab¦il¦ity
im¦per¦meable
im¦per¦miss¦ible
im¦per¦script¦ible
im¦per¦sonal
im¦per¦son¦al¦ity
im¦per¦son¦ally
im¦per¦son¦ate
 (im¦per¦son¦
 at¦ing)
im¦per¦sona¦tion
im¦per¦son¦ator
im¦per¦tin¦ence
im¦per¦tin¦ent
im¦per¦turb¦ab¦il¦
 ity
im¦per¦turb¦able
im¦per¦turb¦ably
im¦per¦vi¦ous
im¦pe¦tig¦in¦ous
im¦pe¦tigo (*pl.*
 im¦pe¦ti¦gos)
im¦pet¦rate
 (im¦pet¦rat¦ing)
im¦petra¦tion
im¦pet¦rat¦ory
im¦petu¦os¦ity
im¦petu¦ous
im¦petus
im¦pi¦ety (*pl.*
 im¦pi¦eties)
im¦pinge
 (im¦pin¦ging)
im¦pi¦ous
imp¦ish
im¦plac¦ab¦il¦ity
im¦plac¦able
im¦plac¦ably
im¦plant
im¦planta¦tion
im¦plaus¦ib¦il¦ity
im¦plaus¦ible
im¦plaus¦ibly
im¦plead
im¦ple¦ment
im¦ple¦menta¦tion
im¦plic¦ate
 (im¦plic¦at¦ing)
im¦plica¦tion
im¦plic¦at¦ive
im¦pli¦cit
im¦plode
 (im¦plod¦ing)
im¦plore
 (im¦plor¦ing)
im¦plo¦sion

im¦plos¦ive
im¦ply (im¦plies,
 im¦plied,
 im¦ply¦ing)
im¦pol¦der
im¦pol¦icy (*pl.*
 im¦poli¦cies)
im¦pol¦ite
 (im¦pol¦itest)
im¦pol¦itic
im¦pol¦it¦icly
im¦pon¦der¦able
im¦pon¦ent
im¦port
im¦port¦able
im¦port¦ance
im¦port¦ant
im¦porta¦tion
im¦porter
im¦por¦tun¦ate
im¦por¦tune
 (im¦por¦tun¦ing)
im¦por¦tun¦ity (*pl.*
 im¦por¦tun¦it¦ies)
im¦pose
 (im¦pos¦ing)
im¦posi¦tion
im¦poss¦ib¦il¦ity
 (*pl.* im¦poss¦ib¦il¦
 it¦ies)
im¦poss¦ible
im¦poss¦ibly
im¦post
im¦postor
im¦pos¦ture
im¦pot¦ence
im¦pot¦ency
im¦pot¦ent
im¦pound
im¦pov¦er¦ish
im¦pov¦er¦ish¦
 ment
im¦prac¦tic¦ab¦il¦
 ity
im¦prac¦tic¦able
im¦prac¦tic¦ably
impractical etc.
 use unpractical
 etc.
im¦prec¦ate
 (im¦prec¦at¦ing)
im¦preca¦tion
im¦prec¦at¦ory
im¦pre¦cise
im¦pre¦ci¦sion
im¦preg¦nab¦il¦ity

im¦preg¦nable
im¦preg¦nably
im¦preg¦nat¦able
im¦preg¦nate
 (im¦preg¦nat¦ing)
im¦preg¦na¦tion
im¦pres¦ario (*pl.*
 im¦pres¦arios)
im¦pre¦script¦ible
im¦press
im¦press¦ible
im¦pres¦sion
im¦pres¦sion¦able
im¦pres¦sion¦ism
im¦pres¦sion¦ist
im¦pres¦sion¦istic
im¦press¦ive
im¦prest
im¦prim¦atur
im¦prim¦at¦ura
 (coloured glaze)
im¦print
im¦prison
im¦pris¦on¦ment
im¦prob¦ab¦il¦ity
im¦prob¦able
im¦prob¦ably
im¦prob¦ity
im¦promptu
im¦proper
im¦pro¦pri¦ate
 (im¦pro¦pri¦
 at¦ing)
im¦pro¦pri¦ation
im¦pro¦pri¦ety (*pl.*
 im¦pro¦pri¦et¦ies)
im¦prov¦ab¦il¦ity
im¦prov¦able
im¦prove
 (im¦prov¦ing)
im¦prove¦ment
im¦prov¦id¦ence
im¦prov¦id¦ent
im¦pro¦visa¦tion
im¦pro¦vis¦at¦ory
im¦pro¦vise
 (im¦pro¦vising)
im¦pru¦dence
im¦pru¦dent
im¦pud¦ence
im¦pud¦ent
im¦pudi¦city
im¦pugn
im¦pu¦is¦sance
im¦pu¦is¦sant
im¦pulse

im|pul|sion
im|puls|ive
im|pun|ity (*pl.*
 im|pun|it|ies)
im|pure
im|pur|ity (*pl.*
 im|pur|it|ies)
im|put|able
im|puta|tion
im|put|at|ive
im|pute
 (im|put|ing)
in|ab|il|ity (*pl.*
 in|ab|il|it|ies)
in ab|sen|tia
in|ac|cess|ib|il|ity
in|ac|cess|ible
in|ac|cess|ibly
in|ac|cur|acy (*pl.*
 in|ac|cur|acies)
in|ac|cur|ate
in|ac|tion
in|ac|tiv|ate
 (in|ac|tiv|at|ing)
in|ac|tiva|tion
in|act|ive
in|ac|tiv|ity
in|ad|equacy (*pl.*
 in|ad|equa|cies)
in|ad|equate
in|ad|miss|ib|il|ity
in|ad|miss|ible
in|ad|miss|ibly
in|ad|vert|ence
in|ad|vert|ency
in|ad|vert|ent
in|ad|vis|able
in|ali|en|ab|il|ity
in|ali|en|able
in|ali|en|ably
in|al|ter|ab|il|ity
in|al|ter|able
in|al|ter|ably
in|am|or|ato (*pl.*
 in|am|or|atos;
 fem. in|am|or|ata,
 pl. in|am|or|atas)
in|ane
in|anga
in|an|im|ate
in|an|ima|tion
in|ani|tion
in|an|ity (*pl.*
 in|an|it|ies)
in|ap|pell|able
in|ap|pet|ence

in|ap|pet|ency
in|ap|pet|ent
in|ap|plic|ab|il|ity
in|ap|plic|able
in|ap|plic|ably
in|ap|pos|ite
in|ap|pre|ciable
in|ap|pre|ciably
in|ap|pre|ci|ation
in|ap|pre|ci|at|ive
in|ap|pre|hens|
 ible
in|ap|pro|pri|ate
in|apt
in|ap|ti|tude
in|arch
in|ar|ticu|late
in|ar|tistic
in|ar|tist|ic|ally
in|as|much
in|at|ten|tion
in|at|tent|ive
in|aud|ib|il|ity
in|aud|ible
in|aud|ibly
in|aug|ural
in|aug|ur|ate
 (in|aug|ur|at|ing)
in|aug|ura|tion
in|aug|ur|ator
in|aug|ur|at|ory
in|aus|pi|cious
in|board
in|born
in|breathe
 (in|breath|ing)
in|breed (in|bred)
in|breed|ing
in-built
Inca
In|caic
in|cal|cul|ab|il|ity
in|cal|cul|able
in|cal|cul|ably
Incan
in|can|desce
 (in|can|des|cing)
in|can|des|cence
in|can|des|cent
in|canta|tion
in|cap|ab|il|ity (*pl.*
 in|cap|ab|il|it|ies)
in|cap|able
in|cap|ably
in|ca|pa|cit|ant

in|ca|pa|cit|ate
 (in|ca|pa|cit|
 at|ing)
in|ca|pa|cita|tion
in|ca|pa|city
in|car|cer|ate
 (in|car|cer|
 at|ing)
in|car|cera|tion
in|car|cer|ator
in|carn|ate
 (in|carn|at|ing)
in|carna|tion
in|cau|tious
in|cen|di|ar|ism
in|cen|di|ary (*pl.*
 in|cen|di|ar|ies)
in|censa|tion
in|cense (as *v.*,
 in|cens|ing)
in|cens|ory (*pl.*
 in|cens|or|ies)
in|cent|ive
in|cept
in|cep|tion
in|cept|ive
in|ceptor
in|cer|ti|tude
in|cess|ancy
in|cess|ant
in|cest
in|ces|tu|ous
in|cho|ate (as *v.*,
 in|cho|at|ing)
in|cho|ation
in|cho|at|ive
in|cid|ence
in|cid|ent
in|cid|ental
in|cid|ent|ally
in|cin|er|ate
 (in|cin|er|at|ing)
in|cin|era|tion
in|cin|er|ator
in|cipi|ence
in|cipi|ency
in|cipi|ent
in|cipit
in|cise (in|cis|ing)
in|cision
in|cis|ive
in|cisor
in|cita|tion
in|cite (in|cit|ing)
in|cite|ment

in|ci|vil|ity (*pl.*
 in|ci|vil|it|ies)
in|civ|ism
in|clem|ency (*pl.*
 in|clem|en|cies)
in|clem|ent
in|clin|able
in|clina|tion
in|cline (as *v.*,
 in|clin|ing)
in|clino|meter
in|clude
 (in|clud|ing)
in|clu|sion
in|clus|ive
in|cog|nito (*pl.*
 in|cog|ni|tos)
in|cog|niz|ance
in|cog|niz|ant
in|co|her|ence
in|co|her|ency
in|co|her|ent
in|com|bust|ib|il|
 ity
in|com|bust|ible
in|come
in|com|ing
in|com|men|sur|
 ab|il|ity
in|com|men|sur|
 able
in|com|men|sur|
 ably
in|com|men|sur|
 ate
in|com|mode
 (in|com|mod|ing)
in|com|mo|di|ous
in|com|mu|nic|
 able
in|com|mu|nic|
 ably
in|com|mu|nic|
 ado
in|com|mu|nic|at|
 ive
in|com|mut|able
in|com|mut|ably
in|com|par|able
in|com|par|ably
in|com|pat|ib|il|
 ity
in|com|patible
in|com|pat|ibly
in|com|pet|ence
in|com|pet|ency

in|com|pet|ent
in|com|plete
in|com|pre|
    hens|ib|il|ity
in|com|pre|hens|
      ible
in|com|pre|hens|
      ibly
in|com|pre|hen|
    sion
in|com|press|ib|il|
    ity
in|com|press|ible
in|con|ceiv|ab|il|
    ity
in|con|ceiv|able
in|con|ceiv|ably
in|con|clus|ive
in|con|dens|able
in|con|dite
in|con|gru|ity (pl.
 in|con|gru|it|ies)
in|con|gru|ous
in|con|sequence
in|con|sequent
in|con|sequen|tial
in|con|sequen|
      tially
in|con|sid|er|able
in|con|sid|er|ate
in|con|sid|era|
    tion
in|con|sist|ency
 (pl. in|con|sist|
    en|cies)
in|con|sist|ent
in|con|sol|able
in|con|sol|ably
in|con|son|ance
in|con|son|ant
in|con|spicu|ous
in|con|stancy (pl.
 in|con|stan|cies)
in|con|stant
in|con|test|able
in|con|test|ably
in|con|tin|ence
in|con|tin|ent
in|con|tro|vert|
    ible
in|con|tro|vert|
    ibly
in|con|veni|ence
(as v.,
 in|con|veni|
    en|cing)

in|con|veni|ent
in|con|vert|ib|il|
    ity
in|con|vert|ible
in|con|vert|ibly
in|co|ord|ina|tion
in|corp|or|ate
 (in|corp|or|
    at|ing)
in|corp|ora|tion
in|corp|or|ator
in|cor|por|eal
in|cor|por|eal|ity
in|cor|por|eally
in|cor|por|eity
in|cor|rect
in|corri|gib|il|ity
in|cor|ri|gible
in|cor|ri|gibly
in|cor|rupt|ib|il|
    ity
in|cor|rupt|ible
in|cor|rupt|ibly
in|cor|rup|tion
in|crass|ate
in|crease (as v.,
 in|creas|ing)
in|cred|ib|il|ity
in|cred|ible
in|cred|ibly
in|credu|lity
in|credu|lous
in|cre|ment
in|crim|in|ate
 (in|crim|in|
    at|ing)
in|crim|ina|tion
in|crim|in|at|ory
in|crusta|tion
in|cub|ate
 (in|cub|at|ing)
in|cuba|tion
in|cub|at|ive
in|cub|ator
in|cub|at|ory
in|cubus (pl.
 in|cubi)
in|cul|cate
 (in|cul|cat|ing)
in|cul|ca|tion
in|cul|cator
in|culp|ate
 (in|culp|at|ing)
in|culpa|tion
in|culp|at|ive
in|culp|at|ory

in|cult
in|cum|bency (pl.
 in|cum|ben|cies)
in|cum|bent
in|cun|able
in|cun|ab|ulum
 (pl.
 in|cun|ab|ula)
incur (in|curred,
 in|cur|ring)
in|cur|ab|il|ity
in|cur|able (not
 curable)
△ incurrable
in|cur|ably
in|curi|os|ity
in|curi|ous
in|cur|rable (able
 to happen)
△ incurable
in|cur|sion
in|curs|ive
in|curva|tion
in|curve
 (in|curv|ing)
in|cus (pl.
 in|cu|des)
in|cuse (as v.,
 in|cus|ing)
in|debted
in|de|cency (pl.
 in|de|cen|cies)
in|de|cent
in|de|ci|pher|able
in|de|ci|sion
in|de|cis|ive
in|dec|lin|able
in|dec|or|ous
in|dec|orum
in|deed
in|de|fat|ig|able
in|de|fat|ig|ably
in|de|feas|ib|il|ity
in|de|feas|ible
in|de|feas|ibly
in|de|fect|ible
in|de|fens|ib|il|ity
in|de|fens|ible
in|de|fens|ibly
in|de|fin|able
in|de|fin|ably
in|def|in|ite
in|de|his|cent
in|del|ib|il|ity
in|del|ible
in|del|ibly

in|del|ic|acy (pl.
 in|del|ic|acies)
in|del|ic|ate
in|dem|ni|fica|
    tion
in|dem|nify
 (in|dem|ni|fies,
 in|dem|ni|fied,
 in|dem|ni|fy|ing)
in|dem|nity (pl.
 in|dem|nit|ies)
in|dem|on|strable
in|dent
in|denta|tion
in|den|tion
in|dentor
in|den|ture (as v.,
 in|den|tur|ing)
in|de|pend|ence
in|de|pend|ency
 (pl. in|de|pend|
    en|cies)
in|de|pend|ent
in|des|crib|able
in|des|crib|ably
in|des|truct|ib|il|
    ity
in|des|truct|ible
in|des|truct|ibly
in|de|term|in|able
in|de|term|in|acy
in|de|term|in|ate
in|de|term|ina|
    tion
in|de|term|in|ism
in|de|term|in|ist
in|de|term|in|istic
in|dex (pl.
 in|dexes, Sci.
 in|di|ces)
in|dexa|tion
in|dex|ical
index-linked
In|dia
In|dia|man (pl.
 In|dia|men)
In|dian
In|di|ana
Indic
in|dic|ate
 (in|dic|at|ing)
in|dica|tion
in|dic|at|ive
in|dic|ator
in|dic|at|ory

in|di|cium (*pl.*
 in|di|cia)
in|dict
in|dict|able
in|dic|tion
in|dict|ment
Ind|ies
in|dif|fer|ence
in|dif|fer|ent
in|di|gence
in|di|gen|ous
in|di|gent
in|di|ges|ted
in|di|gest|ib|il|ity
in|di|gest|ible
in|di|ges|tion
in|di|gest|ive
in|dig|nant
in|dig|na|tion
in|dig|nity (*pl.*
 in|dig|nit|ies)
in|digo (*pl.*
 in|di|gos)
in|dir|ect
in|dir|ec|tion
in|dis|cern|ible
in|dis|cern|ibly
in|dis|cip|line
in|dis|creet
 (unwary)
in|dis|crete (not
 divided)
in|dis|cre|tion
in|dis|crim|in|ate
in|dis|crim|ina|
 tion
in|dis|crim|in|
 at|ive
in|dis|pens|ab|il|
 ity
in|dis|pens|able
in|dis|pens|ably
in|dis|pose
 (in|dis|pos|ing)
in|dis|posi|tion
in|dis|put|ab|il|ity
in|dis|put|able
in|dis|put|ably
in|dis|sol|ub|il|ity
in|dis|sol|uble
in|dis|sol|ubly
in|dis|tinct
in|dis|tinct|ive
in|dis|tin|guish|
 able

in|dis|tin|guish|
 ably
in|dite (in|dit|ing)
in|dium
in|di|vert|ible
in|di|vert|ibly
in|di|vidual
in|di|vidu|al|ism
in|di|vidu|al|ist
in|di|vidu|al|istic
in|di|vidu|al|ity
in|di|vidu|al|iza|
 tion
in|di|vidu|al|ize
 (in|di|vidu|al|iz|
 ing)
in|di|vidu|ally
in|di|vidu|ate
 (in|di|vidu|
 at|ing)
in|di|vidu|ation
in|di|vis|ib|il|ity
in|di|vis|ible
in|di|vis|ibly
Indo-Aryan
Indo-Chinese
in|do|cile
in|do|cil|ity
in|doc|trin|ate
 (in|doc|trin|
 at|ing)
in|doc|trina|tion
Indo-European
in|dole
in|dol|ence
in|dol|ent
In|do|logy
In|do|lo|gist
in|dom|it|able
in|dom|it|ably
In|do|nesia
In|do|ne|sian
in|door *a.*
in|doors *adv.*
indorse etc. *use*
 endorse etc.
in|draught
in|drawn
in|dri
in|dub|it|able
in|dub|it|ably
in|duce
 (in|du|cing)
in|duce|ment
in|du|cible
in|duct

in|duct|ance
in|ductee
in|duc|tion
in|duct|ive
in|ductor
in|dulge
 (in|dul|ging)
in|dul|gence
in|dul|genced
in|dul|gent
in|dult
in|duna
in|dur|ate
 (in|dur|ating)
in|dura|tion
in|dur|at|ive
In|dus
in|du|sial
in|du|sium (*pl.*
 in|du|sia)
in|dus|trial
in|dus|tri|al|ism
in|dus|tri|al|ist
in|dus|tri|al|iza|
 tion
in|dus|tri|al|ize
 (in|dus|tri|al|iz|
 ing)
in|dus|tri|ally
in|dus|tri|ous
in|dus|try (*pl.*
 in|dus|tries)
in|dwell
 (in|dwelt)
in|ebri|ate (as *v.*,
 in|ebri|at|ing)
in|ebri|ation
in|ebri|ety
in|ed|ib|il|ity
in|ed|ible
in|ed|ited
in|ed|uc|ab|il|ity
in|ed|uc|able
in|ef|fable
in|ef|fably
in|ef|face|ab|il|ity
in|ef|face|able
in|ef|face|ably
in|ef|fect|ive
in|ef|fec|tual
in|ef|fec|tu|ally
in|ef|fica|cious
in|ef|fic|acy
in|ef|fi|ci|ency
in|ef|fi|cient
in|el|astic

in|el|ast|ic|ally
in|el|as|ti|city
in|el|eg|ance
in|el|eg|ant
in|el|igib|il|ity
in|el|igible
in|eluct|able
in|eluct|ably
in|ept
in|ept|it|ude
in|equable
in|equal|ity (*pl.*
 in|equal|it|ies)
in|equit|able
in|equit|ably
in|equity (*pl.*
 in|equit|ies)
in|erad|ic|able
in|erad|ic|ably
in|err|ab|il|ity
in|err|able
in|err|ably
in|err|ancy
in|err|ant
in|ert
in|er|tia
in|er|tial
in|es|cap|able
in|es|cap|ably
in|es|cut|cheon
in|es|sen|tial
in|es|tim|able
in|es|tim|ably
in|ev|it|ab|il|ity
in|ev|it|able
in|ev|it|ably
in|ex|act
in|ex|act|it|ude
in|ex|cus|able
in|ex|cus|ably
in|ex|haust|
 ib|il|ity
in|ex|haust|ible
in|ex|haust|ibly
in|ex|or|ab|il|ity
in|ex|or|able
in|ex|or|ably
in|ex|pedi|ency
in|ex|pedi|ent
in|ex|pens|ive
in|ex|peri|ence
in|ex|peri|enced
in|ex|pert
in|ex|pi|able
in|ex|pi|ably
in|ex|plic|ab|il|ity

in|ex|plic|able
in|ex|plic|ably
in|ex|pli|cit
in|ex|press|ible
in|ex|press|ibly
in|ex|press|ive
in|ex|pug|nable
  (impregnable)
in|ex|pun|gible
  (indestructible)
in|ex|tin|guish|
          able
in ex|tremis
in|ex|tric|able
in|ex|tric|ably
in|fal|lib|il|ity
in|fal|lible
in|fal|libly
in|fam|ous
in|famy (*pl.*
  in|fam|ies)
in|fancy
in|fant
in|fanta
in|fanti|cidal
in|fanti|cide
in|fant|ile
in|fant|il|ism
in|fant|ine
in|fan|try (*pl.*
  in|fan|tries)
in|farct
in|farc|tion
in|fatu|ate
  (in|fatu|at|ing)
in|fatu|ation
in|fauna
in|fect
in|fec|tion
in|fec|tious
in|fect|ive
in|fe|li|cit|ous
in|fe|li|city
in|fer (in|fer|ring)
in|fer|able
in|fer|ence
in|fer|en|tial
in|ferior
in|feri|or|ity
in|fernal
in|fern|ally
in|ferno (*pl.*
  in|fer|nos)
in|fer|tile
in|fer|til|ity
in|fest

in|festa|tion
in|fibu|la|tion
in|fi|del
in|fi|del|ity (*pl.*
  in|fi|del|it|ies)
in|field
in|fight|ing
in|fill
in|filt|rate
  (in|filt|rat|ing)
in|filt|rator
in|fin|ite
in|fin|it|es|imal
in|fin|it|es|im|ally
in|fin|it|ival
in|fin|it|ive
in|fin|it|ude
in|fin|ity
in|firm
in|firm|ary (*pl.*
  in|firm|ar|ies)
in|firm|ity (*pl.*
  in|firm|it|ies)
in|fix
in|fixa|tion
in flag|rante
  de|licto
in|flame
  (in|flam|ing)
in|flam|mab|il|ity
in|flam|mable
in|flam|ma|tion
in|flam|mat|ory
in|flat|able
in|flate
  (in|flat|ing)
in|fla|tion
in|fla|tion|ary
in|flect
in|flect|ive
in|flex|ib|il|ity
in|flex|ible
in|flex|ibly
in|flex|ion
in|flex|ional
in|flict
in|flic|tion
in|flor|es|cence
in|flow
in|flu|ence (as *v.,*
  in|flu|en|cing)
in|flu|ent
in|flu|en|tial
in|flu|en|tially
in|flu|enza
in|flux

in|form
in|formal
in|form|al|ity
in|form|ally
in|form|ant
in|forma|tion
in|forma|tional
in|form|at|ive
in|form|at|ory
in|formed
in|former
infra (below)
in|frac|tion
in fra dig.
in|fra|laps|ar|ian
in|fran|gible
infra-red
in|fra|renal
in|fra|sonic
in|fra|son|ic|ally
in|fra|struc|ture
in|fre|quency
in|fre|quent
in|fringe
  (in|frin|ging)
in|fringe|ment
in|fruct|es|cence
in|fula (*pl.*
  in|fu|lae)
in|fund|ibu|lar
in|furi|ate
  (in|furi|at|ing)
in|fus|able (able to
  undergo infusion)
in|fuse
  (in|fus|ing)
in|fus|ib|il|ity
in|fus|ible (not
  fusible or
  meltable)
in|fu|sion
in|gather
in|gem|in|ate
  (in|gem|in|at|ing)
Ingen|housz
in|geni|ous
in génue
in|genu|ity
in|genu|ous
in|gest
in|ges|tion
in|gest|ive
ingle-nook
in|glori|ous
in|go|ing
in|got

ingraft *use*
  engraft
in|grain
in|grained
in|gra|ti|ate
  (in|gra|ti|at|ing)
in|grat|it|ude
in|grav|es|cence
in|grav|es|cent
in|gre|di|ent
In|gres
in|gress
in|grow|ing
in|grown
in|growth
in|guinal
in|gur|git|ate
  (in|gur|git|at|ing)
in|gur|gita|tion
in|habit
  (in|hab|ited,
  in|hab|it|ing)
in|hab|it|able
in|hab|it|ancy
in|hab|it|ant
in|hab|ita|tion
in|hal|ant
in|hala|tion
in|hale
  (in|hal|ing)
in|haler
in|har|monic
in|har|mo|ni|ous
in|here
  (in|her|ing)
in|her|ence
in|her|ent
in|herit
  (in|her|ited,
  in|her|it|ing)
in|her|it|ab|il|ity
in|her|it|able
in|her|it|ance
in|her|itor
in|her|it|ress
in|her|it|rix (*pl.*
  in|her|it|ri|ces)
in|he|sion
in|hibit
  (in|hib|ited,
  in|hib|it|ing)
in|hibi|tion
in|hib|itor
in|hib|it|ory
in|homo|gen|eity
in|homo|gen|eous

in|hos|pit|able
in|hos|pit|ably
in|hos|pit|al|ity
in-house
in|hu|man
in|hu|mane
in|hu|man|ity
in|im|ical
in|imic|ally
in|im|it|able
in|im|it|ably
ini|quit|ous
ini|quity (*pl.*
 ini|quit|ies)
ini|tial (as *v.*,
 ini|tialled,
 ini|tial|ling)
ini|tially
ini|ti|ate (as *v.*,
 ini|ti|at|ing)
ini|ti|ation
ini|ti|at|ive
ini|ti|ator
ini|ti|at|ory
in|ject
in|jec|tion
in|jector
in|ju|di|cious
In|jun
in|junct
in|junc|tion
in|jure (in|jur|ing)
in|juria (*Law*)
in|juri|ous
in|jury (*pl.*
 in|jur|ies)
in|just|ice
ink|ling
ink|stand
ink-well
inky (ink|ier,
 inki|est)
in|land
in-law
in|lay (as *v.*,
 in|laid,
 in|lay|ing)
in|let
in|lier
in loco par|entis
in|ly|ing
in|mate
in me|moriam
in|most
inn|ards
in|nate

in|ner
in|ner|most
in|nerv|ate
 (in|nerv|at|ing)
in|nerva|tion
in|nings (*pl.* same)
inn|keeper
in|no|cence
in|no|cency
in|no|cent
in|nocu|ity
in|nocu|ous
in|nom|in|ate
in|nov|ate
 (in|nov|at|ing)
in|nova|tion
in|nov|at|ive
in|nov|ator
in|nov|at|ory
in|nox|ious
Inns|bruck
in|nu|endo (as *n.*,
 pl. in|nu|en|does;
 as *v.*,
 in|nu|en|doed,
 in|nu|en|do|ing)
In|nuit
in|nu|mer|able
in|nu|mer|ably
in|nu|mer|acy
in|nu|mer|ate
in|nu|tri|tion
in|nu|tri|tious
in|ob|serv|ance
in|ocul|able
in|ocu|late
 (in|ocu|lat|ing)
in|ocu|la|tion
in|ocul|at|ive
in|oculum (*pl.*
 in|ocula)
in|odor|ous
in|of|fens|ive
in|of|fi|cious
in|op|er|able
in|op|er|at|ive
in|op|por|tune
in|or|din|ate
in|or|ganic
in|os|cu|late
 (in|os|cu|lat|ing)
in|os|cu|la|tion
in pro|pria
 per|sona

in|put (as *v.*, in|put
 or in|put|ted,
 in|put|ting)
in|quest
in|qui|et|ude
in|quil|ine
in|quire (in formal
 senses;
 in|quir|ing) See
 also enquire
in|quiry (formal
 investigation; *pl.*
 in|quir|ies) See
 also enquiry
in|quisi|tion
in|quisi|tional
in|quis|it|ive
in|quis|itor
in|quis|it|or|ial
in|quis|it|ori|ally
in|quor|ate
in|road
in|rush
in|sa|lu|bri|ous
in|sa|lu|brity
in|sane
in|san|it|ary
in|san|ity
in|sa|ti|ab|il|ity
in|sa|ti|able
in|sa|ti|ably
in|sa|ti|ate
in|scape
in|scrib|able
in|scribe
 (in|scrib|ing)
in|scrip|tion
in|scrip|tional
in|script|ive
in|scrut|ab|il|ity
in|scrut|able
in|scrut|ably
in|sect
in|sect|ar|ium
in|sect|ary (*pl.*
 in|sect|ar|ies)
in|sect|icidal
in|sect|icide
in|sect|ivore
in|secti|vor|ous
in|secto|logy
in|sec|ure
in|sec|ur|ity (*pl.*
 in|sec|ur|it|ies)
in|sem|in|ate
 (in|sem|in|at|ing)

in|sem|ina|tion
in|sens|ate
in|sens|ib|il|ity
in|sens|ible
in|sens|ibly
in|sens|it|ive
in|sens|it|iv|ity
in|sen|tient
in|sep|ar|ab|il|ity
in|sep|ar|able
in|sep|ar|ably
in|sert
in|ser|tion
in|set (as *v.*, in|set
 or in|set|ted,
 in|set|ting)
in|shal|lah
in|shore
in|side
in|sider
in|si|di|ous
in|sight
in|sight|ful
in|sig|nia *n. pl.*
in|sig|ni|fic|ance
in|sig|ni|fic|ancy
in|sig|ni|fic|ant
in|sin|cere
in|sin|cerely
in|sin|cer|ity (*pl.*
 in|sin|cer|it|ies)
in|sinu|ate
 (in|sinu|at|ing)
in|sinu|ation
in|sinu|at|ive
in|sipid
in|sip|id|ity
in|sist
in|sist|ence
in|sist|ency
in|sist|ent
in situ
in|sob|ri|ety
in|so|far
in|sola|tion
 (exposure to sun)
 △ insulation
in|sole
in|sol|ence
in|sol|ent
in|solu|bil|ity
in|sol|uble
in|sol|ubly
in|solv|ency
in|solv|ent
in|som|nia

in'som|niac
in'so|much
in'sou|ci'ance
in'sou|ci'ant
in'span
 (in|spanned,
 in'span|ning)
in'spect
 (in'spec'ted,
 in'spect|ing)
in'spec'tion
in'spector
in'spect'or|ate
in'spect'or|ial
in'spira|tion
in'spira'tional
in'spira'tion|ism
in'spira'tion|ist
in'spir'ator
in'spir'at'ory
in'spire
 (in'spir'ing)
in'spirit
in'stab'il|ity
in'stall
in'stall|ant
in'stalla'tion
in'stal|ment
in'stance (as v.,
 in'stan|cing)
in'stancy
in'stant
in'stant|an'eous
in'star
in'state
 (in'stat'ing)
in'staura'tion
in'stead
in'step
in'stig|ate
 (in'stig|at'ing)
in'sti'ga|tion
in'stig|ator
in'stil (in'stilled,
 in'still|ing)
in'stilla'tion
in'stil|ment
in'stinct
in'stinc|tive
in'stinct|ual
in'sti|tute (as v.,
 in'sti|tut'ing)
in'sti'tu|tion
in'sti'tu|tional
in'sti'tu|tion'al|
  ism

in'sti'tu'tion'al|ize
 (in'sti'tu|tion'al|
  iz|ing)
in'struct
in'struc'tion
in'struc'tional
in'struc|tive
in'structor
in'struct'ress
in'stru|ment
in'stru'mental
in'stru'ment'al|ist
in'stru'ment'al|ity
in'stru'ment'ally
in'stru'menta|
  tion
in'sub'or|din'ate
in'sub'or'dina|
  tion
in'sub'stan|tial
in'sub'stan'ti|
  al|ity
in'suf'fer|able
in'suf'fer|ably
in'suf'fi|ciency
in'suf'fi|cient
in'suf'flate
 (in'suf'flat'ing)
in'suf'fla|tion
in'suf'flator
in'sular
in'su'lar|ism
in'su'lar|ity
in'su|late
 (in'su|lat'ing)
in'su'la|tion
in'su|lator
in'su'lin
in'sult
in'su'per|ab'il|ity
in'su'per|able
in'su'per|ably
in'sup'port|able
in'sup'port|ably
in'sur|able
in'sur|ance
in'sur|ant
in'sure (of
 insurance;
 in'sur|ing)
△ ensure
in'surer
in'sur'gency (pl.
 in'sur'gen|cies)
in'sur|gent
in'sur'mount|able

in'sur'mount|ably
in'sur'rec|tion
in'sur'rec'tional
in'sur'rec'tion|
  ary
in'sur'rec'tion|ist
in'sus'cept|ib'il|
  ity
in'sus'cept|ible
in'tact
in'tagli|ated
in'taglio (as n., pl.
 in'taglios)
in'take
in'tan'gib|il|ity
in'tan|gible
in'tan|gibly
in'tar|sia
in'te'ger
in'teg'ral
in'teg'ral|ity
in'teg'rally
in'teg'rand
in'teg'rant
in'teg'rate
 (in'teg'rat'ing)
in'teg'ra|tion
in'teg'rat|ive
in'teg'rator
in'teg'rity
in'tegu|ment
in'tegu|mental
in'tegu|ment'ary
in'tel|lect
in'tel'lec'tion
in'tel'lect|ive
in'tel'lec'tual
in'tel'lec'tu'al|ism
in'tel'lec'tu'al|ist
in'tel'lec'tu'al|ity
in'tel'lec'tu'al|ize
 (in'tel'lec'tu'al|iz|
  ing)
in'tel'lec'tu'ally
in'tel'li|gence
in'tel'li|gent
in'tel'li|gent'sia
in'tel'li|gib'il|ity
in'tel'li|gible
in'tel'li|gibly
in'tem'per|ance
in'tem'per|ate
in'tend
in'tend|ancy
in'tend|ant
in'ten'ded

in'tend|ment
in'tense
 (in'tenser,
 in'tens|est)
in'tensi|fica'tion
in'tensi|fier
in'tens|ify
 (in'tensi|fies,
 in'tensi|fied,
 in'tensi|fy'ing)
in'ten|sion
 (intensity)
in'ten|sional
in'tens|ity (pl.
 in'tens|it|ies)
in'tens|ive
in'tent
in'ten|tion
in'ten|tional
in'ten|tion|ally
in'ter (in'terred,
 in'ter|ring)
in'ter|act
in'ter'act|ant
in'ter'ac'tion
in'ter'act|ive
inter alia
in'ter|blend
in'ter|breed
 (in'ter|bred)
in'ter'cal'ary
in'ter'cal|ate
 (in'ter'cal'at|ing)
in'ter'cala|tion
in'ter|cede
 (in'ter|ced'ing)
in'ter|cept
in'ter'cep'tion
in'ter'cept|ive
in'ter|ceptor
in'ter'ces|sion
in'ter|cessor
in'ter'cess'or|ial
in'ter'cess'ory
in'ter|change
 (as v., in'ter|
  chan'ging)
in'ter|change|
  ab'il|ity
in'ter|change|
  able
in'ter|change|
  ably
inter-city
in'ter'col'le'gi'ate
in'ter|com

in¦ter¦
   com¦mun¦ic¦ate
  (in¦ter¦com¦mun¦
      ic¦at¦ing)
in¦ter¦com¦mun¦
     ica¦tion
in¦ter¦
   com¦mu¦nion
in¦ter¦
   com¦mun¦ity
in¦ter¦con¦nect
in¦ter¦
   con¦nec¦tion
in¦ter¦con¦tin¦
      ental
in¦ter¦con¦vert¦
      ible
in¦ter¦costal
in¦ter¦course
in¦ter¦cross
in¦ter¦crural
in¦ter¦cur¦rence
in¦ter¦cur¦rent
in¦ter¦cut
  (in¦ter¦cut,
  in¦ter¦cut¦ting)
in¦ter¦de¦nom¦ina¦
     tional
in¦ter¦de¦part¦
     mental
in¦ter¦de¦pend
in¦ter¦
   de¦pend¦ence
in¦ter¦
   de¦pend¦ency
  (*pl.* in¦ter¦
  de¦pend¦en¦cies)
in¦ter¦de¦pend¦ent
in¦ter¦dict
in¦ter¦dic¦tion
in¦ter¦dict¦ory
in¦ter¦di¦gital
in¦ter¦dis¦cip¦lin¦
     ary
in¦ter¦est
in¦ter¦es¦ted
in¦ter¦est¦ing
in¦ter¦face
  (in¦ter¦fa¦cing)
in¦ter¦fa¦cial
in¦ter¦fe¦moral
in¦ter¦fere
  (in¦ter¦fer¦ing)
in¦ter¦fer¦ence
in¦ter¦fer¦en¦tial
in¦ter¦fero¦meter

in¦ter¦fero¦met¦ric
in¦ter¦fero¦metry
in¦ter¦feron
in¦ter¦fib¦ril¦lar
in¦ter¦flow
in¦ter¦flu¦ent
in¦ter¦fuse
  (in¦ter¦fus¦ing)
in¦ter¦fu¦sion
in¦ter¦gal¦actic
in¦ter¦gla¦cial
in¦ter¦gov¦ern¦
     mental
in¦terim
in¦ter¦ior
in¦teri¦or¦ize
  (in¦teri¦or¦iz¦ing)
in¦ter¦ject
in¦ter¦jec¦tion
in¦ter¦jec¦tional
in¦ter¦jec¦tion¦ary
in¦ter¦ject¦ory
in¦ter¦knit
  (in¦ter¦knit¦ted *or*
  in¦ter¦knit,
  in¦ter¦knit¦ting)
in¦ter¦lace
  (in¦ter¦la¦cing)
in¦ter¦lace¦ment
in¦ter¦lap
  (in¦ter¦lapped,
  in¦ter¦lap¦ping)
in¦ter¦lard
in¦ter¦leaf (*pl.*
  in¦ter¦leaves)
in¦ter¦leave
  (in¦ter¦leav¦ing)
in¦ter¦line
  (in¦ter¦lined,
  in¦ter¦lin¦ing)
in¦ter¦lin¦ear
in¦ter¦lin¦ea¦tion
in¦ter¦link
in¦ter¦lobu¦lar
in¦ter¦lock
in¦ter¦lo¦cu¦tion
in¦ter¦loc¦utor
in¦ter¦loc¦ut¦ory
in¦ter¦lope
  (in¦ter¦lop¦ing)
in¦ter¦loper
in¦ter¦lude
in¦ter¦mar¦ri¦age

in¦ter¦marry
  (in¦ter¦mar¦ries,
  in¦ter¦mar¦ried,
  in¦ter¦
     mar¦ry¦ing)
in¦ter¦me¦di¦ary
  (*pl.* in¦ter¦me¦di¦
     ar¦ies)
in¦ter¦me¦di¦ate
  (as *v.,* in¦ter¦
    me¦di¦at¦ing)
in¦ter¦me¦di¦ation
in¦ter¦me¦di¦ator
in¦ter¦me¦dium
  (*pl.* in¦ter¦me¦dia)
in¦ter¦ment
in¦ter¦mesh
in¦ter¦mezzo (*pl.*
  in¦ter¦mezzi)
in¦ter¦min¦able
in¦ter¦min¦ably
in¦ter¦mingle
  (in¦ter¦ming¦ling)
in¦ter¦mis¦sion
in¦ter¦mit
  (in¦ter¦mit¦ted,
  in¦ter¦mit¦ting)
in¦ter¦mit¦tence
in¦ter¦mit¦tent
in¦ter¦mix
in¦ter¦mix¦ture
in¦ter¦mol¦ecu¦lar
in¦tern
in¦ternal-
internal-
    combustion
  attrib.
in¦tern¦al¦ity
in¦tern¦al¦ize
  (in¦tern¦al¦iz¦ing)
in¦tern¦ally
in¦ter¦na¦tional
In¦ter¦na¦tion¦ale
  (socialist song or
  assoc.)
in¦ter¦na¦tion¦al¦
     ism
inter¦na¦tion¦al¦ist
in¦ter¦na¦tion¦al¦
     ity
in¦ter¦na¦tion¦al¦
     iza¦tion
in¦ter¦na¦tion¦al¦
     ize
  (in¦ter¦na¦tion¦al¦
     iz¦ing)

in¦ter¦na¦tion¦ally
in¦ter¦ne¦cine
in¦ternee
in¦tern¦ist
in¦tern¦ment
in¦ter¦node
in¦ter¦nu¦clear
in¦ter¦nun¦cial
in¦ter¦nun¦cio (*pl.*
  in¦ter¦nun¦cios)
in¦tero¦cept¦ive
in¦ter¦os¦se¦ous
in¦ter¦page
  (in¦ter¦pa¦ging)
in¦ter¦pa¦ri¦etal
in¦ter¦pel¦late
  (in¦ter¦
     pel¦lat¦ing)
in¦ter¦pel¦la¦tion
in¦ter¦pel¦lator
in¦ter¦pen¦et¦rate
  (in¦ter¦pen¦et¦
     rat¦ing)
in¦ter¦pen¦et¦ra¦
     tion
in¦ter¦pen¦et¦rat¦
     ive
in¦ter¦per¦sonal
in¦ter¦plan¦et¦ary
in¦ter¦play
in¦ter¦plead
In¦ter¦pol
in¦ter¦pol¦ate
  (in¦ter¦pol¦at¦ing)
in¦ter¦pola¦tion
in¦ter¦pol¦ator
in¦ter¦posal
in¦ter¦pose
  (in¦ter¦pos¦ing)
in¦ter¦posi¦tion
in¦ter¦pret
  (in¦ter¦preted,
  in¦ter¦pret¦ing)
in¦ter¦pret¦able
in¦ter¦preta¦tion
in¦ter¦pret¦at¦ive
in¦ter¦preter
in¦ter¦pret¦ive
in¦ter¦pret¦ress
in¦ter¦ra¦cial
in¦ter¦ra¦ci¦ally
in¦ter¦reg¦num (*pl.*
  in¦ter¦reg¦nums)
in¦ter¦re¦lated
in¦ter¦re¦la¦tion

in┆ter┆rog┆ate
  (in┆ter┆rog┆at┆ing)
in┆ter┆roga┆tion
in┆ter┆rog┆at┆ive
in┆ter┆rog┆ator
in┆ter┆rog┆at┆ory
in┆ter┆rupt
in┆ter┆rupter
in┆ter┆rup┆tion
in┆ter┆rupt┆ive
in┆ter┆rupt┆ory
in┆ter┆sect
in┆ter┆sec┆tion
in┆ter┆sec┆tional
in┆ter┆septal
in┆ter┆sex
in┆ter┆sexual
in┆ter┆sexu┆al┆ity
in┆ter┆sexu┆ally
in┆ter┆space (as *v.*,
  in┆ter┆spa┆cing)
in┆ter┆spe┆cific
in┆ter┆sperse
  (in┆ter┆spers┆ing)
in┆ter┆sper┆sion
in┆ter┆spinal
in┆ter┆state
in┆ter┆stel┆lar
in┆ter┆stice
in┆ter┆sti┆tial
in┆ter┆tribal
in┆ter┆trigo (*pl.*
  in┆ter┆tri┆gos)
in┆ter┆twine
  (in┆ter┆twin┆ing)
in┆ter┆val
in┆ter┆val┆lic
in┆ter┆vene
  (in┆ter┆ven┆ing)
in┆ter┆ve┆ni┆ent
in┆ter┆ven┆tion
in┆ter┆ven┆tion┆ist
in┆ter┆ver┆teb┆ral
in┆ter┆view
in┆ter┆viewee
in┆ter┆viewer
in┆ter┆weave
  (in┆ter┆wove,
  in┆ter┆woven,
  in┆ter┆weav┆ing)
in┆ter┆wind
  (in┆ter┆wound)
in┆ter┆work
in┆test┆acy
in┆test┆ate
in┆test┆inal

in┆test┆ine
in┆tim┆acy (*pl.*
  in┆tim┆acies)
in┆tim┆ate (as *v.*,
  in┆tim┆at┆ing)
in┆tima┆tion
in┆tim┆id┆ate
  (in┆tim┆id┆at┆ing)
in┆tim┆ida┆tion
in┆tim┆id┆ator
in┆tinc┆tion
in┆tit┆ule
  (in┆tit┆ul┆ing)
into
in┆tol┆er┆able
in┆tol┆er┆ably
in┆tol┆er┆ance
in┆tol┆er┆ant
in┆ton┆ate
  (in┆ton┆at┆ing)
in┆tona┆tion
in┆tone
  (in┆ton┆ing)
in toto
in┆tox┆ic┆ant
in┆tox┆ic┆ate
  (in┆tox┆ic┆at┆ing)
in┆tox┆ica┆tion
in┆tra┆cra┆nial
in┆tract┆ab┆il┆ity
in┆tract┆able
in┆tract┆ably
in┆tra┆dos
in┆tra┆mural
in┆tra┆mus┆cu┆lar
in┆tra┆na┆tional
in┆trans┆igence
in┆trans┆igent
in┆trans┆it┆ive
intra-uterine
in┆tra┆ven┆ous
in-tray
in┆trepid
in┆trep┆id┆ity
in┆tric┆acy (*pl.*
  in┆tric┆acies)
in┆tric┆ate
in┆trig┆ant (*fem.*
  in┆trig┆ante)
in┆trigue
  (in┆trigued,
  in┆tri┆guing)
in┆trinsic
in┆trins┆ic┆ally
in┆tro┆duce
  (in┆tro┆du┆cing)

in┆tro┆duc┆tion
in┆tro┆duct┆ory
in┆tro┆flex┆ion
in┆tro┆gres┆sion
in┆troit
in┆tro┆jec┆tion
in┆tro┆mis┆sion
in┆tro┆mit┆tent
in┆tro┆spect
in┆tro┆spec┆tion
in┆tro┆spect┆ive
in┆tro┆
      sus┆cep┆tion
in┆tro┆vers┆ible
in┆tro┆ver┆sion
in┆tro┆vers┆ive
in┆tro┆vert
in┆tro┆ver┆ted
in┆trude
  (in┆trud┆ing)
in┆truder
in┆tru┆sion
in┆tru┆sion┆ist
in┆trus┆ive
intrust *use*
  entrust
in┆tub┆ate
  (in┆tub┆at┆ing)
in┆tuba┆tion
in┆tuit (in┆tu┆ited,
  in┆tu┆it┆ing)
in┆tu┆ition
in┆tu┆itional
in┆tu┆it┆ive
in┆tu┆mesce
  (in┆tu┆mes┆cing)
in┆tu┆mes┆cence
in┆tu┆mes┆cent
in┆tus┆
      sus┆cep┆tion
intwine *use*
  entwine
in┆unc┆tion
in┆und┆ate
  (in┆und┆at┆ing)
in┆unda┆tion
in┆ure (in┆ur┆ing)
in┆ure┆ment
in utero
in vacuo
in┆vade
  (in┆vad┆ing)
in┆vader
in┆va┆gin┆ate
  (in┆va┆gin┆at┆ing)
in┆va┆gina┆tion

in┆valid (as *v.*,
  in┆val┆ided,
  in┆val┆id┆ing)
in┆val┆id┆ate
  (in┆val┆id┆at┆ing)
in┆val┆ida┆tion
in┆va┆lid┆ity
in┆valu┆able
in┆valu┆ably
in┆vari┆ab┆il┆ity
in┆vari┆able
in┆vari┆ably
in┆vari┆ance
in┆vari┆ant
in┆va┆sion
in┆vas┆ive
in┆vec┆ted
in┆vect┆ive
in┆veigh
in┆veigle
  (in┆veig┆ling)
in┆veigle┆ment
in┆vent
in┆ven┆tion
in┆vent┆ive
in┆ventor
in┆vent┆ory (as *n.*,
  pl. in┆vent┆or┆ies;
  as *v.*,
  in┆vent┆or┆ies,
  in┆vent┆or┆ied,
  in┆vent┆ory┆ing)
In┆ver┆ness
in┆verse
in┆ver┆sion
in┆vers┆ive
invert
in┆ver┆teb┆rate
in┆vest
in┆vest┆ig┆ator
in┆vest┆ig┆ate
  (in┆vest┆ig┆at┆ing)
in┆vest┆iga┆tion
in┆vest┆ig┆at┆ive
in┆vest┆ig┆at┆ory
in┆vest┆it┆ure
in┆vest┆ment
in┆vestor
in┆vet┆er┆acy
in┆vet┆er┆ate
in┆vidi┆ous
in┆vi┆gil┆ate
  (in┆vi┆gil┆at┆ing)
in┆vi┆gila┆tion
in┆vi┆gil┆ator

in͟vig͟or͟ate
 (in͟vig͟or͟at͟ing)
in͟vig͟ora͟tion
in͟vig͟or͟at͟ive
in͟vig͟or͟ator
in͟vin͟cib͟il͟ity
in͟vin͟cible
in͟vin͟cibly
in͟vi͟ol͟ab͟il͟ity
in͟vi͟ol͟able
in͟vi͟ol͟ably
in͟vi͟ol͟acy
in͟vi͟ol͟ate
in͟vis͟ib͟il͟ity
in͟vis͟ible
in͟vis͟ibly
in͟vita͟tion
in͟vit͟at͟ory
in͟vite (in͟vit͟ing)
in͟vitee
in vitro
in vivo
in͟voca͟tion
in͟voc͟at͟ory
in͟voice (as *v.*,
 in͟voicing)
in͟voke
 (in͟vok͟ing)
in͟vol͟uc͟ral
in͟vol͟ucre
in͟vol͟un͟tar͟ily
in͟vol͟un͟tari͟
        ness
in͟vol͟un͟tary
in͟vol͟ute
in͟vol͟uted
in͟volu͟tion
in͟volve
 (in͟vol͟ving)
in͟volve͟ment
in͟vul͟ner͟ab͟il͟ity
in͟vul͟ner͟able
in͟vul͟ner͟ably
in͟ward
in͟wards
in͟weave
 (in͟wove,
 in͟woven,
 in͟weav͟ing)
in͟wrought
in͟yala (*pl.* same)
iod͟ate
iodic
iod͟ide
iod͟in͟ate
 (iod͟in͟at͟ing)

iod͟ina͟tion
iod͟ine
iod͟in͟ize
 (iod͟in͟iz͟ing)
iodo͟form
ion
Ionia
Ion͟ian
ionic (of ions)
Ionic (of Ionia)
ion͟ic͟ally
ion͟ium
ion͟iz͟able
ion͟iza͟tion
ion͟ize (ion͟iz͟ing)
iono͟sphere
iono͟spheric
iota
Iowa
ip͟ecac
ip͟ec͟acu͟anha
ipo͟moea
ip͟si͟lat͟eral
Ip͟swich
Iran
Ira͟nian
Iraq
Iraqi
iras͟cib͟il͟ity
iras͟cible
iras͟cibly
ir͟ate
Ire͟land
irenic
iren͟ical
iri͟da͟ceous
iri͟des͟cence
iri͟des͟cent
iri͟dium
iris
Ir͟ish
Ir͟ish͟man (*pl.*
 Ir͟ish͟men)
Ir͟ish͟wo͟man (*pl.*
 Ir͟ish͟wo͟men)
ir͟itis
irk͟some
iroko (*pl.* iro͟kos)
iron
ironic
iron͟ical
iron͟ic͟ally
iron͟ize
 (iron͟iz͟ing)
iron͟mon͟ger

iron͟mon͟gery (*pl.*
 iron͟mon͟ger͟ies)
Iron͟sides
iron͟stone
iron͟ware
iron͟work
irony (*pl.* iron͟ies)
Iro͟quoian
Iro͟quois (*pl.*
 same)
ir͟radi͟ance
ir͟radi͟ant
ir͟ra͟di͟ate
 (ir͟ra͟di͟at͟ing)
ir͟ra͟di͟ation
ir͟ra͟di͟at͟ive
ir͟ra͟tional
ir͟ra͟tion͟al͟ity
ir͟ra͟tion͟al͟ize
 (ir͟ra͟tion͟al͟iz͟
        ing)
ir͟ra͟tion͟ally
ir͟re͟claim͟able
ir͟re͟claim͟ably
ir͟re͟concil͟ab͟il͟
        ity
ir͟re͟con͟cil͟able
ir͟re͟con͟cil͟ably
ir͟re͟cov͟er͟able
ir͟re͟cov͟er͟ably
ir͟re͟cus͟able
ir͟re͟deem͟able
ir͟re͟deem͟ably
ir͟re͟dent͟ist
ir͟re͟du͟cib͟il͟ity
ir͟re͟du͟cible
ir͟re͟du͟cibly
ir͟re͟frag͟able
 (indisputable)
ir͟re͟frag͟ably
ir͟re͟fran͟gible
 (inviolable)
ir͟re͟fut͟ab͟il͟ity
ir͟re͟fut͟able
ir͟re͟fut͟ably
ir͟regu͟lar
ir͟regu͟lar͟ity (*pl.*
 ir͟regu͟lar͟it͟ies)
ir͟rel͟at͟ive
ir͟rel͟ev͟ance
ir͟rel͟ev͟ancy (*pl.*
 ir͟rel͟ev͟an͟cies)
ir͟rel͟ev͟ant
ir͟re͟li͟gion
ir͟re͟li͟gion͟ist
ir͟re͟li͟gious

ir͟re͟me͟di͟able
ir͟re͟me͟di͟ably
ir͟re͟miss͟ible
ir͟re͟miss͟ibly
ir͟re͟mov͟ab͟il͟ity
ir͟re͟mov͟able
ir͟re͟mov͟ably
ir͟re͟par͟able
ir͟re͟par͟ably
ir͟re͟place͟able
ir͟re͟press͟ible
ir͟re͟press͟ibly
ir͟re͟proach͟ab͟il͟
        ity
ir͟re͟proach͟able
ir͟re͟proach͟ably
ir͟res͟ist͟ib͟il͟ity
ir͟res͟ist͟ible
ir͟res͟ist͟ibly
ir͟res͟ol͟ute
ir͟res͟olu͟tion
ir͟res͟olv͟able
ir͟re͟spect͟ive
ir͟re͟spons͟ib͟il͟
        ity
ir͟re͟spons͟ible
ir͟re͟spons͟ibly
ir͟re͟spons͟ive
ir͟re͟tent͟ive
ir͟re͟triev͟able
ir͟re͟triev͟ably
ir͟rev͟er͟ence
ir͟rev͟er͟ent
ir͟rev͟er͟en͟tial
ir͟re͟vers͟ib͟il͟ity
ir͟re͟vers͟ible
ir͟re͟vers͟ibly
ir͟re͟voc͟ab͟il͟ity
ir͟re͟voc͟able
ir͟re͟voc͟ably
ir͟rig͟able
ir͟rig͟ate
 (ir͟rig͟at͟ing)
ir͟riga͟tion
ir͟rig͟at͟ive
ir͟rig͟ator
ir͟rit͟ab͟il͟ity
ir͟rit͟able
ir͟rit͟ably
ir͟rit͟ancy
ir͟rit͟ant
ir͟rit͟ate
 (ir͟rit͟at͟ing)
ir͟rita͟tion
ir͟rit͟at͟ive

ir'rupt (enter
 forcibly)
ir'rup'tion
 (entering forcibly)
Ir'tysh
Ir'ving|ite
isa'bel|line
isa|go'gic
is'atin
isch|aemia
isch|aemic
is'chi|adic
is'chial
is'chi|atic
is'chium (pl.
 is'chia)
is'en|tropic
Ish|mael
Ish'mael|ite
is'in|glass
Is'lam
Is'lama|bad
Is'lamic
Is'lam|ism
Is'lam|ist
Is'lam|ite
Is'lam|itic
is'land
isle
Isle of Wight
is'let
Is|maili
isn't
iso|bar
iso|baric
Iso'bel
iso|cheim

iso|chro'matic
iso|chron'ous
iso|clinal
iso|clinic
iso|cracy (pl.
 iso|cra'cies)
Iso|cra'tes
iso|cratic
iso|cyc'lic
iso|dyn'amic
iso|geo|therm
iso|gloss
iso|gonic
iso|hel
iso|hyet
isol|able
isol'at|able
isol|ate (as v.,
 isol|at'ing)
isola|tion
isola|tion|ism
isola|tion|ist
isol|at'ive
isol|ator
iso|mer
iso|meric
iso'mer|ism
iso'mer|ize
 (iso'mer|iz|ing)
iso'mer|ous
iso|met'ric
iso|met'rics
iso|metry
iso|morph
iso|morphic
iso|morph|ism
iso|morph|ous

iso|nomy
iso|phote
iso|pleth
iso|pod
iso|sceles
iso|seis'mal
iso|stasy (pl.
 iso|stas'ies)
iso|static
iso|there
iso|therm
iso|thermal
iso|tonic
iso|tope
iso|topic
iso|topy
iso|tropic
iso|trop'ic|ally
iso|tropy
Is|rael
Is|raeli
Is'rael|ite
is|su'able
is'su|ance
is'su|ant
issue (as v.,
 is'su|ing)
Is'tan|bul
Isth|mian
isth|mus
istle
It'al|ian
It'ali|an|ate
it'alic (type)
It'alic (of Italy)
it'al|icize
 (it'ali|ciz|ing)
it'alics

It'al|iot
It'aly
itch
itchy (itch|ier,
 itchi|est)
item
item|ize
 (item|iz|ing)
it'er|ance
it'er|ancy
it'er|ate
 (it'er|at'ing)
it'era|tion
it'er|at|ive
ithy|phal'lic
it'in'er|acy (pl.
 it'in'er|acies)
it'in'er|ancy (pl.
 it'in'er|an'cies)
it'in'er|ant
it'in'er|ary (pl.
 it'in'er|ar'ies)
it'in'er|ate
it'in'era|tion
its (possessive a.)
it's (= it is)
it'self
itsy-bitsy
itty-bitty
Iv'an|hoe (by
 Scott)
ivied
iv'ory (pl.
 iv'or|ies)
ivy (pl. ivies)
ixia
iz'ard
Iz'mir

J

jab (as v., jabbed, jab|bing)
jab|ber
jab|ber|wocky
jab|iru
ja|bo|randi
jabot
jac|ana
ja|ca|randa
ja|cinth
jackal
jack|an|apes
jack|aroo
jack|ass
jack|boot
jack|daw
jacket
jack-in-the-box
jack-knife (as n., pl. jack-knives; as v., jack-knifes, jack-knifed, jack-knifing)
jack-o'-lantern
jack|pot
jack-rabbit
jack|straw
Ja|co|bean
Ja|cobi
jac|obin (pigeon)
Jac|obin (friar; extreme radical)
Jac|ob|ite
Jac|ob|it|ism
jac|onet
Jac|quel|ine
jac|ta|tion
jac|tita|tion
Ja|cuzzi (propr.)
jade (as v., jad|ing)
jade|ite
j'ad|oube (Chess)
jae|ger
Jaffa
jag (as v., jagged, jag|ging)
jag|ger

jaggy (jag|gier, jag|gi|est)
jag|uar
jag|uar|undi
Jahveh use Yahveh
jai alai (game)
jail etc. use gaol etc.
Jain
Jain|ism
Jain|ist
Ja|karta
jalap
ja|lopy (pl. ja|lop|ies)
ja|lou|sie
jam (as v., jammed, jam|ming)
Ja|maica
jamb
jam|ba|laya
jam|boree
James
Jammu
jammy (jam|mier, jam|mi|est)
Jan|áček
Jane Eyre
Janet
jangle (jan|gling)
Jan|ice
jan|itor
jan|it|or|ial
jan|iz|ary (pl. jan|iz|ar|ies)
Janu|ary (pl. Janu|ar|ies)
ja|pan (varnish; as v., ja|panned, ja|pan|ning)
Ja|pan
Jap|an|ese
jape (as v., jap|ing)
Ja|phetic
Jap|lish
ja|pon|ica

jar (as v., jarred, jar|ring)
jar|di|ni|ère
jar|ful (pl. jar|fuls)
jar|gon
jar|gon|elle
jar|gonic
jar|gon|istic
jar|gon|ize (jar|gon|iz|ing)
jarl
jar|rah
Ja|ru|zel|ski
jas|mine
Ja|son
jaspé
jas|per
jato (pl. ja|tos)
jaun|dice (as v., jaun|dicing)
jaunt
jaun|tily
jaun|ti|ness
jaunty (jaun|tier, jaun|ti|est)
Java
Ja|van
Ja|van|ese
jav|elin
Ja|velle (water)
jaw-bone
jay-walk
jay-walker
jazz
jazz|man (pl. jazz|men)
jazzy (jaz|zier, jaz|zi|est)
jeal|ous
jeal|ousy
jean (cloth) △ gene
jeans
Jed|burgh
Je|ho|vah
Je|ho|vist
je|june
je|junum

Jek|yll and Hyde
jell
jellaba
jelly (as n., pl. jel|lies; as v., jel|lies, jel|lied, jel|ly|ing)
jel|ly|fish (pl. usu. same)
jemmy (as n., pl. jem|mies; as v., jem|mies, jem|mied, jem|my|ing)
je ne sais quoi
Jen|ner
jen|net (horse) △ genet
Jen|ni|fer
jenny (pl. jen|nies)
jeop|ard|ize (jeop|ard|iz|ing)
jeop|ardy
je|quir|ity (pl. je|quir|it|ies)
jerbil use gerbil
jer|boa
je|re|miad
Je|re|miah
Jer|icho
jerk|ily
jer|kin
jerki|ness
jerky (jer|kier, jer|ki|est)
je|ro|boam
jerry (pl. jer|ries)
jerry-built
jer|ry|can
jerrymander use gerrymander
jer|sey (cow, jumper)
Jer|sey (island)
Je|ru|sa|lem
Jesse (window)
Jesu
Jes|uit

Jesu|it|ical
Jesus
jet (as v., jetted,
 jet|ting)
jet-black
jeté
jet-propelled
jet|sam
jet|tison
jet|ton
jetty (pl. jet|ties)
Jew
jewel (as v.,
 (jew|elled,
 jew|el|ling)
jew|el|ler
jew|el|lery
jew|elly
Jew|ess
Jew|ish
Jewry
je|zail
Jez|ebel
jib(as v., jibbed,
 jib|bing)
jib|bah
jib|ber
jibe use gibe or
 gybe
Ji|buti
jiff
jiffy
jig (as v., jigged,
 jig|ging)
jig|ger
jiggery-pokery
jiggle (jig|gling)
jig|saw
ji|had
jill|aroo (pl.
 jill|ar|oos)
jilt
Jim|enez
jim-jams
jingle (as v.,
 jing|ling)
jin|gly (jin|glier,
 jin|gli|est)
jingo (pl. jin|goes)
jin|go|ism
jin|go|ist
jin|go|istic
jink
jin|nee (pl. jinn,
 also used as sing.)
jinx

ji|pi|japa
jit|ter
jit|ter|bug
jit|tery
jiu-jitsu use
 ju-jitsu
jive (as v., jiv|ing)
Jo|anne
job (as v., jobbed,
 job|bing)
Job (patriarch)
job|ber
job|bery
job|centre
jockey
jock-strap
joc|ose
joc|os|ity (pl.
 joc|os|it|ies)
joc|ular
jocu|lar|ity
joc|und
joc|und|ity
jodh|purs
joey
jog (as v., jogged,
 jog|ging)
jog|ger
joggle (as v.,
 jog|gling)
jog|trot
Jo|han|nes|burg
johnny (fellow, pl.
 john|nies)
John-o'-Groat's
John|son
John|son|ian
joie de vivre
join|der
joiner
join|ery
jointer
joint|ress
join|ture (as v.,
 join|tur|ing)
joist
jo|joba
joke (as v.,
 jok|ing)
joker
jokey
jol|li|fica|tion
jol|lify (jol|li|fies,
 jol|li|fied,
 jol|li|fy|ing)

jol|lity (pl.
 jol|lit|ies)
jolly (as a., jol|lier,
 jol|li|est; as v.,
 jol|lies, jol|lied,
 jol|ly|ing)
jolty
Jonah
Jon|athan
jon|quil
Jon|son, B.
Jor|dan
Jor|dan|ian
jorum
Jo|seph
Jo|seph|ine
Joshua
joss-stick
jostle (as v.,
 jost|ling)
jot (as v., jot|ted,
 jot|ting)
jot|ter
joule (unit)
Joule (man)
jounce
 (joun|cing)
journal
journ|al|ese
journ|al|ism
journ|al|ist
journ|al|istic
journ|al|ize
 (journ|al|iz|ing)
jour|ney
jour|ney|man
jo|vial
jo|vi|al|ity
jo|vi|ally
Jo|vian
jo|war
jowl
joy|ful
joy|fully
joy|ous
joy-ride
joy|stick
ju|bil|ance
ju|bil|ant
ju|bil|ate
 (ju|bil|at|ing)
ju|bila|tion
ju|bilee
Ju|daean
Judaeo-German
Ju|daic

Ju|da|ism
Ju|da|ist
Ju|da|ize
 (Ju|da|iz|ing)
ju|das (peep-hole)
Ju|das (traitor)
jud|der
judge (as v.,
 judging)
judge|matic
judge|mat|ical
judge|mat|ic|ally
judge|ment
judge|mental
judg|ment (Law)
ju|dic|ature
ju|di|cial
ju|di|ci|ally
ju|di|ciary (pl.
 ju|di|ciar|ies)
ju|di|cious
Ju|dith
judo (pl. ju|dos)
ju|do|ist
ju|doka
Judy (pl. Ju|dies)
jug (as v., jugged,
 jug|ging)
Ju|gend|stil
jug|ful (pl.
 jug|fuls)
jug|ger|naut
 (vehicle)
Jug|ger|naut
 (Hindu idol)
jug|gins
juggle (as v.,
 jug|gling)
jug|gler
jug|glery
Jugoslav etc. use
 Yugoslav etc.
jug|ular
jug|ulate
 (jug|ulat|ing)
juice
juicily
juici|ness
juicy (juicier,
 juici|est)
ju-jitsu
ju-ju
ju|jube
juke-box
ju|lep
Ju|lia

Ju|lian
Ju|lie
ju|li|enne
Ju|liet
Ju|lius Caesar (by
 Shakespeare)
July (*pl.* Ju|lys)
jumble (as *v.*,
 jum|bling)
jum|bly
 (jum|blier,
 jum|bli|est)
jumbo (*pl.*
 jum|bos)
jum|buck
jumper
jump|ily
jumpi|ness
jump-jet
jump-leads
jump-off *n.*
jumpy (jum|pier,
 jum|pi|est)
junco (*pl.* jun|cos
 or jun|coes)

junc|tion
junc|ture
June
Jung
Jung|ian
jungle
jungled
jungly (jun|glier,
 jun|gli|est)
ju|nior
ju|ni|or|ate
ju|ni|or|ity
ju|ni|per
Jun|ker (Ger.
 noble)
jun|ket (as *v.*,
 jun|keted,
 jun|ket|ing)
junkie
junk-shop
Juno (*pl.* Ju|nos)
Ju|no|esque
junta
Ju|piter
jural

Jur|as|sic
jurat
jur|id|ical
jur|is|con|sult
jur|is|dic|tion
jur|is|dic|tional
jur|is|pru|dence
jur|is|pru|dent
jur|is|pru|den|tial
jur|ist
jur|istic
jur|ist|ical
juror
jury (*pl.* jur|ies)
jury-box
jury|man (*pl.*
 jury|men)
jury-mast
jury|wo|man (*pl.*
 jury|wo|men)
juss|ive
just|ice
jus|ti|ci|able
jus|ti|ciar

jus|ti|ci|ary (*pl.*
 jus|ti|ci|ar|ies)
jus|ti|fi|ab|il|ity
jus|ti|fi|able
jus|ti|fi|ably
jus|ti|fica|tion
jus|ti|fic|at|ory
jus|tify (jus|ti|fies,
 jus|ti|fied,
 jus|ti|fy|ing)
jut (as *v.*, jut|ted,
 jut|ting)
jute (fibre)
Jute (Ger. tribe)
Jut|ish
Juv|enal
ju|ven|es|cence
ju|ven|es|cent
ju|ven|ile
ju|ven|ilia
ju|ven|il|ity
jux|ta|pose
 (jux|ta|pos|ing)
jux|ta|posi|tion

K

Ka¦aba
ka|buki
Ka¦bul
Ka¦byle
Kad|dish
Kaf¦fir (S. Afr.
  Bantu)
Kafir (native of
  Kafiristan)
Kafka
kaftan *use* caftan
kain|ite
kaiser
ka¦ke|mono (*pl.*
  ka¦ke|mo¦nos)
kala-azar
kale
kal¦eido|scope
kal¦eido|scopic
kal¦eido|scop¦ical
kali
Kal|muck
kalpa
Kama Sutra
kame
Kamet
ka¦mi|kaze
Kam|pala
kam|pong
Kam|pu|chea
  (Cambodia)
Kan¦ar|ese (*pl.*
  same)
Kan¦chen|junga
Kan|din¦sky
kan¦garoo (*pl.*
  kan¦gar|oos)
kanji
Kan|nada
Kan¦sas
Kan|tian
ka¦olin
kaon
ka¦pell|meis¦ter
  (*pl.* same)
ka¦pok
kappa
ka¦put
ka¦ra|biner

Ka¦ra|chi
Kara|ite
Ka¦ra|koram
ka¦ra|kul (sheep)
kar¦ate
Karen
karma
karmic
Kar|nat¦aka
ka¦roo (*pl.*
  ka¦roos)
karri
karst
ka¦ryo|type
kas¦bah
Kash|mir
kata|batic
kata|
  ther¦mo¦meter
Kath¦ar|ine
Kath¦er|ine
Kath|mandu
ka¦ty|did
Ka¦unda
kauri
kava
kawa-kawa
kayak
kayo (as *n.*, *pl.*
  kayos; as *v.*,
  kay¦oed,
  kayo|ing)
Kaz¦akh|stan
ka¦zoo
kea
ke¦bab
keck
kedge (ked¦ging)
ked¦geree
keel|haul
keen|ness
keep (as *v.*, kept)
keeper
keep|sake
kees|hond
kef¦fi|yeh
Keith
kelp
kel¦pie

kel¦son
kelt (salmon or sea
  trout)
Kelt *use* Celt
kel¦vin (unit)
Kel¦vin (man)
kempt
kempy
ken (as *v.*, kent,
  ken|ning)
ke¦naf
kendo
ken¦nel (as *v.*,
  ken¦nelled,
  ken|el|ling)
ken|osis
ken|otic
ken|ot¦ron
Kent|ish
kent|ledge
Ken|tucky
Kenya
Ken¦yan
kepi
Kep¦ler
Ker¦ala
ker|atin
ker¦at|ose
kerb (stone)
  ⚠ curb
kerb|stone
ker|chief
kerf
ker|fuffle
ker¦mes (insect)
ker¦mis (fair)
kern
ker¦nel
ker|os|ene
Kerry (county,
  cattle; *pl.*
  Ker|ries)
ker¦sey
ker¦sey|mere
ke¦rygma (*pl.*
  ke¦ryg|mata)
ke¦ryg|matic
kes|trel
ketch

ketchup
ke¦tone
kettle
ket¦tle|drum
ket¦tle|ful (*pl.*
  ket¦tle|fuls)
Kevin
kew¦pie
key¦bar
key|board
key|hole
Keynes
Keynes|ian
key|note
key-pad
key-ring
key|stone
key|word
khad|dar
khaki
kham|sin
khan
khan|ate
Khar|toum
Khe|dive
Khmer
Kho|meini
Khrush|chev
ki¦ang
kibble (kib|bling)
kib|butz (*pl.*
  kib|butzim)
kib¦butz|nik
kib¦itz
kib|itzer
kib¦lah
ki¦bosh
kick|back
kick-off *n.*
kick-start
kid (as *v.*, kid¦ded,
  kid|ding)
Kid¦der|min¦ster
kiddie
kid¦nap (as *v.*,
  kid|nap|ping)
kid¦nap|per
kid¦ney
kier

Kier¦ke¦gaard
kies¦el¦guhr
Ki¦gali
Kil¦dare
kil¦der¦kin
Ki¦li¦ma¦njaro
Kil¦kenny
killer
kil¦lick
kil¦li¦fish
kill¦ing
kill¦joy
kiln
kilo (pl. ki¦los)
kilo¦cycle
kilo¦gram
kilo¦hertz
kilo¦litre
kilo¦metre
kilo¦met¦ric
kilo¦ton
kilo¦tonne
kilo¦watt
kilt
kil¦ter
kiltie
ki¦mono (pl.
 ki¦mo¦nos)
kin¦aes¦thesia
kin¦aes¦thetic
kin¦aes¦thet¦ic¦
 ally
kin¦cob
kind¦er¦gar¦ten
kind-hearted
kindle (kind¦ling)
kind¦li¦ness
kindly (kind¦lier,
 kind¦li¦est)
kind¦ness
kind¦red
kin¦ematic
kin¦emat¦ical
kine¦mat¦ic¦ally
kin¦emat¦ics
kin¦es¦ics
kin¦esi¦ology
kin¦etic
kin¦et¦ics
king¦cup
king¦dom
king¦fisher
king¦let
king¦ling
king¦pin
king¦ship

king-size
Kings¦ton
Kings¦town
ki¦nin
kink
kin¦ka¦jou
kin¦ki¦ness
kinky (kink¦ier,
 kinki¦est)
kino (pl. ki¦nos)
Kin¦ross
kins¦folk
Kin¦shasa
kin¦ship
kins¦man (pl.
 kins¦men)
kins¦wo¦man (pl.
 kins¦wo¦men)
ki¦osk
kip (as v., kipped,
 kip¦ping)
kip¦per
kirby-grip
Kir¦ghiz
Kir¦ghizia
Ki¦ri¦bati
kirk
Kirk¦cud¦bright
Kirk¦wall
kirsch
kirsch¦was¦ser
kis¦met
kisser
Ki¦swa¦hili
kit (as v., kit¦ted,
 kit¦ting)
kit¦bag
kit¦chen
kit¦chener
 (cooking)
Kit¦chener (man)
kit¦chen¦ette
kitchen-ware
Kite¦mark
kitsch
kitschy
 (kitsch¦ier,
 kitschi¦est)
kit¦ten
kit¦ten¦ish
kit¦ti¦wake
kittle
kitty (pl. kit¦ties)
kiwi (bird)

Kiwi (New
 Zealander)
Klap¦roth
klaxon
Klee
Klein (bottle)
klepht
klep¦to¦mania
klep¦to¦man¦iac
klieg (light)
klip¦das
klip¦springer
Klon¦dike
kloof
klys¦tron
Klyu¦chev¦skaya
 Sopka
K-meson
knack
knacker
knack¦ery
knag (knot in
 wood)
knaggy
knap (as v., break
 with hammer;
 knapped,
 knap¦ping)
knap¦per
knap¦sack
knap¦weed
knar (knot in
 wood)
knave
knavery
knav¦ish
knawel
knead
knee (as v., kneed,
 knee¦ing)
knee¦cap
knee¦cap¦ping
kneel (kneeled or
 knelt)
knees-up n.
knell
knick¦er¦bock¦ers
knick¦ers
knick-knack
knick-knackery
knick-knackish
knife (as n., pl.
 knives; as v.,
 knifed, knif¦ing)
knife-point
knight

knight¦hood
knish
knit (as v.,
 knit¦ted,
 knit¦ting)
knit¦wear
knob (as v.,
 knobbed,
 knob¦bing)
knobbi¦ness
knobble (small
 knob) △ nobble
knobbly
 (knobbl¦ier,
 knobbli¦est)
knobby
 (knob¦bier,
 knob¦bi¦est)
knob¦ker¦rie
knock
knock¦about a.
 and n.
knock-down a.
knocker
knock-kneed
knock-on n.
knock-out n. & a.
knock-up n.
knoll
knop
Knos¦sos
knot (as v.,
 knot¦ted,
 knot¦ting)
knot¦ter
knot¦tily
knot¦ti¦ness
knotty (knot¦tier,
 knot¦ti¦est)
knout
know (knew,
 known)
know-all
know-how
know¦ledge
know¦ledge¦able
knuckle (as v.,
 knuck¦ling)
knuckle¦duster
knur
knurl
knurled
ko¦ala
koan
ko¦bold
Koch

Ko¦dak (*propr.*)
Ko¦diak (bear)
koel (bird)
koh-i-noor
kohl (powder)
kohl|rabi
koine
Ko|koschka
kol¦in|sky
kol|khoz
ko¦modo (*pl.*
  ko¦mo|dos)
Kom|somol
koodoo *use* kudu
koo¦ka|burra
kopje
Ko¦ran
Kor|anic
Ko¦rea
Kor¦ean
korf|ball

Kos|ciusko
kosher
koto (*pl.* kotos)
kou|miss
kour|bash
kow¦hai
kow¦tow
kraal
kraft (paper)
krait (snake)
Kra¦ka|toa
kraken
krans
Krebs
krem|lin (Russian
  citadel)
Krem|lin (USSR
  government)
krieg|spiel
Krishna
kru¦ger|rand

krumm|horn
Krupp
krypton
K2 (peak in
  Karakoram)
Kuala Lum¦pur
Kub¦lai Khan
Kubla Khan (by
  Coleridge)
ku¦dos
kudu
Kufic
Ku-Klux-Klan
ku¦lak
küm¦mel
kum|quat
kung fu
Kunst|his¦tor|
  isches (Museum)
kur¦chat¦ov|ium
Kurd

Kurd|ish
kur¦ra|jong
kur|saal
kur|tosis
Ku¦wait
kvass
kwashi|or¦kor
ky¦an|ite
ky¦an|ize
  (ky¦an|iz|ing)
kyle
ky¦lin
ky¦loe
ky¦mo|graph
kyph|osis (*pl.*
  kyph|oses)
kyph|otic
Kyp¦ri|anou

L

la (*Mus.*) *use* lah
laa|ger (camp)
△ lager
la|bel (la|belled,
 la|bel|ling)
la|bia (*pl.* of
 labium)
la|bial
la|bi|al|lism
la|bi|al|ize
 (la|bi|al|iz|ing)
la|bi|ate
lab|ile
lab|il|ity
la|bium (*pl.* la|bia)
la|bor|at|ory (*pl.*
 la|bor|at|or|ies)
la|bori|ous
la|bour
la|bourer
Lab|ra|dor (in
 Canada; breed of
 dog)
lab|ret
lab|rum (*pl.*
 labra)
la|burnum
laby|rinth
laby|rinth|ine
lac (resin)
lace (as *v.*, la|cing)
la|cer|ate
 (la|cer|at|ing)
la|cera|tion
lace-up *n.* & *a.*
lace|wing
lace|wood
lacey *use* lacy
la|ches
lach|rymal
lach|ryma|tion
lach|rym|ator
lach|rym|at|ory
 (*pl.* lach|rym|
  at|or|ies)
lach|rym|ose
la|cini|ate
la|cini|ated
lacka|dais|ical

lacka|dais|ic|ally
lackey
lack|land
lack-lustre
La|co|nia
La|co|nian
 (Spartan)
lac|onic
lac|on|ic|ally
lac|on|icism
lac|on|ism
lac|quer
la|crosse
lact|ate (as *v.*,
 lact|at|ing)
lacta|tion
lac|teal
lact|es|cence
lact|es|cent
lactic
lac|to|pro|tein
lact|ose
la|cuna (*pl.*
 la|cu|nas *or*
 la|cu|nae)
la|cunar
la|cun|ary
la|cus|trine
lacy (lacier,
 laci|est)
La|dakh
lad|anum
lad|der
lad|die
laden
la-di-da
la|dies (*pl.* of lady)
la|dies' man
la|dies' room
lad|ing
La|dino (*pl.*
 La|di|nos)
ladle (as *v.*,
 lad|ling)
la|dle|ful (*pl.*
 la|dle|fuls)
La|doga, Lake
lad's love
lady (*pl.* la|dies)

lady|bird
Lady
 Chatter|ley's
 Lover
Lady Day
lady-fern
ladyfy (lady|fies,
 lady|fied,
 lady|fy|ing)
lady-in-waiting
 (*pl.* ladies-in-
  waiting)
lady-killer
lady|like
lady-love
Lady of Sha|lott
lady|ship
lady's maid (*pl.*
 ladies' maids)
lady-smock
lady's slip|per
lae|vo|dopa
lae|vo|ro|tat|ory
lae|vo|tar|taric
lae|vul|ose
La Fon|taine
lag (as *v.*, lagged,
 lag|ging)
lagan
la|ger (beer)
△ laager
Lager|kvist
Lager|löf
lag|gard
lag|ger
lag|ging
la|go|morph
la|goon
La|gos
lah (*Mus.*)
la|har
La|hore
laic
la|ical
la|ic|ally
la|icity
la|iciza|tion
la|icize
 (la|iciz|ing)

laid (*past* and *p.p.*
 of lay) △ lain
laid-back
lain (*p.p.* of lie)
 △ laid
laird
laisser-faire
la|ity (*pl.* la|it|ies)
Lake Dis|trict
lakh
Lak|shad|weep
Lal|lan
Lal|la Rookh
lal|la|tion
L'Al|legro
Lalo
lama
La|marck
la|mas|ery (*pl.*
 la|mas|er|ies)
lam|baste
lambda
lam|bency
lam|bent
lam|bert
Lam|beth
lamb|kin
lam|bre|quin
lamb's fry
lamb|skin
lamb's-tails
lamb's-wool
lame (as *a.*, lamer,
 lamest; as *v.*,
 lam|ing)
lamé
la|mella (*pl.*
 la|mel|lae)
la|mel|lar
lam|el|late
la|mel|li|branch
la|mel|licorn
la|mel|li|form
la|mel|lose
la|ment
lam|ent|able
lam|ent|ably
lam|enta|tion

Lam|enta|tions
(OT book)
lam|ina (*pl.*
lam|inae)
lam|inar
lam|in|ate
(lam|in|at|ing)
lam|ina|tion
lam|in|ose
Lam|mas
lam|mer|geyer
lamp|black
lamp|light
lamp|lighter
lam|poon
lamp-post
lam|prey
lamp|shade
Lan|ark
Lan|ca|shire
Lan|cas|ter
Lan|cas|trian
lance (as *v.*,
lan|cing)
lance-
bombardier
lance-corporal
lance-fish
lance|let
lan|ceo|late
lan|cer
lance-sergeant
lance-snake
lan|cet
lance|wood
Lan|chow
lan|cin|at|ing
Land (Ger. or Aus.
province; *pl.*
Län|der)
land-agent
landau (type of
carriage)
Landau (L., Russ.
physicist)
land|au|let
land-bank
lander
Län|der (*pl.* of
Land)
Landes (in
France)
land|fall
land|holder
land|ing
landing-craft

landing-gear
landing-net
landing-stage
landing-strip
land|lady (*pl.*
land|ladies)
land-law
land-line
land-locked
land|lord
land|lub|ber
land|mark
land-mine
land|owner
land|rail
land|scape
land|scap|ist
Lands|hut
land|slide
land|slip
lands|man (*pl.*
lands|men)
land-tax
land|ward
lang syne
lan|guage
langue d'oc
(language)
Langue|doc (in
France)
lan|guid
lan|guish
lan|guor
lan|guor|ous
lan|gur (monkey)
lani|ary (*pl.*
lani|ar|ies)
lank|ily
lanki|ness
lanky (lank|ier,
lanki|est)
lan|ner
lan|neret
lan|olin
lans|quenet
lan|tern
lantern-slide
lantern-wheel
lan|than|ide
lan|thanum
lan|yard
Laocoön
(sculpture)
Lao|di|cean
Laois

Laokoon (by
Lessing)
Laos
Lao|tian
Lao-tzu
lap (as *v.*, lapped,
lap|ping)
lap|aro|tomy
La Paz
lap-dog
lapel
lap|elled
lap|ful (*pl.*
lap|fuls)
lap|icide
lap|id|ary (*pl.*
lap|id|ar|ies)
lap|id|ate
(lap|id|at|ing)
lap|ida|tion
la|pilli *n. pl.*
lapis lazuli
lap-joint
Lap|land
Lap|lander
Lapp
lap|pet
Lapp|ish
lapse (as *v.*,
laps|ing)
lap|stone
lapsus
lapsus cal|ami
lapsus lin|guae
Lap|tev Sea
La|putan
lap|wing
lar|board
lar|cener
lar|cen|ist
lar|cen|ous
lar|ceny (*pl.*
lar|cen|ies)
larch|wood
larder
larding-needle
larding-pin
lar|don
lardy
lardy-cake
lardy-dardy
lares *n. pl.*
lar|gen
lar|gess
lar|ghetto (*pl.*
lar|ghet|tos)

lar|gish
largo (*pl.* lar|gos)
la|riat
lark|spur
La Roche|fou|
cauld
La Roch|elle
lar|ri|kin
larva (*pl.* lar|vae)
lar|val
lar|vi|cide
la|ryn|geal
lar|yn|ges (*pl. of*
larynx)
lar|yn|gic
lar|yn|gitis
lar|yn|go|logy
la|ryn|go|scope
la|ryn|go|tomy
(*pl.* la|ryng|o|
tom|ies)
lar|ynx (*pl.*
lar|ynges)
la|sagne
Las|car
Las|caux
las|ci|vi|ous
laser
lasher
lash|ing
lash|kar
lash-up *n. & a.*
Las Pal|mas
lasque
Lassa fever
lassie
lassi|tude
lasso (as *n.*, *pl.*
las|sos; as *v.*,
las|soes,
las|soed,
las|so|ing)
last|ing
Las Ve|gas
La|ta|kia (in
Syria; Turk.
tobacco)
latchet
latch|key
la|teen
lateish *use* latish
lately
laten
la|tency
La Tène (culture)
lat|ent

lat|eral
lat|er|ally
Lat|eran
lat|er|ite
lat|er|itic
la|tex (*pl.* la|texes)
lath (thin strip)
lathe (machine)
lather
lathy
la|ti|fun|dia
Latin
Lat|in|ate
lat|ine (in Latin; 3 sylls.)
lat|ish
lat|it|ude
lat|it|ud|inal
lat|it|ud|in|ally
lat|it|ud|in|arian
La|tium
lat|rine
lat|ten
lat|ter
Latter-day Saints
lat|terly
lat|tice
Lat|via
Lat|vian
laud|ab|il|ity
laud|able
laud|ably
laud|anum
lauda|tion
laud|at|ory
laugh|able
laugh|ably
laughing-gas
laughing-stock
laugh|ter
launcher
launch|ing pad
launch|ing site
laun|der
laun|der|ette
laund|ress
laun|dry (*pl.* laun|dries)
laure|ate
Laure|ate (Poet)
laurel
Lau|ren|tian (Mts. etc.)
lau|rus|tinus
Lau|sanne
lava

la|vabo (*pl.* la|va|bos)
lav|age
lava|tion
lav|at|ory (*pl.* lav|at|or|ies)
lav|en|der
laver
lav|er|ock
lav|ish
La|vois|ier
law-abiding
law-breaker
law|court
law|ful
law|fully
law|giver
law|less
Law Lord
law|maker
lawn-mower
Law|rence, D.H.
Law|rence, T.E.
law|ren|cium
law|suit
law-term
law|yer
lax|at|ive
Lax|daela Saga
lax|ity
Lax|ness
lay *v.* (laid)
lay|about
Laya|mon
lay-by (*pl.* lay-bys)
layer
lay figure
lay|man (*pl.* lay|men)
lay-off *n.*
lay|out
lay|shaft
lay|stall
laz|ar|etto (*pl.* laz|ar|et|tos)
laze (laz|ing)
laz|ily
lazi|ness
laz|uli
lazy (laz|ier, lazi|est)
lazy-bones
lea (open land; measure of yarn)
△ lee

lead (to guide; led)
lead (metal; as *v.*, leaded)
leaden
leader
lead|er|ship
lead-in *n.*
lead|ing (foremost; *Printing*)
leads|man (*pl.* leads|men)
lead-work
lead|wort
leaf (*pl.* leaves)
leaf|age
leaf|let
leafy (leaf|ier, leafi|est)
league
leaguer
leak|age
leaki|ness
leaky (leak|ier, leaki|est)
lean (leaned *or* leant)
lean-to (*pl.* lean-tos)
leap (leaped *or* leapt)
leap-frog (leap-frogged, leap-frogging)
leap year
learn (learned *or* learnt)
learned (erudite; 2 sylls.)
learn|ing
lease (as *v.*, leas|ing)
lease|back
lease|hold
lease|holder
least|ways
least|wise
leather
leather-back
leath|er|cloth
leath|er|ette
leather-jacket
leath|ern
leather-neck
leath|er|oid
leath|ery

leave (as *v.*, left, leav|ing)
leaven
leaver
leaves (*pl.* of leaf)
Le Baiser
Leb|an|ese
Leb|anon
le|bens|raum
lecher
lech|er|ous
lech|ery
le|cithin
Le|clan|ché
lec|tern
lec|tion
lec|tion|ary (*pl.* lec|tion|ar|ies)
lector
lec|ture (as *v.*, lec|tur|ing)
lec|turer
lec|turer|ship (at Oxford)
lec|ture|ship
leder|hosen
led|ger
ledgy
lee (shelter given by neighbouring object) △ lea
lee-board
Lee-Enfield (rifle)
Leeu|warden
Leeu|wen|hoek
lee|ward
lee|way
left-hand *a.*
left-handed
left-hander
left|ward
left-wing *a.*
left-winger
lefty (*pl.* left|ies)
leg (as *v.*, legged, leg|ging)
leg|acy (*pl.* leg|acies)
legal
leg|al|ism
leg|al|istic
leg|al|ist|ic|ally
leg|al|ity (*pl.* leg|al|it|ies)
leg|al|ize (leg|al|iz|ing)

leg|ally
leg|ate n.
le'gate v.
leg|atee
leg|at|ine
lega|tion
leg|ato (pl.
  leg|atos)
leg|ator
leg-bye
le'gend
le'gend|ary a.
le'gendry n.
le'ger
le'ger|de|main
legged
leg|gi'ness
leg|gings
leg-guard
leg'gy (leg|gier,
  leg|gi|est)
leg|horn (hat)
Leg|horn
  (=Livorno)
le'gib|il'ity
le'gible
le'gibly
le'gion
le'gion|ary (pl.
  le'gion|ar'ies)
le'gion|naire
le'gion|naires'
  disease
le'gis|late
  (le'gis|lat'ing)
le'gis|la'tion
le'gis|lat'ive
le'gis|lator
le'gis|lat'ure
le'git|im'acy
le'git|im|ate
le'git|ima'tion
le'git|im|iza'tion
le'git|im|ize
  (le'git|im|iz'ing)
leg|man (pl.
  leg|men)
leg-pull
leg-rest
leg-room
leg'ume
leg'um|in|ous
lei (garland)
Leib|niz
Lei'ces|ter
Lei'ces'ter|shire

Lei|den
Lein|ster
Leip|zig
leish'mani|asis
leis|ure
leis|ured
leis|ure'li|ness
leis|urely
leit|motiv
Leit|rim
lemma (pl.
  lemmas; in sense
  'heading of
  annotation',
  lem|mata)
lem|ming
Lem|nos
lemon
lem|on|ade
lem|ony
le'mur
lem|ur|ine
lem|ur|oid
Lena
lend (lent)
lender
lengthen
length|ily
lengthi|ness
length|man (pl.
  length|men)
length|ways
length|wise
lengthy
  (length|ier,
  lengthi|est)
le'ni|ence
le'ni|ency
le'ni|ent
Lenin
Len|in|grad
len|it|ive
len|ity
leno (pl. lenos)
Lent (Ash Wed. to
  Easter)
Lenten
len'ti|cel
len'ti|cular
len|til
len|tisk
lento
lent|oid
Leo (pl. Leos)
León (in Spain)

Le'on|ardo da
  Vinci
Le'onid (a meteor)
le'on|ine (of lions)
Le'on|ine (of Pope
  Leo)
leo|pard
leo|pard|ess
Léo'pold|ville
leo|tard
Le Pen|seur
leper
lep'id|op'teran
lep'id|op'ter|ist
lep'id|op'ter|ous
lep'or|ine
lep|re'chaun
lep|rosy
lep|rous
lep'to|ceph'alic
lep'to|ceph'al|ous
lep'to|dac'tyl
lepton (coin; pl.
  lepta)
lepton (particle;
  pl. lep|tons)
lep'to|spir'osis
Ler|mon|tov
Ler|wick
les|bian
  (homosexual
  woman)
Les|bian (of
  Lesbos)
Les|bos
lèse-majesté
  (treason; Angl. as
  lese-majesty)
le'sion
Les|ley *fem.*
Les|lie *masc.*
Le|so'tho
lessee
lessen
lesser
Less|ing
les'son
lessor
let (let, let|ting)
lethal
leth'al|ity
leth|ally
leth|ar'gic
leth|ar'gic|ally
leth|argy
Le'the

Lett
let'ter
letter-bomb
letter-box
let'ter|press
Lettic
Lett'ish
let|tuce
leu'co|blast
leu'co|cyte
leuc|oma (pl.
  leuc|omas)
leu'cor|rhoea
leu'co|tome
leu'co|tomy (pl.
  leu'co|tom|ies)
leuk|aemia
leuk|aemic
le'vant (abscond)
Le'vant (E.
  Mediterranean)
Le'vant|ine
lev|ator
levee
level (as v.,
  lev'elled,
  lev'el|ling)
level-headed
lev'el|ler
Lev'el|ler (*hist.*)
lev|elly
le'ver
le'ver|age
lev|eret
levi|able
le'vi|athan
lev'ig|ate
  (lev'iga|ting)
lev|iga'tion
lev|ir|ate
Le'vis (*propr.*)
lev'it|ate
  (lev'it|at|ing)
lev|ita'tion
Le'vite
Le'vit'ical
Le'vit'icus (OT
  book)
lev|ity
Lev'kas
levy (as v., lev'ies,
  lev'ied, levy|ing;
  as n., pl. lev'ies)
lewd
Lewes (in E.
  Sussex)

lewis (iron grip)
Lewis (gun)
Lewi|sham
lew'is|ite
lex|ical
lex'ic|ally
lex'ico|grapher
lex'ico|graph'ical
lex'ico|graph'ic|
ally
lex'ico|graphy
lex|icon
lexi|graphy
lexis
ley (land under
grass; line of anc.
track)
Ley|den jar
Lhasa
li'ab'il|ity (pl.
li'ab'il|it'ies)
li'able
li|aise (li'ais|ing)
li|aison
liana
liar
lias (rock)
Lias (Jurassic
strata)
li|assic
liba|tion
li'bel (as v.,
li'belled,
li'bel|ling)
li'bel|lant
li'bel|lee
li'bel|ler
li'bel|list
li'bel|lous
liber
lib|eral
Lib|eral (Party)
lib'er'al|ism
lib'er'al|ist
lib'er'al|istic
lib'er'al|ity
lib'er'al|ize
(lib'er'al|iz|ing)
lib'er|ally
lib'er|ate
(lib'er|at|ing)
lib'era|tion
lib'er|ator
Li|beria
lib'er|tar|ian
lib'er'tin|age

lib'er|tine
lib|erty (pl.
lib'er|ties)
li'bid|inal
li'bid'in|ous
li'bido (pl.
li'bi|dos)
Libra
Lib|ran
lib'rar|ian
lib|rary (pl.
lib'rar'ies)
lib|rate
(lib'rat'ing)
lib'ra|tion
lib'rat'ory
lib'ret'tist
lib|retto (pl.
lib'retti or
lib'ret'tos)
Libre|ville
Lib'rium (propr.)
Libya
Li'byan
li|cence n.
li|cense v.
(li'cens'ing)
li'cens|ee
li|censer
li'cen'ti|ate
li'cen'ti|ous
li'chen (pron. as
liken)
li'cheno|logy
li'chen|ous
Lich|field
lich-gate
li'cit
lick'er|ish
lic'tor
lid'ded
lido (pl. li'dos)
lie (as v., rest
horizontally; lay,
lain, lying)
lie (as v., be
untruthful; lied,
lying)
Lieb|frau|milch
Liech'ten|stein
lied (Ger. song; pl.
lieder)
liege
Li'ège
liege|man (pl.
liege|men)

lien
li'erne
lieu
lieu'ten|ancy
lieu'ten|ant
lieutenant-
colonel
lieutenant-
general
life (pl. lives)
life|belt
life-blood
life|boat
life|buoy
life-guard
Life Guards
(regiment)
life-jacket
life|like
life|line
life|long
lifer
life-raft
life sciences
life-size
life-sized
life-style
life-support
life|time
life-work
Lif|ford
lift-off n.
liga|ment
liga|mental
liga|ment'ary
liga|ment|ous
lig'ate (lig'at'ing)
liga|tion
lig'at|ure (as v.,
lig'at|ur'ing)
li'ger
light (as v., lit or
lighted; attrib.,
lighted)
lighten
lighter
light'er|age
light'er|man (pl.
light'er|men)
light|foot
light-headed
light-hearted
light|house
light|ing
light|ning
light-o'-love

light|ship
light|some
light|weight
light|wood
light-year
lign-aloes
lig|neous
lig'ni|fer|ous
lig'ni|form
lig|nify
(lig'ni|fies,
lig'ni|fied,
lig'ni|fy|ing)
lig|nite
lig'num vitae
lig|roin
ligu|late
lig'ule
Li|guria
like (as v., lik'ing)
like|able
like|ably
like'li|hood
like'li|ness
likely (like|lier,
like'li|est)
liken
like|ness
like|wise
lik'ing
li'lac
li'li|aceous
lilied
lil'li|pu'tian
Li|longwe
lily (pl. lil'ies)
lily-white
lima (bean)
Lima (in Peru)
limb
lim'ber
limbo (pl. lim'bos)
Lim|burg
Lim|burger
lime (as v.,
lim'ing)
lime|ade
lime|light
li'men
lim'er|ick (verse)
Lim'er|ick (in
Ireland)
lime|stone
lime-wort
lim|inal

limit (as v.,
 lim|ited,
 lim|it|ing)
lim|it|ary
lim|ita|tion
lim|it|at|ive
lim|it|less
limi|trophe
lim|no|lo|gical
lim|no|lo|gist
lim|no|logy
Li|mou|sin
lim|ous|ine
lim|pet
limpid
limp|id|ity
limp|kin
limp|wort
lim|ulus (pl.
 lim|uli)
lin|age (number of
 lines) △ lineage
linch|pin
Lin|coln
Lin|coln|shire
Lin|crusta (propr.)
linc|tus
Linda
lind|ane
lin|den
line (as v., lin|ing)
lin|eage (ancestry)
 △ linage
lin|eal
lin|eally
lin|ea|ment
 (feature)
 △ liniment
lin|ear
lin|ear|ity
lin|ear|ize
 (lin|ear|iz|ing)
lin|ea|tion
linen
lin|en|fold
line-out n.
liner
lines|man (pl.
 lines|men)
line-up n.
linger
lin|gerie
lingo (pl. lin|goes)
lin|gua franca
lin|gual

lin|gual|ize
 (lin|gual|iz|ing)
Lin|gua|phone
 (propr.)
lin|gui|form
lin|guist
lin|guistic
lin|guis|tic|ally
lin|guist|ician
lin|guist|ics
lin|guo|dental
lingy
lini|ment
 (embrocation)
 △ lineament
lin|ing
link|age
link|man (pl.
 link|men)
link-up n.
Lin|lith|gow
Lin|naean
Lin|naeus
Lin|nean (Society)
lin|net
lino (pl. li|nos)
li|no|cut
li|no|leum
li|no|leumed
Li|no|type (propr.)
lin|sang
lin|seed
linsey-woolsey
lin|stock
lin|tel
liny
lion
li|on|ess
li|onet
li|on|ize
 (li|on|iz|ing)
lip (as v., lipped,
 lip|ping)
lip|ase
lipid
lipo|graphy
Lippi
Lip|piz|aner
lip-read (lip-read)
lip|salve
lip-service
lip|stick
li|quate
 (li|quat|ing)
li|qua|tion
li|que|fa|cient

li|que|fac|tion
li|que|fact|ive
li|que|fi|able
li|que|fier
li|quefy
 (li|que|fies,
 li|que|fied,
 li|que|fy|ing)
li|ques|cent
li|queur
li|quid
li|quid|ate
 (li|quid|at|ing)
li|quida|tion
li|quid|ator
li|quid|ity
li|quid|ize
 (li|quid|iz|ing)
li|quid|izer
li|quidus
li|quor
li|quor|ice (sweet)
lira (pl. lire)
Lis|bon
lisle
lis|som
lis|ten
lis|tener
Lis|ter
list|less
Liszt
lit|any (pl.
 lit|an|ies)
lit|chi
lit|er|acy
lit|eral
lit|er|al|ize
 (lit|er|al|iz|ing)
lit|er|ally
lit|er|ar|ily
lit|er|ari|ness
lit|er|ary
lit|er|ate
lit|er|ati n. pl.
li|tera|tion
li|ter|ator
lit|er|at|ure
lith|arge
lithe
lithe|some
lithia
lithic
li|tho (pl. li|thos)
litho|graph
li|tho|grapher
li|tho|graphic

li|tho|graph|ic|
 ally
li|tho|graphy
li|tho|lo|gical
li|tho|lo|gist
li|tho|logy
litho|phyte
litho|pone
litho|sphere
li|tho|spheric
li|tho|tom|ist
li|tho|tom|ize
 (li|tho|tom|iz|ing)
li|tho|tomy (pl.
 li|tho|tom|ies)
li|tho|trity (pl.
 li|tho|trit|ies)
Li|thu|ania
Li|thu|an|ian
lit|ig|able
lit|ig|ant
lit|ig|ate
 (lit|ig|at|ing)
lit|iga|tion
li|ti|gi|ous
lit|mus
li|to|tes
litre
litre|age
lit|ter
lit|tér|at|eur
little (lit|tler,
 lit|tlest)
Little Dor|rit
lit|toral
li|tur|gical
li|tur|gic|ally
li|tur|gics
li|tur|gi|ology
li|tur|gist
lit|urgy (pl.
 lit|ur|gies)
live (as v., liv|ing)
live|able
live|li|hood
live|lily
live|li|ness
live|long
lively (live|lier,
 live|li|est)
liven
liver
liv|er|ied
liv|er|ish
Liv|er|pool
Liv|er|pud|lian

liv|er|wort

liv|ery (*pl.*
  liv|er|ies)

liv|ery|man (*pl.*
  liv|ery|men)

live|stock

livid

liv|id|ity

liv|ing

Liv|ing|stone

Livy

lix|ivi|ate
  (lix|ivi|at|ing)

lix|ivi|ation

liz|ard

Ljub|ljana

llama

Llan|drin|dod
  Wells

lla|nero (*pl.*
  lla|neros)

llano (*pl.* lla|nos)

Lloyd's
  (underwriters)

Llu|llai|llaco

loach

load (burden etc.)
  △ lode

loader

loadstar *use*
  lodestar

load|stone

loaf (*pl.* loaves)

loafer (idler)

Loafer (shoe;
  propr.)

loamy (loam|ier,
  loami|est)

loan|able

loanee

loaner

loan-word

loath (averse)

loathe (to hate;
  loath|ing)

loath|some

loaves (*pl.* of loaf)

lob (as *v.*, lobbed,
  lob|bing)

lobar

lob|ate

loba|tion

lobby (as *n.*, *pl.*
  lob|bies; as *v.*,
  lob|bies,
  lob|bied,
  lob|by|ing)

lob|by|ist

lob|ec|tomy (*pl.*
  lob|ec|tom|ies)

lo|belia

lob|lolly (*pl.*
  lob|lol|lies)

lo|bo|tomy (*pl.*
  lo|bo|tom|ies)

lob|scouse

lob|ster

lobu|lar

lob|ule

lob|worm

local

loc|ale

loc|al|ism

loc|al|ity (*pl.*
  loc|al|it|ies)

loc|al|iza|tion

loc|al|ize
  (loc|al|iz|ing)

loc|ally

loc|ate (loc|at|ing)

loca|tion

loc|at|ive

loc|ator

loch

lochan

Loch|gilp|head

lo|chia

lo|chial

Loch Lo|mond

Loch Ma|ree

loci (*pl.* of locus)

lock|age

Locke

locker

locket

lock|jaw

locks|man (*pl.*
  locks|men)

lock|smith

lock-up *n.*

loco (*pl.* lo|cos)

lo|co|mo|tion

lo|co|mot|ive

lo|co|motor

lo|co|mot|ory

locu|lar

locu|lus (*pl.*
  loc|uli)

locum

locum ten|ens (*pl.*
  locum ten|en|tes)

locus (*pl.* loci)

locust

lo|cu|tion

loc|ut|ory (*pl.*
  loc|ut|or|ies)

lode (vein of metal
  ore) △ load

loden

lode|star

lodestone *use*
  loadstone

lodge (as *v.*,
  lodging)

lodge|ment

lodger

lodgings

Łódź

lo|ess

Lo|fo|ten (Islands)

lofter

loft|ily

lofti|ness

lofty (loft|ier,
  lofti|est)

log (as *v.*, logged,
  log|ging)

lo|gan (stone)

Lo|gan

lo|gan|berry (*pl.*
  lo|gan|ber|ries)

lo|ga|oedic

log|ar|ithm

log|ar|ith|mic

log-book

loge

log|ger

log|ger|head

log|gia

lo|gic

lo|gical

lo|gic|al|ity

lo|gic|ally

lo|gi|cian

log|ion (*pl.* logia)

lo|gistic

lo|gist|ics

logo (*pl.* lo|gos)

logo|gram

lo|go|grapher

lo|gor|rhoea

Logos (word of
  God)

logo|type

log|wood

Lo|*hen*|*grin*

loin|cloth

loir (dormouse)

Loire

loiter

loi|terer

Lol|lard

lol|li|pop

lol|lop (lolloped,
  lol|lop|ing)

lolly (*pl.* lol|lies)

Lom|bard

Lom|bardic

Lom|bardy

Lomé

lo|ment

lo|ment|aceous

Lon|don

Lon|don|derry

lone|li|ness

lonely (lone|lier,
  lone|li|est)

loner

lone|some

long|an|im|ity

long|boat

long|bow

lon|geron

lon|gev|ity

Long|ford

long|hand

long|horn

lon|gi|corn

long|ing

lon|git|ude

lon|git|ud|inal

lon|git|ud|in|ally

long ship

long-shoreman
  (*pl.* long-
        shoremen)

long-sighted

long|stop

long|wise

lo|ni|cera

loo|fah

look-alike *n.*

looker

look-out *n.*

loony (as *n.*, *pl.*
  loon|ies; as *a.*,
  loon|ier,
  looni|est)

looper

loop|hole (as v.,
　loop|hol|ing)
loopi|ness
loop-line
loopy (loop|ier,
　loo|pi|est)
loose (as a.,
　looser, loos|est;
　as v., loos|ing)
loose-leaf
loosen
loose|strife
loos|ish
looter
lop (lopped,
　lop|ping)
lope (as v.,
　lop|ing)
lopho|branch
lopho|dont
lopho|phore
lop|sided
lo|qua|cious
lo|qua|city
lo|quat
loral
loran
Lorca
lor|cha
lord
Lord (God)
lord|li|ness
lord|ling
lordly
lor|dosis (pl.
　lor|doses)
lor|dotic
lord|ship
lore
Lor|enz
lor|gnette
lor|gnon
lor|ic|ate
lo|ri|keet
loris
Lor|raine
lorry (pl. lor|ries)
lory (pl. lor|ies)
los|able
Los An|geles
lose (lost, los|ing)
loser
lot (as v., lot|ted,
　lot|ting)
loth use loath

Lo|thario (pl.
　Lo|tharios)
Lothian
lo|tion
lot|tery (pl.
　lot|ter|ies)
lotto
lo|tus
louden
loud|hailer
loud|speaker
lough (Ir., lake)
Lough Neagh
louis (pl. same)
Lou|ise
Loui|si|ana
lounge (as v.,
　loun|ging)
loun|ger
loupe
lour (scowl)
louse|wort
lous|ily
lousi|ness
lousy (lous|ier,
　lousi|est)
Louth
lout|ish
louvre
Louvre (gallery)
louvred
lov|able
lov|ably
lov|age
love (as v., lov|ing)
love-bird
love-child (pl.
　love-children)
love|lily
love|li|ness
love|lock
love|lorn
lovely (as n., pl.
　love|lies; as a.,
　love|lier,
　love|li|est)
love-making
love-match
lover
lov|er|like
love|sick
*Love's Labour's
　Lost*
love|some
love-song

love-story (pl.
　love-stories)
low-born
low-bred
low|brow
low-class
low-down n. & a.
lower
low|er|most
low-grade
low-key
low|land
low|lander
low|lily
low|li|ness
lowly (low|lier,
　low|li|est)
Lowry
loxo|drome
loxo|dromic
loyal
loy|al|ist
loy|ally
loy|alty (pl.
　loy|al|ties)
loz|enge
loz|enged
loz|engy
L-plate
Lu|anda
lub|ber
lub|ric|ant
lub|ric|ate
　(lub|ric|at|ing)
lub|rica|tion
lub|ric|ator
lub|ri|cious
lub|ri|city
Lu|cania
lu|carne (window)
luce (pike)
lu|cency
lu|cent
lu|cerne (plant)
Lu|cerne
*Lu|cia di
　Lam|mer|moor*
Lu|cian
lu|cid
lu|cid|ity
Lu|ci|fer
luck|ily
lucki|ness
lucky (luck|ier,
　lucki|est)
luc|rat|ive

lucre
Lu|crèce Bor|gia
　(by Hugo)
Lu|cre|tius
luc|ub|rate
　(luc|ub|rat|ing)
luc|ub|ra|tion
luc|ub|rator
Lu|cul|lan
Lucy
Lud|dite
lu|dic|rous
lues
lu|etic
Luft|waffe
lug (as v., lugged,
　lug|ging)
luge (toboggan; as
　v., lu|ging)
Lu|ger (gun)
lug|gage
lug|ger
lug|sail
lu|gu|bri|ous
lug|worm
luke|warm
lul|laby (pl.
　lul|la|bies)
lulu
lum|bago (pl.
　lum|ba|gos)
lum|bar (of loin)
lum|ber
lum|berer
lum|ber|jack
lumber-jacket
lum|ber|man (pl.
　lum|ber|men)
lumb|rical
lu|men (unit, pl.
　lu|mens; cavity,
　pl. lu|mina)
Lu|minal (propr.)
lu|min|ance
lu|min|ary (pl.
　lu|min|ar|ies)
lu|min|es|cence
lu|min|es|cent
lu|mini|fer|ous
lu|min|os|ity
lu|min|ous
lum|pen|pro|let|
　　　　　ariat
lump|fish
lump|ily
lumpi|ness

lump|ish
lumpy (lum|pier,
 lum'pi|est)
luna (moth)
lun|acy (pl.
 luna|cies)
lunar
lun'ate
lun|atic
luna|tion
lunch|eon
lunch-hour
lunch-time
lun|ette
lunge (lun'ging)
lung-fish
lung|ful (pl.
 lung|fuls)
lung|wort
luni|solar
lun|ula (pl.
 lun|ulae)
lupi|form
lu'pin
lup|ine
lup'oid
lup'ous
lupus
lurcher
lure (as v., lur'ing)

Lurex (propr.)
lurid
Lu|saka
lus|cious
Lus'it|ania
lust|ful
lust|fully
lust|ily
lusti|ness
lus|tral
lus|trate
 (lus'trat|ing)
lus'tra|tion
lustre
lus|trous
lus|trum (pl.
 lus'tra)
lusty (lus'tier,
 lus'ti|est)
lute (as v., lut'ing)
lut|en|ist
lu|teous
lu'te|tium
Luther
Luth|eran
Luth'er|an|ism
Lu'tine
Lu'ton
lux|ate
 (lux|at'ing)

luxa|tion
Lux'em|burg
lux'uri|ance
lux'uri|ant
lux'uri|ate
 (lux'uri|at'ing)
lux'uri|ous
lux|ury (pl.
 lux|ur'ies)
lyc|an'thrope
lyc|an'thropy
ly'cée
ly'ceum
Ly'ceum (of
 Aristotle)
lychee use litchi
lych|nis
ly'co|pod
ly'co|po'dium
Lyd|ian
lye (alkaline
 substance)
Ly'ell
ly'ing
lyme-grass
lymph
lymph|atic
lympho|cyte
lymphoid
lymph|ous

lyn|cean
lynch
lynchet
lynchpin use
 linchpin
lynx
Lyon (Sc. herald)
Ly'on|nais
Ly'ons
lyo|philic
lyo|phil|ize
 (lyo|phil|iz|ing)
lyo|phobic
lyr|ate
lyre
lyre-bird
lyric
lyr|ical
lyr'ic|ally
lyri|cism
lyr'ist
lyse (lys'ing)
Ly|senko
lys'er|gic
lysin
lysis (pl. lyses)
Lysol (propr.)
lytta (pl. lyt'tae)

M

ma'am
ma|cabre
ma|caco (*pl.*
ma|ca|cos)
mac|adam
mac|ad|amia
mac|ad|am|ize
(mac|ad|am|iz|
ing)
ma|caque
ma|car|oni (*pl.*
ma|car|on|ies)
ma|car|onic
ma|car|oon
Ma|cas|sar
Mac|aulay
ma|caw
Mac|beth
Mac|ca|bean
Mac|ca|bees
Mc|Car|thy
Mc|Car|thy|ism
Mc|Coy
ma|cé|doine
Ma|ce|donia
ma|cer
ma|cer|ate
(ma|cer|at|ing)
ma|cera|tion
ma|cer|ator
Mc|Gon|ag|all
Mach (number)
ma|chete
Ma|chi|avelli
ma|chi|avel|lian
ma|chi|avel|li|an|
ism
ma|chic|ol|ate
(ma|chic|ol|
at|ing)
ma|chic|ola|tion
mach|in|ate
(mach|in|at|ing)
mach|ina|tion
mach|in|ator
ma|chine (as *v.*,
ma|chin|ing)

machine-gun (as
v., machine-
gunned,
machine-
gunning)
machine-
readable
ma|chinery (*pl.*
ma|chiner|ies)
ma|chin|ist
mach|ismo
macho (as *n.*, *pl.*
machos)
macht|pol¦itik
Mac|ken|zie (river
in Canada)
mack|erel
Mc|Kin|ley
mack|in|tosh
mackle (printing
blemish)
macle (twin
crystal, spot in
mineral)
McNagh|ten
(rules)
Mâcon
mac|ramé
mac|ro|bi¦otic
mac|ro|ceph¦alic
mac|ro|
ceph¦al¦ous
mac|ro|cosm
macro-economics
mac|ro|mol¦ec¦ule
mac|ron
mac|ro|
pho¦to¦graphy
mac|ro|scopic
mac|ula (*pl.*
macu|lae)
mac|ula lu¦tea
macu|lar
macu¦la|tion
mad (as *a.*,
mad¦der,
mad¦dest; as *v.*,
mad|ding)
Ma¦da|gas¦car

madam
*Ma¦dama
But¦ter|fly*
Ma¦dame (*pl.*
Mes|dames)
Ma¦dame Bov|ary
mad|cap
mad|den
mad|der
Ma|deira
mad|el¦eine
Ma|dem|ois|elle
(*pl.* Mes|dem¦ois|
elles)
mad|house
Madhya Pra|desh
Mad|ison
Av¦enue
madly
mad|man (*pl.*
mad|men)
ma|donna
ma¦dras (striped
cotton)
Ma¦dras
mad|re|pore
Mad¦rid
mad|rigal
Ma¦dur|ese (*pl.*
same)
mad|wo¦man (*pl.*
mad|wo¦men)
Mae|cenas
mael|strom
maenad
maes¦toso
maes|tro (*pl.*
maes|tros)
Mae|ter|linck
Mae West
maffick
mafia
Mafia (organized
body)
ma¦fi|oso (*pl.*
ma¦fi|osi)
ma|ga¦zine
mag¦da|len

Mag¦da|lenian
(*Archaeol.*)
Mag¦de|burg
Ma¦gel|lan
ma¦genta
mag¦got
mag|goty
magi (*pl.* of
magus)
Magi (the 'wise
men')
ma|gic (as *v.*,
ma|gicked,
ma|gick|ing)
ma|gical
ma|gic|ally
ma|gi|cian
Ma|ginot Line
ma|gis|terial
ma|gis|teri|ally
ma|gis|tracy (*pl.*
ma|gis|tra¦cies)
ma|gis|tral
ma|gis|trate
ma|gis|trate|ship
ma|gis|trat|ure
magma (*pl.*
mag|mata)
mag|matic
Magna Carta
mag|nan|im¦ity
mag|nan|im|ous
mag|nate
mag|ne¦sia
mag|ne¦sian
mag|nes|ium
mag|net
mag|netic
mag|net|ic|ally
mag|net|ism
mag|net|ite
mag|net|iz|able
mag|net|iza|tion
mag|net|ize
(mag|net|iz|ing)
mag|neto (*pl.*
mag|ne¦tos)
magneto-electric
mag|ne¦to|graph

mag|neto|hy|dro|
    dy|namic
mag|ne|to|meter
magneto-motive
mag|neton
mag|neto|sphere
mag|ne|to|
    stric|tion
mag|net|ron
Mag|ni|ficat
 (canticle)
mag|ni|fica|tion
mag|ni|fi|cence
mag|ni|fi|cent
mag|ni|fico (pl.
 mag|ni|fi|coes)
mag|ni|fier
mag|nify
 (mag|ni|fies,
 mag|ni|fied,
 mag|ni|fy|ing)
mag|ni|lo|quence
mag|ni|lo|quent
mag|ni|tude
mag|no|lia
mag|num
mag|num opus
mag|pie
ma|gus (pl. magi)
Mag|yar
ma|ha|leb
ma|ha|raja
ma|ha|ra|nee
Ma|ha|rash|tra
ma|ha|rishi
ma|hatma
Ma|ha|yana
Mahdi
Mahd|ism
Mahd|ist
mah-jong
Mah|ler
ma|hog|any (pl.
 ma|hog|an|ies)
Mahometan use
 Muhammadan
ma|hout
mah|seer
maiden
maid|en|hair
maid|en|head
maid|en|hood
maid|enly
maid|ish
maid|ser|vant
Maid|stone

mai|eutic
maigre
mail|able
mail-bag
mail-boat
mail|box
mail-cart
mail|ing
Maine
main|land
Main|land (in
 Orkney &
 Shetland)
main|line (v.,
 main|lin|ing)
main|mast
main|sail
main|spring
main|stay
main|stream
main|tain
main|tainer
main|tainor (Law)
main|ten|ance
main|top
main-topmast
maiolica use
 majolica
mais|on|ette
ma|jestic
ma|jest|ic|ally
maj|esty (pl.
 maj|est|ies)
Maj|lis
ma|jol|ica
ma|jor
Ma|jorca
major-domo (pl.
 major-domos)
ma|jor|ette
major-general
ma|jor|ity (pl.
 ma|jor|it|ies)
maj|us|cule
mak|able
Ma|kalu
make (as v., made,
 mak|ing)
make-belief
make-believe
make|ready
make|shift
make-up n.
make|weight
mak|ing
mako (pl. ma|kos)

Mal|abar
Ma|labo
Ma|lacca
Mal|achi
mal|ach|ite
mal|aco|derm
ma|la|co|logy
ma|lac|os|tracan
mal|ad|jus|ted
mal|ad|just|ment
mal|ad|min|is|ter
mal|ad|min|is|tra|
    tion
mal|ad|roit
mal|ady (pl.
 mal|ad|ies)
Mal|aga
Ma|la|gasy (pl.
 Ma|la|gas|ies)
mal|aise
mala|mute
mal|aprop
mal|aprop|ism
mal|apro|pos
ma|lar
mal|aria
mal|arial
ma|lar|key
ma|la|thion
Ma|lawi
Ma|lay
Ma|lay|alam
Ma|layan
Ma|lay|sia
mal|con|tent
mal de mer
Mal|dives
Malé
mal|ediction
mal|edict|ive
mal|edict|ory
mal|efac|tion
mal|efactor
mal|efic
mal|efi|cence
mal|efi|cent
mal|evol|ence
mal|evol|ent
mal|feas|ance
mal|feas|ant
mal|forma|tion
mal|formed
mal|func|tion
mali (Ind.
 gardener)
 △ mallee

Mali
malic
mal|ice
ma|li|cious
ma|lign
ma|lig|nancy
ma|lig|nant
ma|lig|nity
ma|lin|ger
mal|ism
mal|lard (pl. same)
mal|le|ab|il|ity
mal|le|able
mal|lee (Austral.
 tree) △ mali
mal|le|muck
mal|le|olus (pl.
 mal|le|oli)
mal|let
mal|leus (pl.
 mal|lei)
mal|low
mal|maison
malm|sey
mal|nour|ish|
       ment
mal|nu|tri|tion
mal|od|or|ous
mal|prac|tice
Malta
mal|ted
Malt|ese (pl. same)
mal|tha
malt-house
Mal|thus
Mal|thu|sian
malt|ing
malt|ose
mal|treat
mal|treat|ment
malt|ster
mal|va|ceous
mal|ver|sa|tion
mal|voisie
mama use
 mamma
mamba (snake)
mambo (dance; pl.
 mam|bos)
mam|elon
Mam|el|uke
ma|milla (pl.
 ma|mil|lae)
ma|mil|lary
ma|mil|late

mamma (mother;
 pl. **mam¦mas**)
mamma (breast;
 pl. **mam¦mae**)
mam¦mal
mam¦ma|lian
mam¦ma¦li|
          fer¦ous
mam¦ma|logy
mam¦mary
mam¦mee (tree)
mam¦mi|form
Mam¦mon
Mam¦mon|ish
Mam¦mon|ism
Mam¦mon|ist
Mam¦mon|ite
mam¦moth
mammy (mother;
 pl. **mam¦mies**)
man (as *n.*, *pl.*
 men; as *v.*,
 manned,
 man¦ning)
mana (power)
 △ manna
man|acle
man¦age
 (man|aging)
man¦age|ab¦il|ity
man¦age|able
man¦age|ably
man¦age|ment
man¦ager
man¦ager|ess
ma¦na¦ger|ial
ma¦na¦geri|ally
man¦ager|ship
man|aging
Ma¦na|gua
man|akin (bird)
 △ manikin,
 mannequin,
 minikin
Ma¦nama
mañ|*ana*
mana|tee
Man|ches¦ter
man¦chin|eel
Man¦chu
Man¦churia
man|ciple
Man|cu¦nian
Man|daean
man|dala
man|da¦mus

man|darin
 (official, orange)
Man|darin
 (language)
man¦dat|ary *n.*
 (*pl.* **man¦dat|**
          ar¦ies)
man|date (as *v.*,
 man¦dat|ing)
man¦dat¦ory *a.*
mand|ible
man|dib|ular
man|dib|ulate
man|dola
man|do¦lin
man|dorla
man|drag|ora
man|drake
man|drel (shaft;
 rod)
man|drill (baboon)
man-eater
man-eating
man¦ège (riding-
 school etc.)
 △ ménage
manes (souls; 2
 sylls.)
Manet
maneuver etc. *use*
 man**œ**uvre etc.
man¦ful
man|fully
man¦ga|bey
man¦gan|ese
man|ganic
man|gan|ous
man|gel
mangel-wurzel
man¦ger
mange-tout
man|gily
man|gi|ness
mangle (as *v.*,
 mang|ling)
mango (*pl.*
 man|goes)
man|gonel
man¦gos|teen
man|grove
mangy (man|gier,
 man¦gi|est)
man|handle
 (man|hand¦ling)
man|hat¦tan
 (cocktail)

Man|hat¦tan
man|hole
man|hood
man-hour
man-hunt
mania
ma|niac
ma|ni|acal
ma¦ni|ac¦ally
manic
manic-depressive
Ma¦ni|chaean
Ma¦ni|chae|ism
Ma¦ni|chee
mani|cure (as *v.*,
 mani|cur¦ing)
mani|cur|ist
mani|fest
ma¦ni|festa¦tion
ma¦ni|fest¦at¦ive
ma¦ni|festo (*pl.*
 ma¦ni|fes¦tos)
mani|fold
man|ikin (dwarf;
 anatomical model)
 △ manakin,
 mannequin,
 minikin
ma¦nila (fibre;
 paper)
Ma¦nila (place;
 cigar)
ma|nilla (Afr.
 bracelet)
ma|nioc
man|iple
ma¦nip|ul|able
ma¦nip|ulate
 (ma¦nip|ulat¦ing)
ma¦nip|ula¦tion
ma¦nip|ulat|ive
ma¦nip|ulator
ma¦nip|ulat¦ory
Ma¦ni|pur
Man|it¦oba
man|itou
man|kind
man¦li|ness
manly
man-made
manna (food)

 △ mana
man|ne¦quin
 (dressmaker's
 model)
 △ manakin,
 manikin,
 minikin
man¦ner
man¦nered
man¦ner|ism
man¦ner|ist
man¦ner|istic
man¦ner¦li|ness
man¦nerly
man|nish
man|œuv|rab¦il|ity
man|œuv|rable
man|œuvre (as *v.*,
 man|œuv|ring)
man|œuvrer
man-of-war (*pl.*
 men-of-war)
mano|meter
ma|no|met¦ric
manor
manor-house
man|orial
man|power
man|*qué*
man|sard
man|ser¦vant (*pl.*
 men|ser¦vants)
man|sion
mansion-house
Man|sion House
 (of Mayor)
man-size
man-sized
man|slaugh¦ter
manta
man¦tel
man¦telet
man¦tel|piece
man¦tel|shelf (*pl.*
 man¦tel|shelves)
mantic
man|tilla
man|tissa
mantle (as *v.*,
 mant|ling)
mant|ling
man¦tra
man¦trap
man¦tua
man|ual

manu|ally
man|u|fact|ory
 (pl. man|u|
  fact|or|ies)
man|u|fac|ture (as
 v., man|u|fac|tur|
  ing)
man|u|fac|turer
ma|nuka
ma|nu|mis|sion
ma|nu|mit
 (ma|nu|mit|ted,
 ma|nu|mit|ting)
ma|nure (as v.,
 ma|nur|ing)
ma|nur|ial
ma|nu|script
Manx|man (pl.
 Manx|men)
many
many|plies
man|zan|illa
man|zan|ita
Mao|ism
Mao|ist
Maori
Maori|land
Mao Ze|dong
 (Mao Tse-tung)
map (as v.,
 mapped,
 map|ping)
maple
maple-leaf (pl.
 maple-leaves)
Ma|puto
ma|quette
Ma|quis
mar (mar|ring)
mara|bou (stork;
 down)
mara|bout
 (Muslim hermit or
  monk)
ma|raca
Ma|ra|caibo, Lake
ma|ras|chino (pl.
 ma|ras|chi|nos)
mar|as|mic
mar|as|mus
Ma|ratha (people)
Ma|rathi
 (language)
mara|thon
ma|raud
ma|rauder

ma|ra|vedi
marble (as v.,
 marb|ling)
marbly
marc (brandy)
Marcan
mar|cas|ite
mar|cato
mar|cel (as v.,
 mar|celled,
 mar|cel|ling)
mar|ces|cence
mar|ces|cent
Marche (in
 France)
marcher
Marches (in Italy)
mar|chion|ess
Mar|coni
Mardi Gras
mare (sea, lunar
 plain; pl. maria)
ma|remma
mare's-tail (marsh
 plant, streak of
  cloud)
Mar|gar|et
mar|gar|ine
mar|gay
Mar|gery
mar|gin
mar|ginal
mar|gin|alia
mar|gin|ally
mar|gin|ate
mar|grave
mar|grav|ine
mar|guer|ite
Mar|ian
mari|gold
ma|ri|juana
ma|rimba
ma|rina
mar|in|ade (as v.,
 mar|in|ad|ing)
mar|in|ate
 (mar|in|at|ing)
ma|rine
mar|iner
Ma|ri|ol|atry
Ma|ri|on
ma|ri|on|ette
mar|ital
mar|it|ally
mari|time
mar|joram

Mar|jor|ie
mark|edly
mark|ed|ness
marker
mar|ket (as v.,
 mar|keted,
 mar|ket|ing)
mar|ket|able
market-day
market-place
mark|hor
mark|ing
marks|man (pl.
 marks|men)
marks|man|ship
mark-up n.
Marl|bor|ough
Marl|burian
mar|lin (fish)
mar|line (Naut.)
mar|lin|spike
marl|ite
Mar|lowe
mar|ma|lade
mar|mite
 (cooking-vesel)
Mar|mite (extract
 of yeast; propr.)
mar|mol|ite
mar|mor|eal
mar|mo|set
mar|mot
ma|ro|cain
Mar|on|ite
ma|roon
mar|plot
marque (make of
 car)
mar|quee (large
 tent)
mar|quetry
mar|quis
mar|quis|ate
mar|quise
mar|quis|ette
Mar|ra|kesh
mar|ram
Mar|rano (pl.
 Mar|ra|nos)
mar|riage
mar|riage|able
mar|ried
mar|ron glacé
 (pl. mar|rons
  gla|cés)

mar|row
mar|row|bone
mar|row|fat
marry (mar|ries,
 mar|ried,
 mar|ry|ing)
Mar|sala
Mar|seil|laise
Mar|seilles
mar|shal (as v.,
 mar|shalled,
 mar|shal|ling)
marshi|ness
marsh|land
marsh|mal|low
 (soft sweet)
marsh mal|low
 (plant, confection)
marshy
 (marsh|ier,
  marshi|est)
mar|sup|ial
mar|ta|gon
Mar|tello (pl.
 Mar|tel|los)
mar|ten (weasel-
 like animal)
△ martin
mar|tens|ite
mar|tial
Mar|tial (poet)
mar|tial|ize
 (mar|tial|iz|ing)
mar|tially
Mar|tian
mar|tin (bird)
△ marten
Mar|tin
Mar|tin
 Chuzzle|wit
mar|tinet
mar|tin|et|tish
mar|tin|gale
Mar|tini (propr.)
Mar|tin|mas
mar|tyr
mar|tyr|dom
mar|tyr|iza|tion
mar|tyro|lo|gical
mar|tyro|lo|gist
mar|tyro|logy (pl.
 mar|tyro|lo|gies)
mar|tyry (pl.
 mar|tyr|ies)

mar'vel (as v.,
 mar'velled,
 mar'vel|ling)
mar'vel|lous
Marx'ian
Marx'ism
Marx'ist
Mary
Mary|bor'ough
Mary|land
mar'zi|pan
Ma'sac'cio
mas|cara
mascle
mas'con
mas'cot
mas'cu|line
mas'cu|lin|ity
Mase|field
maser
Mas'eru
masher
mashie
mas'kin|onge
mas'och|ism
mas'och|ist
mas'och|istic
ma'son
Ma'son
 (Freemason)
Ma|sonic
ma|sonry
Ma|sonry
 (Freemasonry)
Mas|orah
Mas|or|ete
Mas|or|etic
masque
 (entertainment)
mas'quer
mas'quer|ade (as
 v., mas'quer|
  ad'ing)
Mas'sa|chu'setts
mas|sacre (as v.,
 mas|sac'ring)
mas|sage (as v.,
 mas|sa'ging)
mas|sa|sauga
massé
mas|seter
mas|seur (fem.
 mas|seuse)
mas'si|cot
mas'sif
mas|sive
mass|less
mass-produced
mas|taba

mast|ec'tomy (pl.
 mast|ec'tom|ies)
mas'ter
master-at-arms
 (pl. masters-at-
  arms)
mas'ter|ful
mas'ter|fully
mas'ter|li|ness
masterly
master|mind
mas'ter|piece
mas'ter|singer
master-stroke
master-switch
master-work
mas|tery
mast-head
mas'tic
mas'tic|ate
 (mas'tic|at'ing)
mas'tica|tion
mas'tic|ator
mas'tic|at'ory
mas'tiff
mast|itis
mas'to|don
mas'to|dontic
mas'toid
mast|oid|itis
mas'turb|ate
 (mas'turb|at'ing)
mas'turba|tion
mas'turb|at'ory
mat (as v.,
 mat'ted,
 mat'ting)
mat|ador
match|board
match|box
match|less
match|lock
match|maker
match|stick
match|wood
mate (as v.,
 mat'ing)
maté (tea)
mate|lot (sailor)
mate|lote (fish
 stew)
ma'ter
ma'ter|fa'mi'lias
ma'ter|ial
ma'teri|al|ism
ma'teri|al|ist

ma'teri|al|istic
ma'teri|al|ity
ma'teri|al|iza|tion
ma'teri|al|ize
 (ma'teri|al|iz|ing)
ma'teri|ally
ma'teria med'ica
ma'ter|nal
ma'ter|nally
ma'ter|nity
ma'tey (as a.,
 ma'tier,
 ma'ti|est)
ma'tey|ness
math'em'at|ical
math'em'at|ic|ally
math'em'at|ician
math'em'at|ics
ma'tico (pl.
 ma'ti|cos)
Ma|tilda
mat|inée
matiness use
 mateyness
mat|ins
Mat|isse
Mat|lock
mat|rass (glass
 vessel)
mat'ri|arch
mat'ri|archal
mat'ri|archy (pl.
 mat'ri|archies)
ma'tric
ma'tri|cidal
mat'ri|cide
ma'tric|ulate
 (ma'tric|ulat'ing)
ma'tric|ula|tion
ma'tric|ulat|ory
mat'ri|lin|eal
mat'ri|lin|eally
mat'ri|local
mat'ri|mo'nial
mat'ri|mo'ni|ally
mat'ri|mony
mat'rix (pl.
 mat'ri|ces)
mat'ron
mat|ronal
mat|ronly
matt (dull)
mat'ta|more
matte (Smelting)
mat|ter
matter-of-fact a.

mat|tery
Mat|thew
mat|ting
mat|tock
mat|toid
mat|tress
mat|ur'ate
 (mat|ur|at'ing)
mat|ura|tion
mat|urat|ive
ma|ture (as a.,
 ma|turer,
 ma|tur|est; as v.,
 ma|tur|ing)
ma|tur|ity
ma|tu|tinal
maty use matey
matzo (pl.
 mat'zos)
maud|lin
Maugham
maul|stick
Mauna Loa
maun|der
Maundy
Mau'pas|sant
Maur|een
Maur|ist
Mau'ri|ta'nia
Maur|itian
Mau'ri|tius
mau|so|leum
mav'er|ick
mawk|ish
maw|worm
maxi
max|illa (pl.
 max|il|lae)
max|il|lary
maxim
Maxim (gun)
max|imal
max'im|al|ist
max'im|ally
max'im|iza|tion
max'im|ize
 (max'im|iz|ing)
max|imum (pl.
 max'ima)
max|well
may (might)
maya (Hinduism)
Maya (Amer. Ind.)
Mayan
May-apple
maybe

May-bug
May Day (1st
  May)
May|day (signal)
May|fair
May|flower
may'|fly (pl.
  may'|flies)
may'|hem
may'|ing
mayn't
Mayo
may'|on|naise
mayor
may|oral
may'|or|alty (pl.
  may'|or|al'|ties)
may'|or|ess
may|pole
may|weed
maz'|ard
maz'|ar|ine
Maz'|da|ism
maze (as v.,
  maz'|ing)
mazer
ma'|zily
ma'|zi|ness
ma'|zurka
mazy (ma'|zier,
  ma'|zi|est)
Mba|bane
me (Mus.)
meadow
meadow-grass
mead'|ow|sweet
mead|owy
meagre
mealie (maize)
mea'|li|ness
meal|time
mealy (of or like
  meal)
mealy-bug
mealy-mouthed
mean (as v.,
  meant)
me|an'|der
me|and'|rine
meanie
mean|ing
mean'|ing|ful
mean'|ing|fully
mean'|ing|less
mean|time adv.
mean|while adv.

measles
measly
meas'|ur|able
meas'|ur|ably
meas|ure (as v.,
  meas'|ur|ing)
meas'|ured
meas|ure|less
meas|ure|ment
Meath
meat|ily
meati|ness
meat-safe
meatus (pl. same)
meaty (meat|ier,
  meati|est)
Mecca
Mec|cano (propr.)
mech|anic
mech'|an|ical
mech'|an|ic'|al|ism
mech'|an|ic'|ally
mech'|an|ician
mech'|an|ism
mech'|an|ist
mech'|an|istic
mech'|an|iza'|tion
mech'|an|ize
  (mech'|an|iz|ing)
Mech|lin
me'|co|nium
medal
med|alled
me'|dal|lic
med'|al|lion
med'|al|list
meddle
  (med|dling)
med'|dle|some
me'|dia (Phonet. &
  Biol.; pl. me'|diae)
me'|dia (pl. of
  medium)
Media (anc.
  country)
mediaeval use
  medieval
medial
me'|di|ally
me'|dian
Me'|dian (of Media)
me'|di|ant
me'|di|as'|tinal
me'|di|as'|tinum
  (pl. me'|di|as'|tina)

me'|di|ate (as v.,
  me'|di|at'|ing)
me'|di|ation
me'|di|at|iza'|tion
me'|di|ator
me'|di|at|or|ial
me'|di|at'|ory
me'|di|at'|rix (pl.
  me'|di|at'|ri'|ces)
medic (doctor)
med'|ic|able
med'|ical
med'|ic|ally
me'|dic|ament
med'|ic|ate
  (med'|ic|at'|ing)
med'|ica|tion
med'|ic'|at|ive
Me'|di|cean
me'|di|cinal
me'|di|cin|ally
me'|di|cine
medicine-man (pl.
  medicine-men)
med'|ick (plant)
med'|ico (pl.
  med'|icos)
me'|di|eval
me'|di|ev'|al|ism
me'|di|ev'|al|ist
me'|di|ev'|ally
me'|di|ocre
me'|di|oc'|rity (pl.
  me'|di|oc'|rit'|ies)
med'|it|ate
  (med'|it|at'|ing)
me'|di|ta'|tion
med'|it|at'|ive
med'|it|ator
me'|di|ter'|ran'|ean
  (land-locked)
Me'|di|ter'|ran'|ean
  (Sea)
me'|dium (pl.
  me'|dia, in
  spiritualism
  me'|diums)
me'|dium|ism
me'|di|um|istic
med'|lar
med'|ley
Médoc
me'|dulla
me'|dul|lary
me'|dusa (pl.
  me'|du|sae)

me|dusan
meer|kat
meer|schaum
meet (met)
meet|ing
mega|ceph'|alic
mega|cyle
mega|death
mega|lith
mega|lithic
me'|ga|lo|mania
me'|ga|lo|ma'|niac
me'|ga|lo|polis
me'|ga|lo|saurus
me'|ga|phone
me'|ga|pode
mega|scopic
mega|ther'|ium
  (pl. mega|theria)
mega|ton
mega|tonne
Meg'|ger (propr.)
Meg'|ha|laya
meg|ilp
meg|ohm
meg'|rim
Mein Kampf
mei|osis (pl.
  mei|oses)
mei|otic
Meis'|ter|singer
  (pl. same)
*Meis'|ter|singer
  von Nürn|berg*
Me|kong
mel'|am|ine
mel'|an|cho'|lia
mel'|an|cholic
mel'|an|choly
Mel'|an|esian
mélange
mel'|anin
mel'|an|ism
mel'|an|osis (pl.
  mel'|an|oses)
mel'|an|otic
Melba
Mel|bourne
mêlée
melic
meli'|or|ate
  (meli'|or|at'|ing)
meli'|ora'|tion
meli'|or|at'|ive
meli'|or|ism
meli'|or|ist

me|lisma (pl.
 me|lis|mata)
me|lis|matic
mel|li|fer|ous
mel|li|fluence
mel|li|flu|ent
mel|li|flu|ous
mel|low
me|lod|eon
me|lodic
me|lodi|ous
mel|od|ist
mel|od|ize
 (mel|od|iz|ing)
me|lo|drama
me|lo|dra|matic
me|lo|dra|mat|ic|
 ally
me|lo|dram|at|ist
mel|ody (pl.
 mel|od|ies)
melon
melting-point
melting-pot
mel|ton (cloth)
Mel|ton
 Mow|bray
mem|ber
mem|ber|ship
mem|brana|ceous
mem|brane
mem|bran|eous
mem|bran|ous
me|mento (pl.
 me|men|toes)
memo (pl. memos)
mem|oir
mem|oir|ist
mem|or|ab|ilia
mem|or|ab|il|ity
mem|or|able
mem|or|ably
mem|or|andum
 (pl. mem|or|anda
 in sense 'thing to
 be noted',
 mem|or|and|ums
 in sense 'note')
me|mor|ial
me|mori|al|ist
me|mori|al|ize
 (me|mori|al|iz|
 ing)
mem|or|ize
 (mem|or|iz|ing)

mem|ory (pl.
 mem|or|ies)
mem|sahib
men|ace (as v.,
 men|acing)
mén|age
 (household)
△ manège
me|na|gerie
men|ar|che
men|dacious
men|da|city
 (falsehood; pl.
 men|da|cit|ies)
Men|del
men|del|evium
Men|del|eyev
Men|del|ian
Men|dels|sohn
men|dic|ancy
men|dic|ant
men|di|city
 (begging)
mend|ing
men|folk
men|haden
men|hir
me|nial
me|ni|ally
men|in|geal
men|in|gitis
men|in|go|cele
men|inx (pl.
 men|inges)
men|is|cus (pl.
 men|isci)
Men|non|ite
meno|logy (pl.
 meno|lo|gies)
meno|pausal
meno|pause
men|orah
men|or|rha|gia
men|or|rhoea
men|ses
Men|shevik
mens rea
men|strual
men|stru|ate
 (men|stru|at|ing)
men|stru|ation
men|stru|ous
men|struum (pl.
 men|strua)
men|sur|able
men|sural

men|sura|tion
mens|wear
men|tal
men|tal|ism
men|tal|ist
men|tal|ity (pl.
 men|tal|it|ies)
men|tally
men|ta|tion
men|thol
men|thol|ated
men|tion
men|tion|able
mentor
menu
mep|ac|rine
Meph|is|toph|
 elean
Meph|is|toph|eles
meph|itic
meph|itis
mer|cant|ile
mer|cant|il|ism
mer|cant|il|ist
mer|cap|tan
Mer|cator
mer|cen|ari|ness
mer|cen|ary (as
 n., pl.
 mer|cen|ar|ies)
mer|cer
mer|cer|ize
 (mer|cer|iz|ing)
mer|cery
mer|chand|ise (as
 v., merch|and|
 ising)
mer|chant
mer|chant|man
 (pl.
 mer|chant|men)
mer|ci|ful
mer|ci|fully
mer|ci|less
mer|cur|ial
mer|curi|ally
mer|curic
mer|cur|ous
mer|cury (metal)
Mer|cury (god,
 planet)
mercy (pl.
 mer|cies)
mere|tri|cious
mer|gan|ser
merge (mer|ging)

mer|gence
mer|ger
me|ri|dian
me|ri|di|onal
mer|ingue
me|rino (pl.
 me|ri|nos)
mer|is|tem
mer|is|tem|atic
merit (as v.,
 mer|ited,
 mer|it|ing)
mer|ito|cracy (pl.
 mer|ito|cra|cies)
mer|it|ori|ous
mer|lin (falcon)
mer|lon (part of
 parapet)
mer|maid
mer|man (pl.
 mer|men)
mero|blast
mero|hed|ral
Me|ro|vin|gian
mer|rily
mer|ri|ment
merri|ness
merry (as a.,
 mer|rier,
 mer|ri|est; as n.,
 pl. mer|ries)
merry-go-round
merry-maker
merry-making
mer|ry|thought
Mer|sey
Mer|sey|side
Mer|thyr Tyd|fil
més|al|li|ance
mes|cal
mes|cal|ine
mes|em|bry|
 an|themum
mes|en|ceph|alon
mes|en|teric
mes|en|ter|itis
mes|en|tery (pl.
 mes|en|ter|ies)
me|sial
me|si|ally
mesic
mes|meric
mes|mer|ism
mes|mer|ist
mes|mer|ize
 (mes|mer|iz|ing)

meso-American
meso|blast
meso|carp
meso|ceph|alic
meso|derm
meso|gas|ter
meso|lithic
meso|morph
meso|morphic
meso|morphy
meson
mes|onic
meso|phyll
meso|phyte
meso|sphere
meso|tron
Meso|zoic
mes|quite
mes|sage (as v.,
   mes|saging)
mes|sen|ger
Mes|siaen
Mes|siah
Mes|si|anic
Mes|si|an|ism
mes|sily
mes|si|ness
mess|mate
Messrs
mes|suage
messy (mes|sier,
   mes|si|est)
mes|tizo (pl.
   mes|ti|zos)
meta|bolic
meta|bol|ism
meta|bol|ize
   (meta|bol|iz|ing)
meta|carpal
meta|carpus (pl.
   meta|carpi)
meta|centre
meta|cent|ric
met|age
meta|gen|esis
meta|gen|etic
metal (as v.,
   met|alled,
   met|al|ling)
meta|lan|guage
me|tal|lic
me|tal|lic|ally
me|tal|li|fer|ous
met|al|line
me|tal|liza|tion

met|al|lize
   (met|al|liz|ing)
me|tal|lo|graphy
met|al|loid
me|tal|lo|phone
me|tal|lur|gic
me|tal|lur|gical
me|tal|lur|gist
me|tal|lurgy
met|al|work
meta|mer
meta|mere
meta|meric
meta|mer|ism
meta|morphic
meta|morph|ism
meta|morph|ose
   (meta|
      morph|os|ing)
meta|morph|osis
   (pl. meta|
      morph|oses)
meta|phor
meta|phoric
meta|phor|ical
meta|phor|ic|ally
meta|phrase
   (as v., meta|
      phras|ing)
meta|phrastic
meta|physic
meta|physical
meta|phys|ic|ally
meta|physi|cian
meta|physics
meta|plasia
meta|plasm
meta|plastic
meta|pol|it|ics
meta|sta|bil|ity
meta|stable
meta|stasis (pl.
   meta|stases)
meta|static
meta|tarsal
meta|tarsus (pl.
   meta|tarsi)
meta|thesis (pl.
   meta|theses)
meta|thetic
meta|thet|ical
meta|zoan
mete (as v.,
   met|ing)

met|
   em|psy|chosis
   (pl. met|
      em|psy|choses)
met|em|psy|chos|
      ist
met|eor
met|eoric
met|eor|ic|ally
met|eor|ite
met|eoro|graph
met|eor|oid
met|eor|oidal
met|eoro|lo|gical
met|eoro|lo|gic|
      ally
met|eoro|lo|gist
met|eoro|logy
meter (measuring
   device) △ metre
methad|one
meth|amph|et|
      am|ine
meth|ane
meth|anol
Meth|ed|rine
   (propr.)
method
meth|odic
meth|od|ical
meth|od|ic|ally
Meth|od|ism
meth|od|ist
Meth|od|ist
   (religious
   denomination)
Meth|od|istic
Meth|od|ist|ical
meth|od|ize
   (meth|od|iz|ing)
meth|odo|lo|gical
meth|odo|lo|gic|
      ally
meth|odo|logy (pl.
   meth|odo|lo|gies)
Me|thu|selah
methyl
methyl|ate
   (methyl|at|ing)
methyl|ene
me|thylic
metic
me|ticu|lous
mé|tier
metif
metis

metol
Met|onic
met|onym
met|onym|ical
met|onymy (pl.
   met|onym|ies)
met|ope
metre (unit; poetic
   rhythm) △ meter
metre|age
met|ric
met|rical
met|ric|ally
met|ric|ate
   (met|ric|at|ing)
met|rica|tion
met|ri|cian
met|ri|cize
   (met|ri|ciz|ing)
met|rics
met|rist
met|ritis
Metro (pl.
   Met|ros)
met|ro|lo|gic
met|ro|lo|gical
met|ro|logy
met|ro|nome
met|ro|nomic
met|ro|nymic
met|ro|polis
met|ro|pol|itan
met|ro|pol|it|an|
      ate
met|ror|rha|gia
Met|ter|nich
mettle (on one's)
met|tle|some
meu (baldmoney)
mewl (whimper)
Mex|ican
Mex|ico
Meyer
me|zer|eon
me|zu|zah (pl.
   me|zu|zoth)
mez|zan|ine
mezza voce
mezzo (pl.
   mez|zos)
mezzo-rilievo (pl.
   mezzo-rilievos)
mezzo-soprano
   (pl. mezzo-
      sopranos)
mez|zo|tint

mho (*pl.* mhos)
mi (*Mus.*) *use* me
Mi¦ami
mi¦aow
mi¦asma (*pl.*
 mi¦as¦mata)
mi¦as¦mal
mi¦as¦matic
mi¦aul
mica (mineral)
mi¦ca¦ceous
Mi¦cah (OT book)
Mi¦caw¦ber
Mi¦caw¦ber¦ish
mi¦celle
Mi¦chael
Mich¦ael¦mas
Mich¦el¦an¦gelo
Mich¦igan
mickey (take the)
Mickey Finn
Mic¦kie¦wicz
mickle
mi¦crobe
mi¦cro¦bial
mi¦crobic
mi¦cro¦bio¦lo¦gist
mi¦cro¦bio¦logy
Mi¦cro¦card
 (*propr.*)
mi¦cro¦ceph¦alic
mic¦ro¦ceph¦al¦
 ous
mi¦cro¦chip
mi¦cro¦cir¦cuit
mi¦cro¦cli¦mate
mi¦cro¦cline
mi¦cro¦com¦puter
mi¦cro¦cosm
mi¦cro¦cos¦mic
mi¦cro¦crys¦tal¦
 line
mi¦cro¦dot
micro-electronics
mi¦cro¦fiche (*pl.*
 same)
mi¦cro¦film
mi¦cro¦graph
mi¦cro¦groove
mi¦cro¦lith
mi¦cro¦meter
mi¦cro¦
 mi¦ni¦at¦ur¦iza¦
 tion
mi¦cron
Mi¦cro¦nes¦ian

micro-organism
mi¦cro¦phone
mi¦cro¦pho¦to¦
 graph
mi¦cro¦phyte
mi¦cro¦
 pro¦ces¦sor
mi¦cro¦pyle
mi¦cro¦scope
mi¦cro¦scopic
mi¦cro¦scop¦ical
mi¦cro¦scop¦ic¦
 ally
mi¦cro¦scop¦ist
mi¦cro¦scopy
mi¦cro¦seism
mi¦cro¦some
mi¦cro¦spore
mi¦cro¦struc¦ture
mi¦cro¦tech¦nique
mi¦cro¦tome
mi¦cro¦tone
mi¦cro¦wave
mic¦rurgy
mic¦turi¦tion
mid (mid¦most)
Mi¦das
mid¦brain
mid¦day
mid¦den
middle (as *v.*,
 mid¦dling)
middle-aged
middle-brow
mid¦dle¦man (*pl.*
 mid¦dle¦men)
Middles¦brough
Mid¦dle¦sex
middle-sized
mid¦dle¦weight
mid¦dling
middy (*pl.*
 mid¦dies)
mid¦field
mid¦get
midi (dress etc.)
Midi (in France)
mi¦di¦nette
mid¦land
Mid¦lands (of
 England)
mid-line
mid¦night
mid-off
mid-on

Mid¦rash (*pl.*
 Mid¦rashim)
mid¦rib
mid¦riff
mid¦ship
mid¦ship¦man (*pl.*
 mid¦ship¦men)
mid¦sum¦mer
*Mid¦sum¦mer
 Night's Dream*
mid¦way
Mid¦west
mid¦wicket
mid¦wife (*pl.*
 mid¦wives)
mid¦wif¦ery
mid¦win¦ter
mien
might-have-been
 n.
migh¦tily
migh¦ti¦ness
mighty
 (migh¦tier,
 migh¦ti¦est)
mign¦on¦ette
mi¦graine
mi¦grain¦ous
mi¦grant
mi¦grate
 (mi¦grat¦ing)
mi¦gra¦tion
mi¦grator
mi¦grat¦ory
mih¦rab
mi¦kado (*pl.*
 mi¦ka¦dos)
Mi¦kado (by
 Gilbert &
 Sullivan)
mike (as *v.*,
 mik¦ing)
mi¦lady (*pl.*
 mi¦la¦dies)
Mi¦lan
Mil¦an¦ese (*pl.*
 same)
milden
mil¦dew
mil¦dewy
mile¦age
mile-post
miler
Mi¦les¦ian
mile¦stone
Mi¦letus

mil¦foil
mili¦ary
mi¦lieu (*pl.*
 mi¦lieux)
mil¦it¦ancy
mil¦it¦ant
mil¦it¦ar¦ily
mil¦it¦ar¦ism
mil¦it¦ar¦ist
mil¦it¦ar¦istic
mil¦it¦ar¦iza¦tion
mil¦it¦ar¦ize
 (mil¦it¦ar¦iz¦ing)
mil¦it¦ary (as *n.*, *pl.*
 mil¦it¦ar¦ies)
mil¦it¦ate
 (mil¦it¦at¦ing)
mi¦li¦tia
mi¦li¦tia¦man (*pl.*
 mi¦li¦tia¦men)
milk-float
milki¦ness
milk-leg
milk-loaf (*pl.*
 milk-loaves)
milk¦maid
milk¦man (*pl.*
 milk¦men)
milk-powder
milk¦sop
milk-tooth (*pl.*
 milk-teeth)
milk¦weed
milk¦wort
milky (milk¦ier,
 milk¦i¦est)
mill¦board
mille-feuille
mil¦len¦ar¦ian
mil¦len¦ari¦an¦ism
mil¦len¦ary (as *n.*,
 pl. mil¦len¦ar¦ies)
mil¦len¦nial
mil¦len¦nium (*pl.*
 mil¦len¦niums)
mil¦le¦pede
mil¦le¦pore
miller
mil¦les¦imal
mil¦les¦im¦ally
mil¦let
mil¦li¦am¦meter
mil¦li¦am¦pere
mil¦liard
mil¦li¦bar
mil¦li¦gram

mil'li|litre
mil'li|metre
mill|liner
mil'lin|ery
mil'lion
mil'lion|aire
mil'lion|air'ess
mil'lion|fold
mil'lionth
millipede *use*
 millepede
mill-pond
mill-race
mill-rind
mill|stone
mill-wheel
mill|wright
mi'lo|meter
mi'lord
milter
Mil'ton
Mil'ton|ian
Mil'tonic
mim'bar
mime (as *v.*,
 mim'ing)
mi'meo|graph
mi'mesis
mi'metic
mi'met|ic|ally
mimic (as *v.*,
 mim|icked,
 mim'ick|ing)
mim|icry (*pl.*
 mim'ic|ries)
miminy-piminy
mi'mosa
mimu|lus
mina (unit; *pl.*
 minae)
mina (bird; *pl.*
 minas)
mi'na|cious
min|acity (*pl.*
 min|acit'ies)
min|aret
min'at|ory
mince (as *v.*,
 min'cing)
mince|meat
mincer
minded
minder
mind|ful
mind|fully
mind|less

mind-set
mine (as *v.*,
 min'ing)
mine|field
mine|layer
miner
min|eral
min'er'al|ize
 (min'er'al|iz'ing)
min'era|lo'gical
min'er'al|ogist
min'er'al|ogy
min'es|trone
mine|sweeper
mine|worker
mingle
 (ming|ling)
mingy (min|gier,
 min'gi|est)
mini
Mini (car; *propr.*)
mini|ate
 (mini|at'ing)
mini|ature (as *v.*,
 mini|atur'ing)
mini|atur|ist
mini|atur|iza'tion
mini|atur|ize
 (mini|atur|iz'ing)
mini|cab
mini|dress
minify (mini|fies,
 mini|fied,
 mini|fy'ing)
mini|kin
 (diminutive
 person or thing;
 mincing)
 ⚠ manakin,
 manikin,
 mannequin
minim
min|imal
min|im'al|ist
min'im|ally
min'im|iza'tion
min'im|ize
 (min'im|iz'ing)
min|imum (*pl.*
 min'ima)
min'ion
miniscule *use*
 minuscule
mini|skirt
min'is|ter
min'is|ter|ial

min'is'teri|ally
min'is|trant
min'is|tra'tion
min'is|trat'ive
min'is|try (*pl.*
 min'is|tries)
min|iver
minke (whale)
min'ne|singer
Min'ne|sota
min|now
Mi'noan
mi'nor
Min|orca
Mi'nor|ite
mi'nor|ity (*pl.*
 mi'nor|it'ies)
Mi'nos
Mi'no|taur
min'ster
min|strel
min'strelsy
mint|age
Min'ton
minty (min|tier,
 min'ti|est)
minu|end
min'uet
minus
min'us|cu'lar
min'us|cule
min'ute (as *v.*,
 min'ut|ing)
mi'nute *a.*
 (mi|nuter,
 mi'nut|est)
minute-man (*pl.*
 minute-men)
mi'nu'tia (*pl.*
 mi'nu|tiae)
Minya Konka
Mio|cene
mi'osis (*pl.*
 mi'oses)
mi'otic
mi'ra|belle
mir|acle
mi'ra'cu|lous
mi'ra|dor
mir'age
mire (as *v.*,
 mir'ing)
mirepoix
mirk *use* murk
mirky *use* murky
Miró

mir|ror
mirth|ful
mirth|fully
mirth|less
miry
mis|ad'ven|ture
mis|align
mis|align|ment
mis|al'li|ance
mis|an'thrope
mis|an'thropic
mis|an'throp|ical
mis|an'throp|ist
mis|an'thropy
mis|ap'plica|tion
mis|apply
 (mis|ap'plies,
 mis|ap'plied,
 mis|ap'ply|ing)
mis|ap'pre|hend
mis|ap'pre|hen|
 sion
mis|ap'pre|hens|
 ive
mis|ap'pro'pri|ate
 (mis|ap'pro'pri|
 at'ing)
mis|ap'pro'pri|
 ation
mis|be'come
 (mis|be'came,
 mis|be'come,
 mis|be'com|ing)
mis|be'got'ten
mis|be'have
 (mis|be'hav'ing)
mis|be'ha'viour
mis|be'lief
mis|cal'cu|late
 (mis|cal'cu|
 lat'ing)
mis|cal'cu|la'tion
mis|call
mis|car'riage
mis|carry
 (mis|car'ries,
 mis|car'ried,
 mis|car'ry|ing)
mis|cast
 (mis|cast)
mis|ce'gena'tion
mis|cel'la'nea
mis|cel'lan'eous
mis|cel'lan|ist
mis|cel'lany (*pl.*
 mis|cel'lan|ies)

mis|chance
mis|chief
mis|chiev|ous
misch|met|all
mis|cib|il|ity
mis|cible
mis|con|ceive
(mis|con|ceiv|
   ing)
mis|con|cep|tion
mis|con|duct
mis|
 con|struc|tion
mis|con|strue
(mis|con|stru|
   ing)
mis|copy
(mis|cop|ies,
 mis|cop|ied,
 mis|copy|ing)
mis|count
mis|cre|ant
mis|cue (as v.,
 mis|cue|ing)
mis|date
(mis|dat|ing)
mis|deal (as v.,
 mis|dealt)
mis|deed
mis|de|mean|ant
mis|de|mean|our
mis|dir|ect
mis|dir|ec|tion
mis|do|ing
mis|doubt
mise-en-scène
miser
mis|er|able
mis|er|ably
mis|ère (*Cards*)
mis|er|ere
mis|eri|cord
miser|li|ness
miserly
mis|ery (*pl.*
 mis|er|ies)
mis|feas|ance
mis|fire
(mis|fir|ing)
mis|fit
mis|for|tune
mis|give
(mis|gave,
 mis|given,
 mis|giv|ing)
mis|giv|ing

mis|gov|ern
mis|gov|ern|ment
mis|guid|ance
mis|guide
(mis|guid|ing)
mis|guided
mis|handle
(mis|hand|ling)
mis|hap
mis|hear
(mis|heard)
mis|hit (as v.,
 mis|hit,
 mis|hit|ting)
mish|mash
Mish|nah
Mish|naic
mis|in|form
mis|in|forma|tion
mis|in|ter|pret
(mis|in|ter|
   preted,
 mis|in|ter|pret|
   ing)
mis|in|ter|preta|
   tion
mis|judge
(mis|judging)
mis|judge|ment
mis|lay (mis|laid)
mis|lead (misled)
mis|man|age
(mis|man|aging)
mis|man|age|
   ment
mis|match
mis|name
(mis|nam|ing)
mis|nomer
miso|gam|ist
miso|gamy
miso|gyn|ist
miso|gyny
miso|lo|gist
miso|logy
miso|neism
miso|neist
miso|pickel
mis|place
(mis|pla|cing)
mis|place|ment
mis|play
mis|print
mis|pri|sion
mis|prize
(mis|priz|ing)

mis|pro|nounce
(mis|pro|noun|
   cing)
mis|pro|nun|ci|
   ation
mis|quo|ta|tion
mis|quote
(mis|quot|ing)
mis|read
(mis|read)
mis|re|mem|ber
mis|re|port
mis|rep|res|ent
mis|rep|res|enta|
   tion
mis|rule (as v.,
 mis|rul|ing)
miss|able
mis|sal (book)
mis|sel (thrush)
mis|shape
(mis|shap|ing)
mis|shapen
mis|sile
mis|silery
miss|ing
mis|sion
mis|sion|ary (*pl.*
 mis|sion|ar|ies)
mis|sioner
mis|sis
miss|ish
Mis|sis|sippi
mis|sive
Mis|souri
mis|spell
(mis|spelt)
mis|spend
(mis|spent)
mis|state
(mis|stat|ing)
mis|state|ment
mis|step
missy (*pl.*
 mis|sies)
mis|tak|able
mis|tak|ably
mis|take (as v.
 mis|took,
 mis|taken,
 mis|tak|ing)
mis|teach
(mis|taught)
mis|ter
mis|ti|gris
mist|ily

mis|time
(mis|tim|ing)
mis|ti|ness
mis|tle|toe
mist|like
mis|tral
mis|trans|late
(mis|trans|
   lat|ing)
mis|trans|la|tion
mis|treat
mis|treat|ment
mis|tress
mis|trial
mis|trust
mis|trust|ful
mis|trust|fully
misty (mis|tier,
 mis|ti|est)
mis|un|der|stand
(mis|un|der|
   stood)
mis|un|der|stand|
   ing
mis|us|age
mis|use (as v.,
 mis|us|ing)
Mith|raic
Mith|ra|ism
Mith|ra|ist
Mith|ras
mit|ig|able
mit|ig|ate
(mit|ig|at|ing)
mit|iga|tion
mit|ig|at|ory
mi|to|chon|drion
(*pl.* mi|to|
   chon|dria)
mi|tosis (*pl.*
 mi|toses)
mi|totic
mit|rail|leuse
mi|tral
mitre (as v.,
 mi|tring)
mitre-block
mitre-board
mitre-box
mitred
mitt
mit|ten
mit|tened
Mit|ter|rand
mit|ti|mus
Mitty (*pl.* Mit|tys)

mity (of mites)
mixer
mix|ture
mix-up *n*.
mizen
mizen-mast
mizen-sail
Mi|zoram
mizzle (as *v*.,
 mizz|ling)
mizzly
mne|monic
mne|mon|ist
mo (*sl.*, = moment;
 pl. mos)
moa (bird)
moan|ful
mob (as *v*.,
 mobbed,
 mob|bing)
mob|bish
mob-cap
mo|bile
mo|bili|ary
mo|bil|ity
mo|bil|iz|able
mo|bil|iza|tion
mo|bil|ize
 (mo|bil|iz|ing)
Mö|bius (strip etc.)
mob|oc|racy (*pl.*
 mob|oc|ra|cies)
mob|ster
moc|casin
mocha (coffee,
 sheepskin)
Mocha (moss
 agate)
mocker
mock|ery (*pl.*
 mock|er|ies)
mocking-bird
mock-up
mod (modification;
 modern; Gaelic
 congress)
Mod (teenager)
modal
mod|al|ity (*pl.*
 mod|al|it|ies)
mod|ally
model (as *v*.,
 mod|elled,
 mod|el|ling)
mo|dem

mod|er|ate (as *v*.,
 mod|er|at|ing)
mod|era|tion
Mod|era|tions
 (examination)
mod|er|at|ism
mod|er|ato
mod|er|ator
mod|er|at|or|ship
mod|ern
mod|ern|ism
mod|ern|ist
mod|ern|istic
mod|ern|ity
mod|ern|iza|tion
mod|ern|ize
 (mod|ern|iz|ing)
mod|est
mod|esty
mod|icum
modi|fi|able
mo|di|fica|tion
modi|fic|at|ory
modi|fier
mod|ify
 (modi|fies,
 modi|fied,
 modi|fy|ing)
Modi|gliani
mo|dil|lion
mod|ish
mod|iste
modu|lar
modu|late
 (modu|lat|ing)
modu|la|tion
modu|lator
mod|ule
mod|ulo
modu|lus (*pl.*
 mod|uli)
modus op|er|andi
modus vi|vendi
mo|fette
Mo|ga|di|shu
mog|gie
mo|gul (important
 person)
Mo|gul
 (Mongolian)
mo|hair
Mohammedan
 use
 Muhammadan
Mo|hawk (N.
 Amer. Indian)

moho (*pl.* mo|hos)
Mo|hock (ruffian)
mo|hole
moi|ety (*pl.*
 moi|et|ies)
moire (watered
 fabric)
moiré (watered)
moisten
mois|ture
mois|tur|ize
 (mois|tur|iz|ing)
mois|tur|izer
moko (*pl.* mo|kos)
moksa
molal
molar
mol|ar|ity (*pl.*
 mol|ar|it|ies)
mo|lasses
Mol|da|via
mo|lecu|lar
mo|lecu|lar|ity
mole|hill
mole|skin
mo|lest
mo|les|ta|tion
Mol|ière
mo|line
Mo|lise
mol|li|fica|tion
mol|lify
 (mol|li|fies,
 mol|li|fied,
 mol|li|fy|ing)
mol|lusc
mol|luscan
mol|lusc|oid
mol|lusc|ous
molly (*pl.*
 mol|lies)
mol|ly|coddle
 (as *v*.,
 mol|ly|cod|dling)
mo|loch (reptile)
Mo|loch (idol)
mo|los|sus (*pl.*
 mo|lossi)
Mol|otov
mol|ten
molto
Mo|lucca (Islands)
moly (*pl.* molies)
mol|yb|den|ite
mol|yb|denum
Mom|basa

mo|ment
mo|ment|ar|ily
mo|ment|ar|iness
mo|ment|ary
mo|mently
mo|ment|ous
mo|mentum (*pl.*
 mo|menta)
Mo|mus
mon|achal
mon|ach|ism
Mon|aco
monad
mon|adelph|ous
mon|adic
mon|ad|ism
Mon|ag|han
Mona Lisa
mon|and|rous
mon|andry
mon|arch
mon|archal
mon|archic
mon|arch|ical
mon|arch|ism
mon|arch|ist
mon|archy (*pl.*
 mon|arch|ies)
mon|as|tery (*pl.*
 mon|as|ter|ies)
mon|astic
mon|ast|ic|ally
mon|asti|cism
mon|asti|cize
 (mon|asti|ciz|ing)
mon|atomic
mon|aural
mon|az|ite
mon|daine
Mon|day
mon|dial
Monel (metal)
Monet
mon|et|ar|ism
mon|et|ar|ist
mon|et|ary
mon|et|iza|tion
mon|et|ize
 (mon|et|iz|ing)
money
moneyed
moneyer
money's-worth
money|wort
mon|ger

mon'gol (person
with Down's
syndrome)
Mon|gol (member
of Asian people)
Mon|go'lia
Mon|go'lian
mon'gol|ism
Mon|gol|oid
mon|goose
mon|grel
mon'grel|ism
mon'grelly
mo'nial
mon|iker
mo'ni'li|form
mon'ism
mon'ist
mon|istic
moni|tion
mon|itor
mon'it|or|ial
mon'it|ory (pl.
mon'it|or|ies)
mon'it|ress
monk|ery
mon'key
monkey-nut
monkey-puzzle
monk|fish
monk|ish
monks|hood
Mon|mouth
mono (pl. monos)
mono|basic
mono|carpic
mono|carp'ous
mono|ceph'al|ous
mono|chord
mono|chro'matic
mono|chrome
mon|ocle
mono|clinal
mono|cline
mono|clinic
mono|coque
mono|cot
mono|co'ty|ledon
mono|cracy (pl.
mono|cra'cies)
mono|crotic
mon|ocular
mono|cul'ture
mono|cyte
mono|dac'tyl|ous
mon'odic

mon'od|ist
mono|drama
mon'ody (pl.
mon'od|ies)
mon|oeci'ous
mono|gam'ist
mono|gam'ous
mono|gamy
mono|gen'esis
mono|ge'netic
mono|geny
mono|glot
mono|gram
mono|gram'matic
mono|grammed
mono|graph
mono|grapher
mono|graphic
mono|graph|ist
mono|gyn'ous
mono|gyny
mono|hull
mono|hy'|brid
mono|hyd'ric
mono|latry
mono|layer
mono|lin'gual
mono|lith
mono|lithic
mono|logic
mono|log'ical
mono|log|ist
mono|logue
mono|ma'nia
mono|ma'niac
mono|ma'ni|acal
mono|mark
mono|mer
mono|meric
mono|met'al|lism
mon|omial
mono|mo'lecu|lar
mono|morphic
mono|morph'ous
mono|nuc'leosis
mono|pet'al|ous
mono|phonic
mon'oph|thong
mono'ph|thongal
Mono|phys'ite
mono|plane
mono|pol'ist
mono|pol'istic
mono|pol'iza'tion
mono|pol'ize
(mono'pol|iz|ing)

mono|poly (pl.
mono|pol'ies)
Mono|poly (game;
propr.)
mon|op'sony
mono|psych'ism
mono|rail
mono|rhyme
mono|sac'char|
ide
mono|so'dium
glu'tam|ate
mono|sperm'ous
mono|stich'ous
mono|strophic
mono|syl'labic
mono|syl'lable
mono|the'ism
mono|the'ist
mono|the'istic
mono|tint
mono|tone (as v.,
mono|ton'ing)
mono|tonic
mono|ton'ic|ally
mono|ton|ize
(mono'ton|iz|ing)
mono|ton'ous
mono|tony
mono|treme
mono|type
(impression)
Mono|type
(machine; propr.)
mono|typic
mono|val'ent
mon|ox'ide
Mon'roe
(Doctrine)
Mon|ro'via
Mon|seign'eur (pl.
Mes|seign'eurs)
Mon|sieur (pl.
Mes|sieurs)
Mon|signor (pl.
Mon|sign'ori)
mon|soon
mon|soonal
mon|ster
mon|strance
mon'stros|ity (pl.
mon'stros|it'ies)
mon|strous
mons Ven|eris
mont|age
Mon|taigne

Mon|tana
mont|ane
Mont Blanc
mont|bre'tia
monte (Sp. game)
Monte Carlo
Mon'te|neg'rin
Mon'te|negro
Mon'tes|quieu
Mon'tes|sori
Monte|verdi
Mon'te|video
monthly (as n., pl.
month|lies)
mon'ti|cule
Mont|mar'tre
Mont|real
Mont'ser|rat
monu|ment
mo'nu|mental
mo'nu|ment|ally
mooch
moo-cow
mood|ily
moodi|ness
moody (mood|ier,
moodi|est)
moo'lah
moolvi
moon|beam
moon|calf (pl.
moon|calves)
moon-face
moon-fish
moon-flower
moon|less
moon|light
moon|lit
moon|quake
moon|rise
moon|scape
moon|set
moon|shee
moon|shine
moon-shot
moon|stone
moon|struck
moony (moon|ier,
mooni|est)
moor|age
moor|cock
moor|fowl
moor|hen
moor|ing
moor|ish

Moor|ish (of
  Moors)
moor|land
Moor|man (*pl.*
  Moor|men)
moory
moose (*pl.* same)
mop (as *v.*
  mopped,
  mop|ping)
mope (mop|ing)
mo|ped (cycle)
mop|head
mop|ish
mo|poke
mop|pet
moppy
mo|quette
mora (It. game)
mo|rainal
mo|raine
mo|rainic
moral
mor|ale
mor|al|ism
mor|al|ist
mor|al|istic
mor|al|ist|ic|ally
mor|al|ity (*pl.*
  mor|al|it|ies)
mor|al|iza|tion
mor|al|ize
  (mor|al|iz|ing)
mor|ally
mor|ass
mo|ra|tor|ium (*pl.*
  mo|ra|tor|iums)
Mo|ra|via
Mo|ra|vian
moray
mor|bid
mor|bid|ity
mor|bi|fic
mor|billi
mor|da|cious
mor|da|city
mord|ancy
mord|ant (caustic)
mord|ent (*Mus.*)
mo|reen
more|ish
mo|rel
mo|rello (*pl.*
  mo|rel|los)
more|over
mores

Mor|esque
Mor|gan
mor|gan|atic
mor|gan|at|ic|ally
mor|gen
morgue
mori|bund
morion
Mor|isco (*pl.*
  Mor|is|cos)
Mor|mon
Mor|mon|ism
mor|nay
morn|ing
Moro (*pl.* Moros)
Mo|roc|can
mo|rocco (leather,
  pl. mo|roc|cos)
Mo|rocco
moron
Mo|roni
mor|onic
mor|ose
Mor|peth
morph|eme
morph|emic
morph|em|ics
Mor|pheus
mor|phia
mor|phine
mor|phin|ism
mor|pho|gen|esis
mor|pho|lo|gical
mor|pho|lo|gist
mor|pho|logy
mor|ris (dance)
Mor|ris (chair etc.)
mor|row
morse (walrus,
  clasp)
Morse (code; as *v.*,
  Mors|ing)
mor|sel
mor|tal
mor|tal|ity
mor|tally
mor|tar
mortar-board
mor|tary
mort|gage (as *v.*,
  mort|ga|ging)
mort|ga|gee
  (creditor in
  mortgage)

mort|ga|ger
  (debtor in
  mortgage)
mort|ga|gor (*Law*)
mor|ti|fica|tion
mor|tify
  (mor|ti|fies,
  mor|ti|fied,
  mor|ti|fy|ing)
mor|tise (as *v.*,
  mor|tis|ing)
mort|main
mor|tu|ary (as *n.*,
  pl. mor|tu|ar|ies)
mor|ula (*pl.*
  mor|ulae)
mor|wong
mo|saic (as *v.*,
  mo|sa|icked,
  mo|sa|ick|ing)
Mo|saic (of Moses)
mo|sa|icist
mo|sa|saurus
mos|chat|el
Mos|cow
mos|elle (wine)
Mos|elle (river)
Moses
mo|sey
mo|shav (*pl.*
  mo|shavim)
Moslem *use*
  Muslim
mos|quito (*pl.*
  mos|qui|toes)
mos|si|ness
mosso
moss|trooper
mossy (mos|sier,
  mos|si|est)
mo|tel
mo|tet
moth|ball
moth-eaten
mother
moth|er|craft
moth|er|hood
Moth|er|ing
  Sun|day
mother-in-law (*pl.*
  mothers-in-law)
moth|er|land
moth|er|less
moth|er|like
moth|er|li|ness
moth|erly

mother-of-pearl
moth|proof
mothy (moth|ier,
  mothi|est)
mo|tif
mot|ile
mot|il|ity
mo|tion
mo|tional
mo|tion|less
mo|tiv|ate
  (mo|tiv|at|ing)
mo|tiva|tion
mo|tive (as *v.*,
  mo|tiv|ing)
mo|tive|less
mo|tiv|ity
mot juste
mot|ley
moto-cross
mo|tor
mo|tor bike
mo|tor boat
mo|tor|cade
mo|tor car
mo|tor cycle
motor-cyclist
mo|tor|ist
mo|tor|iza|tion
mo|tor|ize
  (mo|tor|iz|ing)
mo|tor|man (*pl.*
  mo|tor|men)
mo|tor|way
mottle (as *v.*,
  mot|tling)
motto (*pl.*
  mot|toes)
mouf|flon
mou|jik
mould
moulder
moul|di|ness
mould|ing
mouldy
  (moul|dier,
  moul|di|est)
moult
moun|tain
moun|tain|eer
moun|tain|eer|ing
moun|tain|ous
moun|tain|side
moun|te|bank
Mountie
mourner
mourn|ful
mourn|fully

mourn|ing
mouse (as v.,
 mous|ing)
mouser
mouse|trap
mou'si|ness
mous|saka
mous'sel|ine
mous|tache
Mous'ter|ian
mousy (mous|ier,
 mou'si|est)
mouth|ful (pl.
 mouth|fuls)
mouth-organ
mouth|piece
mouth|wash
mouthy
 (mouth|ier,
 mouthi|est)
mov'ab|il|ity
mov'able
move (as v.,
 mov'ing)
move|ment
mover
movie
mov'ing
mow|burnt
mower
moxa
moya
Mo'zam|bique
Moz|arab
Moz|ar'abic
Moz'art
Mu|barak
muchly
much|ness
mu'cil|age
mu'cil'agin|ous
mucker
mucki|ness
muckle
muck-rake (as v.,
 muck-raking)
muck|worm
mucky (muck|ier,
 mucki|est)
mu'cosa
mu'cos|ity
mu'cous a.
mu'cro (pl.
 mu'cro'nes)
mu'cron|ate
mu'cus n.

mud-bath
mud|dily
mud'di|ness
muddle (as v.,
 mud|dling)
muddle-headed
mud|dler
muddy (as a.,
 mud|dier,
 mud'di|est; as v.,
 mud|dies,
 mud|died,
 mud'dy|ing)
Mud|éjar
mud|fish
mud-flap
mud-flat
mud|guard
mud|lark
muesli
mu'ez|zin
muf|fetee
muf'fin
muf'fin|eer
muffin-man (pl.
 muffin-men)
muff|ish
muffle (as v.,
 muf|fling)
muf|fler
mufti
mug (as v.,
 mugged,
 mug|ging)
Mu'gabe
mug|ger
mug'gi|ness
mug|gins
muggy (mug|gier,
 mug'gi|est)
mug|wort
Mu'ham|mad
Mu'ham|madan
Mu'ham|mad'an|
 ism
Muk|den
mu|latto (pl.
 mu'lat|tos)
mul|berry (pl.
 mul|ber'ries)
mule v. use mewl
mu'leteer
mulga
mu'li|eb'rity
mul|ish
mul|lah

mul|lein
muller
mul|let
mul'li|ga|tawny
mul'li|grubs
Mul'lin|gar
mul|lion
mul|lioned
mul|lock
mul|lo|way
mult|an'gu|lar
mul'ti|col'our
mul'ti|col|oured
mul'ti|fari|ous
mul'ti|fid
mul'ti|foil
mul'ti|form
mul'ti|form|ity
mul'ti|lat'eral
mul'ti|lin'gual
mul'ti|mil'lion|
 aire
mul'ti|na'tional
mul'ti|no'mial
mul'ti|par'ous
mul'ti|part'ite
mul'ti|phase
mul|tiple
multiple-choice
mul'ti|plex
mul'ti|pli'able
mul'ti|plic|able
mul'ti|plic'and
mul'ti|plica'tion
mul'ti|plic'ative
mul'ti|pli'city (pl.
 mul'ti|pli'cit'ies)
mul'ti|plier
mul'ti|ply (as v.,
 mul'ti|plies,
 mul'ti|plied,
 mul'ti|ply'ing)
mul'ti|polar
multi-purpose
mul'ti|ra'cial
multi-role
multi-stage
multi-storey
mul'ti|tude
mul'ti|tud'in|ous
mul'ti|va'lent
mul'ti|valve
mul'ti|ver'sity (pl.
 mul'ti|ver'sit|ies)
mul'ti|vocal
multi-way

mul|ture
mum (as v.,
 mummed,
 mum|ming)
mumble (as v.,
 mum|bling)
mum|bler
mumbo-jumbo
 (pl. mumbo-
 jumbos)
mum|chance
mu-meson
mum|mer
mum|mery (pl.
 mum|mer|ies)
mum'mi|fica|tion
mum|mify
 (mum'mi|fies,
 mum'mi|fied,
 mum'mi|fy'ing)
mummy (pl.
 mum|mies)
mump|ish
Munch|ausen
mun|dane
mungo (pl.
 mun|gos)
Mun|ich
mu'ni|cipal
mu'ni|cip'al|ity
 (pl. mu'ni|cip'al|
 it|ies)
mu'ni|cip'al|ize
 (mu'ni|cip'al|iz|
 ing)
mu'ni|cip|ally
mu'ni|fi'cence
mu'ni|fi'cent
mu'ni|ment
mu'ni|tion
mu'ni|tioner
munt|jak
muon
mur'age
mural
Mur'cia
mur'der
mur'derer
mur'der|ess
mur'der|ous
mure (mur'ing)
murex (pl.
 mur|ices)
Mur|illo
mur'ine
murk

murk|ily
murki|ness
murky (mur|kier,
  mur|ki|est)
murmur
mur|mur|ous
murphy (pl.
  mur|phies)
Mur|ray
mur|rhine
mus|cad|ine
  (grape)
mus|car|ine
mus|cat (grape,
  wine)
Mus|cat
mus|ca|tel (grape,
  wine, raisin)
muscle (as v.,
  muscl|ing)
muscle|man (pl.
  muscle|men)
mus|co|lo|gist
mus|co|logy
mus|co|vado (pl.
  mus|co|va|dos)
mus|cov|ite (mica)
Mus|cov|ite
  (citizen of
  Moscow)
Mus|covy
mus|cu|lar
mus|cu|lar|ity
mus|cu|lat|ure
muse (as v.,
  mus|ing)
mu|seo|logy
mus|ette
mu|seum
mush|room
mushy (mush|ier,
  mushi|est)
music
mu|sical
mu|sic|al|ity
mu|sic|ally
music-hall
mu|si|cian
mu|si|co|lo|gical
mu|si|co|lo|gist

mu|si|co|logy
mus|keg
mus|ket
mus|ket|eer
mus|ket|oon
mus|ketry
musk-ox (pl.
  musk-oxen)
musk-rat
musk-rose
musky (mus|kier,
  mus|ki|est)
Mus|lim
mus|lin
mus|lined
mus|mon
mus|quash
mus|sel
Mus|so|lini
Mus|sorg|sky
mus|tang
mus|tard
mus|ter
mus|ti|ness
musty (mus|tier,
  mus|ti|est)
mut|ab|il|ity
mut|able
mu|ta|gen
mu|ta|genic
mut|ant
mut|ate
  (mut|at|ing)
muta|tion
mu|ta|tis
  mut|andis
mute (as v.,
  mut|ing)
mu|til|ate
  (mu|til|at|ing)
mu|tila|tion
mu|til|ator
mu|tin|eer
mu|tin|ous
mu|tiny (as n., pl.
  mu|tin|ies; as v.,
  mu|tin|ies,
  mu|tin|ied,
  mu|tiny|ing)
mut|ism

mut|ter
mut|ton
mut|tony
mu|tual
mu|tu|al|ism
mu|tu|al|ist
mu|tu|al|ity
mu|tu|ally
mut|ule
muu-muu
Muzak (propr.)
muz|zily
muz|zi|ness
muzzle (as v.,
  muzz|ling)
muzzy (muz|zier,
  muz|zi|est)
my|al|gia
my|al|ism (W.
  Indian witchcraft)
my|all (acacia)
my|as|thenia
my|celial
my|celium (pl.
  my|celia)
My|cen|ae
My|cen|aean
my|co|lo|gist
my|co|logy
my|cor|rhiza (pl.
  my|cor|rhizae)
my|cor|rhizal
my|cosis (pl.
  my|coses)
my|co|trophy
myd|ri|asis
my|elin
my|el|itis
my|el|oma
my|lo|don
mynah use mina
myn|heer
myo|car|dium
myo|logy
my|ope
my|opia
my|opic
myosis use miosis
myo|sote
myo|sotis

myriad
myria|pod
myr|midon
my|ro|balan
myrrh
myrrhic
myrrhy
myr|ta|ceous
myrtle
my|self
mys|ta|go|gic
mys|ta|go|gical
mys|ta|gogue
mys|ter|ious
mys|tery (pl.
  mys|ter|ies)
mystic
mys|tical
mys|tic|ally
mys|ti|cism
mys|ti|fica|tion
mys|tify
  (mys|ti|fies,
  mys|ti|fied,
  mys|ti|fy|ing)
mys|tique
mythic
myth|ical
myth|ic|ally
mythi|cism
mythi|cist
mythi|cize
  (mythi|ciz|ing)
mytho|gen|esis
mytho|grapher
mytho|graphy
mytho|loger
mytho|lo|gical
mytho|lo|gist
mytho|lo|gize
  (mytho|
      lo|giz|ing)
mytho|logy (pl.
  mytho|lo|gies)
mytho|mania
mytho|poeia
mytho|poeic
myx|oedema
myx|oma
myx|oma|tosis

N

Naas
nab (nabbed,
 nab|bing)
na|bob
Na|bo|kov
nac|arat
na|celle
nacre
nac|re|ous
na|dir
naevus (pl. naevi)
nag (as v., nagged,
 nag|ging)
Naga
Na|ga|land
na|gana
Nagar
nag|ger
na|gor
Na|huatl
Na|huat|lan
Na|hum (OT book)
naiad
nail-brush
nailer
nail|ery (pl.
 nail|er|ies)
nail-file
nain|sook
Nairn
Nai|robi
naïve
naïv|ety
naked
namby-pamby
 (as n., pl.
 namby-pambies)
Nam|cha Barwa
name (as v.,
 nam|ing)
name|able
name-day
name|less
namely
name-plate
name|sake
name-tape
Na|mi|bia
Namur

nancy (pl.
 nan|cies)
Nanda Devi
Nanga Par|bat
nan|keen
nanny (pl.
 nan|nies)
nanny-goat
na|no|sec|ond
naos (pl. naoi)
nap (as v.,
 napped,
 nap|ping)
nap|alm
naph|tha
naph|thal|ene
naph|thalic
naph|thene
naph|thenic
Na|pier
nap|kin
Naples
na|po|leon (coin;
 game)
Na|po|leon
Na|po|leonic
nappa
nap|per
nappy (as n., pl.
 nap|pies)
nar|ceine
nar|ciss|ism
nar|ciss|istic
nar|cissus (pl.
 nar|cissi)
nar|co|lepsy
nar|co|leptic
nar|cosis (pl.
 nar|coses)
nar|cotic
nar|cot|ic|ally
nar|cot|ism
nar|cot|ize
 (nar|cot|iz|ing)
nar|doo
nares
nar|ghile
nar|ial

narky (nar|kier,
 nar|ki|est)
nar|rate
 (nar|rat|ing)
nar|ra|tion
nar|rat|ive
nar|rator
nar|row
narrow-minded
nar|thex
nar|whal
nary
nasal
nas|al|ity
nas|al|ize
 (nas|al|iz|ing)
nas|ally
nas|cency
nas|cent
nase|berry (pl.
 nase|ber|ries)
naso-frontal
Nas|sau
nastic
nas|tily
nas|ti|ness
nas|tur|tium
nasty (nas|tier,
 nas|ti|est)
natal
nat|al|ity
na|ta|tion
na|ta|tor|ial
na|ta|tor|ium
na|tat|ory
na|tes
na|tion
na|tional
na|tion|al|ism
na|tion|al|ist
na|tion|al|istic
na|tion|al|ity (pl.
 na|tion|al|it|ies)
na|tion|al|iza|tion
na|tion|al|ize
 (na|tion|al|iz|ing)
na|tion|ally
nation-wide
nat|ive

nat|iv|ism
nat|iv|ist
na|tiv|ity (pl.
 na|tiv|it|ies)
nat|ron
nat|ter
nat|ter|jack
nat|tier (blue)
nat|tily
nat|ti|ness
natty (nat|tier,
 nat|ti|est)
nat|ural
nat|ur|al|ism
nat|ur|al|ist
nat|ur|al|istic
nat|ur|al|ist|ic|
 ally
nat|ur|al|iza|tion
nat|ur|al|ize
 (nat|ur|al|iz|ing)
nat|ur|ally
na|ture
na|tur|ism
na|tur|ist
na|turo|path
na|turo|pathic
na|turo|pathy
naugh|tily
naugh|ti|ness
naughty
 (naugh|tier,
 naugh|ti|est)
nau|plius (pl.
 nau|plii)
Na|uru
nausea
naus|eate
 (naus|eat|ing)
naus|eous
nautch
nautch-girl
naut|ical
naut|ic|ally
naut|ilus
Na|vaho (pl.
 Na|va|hos)
naval
nav|ally

nav|arin
Na|varre
na|vel
navel|wort
na|vic|ular
nav|ig|ab|il|ity
nav|ig|able
nav|ig|ate
(nav|ig|at|ing)
nav|iga|tion
nav|iga|tional
nav|ig|ator
navvy (as n., pl.
nav|vies; as v.,
nav|vies,
nav|vied,
nav|vy|ing)
navy (pl. na|vies)
na|wab
nay|say
(nay|said)
Naz|ar|ene
Naz|ar|eth
Naz|ar|ite (native
of Nazareth)
Nazi
Nazi|dom
Nazify (Nazi|fies,
Nazi|fied,
Nazi|fy|ing)
Naz|ir|ite (Hebrew
who had taken
vows of
abstinence)
Naz|ism
Ndja|mena
né (fem. née)
Ne|an|der|thal
Nea|pol|itan
neap-tide
nearby a.
Ne|arc|tic
nearly
near-sighted
neaten
neb|bish
Neb|raska
Ne|bu|chad|
     nez|zar
neb|ula (pl.
   neb|ulae)
neb|ular
nebu|los|ity
neb|ulous
neb|uly
ne|ces|sar|ily

ne|ces|sary (as n.,
   pl. ne|ces|sar|ies)
ne|ces|sit|ar|ian
ne|ces|sit|ate
   (ne|ces|sit|at|ing)
ne|ces|sit|ous
ne|ces|sity
   (pl.ne|ces|sit|ies)
Neckar
neck|band
neck|cloth
neck|er|chief
neck|ing
neck|lace
neck|let
neck|line
neck|tie
neck|wear
nec|ro|bi|osis
nec|ro|genic
nec|ro|latry
nec|ro|logy (pl.
   nec|ro|lo|gies)
nec|ro|man|cer
nec|ro|mancy
nec|ro|mantic
nec|ro|phag|ous
nec|ro|phile
nec|ro|philia
nec|ro|philiac
nec|ro|phil|ism
nec|ro|phily
nec|ro|polis
nec|ropsy (pl.
   nec|rop|sies)
nec|ro|scopic
nec|ro|scopy (pl.
   nec|ro|scop|ies)
nec|rose
   (nec|ros|ing)
nec|rosis (pl.
   nec|roses)
nec|rotic
nec|rot|ize
   (nec|rot|iz|ing)
nec|tar
nec|tar|ean
nec|tared
nec|tar|eous
nec|tari|fer|ous
nec|tar|ine
nec|tar|ous
nec|tary (pl.
   nec|tar|ies)
neddy (donkey; pl.
   ned|dies)

Neddy (National
Economic
Development
Council)
need|fire
need|ful
needi|ness
needle (as v.,
   need|ling)
needle|cord
needle|craft
needle-lace
needle-point
need|less
needle|wo|man
   (pl.
   needle|wo|men)
needle|work
need|ments
needy (need|ier,
   needi|est)
ne'er-do-weel
ne'er-do-well
ne|fari|ous
neg|ate
   (neg|at|ing)
nega|tion
nega|tion|ist
neg|at|ive (as v.,
   neg|at|iv|ing)
neg|at|iv|ism
neg|at|iv|ist
neg|at|iv|istic
neg|at|iv|ity
neg|at|ory
neg|lect
neg|lect|ful
neg|lect|fully
nég|ligé
neg|li|gence
neg|li|gent
neg|li|gible
neg|li|gibly
ne|go|ti|able
ne|go|ti|ant
ne|go|ti|ate
   (ne|go|ti|at|ing)
ne|go|ti|ation
ne|go|ti|ator
Neg|rillo (pl.
   Neg|ril|los)
Neg|rito (pl.
   Neg|ri|tos)
Neg|rit|ude

Ne|gro (pl.
   Ne|groes; fem.
   Ne|gress)
Ne|groid
Ne|groidal
Ne|gro|ism
Ne|gro|phile
Ne|gro|pho|bia
ne|gus (drink)
Ne|gus (hist., ruler
   of Ethiopia)
Ne|he|miah (OT
   book)
Nehru
neigh|bour
neigh|bour|hood
neigh|bour|li|ness
neigh|bourly
nei|ther
nek|ton
nelly (pl. nel|lies)
nel|son
ne|lumbo (pl.
   ne|lum|bos)
nem|ato|cyst
nem|at|ode
Nem|butal
   (sedative; propr.)
Ne|mean
ne|mert|ine
ne|me|sia
nem|esis (pl.
   nem|eses)
nene
nenu|phar
neo-Cambrian
neo-clas|sic
neo|clas|sical
neo|clas|si|cism
neo|clas|si|cist
neo-colonialism
neo|dy|mium
neo-Hellenism
neo|lithic
neo|lo|gian
neo|lo|gism
neo|lo|gist
neo|lo|gize
   (neo|lo|giz|ing)
neo|logy (pl.
   neo|lo|gies)
neo|my|cin
neon
neo|natal
neo|nate
ne|onto|lo|gist

ne|onto|logy
neo|pen|tane
neo|phron
neo|phyte
neo|plasm
neo|plastic
Neo|pla|ton|ism
neo|prene
neo|teny
neo|teric
neo|trop|ical
Neo|zoic
Ne|pal
Nep|al|ese (*pl.*
  same)
Nep|ali
ne|pen|the
ne|pen|thes
neph|elo|meter
neph|elo|met|ric
neph|elo|metry
nephew
nepho|logy
neph|rec|tomy
  (*pl.* neph|rec|
       tomies)
neph|rite
neph|ritic
neph|ritis
neph|ro|logy
neph|ro|tomy (*pl.*
  neph|ro|tom|ies)
nep|ot|ism
nep|ot|ist
Nep|tune
Nep|tun|ian
Nep|tun|ist
nep|tun|ium
ner|eid
ner|ine
nerka
Nero
ner|oli
Ner|on|ian
nerv|ate
nerva|tion
nerve (as *v.*,
  nerv|ing)
nerve-cell
nerve-centre
nerve-racking
nerv|ine
nerv|ous
nerv|ure
nervy (ner|vier,
  ner|vi|est)

nes|ci|ence
nes|ci|ent
nest-egg
nestle (nest|ling)
nest|ling
Nes|tor
Nes|tor|ian
net (as *v.*, net|ted,
  net|ting)
net|ball
nether
Neth|er|lander
Neth|er|land|ish
Neth|er|lands
neth|er|most
net|suke
nett *use* net
net|ting
nettle (as *v.*,
  net|tling)
net|work
Neu|châtel
neume
neural
neur|al|gia
neur|al|gic
neur|as|thenia
neur|as|thenic
neura|tion
neur|itic
neur|itis
neur|oglia
neuro|lo|gical
neuro|lo|gist
neuro|logy
neur|oma
neuro-muscular
neur|onal
neur|one
neur|onic
neuro|path
neuro|pathic
neuro|patho|logy
neuro|pathy
neuro|physi|
         ology
neur|op|ter|ous
neur|osis (*pl.*
  neur|oses)
neuro|surgery
neuro|surgical
neur|otic
neur|ot|ic|ally
neur|ot|ic|ism
neuro|tomy (*pl.*
  neuro|tom|ies)

neu|ter
neut|ral
neut|ral|ity
neut|ral|iza|tion
neut|ral|ize
  (neut|ral|iz|ing)
neut|rally
neut|rino (*pl.*
  neut|ri|nos)
neut|ron
Ne|vada
névé (snow)
never
nev|er|more
never-never
  (hire-purchase)
Never Never
  Land (Utopia; in
  Australia)
nev|er|the|less
Nevis
new-born
New|burg
New|castle
new-come
new|comer
newel
new|fangled
New|found|land
new|ish
new-laid
newly
newly-wed
New|mar|ket
New Or|leans
New|port
Newry
news|agent
news|cast
news|caster
news|let|ter
news|pa|per
news|pa|per|man
  (*pl.* news|pa|per|
        men)
New|speak
news|print
news-reader
news|reel
news-room
news-sheet
news-stand
news|wor|thi|
        ness
news|worthy
newsy

new|ton (unit)
New|ton (man)
New|ton|ian
New|town|ab|bey
New Zea|land
next-best
nexus
ngaio (*pl.* ngaios)
ni|acin
Ni|ag|ara
Ni|amey
nib (as *v.*, nibbed,
  nib|bing)
nibble (as *v.*,
  nib|bling)
nib|lick
Ni|caea
Ni|car|agua
nice (nicer,
  nicest)
Ni|cene
ni|cety (*pl.*
  ni|cet|ies)
niche (as *v.*,
  nich|ing)
Nich|olas
Ni|chrome (*propr.*)
nicish
nickel (as *v.*,
  nick|elled,
  nick|el|ling)
nick|elic
nick|el|odeon
nick|el|ous
nickel-plate
  (nickel-plating)
nicker
nick|name (as *v.*,
  nick|nam|ing)
Ni|co|bar (Islands)
nicol
Nic|ola
Ni|co|sia
nic|ot|ine
ni|co|tinic
nic|ot|in|ism
nic|ot|in|ize
  (nic|ot|in|iz|ing)
nic|tit|ate
  (nic|tit|at|ing)
nic|tita|tion
ni|da|mental
ni|di|fic|ate (ni|di|
    fic|at|ing)
ni|di|fica|tion

nid¦ify (nidi¦fies,
 nidi¦fied,
 nidi¦fy¦ing)
nidus (*pl.* nidi)
niece
niello (*pl.* ni¦elli)
ni¦el¦loed
Niel¦sen
Ni¦er¦steiner
Nietz¦sche
Nietz¦schean
niffy (nif¦fier,
 nif¦fi¦est)
nif¦tily
nif¦ti¦ness
nifty (nif¦tier,
 nif¦ti¦est)
Ni¦gel
Ni¦ger
Ni¦geria
nig¦gard
nig¦gard¦li¦ness
nig¦gardly
nig¦ger
nig¦ger¦head
niggle (nig¦gling)
nig¦gly
night-bird
night¦cap
night-clothes
night-club
night-dress
night¦fall
night-glass
night-gown
nightie
night¦in¦gale
night¦jar
night-life
night-light
night-line
night-long
nightly
night¦man (*pl.*
 night¦men)
night¦mare
night¦mar¦ish
night-night
night-owl
night-school
night¦shade
night-shirt
night-spot
night-time
night-watch

night-watchman
 (*pl.* night-
 watchmen)
night-work
ni¦gres¦cence
ni¦gres¦cent
nig¦rit¦ude
ni¦hil¦ism
ni¦hil¦ist
ni¦hil¦istic
ni¦hil¦ity
ni¦hil ob¦stat
 (authorization)
Ni¦jin¦sky
Nile
nil¦gai
Nilo¦meter
Nil¦otic
nimble (nim¦bler,
 nim¦blest)
nimbly
nimbo-stratus (*pl.*
 nimbo-strati)
nim¦bus (*pl.*
 nimbi)
nim¦bused
niminy-piminy
Nim¦rod
nin¦com¦poop
nine¦fold
nine¦pins
nine¦teen
nine¦teenth
nineti¦eth
ninety (*pl.*
 nine¦ties)
Nin¦eveh
Nin¦ev¦ite
ninny (*pl.*
 nin¦nies)
ni¦non
ninth
Ni¦obe
Ni¦obean
ni¦obic
ni¦obium
ni¦ob¦ous
nip (as *v.*, nipped,
 nip¦ping)
nipa
nip¦per
nip¦pily
nip¦pi¦ness
nipple
nipple-wort
Nip¦pon

Nip¦pon¦ese (*pl.*
 same)
Nip¦pon¦ian
nippy (nip¦pier,
 nip¦pi¦est)
nir¦vana
nisi (subject to
 conditions)
Nis¦sen
nitid
nit-picking
ni¦trate (as *v.*,
 ni¦trat¦ing)
ni¦tra¦tion
nitre
ni¦tric
ni¦tride
ni¦tri¦fica¦tion
ni¦trify (ni¦tri¦fies,
 ni¦tri¦fied,
 ni¦tri¦fy¦ing)
ni¦trile
ni¦trite
nitro-acid
nitro¦ben¦zene
nitro-cellulose
Nitro-chalk
 (*propr.*)
nitro-compound
nitro-explosive
ni¦tro¦gen
ni¦tro¦gen¦ous
nitro-glycerine
nitro-group
nitro-lime
nitro-powder
ni¦trous
nitty-gritty
nit¦wit
nit¦wit¦ted
Ni¦ver¦nais
nixie
no (as *n.*, *pl.* noes)
No¦achian
No¦achic
Noah
nob (as *v.*,
 nobbed,
 nob¦bing)
no-ball
nobble
 (nob¦bling)
No¦bel
no¦be¦lium
no¦bili¦ary

no¦bil¦ity (*pl.*
 no¦bil¦it¦ies)
noble (no¦bler,
 no¦blest)
noble¦man (*pl.*
 noble¦men)
no¦blesse ob¦lige
noble¦wo¦man (*pl.*
 noble¦wo¦men)
nobly
no¦body (as *n.*, *pl.*
 no¦bod¦ies)
no-claims bonus
noct¦am¦bu¦lant
noct¦am¦bu¦list
noct¦am¦bu¦lous
noc¦ti¦vag¦ant
noc¦ti¦vag¦ous
noc¦tule
noc¦turn (part of
 matins)
noc¦turnal
noc¦turn¦ally
noc¦turne (piece of
 music; painting)
nocu¦ous
nod (as *v.*,
 nodded,
 nod¦ding)
nodal
noddle (as *v.*,
 nod¦dling)
noddy (*pl.*
 nod¦dies)
nod¦ical
nod¦ose
nod¦os¦ity
nodu¦lar
nodu¦lated
nodu¦la¦tion
nod¦ule
nodu¦lose
nodu¦lous
nodus (*pl.* nodi)
Noel
no¦etic
nog (as *v.*, nogged,
 nog¦ging)
nog¦gin
Noh (Jap. drama)
no¦how
noise (as *v.*,
 nois¦ing)
nois¦ette
nois¦ily
noisi¦ness

noi|some
noisy (nois|ier,
  noisi|est)
no|mad
no|madic
no|mad|ic|ally
no|mad|ism
no|mad|ize
  (no|mad|iz|ing)
nom|bril
nom de guerre
  (*pl. noms de*
  guerre)
nom de plume (*pl.*
  noms de plume)
nomen
no|men|clat|ive
no|men|clator
no|men|clat|ure
nom|inal
nom|in|al|ism
nom|in|al|ist
nom|in|al|istic
nom|in|ally
nom|in|ate
  (nom|in|at|ing)
nom|ina|tion
nom|in|at|ival
nom|in|at|ive
nom|in|ator
nom|inee
nomo|gram
nomo|graphic
nomo|graphy
nomo|thetic
non-access
non|age
nona|gen|ar|ian
non|agon
non-aligned
non-alignment
non|ary (as *n.*, *pl.*
  non|ar|ies)
non-attendance
nonce-word
non|chal|ance
non|chal|ant
non-combatant
non-
  commissioned
non-committal
non-committally
non com|pos
  men|tis
non-conducting
non-conductor

non|con|form|ism
non|con|form|ist
  (*gen.*)
Non|con|form|ist
  (*Relig.*)
non|con|form|ity
non-content
non-contributory
non-co-operation
nonda (fruit)
non-
  denominational
non|des|cript
non-effective
non|ent|ity (*pl.*
  non|ent|it|ies)
none-so-pretty
  (plant)
nonesuch *use*
  nonsuch
nonet
none the less
non-event
non-existence
non-existent
non-feasance
non-fiction
non-flammable
non-interference
non-intervention
non-iron
non|ius
non|juror
non-member
non-net
no-nonsense *a.*
non|par|eil
non-person
non|plus (as *v.*,
  non|plusses,
  non|plussed,
  non|plus|sing)
non-residence
non-resident
non|sense
non|sens|ical
non|sens|ic|ally
non sequitur
non-smoker
non-smoking
non-starter
non-stick
non-stop
non|such
non|suit
non-U

non-union
non-usage
non-use
non-user
non-violence
non-violent
non-voting
non-white
noodle
noon|day
no one
noon|tide
noon|time
noose (as *v.*,
  noos|ing)
nopal
no|palry (*pl.*
  no|pal|ries)
Nor|bert|ine
Nordic
Nor|folk
nor|land
nor|mal
nor|malcy
nor|mal|ity
nor|mal|iza|tion
nor|mal|ize
  (nor|mal|iz|ing)
norm|ally
Nor|man
Nor|mandy
Nor|man|esque
norm|at|ive
Nor|roy
Norse|land
Norse|man (*pl.*
  Norse|men)
North|al|ler|ton
North|amp|ton
North|amp|ton|
        shire
North|an|ger
  Ab|bey
north|bound
North-
      countryman
  (*pl.* North-
      countrymen)
north-east
north|easter
north-eastern
north|erly (as *n.*,
  pl. north|er|lies)
north|ern
north|erner
north|ing

North|land
North|man (*pl.*
  North|men)
North|um|ber|
        land
North|um|brian
north|ward
north|wards
north-west
north|wester
north-western
Nor'|way
Nor|we|gian
nor'-wester
Nor|wich
nose (as *v.*,
  nos|ing)
nose|bag
nose|band
nose|bleed
nose-cone
nose|dive (as *v.*,
  nose|div|ing)
nose|gay
nose-piece
nose|pipe
noser
nose-rag
nose|ring
nose-wheel
nosey *use* nosy
nosh|ery (*pl.*
  nosh|er|ies)
no-show
nosh-up *n.*
nos|ily
nosi|ness
nos|ing
noso|graphy
noso|logy
nos|tal|gia
nos|tal|gic
nos|tal|gic|ally
nos|toc
Nos|tra|damus
nos|tril
nos|trilled
nos|trum
nosy (as *n.*, *pl.*
  nos|ies; as *a.*,
  no|sier, no|si|est)
not|ab|il|ity (*pl.*
  not|ab|il|it|ies)
not|able
not|ably
not|ar|ial

not|ari|ally
not|ar|ize
　(not|ar|iz|ing)
not|ary (pl.
　not|ar|ies)
not|ate
　(not|at|ing)
nota|tion
notchy
note (as v.,
　not|ing)
note|book
note|case
note|let
note|paper
note-row
note|worthy
noth|ing
noth|ing|ness
no|tice (as v.,
　no|ti|cing)
no|tice|able
no|tice|ably
notice-board
no|ti|fi|able
no|ti|fica|tion
no|tify (no|ti|fies,
　no|ti|fied,
　no|ti|fy|ing)
no|tion
no|tional
no|tion|al|ist
no|tion|ally
no|to|chord
no|tori|ety
no|tori|ous
not|or|nis
Not|ting|ham
Not|ting|ham|
　　　　shire
not|with|
　　　stand|ing
Nou|ak|chott
nou|gat
nou|menal
nou|men|ally
nou|menon (pl.
　nou|mena)
nounal
nour|ish
nour|ish|ment
nou|veau riche
　(pl. nou|veaux
　riches)
nou|velle vague
nova (pl. no|vae)

No|va|lis
Nova Scotia
nova|tion
novel
nov|el|ese
nov|el|esque
nov|el|ette
nov|el|et|tish
nov|el|ist
nov|el|istic
nov|el|iza|tion
nov|el|ize
　(nov|el|iz|ing)
no|vella
nov|elty (pl.
　nov|el|ties)
No|vem|ber
no|vena
nov|ice
no|vi|ci|ate
No|vo|caine
　(propr.)
now|aday
now|adays
no|ways
no|where
no|whither
no|wise
nox|ious
noyau (liqueur; pl.
　noy|aux)
Nozze di Fi|garo
nozzle
nu|ance (as v.,
　nu|an|cing)
nub|bin
nubble
nub|bly
nu|bile
nu|bil|ity
nuchal
nu|ci|fer|ous
nu|ci|vor|ous
nuc|lear
nucle|ase
nucle|ate
　(nuc|le|at|ing)
nuc|le|ation
nuc|leic
nuc|le|olar
nuc|le|olus (pl.
　nuc|le|oli)
nuc|leon
nuc|le|onic
nucleo-protein
nuc|le|os|ide

nuc|le|ot|ide
nuc|leus (pl.
　nuc|lei)
nuc|lide
nuc|lidic
nudge (as v.,
　nudging)
nud|ism
nud|ist
nud|ity (pl.
　nud|it|ies)
nu|gat|ory
nug|gar
nug|get
nuis|ance
Nu|ku'alofa
nulla-nulla
nul|li|fica|tion
nul|li|fidian
nul|lify
　(nul|li|fies,
　nul|li|fied,
　nul|li|fy|ing)
nul|li|para
nul|li|par|ous
nul|li|pore
null|ity (pl.
　null|it|ies)
num|bat
number (compar.
　of numb)
num|ber n. & v.
number-plate
numb-fish
numbskull use
　numskull
num|dah
nu|men (pl.
　nu|mina)
nu|mer|able
nu|mer|acy
nu|meral
nu|mer|ate
nu|mera|tion
nu|mer|ator
nu|mer|ical
nu|mer|ic|ally
nu|mero|lo|gical
nu|mero|lo|gist
nu|mero|logy
nu|mer|ous
nu|min|ous
nu|mis|matic
nu|mis|mat|ic|ally
nu|mis|mat|ist
nu|mis|mato|logy

num|mary
num|mu|lite
num|nah
num|skull
nun|atak
nun-buoy
Nunc Di|mit|tis
　(canticle)
nun|ci|at|ure
nun|cio (pl.
　nun|cios)
nun|cu|pate
　(nun|cu|pat|ing)
nun|cu|pa|tion
nun|cu|pat|ive
nun|like
nun|nery (pl.
　nun|ner|ies)
nun|nish
nup|tial
Nur|eyev
nurse (as v.,
　nurs|ing)
nurse|ling
nurse|maid
nursery (pl.
　nurs|er|ies)
nurs|ery|man (pl.
　nurs|ery|men)
nur|ture (as v.,
　nur|tur|ing)
nut (as v., nut|ted,
　nut|ting)
nut|ant
nu|ta|tion
nut-brown
nut-butter
nut-case
nut|cracker
nut-gall
nut|hatch
nut-house
nut|let
nut-meat
nut|meg
nut-oil
nut-palm
nut-pine
nu|tria
nu|tri|ent
nu|tri|ment
nu|tri|mental
nu|tri|tion
nu|tri|tional
nu|tri|tion|ist
nu|tri|tious

nu'trit|ive
nut|shell
nut'ter
nut'ti|ness
nut-tree
nutty (nut|tier,
 nut'ti|est)
nux vom'ica

nuzzle (nuzz|ling)
nyala
nyct'al|opia
nyc'ti|tropic
Ny'er|ere
Nyira|gongo
ny'lon

nymphae *n. pl.*
nymphal
nymph|ean
nymphet
nymph|like
nym'pho (*pl.*
 nym|phos)

nym'pho|lepsy
nym'pho|lept
nym'pho|leptic
nym'pho|mania
nym'pho|ma'niac
nys'tag|mic
nys'tag|mus

O

oaf (*pl.* oafs)
oak-apple
oaken
oak-gall
Oak|ham
oakum
oars|man (*pl.*
 oars|men)
oars|man|ship
oars|wo|man (*pl.*
 oars|wo|men)
oar|weed
oasis (*pl.* oases)
oast-house
oat|cake
oaten
oath
oat|meal
ob'bli|gato (*pl.*
 ob'bli|ga'tos)
ob|con|ical
ob|cor'date
ob|dur'acy
ob|dur'ate
ob'eah
obedi|ence
obedi|ent
obeis|ance
obeis|ant
ob'el|isk
ob'el|ize
 (ob'el|iz|ing)
ob'elus (*pl.* ob'eli)
obese
obes|ity
obey
ob|fus'cate
 (ob|fus|cat'ing)
ob|fus|ca'tion
ob|fus'cat|ory
ob'*iter dictum* (*pl.*
 ob'*iter dicta*)
ob'itu|ar|ist
ob'itu|ary (*pl.*
 ob'itu|ar'ies)
ob|ject
ob'jec'ti|fica'tion

ob'jec|tify
 (ob'jec'ti|fies,
 ob'jec'ti|fied,
 ob'jecti|fy'ing)
ob'jec'tion
ob'jec'tion|able
ob'jec'tion|ably
ob'jec|tival
ob|ject|ive
ob'jec'tiv|ism
ob'jec'tiv|ist
ob'jec'tiv|ity
ob|jector
ob'*jet d'art* (*pl.*
 ob'*jets d'art*)
ob|lan'ceol|ate
ob|late
ob|la'tion
ob|la'tional
ob|lat'ory
ob|lig'ate
 (ob|lig|at'ing)
ob|liga'tion
ob|lig|at'ory
ob|lige
 (ob|li'ging)
ob|li'gee
ob|ligor
ob|lique
ob|li'quity
ob|lit'er|ate
 (ob|lit'er|at'ing)
ob|lit|era'tion
ob|li'vion
ob|li'vi|ous
ob|long
ob|lo'quy
ob|nox|ious
oboe
obo'ist
obol
ob|ov'ate
ob|scene
ob'scen|ity (*pl.*
 ob'scen|it'ies)
ob'scur|ant
ob'scur|ant|ism
ob'scur|ant|ist
ob'scura'tion

ob|scure
 (ob|scur'ing)
ob|scur|ity (*pl.*
 ob|scur'it'ies)
ob|sec'ra'tion
ob|sequial
ob|sequies *n. pl.*
ob|sequi|ous
ob|serv|able
ob|serv|ably
ob|serv|ance
ob|serv|ant
ob|ser'va'tion
ob|ser'va'tional
ob|ser'va'tion|
 ally
ob|ser'vat|ory (*pl.*
 ob|ser'vat|or'ies)
ob|serve
 (ob|serv|ing)
ob|ser|ver
ob|sess
ob|ses|sion
ob|ses|sional
ob|sess|ive
ob|si|dian
ob|sol'es|cence
ob|sol'es|cent
ob|sol|ete
ob|sol'et|ism
obs|tacle
ob'stet|ric
ob'stet|rical
ob'stet|ri|cian
ob'stet|rics
ob'stin|acy
ob'stin|ate
ob|strep'er|ous
ob|struct
ob|struc'tion
ob|struc'tion|ism
ob|struc'tion|ist
ob|struct|ive
ob|stu'pe|fac'tion
ob|stu'pefy
 (ob|stu'pe|fies,
 ob|stu'pe|fied,
 ob|stu'pe|fy'ing)
ob|tain

ob'tain|able
ob|ten'tion
ob|trude
 (ob|trud|ing)
ob|tru'sion
ob|trus|ive
ob|tund
ob|tur'ate
 (ob|tur|at'ing)
ob|tura'tion
ob|tur'ator
ob|tuse
ob|tus|ity
ob|verse
ob|ver'sion
ob|vert
ob'vi|ate
 (ob'vi|at'ing)
ob'vi|ation
ob'vi|ous
oc'ar|ina
Oc'cam's razor
oc'ca|sion
oc'ca|sional
oc'ca|sion|al|ism
oc'ca|sion|al|ist
oc'ca|sion|al|ity
oc'ca|sion|ally
Oc'ci|dent
oc'ci|dental *a.*
Oc'ci|dental *n.*
oc'ci|dent|al|ize
 (oc'ci|dent|al|iz|
  ing)
oc'ci|dent|ally
oc'ci|pital
oc'ci|put
Oc|citan
Oc|cit'an|ian
oc|clude
 (oc|clud|ing)
oc|clu|sion
oc|clus|ive
oc|cult
oc|culta'tion
oc|cult|ism
oc|cult|ist
oc|cu|pancy (*pl.*
 oc'cu|pan'cies)

oc|cu|pant
oc|cu|pa|tion
oc|cu|pa|tional
oc|cu|pier
oc|cupy
 (oc|cu|pies,
 oc|cu|pied,
 oc|cu|py|ing)
oc|cur (oc|curred,
 oc|cur|ring)
oc|cur|rence
oc|cur|rent
ocean
ocean|arium (pl.
 ocean|ari|ums)
ocean-going
Oceania
Ocean|ian
oceanic (of the
 ocean)
Oceanic (of
 Oceania)
Oceanid (pl.
 Ocean|ids or
 Ocean|ides)
oceano|grapher
oceano|graphic
oceano|
        graph|ical
oceano|graphy
ocel|late a.
ocel|lated a.
ocel|lus (pl. ocelli)
ocelot
och|lo|cracy (pl.
 och|lo|cra|cies)
och|lo|crat
och|lo|cratic
och|one
ochre
ochre|ish
ochre|ous
ochry
ocker
o'clock
oc|ta|chord
octad
oc|ta|gon
oc|ta|gonal
oc|ta|hed|ral
oc|ta|hed|ron (pl.
 oc|ta|hed|rons)
octal
oct|am|er|ous
oc|ta|meter
oct|ane

oct|ant
oct|archy (pl.
 oct|arch|ies)
oc|ta|style
Oc|ta|teuch
oc|ta|va|lent
oct|ave
oc|tavo (pl.
 oc|ta|vos)
oct|en|nial
oct|en|ni|ally
octet
Oc|to|ber
Oc|to|brist
oc|to|de|cimo (pl.
 oc|to|de|ci|mos)
oc|to|gen|arian
oc|ton|arian
oc|ton|arius (pl.
 oc|ton|arii)
oc|ton|ary (pl.
 oc|ton|ar|ies)
oc|to|pod
oc|to|pus (pl.
 oc|to|puses)
oc|to|roon
oc|to|syl|labic
oc|to|syl|lable
oc|troi
oc|tuple (as v.,
 oc|tu|pling)
ocu|lar
ocu|lar|ist
ocu|late
ocu|list
ocu|listic
ocu|lo|nasal
odal|isque
odd|ball
Odd|fel|low
odd|ity (pl.
 odd|it|ies)
odd|ment
odds-on
Oder
Odessa
odeum (pl.
 odeums)
odi|ous
odium
odo|meter
odon|to|glos|sum
odont|oid
odon|to|lo|gical
odon|to|lo|gist
odon|to|logy

odon|to|rhynch|
        ous
odori|fer|ous
odor|ous
odour
odys|sey
oe|cist
oed|ema
oede|mat|ose
oede|mat|ous
Oed|ipal
Oed|ipus
oeno|lo|gical
oeno|lo|gist
oeno|logy
oeno|phile
oeno|phil|ist
oer|sted
oe|so|pha|geal
oe|so|phagus (pl.
 oe|so|phagi)
oes|tral
oes|tro|gen
oes|tro|genic
oes|trous a.
oes|trum
oes|trus n.
œuvre
of|fal
Of|faly
off-beat
off-centre
off|cut n.
off-day
off|drive (as v.,
 off|drove,
 off|driven,
 off|driv|ing)
of|fence
of|fend
of|fender
of|fens|ive
of|fer
of|fer|tory
off|hand
of|fice
of|ficer
of|fi|cial
of|fi|cial|dom
of|fi|cial|ese
of|fi|cial|ism
of|fi|ci|ally
of|fi|ci|ant
of|fi|ci|ate
 (of|fi|ci|at|ing)
of|fi|cinal

of|fi|cin|ally
of|fi|cious
off|ing
off-key a.
off-licence
off-line
off-load
off-peak
off|print
off-putting
off-season
off|set (as v.,
 off|set,
 off|set|ting)
off|shoot
off|shore
off|side
off|spring
off-stage
of|ten
og|doad
ogee
ogee'd
og|ham
ogival
ogive
ogle (as v., og|ling)
ogre
og|ress
og|rish
Ogy|gian
Ohio
ohm
ohm|age
ohmic
ohm|meter
oi|dium (pl. oi|dia)
oil|cake
oil|can
oil|cloth
oil|field
oil-fired
oil-gauge
oil-gland
oil|ily
oili|ness
oil|man (pl.
 oil|men)
oil|skin
oil-slick
oil-tanker
oily (oil|ier,
 oili|est)
oint|ment
Oire|ach|tas
Ojos del Sa|lado

OK
okapi
okay *use* OK
Ok|hotsk, Sea of
Ok|la|homa
okra
old-age *a.*
old-boy *a.*
olden
old-fashioned
Old|ham
oldie
old|ish
old|ster
old-time
old-timer
old-world *a.*
olea|ceous
olea|gin|ous
olean|der
oleas|ter
oleate
ole|cranon
ol|efin
oleic (acid)
olei|fer|ous
oleo|graph
oleo|mar|gar|ine
oleo|meter
oleo-resin
oleum
ol|fac|tion
ol|fact|ive
ol|fact|ory
olib|anum
ol|ig|arch
ol|ig|archic
ol|ig|arch|ical
ol|ig|archy (*pl.*
  ol|ig|arch|ies)
oli|go|carp|ous
Oli|go|cene
oli|go|mer
oli|go|poly (*pl.*
  oli|go|pol|ies)
olio (*pl.* olios)
oli|va|ceous
oliv|ary
ol|ive
Oliv|ier
ol|iv|ine
ol|or|oso (*pl.*
  ol|or|osos)
Olym|piad
Olym|pian
Olym|pic

Olym|pus
oma|dhaun
Omagh
Oman
Omar Khay|yám
oma|sum (*pl.*
  omasa)
ombre (game)
ombré (of fabric
  etc.)
om|bro|logy
om|bro|meter
om|buds|man (*pl.*
  om|buds|men)
omega
om|elette
omen
omental
omen|tum (*pl.*
  omenta)
omic|ron
om|in|ous
omis|sible
omis|sion
omis|sive
omit (omit|ted,
  omit|ting)
om|ni|bus
om|ni|com|pet|ent
om|ni|
            di|rec|tional
om|ni|far|ious
om|ni|fic
om|ni|gen|ous
om|ni|po|tence
om|ni|po|tent
om|ni|pres|ence
om|ni|pres|ent
om|ni|sci|ence
om|ni|sci|ent
om|ni|vor|ous
om|phalos
om|phalo|tomy
  (*pl.* om|phalo|
            tom|ies)
on|ager
on|an|ism
on|an|ist
on|an|istic
once
once-over
on|co|gene
on|co|genic
on|co|gen|ous
on|co|lo|gist
on|co|logy

on|com|ing
on|eiric
on|eiro|critic
on|eiro|logy
on|eiro|mancy
on|er|ous
one|self
one|step (foxtrot)
one-upmanship
on|flow
on|go|ing
on|ion
on|iony
on-line
on|looker
on|look|ing
only
ono|mas|tic
ono|ma|to|poeia
ono|ma|to|poeic
ono|ma|to|po|etic
on|rush
on|set
on|shore
on|side
on|slaught
on-stage *a.*
On|tario
onto *use* on to
on|to|gen|esis
on|to|gen|etic
on|to|gen|et|ic|
            ally
on|to|geny
on|to|lo|gical
on|to|lo|gic|ally
on|to|lo|gist
on|to|logy
onus
on|ward
onym|ous
onyx
oo|cyte
oodles
oo|gam|ous
oo|gamy
oo|gen|esis
oo|gen|etic
oo|lite
oo|litic
oo|lo|gist
oo|logy
oo|long
oo|miak
oom|pah

oo|phor|ec|tomy
  (*pl.* oo|phor|
            ec|tom|ies)
oo|sperm
ooze (as *v.,*
  ooz|ing)
oozy (ooz|ier,
  oozi|est)
opa|city
opah
opal
opal|es|cence
opal|es|cent
opal|ine
opaque (opaquer,
  opaquest)
open
opener
open|ing
open|ness
op|era
op|er|able
op|er|and
op|er|ate
  (op|er|at|ing)
op|er|atic
op|er|at|ic|ally
op|er|at|ics
op|era|tion
op|era|tional
op|era|tion|ally
op|er|at|ive
op|er|ator
oper|cu|lar
oper|cu|late
oper|cu|lum (*pl.*
  oper|cula)
op|er|etta
ophid|ian
ophio|latry
ophio|logy
oph|ite
oph|itic
oph|thal|mia
oph|thal|mic
oph|thal|mitis
oph|thal|mo|
            lo|gical
oph|thal|mo|
            lo|gist
oph|thal|mo|logy
oph|thal|mo|
            scope
oph|thal|mo|
            scopic

oph¦thal¦mo¦
    scop¦ic¦ally
oph¦thal¦mo¦
    scopy
opi¦ate (as v.,
  opi¦at¦ing)
opine (opin¦ing)
opin¦ion
opin¦ion¦ated
opin¦ion¦at¦ive
opi¦so¦meter
opis¦tho¦graph
opis¦tho¦graphy
opium
opi¦um¦ize
  (opi¦um¦iz¦ing)
opo¦del¦doc
opop¦anax
Oporto
opos¦sum
Op¦pen¦heimer
op¦pidan
op¦pon¦ency
op¦pon¦ent
op¦por¦tune
op¦por¦tun¦ism
op¦por¦tun¦ist
op¦por¦tun¦ity (pl.
  op¦por¦tun¦it¦ies)
op¦pos¦able
op¦pose
  (op¦pos¦ing)
op¦poser
op¦pos¦ite
op¦posi¦tion
Op¦posi¦tion
  (party)
op¦pos¦it¦ive
op¦press
op¦pres¦sion
op¦press¦ive
op¦pressor
op¦probri¦ous
op¦pro¦brium
op¦pugn
op¦pug¦nance
op¦pug¦nancy
op¦pug¦nant
op¦pugna¦tion
op¦sonic
op¦sonin
opt¦ant
opt¦at¦ive
op¦tic (of eye)
Op¦tic (measure
  for spirits; propr.)

op¦tical
op¦tic¦ally
op¦ti¦cian
op¦tics
op¦timal
op¦tim¦ally
op¦tim¦ism
op¦tim¦ist
op¦tim¦istic
op¦tim¦ist¦ic¦ally
op¦tim¦iza¦tion
optim¦ize
  (op¦tim¦iz¦ing)
op¦timum (pl.
  op¦tima)
op¦tion
op¦tional
op¦tion¦ally
op¦to¦meter
op¦to¦met¦rist
op¦to¦metry
op¦to¦phone
opu¦lence
opu¦lent
opun¦tia
opus (pl. op¦era)
opus¦cule
or¦ache
or¦acle
orac¦ular
oracu¦lar¦ity
oracy
oral
or¦ally
or¦ange
Or¦ange (of Ir.
  Protestants)
or¦ange¦ade
Or¦ange¦ism
Or¦ange¦man (pl.
  Or¦ange¦men)
or¦an¦gery (pl.
  or¦an¦ger¦ies)
orang-utan
orate (or¦at¦ing)
ora¦tion
or¦ator
ora¦tor¦ian
ora¦tor¦ical
ora¦torio (pl.
  ora¦tor¦ios)
ora¦tory (pl.
  ora¦tor¦ies)
or¦bicu¦lar
or¦bicu¦lar¦ity
or¦bicu¦late

or¦bit (as v.,
  or¦bited,
  or¦bit¦ing)
or¦bital
or¦biter
orc (cetacean)
Or¦ca¦dian
orch¦ard
or¦chestic
or¦ches¦tra
or¦ches¦tral
or¦ches¦trally
or¦ches¦trate
  (or¦ches¦trat¦ing)
or¦ches¦tra¦tion
or¦ches¦trator
or¦ches¦trina
orchid
orch¦ida¦ceous
orch¦id¦ist
orch¦ido¦logy
orchil
orchis
orch¦itis
or¦cin
or¦cinol
or¦dain
or¦dainer
or¦dain¦ment
or¦deal
or¦der
or¦der¦li¦ness
or¦derly (as n., pl.
  or¦der¦lies)
or¦dinal
or¦din¦ance
  (decree etc.)
△ ordnance
or¦din¦and
or¦din¦ar¦ily
or¦din¦ari¦ness
or¦din¦ary (as n.,
  pl. or¦din¦ar¦ies)
or¦din¦ate
or¦dina¦tion
ord¦nance (govt.
  service)
△ ordinance
or¦don¦nance
Or¦do¦vi¦cian
ord¦ure
or¦ead
orectic
oreg¦ano
Oregon
orfe

or¦gan
or¦gan¦die
or¦gan¦elle
or¦ganic
or¦gan¦ic¦ally
or¦gan¦ism
or¦gan¦ist
or¦gan¦iz¦able
or¦gan¦iza¦tion
or¦gan¦iza¦tional
or¦gan¦ize
  (or¦gan¦iz¦ing)
or¦gan¦izer
or¦gano¦lep¦tic
or¦gano¦met¦al¦lic
or¦ganon
or¦gano¦ther¦apy
or¦ganza
or¦gan¦zine
or¦gasm
or¦gas¦mic
or¦gastic
or¦geat
or¦gi¦astic
orgy (pl. or¦gies)
oribi
oriel
ori¦ent a. & v.
Ori¦ent n.
ori¦ental
Ori¦ental (native)
ori¦ent¦al¦ism
ori¦ent¦al¦ist
oriental¦ize
  (ori¦ent¦al¦iz¦ing)
ori¦ent¦ally
ori¦ent¦ate
  (ori¦ent¦at¦ing)
ori¦enta¦tion
ori¦ent¦eer¦ing
ori¦fice
ori¦flamme
ori¦gami
ori¦gan
Ori¦gen
ori¦gin
ori¦ginal
ori¦gin¦al¦ity
ori¦gin¦ally
ori¦gin¦ate
  (ori¦gin¦at¦ing)
ori¦gina¦tion
ori¦gin¦at¦ive
ori¦gin¦ator
ori¦nasal
ori¦ole

Orion
Orissa
Oriya
Ork|ney
orle (*Her.*)
Or'lé'an|ais
or'lop
or'mer
or'molu
or'na|ment
or'na|mental
or'na|ment'al|ism
or'na|ment'al|ist
or'na|ment|ally
or'na|menta|tion
or'nate
or|nithic
or'ni'tho|lo'gical
or'ni'tho|lo'gist
or'ni'tho|logy
or'ni'tho|mancy
or'ni'tho|
          rhyn'chus
or'ni'tho|scopy
oro|gen'esis
oro|gen'etic
oro|genic
oro'geny
oro|graphic
oro|graph'ical
oro|graphy
oro'ide
oro|lo'gical
oro|lo'gist
oro|logy
oro|tund
orphan
orph'an|age
orph'an|ize
 (orph'an|iz|ing)
Orph|ean
Orphic
Orph|ism
or|phrey
or'pi|ment
or'pine
Or'ping|ton
or'rery
or'ris
or'tho|ceph'alic
or'tho|chro'matic
or'tho|clase
or'tho|don'tia
or'tho|dontic
or'tho|dont'ics
or'tho|dont'ist

or'tho|dox
or'tho|doxy
or'tho|epic
or'tho|ep'ist
or'tho|epy
or'tho|gen'esis
or'tho|gen'etic
or'tho|gnath'ous
or'tho|gonal
or'tho|gon'ally
or'tho|graphic
or'tho|graph'ical
or'tho|graph'ic|
                    ally
or'tho|graphy
ortho-hydrogen
or'tho|paedic
or'tho|paed'ics
or'tho|paed'ist
or'tho|pter'ous
orth|op'tic
orth|op'tics
orth|op'tist
or'tho|rhom'bic
or'tho|tone
or'to|lan
Or'vi|eto (*pl.*
 Or'vi|etos)
Or'wel|lian
oryx
Osaka
Os|borne
Os'can
Os'car
os'cil|late
 (os'cil|lat'ing)
os'cil|la|tion
os'cil|lator
os'cil'lat|ory
os'cil'lo|graph
os'cil'lo|scope
os'cine
os'cin|ine
os'cita|tion
os'cu|lant
os'cu|lar
os'cul|ate
 (os'cu|lat'ing)
os'cu|la'tion
os'cu|lat'ory
os'cu|lum (*pl.*
 os'cula)
os'ier
Oslo
Os|manli
os'mium

os|mosis (*pl.*
 os|moses)
os|motic
os'mot'ic|ally
os'mund
os'prey
os'sein
os|se|ous
os'sia
Os'si|anic
oss|icle
os'si|fic
os|si'fica|tion
os|si|frage
os|sify (os'si|fies,
 os'si|fied,
 os'si|fy'ing)
os'su|ary (*pl.*
 os'su|ar'ies)
os'te|itis
Ost|end
os'tens|ible
os'tens|ibly
os'tens|ive
os'tens|ory (*pl.*
 os'tens|or'ies)
os'ten'ta|tion
os'ten'ta'tious
osteo-arthritis
os'teo|gen'esis
os'teo|geny
os'teo|graphy
os'teo|logy
os'teo|ma'la'cia
os'teo|my'el'itis
os'teo|path
os'teo|pathic
os'teo|pathy
os'teo|phyte
os'teo|por'osis
os'tin|ato (*pl.*
 os'tin|atos)
ost'ler
Ost|pol'itik
os'tra|cism
os'tra|cize
 (os'tra|ciz|ing)
os|tracon (*pl.*
 os|traca)
os|trich
Os'tro|goth
Os'tro|gothic
ot'ary (*pl.*
 ot'ar|ies)
Ot'ello (by Verdi)

Oth'|ello (by
 Shakespeare)
other
oth'er|wise
other-worldly
otic
oti'ose
ot'itis
oto|laryn'go'logy
oto|lith
oto|lo'gist
oto|logy
oto'rhino|
          laryn'go'logy
oto|scope
Ot'tawa
ot'ter
ot'to|man (seat; *pl.*
 ot'to|mans)
Ot'to|man
 (Turk(ish); as *n.*,
 pl. Ot'to|mans)
Ou'aga|dou'gou
ou|bli|ette
ought
oughtn't
Ouija (*propr.*)
ounce
our|self
our|selves
Ouse
ousel
out'age
out|back
out|bid (out'bid,
 out|bid'ding)
out|bid'der
out|board
out|bound
out|brave
 (out|brav'ing)
out|break
out|breed'ing
out|build'ing
out|burst
out|cast (person
 cast out)
out|caste (Indian
 without caste)
out|class
out|come
out|crop (as *v.*,
 out|cropped,
 out|crop'ping)
out|cry (*pl.*
 out|cries)

out|dated
out|dis|tance
 (out|dis|tan|cing)
outdo (out|does,
 out|did,
 out|done,
 out|do|ing)
out|door
out|doors
outer
out|er|most
out|er|wear
out|face
 (out|fa|cing)
out|fall
out|field
out|fielder
out|fight|ing
out|fit
out|fit|ter
out|flank
out|flow
out|fox
out|go|ing
out|go|ings
out|grow
 (out|grew,
 out|grown)
out|growth
out|house
out|ing
out|land|ish
out|last
out|law
out|lawry
out|lay
out|let
out|lier
out|line (as v.,
 out|lin|ing)
out|live
 (out|liv|ing)
out|look
out|ly|ing
out|man|œuvre
 (out|man|œuv|
 ring)
out|match
out|moded
out|most
out|num|ber
out-patient
out|post
out|pour|ing

out|put (as v.,
 out|put or
 out|put|ted,
 out|put|ting)
out|rage (as v.,
 out|ra|ging)
out|ra|geous
out|rank
outré
out|reach
out|ride
 (out|rode,
 out|rid|den,
 out|rid|ing)
out|rider
out|rigged
out|rig|ger
out|right
out|ri|val
 (out|ri|valled,
 out|ri|val|ling)
out|run (out|ran,
 out|run,
 out|run|ning)
out|rush
out|set
out|shine
 (out|shone,
 out|shin|ing)
out|side
out|sider
out|sight
out|size
out|skirts
out|smart
out|span (as v.,
 out|spanned,
 out|span|ning)
out|spoken
out|spread (as v.,
 out|spread)
out|stand|ing
out|stare
 (out|star|ing)
out|sta|tion
out|stay
out|stretched
out|strip
 (out|stripped,
 out|strip|ping)
out-swinger
out-talk
out-tray
out-turn
out|vote
 (out|vot|ing)

out|ward
out|wards
out|wash
out|wear
 (out|wore,
 out|worn)
out|weigh
out|wit
 (out|wit|ted,
 out|wit|ting)
out|with
out|work
out|worker
ou|zel
ouzo (pl. ou|zos)
oval
oval|ity
ovally
ovarian
ova|ri|ec|tomy (pl.
 ova|ri|ec|tom|ies)
ova|ri|otomy (pl.
 ova|ri|otom|ies)
ovar|itis
ovary (pl.
 ovar|ies)
ovate
ova|tion
oven
ov|en|ware
over-abundance
over-abundant
over|achieve
 (over|achiev|ing)
over|act
over-active
over-activity
over-age
over|all
over|alls
over-anxiety
over-anxious
over|arch
over|arm
over|awe
 (over|aw|ing)
over|bal|ance
 (over|
 bal|an|cing)
over|bear
 (over|bore,
 over|borne)
over|bear|ing
over|bid
 (over|bid,
 over|bid|ding)

over|bid|der
over|blouse
over|blow
 (over|blew,
 over|blown)
over|board
over|book
over|boot
over|brim
 (over|brimmed,
 over|brimming)
over|build
 (over|built)
over|bur|den
over|call
over-careful
over|cast (as v.,
 over|cast)
over-cautious
over|charge
 (over|char|ging)
over|check
over|cloud
over|coat
over|come
 (over|came,
 over|com|ing)
over-compensate
 (over-
 compensating)
over-
 compensation
over-confidence
over-confident
over-cooked
over|crop
 (over|cropped,
 over|crop|ping)
over|crowd
over|de|velop
 (over|
 de|veloped,
 over|
 de|vel|op|ing)
overdo
 (over|does,
 over|did,
 over|done,
 over|do|ing)
over|dose
over|draft
over|draw
 (over|drew,
 over|drawn)
over|dress
over|drive

overdue
over-eager
over|eat
 (over|ate,
 over|eaten)
over-emphasis
over-emphasize
 (over-
 emphasizing)
over|es|tim|ate
 (as *v.*, over|
 es|tim|at|ing)
over|es|tima|tion
over-excite
 (over-exciting)
over-exert
over-exertion
over-expose
 (over-exposing)
over-exposure
over|fall
over|feed
 (over|fed)
over|fill
over|flight
over|flow
over|fly
 (over|flies,
 over|flew,
 over|flown,
 over|fly|ing)
over|fold
over|fond
over|ful|fil
 (over|ful|filled,
 over|ful|fill|ing)
over|ful|fil|ment
over|full
over|glaze
over|ground
over|grow
 (over|grew,
 over|grown)
over|growth
over|hand
over|hang (as *v.*,
 over|hung)
over-haste
over-hastily
over-hasty
over|haul
over|head
over|heads
over|hear
 (over|heard)
over|heat

Over|ijs|sel
over-indulge
 (over-indulging)
over-indulgence
over-indulgent
over-insurance
over|joyed
over|kill
over|laden
over|land
over|lander
over|lap (as *v.*,
 over|lapped,
 over|lap|ping)
over-large
over|lay (as *v.*,
 over|laid)
over|leaf
over|lie (overlay,
 over|lain,
 over|ly|ing)
over|load
over|long
over|look
over|lord
overly
over|man (as *n.*,
 pl. over|men; as
 v., over|manned,
 over|man|ning)
over|man|tel
over-much
over|night
over|pass
over|pay
 (over|paid)
over|pay|ment
over|per|suade
 (over|
 per|suad|ing)
over|pitch
over|play
over-populated
over-population
over|power
over|praise
 (over|prais|ing)
over|print
over-produce
 (over-producing)
over-production
over|proof
over-protect
over-protection
over-protective

over|rate
 (over|rat|ing)
over|reach
over-react
over-reaction
over-refine
 (over-refining)
over|ride
 (over|rode,
 over|rid|den,
 over|rid|ing)
over|rider
over|ripe
over|rule
 (over|rul|ing)
over|run
 (over|ran,
 over|run|ning)
over|sail|ing
over|sea
over|see
 (over|saw,
 over|seen)
over|seer
over|sell
 (over|sold)
over-sensitive
over-sensitivity
over|set (as *v.*,
 over|set,
 over|set|ting)
over|sew
 (over|sewed,
 over|sewn)
over-sexed
over|shadow
over|shoe
over|shoot (as *v.*,
 over|shot)
over|side
over|sight
over-
 simplification
over-simplify
 (over-simplifies,
 over-simplified,
 over-
 simplifying)
over|size
over|sized
over|skirt
over|slaugh
over|sleep
 (over|slept)
over|sleeve
over-solicitous

over-solicitude
over|spend
 (over|spent)
over|spill
over|spread
over|staff
over|state
 (over|stat|ing)
over|state|ment
overstay
over|steer
over|step
 (over|stepped,
 over|step|ping)
over|stock
over|strain
over|stress
over|stretch
over|strong
over|strung
over-subscribe
 (over-
 subscribing)
over|subtle
over|supply
 (over|sup|plies,
 over|sup|plied,
 over|sup|ply|ing)
overt
over|take
 (over|took,
 over|taken,
 over|tak|ing)
over|tax
over|throw
 (over|threw,
 over|thrown)
over|thrust
over|time
over|tire
 (over|tir|ing)
over|tone
over|top
 (over|topped,
 over|top|ping)
over|train
over|trick
over|trump
over|ture
over|turn
over-use
 (over-using)
over|valu|ation
over|value
 (over|val|ued,
 over|valu|ing)

over|view
over|ween|ing
over|weight
over|whelm
over|wind
 (over|wound)
over|winter
over|work
over|write
 (over|wrote,
 over|writ|ten,
 over|writ|ing)
over|wrought
over-zealous
ovi|bov|ine
ovi|cide
Ovid
ovi|duct
ovi|form
ovine
ovi|par|ity
ovi|par|ous
ovi|posit
ovi|posi|tion

ovi|pos|itor
ovoid
ovolo (*pl.* ovoli)
ovo|tes|tis (*pl.*
 ovo|tes|tes)
ovo|vi|vi|par|ous
ovu|lar
ovu|late
 (ovu|lat|ing)
ovu|la|tion
ovu|lat|ory
ovule
ovum (*pl.* ova)
owe (ow|ing)
owl|ery (*pl.*
 owl|er|ies)
ow|let
owl|ish
owner
owner-occupier
own|er|ship
ox (*pl.* oxen)
ox|al|ate
ox|alic

Ox|bridge
Ox|fam
Ox|ford
Ox|ford|shire
ox|herd
ox|hide
ox|id|ant
ox|id|ate
 (ox|id|at|ing)
ox|ida|tion
ox|id|at|ive
ox|ide
ox|id|iz|able
ox|id|iza|tion
ox|id|ize
 (ox|id|iz|ing)
ox|id|izer
ox|lip
Oxo|nian
ox|tail
ox|ter
oxy-acetylene
oxy|acid
oxy|carp|ous

oxy|gen
oxy|gen|ate
 (oxy|gen|at|ing)
oxy|gena|tion
oxy|gen|ize
 (oxy|gen|iz|ing)
oxy|gen|ous
oxy|hae|mo|
             glo|bin
oxy-hydrogen
oxy|moron
oxy|opia
oxy|salt
oxy|to|cin
oxy|tone
oyer
oys|ter
oyster-catcher
ozo|cer|ite
ozone
ozonic
ozon|ize
 (ozon|iz|ing)

P

pab|ulum
paca
pace (as *v.*,
 pa|cing)
pace|maker
pacer
pa|chy|derm
pa|chy|dermal
pa|chy|derm|at|
              ous
pa|ci|fic (peaceful)
Pa|ci|fic (ocean)
pa|ci|fic|ally
pa|ci|fica|tion
pa|ci|fic|at|ory
pa|ci|fier
pa|ci|fism
pa|ci|fist
pa|cify (pa|ci|fies,
 pa|ci|fied,
 pa|ci|fy|ing)
pack|age (as *v.*,
 pack|aging)
packer
packet
pack-horse
pack-ice
packing-case
pad (as *v.*,
 pad|ded,
 pad|ding)
pad|ded
pad|ding
paddle (as *v.*,
 pad|dling)
pad|dler
pad|dock
paddy (rage, rice;
 pl. pad|dies)
Paddy (Irishman;
 pl. Pad|dies)
paddy-field
pad|dy|whack
Pa|di|shah
pad|lock
padre
paean
pae|di|at|ric
pae|di|at|ri|cian

pae|di|at|rics
pae|di|at|rist
pae|do|phile
pae|do|philia
pae|do|philiac
pa|ella
paeon
pae|onic
pa|gan
Pa|ga|nini
pa|gan|ish
pa|gan|ism
pa|geant
pa|geantry
page (as *v.*,
 pa|ging)
page-boy
pa|ginal
pa|gin|ary
pa|gin|ate
 (pa|gin|at|ing)
pa|gina|tion
pa|goda
pa|gur|ian
Pah|lavi
paid-up
pail|ful (*pl.*
 pail|fuls)
pail|lette (spangle)
pain|ful
pain|fully
pain-killer
pain-killing
pain|less
pains|tak|ing
paint|box
paint|brush
painter
paint|ing
paint|work
painty
paisa (*pl.* paise)
Pais|ley
pa|keha
Pak|is|tan
Pa|ki|stani
pal (as *v.*, palled,
 pall|ing)
pal|ace

pal|adin
Pal|ae|arctic
pal|aeo|bot|any
Pal|aeo|cene
pal|aeo|grapher
pal|aeo|graphic
pal|aeo|
          graph|ical
pal|aeo|graphy
pal|aeo|lithic
pal|ae|on|to|
          lo|gical
pal|ae|on|to|
          lo|gist
pal|ae|on|to|logy
Pal|aeo|zoic
pa|laes|tra
pala|fitte
pal|ais
pa|lan|quin
pa|lat|ab|il|ity
pa|lat|able
pal|at|ably
pal|atal
pal|ate (part of
 mouth) △ palette,
 pallet
pa|la|tial
pa|la|tially
pa|lat|in|ate
 (colour)
Pa|lat|in|ate
 (region)
pal|at|ine (of the
 palate)
Pal|at|ine (count)
pa|la|ver
pale (as *a.*, paler,
 palest; as *v.*,
 pal|ing)
palea (*pl.* paleae)
pale-face
palely
Pal|es|tine
Pal|es|tin|ian
Pal|es|trina
pa|le|tot

pal|ette (in
 painting)
 △ palate, pallet
palette-knife (*pl.*
 palette-knives)
pal|frey
pal|imp|sest
pal|in|drome
pal|in|dromic
pal|ing
pal|in|gen|esis
pal|in|gen|etic
pal|in|ode
pal|is|ade
 (palis|ad|ing)
pal|ish
Pal|la|dian
pal|la|dium
pall|bearer
pal|let (mattress,
 platform, etc.)
 △ palate, palette
pal|lial
pal|li|asse
pal|li|ate
 (pal|li|at|ing)
pal|li|ation
pal|li|at|ive
pal|lid
pal|lid|ity
pal|lium (*pl.*
 pal|lia)
pal|lor
pally
palm
pal|ma|ceous
pal|mar
pal|mary
pal|mate
palmer
Pal|mer|ston
pal|mette
pal|metto (*pl.*
 pal|met|tos)
palm|ful (*pl.*
 palm|fuls)
pal|mi|ped
palm|ist
palm|istry

palmy
pal|myra
pa|lolo (pl.
  pa|lo|los)
pa'lo|mino (pl.
  pa'lo|mi'nos)
pa'lo|verde
palp|ab'il|ity
palp|able
palp|ably
palp|ate
  (palp|at'ing)
palpa'tion
pal|pebral
pal'pit|ate
  (pal'pit|at'ing)
pal'pita|tion
palpus (pl. palpi)
pal|stave
palsy (as a v.,
  pal|sies, pal|sied,
  pal'sy|ing)
pal'ter
pal'tri|ness
pal'try (pal'trier,
  pal|tri|est)
pal|udal
pa'lyno|lo'gical
pa'lyno|lo'gist
pa'lyno|logy
Pam'ela
Pa'mir
pam'pas
pam'per
pam'pero (pl.
  pam|peros)
pamph|let
pamph|let|eer
pan (as a v.,
  panned,
  pan|ning)
pana|cea
pan|ache
pa'nada
pan'ama (hat)
Pan'ama (in C.
  Amer.)
Pa'na|ma'nian
pan-American
pan-Anglican
pa'na|tella
pan|cake (as a v.,
  pan|cak'ing)
pan|chro'matic
pan|cos'mism
pan|creas

pan'cre|atic
pan'cre|atin
pan'cre'at|itis
panda
pan|da'nus
Pan|dean
pan|dect
pan|demic
pan|de'mon|ium
pan'der
pan|dora (lute)
Pan|dora's box
pan|egyric
pan'egyr|ical
pan'egyr|ist
pan'egyr|ize
  (pan'egyr|iz|ing)
panel (as a v.,
  panelled,
  pan'el|ling)
pan|el'ling
pan|el|list
pan|ful (pl.
  pan|fuls)
panga
pan|go|lin
pan|handle
pan-Hellenism
panic (as a v.,
  pan|icked,
  pan|ick|ing)
pan|icky
pan|icle
pan'jan|drum
pan|nage
panne (velvet)
pan|nier
pan'ni|kin
pan|op'lied
pan|oply (pl.
  pan|op'lies)
pan|op'tic
pan|or'ama
pan|or'amic
pan-pipes
pansy (pl.
  pan|sies)
pan'ta|loons
pan|tech'nicon
pan|the'ism
pan|the'ist
pan|the'istic
pan|theon
Pan|theon
pan|ther
pant'ies

pan'ti|hose
pan|tile
panto (pl. pan'tos)
panto|graph
pan'to|graphic
pan'to|lo'gic
pan'to|logy
pan'to|mime (as
  a v.,
  pan'to|mim'ing)
pan'to|mimic
pan'to|mim'ist
pan'to|morphic
pan'to|scopic
pan'to|thenic
  (acid)
pan'try (pl.
  pan|tries)
pan'zer
papa
pap'acy (pl.
  pap'acies)
pa'pain
papal
pap'al|ism
pap'al|ist
pap|ally
Pap'an|dreou
pa'pa'ver|ous
pa'paw
pa'paya
pa'per
pa'per|back
paper-chase
paper-clip
paper-mill
pa'per|weight
pa'per|work
pa'pery
pa'pier mâché
pa'pilla (pl.
  pa'pil|lae)
pap'il|lary
pap'il|late
pa'pil|loma
pa'pil|lon
pap'il|lose
pap'ist
pap|istic
pap'ist|ical
pap|istry
pa'poose
pap|pose
pap'pus (pl.
  pappi)

pappy (pap'pier,
  pap'pi|est)
pap|rika
Papua New
  Guinea
pap|ula (pl.
  pap|ulae)
pap|ular
papu|lose
papu|lous
pa'py|ra'ceous
pa'pyro|lo'gical
pa'pyro|lo'gist
pa'pyro|logy
pa'pyrus (pl.
  pa'pyri)
para (colloq.)
para|basis (pl.
  para|bases)
para|bi'osis (pl.
  para|bi'oses)
para|bi'otic
par|able
para|bola
para|bolic
para|bol'ical
para|bol'ic|ally
para|bol|oid
para|bol'oidal
Pa'ra|cel'sus
par|acet|amol
para|chron'ism
para|chute (as a v.,
  para|chut'ing)
para|chut'ist
para|clete
par'ade (as a v.,
  par|ad'ing)
para|di'chloro|
          ben'zene
para|diddle
para|digm
para|dig'matic
para|disa'ical
para|dise
para|dos
para|dox
para|dox'ical
para|dox'ic|ally
para|dox'ure
para|doxy
par'af|fin
par|agoge
par|ago'gic
par|agon
para|graph

para¦graph¦ist
Pa¦ra¦guay
para-hydrogen
para¦keet
par¦al¦de¦hyde
para¦lip¦om¦ena
para¦lip¦sis (pl.
 pa¦ra¦lip¦ses)
par¦al¦lac¦tic
par¦al¦lax
par¦al¦lel (as v.,
 par¦alleled,
 par¦al¦lel¦ing)
par¦al¦lel¦epi¦ped
par¦al¦lel¦ism
par¦al¦lelo¦gram
para¦lo¦gism
para¦lo¦gist
para¦lysa¦tion
para¦lyse
 (para¦lys¦ing)
para¦lysis (pl.
 para¦lyses)
para¦lytic
para¦lyt¦ic¦ally
para¦mag¦netic
para¦mag¦net¦ism
Pa¦ra¦ma¦ribo
para¦me¦cium
para¦med¦ical
para¦meter
para¦met¦ric
para¦mil¦it¦ary
par¦am¦ne¦sia
par¦amo (pl.
 par¦amos)
para¦mount
para¦mountcy
par¦amour
Pa¦raná (river)
par¦ang
para¦noia
para¦noiac
para¦noic
pa¦ra¦noid
para¦nor¦mal
para¦nor¦mally
para¦pet
para¦peted
par¦aph
para¦pher¦na¦lia
para¦phrase (as
 v., para¦
  phras¦ing)
para¦phrastic
para¦ple¦gia

para¦ple¦gic
para¦psy¦cho¦
  lo¦gical
para¦psy¦cho¦
  lo¦gist
para¦psy¦cho¦logy
para¦quat
para¦se¦lene (pl.
 para¦se¦lenae)
para¦site
para¦sitic
para¦sit¦ical
para¦siti¦cide
para¦sit¦ism
pa¦ra¦sit¦ize
 (para¦sit¦iz¦ing)
para¦sito¦logy
para¦sol
para¦sym¦path¦
           etic
para¦syn¦thesis
 (pl. para¦
       syn¦theses)
para¦syn¦thetic
para¦tactic
para¦taxis
para¦thion
para¦thy¦roid
para¦trooper
para¦troops
para¦ty¦phoid
para¦vane
par¦boil
par¦buckle (as v.,
 par¦buck¦ling)
par¦cel (as v.,
 par¦celled,
 par¦cel¦ling)
par¦cen¦ary (pl.,
 par¦cen¦ar¦ies)
par¦cener
parch¦ment
par¦close
par¦da¦lote
par¦don
par¦don¦able
par¦don¦ably
pare (par¦ing)
par¦egoric
par¦eira
par¦en¦chyma
par¦en¦chy¦mal
par¦en¦chy¦mat¦
           ous
par¦ent
par¦ent¦age

par¦ental
par¦en¦teral
par¦en¦thesis (pl.
 par¦en¦theses)
par¦en¦thes¦ize
 (par¦en¦thes¦iz¦
           ing)
par¦en¦thetic
par¦en¦thet¦ical
par¦en¦thet¦ic¦ally
par¦ent¦hood
parer
par¦er¦gon (pl.
 par¦erga)
par¦esis (pl.
 par¦eses)
par¦etic
par ex¦cel¦lence
par¦fait
par¦get (as v.,
 par¦geted,
 par¦get¦ing)
par¦he¦li¦acal
par¦he¦lic
par¦he¦lion (pl.
 par¦he¦lia)
pa¦ri¦ah
Par¦ian
pa¦ri¦etal
par¦ing
Paris
par¦ish
pa¦rish¦ioner
Pa¦ris¦ian
par¦ison
pa¦ri¦syl¦labic
par¦ity (pl.
 par¦it¦ies)
parka
par¦kin
Par¦kin¦son
Par¦kin¦son¦ism
park¦land
par¦lance
par¦ley (as v.,
 par¦leys,
 par¦leyed,
 par¦ley¦ing)
par¦lia¦ment
par¦lia¦ment¦
          arian
par¦lia¦ment¦ary
par¦lour
par¦lour¦maid
par¦lous
Parma

Par¦mesan
Par¦nas¦sian
Par¦nell
pa¦ro¦chial
pa¦ro¦chi¦al¦ism
pa¦ro¦chial¦ity
pa¦ro¦chi¦ally
par¦odic
par¦od¦ist
par¦ody (as n., pl.
 par¦od¦ies; as v,
 par¦od¦ies,
 par¦od¦ied,
 par¦ody¦ing)
pa¦rol (Law, oral
 declaration)
pa¦role (word of
 honour etc.; as v.,
 pa¦rol¦ing)
pa¦rolee
par¦ono¦masia
par¦onym
par¦onym¦ous
pa¦rotid
pa¦rot¦itis
Par¦ou¦sia
par¦ox¦ysm
par¦ox¦ys¦mal
par¦oxy¦tone
par¦pen
par¦quet
par¦quetry
parr (salmon)
par¦ra¦matta
par¦ri¦cidal
par¦ri¦cide
par¦rot
parry (as n., pl.
 par¦ries; as v.,
 par¦ries,
 par¦ried,
 par¦ry¦ing)
parse (pars¦ing)
par¦sec
Par¦see
Par¦see¦ism
Par¦si¦fal
par¦si¦mo¦ni¦ous
par¦si¦mony
pars¦ley
pars¦nip
par¦son
par¦son¦age

par|take
 (par|took,
 par|taken,
 par|tak|ing)
par|tan
par|terre
part-exchange (as
 v., part-
 exchanging)
par|theno|
   gen|esis
par|theno|
   gen|etic
Par|thenon
Par|thian
parti
par|tial
par|ti|al|ity (*pl.*
 par|ti|al|it|ies)
par|tially
part|ible
par|ti|cip|ant
par|ti|cip|ate
 (par|ti|cip|at|ing)
par|ti|cipa|tion
par|ti|cip|ator
par|ti|cip|at|ory
par|ti|ci|pial
par|ti|ciple
par|ticle
par|ti|col|oured
par|ticu|lar
par|ti|cular|ism
par|ti|cular|ist
par|ti|cu|lar|ity
par|tic|ular|iza|
      tion
par|ti|cular|ize
 (par|tic|ular|iz|
      ing)
par|tic|ulate
part|ing
par|tisan
par|tis|an|ship
par|tita (*pl.*
 par|tite)
par|tite
par|ti|tion
par|ti|tioned
par|tit|ive
part|ner
part|ner|ship
part|ridge
part-time
par|turi|ent
par|turi|tion

party (*pl.* par|ties)
par|venu (*fem.*
 par|venue)
par|vis
pas|cal (unit)
Pas|cal (scientist;
 Comp. lang.)
pas|chal (of
 Easter)
pas de deux
pasha
pash|alic
Pashto
paso doble
pas|quin|ade
pass|able (in
 senses of *pass*)
△ passible
pass|ably
pas|sa|caglia
pas|sage (as *v.*,
 pas|sa|ging)
pas|sage|way
pass|ant
pass|book
passé (*fem.*
 pas|sée)
pas|sen|ger
passe-partout
passer-by
pas|ser|ine
pass|ib|il|ity
pass|ible (*Theol.*)
△ passable
passim
pas|sion
Pas|sion (of
 Christ)
pas|sional
pas|sion|ate
Pas|sion|ist (RC
 order)
Pas|sion|tide
pas|siv|ate
 (pas|siv|at|ing)
pas|siva|tion
pass|ive
pas|siv|ity
pass|key
pass-mark
Pass|over
pass|port
pass|word
pasta
paste (as *v.*,
 past|ing)

paste|board
pas|tel
pas|tel|list
pas|tern
Pas|ter|nak
paste-up
Pas|teur
pas|teur|iza|tion
pas|teur|ize
 (pas|teur|iz|ing)
pas|tic|cio (*pl.*
 pas|tic|cios)
pas|tiche
pas|tille
pas|time
pas|tor
pas|toral
pas|tor|ale (*pl.*
 pas|tor|ali)
pas|tor|al|ism
pas|tor|al|ist
pas|tor|al|ity
pas|tor|ally
pas|tor|ate
pas|trami
pas|try (*pl.*
 pas|tries)
pas|tur|age
pas|ture (as *v.*,
 pas|tur|ing)
pasty *a.* (pas|tier,
 pas|ti|est)
pasty *n.* (*pl.*
 pas|ties)
pat (as *v.*, pat|ted,
 pat|ting)
pat-a-cake
pa|ta|gium (*pl.*
 pa|ta|gia)
pa|ta|vin|ity
patch|ily
patchi|ness
patch|ouli
patch|work
patchy (patch|ier,
 patchi|est)
pâté
pâté de foie gras
pa|tel|la (*pl.*
 pa|tel|lae)
pa|tel|lar
pa|tel|late
paten
pa|tency
pa|tent
pa|tent|able

pa|tentee
pa|ter
pa|ter|fa|mi|lias
pa|ter|nal
pa|ter|nal|ism
pa|ter|nal|ist
pa|ter|nal|istic
pa|tern|ally
pa|tern|ity (*pl.*
 pa|tern|it|ies)
pa|ter|nos|ter
Pa|than
path|etic
path|et|ic|ally
path|finder
pathic
patho|gen
pa|tho|gen|esis
pa|tho|gen|etic
pa|tho|genic
pa|tho|gen|ous
pa|tho|geny
pa|tho|gno|monic
pa|tho|gnomy
pa|tho|lo|gical
pa|tho|lo|gic|ally
patho|lo|gist
patho|logy
pathos
path|way
pa|tience
pa|tient
pat|ina
pat|in|ated
pat|ina|tion
pat|in|ous
patio (*pl.* patios)
pa|tis|serie
Patna (rice)
pat|ois
pat|rial
pat|ri|al|ity
pat|ri|arch
pat|ri|archal
pat|ri|arch|ate
pat|ri|arch|ism
pat|ri|archy (*pl.*
 pat|ri|arch|ies)
Pat|ri|cia
pa|tri|cian
pa|tri|ci|ate
pat|ri|cidal
pat|ri|cide
Pat|rick
pat|ri|lin|eal
pat|ri|mo|nial

pat|ri|mony
pat|riot
pat|ri|otic
pat|ri|ot|ism
pa|tristic
pa|trol (as v.,
 pa|trolled,
 pa|trol|ling)
pa|trol|man (pl.
 pa|trol|men)
pat|ro|lo|gical
pat|ro|lo|gist
pa|tro|logy
pat|ron
pat|ron|age
pat|ron|ess
pat|ron|ize
 (pat|ron|iz|ing)
pat|ronymic
pat|tee
pat|ten
pat|ter
pat|tern
patty (pl. pat|ties)
patu|lous
paua
pau|city (pl.
 pau|cit|ies)
Paul|ine
Paul|ing
paul|ow|nia
paunch
paunchy
pau|per
pause (as v.,
 paus|ing)
pav|age
pavan
pave (pav|ing)
pavé
pave|ment
pa|vil|ion
pa|vior
Pav|lov
pav|lova
pav|on|ine
pawl (lever etc.)
pawn
pawn|broker
pawn|shop
pawpaw use
 papaw
pay (as v., paid,
 pay|ing)
pay|able
pay-claim

pay-day
payee
payer
pay|load
pay|mas|ter
pay|ment
pay-off
pay|ola
pay-packet
pay|roll
pays|age
peace
peace|able
peace|ably
peace|ful
peace|fully
peace|maker
peace-pipe
peace|time
peach
pea-chick
peach Melba
peachy
 (peach|ier,
 peachi|est)
pea|cock
pea|cock|ery
pea|fowl
pea|hen
peak (summit)
 △ peek
peaky (peak|ier,
 peaki|est)
peal (ring) △ peel
pea|nut
pear-drop
pearl
pearly (as n., pl.
 pearlies; as a.,
 pearl|ier,
 pearli|est)
pear|main
peas|ant
peas|antry
pease
pea-shooter
pea-stick
peat
peat|bog
peaty
peau-de-soie
 (fabric)
pebble
pebble-dash
pebbly (peb|blier,
 peb|bli|est)

pe|can (nut)
 △ pekan
pec|cab|il|ity
pec|cable
pec|ca|dillo (pl.
 pec|ca|dil|loes)
pec|cancy
pec|cant
pec|cary (pl.
 pec|car|ies)
pec|cavi
pecker
peck|ish
pec|or|ino (pl.
 pec|or|inos)
pec|ten (Zool.; pl.
 pec|tens or
 pec|tines)
pec|tic
pec|tin (Chem.)
pec|tin|ate
pec|tina|tion
pec|toral
pec|tose
pecu|late
 (pecu|lat|ing)
pecu|la|tion
pecu|lator
pe|cu|liar
pe|cu|li|ar|ity (pl.
 pe|cu|li|ar|it|ies)
pe|cu|ni|ar|ily
pe|cu|ni|ary
ped|ago|gic
ped|ago|gical
ped|ago|gics
ped|ago|gism
ped|agogue
ped|agogy
pedal (as v.,
 ped|alled,
 ped|al|ling)
ped|alo (pl.
 ped|alos)
ped|ant
pe|dantic
ped|antry
ped|ate
peddle
 (ped|dling)
ped|dler
ped|er|ast
ped|er|asty
ped|es|tal (as v.,
 ped|es|talled,
 ped|es|tal|ling)

ped|es|trian
ped|es|tri|an|ism
ped|es|tri|an|ize
 (ped|es|tri|an|iz|
 ing)
pediatric etc. use
 paediatric etc.
pedi|cab
pedi|cel
pedi|cel|late
pe|di|cu|lar
pe|di|cu|late
pe|di|cu|losis
pe|di|cu|lous
pedi|cure (as v.,
 pedi|cur|ing)
pedi|gree
pedi|greed
pedi|ment
pedi|mental
pedi|men|ted
ped|lar
ped|lary
pe|do|lo|gical
pe|do|lo|gist
pe|do|logy
pe|do|meter
ped|uncle
ped|un|cu|lar
ped|un|cu|late
pee (urine; as v.,
 peed, pee|ing)
Peebles
peek (peep)
 △ peak
peek|aboo
peel (rind etc.)
 △ peal
Peel
peeler
peen
peep-hole
peep-show
peer (a noble, an
 equal, to look)
 △ pier
peer|age
peer|ess
Peer Gynt
peer|less
peeve (as v.,
 peev|ing)
peev|ish
pee|wit
peg (as v., pegged,
 peg|ging)

Peg|as|ean
Peg|asus
peg-leg
peg|mat|ite
peignoir
pe|jor|at|ive
pekan (animal)
△ pecan
peke (dog)
Pe|kin|ese (dog)
Pe|king
Pe|king|ese
 (inhab. of Peking)
pe|koe
pel|age
pe|la|gian
pe|la|gic
pel|ar|go|nium
Pe|las|gic
Pe|lée
pel|er|ine
pelf (money)
pel|ham
pel|ican
pe|lisse
pel|lagra
pel|lag|rous
pel|let
pel|licle
pel|li|cu|lar
pel|lit|ory (pl.
 pel|lit|or|ies)
pell-mell
pel|lu|cid
pel|lu|cid|ity
Pel|man|ism
pel|met
pe|lorus
pe|lota
pelta (pl. pel|tae)
pelt|ate
pel|vic
pel|vis (pl. pel|ves
 or pel|vises)
Pem|broke
pem|mican
pem|phig|oid
pem|phig|ous
pem|phigus
pen (as v.,
 penned,
 pen|ning)
penal
pen|al|ize
 (pen|al|iz|ing)
pen|ally

pen|alty (pl.
 pen|al|ties)
pen|ance (as v.,
 pen|an|cing)
pen|an|nu|lar
pe|na|tes
pence (pl. of
 penny)
pen|chant
pen|cil (as v.,
 pen|cilled,
 pen|cil|ling)
pencil-case
pen|cil|ler
pen|dant n.
pen|dency
pen|dent a.
pen|dent|ive
pend|ing
pen|dragon
pen|du|late
 (pen|du|lat|ing)
pen|du|line
pen|du|lous
pen|du|lum
Pe|nel|ope
pe|ne|plain
pen|et|rab|il|ity
pen|et|rable
pe|ne|tra|lia
pen|et|rate
 (pen|et|rat|ing)
pen|et|ra|tion
pen|et|rat|ive
pen|et|rator
pen-friend
pen|guin
pen|holder
pe|nial
peni|cil|late
pe|ni|cil|lin
pen|ile
pen|in|sula
pen|in|su|lar
penis (pl.
 pen|ises)
pen|it|ence
pen|it|ent
pen|it|en|tial
pen|it|en|tiary (pl.
 pen|it|en|tiar|ies)
pen|knife (pl.
 pen|knives)
pen-name
pen|nant

pen|nies (pl. of
 penny)
pen|ni|less
pen|nill (pl.
 pen|nil|lion)
pen|non
Penn|syl|va|nia
Penn|syl|va|nian
penny (pl.
 pen|nies for coins,
 pence for sum)
penny|royal
penny|weight
penny|wort
penny|worth
peno|lo|gical
peno|lo|gist
peno|logy
pen|sée
pens|ile
pen|sion
pen|sion|able
pen|sion|ary (as
 n., pl.
 pen|sion|ar|ies)
pen|sioner
pens|ive
pen|stock
pen|ta|chord
pent|acle
pentad
penta|gon
Pen|ta|gon (US
 defence HQ)
pen|ta|gonal
pen|ta|gram
pen|ta|gyn|ous
pen|ta|hed|ron
 (pl. pen|ta|hedra)
pent|amer|ous
pen|ta|meter
pent|and|rous
pent|ane
pent|angle
pen|ta|prism
Pen|ta|teuch
pen|ta|teuchal
pent|ath|lete
pent|ath|lon
pent|atomic
pen|ta|tonic
pen|ta|val|ent
Pente|cost
pente|costal
pent|house

pen|ti|mento (pl.
 pen|ti|menti)
pen|to|bar|bital
pen|to|bar|bit|one
pent|ode
pent|ste|mon
pen|tyl
pen|ult
pen|ul|tim|ate
pen|um|bra (pl.
 pen|um|brae)
pen|umb|ral
pen|uri|ous
pen|ury
peon
pe|on|age
pe|ony (pl.
 pe|on|ies)
people (as v.,
 peopling)
pep (as v.,
 pepped,
 pep|ping)
pep|er|ino
pep|lum
pepo (pl. pe|pos)
pep|per
pep|per|corn
pepper-mill
pep|per|mint
pepper-pot
pep|per|wort
pep|pery
peppy
pep|sin
pep|tic
pep|tide
pep|tone
Pepys
per|ad|ven|ture
per|am|bul|ate
 (per|am|bu|
        lat|ing)
per|am|bu|la|tion
per|am|bu|lator
per|am|bu|lat|ory
per an|num
per|cale
per cap|ita
per caput
per|ceive
 (per|ceiv|ing)
per cent
per|cent|age
per|cent|ile
per|cept

per'cept|ib'il|ity
per'cept|ible
per'cept|ibly
per'cep'tion
per'cept|ive
per'cep'tiv|ity
per'chance
per'cheron
per'chlor'ate
per'chloric
per'cipi|ence
per'cipi|ent
per'col|ate
 (per'col|at'ing)
per'cola'tion
per'col|ator
per'cuss
per'cus'sion
per'cuss|ive
per'cu'tan|eous
per diem
per'di'tion
perdu (concealed,
 lost; *fem.* per'due)
per'dur'ab'il|ity
per'dur'able
per'dur'ably
père
per'eg'rin|ate
 (per'eg'rin|
                at'ing)
per'eg'rina'tion
per'eg'rin|ator
per'eg'rine
per'emp'tor'ily
per'emp'tori|ness
per'emp'tory
per'en'nial
per'en'ni|al'ity
per'en'ni|ally
per'fect
per'fect|ib'il|ity
per'fect|ible
per'fec'tion
per'fec'tion|ism
per'fec'tion|ist
per'fect|ive
per'fer'vid
per'fi'di|ous
per'fidy (*pl.*
 per'fid|ies)
per'fo'li|ate
per'for|ate
 (per'for|at'ing)
per'fora'tion
per'for'at|ive

per'for|ator
per'force
per'form
per'form|able
per'form|ance
per'form'at|ive
per'former
per'fume (as *v.*,
 per'fum|ing)
per'fumer
per'fumery (*pl.*
 per'fumer|ies)
per'func'tor|ily
per'func'tori|ness
per'func'tory
per'fuse
 (per'fus|ing)
per'fu'sion
per'fus|ive
per'gola
Per'go|lesi
per'haps
peri
peri|anth
peri|apt
peri|car'diac
peri|car'dial
peri|card'itis
peri|car'dium (*pl.*
 peri|car'dia)
peri|carp
peri|chon'drium
 (*pl.* peri|
              chon'dria)
peri|clase
peri|clinal
peri|cope
peri|cra'nium
peri|dot
peri|gean
peri|gee
peri|gla'cial
peri|gyn'ous
peri|he'lion (*pl.*
 peri|he'lia)
peril (as *v.*,
 per'illed,
 per'il|ling)
per'il|ous
peri|lune
peri|lymph
peri|meter
peri|natal
peri|neal
peri|neum
period

peri'od|ate
peri|odic
peri|od|ical
peri'od'ic|ally
peri'od|icity (*pl.*
 peri|od|icit'ies)
peri'od|iza'tion
peri|od|ontal
peri'od'ont|ics
peri'od'ont|ist
peri'od'on'to|logy
peri|os'teal
peri|os'teum (*pl.*
 peri|os'tea)
peri|ost'itis
peri|pat'etic
peri|pat'et'ic|ally
peri|pet'eia
peri|pheral
peri|pher|ally
peri|phery (*pl.*
 peri|pher|ies)
peri|phrasis (*pl.*
 peri|phrases)
peri|phrastic
per'ip|teral
per|ique
peri|scope
peri|scopic
per|ish
per|ish|able
per|isher
peri|sperm
peri|sta'lith
peri|stal'sis
peri|staltic
peri|stalt'ic|ally
peri|stome
peri|style
peri'ton|eal
peri'ton|eum (*pl.*
 peri'ton|eums)
peri'ton|itis
peri|wig
peri|wigged
peri|winkle
per|jure
 (per'jur|ing)
per|jurer
per'juri|ous
per|jury (*pl.*
 per'jur|ies)
per|kily
per'ki|ness
perky (per|kier,
 per'ki|est)

perl|ite
per'ma|frost
perm|al'loy
per'man|ence
per'man|ency
per'man|ent
per'man'gan|ate
per'man|ganic
per'meab'il|ity
 (*pl.* per'meab'il|
              it'ies)
per'meable
per'meance
per'meant
per'meate
 (per'meat|ing)
per'mea'tion
Per'mian
per'miss'ib'il|ity
per'miss|ible
per'miss|ibly
per'mis|sion
per'miss|ive
per'mit (as *v.*,
 per'mit|ted,
 per'mit|ting)
per'mit|tiv'ity
per'mu'ta'tion
per'mute
 (per|mut'ing)
per|ni'cious
per|nick|ety
per'noct|ate
 (per'noct|at'ing)
per'noc'ta'tion
Perón
pe'ro|neal
per'or|ate
 (per'or|at'ing)
per'ora'tion
per'ox|ide (as *v.*,
 per'ox'id|ing)
per'pend
per'pen'dic|ular
per'pen'dic|ular|
                ity
per'pet|rable
per'pet|rate
 (per'pet|rat'ing)
per'pet|rat|ion
per'pet|rator
per'petual
per'petu|ally
per'petu|ance
per'petu|ate
 (per'petu|at'ing)

per¦petu¦ation
per¦petu¦ator
per¦petu¦ity
per¦plex
per¦plex|ity (*pl.*
 per¦plex|it¦ies)
per pro (by proxy)
per¦quis¦ite
Per¦rier (*propr.*)
per¦ron
perry (*pl.*
 per¦ries)
per se
per¦se¦cute
 (per¦se¦cut¦ing)
per¦se¦cu¦tion
per¦se¦cutor
per¦se¦ver¦ance
per¦sev¦er¦ate
 (per¦sever¦at¦ing)
per¦sev¦era¦tion
per¦se¦vere
 (per¦se¦ver¦ing)
Per¦sian
per¦si¦ennes
per¦si¦flage
per¦sim¦mon
per¦sist
per¦sist¦ence
per¦sist¦ency
per¦sist¦ent
per¦son
per¦sona (*pl.*
 per¦sonae)
per¦son¦able
per¦son¦age
per¦sona grata
per¦sonal
per¦son¦al¦ity (*pl.*
 per¦son¦al¦it¦ies)
per¦son¦al¦iza¦tion
per¦son¦al¦ize
 (per¦son¦al¦iz
  ing)
per¦son¦ally
per¦son¦alty (*pl.*
 per¦son¦al¦ties)
*per|sona non
 grata*
per¦son¦ate
 (per¦son¦at¦ing)
per¦sona¦tion
per¦son¦ator
per¦soni¦fica¦tion

per¦son¦ify
 (per¦soni¦fies,
 per¦soni¦fied,
 per¦soni¦fy¦ing)
per¦son¦nel
per¦spec¦tival
per¦spect¦ive
per¦spect¦ively
Per¦spex (*propr.*)
per¦spic¦acious
per¦spi¦ca¦city
per¦spi¦cu¦ity
per¦spic¦uous
per¦spira¦tion
per¦spir¦at¦ory
per¦spire
 (per¦spir¦ing)
per¦suad¦able
per¦suade
 (per¦suad¦ing)
per¦suader
per¦suas¦ible
per¦sua¦sion
per¦suas¦ive
per¦tain
Perth
per¦ti¦na¦cious
per¦ti¦na¦city
per¦tin¦ence
per¦tin¦ency
per¦tin¦ent
per¦turb
per¦turba¦tion
per¦turb¦at¦ive
per¦tussis
Peru
per¦uke
per¦usal
per¦use
 (per¦us¦ing)
Pe¦ru¦vian
per¦vade
 (per¦vad¦ing)
per¦va¦sion
per¦vas¦ive
per¦verse
per¦ver¦sion
per¦vers¦ity (*pl.*
 per¦vers¦it¦ies)
per¦vers¦ive
per¦vert
per¦vi¦ous
Pe¦sach
pe¦seta
Pe¦shito

pesky (pes¦kier,
 pes¦ki¦est)
peso (*pl.* pesos)
pess¦ary (*pl.*
 pess¦ar¦ies)
pess¦im¦ism
pess¦im¦ist
pess¦im¦istic
pess¦im¦ist¦ic¦ally
pes¦ter
pes¦ti¦cide
pes¦ti¦fer¦ous
pes¦ti¦lence
pes¦ti¦lent
pes¦ti¦len¦tial
pes¦ti¦len¦tially
pestle (as *v.*,
 pest¦ling)
pes¦to¦lo¦gical
pes¦to¦lo¦gist
pesto¦logy
pet (as *v.*, pet¦ted,
 pet¦ting)
petal
pet¦al¦ine
pet¦alled
pet¦al¦oid
pet¦alon
pe¦tard
pet¦asus
pe¦taur¦ist
peter (out)
Peter
Pet¦er¦bor¦ough
peter¦sham
peth¦id¦ine
peti¦olar
peti¦ol¦ate
peti¦ole
petit bour¦geois
*pe¦tite
 bour¦geoisie*
petit four
pe¦ti¦tion
pe¦ti¦tion¦ary
pe¦ti¦tioner
petit mal
petits pois
Pet¦rarch
pet¦rel
Petri (dish)
pet¦ri¦fac¦tion
pet¦rify
 (pet¦ri¦fies,
 pet¦ri¦fied,
 pet¦ri¦fy¦ing)

pet¦ro¦chem¦ical
pet¦ro¦chem¦istry
pet¦ro¦dol¦lar
pet¦ro¦gen¦esis
pet¦ro¦glyph
pet¦ro¦graphic
pet¦ro¦graph¦ical
pet¦ro¦graphy
pet¦rol
pet¦ro¦leum
pet¦rolic
pet¦ro¦lo¦gic
pet¦ro¦lo¦gical
pet¦ro¦lo¦gist
pet¦ro¦logy
pet¦ronel
pet¦rous
Pet¦rushka
pet¦ti¦coat
pet¦ti¦fog
 (pet¦ti¦fogged,
 pet¦ti¦fog¦ging)
pet¦ti¦fog¦ger
pet¦ti¦fog¦gery
pet¦tily
pet¦ti¦ness
pet¦tish
pet¦ti¦toes
petty (pet¦tier,
 pet¦ti¦est)
pet¦ulance
pet¦ulant
pe¦tu¦nia
pe¦tuntse
pew¦ter
pew¦terer
pey¦ote
pey¦ot¦ism
pfen¦nig
phaeton
pha¦ged¦aena
pha¦ged¦aenic
pha¦go¦cyte
pha¦go¦cytic
pha¦go¦cyt¦osis
phal¦ange
pha¦lan¦geal
pha¦lan¦ger
phal¦an¦sterian
phal¦an¦stery (*pl.*
 phal¦an¦ster¦ies)
phal¦anx
phala¦rope
phal¦lic
phal¦li¦cism
phal¦lism

phal|lus (*pl.*
 phal|luses *or*
 phalli)
phan|ariot
phan|ero|gam
phan|ero|gamic
phan|ero|
          gam|ous
phant|asm
phant|as|ma|
          goria
phant|as|ma|
          goric
phant|as|mal
phant|as|mic
phantom
Phar|aoh
Phar|aonic
Phar|isaic
Phar|isa|ical
Phar|isa|ism
Phar|isee
phar|ma|ceut|ical
phar|ma|ceut|ic|
          ally
phar|ma|ceut|ics
phar|ma|cist
phar|ma|co|
          lo|gical
phar|ma|co|
          lo|gist
phar|ma|co|logy
phar|ma|co|poeia
phar|ma|co|
          poeial
phar|macy (*pl.*
 phar|ma|cies)
pharos
pha|ryn|geal
pha|ryn|gitis
pha|ryn|go|cele
pha|ryn|go|scope
pha|ryn|go|tomy
 (*pl.* pha|ryn|go|
          tom|ies)
pharynx
phase (as *v.*,
 phas|ing)
phasic
phatic
pheas|ant
pheas|antry
phen|acetin
phe|no|bar|bital
phe|no|
          bar|bit|one

phe|no|cryst
phenol
phen|olic
pheno|lo|gical
pheno|lo|gist
pheno|logy
phe|nom|enal
phe|nom|en|al|
          ism
phe|nom|en|al|
          istic
phe|no|men|ally
phe|no|meno|
          lo|gical
phe|nom|eno|logy
phe|nom|enon (*pl.*
 phe|nom|ena)
pheno|type
pheno|typic
phenyl
phero|monal
phero|mone
phial (small bottle)
Phil|adel|phia
phil|adel|phus
phil|an|der
phil|an|derer
phil|an|thrope
phil|an|thropic
phil|an|throp|ic|
          ally
phil|an|throp|ism
phil|an|throp|ist
phil|an|throp|ize
 (phil|an|throp|iz|
          ing)
phil|an|thropy
phil|atelic
phil|atel|ist
phil|ately
phil|har|monic
phil|hel|lene
phil|hel|lenic
Philip
phil|ip|pic
phil|ip|pina
Phil|ip|pine
Phil|ip|pines
Phil|is|tine
phil|is|tin|ism
phil|lu|men|ist
phil|lu|meny
philo|den|dron
philo|lo|ger
philo|lo|gian
philo|lo|gical

philo|lo|gist
philo|logy
Philo|mel
Philo|mela
philo|pro|gen|it|
          ive
philo|soph|as|ter
philo|sopher
philo|sophic
philo|soph|ical
philo|soph|ic|ally
philo|soph|ize
 (philo|soph|iz|
          ing)
philo|sophy (*pl.*
 philo|soph|ies)
philtre (love
 potion)
phi|mo|sis (*pl.*
 phi|mo|ses)
phle|bitic
phle|bitis
phle|bot|om|ist
phle|bot|omy
phlegm
phleg|matic
phleg|mat|ic|ally
phlegmy
phloem
phlo|gistic
phlo|gis|ton
phlox
Phnom Penh
pho|bia
phobic
phoebe
Phoebus
Phoe|ni|cian
phoenix
Phoenix
pho|las
phon (unit)
phon|at|ory
phon|au|to|graph
phone (as *v.*,
 phon|ing)
phone-in *n.*
phon|eme
phon|emic
phon|em|ics
phon|en|do|scope
phon|etic
phon|et|ic|ally
phon|eti|cian
phon|eti|cist
phon|et|ics

phon|et|ist
pho|ney (as *n.*, *pl.*
 pho|neys; as *a.*,
 pho|nier,
 pho|ni|est)
phonic
pho|nily
pho|ni|ness
phono|gram
phono|graph
phono|graphic
phono|graphy
phon|ol|ite
phono|lo|gical
phono|lo|gist
phono|logy
phono|meter
phonon
phono|scope
phooey
phor|mium
phos|gene
phos|phate
phos|phatic
phos|phene (of
 eye)
phos|phide
phos|phine (gas)
phos|phite
phos|phor
phos|phor|ate
 (phos|phor|
          at|ing)
phos|phor|esce
 (phos|phor|
          es|cing)
phos|phor|
          es|cence
phos|phor|es|cent
phos|phoric
phos|phor|ism
phos|phor|ite
phos|phor|ous *a.*
phos|phorus *n.*
phot (unit)
photic
phot|ism
photo (*pl.* pho|tos)
pho|to|cell
pho|to|chem|istry
pho|to|com|posi|
          tion
pho|to|con|duct|
          iv|ity
pho|to|copier

pho'to|copy
(as *n.*, *pl.*
pho'to|cop'ies; as
v., pho'to|cop'ies,
pho'to|cop'ied,
pho'to|copy'ing)
pho'to|di'ode
pho'to|el'ec'tric
pho'to|el'ec'tri|
   city
pho'to|fit
pho'to|genic
pho'to|gram
pho'to|
  gram'metry
pho'to|graph
pho'to|grapher
pho'to|graphic
pho'to|graph'ic|
   ally
pho'to|graphy
pho'to|grav'ure
pho'to|litho|
   graphy
pho'to|meter
pho'to|met'ric
pho'to|metry
pho'to|mic'ro|
   graph
pho'to|mic'ro|
   graphy
photon
photo-offset
pho'to|pho'bia
pho'to|sens'it|ive
pho'to|set'ting
pho'to|sphere
pho'to|spheric
pho'to|stat *v.*
(pho'to|stated,
pho'to|stat'ing)
Pho'to|stat *n.*
(*propr.*)
pho'to|syn'thesis
pho'to|syn'thetic
pho'to|tropic
pho'to|trop'ism
pho'to|vol'taic
phrasal
phrase (as *v.*,
phras'ing)
phrase-book
phras'eo|gram
phras'eo|lo'gical
phras'eo|logy (*pl.*
phras'eo|lo'gies)

phre|atic
phren|etic
phren|et'ic|ally
phrenic
phreno|lo'gical
phreno|lo'gist
phreno|logy
Phry|gian
phthal|ate
phthalic
phthisic
phthis|ical
phthisis
phut
phyl'ac|tery (*pl.*
 phyl',ac|ter'ies)
phy|letic
phyl|lode
phyl'lo|phag'ous
phyl'lo|pod
phyl'lo|stome
phyl'lo|taxis
phyl'lo|taxy
phyl'lox|era
phylo|gen'esis
phylo|gen'etic
phylo|genic
phylo|geny
phylum (*pl.*
 phyla)
physic (as *v.*,
 phys|icked,
 phys|ick|ing)
phys|ical
phys'ic|ally
physi|cian
physi|cist
phys|icky
physico-chemical
phys|ics
physi|ocracy (*pl.*
 physi|ocra'cies)
physio|crat
physio|gnomic
physio|gnom|ical
physi|ognom|ist
physi|ognomy
 (*pl.* physi|
  ognom'ies)
physio|grapher
physio|graphic
physio|graph'ical
physio|graphy
physio|lo'gical
physio|lo'gic|ally
physi|olo'gist

physi|ology
physio|ther'ap|ist
physio|ther'apy
phys|ique
phyto|gen'esis
phyto|geny
phyto|graphy
phyto|mer
phyto|patho|logy
phyto|phag'ous
phyto|plank'ton
phyto|tomy
phyto|toxic
phyto|zoon
pi'ac|ular
pi'affe (pi'aff|ing)
pi|affer
pia ma'ter
pi'an|ism
pi'an'is|simo
pi'an|ist
pi'an|istic
piano (*pl.* pi'anos)
pi'ano|forte
Pi'an|ola (*propr.*)
pi'as|sava
pi|astre
pi'azza
pib|roch
pica (type; *Path.*)
 △ pika
pic|ador
Pic|ardy
pi'car|esque
pi'car|oon
Pi|casso
Pic'ca|dilly
pic'ca|lilli
pic'ca|ninny (*pl.*
 pic'ca|nin'nies)
Pic|card
pic|colo (*pl.*
 pic'co|los)
pick|axe
pick|erel
picket (as *v.*,
 pick|eted,
 pick'et|ing)
pickle (as *v.*,
 pick|ling)
pick|lock
pick|pocket
pick-up *n.*
Pick'wick|ian
picky

pic|nic (as *v.*,
 pic|nicked,
 pic|nick|ing)
pic|nicker
pi'cot
pi|cotee
pic|rate
pic'ric (acid)
Pict
Pict|ish
pic'to|gram
pic'to|graph
pic'to|graphic
pic'to|graphy
pic|tor'ial
pic|tori|ally
pic|ture (as *v.*,
 pic'tur|ing)
pic'tur|esque
piddle (as *v.*,
 pid'dling)
pid|dock
pid'gin
pie|bald
piece (as *v.*,
 pie'cing)
*pièce de
 rés'ist|ance*
 (*pl.* **pièces de
 rés'ist|ance**)
piece|meal
piece-work
pie|crust
pied
pied-à-terre (*pl.*
 pieds-à-terre)
Pied|mont
pie-eyed
pier (at seaside)
 △ peer
pierce (pier|cing)
Pi'er|ian
pier|rot (*fem.*
 pier|rette)
pietà
piety
piezo-electric
piezo-electricity
pi'ezo|meter
piffle (as *v.*,
 piff|ling)
piff|ler
pig (as *v.*, pigged,
 pig|ging)
pi'geon

pigeon-hole (as v.,
 pigeon-holing)
pi'geonry
pigeon-toed
pig'gery (pl.,
 pig'ger'ies)
pig|gish
piggy (as n., pl.
 pig'gies)
pig'gy|back
pig|headed
pig-iron
pig'let
pig|like
pig|ment
pig|ment'ary
pig'menta|tion
pig|nut
pig|pen
pig|skin
pig|stick'ing
pig'sty (pl.,
 pig|sties)
pig|swill
pig|tail
pig|wash
pig|weed
pika (animal)
 △ pica
pike (fish; pl.
 same)
pike (as v.,
 pik'ing)
pike|let
pike|man (pl.
 pike|men)
piker
pike|staff
Pik
 Kom'mun|izma
Pik Po'bedy
pi|laff
pi'las|ter
pilau use pilaff
pilch
pilch|ard
pile (as v., pil'ing)
pil|eate
pile-driver
pile-up n.
pi'leus (pl. pi'lei)
pil|fer
pil|ferer
pil|grim
pil'grim|age (as v.,
 pil'grim|aging)

pi'li|fer'ous
pi'li|form
pil|lage (as v.,
 pil|la'ging)
pil|la'ger
pil'lar
pillar-box
pill|box
pil|lion
pil|lory (as n., pl.
 pil'lor|ies; as v.,
 pil'lor|ies,
 pil'lor|ied,
 pil'lory|ing)
pil'low
pil'low|case
pil'low|slip
pil'lowy
pill|wort
pil'ose
pil'os|ity
pi'lot (as v.,
 pi'loted,
 pi'lot|ing)
pi'lot|age
pilot-light
pil'ous
Pil|sener
pil|ular
pil'ule
pilu|lous
pi|mento (pl.
 pi'men|tos)
pim'per|nel
pimple
pimpled
pimply
 (pimp|lier,
 pimp'li|est)
pin (as v., pinned,
 pin|ning)
pin|afore
pin|as'ter
pin-ball
pince-nez
pin|cers
pin|cette
pinch|beck
pin|cush'ion
Pin'dar
Pin|daric
pine (as v.,
 pin'ing)
pin'eal
pine|apple
pine-cone

pinery (pl.
 piner|ies)
pin'etum (pl.
 pin'eta)
pin|fold
pinger
ping-pong
pin|guid
pin|guin
pin-head
pin-hole
pin'ion
pink-eye
pinkie n.
pink|ish
pinko (pl. pinkos)
pinky (pin|kier
 pin'ki|est)
pin-money
pinna (pl.
 pin'nae)
pin|nace
pin|nacle (as v.,
 pin'nac|ling)
pin|nate
pin|nated
pin'ni|grade
pin'ni|ped
pin'nu|lar
pin|nule
pinny (pl.
 pin|nies)
Pi'no|chet
piñon
pin-point
pin|prick
pin-stripe
pinta
pin|tado (pl.
 pin|ta'dos)
pin|tail
pintle
pin-tuck
pin-up n.
piny
pio'let
pion
pi'on|eer
pionic
pi'ous
pip (as v., pipped,
 pip|ping)
pipa (toad)
pipal (fig-tree)
pipe (as v.,
 pip'ing)

pipe-dream
pipe|ful (pl.
 pipe|fuls)
pipe|line
pip emma
piper
pi'per'id|ine
pip|ette
pip'ing
pip'is|trelle
pipit
pip'kin
pip'pin
pip-squeak
pipy (f. pipe)
pi'quancy
pi'quant
pique (as v.,
 piqued, piquing)
pi'quet
pir'acy (pl.
 pir|acies)
pi'ra|gua
pi|ranha
pi'ra|rucu
pir|ate (as v.,
 pir'at|ing)
pir|atic
pir'at|ical
pi'rou|ette (as v.,
 pi'rou'et|ting)
pis'cary
pis'cat|orial
pis'cat|ory
Pis|cean
Pis|ces
pis'ci|cul'tural
pis'ci|cul'ture
pis'ci|cul'tur|ist
pis|cina (pl.
 pis|ci|nae)
pis|cine
pis'ci|vor'ous
pisé
Pis|gah
pisi|form
piss (as v., pissed,
 piss|ing)
Pis|sarro
pis|soir
pis'ta'chio (pl.
 pis|ta'chios)
piste
pis'til (of flower)
pis'til|late

pis|tol (as v.,
 pis|tolled,
 pis|tol|ling)
pis|tole (coin)
pis|ton
piston-ring
piston-rod
pit (as v., pitted,
 pit|ting)
pit-a-pat
Pit|cairn (Islands)
pitch|blende
pitcher
pitch|fork
pitch-pine
pitchy (pitch|ier,
 pitchi|est)
pit|eous
pit|fall
pit-head
pi|thec|an|thrope
pith|ec|oid
pith|ily
pithi|ness
pithos (pl. pithoi)
pithy (pith|ier,
 pithi|est)
pi|ti|able
pi|ti|ably
pi|ti|ful
pi|ti|fully
pi|ti|less
Pit|man
piton
Pitot (tube)
pit|tance
pitter-patter
pit|to|sporum
Pitts|burgh
pi|tu|it|ary (pl.
 pi|tu|it|ar|ies)
pit|uri
pity (as v., pit|ies,
 pit|ied, pity|ing)
pi|ty|ri|asis (pl.
 pi|ty|ri|ases)
pivot (as v.,
 pivoted,
 piv|ot|ing)
piv|otal
pixie
pix|il|ated
pizza
piz|zeria

piz|zi|cato (pl.
 piz|zi|ca|tos,
 piz|zi|cati)
plac|ab|il|ity
plac|able
plac|ably
plac|ard
pla|cate
 (pla|cat|ing)
pla|cat|ory
place (as v.,
 pla|cing)
pla|cebo (pl.
 pla|cebos)
place|ment
pla|centa (pl.
 pla|cen|tae)
pla|cen|tal
pla|cer
pla|cid
pla|cid|ity
placket
plac|oid
pla|fond
plagal
plage (beach)
pla|gi|ar|ism
pla|gi|ar|ist
pla|gi|ar|ize
 (pla|gi|ar|iz|ing)
pla|gio|ceph|alic
pla|gio|clase
pla|gio|clastic
pla|gio|stome
plague (as v.,
 plagued,
 plaguing)
plague|some
pla|guy
plaice (fish)
plaid
plain (simple; flat
 land) △ plane
plain|ness
plains|man (pl.
 plains|men)
plaint
plaint|iff
plaint|ive
plait (interlacing)
plan (as v.,
 planned,
 plan|ning)
planar
plan|ar|ian

plan|chet (coin-
 blank)
planch|ette (board
 at seance)
Planck
plane (tool, tree
 etc.; as v.,
 plan|ing) △ plain
planet
plan|et|arium (pl.
 plan|et|ari|ums)
plan|et|ary
plan|et|esimal
plan|et|oid
plan|eto|logy
plan|gency
plan|gent
pla|ni|meter
pla|ni|met|ric
pla|ni|metry
plan|ish
plan|isher
plani|sphere
plani|spheric
plank|ton
plank|tonic
plan|ner
pla|no|con|cave
pla|no|con|vex
pla|no|meter
plant|able
Plan|ta|genet
plan|tain
plantar (Anat.)
planta|tion
planter
plan|ti|grade
plaque
plasm
plasma
plas|matic
plas|mod|ium (pl.
 plas|modia)
plas|mo|lyse
 (plas|mo|lys|ing)
plas|mo|lysis
plas|ter
plas|ter|board
plas|terer
plas|tery
plas|tic
plas|tic|ally
Plas|ti|cine
 (propr.)
plas|ti|city

plas|ti|cize
 (plas|ti|ciz|ing)
plas|ti|cizer
plastid
plas|tron
platan
plate (as v.,
 plat|ing)
plat|eau (pl.
 plat|eaux)
plate|ful (pl.
 plate|fuls)
plate|layer
plate|let
platen
plater
plat|er|esque
plat|form
pla|tinic
plat|in|ize
 (plat|in|iz|ing)
plat|in|oid
plat|ino|type
plat|inum
plat|it|ude
plat|it|ud|in|arian
plat|it|ud|in|ous
Plato
pla|tonic (of
 friendship)
Pla|tonic (of Plato)
pla|ton|ic|ally
Pla|ton|ism
Pla|ton|ist
pla|toon
plat|ter
platy|hel|minth
platy|pus
platyr|rhine
plaudit
plaus|ib|il|ity
plaus|ible
plaus|ibly
Plautus
playa
play-back n.
play|bill
play|boy
player
play|ful
play|fully
play|girl
play|goer
play|ground
play|house
play|let

play|mate
play-off *n.*
play-pen
play-suit
play|thing
play|time
play|wright
plaza
plea
pleach
plead (pleaded)
plead|able
pleas|ant
 (pleas|anter,
 pleas|ant|est)
pleas|antry (*pl.*
 pleas|ant|ries)
please (pleas|ing)
pleas|ur|able
pleas|ur|ably
pleas|ure (as *v.*,
 pleas|ur|ing)
pleat
ple|beian
ple|bis|cit|ary
pleb|is|cite
plec|trum (*pl.*
 plec|tra)
pledge (as *v.*,
 pledging)
pledge|able
pledgee
pledger
pledget
Pleiad (*pl.*
 Plei|ades)
plein|air|ist
Pleis|to|cene
plen|ary
ple|ni|po|ten|ti|
 ary
 (*pl.* ple|ni|
 po|ten|ti|ar|ies)
plen|it|ude
plent|eous
plen|ti|ful
plenty
plenum
pleo|chroic
pleo|chro|ism
pleo|morphic
ple|on|asm
ple|on|astic
ple|sio|saurus
pleth|ora

pleura (*pl.*
 pleurae)
pleural
pleur|isy
pleur|itic
pleur|odynia
pleuro-
 pneumonia
plexi|form
Plexi|glas (*propr.*)
plexor
plexus
pli|ab|il|ity
pli|able
pli|ably
pli|ancy
pli|ant
pli|cate
pli|cated
pli|ca|tion
plié
pli|ers
plight
plim|soll (shoe)
Plim|soll (line)
Pliny
Plio|cene
plissé
plod (plod|ded,
 plod|ding)
plod|der
ploidy (*pl.*
 ploi|dies)
plop (as *v.*,
 plopped,
 plop|ping)
plo|sion
plo|sive
plot (as *v.*,
 plot|ted,
 plot|ting)
plot|ter
plough
plough|man (*pl.*
 plough|men)
plough|share
plover
plucker
pluck|ily
plucki|ness
plucky (pluck|ier,
 plucki|est)
plug (as *v.*,
 plugged,
 plug|ging)
plug-in *a.*& *n.*

plum (fruit)
 △ plumb
plum|age
plum|aged
plu|mas|sier
plumb (work as
 plumber, sound
 depth) △ plum
plum|ba|gin|ous
plum|bago (*pl.*
 plum|ba|gos)
plum|bate
plum|be|ous
plumber
plumb|ery (*pl.*
 plumb|er|ies)
plum|bic
plum|bi|fer|ous
plumb|ing
plum|bism
plumb-line
plumb-rule
plume (as *v.*,
 plum|ing)
plumery
plu|mi|corn
plummer-block
plum|met
 (plummeted,
 plum|met|ing)
plummy
 (plum|mier,
 plum|mi|est)
plum|ose
plumu|lar
plum|ule
plumy (plu|mier,
 plu|mi|est)
plun|der
plunge (as *v.*,
 plun|ging)
plun|ger
plu|per|fect
plural
plur|al|ism
plur|al|ist
plur|al|istic
plur|al|ity
plur|al|ize
 (plur|al|iz|ing)
plur|ally
plu|ri|pres|ence
plus (*pl.* pluses)
plus-fours
plushy (plush|ier,
 plushi|est)

Plut|arch
plut|archy (*pl.*
 plut|arch|ies)
Pluto
plu|to|cracy (*pl.*
 plu|to|cra|cies)
plu|to|crat
plu|to|cratic
plu|to|latry
pluton
Plu|to|nian
plu|tonic
Plu|ton|ist
plu|to|nium
plu|vial
plu|vi|ous
plu|vi|ometer
plu|vio|met|ric
plu|vio|met|rical
ply *n.*(*pl.* plies)
ply *v.*(plies, plied,
 ply|ing)
Ply|mouth
ply|wood
pneu|matic
pneu|mat|ic|ally
pneu|ma|ti|city
pneu|ma|to|cyst
pneu|ma|to|
 lo|gical
pneu|ma|to|logy
pneu|ma|to|phore
pneu|mo|coni|
 osis
pneu|mo|gas|tric
pneu|mon|
 ec|tomy
 (*pl.* pneu|mon|
 ec|tom|ies)
pneu|mo|nia
pneu|monic
pneu|mon|itis
pneu|mo|thorax
poacher
po|chard
pocket (as *v.*,
 pock|eted,
 pock|et|ing)
pocket-book
pock|et|ful (*pl.*
 pock|et|fuls)
pocket-knife (*pl.*
 pocket-knives)
pocket-money
pock-marked
po|co|cur|ante

po|co|cur|ant|ism
pod (as v.,
 pod|ded,
 pod|ding)
pod|agra
pod|ag|ral
pod|ag|ric
pod|ag|rous
po|destà
podgy (podgier,
 podgi|est)
po|dium (pl.
 podia)
po|do|phyl|lin
pod|zol
poem
poet
po|et|as|ter
po|et|ess
po|etic
po|et|ical
po|et|ic|ally
po|et|icize
 (po|et|iciz|ing)
po|etry
po-faced
pogo (pl. po|gos)
pog|rom
poign|ancy
poign|ant
poi|ki|lo|therm
poi|ki|lo|thermal
poi|ki|lo|thermic
poin|ci|ana
poin|set|tia
point-blank
poin|ted
point|edly
pointer
poin|til|lism
poin|til|list
point|less
poise (as v.,
 pois|ing)
poison
poisoner
pois|on|ous
Poi|tou
poke (as v.,
 pok|ing)
poker
poker-face
poke|weed
poky (po|kier,
 po|ki|est)
po|lacre

Pol|and
po|lar
po|lari|meter
po|lari|met|ric
po|lari|metry
po|lari|scope
po|lari|scopic
po|lar|ity (pl.
 po|lar|it|ies)
po|lar|iz|able
po|lar|iza|tion
po|lar|ize
 (po|lar|iz|ing)
po|lar|izer
po|laro|graphic
po|laro|graphy
po|la|touche
pol|der
pole (as v.,
 pol|ing)
Pole (Polish
 person)
pole-axe (as v.,
 pole-axing)
pole|cat
po|lemic
po|lem|ical
po|lem|ic|ally
pol|em|ize
 (pol|em|iz|ing)
po|lenta
pole-star
pole|wards
po|lice (as v.,
 po|li|cing)
po|lice|man (pl.
 po|lice|men)
police-officer
po|lice|wo|man
 (pl.
 po|lice|wo|men)
po|li|clinic
pol|icy (pl.
 pol|icies)
po|lio
po|lio|my|el|itis
pol|ish
Pol|ish
pol|isher
pol|it|buro (pl.
 pol|it|buros)
po|lite (po|liter,
 po|litest)
po|lit|esse

pol|itic (as v.,
 pol|it|icked,
 pol|it|ick|ing)
po|lit|ical
po|lit|ic|ally
po|li|ti|cian
po|li|ti|cize
 (po|li|ti|ciz|ing)
po|li|tic|iza|tion
po|lit|ico (pl.
 po|lit|icos)
politico-
 economical
pol|it|ics
pol|ity (pl.
 pol|it|ies)
polka (as v.,
 pol|kaed)
pol|lack
pol|lan
pol|lard
pol|len
pol|lex (pl.
 pol|li|ces)
pol|li|cita|tion
pol|lin|ate
 (pol|lin|at|ing)
pol|lina|tion
poll|ster
pol|lut|ant
pol|lute
 (pol|lut|ing)
pol|lu|tion
Pol|ly|anna
polo
po|lo|crosse
pol|on|aise
polo-neck
po|lo|nium
po|lony (pl.
 po|lon|ies)
pol|ter|geist
pol|troon
pol|troon|ery
poly (colloq., pl.
 polys)
poly|adelph|ous
poly|and|rous
poly|andry
poly|anthus
poly|atomic
poly|basic
Poly|bius
poly|chaetan
poly|chaete
poly|chaet|ous

poly|chro|matic
poly|chrome
poly|chromic
poly|chrom|ous
poly|chromy
poly|clinic
poly|crys|tal
poly|crys|tal|line
poly|dac|tyl
poly|dae|mon|ism
poly|es|ter
poly|ethyl|ene
poly|gamic
poly|gam|ist
poly|gam|ous
poly|gamy
poly|gene
poly|gen|esis
poly|gen|etic
poly|genic
poly|gen|ism
poly|gen|ist
poly|geny
poly|glot
poly|glot|tal
poly|glot|tic
poly|glot|tism
poly|gon
poly|gonal
poly|graph
poly|gyn|ous
poly|gyny
poly|hed|ral
poly|hed|ric
poly|hed|ron (pl.
 poly|hedra)
poly|math
poly|mathy
poly|mer
poly|meric
poly|mer|ism
poly|mer|ize
 (poly|mer|iz|ing)
poly|mer|ous
poly|morphic
poly|morph|ism
poly|morph|ous
Poly|ne|sia
Poly|ne|sian
poly|neur|itic
poly|neur|itis
poly|no|mial
po|lynya
poly|opia
polyp

pol'yp|ary (*pl.*
 pol'yp|ar'ies)
poly|pep'tide
poly|phag'ous
poly|phase
poly|phone
poly|phonic
poly|phon'ous
poly|phony
poly|phyl'etic
poly|ploid
poly|ploidy
poly|pod
poly|pody (*pl.*
 poly|pod'ies)
polyp|oid
polyp'oid|ous
po'lyp|tych
poly|pus (*pl.*
 polypi)
poly|sac'char|ide
poly|se'mic
poly|se'mous
poly|semy
poly|sty'rene
poly|syl'labic
poly|syl'lab|
    ic'ally
poly|syl'lable
poly|syn'thetic
poly|tech'nic
poly|the'ism
poly|the'ist
poly|the'istic
poly|thene
poly|tonal
poly|un'sat'ur|
    ated
poly|ureth'ane
poly|val'ent
poly|vi'nyl
poly|zoan
pom'ace
po'made (as *v.*,
 po'mad'ing)
po'man|der
pombe (drink)
pome (fruit)
pom'egran|ate
pom'elo (*pl.*
 pom|elos)
Pom'er|anian
pom|fret
po'mi|cul'ture
po'mi|fer'ous
Pom|mard

pom'mel (as *v.*,
 pom|melled,
 pom|mel'ling)
pommy (*pl.*
 pom|mies)
po'mo|lo'gical
po'mo|lo'gist
po'mo|logy
pom'pa|dour
pom'pano (*pl.*
 pom'pa|nos)
Pom|peii
Pom'pey
pom-pom (gun)
pom'pon
 (ornament)
pom'pos'ity
pom|pous
ponce (as *v.*,
 pon'cing)
pon|ceau
pon'cho (*pl.*
 pon'chos)
pond|age
ponder
pon'der|ab'il|ity
pon'der|able
pon|dera'tion
pon'der|osa
pon'der|os'ity
pon'der|ous
Pon'di|cherry
pond|weed
pon'gee
pon'gid
pongo (*pl.*
 pon'gos)
pon'iard
pons as'in|orum
Ponte Vec|chio
pon'ti|fex (*pl.*
 pon'ti|fi'ces)
pon|tiff
pon'ti|fical
pon'ti|fic|alia
pon'ti|fic|ally
pon'ti|fic|ate (as
 v., pon'ti|fic|
        at'ing)
pon'tify
 (pon'ti|fies,
 pon'ti|fied,
 pon'ti|fy'ing)
pon|toon
pony (*pl.* po'nies)
pony-tail

poodle
poof (*derog.*, male
 homosexual; *pl.*
 pooves) △ pouffe
poof|ter
Pooh-Bah
pooh-pooh
pool|hall
poorly
pop (as *v.*,
 popped,
 pop|ping)
pop|corn
popery
pop-eyed
pop'gun
pop|in'jay
pop|ish
pop'lar
pop'lin
pop'lit|eal
Po'po|ca'te|petl
pop'pa|dam
pop'per
pop'pet
pop|pied
popple (as *v.*,
 pop|pling)
pop'ply
poppy (*pl.*
 pop|pies)
pop'py|cock
pop|ulace
pop|ular
popu|lar'ity
pop'ular|iza'tion
pop'ular|ize
 (pop'ular|iz'ing)
popu|larly
popu|late
 (popu|lat'ing)
popu|la'tion
popu|lism
popu|list
popu|listic
popu|lous
pop-up *a.*
por|beagle
por'cel|ain
por|cine
por'cu|pine
pore (as *v.*,
 por'ing)
pori|fer
por'ism
por'is|matic

por|istic
porker
pork'ling
porky (pork|ier,
 porki|est)
por'no|grapher
por'no|graphic
por'no|graph'ic|
        ally
por'no|graphy
poro|plastic
por'os|ity
por'ous
por'phyria
por'phy|ritic
por'phyro|gen'ite
por'phyry
por|poise
por|rect
por|ridge
por'rin|ger
port|ab'il|ity
port|able
port'age (as *v.*,
 port'aging)
portal
por'ta|mento (*pl.*
 por'ta|menti)
port|at'ive
Port au Prince
port|cul'lis
por|tend
por|tent
por|tent'ous
porter
port'er|age
port'er|house
 (steak)
port|fire
port|fo'lio (*pl.*
 port|fo'lios)
port|hole
por|tico (*pl.*
 por'ti|coes)
por'ti|coed
por'ti|ère
por|tion
Port|land
port|li|ness
Port Louis
portly
port|man'teau (*pl.*
 port|man'teaus)
Port Moresby
Pôrto Alegre
Porto Novo

por|trait
por|trait|ist
por|trait|ure
por|tray
por|trayal
Port Said
Ports|mouth
Por|tu|gal
Por|tu|guese
pose (as v.,
 pos|ing)
poser (problem)
pos|eur (person;
 fem. pos|euse)
posit (pos|ited,
 pos|it|ing)
po|si|tion
po|si|tional
pos|it|ive
pos|it|iv|ism
pos|it|iv|ist
pos|it|iv|istic
po|si|tiv|ity
posi|tron
po|si|tro|nium
po|so|lo|gical
po|so|logy
posse
pos|sess
pos|ses|sion
pos|sess|ive
pos|sessor
pos|set
poss|ib|il|ity (pl.
 poss|ib|il|it|ies)
poss|ible
poss|ibly
pos|sum
post|age
postal
post-bag
post-box
post-boy
post|card
post-chaise
post-classical
post|code
post-coital
post-date
 (post-dating)
poster
poste rest|ante
pos|ter|ior
pos|teri|or|ity
pos|ter|ity
pos|tern

post|face
post-free
post|gradu|ate
post-haste
post-horn
post|hum|ous
pos|tiche
pos|til|ion
Post-
 Impressionism
Post-
 Impressionist
post|lim|iny (pl.
 post|lim|in|ies)
post|man (pl.
 post|men)
post|mark
post|mas|ter
post-millennial
post|mis|tress
post-mortem
post|natal
post-obit
post-paid
post-partum
post|pone
 (post|pon|ing)
post|pone|ment
post|pos|it|ive
post|pran|dial
post|script
post-tax
pos|tu|lant
pos|tu|late (as v.,
 pos|tu|lat|ing)
pos|tu|la|tion
pos|tu|lator
pos|tural
pos|ture (as v.,
 pos|tur|ing)
pos|turer
post-war
posy (pl. po|sies)
pot (as v., pot|ted,
 pot|ting)
pot|ab|il|ity
pot|able
pot|age
pot|amic
pot|amo|logy
pot|ash
po|tas|sic
pot|as|sium
po|ta|tion
po|tato (pl.
 po|ta|toes)

pot|at|ory
pot-belly
 (pl. pot-bellies)
pot-boiler
po|teen
po|tence
po|tency
po|tent
po|tent|ate
po|ten|tial
po|ten|ti|al|ity (pl.
 po|ten|ti|al|it|ies)
po|ten|tially
po|ten|ti|ate
 (po|ten|ti|at|ing)
po|ten|tilla
po|ten|ti|ometer
po|ten|tio|met|ric
pot|ful (pl.
 pot|fuls)
pother
pot-hole (as v.,
 pot-holing)
pot-holer
po|tion
pot-pourri
pot-roast
pot|sherd
pot-shot
pot|stone
pot|ter
pot|tery (pl.
 pot|ter|ies)
pottle
potto (pl. pot|tos)
potty (as a.,
 pot|tier,
 pot|ti|est; as n.,
 pl. pot|ties)
pouchy
pouffe (seat)
 △ poof
poul|lard
Pou|lenc
poult
poult-de-soie
poulter
poult|erer
poult|ice (as v.,
 poult|icing)
poultry
pounce (as v.,
 poun|cing)
pound|age
poundal
pounder

pour|boire
pourer
pous|sette (as v.,
 pous|set|ting)
pous|sin
pov|erty
powan
pow|der
powder-keg
powder-puff
powder-room
pow|dery
power
power|ful
power|fully
power|house
power|less
power-station
pow|wow
Powys
poxy (pox|ier,
 poxi|est)
poz|zo|lana
prac|tic|ab|il|ity
prac|tic|able
prac|tic|ably
prac|tical
prac|tic|al|ity (pl.
 prac|tic|al|it|ies)
prac|tic|ally
prac|tice n.
prac|ti|cian
prac|tise v.
 (prac|tis|ing)
prac|tiser
prac|ti|tioner
Prado
prae|co|cial
prae|no|men
prae|tor
praet|or|ial
prag|matic
prag|mat|ic|al|ity
prag|mat|ic|ally
prag|mat|ism
prag|mat|ist
prag|mat|istic
prag|mat|ize
 (prag|mat|iz|ing)
Prague
Praia
prairie
praise (as v.,
 prais|ing)
praise|ful

praise|wor|thi|ness
praise|worthy
Prak|rit
pra|line
prall|triller
prance (as *v.*,
 pran|cing)
pran|dial
prank|ish
prank|ster
prase (quartz)
pra|seo|dy|mium
prate (as *v.*,
 prat|ing)
prat|in|cole
prat|ique
prattle (as *v.*,
 prat|tling)
prat|tler
praxis
prayer
prayer-book
pray|er|ful
prayer-mat
preacher
preach|ify
 (preachi|fies,
 preachi|fied,
 preachi|fy|ing)
preachi|ness
preachy
pre|amble (as *v.*,
 pre|am|bling)
pre-arrange
 (pre-arranging)
pre-arrangement
preb|end
preb|endal
preb|end|ary (*pl.*
 preb|end|ar|ies)
Pre|cam|brian
pre|car|ious
pre-cast
prec|at|ive
prec|at|ory
pre|cau|tion
pre|cau|tion|ary
pre|cede
 (pre|ced|ing)
pre|ced|ence
pre|ced|ency
pre|ced|ent
pre|ced|en|ted
pre|cent
pre|centor

pre|cent|rix (*pl.*
 pre|cent|rices)
pre|cept
pre|cept|ive
pre|ceptor
pre|cept|orial
pre|ces|sion
pre|ces|sional
pre|cinct
pre|ci|os|ity
pre|cious
pre|cip|ice
pre|cip|it|ab|il|ity
pre|cip|it|able
pre|cip|it|ance
pre|cip|it|ancy
pre|cip|it|ant
pre|cip|it|ate
 (as *v.*, pre|cip|it|at|ing)
pre|cip|ita|tion
pre|cip|it|ator
pre|cip|it|ous
pré|cis (*pl.* same)
pre|cise
pre|ci|sian
 (precise person)
pre|ci|sian|ism
pre|ci|sion
 (accuracy)
pre|ci|sion|ist
pre|clude
 (pre|clud|ing)
pre|clus|ive
pre|co|cious
pre|co|city
pre|cog|ni|tion
pre|con|ceive
 (pre|con|ceiv|ing)
pre|con|cep|tion
pre-condition
pre|con|iza|tion
pre|con|ize
 (pre|con|iz|ing)
pre-cook
pre|curs|ive
pre|cursor
pre|curs|ory
pre|da|cious
pre|da|city
pre-date
 (pre-dating)
pred|ator
pred|at|ory

pre|de|cease
 (pre|de|ceas|ing)
pre|de|ces|sor
pre|della
pre|des|tin|arian
pre|des|tin|ate
 (pre|des|tin|at|ing)
pre|des|tina|tion
pre|des|tine
 (pre|des|tin|ing)
pre|de|ter|min|ate
pre|de|ter|mina|tion
pre|de|ter|mine
 (pre|de|ter|min|ing)
pre|dial
pre|dic|ab|il|ity
pre|dic|able
pre|dica|ment
pre|dic|ant
pre|dic|ate (as *v.*,
 pre|dic|at|ing)
pre|dica|tion
pre|dic|at|ive
pre|dic|at|ory
pre|dict
pre|dict|ab|il|ity
pre|dict|able
pre|dict|ably
pre|dic|tion
pre|dict|ive
pre|dictor
pre|di|gest
pre|di|ges|tion
pre|di|lec|tion
pre|dis|pose
 (pre|dis|pos|ing)
pre|dis|posi|tion
pred|nis|one
pre|dom|in|ance
pre|dom|in|ant
pre|dom|in|ate
 (pre|dom|in|at|ing)
pre-elect
pre-election
pre-eminence
pre-eminent
pre-empt
pre-emption
pre-emptive
pre-establish
pre-exist
pre-existence

pre|fab
pre|fab|ric|ate
 (pre|fab|ric|at|ing)
pre|fab|rica|tion
pre|face (as *v.*,
 pre|fa|cing)
pre|fat|orial
pre|fat|ory
pre|fect
pre|fect|oral
pre|fect|orial
pre|fec|tural
pre|fec|ture
pre|fer
 (pre|ferred,
 pre|fer|ring)
pre|fer|able
pre|fer|ably
pref|er|ence
pref|er|en|tial
pref|er|en|tially
pre|fig|ura|tion
pre|fig|ure
 (pre|fig|ur|ing)
pre|fix
pre|fixa|tion
pre|fix|ion
pre|fix|ture
pre|form
pre|forma|tion
pre|form|at|ive
preg|nable
preg|nancy (*pl.*
 preg|nan|cies)
preg|nant
pre-heat
pre|hens|ile
pre|hens|il|ity
pre|hen|sion
pre|his|tor|ian
pre|his|toric
pre|his|tor|ic|ally
pre|his|tory
pre-ignition
pre|judge
 (pre|judging)
pre|judge|ment
pre|ju|di|ca|tion
pre|ju|dice (as *v.*,
 pre|ju|dicing)
pre|ju|di|cial
pre|ju|di|cially
prel|acy (*pl.*
 prel|acies)
prel|ate

pre|lect
pre|lec'tion
pre|lector
pre|li'ba|tion
pre|lim
pre|lim'in|ar'ily
pre|lim'in|ary
  (as *n.*, *pl.*
  pre|lim'in|ar'ies)
pre|lude (as *v.*,
  pre|lud'ing)
pre|lu'sion
pre|lus'ive
pre|mar'ital
pre|ma'ture
pre|ma'tur|ity
pre-med
pre-medication
pre|med'it|ate
  (pre|med'it|
            at'ing)
pre|med'ita|tion
pre|men'strual
prem|ier (first in
  importance etc.)
premi|ère (first
  performance)
pre|mise *v.*
  (pre|mis'ing)
pre|mises (house
  etc.)
prem|iss (in logic)
pre|mium
pre|molar
pre|moni'tion
pre|mon'itor
pre|mon'it|ory
pre|morse
pre|mo'tion
pre-natal
pre|oc'cu'pa|tion
pre|oc'cupy
  (pre|oc'cu'pies,
  pre|oc'cu'pied,
  pre|oc'cu'py|ing)
pre-ordain
pre-pack
pre-package
  (pre-packaging)
pre|para|tion
pre|par'at|ive
pre|par'at|or'ily
pre|par'at|ory
pre|pare
  (pre|par'ing)

pre|pay
  (pre|paid)
pre|pay'able
pre|pay'ment
pre|pense
pre|pon'der|ance
pre|pon'der|ant
pre|pon'der|ate
  (pre|pon'der|
            at'ing)
pre'posi'tion
pre'posi|tional
pre'pos'it|ive
pre'pos'sess
pre'pos'ses|sion
pre'pos'ter|ous
pre|po'tence
pre|po'tency
pre|po'tent
pre|pran'dial
pre'print
pre'puce
pre|pu'tial
Pre-Raphaelism
Pre-Raphaelite
Pre-Raphaelitism
pre-record
pre|requis'ite
pre|rog'at|ive
pres'age (as *v.*,
  pres'aging)
pres'by|opia
pres'by|opic
pres'by|ter
pres'by|teral
pres'by|ter'ial
Pres'by'ter'ian
Pres'by'teri|an|
                ism
pres'by'tery (*pl.*
  pres'by|ter'ies)
pre-school
pres'ci|ence
pres'ci|ent
pre|scind
pre|scribe
  (pre|scrib'ing)
pre|script
pre|scrip'tion
pre|script'ive
pre-select
pre|sel'ect|ive
pre|sel'ector
pres|ence
pres'ent *n.* & *a.*
pre|sent *v.*

pre'sent|ab'il|ity
pre'sent|able
pre'sent|ably
pre|senta'tion
pre|senta'tional
pre|sentee
pre|sen'tient
pre|sen'ti|ment
pres'ently
pre|serv|able
pre|ser'va'tion
pre|ser'vat|ive
pre|serve
  (pre|serv'ing)
pre|server
pre-set
pre-setting
pre-shrink
  (pre-shrunk)
pres|ide
  (pres|id'ing)
pres'id|ency (*pl.*
  pres'id|en'cies)
pres'id|ent
pres'id'en|tial
pre|si'di|ary
pre|si'dio (*pl.*
  pre|si'dios)
pre|si'dium
press-gang
press'ing
press'man (*pl.*
  press'men)
press'mark
press-stud
press-up *n.*
pres'sure (as *v.*,
  pres'sur'ing)
pres'sur|iza'tion
pres'sur|ize
  (pres'sur|iz|ing)
Pres'teigne
pres'ti|di'gita|tion
pres'ti|di'git|ator
pres'tige
pres'ti'gi|ous
pres'tis'simo (*pl.*
  pres'tis|si'mos)
presto (*pl.*
  pres'tos)
Pres'ton
pre|sum'able
pre|sum'ably
pre|sume
  (pre|sum'ing)
pre|sump'tion

pre|sumpt'ive
pre|sump'tu|ous
pre|sup'pose
  (pre|sup'pos'ing)
pre|sup'posi|tion
pre|tence
pre|tend
pre|tender
pre|ten'sion
pre|ten'tious
pre|ter|hu'man
pret'er|ite
pre|ter|ition
pre|ter|mis'sion
pre|ter|mit
  (pre'ter|mit'ted,
  pre'ter|mit'ting)
pre|ter|nat'ural
pre|text
pre|tone
pre|tonic
Pre|toria
pret'ti|fica|tion
pret'tify
  (pret'ti|fies,
  pret'ti|fied,
  pret'ti|fy'ing)
pret'tily
pret'ti|ness
pretty (pret'tier,
  pret'ti|est)
pretty|ish
pret'zel
pre|vail
pre|val'ence
pre|val'ent
pre|var'ic|ate
  (pre|var'ic|
            at'ing)
pre|var'ica|tion
pre|var'ic|ator
pre|veni|ent
pre|vent
pre|vent|able
pre|ven'tion
pre|vent|ive
pre|view
pre|vi|ous
pre-war
pri|apic
pri|ap'ism
price (as *v.*,
  pri'cing)
price|less
price-list

pricey (pri¦cier,
  pri¦ci¦est)
pricker
pricket
prickle (as v.,
  prick¦ling)
prick¦li¦ness
prickly
  (prick¦lier,
  prick¦li¦est)
pricy use pricey
pride (as v.,
  prid¦ing)
priest
priest¦ess
priest¦hood
Priest¦ley
priest¦li¦ness
priest¦ling
priestly
prig
prig¦gery
prig¦gish
prig¦gism
prim (as a.,
  prim¦mer,
  prim¦mest; as v.,
  primmed,
  prim¦ming)
prima bal¦ler¦ina
pri¦macy (pl.
  pri¦ma¦cies)
prima donna
primaeval use
  primeval
prima facie
primal
prim¦ally
prim¦ar¦ily
prim¦ary (as n., pl.
  prim¦ar¦ies)
prim¦ate
prima¦tial
prim¦ato¦logy
pri¦ma¦vera
prime (as v.,
  prim¦ing)
primer
prim¦eval
prim¦ev¦ally
pri¦mi¦gra¦vida
  (pl. pri¦mi¦
      gra¦vidae)
pri¦mi¦para (pl.
  pri¦mi¦parae)
pri¦mi¦par¦ous

prim¦it¦ive
prim¦it¦iv¦ism
primo (pl.
  pri¦mos)
pri¦mo¦gen¦ital
pri¦mo¦gen¦it¦ary
pri¦mo¦gen¦itor
pri¦mo¦gen¦it¦ure
prim¦or¦dial
prim¦or¦di¦al¦ity
prim¦or¦di¦ally
prim¦or¦dium (pl.
  prim¦or¦dia)
prim¦rose
prim¦ula
primus (bishop)
Primus (stove;
  propr.)
prince¦dom
prince¦li¦ness
prince¦ling
princely
prin¦cess
Prince¦town
prin¦cipal (chief)
prin¦cip¦al¦ity (pl.
  prin¦cip¦al¦it¦ies)
prin¦cip¦ally
prin¦cip¦ate
Príncipe
prin¦ciple
  (fundamental
  truth etc.)
prin¦cipled
print¦able
printer
print¦out
prior
pri¦or¦ate
pri¦or¦ess
pri¦or¦ity (pl.
  pri¦or¦it¦ies)
pri¦ory (pl.
  pri¦or¦ies)
prise (force open,
  pris¦ing) △ prize
prism
pris¦matic
pris¦mat¦ic¦ally
pris¦moid
pris¦moidal
prison
prisoner
pris¦sily
prissy (pris¦sier,
  pris¦si¦est)

pris¦tine
pri¦thee
priv¦acy
pri¦vate
pri¦vat¦eer
pri¦vat¦eer¦ing
pri¦va¦tion
priv¦at¦ive
privet
priv¦il¦ege (as v.,
  priv¦il¦eging)
priv¦ily
priv¦ity (pl.
  priv¦it¦ies)
privy (as n., pl.
  priv¦ies)
prize (as v.,
  priz¦ing) △ prise
prize-fighter
proa (boat)
pro-am
prob¦ab¦ili¦or¦ism
prob¦ab¦il¦ism
prob¦ab¦il¦ity (pl.
  prob¦ab¦il¦it¦ies)
prob¦able
prob¦ably
prob¦and
pro¦bang
pro¦bate (as v.,
  pro¦bat¦ing)
pro¦ba¦tion
pro¦ba¦tional
pro¦ba¦tion¦ary
pro¦ba¦tioner
pro¦bat¦ive
probe (as v.,
  prob¦ing)
probe¦able
probit
prob¦ity
prob¦lem
prob¦lem¦atic
prob¦lem¦at¦ical
prob¦lem¦at¦ic¦
      ally
prob¦lem¦ist
pro¦bos¦cid¦ean
pro¦bos¦cidi¦form
pro¦bos¦cis
pro¦ced¦ural
pro¦ced¦ure
pro¦ceed
pro¦ceed¦ing
pro¦ceed¦ings
pro¦ceeds

pro¦cel¦eus¦matic
pro¦cess
pro¦ces¦sion
pro¦ces¦sional
pro¦ces¦sion¦ary
pro¦ces¦sion¦ist
pro¦cessor
pro¦chron¦ism
pro¦claim
pro¦clama¦tion
pro¦clam¦at¦ory
pro¦clitic
pro¦cliv¦ity (pl.
  pro¦cliv¦it¦ies)
pro¦con¦sul
pro¦con¦su¦lar
pro¦con¦su¦late
pro¦cras¦tin¦ate
  (pro¦cras¦tin¦
        at¦ing)
pro¦cras¦tina¦tion
pro¦cras¦tin¦ator
pro¦cras¦tin¦
        at¦ory
pro¦cre¦ant
pro¦cre¦ate
  (pro¦cre¦at¦ing)
pro¦cre¦ation
pro¦cre¦at¦ive
Pro¦crus¦tean
proc¦tor
proc¦torial
pro¦cumb¦ent
pro¦cur¦able
pro¦cural
pro¦cur¦ance
pro¦cura¦tion
pro¦cur¦ator
pro¦cur¦at¦orial
pro¦cur¦at¦ory
pro¦cure
  (pro¦cur¦ing)
pro¦cure¦ment
pro¦curer
pro¦curess
prod (as v.,
  prod¦ded,
  prod¦ding)
prod¦el¦ision
prod¦igal
prod¦ig¦al¦ity (pl.
  prod¦ig¦al¦it¦ies)
prod¦ig¦al¦ize
  (prod¦ig¦al¦iz¦ing)
prod¦ig¦ally
pro¦di¦gi¦ous

prod|igy (*pl.*
  prod'i|gies)
pro|dromal
pro|drome
pro|dromic
pro|duce (as *v.*,
  pro'du|cing)
pro'du|cer
pro'du|cible
prod|uct
pro|duc'tion
pro|duct|ive
pro|duc'tiv|ity (*pl.*
  pro'duc'tiv|it|ies)
proem
pro|emial
prof'ana|tion
pro|fane (as *v.*,
  pro|fan'ing)
pro|fan|ity (*pl.*
  pro|fan|it|ies)
pro|fess
pro|fes|sion
pro|fes|sional
pro|fes|sion|
    al|ism
pro|fes|sion|al|ize
  (pro|fes|sion|al|
    iz|ing)
pro|fes|sion|ally
pro|fessor
pro'fess'or|ial
pro'fess'ori|ate
prof|fer
pro|fi|ciency (*pl.*
  pro|fi|cien|cies)
pro|fi|cient
pro|file (as *v.*,
  pro|fil'ing)
pro|fil|ist
profit (as *v.*,
  prof|ited,
  prof'it|ing)
prof'it|ab|il|ity
  (*pl.* prof'it|ab'il|
    it|ies)
prof'it|able
prof'it|ably
prof'it|eer
pro'fit'er|ole
prof'it|less
prof'lig|acy
prof'lig|ate
pro forma

pro|found
  (pro|founder,
  pro|found|est)
pro|fund|ity (*pl.*
  pro|fund|it|ies)
pro|fuse
pro|fu'sion
pro|gen'it|ive
pro|gen'itor
pro|gen'it|orial
pro|gen'it'ress
pro|gen'it'rix (*pl.*
  pro|gen'it'ri|ces)
pro|gen'it|ure
pro|geny
pro'ges'ter|one
pro'ges'to|gen
pro|glot'tis (*pl.*
  pro|glot'tides)
pro|gnathic
pro|gnath|ism
pro|gnath|ous
pro|gnosis (*pl.*
  pro|gnoses)
pro|gnostic
pro'gnost'ic|ate
  (pro'gnost'ic|
    at'ing)
pro'gnost'ica'tion
pro'gnost'ic|ator
pro|gram (*Comp.*;
  as *v.*,
  pro'grammed,
  pro'gram|ming)
pro'gram|matic
pro|gramme
  (as *v.*,
  pro'gram|ming)
pro'gram|mer
pro|gress
pro|gres|sion
pro|gres|sional
pro|gres|sion|ist
pro|gress|ive
pro|gress|iv'ism
pro|hibit
  (pro|hib|ited,
  pro|hib'it|ing)
pro|hibi|tion
pro|hibi|tion|ist
pro|hib'it|ive
pro|hib'itor
pro|hib'it|ory
project
pro|ject'ile
pro|jec'tion

pro|jec'tion|ist
pro|ject|ive
projector
Pro|kofiev
pro|lapse (as *v.*,
  pro|lap'sing)
pro|lap'sus
pro|late
pro|lat|ive
pro'leg
pro'leg|om'ena
pro|lep'sis (*pl.*
  pro|lep'ses)
pro|lep'tic
pro|let|arian
pro|let|ari'an|ism
pro|let|ariat
pro|lif'er|ate
  (pro|lif'er|ating)
pro|lif'era'tion
pro|lif'er|at|ive
pro|lif'er|ous
pro|lific
pro|lif'ic|acy
pro|li|fi|city
pro|lix
pro|lix|ity
pro|locu'tor
pro|lo'gize
  (pro|lo'giz|ing)
pro|logue (as *v.*,
  pro|logued,
  pro|loguing)
pro|long
pro|longa'tion
pro|lu'sion
pro|lus'ory
prom'en|ade
  (as *v.*,
  prom'en|ad'ing)
prom'en|ader
pro|meth'az|ine
Pro|meth'ean
Pro|meth'eus
pro|meth'ium
prom'in|ence
prom'in|ency
prom'in|ent
pro|mis'cu|ity
pro|mis'cu|ous
prom'ise (as *v.*,
  prom'is|ing)
prom'isee
prom'iser
prom'isor
prom'is|sory

prom'on|tory (*pl.*
  prom'on|tor|ies)
pro|mote
  (pro|mot'ing)
pro|moter
pro|mo'tion
pro|mo'tional
pro|mot'ive
prompter
prompt'it|ude
pro|mul|gate
  (pro|mul'gat'ing)
pro|mul'ga'tion
pro|mul'gator
pro|mulge
  (pro|mul'ging)
pro|naos (*pl.*
  pro|naoi)
pro|nate
  (pro|nat'ing)
prona'tion
pron'ator
pro|nom'inal
pro|nom'in|ally
pro|noun
pro|nounce
  (pro|noun'cing)
pro|nounce|able
pro|nounce|ment
pronto
pro|nun'ci|
    amento
  (*pl.* pro|nun'ci|
    amen'tos)
pro|nun'ci|ation
proof-read
  (proof-read)
proof-reader
prop (as *v.*,
  propped,
  prop|ping)
pro|pae'deutic
pro|pae'deut|ical
pro|pa'ganda
pro|pa'gand|ism
pro|pa'gand|ist
pro|pa'gand|istic
pro|pa'gand|ize
  (pro|pa'gand|iz|
    ing)
prop|ag|ate
  (prop'ag|at'ing)
pro|pa'ga'tion
prop'ag|at|ive
prop'ag|ator
pro|pane

pro|par|oxy|tone
pro|pel
 (pro|pelled,
 pro|pel|ling)
pro|pel|lant
pro|pel|lent
pro|pel|ler
pro|pen|sity (pl.
 pro|pen|sit|ies)
proper
pro|peri|
      spo|menon
(pl. pro|peri|
      spo|mena)
prop|er|tied
Pro|per|tius
prop|erty (pl.
 prop|er|ties)
proph|ecy n. (pl.
 proph|ecies)
proph|esier
proph|esy v.
 (proph|es|ies,
 proph|es|ied,
 proph|esy|ing)
prophet
proph|et|ess
proph|etic
proph|et|ical
proph|et|ic|ally
proph|et|icism
proph|et|ism
pro|phy|lactic
pro|phy|laxis (pl.
 pro|phy|laxes)
pro|pin|quity (pl.
 pro|pin|quit|ies)
pro|pi|on|ate
pro|pi|onic
pro|pi|ti|ate
 (pro|pi|ti|at|ing)
pro|pi|ti|ation
pro|pi|ti|at|or|ily
pro|pi|ti|at|ory
pro|pi|tious
prop-jet
pro|polis
pro|ponent
pro|por|tion
pro|por|tion|able
pro|por|tion|ably
pro|por|tional
pro|por|tion|al|ist
pro|por|tion|al|ity
pro|por|tion|ally
pro|por|tion|ate

pro|posal
pro|pose
 (pro|pos|ing)
pro|poser
pro|posi|tion
pro|posi|tional
pro|pound
pro|pounder
pro|praetor
pro|pri|et|ary
pro|pri|etor
pro|pri|et|or|ial
pro|pri|et|or|ship
pro|pri|et|ress
pro|pri|ety (pl.
 pro|pri|et|ies)
prop|rio|cept|ive
pro-proctor
prop|tosis (pl.
 prop|toses)
pro|pul|sion
pro|puls|ive
pro|pyl
pro|pyl|aeum (pl.
 pro|pyl|aea)
pro|pylon (pl.
 pro|pylons)
pro rata
pro|rate
 (pro|rat|ing)
pro|roga|tion
pro|rogue
 (pro|rogued,
 pro|roguing)
pro|saic
pro|sa|ic|ally
pro|sa|ism
pro|sa|ist
pro|scen|ium (pl.
 pro|sceni|ums)
pros|ciutto (pl.
 pros|ciut|tos)
pro|scribe
 (pro|scrib|ing)
pro|scrip|tion
pro|script|ive
prose (as v.,
 pros|ing)
pro|sector
pro|sec|ute
 (pro|sec|ut|ing)
pro|secu|tion
pro|secu|tor
pro|secu|trix (pl.
 pro|secu|trices)
pros|elyte

pros|elyt|ism
pros|elyt|ize
 (pros|elyt|iz|ing)
pros|en|chyma
pros|en|chymal
pros|en|chym|at|
           ous
proser
pros|ify
 (prosi|fies,
 prosi|fied,
 prosi|fy|ing)
pro|sily
pro|si|ness
pros|odic
pros|od|ist
pros|ody
pros|opo|grapher
pros|opo|
        graph|ical
pros|opo|graphy
pros|opo|poeia
pro|spect
pro|spect|ive
pro|spector
pro|spectus
pros|per
pros|per|ity
pros|per|ous
pros|ta|glandin
pro|state
pro|static
pros|thesis (pl.
 pros|theses)
pros|thetic
pros|thet|ics
pros|ti|tute (as v.,
 pros|ti|tut|ing)
pros|ti|tu|tion
pros|trate (as v.,
 pros|trat|ing)
pros|tra|tion
pro|style
prosy (pro|sier,
 pro|si|est)
prot|ac|tin|ium
prot|ag|on|ist
prot|am|ine
prot|asis (pl.
 prot|ases)
pro|tatic
pro|tea
pro|tean
pro|tease
pro|tect
pro|tec|tion

pro|tec|tion|ism
pro|tec|tion|ist
pro|tect|ive
pro|tector
pro|tect|oral
pro|tect|or|ate
pro|tect|ress
pro|tégé (fem.
 pro|té|gée)
pro|tei|form
pro|tein
pro|tein|aceous
pro|teinous
pro tem
pro|teo|lysis (pl.
 pro|teo|lyses)
pro|teo|lytic
Prot|ero|zoic
pro|test
prot|est|ant (gen.)
Prot|est|ant
 (Relig.)
Prot|est|ant|ism
prot|esta|tion
pro|tester
pro|teus
 (bacterium;
 pl. pro|tea)
Pro|teus
 (changing person
 etc.)
pro|tha|lam|ium
 (pl.
 pro|tha|lamia)
pro|thal|lium (pl.
 pro|thal|lia)
pro|thal|lus (pl.
 pro|thalli)
pro|thesis (pl.
 pro|theses)
pro|thetic
prot|ist
prot|isto|logy
pro|tium
pro|to|col (as v.,
 pro|to|colled,
 pro|to|col|ling)
pro|ton
pro|tonic
pro|to|not|ary (pl.
 pro|to|not|ar|ies)
pro|to|pectin
pro|to|phyte
pro|to|plasm
pro|to|plas|mal
pro|to|plas|mic

pro|to|plast
pro|to|plastic
pro|to|theria
pro|to|typal
pro|to|type
pro|to|typic
pro|to|typ|ical
pro|to|zoal
pro|to|zoan
pro|to|zoic
pro|to|zo|ology
pro|to|zoon (pl.
  pro|to|zoa)
pro|tract
pro|tract|ile
pro|trac|tion
pro|tractor
pro|trude
  (pro|trud|ing)
pro|trudent
pro|trus|ible
pro|trus|ile
pro|tru|sion
pro|trus|ive
pro|tu|ber|ance
pro|tu|ber|ant
Proud|hon
Proust
prove (proved,
  proved or
  proven,
  prov|ing)
prov|en|ance
Pro|ven|çal
Pro|vence
prov|ender
pro|veni|ence
pro|verb
pro|ver|bial
pro|ver|bi|al|ity
pro|ver|bi|ally
pro|vide
  (pro|vid|ing)
prov|id|ence
prov|id|ent
prov|id|en|tial
pro|vider
prov|ince
pro|vin|cial
prov|in|cial|ism
pro|vin|cial|ist
pro|vin|ci|al|ity
  (pl. pro|vinci|
    al|it|ies)

pro|vin|cial|ize
  (pro|vin|cial|iz|
    ing)
pro|vin|cially
pro|vi|sion
pro|vi|sional
pro|vi|sion|al|ity
pro|vi|sion|ally
pro|viso (pl.
  pro|visos)
pro|vis|or|ily
pro|vis|ory
pro|voca|tion
pro|voc|at|ive
pro|voke
  (pro|vok|ing)
prov|ost
prow|ess
prowler
prox|imal
prox|im|ally
prox|im|ate
prox|im|ity (pl.
  prox|im|it|ies)
prox|imo
proxy (pl.
  prox|ies)
pru|dence
pru|dent
pruden|tial
pruden|tial|ism
pruden|tial|ist
pruden|tially
prudery
prud|ish
pru|in|ose
prune v.
  (prun|ing)
prunella
pruri|ence
pruri|ency
pruri|ent
pruri|gin|ous
prur|igo
prur|itus
Prus|sian
prussic
pry (pries, pried,
  pry|ing)
psalm
psalm|ist
psalm|odic
psalm|od|ist
psalm|ody
psal|ter
psal|ter|ium

psal|tery (pl.
  psal|ter|ies)
psepho|lo|gical
psepho|lo|gist
psepho|logy
pseud
pseud|epi|grapha
pseudo (pl.
  pseudos)
pseudo|carp
pseudo|graph
pseudo|morph
pseudo|morphic
pseud|onym
pseud|onym|ity
pseud|onym|ous
pseudo|pod
pseudo|pod|ium
  (pl.
  pseudo|po|dia)
psi (Gr. letter)
psil|an|thropic
psil|an|throp|ism
psil|an|throp|ist
psilo|cybin
psil|osis (pl.
  psil|oses)
psit|ta|cine
psit|tac|osis (pl.
  (psit|tac|oses)
psoas
psori|asis (pl.
  psori|ases)
psy|che
psy|che|de|lia
psy|che|delic
psy|che|del|ic|ally
psy|chi|at|ric
psy|chi|at|rical
psy|chi|at|rist
psy|chi|atry
psychic
psych|ical
psych|ic|ally
psych|icism
psych|icist
psy|cho (pl.
  psy|chos)
psycho-active
psy|cho|ana|lyse
  (psy|cho|ana|lys|
    ing)
psy|cho|ana|lysis
psy|cho|ana|lyst
psy|cho|ana|lytic

psy|cho|
  ana|lyt|ical
psycho-dynamic
psy|cho|gen|esis
psy|cho|graph
psy|cho|kin|esis
psy|cho|
  lin|guist|ics
psy|cho|lo|gical
psy|cho|lo|gic|
    ally
psy|cho|lo|gist
psy|cho|lo|gize
  (psy|cho|lo|giz|
    ing)
psy|cho|logy
psy|cho|met|ric
psy|cho|met|rist
psy|cho|metry
psy|cho|mo|tor
psy|cho|neur|osis
  (pl. psy|cho|
    neur|oses)
psy|cho|path
psy|cho|pathic
psy|cho|patho|
    logy
psy|cho|pathy
psy|cho|phys|ics
psy|cho|physi|
    ology
psych|osis (pl.
  psych|oses)
psycho|so|matic
psy|cho|sur|gery
psy|cho|ther|apy
psych|otic
psy|cho|tropic
psych|ro|meter
ptar|migan
pter|ido|lo|gical
pter|ido|lo|gist
pter|ido|logy
pter|ido|phyte
ptero|dac|tyl
ptero|pod
ptero|saur
pteryg|oid
  (process)
ptisan
Ptol|em|aic
Ptol|emy
pto|maine
ptosis (pl. ptoses)
pty|alin
pu|ber|tal

pu|berty
pubes
pu|bes|cence
pu|bes|cent
pu|bic
pu|bis (*pl.* pu|bes)
pub|lic
pub|lican
pub|lica|tion
pub|li|cism
pub|li|cist
pub|li|city
pub|li|cize
 (pub|li|ciz|ing)
pub|lish
pub|lisher
puc|coon
pucker
puckery
pud|ding
pud|dingy
puddle (as *v.*,
 pud|dling)
pud|dly
pu|dency
pu|dendal
pu|dendum (*pl.*
 pu|denda)
pudgy (pudgier,
 pudgi|est)
pu|dic
pueblo (*pl.*
 pueb|los)
pu|er|ile
pu|er|il|ity
pu|er|peral
Puerto Rico
puff-adder
puff-ball
puffer
puf|fin
puf|fi|ness
puffy (puf|fier,
 puf|fi|est)
pug (as *v.*,
 pugged,
 pug|ging)
pug|garee
pug|gish
puggy
pu|gil|ism
pu|gil|ist
pu|gil|istic
pug|na|cious
pug|na|city
pug-nosed

puisne (judge)
puis|sance
puis|sant
puja
puke (as *v.*,
 puk|ing)
pukka
puku
pulch|rit|ude
pulch|rit|ud|in|
 ous
pule (pul|ing)
Pul|it|zer (prize)
pul|let
pul|ley
pull-in *n.*
Pull|man
pull-out *n.*
pull|over
pul|lu|lant
pul|lu|late
 (pul|lu|lat|ing)
pul|lu|la|tion
pul|mon|ary
pul|mon|ate
pul|monic
pul|pit
pul|pit|eer
pulp|ous
pulp|wood
pulpy (pul|pier,
 pul|pi|est)
pul|que
pulsar
puls|ate
 (puls|at|ing)
puls|at|ile
pulsa|tion
puls|ator
puls|at|ory
pulse (as *v.*,
 puls|ing)
pul|si|meter
Pul|so|meter
 (*propr.*)
pul|ver|iza|tion
pul|ver|iz|ator
pul|ver|ize
 (pul|ver|iz|ing)
pul|ver|izer
pul|veru|lent
pul|vin|ate
pul|vin|ated
puma
pum|ice (as *v.*,
 pum|icing)

pum|mel
 (pum|melled,
 pum|mel|ling,
 pum|per|nickel
pump|kin
pun (as *v.*,
 punned,
 pun|ning)
puna
punch-ball
punch-bowl
pun|cheon
Pun|chin|ello (*pl.*
 Pun|chin|el|los)
punch-up *n.*
punchy
 (punch|ier,
 punchi|est)
punct|ate
puncta|tion
punc|tilio (*pl.*
 punc|til|ios)
punc|tili|ous
punc|tual
punc|tu|al|ity
punc|tu|ally
punc|tu|ate
 (punc|tu|at|ing)
punc|tu|ation
punctum (*pl.*
 puncta)
punc|ture (as *v.*,
 punc|tur|ing)
pun|dit
pun|ditry
pun|gency
pun|gent
Punic
pu|ni|ness
pun|ish
pun|ish|able
pun|ish|ment
pun|it|ive
pun|it|ory
Pun|jab
Pun|jabi
pun|kah
pun|ner
pun|net
pun|ster
punter
puny (pu|nier,
 pu|ni|est)
pup (as *v.*,
 pupped,
 pup|ping)

pupa (*pl.* pu|pae)
pu|pal
pu|pate
 (pu|pat|ing)
pu|pa|tion
pu|pil
pu|pil|lage
pu|pil|lar
pu|pil|lar|ity
pu|pil|lary
pu|pi|par|ous
pup|pet
pup|pet|eer
pup|petry
puppy (*pl.*
 pup|pies)
pup|py|ish
Pur|ana
Pur|anic
Pur|beck
pur|blind
Pur|cell
pur|chas|able
pur|chase (as *v.*,
 pur|chas|ing)
pur|chaser
pur|dah
pure (purer,
 purest)
purée (as *v.*,
 pur|éed,
 pur|ée|ing)
purfle (as *v.*,
 purf|ling)
pur|ga|tion
pur|gat|ive
pur|gat|orial
pur|gat|ory
purge (as *v.*,
 pur|ging)
puri|fica|tion
puri|fic|ator
puri|fic|at|ory
puri|fier
pur|ify (puri|fies,
 puri|fied,
 puri|fy|ing)
Purim
pur|ine
pur|ism
pur|ist
pur|istic
pur|itan (*gen.*)
Pur|itan (*hist.*)
pur|it|anic
pur|it|an|ical

pur¦ity
purl
purler
pur¦lieu
pur¦lin
pur¦loin
purple (as v.,
  pur¦pling)
purp¦lish
purply
pur¦port
pur¦pose (as v.,
  pur¦pos¦ing)
pur¦pose¦ful
pur¦pose¦fully
pur¦pos¦ive
pur¦pura
pur¦puric
pur¦purin
purr
purse (as v.,
  purs¦ing)
purser
purs¦lane
pur¦su¦able
pur¦su¦ance
pur¦su¦ant
pur¦sue
  (pur¦su¦ing)
pur¦suer
pur¦suit
puru¦lence
puru¦lent
pur¦vey
pur¦vey¦ance
pur¦veyor
pur¦view
pus (Med.)
push-bike
push-chair
pusher
push¦ily
pushi¦ness
Push¦kin
push-over n.
Pushtu use
  Pashto

push-up n.
pushy (push¦ier,
  pushi¦est)
pu¦sil¦lan¦im¦ity
pu¦sil¦lan¦im¦ous
pussy (pl.
  puss¦ies)
pussy-cat
pussy¦foot
pus¦tu¦lar
pus¦tu¦late (as v.,
  pus¦tu¦lat¦ing)
pus¦tu¦la¦tion
pus¦tule
pus¦tu¦lous
put (put, put¦ting)
pu¦tat¦ive
put-down n.
put¦log
put-on n.
put-put (as v.,
  put-putted,
  put-putting)
pu¦tre¦fa¦cient
pu¦tre¦fac¦tion
pu¦tre¦fact¦ive
pu¦trefy
  (pu¦tre¦fies,
  pu¦tre¦fied,
  pu¦tre¦fy¦ing)
pu¦tres¦cence
pu¦tres¦cent
pu¦tres¦cible
pu¦trid
pu¦trid¦ity
putsch
putt (*Golf*)
put¦tee (shin cloth)
putter
putto (pl. putti)
putty (cement; as
  v., put¦ties,
  put¦tied,
  put¦ty¦ing)
put-up a.
puy (volcanic cone)

puzzle (as v.,
  puzz¦ling)
puz¦zle¦ment
puzz¦ler
py¦aemia
py¦aemic
pye-dog
py¦el¦itis
py¦elo¦gram
Pyg¦ma¦lion
pygmy (pl.
  pyg¦mies)
py¦ja¦mas
pyk¦nic
py¦lon
pyl¦oric
pyl¦orus (pl.
  pyl¦ori)
Pyong¦yang
py¦or¦rhoea
pyr¦acan¦tha
pyr¦amid
pyr¦am¦idal
pyre
Pyr¦en¦ees
pyr¦eth¦rum
pyr¦etic
pyr¦exia
pyr¦exial
pyr¦exic
pyr¦ex¦ical
pyr¦hel¦io¦meter
pyr¦id¦ine
pyr¦ites
pyr¦itic
pyr¦iti¦fer¦ous
pyr¦it¦ize
  (pyr¦it¦iz¦ing)
pyr¦it¦ous
pyro-electric
pyro-electricity
pyro¦gal¦lic
pyro¦gal¦lol
pyro¦genic
pyro¦gen¦ous
pyro¦graphy
pyro¦latry

pyro¦lig¦neous
pyro¦lyse
  (pyro¦lys¦ing)
pyro¦lysis (pl.
  pyro¦lyses)
pyro¦lytic
pyro¦mancy
pyro¦mania
pyro¦ma¦niac
pyro¦meter
pyro¦met¦ric
pyro¦metry
pyr¦ope
pyro¦phoric
pyr¦osis
pyro¦tech¦nic
pyro¦tech¦nical
pyro¦tech¦nics
pyro¦tech¦nist
pyro¦techny
pyr¦ox¦ene
pyr¦oxy¦lin
pyr¦rhic (metre)
Pyr¦rhic (victory)
Pyr¦rhon
Pyr¦rhon¦ian
Pyr¦rhonic
Pyr¦rhon¦ism
Pyr¦rhon¦ist
pyr¦uvic (acid)
Py¦thag¦oras
Py¦thag¦oras'
  (theorem)
Py¦thag¦or¦ean
Pyth¦ian
py¦thon
py¦thon¦ess
py¦thonic
py¦uria
pyx (vessel etc.)
pyx¦idium (pl.
  pyx¦idia)
pyxis (pl.
  pyx¦ides)

Q

Qatar
Q-boat
Q-ship
quack|ery
quack|ish
quad|ra|
      gen|arian
Quad|ra|ges|ima
quad|ra|ges|imal
quad|rangle
quad|ran|gu|lar
quad|rant
quad|rantal
quad|ra|phonic
quad|ra|phon|ic|
      ally
quad|ra|phony
quad|rat
quad|rate (as v.,
 quad|rat|ing)
quad|ratic
quad|rat|ure
quad|ren|nial
quad|ren|ni|ally
quad|ren|nium
quad|ric
quad|ri|ceps
quad|ri|fid
quad|riga (pl.
 quad|rigae)
quad|ri|lat|eral
quad|ri|lin|gual
quad|rille
quad|ril|lion
quad|ri|no|mial
quad|ri|par|tite
quad|ri|ple|gia
quad|ri|ple|gic
quad|ri|reme
quad|ri|syl|labic
quad|ri|syl|lable
quad|ri|val|ent
quad|ri|vium
quad|roon
quad|ru|man|ous
quad|ru|ped
quad|ru|pedal
quad|ruple (as v.,
 quad|ru|pling)

quad|ru|plet
quad|ru|plic|ate
 (as v., quad|ru|
    plic|at|ing)
quad|ru|plica|
        tion
quad|ru|pli|city
quad|ruply
quad|ru|pole
quaes|tor
quaes|tor|ial
quaes|tor|ship
quaff
quag
quagga
quaggy
 (quag|gier,
 quag|gi|est)
quag|mire
quail|ery (pl.
 quail|er|ies)
quake (as v.,
 quak|ing)
Quaker
Quaker|ess
Quaker|ish
Quaker|ism
Quakerly
quaky (qua|kier,
 qua|ki|est)
quali|fica|tion
quali|fic|at|ory
quali|fier
qual|ify
 (quali|fies,
 quali|fied,
 quali|fy|ing)
qual|it|at|ive
qual|ity (pl.
 qual|it|ies)
qualm|ish
quan|dary (pl.
 quan|dar|ies)
quand même
quango (pl.
 quan|gos)
quantic
quan|ti|fi|able
quan|ti|fica|tion

quan|ti|fier
quant|ify
 (quan|ti|fies,
 quan|ti|fied,
 quan|ti|fy|ing)
quant|it|at|ive
quant|ity (pl.
 quant|it|ies)
quant|iza|tion
quant|ize
 (quant|iz|ing)
quantum (pl.
 quanta)
qua|qua|versal
quar|ant|ine (as
 v., quar|ant|
     in|ing)
quar|en|den
quark
quar|rel
 (quar|relled,
 quar|rel|ling)
quar|rel|some
quarry (as n., pl.
 quar|ries; as v.,
 quar|ries,
 quar|ried,
 quar|ry|ing)
quar|ry|man (pl.
 quar|ry|men)
quart
quartan
quarta|tion
quar|ter
quar|ter|age
quarter-day
quar|ter|deck
quarter-final
quarter-hour
quar|ter|ing
quarter-light
quar|terly (as n.,
 pl. quar|ter|lies)
quar|ter|mas|ter
quar|ter|staff
quar|tet
quartic
quart|ile

quarto (pl.
 quar|tos)
quartz|ite
quasar
quasi
quas|sia
quat|er|
    cen|ten|ary
 (as n., pl. quat|er|
  cen|ten|ar|ies)
qua|tern|ary (as
 n., pl. qua|tern|
    ar|ies)
Qua|tern|ary
 (Geol.)
qua|ter|nion
qua|tern|ity (pl.
 qua|tern|it|ies)
quat|orz|ain
quat|orze
quat|rain
quatre|foil
quat|tro|cent|ist
quat|tro|cento
qua|ver
qua|very
quay
quay|age
quay|side
queas|ily
queasi|ness
queasy
 (quea|sier,
 quea|si|est)
Que|bec
que|bra|cho (pl.
 que|bra|chos)
Que|chua
Que|chuan
queen
queenie
queen|li|ness
queenly
Queens|berry
queen|ship
Queens|land
que|nelle
quer|ist
quern-stone

queru|lous
query (as *n.*, *pl.*
 quer|ies; as *v.*,
 quer|ies,
 quer|ied,
 query|ing)
ques|tion
ques|tion|able
ques|tion|ably
ques|tion|ary (*pl.*
 ques|tion|ar|ies)
question-master
ques|tion|naire
quet|zal
queue (as *v.*,
 queued,
 queu|ing)
Que|vedo y
 Vil|legas
Que|zon City
quibble (as *v.*,
 quib|bling)
quiche
quicken
quick-freeze (as
 v., quick-froze,
 quick-frozen,
 quick-freezing)
quickie
quick|lime
quick|sand
quick|set
quick|sil|ver
quick|step (dance)
quick|thorn
quid|dity (*pl.*
 quid|dit|ies)
quid|nunc
qui|es|cence
qui|es|cency
qui|es|cent

quiet (as *a.*,
 quieter,
 qui|et|est; as *v.*,
 qui|eted,
 qui|et|ing)
qui|eten
quiet|ism
quiet|ist
quiet|istic
quiet|ude
qui|etus
quill
Quiller-Couch
quill|ing
quilter
quilt|ing
quin|ac|rine
quin|ary
quin|ate
quin|cen|ten|ary
 (as *n.*, *pl.* quin|
  cen|ten|ar|ies)
quinc|un|cial
quinc|unx
quin|gent|en|ary
 (as *n.*, *pl.*
  quin|gent|
   en|ar|ies)
quin|ine
quinol
quin|ol|ine
quin|qua|
  gen|arian
quin|qua|gen|ary
 (as *n.*, *pl.*
  quin|qua|
   gen|ar|ies)
Quin|qua|ges|ima
quin|que|
   cent|en|nial
quin|que|lat|eral

quin|quen|nial
quin|quen|ni|ally
quin|quen|nium
quin|que|reme
quin|que|val|ent
quins|ied
quinsy (*pl.*
 quins|ies)
quint (in piquet)
quinta (house)
quint|ain
quin|tal
quin|tan
quinte (in fencing)
quint|es|sence
quint|es|sen|tial
quint|es|sen|tially
quin|tet
quin|til|lion
quin|tuple (as *v.*,
 quin|tu|pling)
quin|tu|plet
quin|tu|plic|ate
 (as *v.*,
 quin|tu|plic|
         at|ing)
quin|tu|plica|tion
quin|tuply
quip (as *v.*,
 quipped,
 quip|ping)
quire (paper)
quirk|ily
quirki|ness
quirky (quir|kier,
 quir|ki|est)
quis|ling
quit (as *v.*,
 quit|ted,
 quit|ting)
quit|claim

Quito
quit|rent
quit|tance
quit|ter
quiver
qui vive (on the)
Quix|ote
quix|otic
quix|ot|ic|ally
quix|ot|ism
quix|ot|ize
 (quix|ot|iz|ing)
quix|otry
quiz (as *n.*, *pl.*
 quizzes; as *v.*,
 quizzes, quizzed,
 quizz|ing)
quiz-master
quiz|zical
quiz|zic|ally
quod (prison etc.;
 as *v.*, quod|ded,
 quod|ding)
quod|libet
quoin
quoin|ing
quoit
quon|dam
quor|ate
quorum
quota
quot|able
quo|ta|tion
quot|at|ive
quote (as *v.*,
 quot|ing)
quo|ti|dian
quo|tient

R

Ra|bat
rab|bet (groove; as
 v., rab|beted,
 rab|bet|ing)
rabbi
rabbin
rab|bin|ate
rab|bin|ical
rab|bin|ism
rab|bin|ist
rab|bit (animal,
 dish; as v.,
 rab|bited,
 rab|bit|ing)
rab|bity
rabble
rabble-rouser
Rab|el|ais
Rab|el|ais|ian
rabi (grain
 harvest)
ra|bid
ra|bid|ity
ra|bies
race (as v.,
 ra|cing)
race|card
race|course
race|goer
race|horse
race|mate
ra|ceme
ra|cemic
ra|cem|ize
 (ra|cem|iz|ing)
ra|cem|ose
ra|cer
race-riot
race-track
race|way
ra|chel
ra|chis (pl.
 ra|chides)
rach|itic
rach|itis
Rach|man|inov
Rach|man|ism
ra|cial
ra|cial|ism

ra|cial|ist
ra|cially
ra|cily
Ra|cine
ra|ci|ness
ra|cism
ra|cist
racket (as v.,
 rack|eted,
 rack|et|ing)
rack|et|eer
rack|et|eer|ing
rack|ety
rack-rent
ra|con|teur (fem.
 ra|con|teuse)
ra|coon
racy (ra|cier,
 ra|ci|est)
ra|dar
raddle (as v.,
 rad|dling)
ra|dial
ra|di|ally
ra|dian
ra|di|ance
ra|di|ancy
ra|di|ant
ra|di|ate (as v.,
 ra|di|at|ing)
ra|di|ation
ra|di|at|ive
ra|di|ator
rad|ical
rad|ic|al|ism
rad|ic|al|ize
 (rad|ic|al|iz|ing)
rad|ic|ally
rad|icle (Bot.)
ra|dicu|lar
ra|dio (as n., pl.
 ra|dios)
ra|dio|act|ive
ra|dio|ac|tiv|ity
radio-assay
radio-biology
radio-caesium
radio-carbon
radio-carpal

radio-chemistry
radio-cobalt
radio-element
radio-frequency
 (pl. radio-
  frequencies)
ra|dio|genic
ra|dio|gen|ic|ally
radio-goniometer
ra|dio|gram
ra|dio|graph
ra|dio|grapher
ra|dio|graphic
ra|dio|graphy
ra|dio|iso|tope
ra|dio|larian
ra|dio|loca|tion
ra|dio|lo|gic
ra|dio|lo|gical
ra|di|olo|gist
ra|di|ology
ra|dio|meter
radio-nuclide
ra|di|opaque
ra|dio|phonic
ra|dio|scopy
ra|dio|sonde
radio-telegraphy
radio-therapy
rad|ish
ra|dium
ra|dius (pl. ra|dii)
ra|dix (pl.
 ra|di|ces)
ra|dome
ra|don
rad|ula (pl.
 rad|ulae)
raf|fia
raf|fin|ate
raff|ish
raffle (as v.,
 raff|ling)
raf|ter
rafts|man (pl.
 rafts|men)
rag (as v., ragged,
 rag|ging)
raga

rag|amuf|fin
rag-bag
rage (as v.,
 ra|ging)
ragee
rag|ged a.
rag|gedy
rag|lan
rag|out
rag|stone
rag|tag
rag|time
rag|uly
rag|weed
rag-wheel
rag|wort
raider
rail|age
rail|car
rail|head
rail|ing
rail|lery (pl.
 rail|ler|ies)
rail|man (pl.
 rail|men)
rail|road
rail|way
rail|way|man (pl.
 rail|way|men)
rai|ment
rain|bow
rain-check
rain|coat
rain|drop
rain|fall
rain|ily
raini|ness
rain|proof
rain|tight
rain-wash
rain-water
rainy (rain|ier,
 raini|est)
raise (as v.,
 rais|ing)
raisin
raison d'être (pl.
 rais|ons d'être)
raja

Ra|jas|than
Raj|put
rake (as v.,
  rak|ing)
rake-off n.
rak|ish
râle
Ral|eigh
ral|lent|ando (pl.
  ral|lent|an|dos)
rall|ine
rally (as n., pl.
  ral|lies; as v.,
  ral|lies, ral|lied,
  ral|ly|ing)
rally-cross
ram (as v.,
  rammed,
  ram|ming)
Ram|adan
ramal
Ra|man
ramble (as v.,
  ram|bling)
ram|bler
ram|bling
ram|bu|tan
ram|ekin
ramie
ra|mi|fica|tion
ram|ify (rami|fies,
  rami|fied,
  rami|fy|ing)
ram-jet
ram|mer
ram|ose
ram|page (as v.,
  ram|pa|ging)
ram|pa|geous
ramp|ancy
ramp|ant
ram|part
ram|pion
Ram|pur
ram|rod
ram|shackle
ram|son
rancher
ran|cid
ran|cid|ity
ran|cor|ous
ran|cour
ran|dan
ran|di|ness
ran|dom

ran|dom|ize
  (ran|dom|iz|ing)
randy (ran|dier,
  ran|di|est)
ranee
ran|ga|tira
range (as v.,
  ran|ging)
range-finder
ranger
Ran|goon
rangy (ran|gier,
  ran|gi|est)
ranker
rankle (rank|ling)
ran|sack
ran|som
ranter
ran|ti|pole
ra|nun|cu|
        la|ceous
ra|nun|cu|lus
rap (as v., rapped,
  rap|ping)
ra|pa|cious
ra|pa|city
rape (as v.,
  rap|ing)
Raph|ael
raph|ide
rapid (rap|ider,
  rap|id|est)
ra|pid|ity
ra|pier
ra|pine
rap|ist
rap|paree
rap|pee
rap|pel (as v.,
  rap|pelled,
  rap|pel|ling)
rap|port
rap|por|teur
rap|proche|ment
rap|scal|lion
rap|tor
rap|tor|ial
rap|ture
rap|tured
rap|tur|ous
rara avis
rare (rarer,
  rarest)
rarebit *use* rabbit
raree-show
rar|efac|tion

rar|efact|ive
rar|efy (rar|efies,
  rar|efied,
  rar|efy|ing)
rar|ing
rar|ity (pl.
  rar|it|ies)
ras|cal
ras|cal|ity
ras|cally
ras|chel
rasher
rasp|at|ory (pl.
  rasp|at|or|ies)
rasp|berry (pl.
  rasp|ber|ries)
rasper
Ras|ta|far|ian
ras|ter
rat (as v., rat|ted,
  rat|ting)
ratable *use*
  rateable
ra|ta|fia
ra|ta|plan (as v.,
  ra|ta|plan|ning)
ra|ta|tat
ra|ta|touille
rat|bag
ratchet (as v.,
  ratch|eted,
  ratch|et|ing)
rate (as v., rat|ing)
rate|ab|il|ity
rate|able
rate|ably
ra|tel
rate|payer
ra|ther
rati|fica|tion
rat|ify (rati|fies,
  rati|fied,
  rati|fy|ing)
rat|ing
ra|tio (pl. ra|tios)
ra|ti|ocin|ate
  (ra|ti|ocin|at|ing)
ra|ti|ocina|tion
ra|ti|ocin|at|ive
ra|tion
ra|tional
ra|tion|ale
ra|tion|al|ism
ra|tion|al|ist
ra|tion|al|istic
ra|tion|al|ity

ra|tion|al|iza|tion
ra|tion|al|ize
  (ra|tion|al|iz|ing)
ra|tion|ally
rat|ite
rat|line
ra|toon
rats|bane
rat's-tail (file)
rat-tail (fish,
  horse)
rat|tan
rat-tat
rat|ter
rattle (as v.,
  rat|tling)
rat|tler
rattle|snake
rattle|trap
rat|tling
ratty (rat|tier,
  rat|ti|est)
rauc|ous
raunch|ily
raunchi|ness
raunchy
  (raun|ch|ier,
  raun|chi|est)
rav|age (as v.,
  rav|aging)
rave (as v.,
  rav|ing)
ravel (ravelled,
  rav|el|ling)
Ravel
rav|elin
raven
rav|en|ous
raver
rave-up n.
ra|vine
ra|vined
rav|ing
ra|vi|oli
rav|ish
rav|ish|ment
raw|hide
raw|ish
ray (Mus.)
rayah
ray|let
Ray|mond
rayon
raze (raz|ing)
razee (hist.; as v.,
  raz|eed)

razor
razor-back
razor-bill
razor-blade
razor-edge
raz'zia
razzle
razz|ma'tazz
re (*Mus.*) *use* ray
re|ab'sorb
reach|able
re'act
re-act (act again)
re'act|ance
re'act|ant
re|ac'tion
re|ac'tion|ary (as
  n., pl. re'ac'tion|
              ar'ies)
re'ac'tion|ist
re|act'iv|ate
  (re|act'iv|at'ing)
re|act'iva'tion
re|act'ive
re|act'iv'ity (*pl.*
  re'act'iv'it|ies)
re|actor
read (as *v.*, read)
read|ab'il'ity
read|able
read|ably
re|ad'dress
reader
read'er|ship
read|ily
read-in *n.*
readi|ness
read|ing
Read|ing
re|ad'just
re|ad'just|ment
re|ad'mit
  (re|ad'mit'ted,
  re|ad'mit|ting)
re|ad'mit|tance
read-out *n.*
ready (as *a.*,
  read|ier,
  readi|est; as *v.*,
  read|ies,
  read|ied,
  ready|ing)
ready-made
re|af'firm
re|af'firma|tion
re|af'for'est

re|af'for|esta|tion
Rea'gan
re|agency (*pl.*
  re|agen'cies)
re|agent
real
re|al'gar
re|align
re|align|ment
real|ism
real|ist
real|istic
real|ist'ic|ally
real|ity (*pl.*
  real|it'ies)
real|iz|able
real|iza|tion
real|ize
  (real|iz'ing)
really
re|alty
reamer
re|an'im|ate
  (re|an'im|at'ing)
re|an'ima|tion
re|appear
re|appear|ance
re|applica|tion
re|apply
  (re|applies,
  re|applied,
  re|apply|ing)
re|appoint
re|appoint|ment
re|appraisal
re|appraise
  (re|apprais|ing)
rear-admiral
rear-arch
rear'guard
re'arm
re|arma|ment
rear|most
re|arrange
  (re|arran'ging)
re|arrange|ment
rear|ward
rear|wards
re|as'cend
reason
reas'on|able
reas'on|ably
re|as'semble
  (re|as'semb|ling)
re|as'sembly
re|as'sert

re|as'ser'tion
re|as'sess
re|as'sess|ment
re|as'sign
re|as'sign|ment
re|as'sume
  (re|as'sum'ing)
re|as'sump|tion
re|as'sur'ance
re|as'sure
  (re|as'sur'ing)
Ré'au|mur (scale)
re|bap'tize
  (re|bap'tiz'ing)
re|barb'at|ive
re'bate
re'bec
Re|becca
rebel (as *v.*,
  re|belled,
  re'bel'ling)
re'bel|lion
re'bel'li|ous
re'bid (as *v.*,
  re'bid,
  re'bid'ding)
re|bind
  (re|bound)
re|birth
re'bore (as *v.*,
  re|bor'ing)
re|born
re|bound
re|buff
re|build (re|built)
re'buke (as *v.*,
  re|buk'ing)
re'bus
re'but (re|but'ted,
  re'but|ting)
re'but|ment
re'but|table
re'but|tal
re'but|ter
re'cal'cit|rance
re'cal'cit|rant
re|cal'esce
  (re|cal'es|cing)
re|cal'es|cence
re'call
re'cant
re|canta|tion
re'cap (as *v.*,
  re'capped,
  re'cap|ping)

re|cap'itu|late
  (re|cap'itu|
              lat'ing)
re|cap'itu|la'tion
re|cap'itu|lat'ive
re|cap'itu|lat'ory
re|cap'ture (as *v.*,
  re|cap'tur'ing)
re'cast (as *v.*,
  re'cast)
recce (as *v.*,
  recced,
  recce|ing)
re'cede (withdraw;
  re|ced'ing)
re-cede (cede back;
  re-ceding)
re|ceipt
re|ceiv|able
re|ceive
  (re|ceiv|ing)
re|ceiver
re|ceiv'er|ship
re|cency
re|cen|sion
re|cent
re|cept|acle
re|cep|tion
re|cep'tion|ist
re|cept|ive
re|cep'tiv|ity
re|cep|tor
re'cess
re|ces|sion
re|ces|sional
re|ces|sion|ary
re|cess|ive
Rech'ab|ite
re|charge (as *v.*,
  re|char'ging)
ré*chauffé*
re|cher|ché
re|christen
re'cid'iv|ism
re'cid'iv|ist
re|cipe
re|cipi|ency
re|cipi|ent
re|cip'rocal
re|cip'roc|ally
re|cip'roc|ate
  (re|cip'roc|
              at'ing)
re|cip'roca|tion
re|ci|pro'city
re|cital

re|cit|al|ist
re|cita|tion
re|cit|at|ive
re|cite (re|cit|ing)
reck|less
reckon
reck|on|ing
re|claim
re|claim|able
re|clama|tion
ré|clame
(notoriety)
re|clin|ate
re|cline
(re|clin|ing)
re|cluse
re|clus|ive
re|cog|ni|tion
re|cog|nit|ory
re|cog|niz|ab|il|ity
re|cog|niz|able
re|cog|niz|ably
re|cog|niz|ance
re|cog|niz|ant
re|cog|nize
(re|cog|niz|ing)
re|coil
re|coin
re|col|lect
(remember)
re-collect (collect
again)
re|col|lec|tion
re|col|lect|ive
re|col|on|iza|tion
re|col|on|ize (re|
col|on|iz|ing)
re|col|our
re|com|bin|ant
re|comb|ina|tion
re|com|bine
(re|com|bin|ing)
re|com|mence (re|
com|men|cing)
re|com|mence|
ment
re|com|mend
re|com|mend|able
re|com|menda|
tion
re|com|mend|at|
ory
re|com|mit
(re|com|mit|ted,
re|com|mit|ting)
re|com|mit|ment

re|com|mit|tal
re|com|pense (as
v., re|com|pens|
ing)
re|com|pose
(re|com|pos|ing)
re|con|cil|ab|il|ity
re|con|cil|able
re|con|cile
(re|con|cil|ing)
re|con|cile|ment
re|con|cili|ation
re|con|dite
re|con|di|tion
re|con|nais|sance
re|con|noitre (as
v., re|con|noit|
ring)
re|con|quer
re|con|quest
re|con|sider
re|con|sid|era|
tion
re|con|sol|id|ate
(re|con|sol|id|
at|ing)
re|con|sol|ida|
tion
re|con|stit|ute (re|
con|stit|ut|ing)
re|con|stitu|tion
re|con|struct
re|con|struc|tion
re|con|vene
(re|con|ven|ing)
re|con|ver|sion
re|con|vert
rec|ord *n.*
re|cord *v.*
re|cord|able
re|corder
re|cord|ing
re|cord|ist
record-player
re-count (count
again)
re|count (narrate)
re|coup
re|coup|ment
re|course
re|cover
re-cover (cover
again)
re|cov|er|able
re|cov|ery (*pl.*
re|cov|eries)

rec|re|ancy
rec|re|ant
re|cre|ate (refresh;
re|cre|at|ing)
re-create
(create again;
re-creating)
re|cre|ation
re|cre|ational
re|cre|at|ive
re|crim|in|ate
(re|crim|in|
at|ing)
re|crim|ina|tion
re|crim|inat|ive
re|crim|in|at|ory
re|cross
re|cru|desce
(re|cru|des|cing)
re|cru|des|cence
re|cru|des|cent
re|cruit
re|cruital
re|cruit|ment
rectal
rect|angle
rect|an|gu|lar
rect|an|gu|lar|ity
rec|ti|fi|able
rec|ti|fica|tion
rec|ti|fier
rect|ify
(rec|ti|fies,
rec|ti|fied,
rec|ti|fy|ing)
rec|ti|lin|eal
rec|ti|lin|ear
rec|ti|lin|ear|ity
rect|it|ude
recto (*pl.* rec|tos)
rector
rect|or|ate
rect|orial
rect|or|ship
rect|ory
(*pl.*rect|or|ies)
rect|rix (*pl.*
rect|ri|ces)
rectum
rectus (*pl.* recti)
re|cum|bency
re|cum|bent
re|cu|per|ate
(re|cu|per|at|ing)
re|cu|pera|tion
re|cu|per|at|ive

re|cur (re|curred,
re|cur|ring)
re|cur|rence
re|cur|rent
re|cur|sion
re|curs|ive
re|curv|ate
re|curv|at|ure
re|curve
(re|curv|ing)
re|cus|ance
re|cus|ancy
re|cus|ant
re|cycle
(re|cyc|ling)
red (red|der,
red|dest)
Red (Communist)
re|dact
re|dac|tion
re|dactor
re|dan
red|breast
red|brick
red|bud
red|cap
red|coat
redd (to tidy etc.;
redd)
red|den
red|dish
reddle
reddy
re|dec|or|ate
(re|dec|or|at|ing)
re|dec|ora|tion
re|deem
re|deem|able
re|demp|tion
re|dempt|ive
Re|demp|tor|ist
(*fem.*
Re|demp|tor|
ist|ine)
re|deploy
re|deploy|ment
re|des|cend
re|design
re|develop
(re|developed,
re|develop|ing)
re|devel|op|ment
red-eye
red-fish
red-handed
red|head

red-hot
re|dial
  (re|di|alled,
  re|di|al|ling)
re|dif|fu|sion
red|in|gote
red|in|teg|rate
  (red|in|teg|
      rat|ing)
red|in|teg|ra|tion
re|dir|ect
re|dir|ec|tion
re|dis|cover
re|dis|cov|ery (pl.
  re|dis|cov|er|ies)
re|dis|solu|tion
re|dis|solve
  (re|dis|solv|ing)
re|dis|trib|ute (re|
    dis|trib|ut|ing)
re|dis|tribu|tion
re|dis|trib|ut|ive
re|div|ide
  (re|div|id|ing)
re|di|vi|sion
re|di|vivus
redo (re|does,
  re|did, re|done)
red|ol|ence
red|ol|ent
re|double (as v.,
  re|doub|ling)
re|doubt
re|doubt|able
re|dound
redox
red|poll
re|draw (re|drew,
  re|drawn)
re|dress
re|dressal
re|dress|ment
red|shank
red-shift
red|skin
red|start
re|duce
  (re|du|cing)
re|du|cer
re|du|cible
re|*duc*|*tio ad*
  ab|*surdum*
re|duc|tion
re|duc|tion|ism
re|duc|tion|ist
re|duc|tion|istic

re|duct|ive
re|dund|ance
re|dund|ancy (pl.
  re|dund|an|cies)
re|dund|ant
re|du|plic|ate (re|
    du|plic|at|ing)
re|du|plica|tion
re|du|plic|at|ive
red|wing
red|wood
re|dye (re|dyed,
  re|dye|ing)
ree|bok
re-echo
reedi|ness
reed|ing
re-edit (re-edited,
  re-editing)
re-edition
reed|ling
re-educate
  (re-educating)
re-education
reedy (reed|ier,
  reedi|est)
reefer
reef-knot
reeky (reek|ier,
  reeki|est)
re-elect
re-election
re-eligible
re-embark
re-embarkation
re-emerge
  (re-emerging)
re-emergence
re-emergent
re-enact
re-enactment
re-enforce
  (enforce again;
  re-enforcing)
△ reinforce
re-enforcement
re-enter
re-entrance
re-entrant
re-entry
  (pl. re-entries)
re-establish
re-establishment
reeve (as v., rove,
  reev|ing)
re-examination

re-cxamine
  (re-examining)
re-export
re|face
  (re|fa|cing)
re|fash|ion
re|fec|tion
re|fect|ory (pl.
  re|fect|or|ies)
re|fer (re|ferred,
  re|fer|ring)
re|fer|able
ref|eree (as v.,
  ref|er|eed)
ref|er|ence (as v.,
  ref|er|en|cing)
ref|er|en|dum (pl.
  ref|er|en|dums)
ref|er|ent
ref|er|en|tial
ref|er|en|tially
re|fer|ral
re|fill
re|fine (re|fin|ing)
re|fine|ment
re|finer
re|finery (pl.
  re|finer|ies)
re|fit (as v.,
  re|fit|ted,
  re|fit|ting)
re|fit|ment
re|flate
  (re|flat|ing)
re|fla|tion
re|flect
re|flec|tion
re|flec|tional
re|flect|ive
re|flector
re|flex
re|flexed
re|flex|ib|il|ity
re|flex|ible
reflexion *use*
  reflection
re|flex|ive
re|flexo|logy
re|float
re|flu|ence
re|flu|ent
re|flux
re|form
re-form (form
  again)
Re|form (Judaism)

re|form|able
re|forma|tion (f.
  reform)
re-formation
Re|forma|tion
  (*Hist.*)
re|forma|tional
re|form|at|ive
re|form|at|ory (pl.
  re|form|at|or|ies)
Re|formed
  (Calvinist, of
  Reform Judaism)
re|former
re|form|ism
re|form|ist
re|fract
re|frac|tion
re|fract|ive
re|frac|to|meter
re|fractor
re|fract|or|ily
re|fract|ori|ness
re|fract|ory
  (as n., pl.
  re|fract|or|ies)
re|frain
re|fran|gib|il|ity
re|fran|gible
re|fresh
re|fresher
re|fresh|ment
re|fri|ger|ant
re|fri|ger|ate
  (re|fri|ger|at|ing)
re|fri|gera|tion
re|fri|ger|ator
re|fri|ger|at|ory
  (as n., pl.
  re|fri|ger|at|
            or|ies)
re|frin|gence
re|frin|gency
re|frin|gent
re|fuel
  (re|fu|elled,
  re|fu|el|ling)
ref|uge
re|fu|gee
re|ful|gence
re|ful|gent
re|fund (pay back,
  repayment)
re-fund (fund
  afresh)
re|fund|ment

re|fur|bish
re|furn|ish
re|fus|able
re|fusal
re|fuse (say no,
 rubbish; as *v.*,
 re|fus|ing)
re-fuse (fuse
 again; re-fusing)
re|fut|able
re|futal
re|futa|tion
re|fute (re|fut|ing)
re|gain
regal
re|gale
 (re|gal|ing)
re|gale|ment
re|galia
re|gal|ism
re|gal|ity (*pl.*
 re|gal|it|ies)
reg|ally
re|gard
re|gard|ant
re|gard|ful
re|gard|ing
re|gard|less
re|gatta
re|gel|ate
 (re|gel|at|ing)
re|gela|tion
re|gency (*pl.*
 re|gen|cies)
re|gen|er|ate
 (re|gen|er|at|ing)
re|gen|era|tion
re|gen|er|at|ive
re|gen|er|ator
re|gen|esis (*pl.*
 re|gen|eses)
re|gent
re|ger|min|ate (re|
 ger|min|at|ing)
re|ger|mina|tion
reg|gae
re|gi|cidal
re|gi|cide
ré|gie (monopoly)
re|gild
re|gime
re|gi|men
re|gi|ment
re|gi|mental
re|gi|ment|ally
re|gi|menta|tion

Re|gina (queen)
re|gion
re|gional
re|gion|al|ism
re|gion|al|ize
 (re|gion|al|iz|ing)
re|gis|seur
re|gis|ter
re|gis|trable
re|gis|trar
Re|gis|trary (*pl.*
 Re|gis|trar|ies)
re|gis|tra|tion
re|gis|try (*pl.*
 re|gis|tries)
Re|gius
re|glet
reg|nal
reg|nant
re|gorge
 (re|gor|ging)
re|grate
 (re|grat|ing)
re|gress
re|gres|sion
re|gress|ive
re|gret (as *v.*,
 re|gret|ted,
 re|gret|ting)
re|gret|ful
re|gret|fully
re|gret|table
re|gret|tably
re|group
re|group|ment
regu|lable
regu|lar
re|gu|lar|ity (*pl.*
 re|gu|lar|it|ies)
regu|lar|ize
 (regu|lar|iz|ing)
regu|late
 (regu|lat|ing)
re|gu|la|tion
regu|lat|ive
regu|lator
regu|line
regu|lus (*pl.*
 reguli)
re|gur|git|ate
 (re|gur|git|at|ing)
re|gur|gita|tion
re|hab|il|it|ate (re|
 hab|il|it|at|ing)
re|hab|il|ita|tion

re|handle
 (re|hand|ling)
re|hang (re|hung)
re|hash
re|hear (re|heard)
re|hearsal
re|hearse
 (re|hears|ing)
re-heat
re|ho|boam
re|house
 (re|hous|ing)
Reich
Reichs|tag
re|ifica|tion
re|ific|at|ory
re|ify (re|ifies,
 re|ified,
 re|ify|ing)
Rei|gate
reign (rule)
re|ignite
 (re|ignit|ing)
re|im|burse
 (re|im|burs|ing)
re|im|burse|ment
re|im|port
re|im|pose
 (re|im|pos|ing)
re|im|posi|tion
Reims
rein (in riding etc.)
re|in|carn|ate
 (as *v.*, re|in|carn|
 at|ing)
re|in|carna|tion
re|in|cor|por|ate
 (re|in|cor|por|
 at|ing)
re|in|cor|pora|
 tion
rein|deer
re|in|force
 (strengthen;
 re|in|for|cing)
△ re-enforce
re|in|force|ment
re|in|sert
re|in|ser|tion
re|in|state
 (re|in|stat|ing)
re|in|state|ment
re|in|sur|ance
re|in|sure
 (re|in|sur|ing)

re|in|ter
 (re|in|terred,
 re|in|ter|ring)
re|in|ter|pret
 (re|in|ter|preted,
 re|in|ter|pret|
  ing)
re|in|ter|preta|
  tion
re|in|vest
re|in|vest|ment
re|in|vig|or|ate
 (re|in|vig|or|
  at|ing)
re|in|vig|ora|tion
re|is|sue (as *v.*,
 re|is|su|ing)
re|it|er|ate
 (re|it|er|at|ing)
re|it|era|tion
re|it|er|at|ive
reive (reiv|ing)
re|ject
re|ject|able
re|jec|ta|menta
re|jec|tion
re|jector
re|jig (re|jigged,
 re|jig|ging)
re|joice
 (re|joi|cing)
re|join
re|join|der
re|ju|ven|ate
 (re|ju|ven|at|ing)
re|ju|vena|tion
re|ju|ven|ator
re|ju|ven|esce
 (re|ju|ven|es|
  cing)
re|ju|ven|es|cence
re|ju|ven|es|cent
re|kindle
 (re|kind|ling)
re|la|bel
 (re|la|belled,
 re|la|bel|ling)
re|lapse (as *v.*,
 re|laps|ing)
re|late (re|lat|ing)
re|later (*gen.*)
re|la|tion
re|la|tional
re|la|tion|ship
re|lat|ival
rel|at|ive

rel|at|iv|ism
rel|at|iv|ist
re|lat|iv|istic
re|lat|iv|ity (*pl.*
  re|lat|iv|it|ies)
re|la|tiv|iza|tion
re|la|tiv|ize
  (re|la|tiv|iz|ing)
re|lator (*Law*)
re|lax
re|lax|ant
re|laxa|tion
re|lay (pass on,
  arrange in relays)
re-lay (lay again;
  re-laid)
re|leas|able
re|lease
  (re|leas|ing)
re|leasee (*Law*)
re|leasor (*Law*)
re|leg|able
re|leg|ate
  (re|leg|at|ing)
re|lega|tion
re|lent
re|lent|less
rel|ev|ance
rel|ev|ancy
rel|ev|ant
re|li|ab|il|ity
re|li|able
re|li|ably
re|li|ance
re|li|ant
relic
rel|ict
re|lief
re|liev|able
re|lieve
  (re|liev|ing)
re|lievo (*pl.*
  re|lievos)
re|li|gion
re|li|gioner
re|li|gion|ism
re|li|gion|ist
re|li|gi|ose
re|li|gi|os|ity
re|li|gious (as *n.*,
  pl. same)
re|line (re|lin|ing)
re|lin|quish
re|lin|quish|ment
rel|iquary (*pl.*
  rel|iquar|ies)

re|*li*|*quiae* (*pl.*,
  remains)
rel|ish
re|live (re|liv|ing)
re|load
re|lo|cate
  (re|lo|cat|ing)
re|lo|ca|tion
re|lu|cent
re|luct|ance
re|luct|ant
rely (re|lies,
  re|lied, re|ly|ing)
re|main
re|main|der
re|mains *pl.*
re|make (as *v.*,
  re|made,
  re|mak|ing)
re|man
  (re|manned,
  re|man|ning)
re|mand
re|man|ence
re|man|ent
re|mark
re|mark|able
re|mark|ably
re|mar|riage
re|marry
  (re|mar|ries,
  re|mar|ried,
  re|mar|ry|ing)
rem|blai
Rem|brandt
re|medi|able
re|med|ial
re|medi|ally
rem|edy (as *n.*, *pl.*
  rem|ed|ies; as *v.*,
  rem|ed|ies,
  rem|ed|ied,
  rem|edy|ing)
re|mem|ber
re|mem|ber|able
re|mem|brance
re|mem|bran|cer
re|mex (*pl.*
  rem|iges)
re|mind
re|minder
re|mind|ful
re|min|isce
  (re|min|is|cing)
re|min|is|cence
re|min|is|cent

re|min|is|cen|tial
re|mint
re|mise (as *v.*,
  re|mis|ing)
re|miss
re|miss|ible
re|mis|sion
re|miss|ive
re|mit (as *v.*,
  re|mit|ted,
  re|mit|ting)
re|mit|tal
re|mit|tance
re|mit|tee
re|mit|tent
re|mit|ter
rem|nant
re|model
  (re|mod|elled,
  re|mod|el|ling)
re|mon|et|iza|tion
re|mon|et|ize
  (re|mon|et|iz|ing)
re|mon|strance
re|mon|strant
re|mon|strate
  (re|mon|
        strat|ing)
re|mon|stra|tion
re|mon|strat|ive
re|mon|strator
re|mont|ant
rem|ora
re|morse
re|morse|ful
re|morse|fully
re|morse|less
re|mote
  (re|moter,
  re|motest)
re|mould
re|mount
re|mov|ab|il|ity
re|mov|able
re|moval
re|mov|al|ist
re|move (as *v.*,
  re|mov|ing)
re|mover
re|mu|ner|ate
  (re|mu|ner|
        at|ing)
re|mu|nera|tion
re|mu|nerat|ive
re|mu|ner|at|ory

re|nais|sance
  (revival)
Re|nais|sance
  (*hist.*)
renal
re|name
  (re|nam|ing)
re|nas|cence
  (rebirth)
re|nas|cent
rend (rent)
ren|der
ren|der|ing
ren|dez|vous (as
  n., *pl.* same; as *v.*,
  ren|dez|vouses,
  ren|dez|voused,
  ren|dez|vous|ing)
ren|di|tion
ren|eg|ade (as *v.*,
  ren|eg|ad|ing)
re|nege
  (re|neging)
re|new
re|new|able
re|newal
reni|form
re|nit|ence
re|nit|ency
re|nit|ent
ren|net
Ren|oir
re|nounce
  (re|noun|cing)
re|nounce|ment
ren|ov|ate
  (ren|ov|at|ing)
re|nova|tion
ren|ov|ator
re|nown
re|nowned
rent|ab|il|ity
rent|able
rental
renter
rent-free
ren|*tier*
re|num|ber
re|nun|ci|ant
re|nun|ci|ation
re|nun|ci|at|ive
re|nun|ci|at|ory
re|oc|cu|pa|tion

re|oc|cupy
(re|oc|cu|pies,
re|oc|cu|pied,
re|oc|cu|py|ing)
re|open
re|order
re|or|gan|iza|tion
re|or|gan|ize (re|
or|gan|iz|ing)
re|ori|ent
re|ori|ent|ate (re|
ori|ent|at|ing)
re|ori|enta|tion
re|paint
re|pair
re|pair|able (that
can be repaired)
re|pair|man (*pl.*
re|pair|men)
re|pand
re|pa|per
rep|ar|able (that
can be put right)
re|para|tion
rep|ar|at|ive
re|par|tee
re|par|ti|tion
re|pass
re|past
re|pat|ri|ate (as *v.*,
re|pat|ri|at|ing)
re|pat|ri|ation
re|pay (re|paid)
re|pay|able
re|pay|ment
re|peal
re|peal|able
re|peat
re|peat|able
re|peater
re¦pêch¦age
re|pel (re|pelled,
re|pel|ling)
re|pel|lent
re|pent
re|pent|ance
re|pent|ant
re|people
(re|peop|ling)
re|per|cus|sion
re|per|cuss|ive
rep|er|toire
rep|er|tory (*pl.*
rep|er|tor|ies)
rep|et|end

ré¦pét¦it¦eur
(*Mus.*)
re|pe|ti|tion
re|pe|ti|tional
re|pe|ti|tion|ary
re|pe|ti|tious
re|pet|it|ive
re|pine
(re|pin|ing)
re|pique (as *v.*,
re|piqued,
re|piquing)
re|place
(re|pla|cing)
re|place|able
re|place|ment
re|plant
re|play
re|plen|ish
re|plen|ish|ment
re|plete
re|ple|tion
re|plevin
re|plevy
(re|plev|ies,
re|plev|ied,
re|plevy|ing)
rep|lica
replicable
rep|lic|ate (as *v.*,
rep|lic|at|ing)
rep|lica|tion
re|ply (as *n.*, *pl.*
re|plies; as *v.*,
re|plies, re|plied,
re|ply|ing)
re|point
re|pol|ish
re|popu|late
(re|popu|lat|ing)
re|popu|lation
re|port
re|port|able
re|port|age
re|porter
re|port|orial
re|port|ori|ally
re|posal
re|pose (as *v.*,
re|posed,
re|pos|ing)
re|pose|ful
re|pose|fully
re|pos|it|ory (*pl.*
re|pos|it|or|ies)
re|pos|sess

re|pos|ses|sion
re|pot (re|pot|ted,
re|pot|ting)
re|poussé
rep|re|hend
rep|re|hens|ible
rep|re|hens|ibly
rep|re|hen|sion
rep|res|ent
rep|res|ent|able
rep|res|enta|tion
rep|res|enta|
tional
rep|res|ent|at|ive
re|press
re|pres|sion
re|press|ive
re|prieve (as *v.*,
re|priev|ing)
rep|rim|and
re|print
re|prisal
re|prise
re|proach
re|proach|ful
re|proach|fully
rep|rob|ate (as *v.*,
rep|rob|at|ing)
rep|roba|tion
re|pro|duce
(re|pro|du|cing)
re|pro|du|cib|
il|ity
re|pro|du|cible
re|pro|du|cibly
re|pro|duc|tion
re|pro|duct|ive
re|pro|graphic
re|pro|graphy
re|proof
re|prove
(re|prov|ing)
re|pro|vi|sion
rept|ant
rep|tile
rep|ti|lian
re|pub|lic
re|pub|lican
re|pub|lic|an|ism
re|pub|lica|tion
re|pub|lish
re|pu|di|ate
(re|pu|di|at|ing)
re|pu|di|ation
re|pu|di|ator
re|pug|nance

re|pug|nant
re|pulse (as *v.*,
re|puls|ing)
re|pul|sion
re|puls|ive
re|pur|chase (as
v., re|pur|chas|
ing)
re|puri|fica|tion
re|pur|ify
(re|puri|fies,
re|puri|fied,
re|puri|fy|ing)
rep|ut|able
rep|ut|ably
re|pu|ta|tion
re|pute (as *v.*,
re|put|ing)
re|putedly
re|quest
re|quicken
re|quiem
re|qui|es|cat
re|quire
(re|quir|ing)
re|quire|ment
re|quis|ite
re|quisi|tion
re|quital
re|quite
(re|quit|ing)
re|read (re|read)
rere|dos
re-route
(re-routeing)
re|run (as *v.*,
re|ran, re|run,
re|run|ning)
re|sale
res|cind
res|cis|sion
re|script
res|cue (as *v.*,
res|cued,
res|cu|ing)
res|cuer
re|search
re|seat
re|sect
re|sec|tion
res|eda
re|sell (re|sold)
re|semb|lance
re|semb|lant
re|semble
(re|sem|bling)

re|sent
re|sent|ful
re|sent|fully
re|sent|ment
re|ser|pine
re|serv|able
re|ser|va|tion
re|serve (as *v.*,
  re|serv|ing)
re-serve (serve
  again;
  re-serving)
re|serv|ist
res|er|voir
re|set (re|set,
  re|set|ting)
re|settle
  (re|set|tling)
re|set|tle|ment
re|shape
  (re|shap|ing)
re|ship
  (re|shipped,
  re|ship|ping)
re|shuffle (as *v.*,
  re|shuff|ling)
res|ide
  (res|id|ing)
res|id|ence
res|id|ency (*pl.*
  res|id|en|cies)
res|id|ent
res|id|en|tial
res|id|en|tiary (*pl.*
  res|id|en|tiar|ies)
res|id|ent|ship
re|sid|ual
re|sid|uary
res|idue
re|siduum (*pl.*
  re|sidua)
resign
re-sign (sign
  again)
resig|na|tion
resigned
re|sile (re|sil|ing)
re|si|li|ence
re|si|li|ency
re|si|li|ent
resin
res|in|ate
  (res|in|at|ing)
res|ini|fer|ous
res|ini|fica|tion
res|ini|form

res|in|ify
  (res|ini|fies,
  res|ini|fied,
  res|ini|fy|ing)
res|in|oid
res|in|ous
res|ist
res|ist|ance
res|ist|ant
res|ister (person)
res|ist|ib|il|ity
res|ist|ible
res|ist|ive
res|is|tiv|ity
res|istor (thing)
re|sit (as *v.*, re|sat,
  re|sit|ting)
re|sole (re|sol|ing)
re|sol|uble (that
  can be resolved)
re-soluble (that
  can be dissolved
  again)
res|ol|ute
res|olu|tion
res|ol|ut|ive
re|solv|able
re|solve (as *v.*,
  re|solv|ing)
re|sol|vent
res|on|ance
res|on|ant
res|on|ate
  (res|on|at|ing)
res|on|ator
re|sorb
re|sorb|ence
re|sorb|ent
re|sor|cin
re|sor|cinol
re|sorp|tion
re|sort
re-sort (sort again)
re|sound
re|sound|ing
re|source
re|source|ful
re|source|fully
re|source|less
re|spect
re|spect|ab|il|ity
re|spect|able
re|spect|ably
re|specter
re|spect|ful
re|spect|fully

re|spect|ing
re|spect|ive
re|spect|ively
re|spell (re|spelt)
res|pir|able
res|pira|tion
res|pir|ator
res|pir|at|ory
re|spire
  (re|spir|ing)
res|pite (as *v.*,
  res|pit|ing)
re|splen|dence
re|splen|dency
re|splen|dent
re|spond
re|spond|ent
re|sponse
re|spons|ib|il|ity
  (*pl.* re|spons|ib|il|
         it|ies)
re|spons|ible
re|spons|ibly
re|spons|ive
re|spons|ory (*pl.*
  re|spons|or|ies)
re|spray
re|start
re|state
  (re|stat|ing)
re|state|ment
res|taur|ant
res|taur|at|eur
rest-cure
rest-day
rest|ful
rest|fully
rest-home
rest-house
res|ti|tu|tion
rest|ive
rest|less
re|stock
re|stor|able
res|tora|tion
res|tora|tion|ism
res|tora|tion|ist
res|tor|at|ive
re|store
  (re|stor|ing)
re|storer
re|strain
re-strain (strain
  again)
re|strain|able
re|straint

re|strict
re|stric|tion
re|strict|ive
rest-room
re|struc|ture
  (re|struc|tur|ing)
re|study
  (re|stud|ies,
  re|stud|ied,
  re|study|ing)
re|style
  (re|styl|ing)
res|ult
res|ult|ant
res|ult|ful
res|ult|less
re|sume
  (re|sum|ing)
ré|sumé
re|sump|tion
re|sumpt|ive
re|su|pin|ate
re|sur|face
  (re|sur|fa|cing)
re|sur|gence
re|sur|gent
re|sur|rect
re|sur|rec|tion
re|sur|vey
re|sus|cit|ate
  (re|sus|cit|at|ing)
re|sus|cita|tion
re|sus|cit|at|ive
re|sus|cit|ator
ret (ret|ted,
  ret|ting)
re|table
re|tail
re|tain|able
re|tainer
re|take (as *v.*,
  re|took,
  re|taken,
  re|tak|ing)
re|tali|ate
  (re|tali|at|ing)
re|tali|ation
re|tali|at|ive
re|tali|at|ory
re|tard
re|tard|ant
re|tard|ate
re|tarda|tion
re|tard|at|ive
re|tard|at|ory

re|tard|ment
retch (vomit)
△ wretch
re|tell (re|told)
re|ten|tion
re|tent|ive
re|think (as v.,
 re|thought)
re|ti|arius (pl.
 re|ti|arii)
re|tiary (pl.
 re|tiar|ies)
re|ti|cence
re|ti|cent
ret|icle
re|ticu|lar
re|ticu|late (as v.,
 re|ticu|lat|ing)
re|ticu|la'tion
ret|ic'ule
re|tic|ulo|cyte
re|ticu|lose
re|ticu|lum (pl.
 re|tic|ula)
re|ti|form
ret|ina (pl.
 ret|inas or
 ret|inae)
ret|inal
ret|in|itis
ret|inol
ret|inue
re|tir|acy
re|tiral
re|tire (re|tir|ing)
re|tiree
re|tire|ment
re|tir'ing
re|tool
re|tort
re|tor'tion
re|touch
re|trace
 (re|tra'cing)
re|tract
re|tract|able
re|trac'ta|tion
re|tract|ile
re|tract|il'ity
re|trac'tion
re|tract|ive
re|tractor
re|train
ret|ral
re|trans|late
 (re|trans|lat'ing)

re|trans|la'tion
re|tread (tread
 again; re|trod,
 re|trod'den,
re|tread (give new
 tread to;
 re|treaded)
re|treat
re|trench
re|trench|ment
re|trial
re|tri'bu|tion
re|tribu|tive
re|triev|able
re|trieval
re|trieve
 (re|triev'ing)
re|triever
re|trim
 (re|trimmed,
 re|trim'ming)
ret|ro|act
ret|ro|ac'tion
ret|ro|act'ive
ret|ro|cede
 (ret|ro|ced'ing)
ret|ro|cedence
ret|ro|cedent
ret|ro|ces'sion
ret|ro|cess'ive
ret|ro|choir
ret|ro|flex
ret|ro|flexed
ret|ro|flex'ion
ret|ro|grada'tion
ret|ro|grade (as v.,
 ret|ro|grad'ing)
ret|ro|gress
ret|ro|gres'sion
ret|ro|gress'ive
ret|ro|ject
retro-rocket
ret'rorse
ret|ro|spect
ret|ro|spec'tion
ret|ro|spect'ive
ret|ro|sternal
re|troussé
ret|ro|ver'sion
ret|ro|vert
re|try (re|tries,
 re|tried,
 re|try'ing)
ret|sina
ret|tery (pl.
 ret|ter'ies)

re|turf
re|turn
re|turn|able
re|turn|less
re|tuse
re|type
 (re|typ'ing)
re|union
Ré|union
re|unite
 (re|unit'ing)
re|urge
 (re|urging)
re|usable
re|use (as v.,
 re|using)
rev (as v., revved,
 rev|ving)
re|vac'cin|ate (re|
 vac'cin|at'ing)
re|vac'cina'tion
re|val'or|iza'tion
re|val'or|ize
 (re|val'or|iz|ing)
re|valu|ation
re|value
 (re|valued,
 re|valu'ing)
re|vamp
re|vanch|ism
re|vanch|ist
re|veal
re|veal|able
re|veal|ing
re|veille
revel (as v.,
 rev'elled,
 rev'el|ling)
rev|ela'tion
rev|el'ler
rev|elry
re|ven|ant
re|ven'dica'tion
re|venge (as v.,
 re|ven'ging)
re|venge|ful
rev|enue
re've|ver'ber|ant
re've|ver'ber|ate
 (re've|ver'ber|
                at'ing)
re've|ver'bera'tion
re've|ver'ber|at'ive
re've|ver'ber|ator

re've|ver'ber|at|ory
 (pl. re've|ver'ber|at|
                or'ies)
re|vere
 (re|ver'ing)
rev'er|ence (as v.,
 rev'er|en'cing)
rev'er|end
rev'er|ent
rev'er|en'tial
rev'er|en'tially
rev|erie
re|vers (pl. same)
re|versal
re|verse (as v.,
 re|vers'ing)
re|vers'ib'il'ity
re|vers|ible
re|vers|ibly
re|ver|sion
re|ver|sional
re|ver|sion'ary
re|ver|sioner
re|vert
re|verter
re|vert|ible
re|vet (re|vet'ted,
 re|vet'ting)
re|vet|ment
re|victual
 (re|victualled,
 re|victual|ling)
re|view
re|view|able
re|viewal
re|viewer
re|vile (re|vil'ing)
re|vile|ment
re|vis'able
re|visal
re|vise (re|vis'ing)
re|vi'sion
re|vi'sion|ism
re|vi'sion|ist
re|visit
re|vis'ory
re|vit'al|ize
 (re|vit'al|iz'ing)
re|viv'able
re|vival
re|viv'al|ism
re|viv'al|ist
re|vive
 (re|viv'ing)
re|viver
re|vivi|fica'tion

re|viv|ify
(re|vivi|fies,
re|vivi|fied,
re|vivi|fy|ing)
re|viv|is|cence
re|viv|is|cent
re|vivor (*Law*)
re|voc|able
re|voca|tion
re|voc|at|ory
re|voke
(re|vok|ing)
re|volt
re|volt|ing
re|volute
re|volu|tion
re|volu|tion|ary
(as *n., pl.* re|volu|
tion|ar|ies)
re|volu|tion|ism
re|volu|tion|ist
re|volu|tion|ize
(re|volu|tion|iz|
ing)
re|volve
(re|volv|ing)
re|volver
re|vue
re|vul|sion
re|vuls|ive
re|ward
re|ward|ing
re|ward|less
re|wind
(re|wound)
re|wire
(re|wir|ing)
re|word
re|write (as *v.,*
re|wrote,
re|writ|ten,
re|writ|ing)
Rex (king)
Rex|ine (*propr.*)
Rey|kja|vik
Rey|nard
Reyn|olds
rhab|do|mancy
Rha|da|manth|
ine
Rha|da|manthus
Rhae|tian
Rhaetic
rhaps|ode
rhaps|odic
rhaps|od|ical

rhaps|od|ist
rhaps|od|ize
(rhaps|od|iz|ing)
rhaps|ody (*pl.*
rhaps|od|ies)
rhat|any
rhea
Rhem|ish (of
Reims)
Rhen|ish (of the
Rhine)
rhe|nium
rhe|olo|gical
rhe|olo|gist
rhe|ology
rheo|stat
rheo|tropic
rheo|trop|ism
rhesus
rhetor
rhet|oric
rhet|or|ical
rhet|or|ic|ally
rhet|or|ician
rheum|atic
rheum|at|ic|ally
rheum|at|icky
rheum|at|ism
rheum|at|oid
rheum|ato|
lo|gical
rheum|ato|lo|gist
rheum|ato|logy
rhinal
Rhine
Rhine|land
rhine|stone
rhin|itis
rhino (*pl.* rhi|nos)
rhi|no|ceros
rhi|no|cer|otic
rhi|no|
pharyn|geal
rhi|no|plas|tic
rhi|no|plasty
rhi|no|scope
rhi|zo|carp
rhiz|oid
rhiz|ome
rhi|zo|pod
rho (Gr. letter)
rhod|am|ine
Rhode (Island)
Rhodes
Rho|dian
rho|dium

rho|do|chros|ite
rho|do|den|dron
rhod|op|sin
rhod|ora
rhom|bic
rhom|bo|hedral
rhom|bo|hed|ron
(*pl.*
rhom|bo|hedra)
rhomb|oid
rhomb|oidal
rhomb|oid|ally
rhom|boid|eus
(*pl.* rhom|boidei)
rhom|bus (*pl.*
rhom|buses)
Rhône
rhu|barb
rhumba *use*
rumba
rhumb-line
rhyme (as *v.,*
rhym|ing)
rhyme|ster
rhym|ist
rhy|ol|ite
rhythm
rhyth|mic
rhyth|mical
rhythm|ist
ria
Ri|alto
ri|ant
rib (as *v.,* ribbed,
rib|bing)
rib|ald
rib|aldry
rib|and
ribbed
rib|bing
rib|bon
rib-cage
rib|less
ri|bo|flavin
ri|bo|nuc|leic
rib|ose
ri|bo|somal
ri|bo|some
rib|wort
rice-bowl
rice-paper
ri|cer|car
Rich|ard
Riche|lieu
richen
riches

Richter (scale)
rick|eti|ness
rick|ets
rick|ett|sia (*pl.*
rick|ett|siae)
rick|ett|sial
rick|ety
rickey
rick|shaw
ri|co|chet (as *v.,*
ri|co|cheted,
ri|co|chet|ing)
ric|rac
ric|tal
ric|tus
rid (rid, rid|ding)
rid|able
rid|dance
riddle (as *v.,*
rid|dling)
rid|dling
ride (as *v.,* rode,
rid|den, rid|ing)
rider
rider|less
ridge (as *v.,*
ridging)
ridge|way
ridgy (ridgier,
ridgi|est)
ri|di|cule (as *v.,*
ri|di|cul|ing)
ri|dicu|lous
rid|ing
Ries|ling
riffle (as *v.,*
riff|ling)
riff-raff
rifle (as *v.,* rif|ling)
rifle|man (*pl.*
rifle|men)
rifle|scope
rifle-shot
rif|ling
rifty (rif|tier,
rif|ti|est)
rig (as *v.,* rigged,
rig|ging)
Riga
ri|ga|doon
rig|ger
rig|ging
right|able
right-angled
righten
right|eous

right|ful
right|fully
right-hand a.
right-handed
right-hander
right|ish
right|ism
right|ist
right|most
righto
right|ward
right|wards
right-wing a.
right-winger
ri|gid
ri|gid|ify
 (ri|gidi|fies,
 ri|gidi|fied,
 ri|gid|fy|ing)
ri|gid|ity (pl.
 ri|gid|it|ies)
rig|mar|ole
Ri|go|letto
rigor (*Path.*)
rig|or|ism
rig|or|ist
rigor mor|tis
rig|or|ous
rig|our (severity)
rig-out n.
Rig-Veda
Rijks|mu|seum
rile (ril|ing)
Ri|ley (life of)
ri|li|evo (pl.
 ri|li|evi)
Rilke
rill (small stream)
rille (valley on
 moon)
ril|let
rim (as v.,
 rimmed,
 rim|ming)
rime (as v.,
 rim|ing)
Rim|mon
rim|ose
rim|ous
Rimsky-
 Korsakov
rimu
rimy (ri|mier,
 ri|mi|est)
rin|der|pest
ring (encircle etc.,
 ringed)

ring (to sound,
 rang, rung)
ring-cut (ring-cut,
 ring-cutting)
Ring des
 Nib|el|ungen
rin|gent
ringer
ring|hals
ring|leader
ring|let
ring|leted
ring|lety
ring-lock
ring|mas|ter
ring|side a.
ring|ster
ring|tail
ring-tailed
ring-wall
ring|worm
rinse (as v.,
 rins|ing)
Rio de Ja|neiro
Rio Grande
riot
ri|ot|ous
rip (as v., ripped,
 rip|ping)
ri|par|ian
rip-cord
ripe (riper, ripest)
ripen
ri|pi|eno (pl.
 ri|pi|enos)
rip-off n.
ri|poste (as v.,
 ri|post|ing)
rip|per
ripple (as v.,
 rip|pling)
rip|plet
rip|ply (rip|plier,
 rip|pli|est)
rip-roaring
rip-saw
rip-tide
Ri|pu|arian
Rip van Winkle
rise (as v., rose,
 risen, ris|ing)
riser
ri|shi
ris|ib|il|ity
ris|ible
ris|ing

risk|ily
riski|ness
risky (ris|kier,
 ris|ki|est)
Ri|sor|gi|mento
ris|otto (pl.
 ris|ot|tos)
risqué
ris|sole
ri|tard|ando (pl.
 ri|tard|andos)
ri|ten|uto (pl.
 ri|ten|utos)
ritornello (pl.
 ritornellos)
rit|ual
ritu|al|ism
ritu|al|ist
ritu|al|istic
ritu|al|ize
 (ritu|al|iz|ing)
ritu|ally
ritzy (rit|zier,
 rit|zi|est)
riv|age
ri|val (as v.,
 ri|valled,
 ri|val|ling)
ri|valry (pl.
 ri|val|ries)
rive (rived, riven,
 riv|ing)
river
riv|er|ain
rivered
river-head
riv|er|ine
riv|er|less
riv|er|side
rivet (as v.,
 riv|eted,
 riv|et|ing)
ri|vi|era
Ri|vi|era
ri|vi|ère (necklace)
rivu|let
Riy|adh
roach (fish, pl.
 same)
road-block
road-hog
roadie
road|less
road|man (pl.
 road|men)
road-map

road|run'ner
road|side
road|stead
road|ster
road|way
road-works
road|wor|thi|ness
road|wor|thy
roar|ing
roaster
rob (robbed,
 rob|bing)
rob|ber
rob|bery (pl.
 rob|ber|ies)
robe (as v.,
 rob|ing)
Rob|ert
Robes|pierre
robin
ro|binia
Ro|bin|son
 Cru|soe
ro|bor|ant
ro|bot
ro|bust
 (ro|buster,
 ro|bust|est)
ro|bus|tious
roc (myth. bird)
ro|caille
roc|am|bole
Roch|dale
Ro|ches|ter
rochet
rock-bed
rock-bottom
rock-cake
rocker
rock|ery (pl.
 rock|er|ies)
rocket (as v.,
 rock|eted,
 rock|et|ing)
rock|et|eer
rock|etry
Rock|ies
rock|ily
rocki|ness
rocking-chair
rocking-horse
rock|less
rock|let
rock|like
rock|ling

rocky (rock|ier,
  rocki|est)
ro|coco (pl.
  ro|co|cos)
ro|dent
ro|den|tial
ro|den|ti|cide
ro|deo (pl.
  ro|deos)
Rodin
rod|less
rod|let
rod|like
ro|do|mont|ade
  (as v.,
  ro|do|mont|
        ad|ing)
roe|buck
roe-deer
roent|gen (unit)
roent|geno|
      graphy
roent|geno|logy
roe-stone
roga|tion
roga|tional
roger (signal etc.)
Roger (name)
rogue (as v.,
  rogued, roguing)
roguery (pl.
  roguer|ies)
roguish
rois|ter
rois|terer
Ro|land
role
roll|able
roll-bar
roll-call
roller
roller-coaster
roller-skate
rol|lick
roll|ing
rolling-pin
rolling-stock
roll|mop
roll-neck
roll-on n. & a.
roll-top
roly-poly (as n., pl.
  roly-polies)
Rom (male gypsy;
  pl. Roma)
Ro|maic

ro|maine
ro|maji
ro|man (type)
Ro|man
roman-à-clef (pl.
  romans-à-clef)
ro|mance (as v.,
  ro|man|cing)
Ro|mance
  (languages)
ro|man|cer
Ro|manes
Ro|man|esque
roman-fleuve (pl.
  romans-fleuves)
Ro|mania
Ro|ma|nian
Ro|manic
Ro|man|ish
Ro|man|ism
Ro|man|ist
ro|man|iza|tion
ro|man|ize
  (ro|man|iz|ing)
Ro|mansh
ro|man|tic
ro|man|tic|ally
ro|man|ti|cism
ro|man|ti|cist
ro|man|ti|cize
  (ro|man|ti|ciz|
        ing)
Ro|many
Rome
Ro|meo (pl.
  Ro|meos)
Rom|ish
rom|neya
romper
rompy (romp|ier,
  rom|pi|est)
ron|deau (pl.
  ron|deaux)
ron|del
rondo (pl.
  ron|dos)
ro|neo v.
  (ro|neoes,
  ro|neoed,
  ro|neo|ing)
Ro|neo n. (pl.
  Ro|neos)
rong|geng
ronin
röntgen (unit) use
  roentgen

Rönt|gen
Rönt|gen (rays)
rood (crucifix)
rood-screen
roof|age
roofer
roof|ing
roof-rack
roof-top
rooi|nek
rook|ery (pl.
  rook|er|ies)
rookie n.
rook|let
rook|ling
roomer
room|ette
room|ful (pl.
  room|fuls)
room|ily
roomi|ness
rooming-house
room-mate
roomy (room|ier,
  roomi|est)
Roose|velt
rooster
root|age
rootle (root|ling)
root|less
root|let
root-stock
rooty (root|ier,
  rooti|est)
rope (as v.,
  rop|ing)
rope|able
rope|man|ship
rope-walk
rope|way
ro|pi|ness
rop|ing
ropy (ro|pier,
  ro|pi|est)
Roque|fort
ro|que|laure
ro|quet (as v.,
  ro|queted,
  ro|quet|ing)
ror|qual
Rorschach (test)
rorty (ror|tier,
  ror|ti|est)
ros|ace
ros|aceous
ros|an|il|ine

ros|ar|ian
ros|ar|ium
ros|ary (beads etc.;
  pl. ro|sar|ies)
Ros|cian
Ros|com|mon
rose (as v.,
  ros|ing)
rosé
ros|eate
Ro|seau
rose-bowl
rose-bud
rose-bush
rose-hip
rose-leaf
  (pl. rose-leaves)
rose|like
ro|sella
rose|mary
Ros|en|ka|va|lier
ros|eola
ros|eo|lar
ros|eol|ous
rose-red
rosery (rose-
  garden; pl.
  roser|ies)
ros|ette
ros|et|ted
rose-water
rosewood
Rosh Hash|anah
Ro|si|cru|cian
Ro|si|cru|cian|
        ism
ros|ily
rosin
Ros|in|ante
rosi|ness
ros|iny
ro|solio (pl.
  ro|solios)
Ros|sini
ros|ter
rost|ral
rost|rate
rost|rated
rost|ri|fer|ous
rost|ri|form
rost|rum (pl.
  rostra)
rosy (ro|sier,
  ro|si|est)
rot (rot|ted,
  rot|ting)

rota
Ro|tar|ian
ro|tary (as *n., pl.*
  ro|tar|ies)
Ro|tary (society)
ro|tat|able
ro|tate (as *v.*,
  ro|tat|ing)
ro|ta|tion
ro|ta|tional
ro|tat|ive
ro|tator
ro|tat|ory
ro|ta|vate
  (ro|ta|vat|ing)
Ro|ta|vator
  (*propr.*)
rotche (auk)
rot-gut
Roth|er|ham
Rothe|say
Roths|child
ro|ti|fer
ro|tis|serie
ro|to|grav|ure
ro|tor
rot-proof
rot|ten (rot|tener,
  rot|ten|est)
rotten-stone
rot|ter
Rot|ter|dam
Rott|weiler
ro|tund
ro|tunda
ro|tund|ity
ro|tur|ier
rouble
rou|cou
roué
Rouen
rouge (as *v.*,
  rou|ging)
rough|age
rough-and-ready
rough-and-
            tumble
rough|cast (as *v.*,
  rough|cast)
roughen
rough|ish
rough|neck
rough|shod
roul|ade
roul|eau (*pl.*
  roul|eaux)

roul|ette
roul|et|ted
round|about
  n. & a.
roun|ded
roundel
round|elay
rounder
round|ers
Round|head
  (*hist.*)
round|ish
roundly
rounds|man (*pl.*
  rounds|men)
round-up *n.*
round|worm
rouse (rous|ing)
rous|ing
Rous|seau
Rous|sil|lon
roust|about
route (as *v.*,
  routed,
  route|ing)
router
rou|tine
rou|tin|ism
rou|tin|ist
roux (*pl.* same)
rove (as *v.*,
  rov|ing)
rover
rowan
row-boat
row|di|ness
rowdy (row|dier,
  row|di|est)
row|dy|ism
rowel (as *v.*,
  row|elled,
  row|el|ling)
rowing-boat
row|lock
Rowton (house)
royal
roy|al|ism
roy|al|ist
roy|al|istic
roy|ally
roy|alty (*pl.*
  roy|al|ties)
Roy|ston
roz|zer
rub (as *v.*, rubbed,
  rub|bing)

rub-a-dub
  (rub-a-dubbed,
  rub-a-dubbing)
Ru|bá|iyát of
  Omar Khay|yám
ru|bato (*pl.*
  ru|ba|tos)
rub|ber
rub|ber|ize
  (rub|ber|iz|ing)
rubber-neck
rubber-stamp *v.*
rub|bery
rub|bing
rub|bish
rub|bishy
rubble
rub|bly
ru|be|fa|cient
ru|be|fac|tion
ru|befy
  (ru|be|fies,
  ru|be|fied,
  ru|be|fy|ing)
ru|bella
ru|bel|lite
Ru|bens
ru|beola
ru|bi|con (*Cards*)
Ru|bi|con
  (crossing)
rubi|cund
rubi|cund|ity
ru|bid|ium
ru|bi|gin|ous
ru|bi|ous
rub|ric
rub|rical
rub|ric|ate
  (rub|ric|at|ing)
rub|rica|tion
rub|ric|ator
rub|ri|cian
rub|ri|cism
rub|ri|cist
ruby (as *n., pl.*
  ru|bies; as *v.*,
  ru|bies, ru|bied,
  ru|by|ing)
ruche (frill)
ruched
ruch|ing
ruckle (ruck|ling)
ruck|sack
ruckus
ruc|tion

rud|beckia
rudd (fish; *pl.*
  same)
rud|der
rud|der|less
Rud|di|gore
rud|dily
rud|di|ness
ruddle (as *v.*,
  rud|dling)
rud|dock
ruddy (as *a.*,
  rud|dier,
  rud|di|est; as *v.*,
  rud|dies,
  rud|died,
  rud|dy|ing)
rude (ruder,
  rudest)
rudery (*pl.*
  ruder|ies)
Rüd|es|heimer
ru|di|ment
ru|di|ment|ary
rud|ish
rue (as *v.*, ru|ing)
rue|ful
rue|fully
ruf|es|cence
ruf|es|cent
ruff (frill, bird)
ruf|fian
ruf|fi|an|ism
ruf|fi|anly
ruffle (as *v.*,
  ruff|ling)
ruf|ous
Rug|beian
Rugby
rug|ged
rug|ger
rug|ose
ru|gos|ity
ruin (as *v.*,
  ru|ined,
  ru|in|ing)
ru|ina|tion
ru|in|ous
Ruis|lip
rule (as *v.*, rul|ing)
ruler
ruler|ship
rul|ing
rum *a.* (rum|mer,
  rum|mest)

Rumanian *use*
 Romanian
rumba
rumble (as *v.*,
 rum|bling)
rum|bus|tious
ru|men
ru|min|ant
ru|min|ate
 (ru|min|at|ing)
ru|mina|tion
ru|min|at|ive
ru|min|ator
rum|mage (as *v.*,
 rum|ma|ging)
rum|mer
rummy (as *a.*,
 rum|m|ier,
 rum|mi|est)
ru|mour
rumple
 (rump|ling)
rum|pus
rumpy (*pl.*
 rum|pies)
run (as *v.*, ran,
 run, run|ning)
run|about *n.*
run-around *n.*

run|away *n.* & *a.*
run|cible
run|cin|ate
run|dale
run-down *n.* & *a.*
ru|nic
run-in *n.*
run|let
run|nable
run|nel
run|ner
runner-up (*pl.*
 runners-up)
run|ning
runny (run|nier,
 run|ni|est)
run-up *n.*
run|way
ru|pee
ru|piah
rup|ture (as *v.*,
 rup|tur|ing)
rural
rur|al|ity (*pl.*
 rur|al|it|ies)
rur|al|ize
 (rur|al|iz|ing)
rur|ally
ruri|dec|anal

Ru|ri|ta|nia
Ru|ri|ta|nian
rusa
rush-hour
rush|light
rush|like
rushy (rush|ier,
 rushi|est)
Rus|kin
Rus|sell
rus|set
rus|sety
Rus|sia
Rus|sian
Rus|si|fica|tion
Rus|sify
 (Rus|si|fies,
 Rus|si|fied,
 Rus|si|fy|ing)
Russki
Rus|so|phile
Rus|so|phobe
Rus|so|phobia
rus|tic
rus|tic|ally
rus|tic|ate
 (rus|tic|at|ing)
rus|tica|tion
rus|ti|city

rust|ily
rusti|ness
rustle (as *v.*,
 rust|ling)
rust|ler
rust|less
rust-proof
rustre
rusty (rus|tier,
 rus|ti|est)
rut (as *v.*, rut|ted,
 rut|ting)
ru|ta|baga
ruth|enium
Ruth|er|ford
ruth|er|fordium
Ru|thin
ruth|less
ru|tile
rut|tish
rutty (rut|tier,
 rut|ti|est)
Rwanda
rye-grass
ry|okan
ryot

S

Saar|land
sa'ba|dilla
Sa|baean (of anc.
 Yemen)
Sa'ba|ism
Sa'ba|oth
Sab'bat|arian
Sab'bat|ari'an|
    ism
sab|bath
sab|batic
sab'bat|ical
sab'bat'ic|ally
sab'bat|ize
 (sab'bat|iz|ing)
Sa'bel|lian
Sa'bian
sab'icu
Sab'ine
sable
sabled
sa'bly
sabot
sab'ot|age (as v.,
 sab'ot|aging)
sab|oted
sa'bot|eur
sabra
sabre (as v.,
 sab'ring)
sab're|tache
sab|reur
sac|cade
sac|cadic
sac|cate
sac'char|ide
sac'chari|meter
sac'chari|metry
sac'charin n.
sac'char|ine a.
sac'charo|genic
sac'charo|meter
sac'charo|metry
sac'char|ose
sac'ci|form
sac'cu|lar
sac'cu|late
sac'cu|la'tion
sac|cule

sa'cer|dot'age
sa'cer|dotal
sa'cer|dot'al|ism
sa'cer|dot'al|ist
sa'cer|dot'ally
sa'chem
sachet
sack|but
sack|cloth
sack|ful (pl.
 sack|fuls)
sack|ing
sac'ral
sac'ra|ment
sac'ra|mental
sac'ra|ment'al|
    ism
sac'ra|ment'al|ist
sac'ra|ment'al|ity
sac'ra'ment|ally
sac'ra|ment|arian
Sac'ra|mento
sac'rar|ium (pl.
 sac|raria)
sac|red
sac'ri|fice (as v.,
 sac'ri|fi'cing)
sac'ri|fi'cial
sac'ri|fi'cially
sac'ri|lege
sac'ri|le'gious
sac|rist
sac|ristan
sac|risty (pl.
 sac'rist|ies)
sac'ro|sanct
sac'ro|sanct|ity
sac'rum
sad (sad'der,
 sad|dest)
sad'den
sad|dish
saddle (as v.,
 sad|dling)
sad'dle|back
sad'dle|backed
saddle-bag
saddle-cloth
sad|dler

sad|dlery (pl.
 sad'dler|ies)
Sad'du|cean
Sad'du|cee
Sad'du|cee|ism
sadhu
sad'ism
sad'ist
sad|istic
sad'ist'ic|ally
sado-masochism
sado-masochist
sado-masochistic
saeter
sa'fari (pl.
 sa'fa'ris)
safe (as a., safer,
 safest)
safe|guard
safety (pl.
 safe|ties)
safety-belt
safety-catch
safety-glass
safety-pin
safety-valve
saf|flower
saf|fron
saf|frony
saf|ranin
sag (as v., sagged,
 sag|ging)
saga
sa'ga|cious
sa'ga|city
saga|more
sag'gar
saggy (sag|gier,
 sag'gi|est)
sag|itta
sa'git|tal
Sa'git|tarian
Sa'git|tarius
sa'git|tate
sago (pl. sa'gos)
sa|guaro (pl.
 sa|guaros)
sagy
Sa|hara
Sa|haran

sahib
saiga
sail-arm
sail|boat
sail|cloth
sailer (ship)
sailing-ship
sail|less
sailor (seaman)
sail'or|ing
sail'orly
sailor-man (pl.
 sailor-men)
sail|plane
sain|foin
St Alb'ans
St Ber|nard (dog)
St Chris'to|pher
saint|dom
Sainte-Beuve
St Elias
Saint-Gall
St George's
 (Cross, Day)
St Hel'ena
St Hel'ens
saint|hood
St Ives
St Kitts
St Law|rence
saint|like
saint'li|ness
saint|ling
St Louis
St Lu'cia
saintly (saint|lier,
 saint'li|est)
St Neot (in
 Cornwall)
St Neots (in
 Cambridgeshire)
Sain|tonge
saint|paulia
St Peter Port
Saint-Saëns
saint'ship
St Vin'cent
Sa'jama

sake (Jap. liquor; 2
 sylls.)
saker
sakeret
saki
sa|laam
salable *use*
 saleable
sa|la|cious
sa|la|city
salad
sala|mander
sa|la|man|drian
sa|la|man|drine
sa|la|man|droid
sa|lami
sal am'mo|niac
sal'an|gane
sa|lar|iat
sal'ary (as *n., pl.*
 sal|ar'ies)
sal|ar'ied
sale|ab'il|ity
sale|able
salep
sale-room
sales|girl
Sa|lesian
sales|lady (*pl.*
 sales|la'dies)
sales|man (*pl.*
 sales|men)
sales'man|ship
sales|per'son
sales|wo'man (*pl.*
 sales|wo'men)
Sal|ford
Sa|lian
Salic (law)
sali|cet
sali|cin
sa|li|cional
sa|li'cyl|ate
sa|li'cylic
sa|li|ence
sa|li|ency
sa|li|ent
sa|li|en'tian
sa|li'fer|ous
sa|lina
sa|line
sa|lin|ity
sa|lino|meter
Salis|bury
sa|liva
sa|liv|ary

sal'iv|ate
 (sal'iv|at'ing)
sal'iva|tion
sal|lee
sal|len|ders
sal|let
sal|low
sal|low|ish
sal|lowy
sally (as *n., pl.*
 sal|lies; as *v.,*
 sal|lies, sal|lied,
 sal'ly|ing)
Sally
sally-hole
Sally Lunn
sally-port
sal'ma|gundi
salmi
sal'mon
sal'mon|ella
sal'mon|el|losis
sal'mon|oid
salon
Salon (exhibition)
sa|loon
Sa'lo|pian
sal'pi|glos'sis
sal'ping|ec'tomy
 (*pl.* sal'ping|
 ec'tom|ies)
sal'ping|itis
sal|sify
sal'tar|ello (*pl.*
 sal'tar|el'los)
sal'ta|tion
salt'at|orial
salt'at|ory
salt|bush
salt-cat
salt-cellar
salter
salt|ern
sal'ti|grade
sal'ti|ness
salt|ing
sal|tire
salt|ish
Salt Lake City
salt|less
salt-lick
salt-marsh
salt-mine
salt-pan
salt'petre
sal'tus

salt-water *a.*
salt-works
salt|wort
salty (sal|tier,
 sal'ti|est)
sa|lu|bri'ous
sa|lu|brity
sa|luki
sal'ut|ar'ily
sal'ut|ary
sa|lu'ta|tion
sa|lu'ta|tional
sa|lut|at'ory
sa|lute (as *v.,*
 sa|lut'ing)
salv|able
sal|vage (as *v.,*
 sal|va'ging)
sal'vage|able
sal|va|tion
sal'va|tion|ism
sal'va|tion|ist
salve (as *v.,*
 salv|ing)
salver (tray)
sal|via
salvo (of guns etc.,
 pl. salvoes)
salvo (excuse etc.,
 pl. salvos)
sal vo'la|tile
salvor (one who
 salvages)
Sal|ween
Salz|burg
sa|madhi
sam'ara
Sa'mar|itan
Sa'mar'it|an'ism
sa'mar|ium
Sam'ar|kand
samba
sambo (half-breed;
 pl. sam'bos)
Sambo (*derog.,*
 Negro; *pl.*
 Sam'bos)
Sam Browne
sam'bur
samel
samfu
Sa'mian
sam|isen
sam|ite
sam'iz|dat
sam'let

Sam|nite
Sa'moa
Sa'moan
Sa'mos
samo|var
Sam|oyed
Sam'oy|edic
sam|pan
sam|phire
sample (as *v.,*
 sam|pling)
sam|pler
Sam|son
Samuel
sam|urai (*pl.*
 same)
Sa'na'a
san'at|ive
san|at|orium
san'at|ory
 (healing)
⚠ sanitary
san|ben'ito (*pl.*
 san|ben'itos)
sanc'ti|fica|tion
sanc'ti|fier
sanc|tify
 (sanc'ti|fies,
 sanc'ti|fied,
 sanc'ti|fy'ing)
sanc'ti|mo'ni|ous
sanc'ti|mony
sanc|tion
sanc|tity
sanc'tu|ary (*pl.*
 sanc'tu|ar'ies)
sanc|tum (*pl.*
 sanc|tums)
sanc|tus
san|dal
san|dalled
san|dal'wood
san|darac
sand|bag (as *v.,*
 sand|bagged,
 sand|bag|ging)
sand|bank
sand-bar
sand-bath
sand-bed
sand-blast
sand-box
sand|boy
sand-castle
sand-dune
sander

san|der|ling
sanders
sand-fly (*pl.*
 sand-flies)
san|dhi
sand-hill
sand-hopper
San Diego
sandi|ness
san|di|ver
sand|man
sand|pa|per
sand|piper
sand-pit
sand|stone
sand|storm
sand|wich
sand|wort
sandy (san|dier,
 san|di|est)
Sandy (Scotsman)
san|dy|ish
sane (saner,
 sanest)
San Fran|cisco
san|gar
san|garee
sang-de-bœuf
sang-froid
san|grail
san|gría
san|gui|fica|tion
san|guin|ar|ily
san|guin|ari|ness
san|guin|ary
san|guine
san|guin|eous
San|hed|rin
san|icle
sa|nies (*pl.* same)
san|ify (sani|fies,
 sani|fied,
 sani|fy|ing)
sa|ni|ous
san|it|arian
san|it|ar|ily
san|it|ari|ness
sanitarium *use*
 sanatorium
san|it|ary (healthy
 etc.) △ sanatory
san|it|ate
 (san|it|at|ing)
san|ita|tion
san|it|ize
 (san|it|iz|ing)

san|ity
San José
San Ma|rino
san|nyasi
San Sal|va|dor
sans|cu|lotte
san|serif
Sans|krit
Sans|kritic
Sans|krit|ist
Santa Claus
Santa Fe
San|tan|der
San|ti|ago
Santo Dom|ingo
san|to|lina
san|ton|ica
san|tonin
São Fran|cisco
São Paulo
São Tomé
sap (as *v.*, sapped,
 sap|ping)
sapa|jou
sapan
sa|pele
sap|ful
sap-green
sapid
sa|pid|ity
sapi|ence
sapi|ent
sa|pi|en|tial
sap|less
sap|ling
sa|po|dilla
sa|po|na|ceous
sa|poni|fi|able
sa|poni|fica|tion
sa|pon|ify
 (sa|poni|fies,
 sa|poni|fied,
 sa|poni|fy|ing)
sap|onin
sapor
sap|per
sap|phic (metre)
Sap|phic (of
 Sappho)
sap|phire
sap|phir|ine
Sap|phism
Sap|pho
sappy (sap|pier,
 sap|pi|est)
sap|ro|genic

sap|ro|phagous
sap|ro|phile
sap|ro|phyte
sap|ro|phytic
sap|wood
Sara
sara|band
Sara|cen
Sa|ra|cenic
Sar|ah
Sa|ra|jevo
sa|rangi
sar|casm
sar|castic
sar|cast|ic|ally
sar|celle
sar|coma (*pl.*
 sar|co|mata)
sar|co|mat|osis
sar|co|mat|ous
sar|co|phagus (*pl.*
 sar|co|phagi)
sar|co|plasm
sar|cous
Sar|da|na|pa|lian
Sar|da|nap|alus
sar|delle
sar|dine
Sar|dinia
Sar|din|ian
sar|dius
sar|donic
sar|don|ic|ally
sard|onyx
sar|gasso (*pl.*
 sar|gas|sos)
sari
sark|ing
Sar|ma|tian
sar|ment|ose
sar|ment|ous
sa|rong
saros
sar|ruso|phone
sar|sa|par|illa
sar|sen
sar|senet
sar|tor|ial
sar|tor|ius
Sar|tre
Sarum
sashay
sash-cord
sash|imi
sash-window
sasin (antelope)

sas|ine (*Sc. Law*)
Sas|katch|ewan
sas|quatch
sas|saby (*pl.*
 sas|sa|bies)
sas|sa|fras
Sas|sa|nian
Sas|sanid
Sas|sen|ach
sass|ily
sassi|ness
sassy (sas|sier,
 sas|si|est)
sas|trugi
Satan
sa|tanic
sa|tan|ic|ally
Sa|tan|ism
Sa|tan|ist
Sa|tan|ize
 (Sa|tan|iz|ing)
Sa|tano|logy
satchel
sate (sat|ing)
sat|een
sate|less
sat|el|lite
sat|el|litic
sa|tiate
 (sa|ti|at|ing)
sa|ti|ation
Satie
sa|ti|ety
satin
sat|inet
sat|in|wood
sat|iny
sat|ire
sa|tiric
sa|tir|ical
sa|tir|ic|ally
sat|ir|ist
sat|ir|ize
 (sat|ir|iz|ing)
sat|is|fac|tion
sat|is|fact|or|ily
sat|is|fact|ori|
 ness
sat|is|fact|ory
sat|is|fi|able
sat|isfy
 (sat|is|fies,
 sat|is|fied,
 sat|is|fy|ing)
sa|tori
sat|rangi

sat|rap
sat|rapy (*pl.*
  sat|rap|ies)
sat|suma (orange)
Sat|suma (pottery)
sat|ur|able
sat|ur|ant
sat|ur|ate
  (sat|ur|at|ing)
sat|ura|tion
Sat|ur|day
Sat|urn
sat|ur|na|lia
  (revelry)
Sat|ur|na|lia
  (festival)
sat|ur|na|lian
Sat|ur|nian
sat|urnic
sat|ur|nine
sat|urn|ism
sat|ya|graha
satyr
sa|tyri|asis (*pl.*
  sa|tyri|ases)
sa|tyric
satyrid
sauce (as *v.*,
  sau|cing)
sauce-boat
saucebox
sauce|pan
sau|cer
sau|cer|ful (*pl.*
  sau|cer|fuls)
sau|cily
sau|ci|ness
saucy (sau|cier,
  sau|ci|est)
Saudi
Saudi Ara|bia
sauer|kraut
sau|ger
Sau|mur
sauna
saun|ter
saur|ian
saury (*pl.*
  saur|ies)
saus|age
sauté (as *v.*,
  sautéd)
Sau|ternes
sav|able
sav|age (as *v.*,
  sav|aging)

sav|age|dom
sav|agery (*pl.*
  sav|age|ries)
sa|van|nah
sav|ant (*fem.*
  sav|ante)
sa|vate
save (as *v.*,
  sav|ing)
save-all
sav|eloy
saver
savin
sav|ing
sa|viour
savoir-faire
Sa|von|ar|ola
sa|vory (herb)
sa|vour
sa|vour|ily
sa|vouri|ness
sa|voury (as *n.*, *pl.*
  sa|vour|ies)
sa|voy (cabbage)
Sa|voy (region)
Sa|voy|ard
savvy (as *v.*,
  sav|vies,
  sav|vied,
  sav|vy|ing)
saw (as *v.*, sawn)
saw-bill
saw|bones
saw|buck
saw|der
saw-doctor
saw|dust
saw-edged
saw|fish
saw|mill
Saw|ney
saw|tooth
saw|toothed
saw|yer
sax|at|ile
sax|board
saxe (blue)
sax|horn
saxi|col|ine
saxi|col|ous
saxi|frage
Saxon
saxony (wool etc.)
Sax|ony
saxo|phone
saxo|phon|ist

sax|tuba
say (as *v.*, said)
say|ing
say-so
scab (as *v.*,
  scabbed,
  scab|bing)
scab|bard
scabby
  (scab|bier,
  scab|bi|est)
sca|bies
sca|bi|ous
scab|rous
Sca Fell
Sca|fell Pike
scaf|fold
scaf|folder
scaf|fold|ing
scagli|ola
scal|able
scalar
scal|ari|form
scalder
scald-head
scale (as *v.*,
  scal|ing)
sca|lene
sca|lenus (*pl.*
  sca|leni)
scale-pan
scaler
scal|lion
scal|lop
scal|lop|ing
scal|ly|wag
scal|pel
scalper
scal|pri|form
scaly (sca|lier,
  sca|li|est)
scam|mony
scamper
scampi
scamp|ish
scan (as *v.*,
  scanned,
  scan|ning)
scan|dal
scan|dal|ize
  (scan|dal|iz|ing)
scan|dal|monger
scan|dal|ous
Scan|din|avia
Scan|din|avian
scan|dium

scan|ner
scan|sion
scan|sorial
scant|ies
scant|ily
scanti|ness
scant|ling
scanty (scan|tier,
  scan|ti|est)
scape|goat
scape|grace
scaph|oid
scap|ula (*pl.*
  scapu|lae)
scapu|lar
scapu|lary
scar (as *v.*,
  scarred,
  scar|ring)
scarab
sca|ra|baeid
Scar|bor|ough
scarce (scar|cer,
  scar|cest)
scarcely
scar|city
scare (as *v.*,
  scar|ing)
scare|crow
scare|mon|ger
scarf (as *n.*, *pl.*
  scarves)
scari|fica|tion
scari|fic|ator
scari|fier
scar|ify
  (scari|fies,
  scari|fied,
  scari|fy|ing)
scar|ious
scar|lat|ina
Scar|latti
scar|let
scar|oid
scarper
scarus
scary (scar|ier,
  scari|est)
scat (as *v.*,
  scat|ted,
  scat|ting)
scathe (scath|ing)
scathe|less
scato|lo|gical
scato|logy
sca|to|phag|ous

scat|ter
scatter-brain
scatter-brained
scat|tily
scat|ti|ness
scatty (scat|tier,
  scat|ti|est)
scav|enge
  (scav|en|ging)
scav|en|ger
scav|engery
scazon
scena (*Mus.*)
scen|ario (*pl.*
  scen|arios)
scen|ar|ist
scenery
scenic
scen|ic|ally
scen|ted
scent|less
scep|sis
scep|tic
scep|tical
scep|tic|ally
scep|ti|cism
sceptre
sceptred
schad|en|freude
Schaff|hausen
sched|ule (as *v.*,
  sched|ul|ing)
scheel|ite
Sche'her|az'ade
Schel|ling
schema (*pl.*
  sche|mata)
schem|atic
schem'at|ic|ally
schem'at|ism
schem'at|iza|tion
schem'at|ize
  (schem'at|iz|ing)
scheme (as *v.*,
  schem'ing)
scherz|ando (*pl.*
  scherz|an'dos)
scherzo (*pl.*
  scherzos)
Schie|dam
Schil|ler
schil|ling
  (Austrian coin)
schip|perke
schism
schis|matic

schis'mat|ical
schis'mat|ic|ally
schis'mat|ize
  (schis'mat|iz|ing)
schist|ose
schis|to|some
schis'to|so'mi|asis
  (*pl.* schis'to|
    so'mi|ases)
schiz|an'thus
schizo (*pl.*
  schizos)
schizo|carp
schiz|oid
schizo|my'cete
schizo|phre'nia
schizo|phrenic
schizo|thy'mia
schizo|thy'mic
Schle|gel
schle|miel
Schleswig-
           Holstein
schlieren
schmaltz
schmaltzy
  (schmalt|zier,
  schmalt'zi|est)
schnapps
schnauzer
schnit|zel
schnorkel *use*
  snorkel
schnor|rer
Schoen|berg
scholar
schol|arly
schol'ar|ship
schol|astic
schol'ast|ic|ally
schol|as'ti|cism
scho|li|ast
scho|li|astic
scho|lium (*pl.*
  scho|lia)
school|able
school|boy
school|child (*pl.*
  school|chil'dren)
school-days
school|fel'low
school|girl
school|house
school|ing
school|man (*pl.*
  school|men)

school|mas'ter
school|mas'ter|
           ing
school|mate
school|mis'tress
school|mis'tressy
school|room
school|teacher
schooner
Schop'en|hauer
schot|tische
Schröd|inger
Schu|bert
Schu|mann
schwa
Schweit'zer
Schwyz
scia|gram
scia|graph
scia|graphic
scia|graphy
scia|machy
sci|atic
sci|at|ica
sci|at|ic|ally
sci|ence
sci|en'ter
sci|en|tial
sci|ent|if'ic
sci|en'tif|ic|ally
sci|ent|ism
sci|ent|ist
sci|ent|istic
sci|ento|lo'gist
sci|ento|logy
sci-fi
sci|li'cet
scilla
Scil|lo'nian
Scilly, Isles of
scim|itar
scin'ti|graphy
scin|tilla
scin'til|lant
scin'til|late
  (scin'til|lat'ing)
scin'til|la'tion
sci|ol|ism
sci|ol|ist
sci|ol|istic
scion
scir|rhoid
scir|rhos|ity
scir|rhous
scir|rhus (*pl.*
  scir|rhi)

scis|sel
scis|sile
scis|sion
scis|sor
scis|sors
scis|sor|wise
sci'ur|ine
sci'ur|oid
sclera
scler|en|chyma
scler|itis
scler|oid
scler|oma (*pl.*
  scler|omata)
sclero|meter
sclero|phyll
sclero|phyte
scler|osed
scler|osis (*pl.*
  scler|oses)
scler|otic
scler|ot|itis
sclero|tomy (*pl.*
  sclero|tom|ies)
scler|ous
scold|ing
sco|lex (*pl.*
  sco|leces)
sco|li|osis (*pl.*
  sco|li|oses)
sco|li|otic
scollop *use*
  scallop
sco|lo|pen|drium
scom|ber
scom|brid
scom|broid
sconce (as *v.*,
  scon|cing)
scooper
scooter
scoot'er|ist
scopa (*pl.*
  sco|pae)
sco|pol|am|ine
scop|ula (*pl.*
  scopu|lae)
scor|bu'tic
scor'bu'tic|ally
scorcher
score (as *v.*,
  scor'ing)
score-board
score-book
score-card
scorer

score-sheet
scoria (*pl.*
  scor|iae)
scori|aceous
scori|fica|tion
scori|fier
scor|ify
  (scori|fies,
  scori|fied,
  scori|fy|ing)
scorn|ful
scorn|fully
scorper
Scor|pian
Scor|pio (*pl.*
  Scor|pios)
scor'pi|oid
scor|pion
scorz'on|era
scoter
scot-free
sco'tia
Scot|ism
Scot|ist
Scot|land
sco'to|dinia
scot|oma (*pl.*
  scot|omata)
Scots|man (*pl.*
  Scots|men)
Scots|wo'man (*pl.*
  Scots|wo'men)
scot|tice
Scot'ti|cism
Scot|tie
Scot|tish
scoun|drel
scoun'drelly
scourer
scourge (as *v.*,
  scour|ging)
scouse
Scout (boy)
Scouter
scout|mas'ter
scrabble
  (scrab|bling)
Scrabble (game,
  propr.)
scrag (as *v.*,
  scragged,
  scrag|ging)
scrag'gi|ness
scraggy
  (scrag|gier,
  scrag'gi|est)

scram
  (scrammed,
  scram|ming)
scramble (as *v.*,
  scram|bling)
scrambler
scrap (as *v.*,
  scrapped,
  scrap|ping)
scrap-book
scrape (as *v.*,
  scrap'ing)
scraper
scraper|board
scra|pie
scrap'ing
scrap|pily
scrap'pi|ness
scrappy
  (scrap|pier,
  scrap'pi|est)
scrap-yard
scratch|board
scratch|ily
scratchi|ness
scratchy
  (scratch|ier,
  scratchi|est)
scrawny
  (scraw|nier,
  scraw'ni|est)
screamer
screech-owl
screechy
  (screechi|er,
  screechi|est)
screen|ing
screen|play
screen-print *v.*
screw|ball
screw-cap
screw|driver
screw-top
screwy
  (screw|ier,
  screwi|est)
scribal
scribble (as *v.*,
  scrib|bling)
scrib|bler
scrib|bly
scribe (as *v.*,
  scrib'ing)
scriber
scrim|mage (as *v.*,
  scrim|ma'ging)

scrimpy
  (scrim|pier,
  scrim'pi|est)
scrim|shank
scrim|shaw
scrip|torial
scrip|torium (*pl.*
  scrip|toria)
scrip|tural
scrip'tur|al|ism
scrip'tur|al|ist
scrip'tur|ally
scrip|ture
Scrip|tures (Bible)
scriv|ener
scro'bicu|late
scrof|ula
scrofu|lous
scroll-head
scroll|ing
scroll-lathe
scroll-saw
scroll-work
scro|tal
scrot|itis
scro'to|cele
scro|tum (*pl.*
  scrota)
scrounge
  (scroun|ging)
scrub (as *v.*,
  scrubbed,
  scrub|bing)
scrub|ber
scrubby
  (scrub|bier,
  scrub'bi|est)
scruff|ily
scruf'fi|ness
scruffy
  (scruf|fier,
  scruf'fi|est)
scrum-half (*pl.*
  scrum-halves)
scrum|mage
scrump|tious
scrumpy
scruple (as *v.*,
  scru|pling)
scru'pu|los|ity
scru'pu|lous
scru|tator
scru'tin|eer
scru'tin|ize
  (scru'tin|iz|ing)

scrutiny (*pl.*
  scru'tin|ies)
scry (scries,
  scried, scry|ing)
scryer
scuba
scud (as *v.*,
  scud'ded,
  scud|ding)
scuffle (as *v.*,
  scuff|ling)
sculler
scull|ery (*pl.*
  scull|er|ies)
scul|pin
sculptor
sculp|tress
sculp|tural
sculp'tur|ally
sculp|ture (as *v.*,
  sculp|tur|ing)
sculp'tur|esque
scum (as *v.*,
  scummed,
  scum|ming)
scumble (as *v.*,
  scum|bling)
scummy
  (scum|mier,
  scum'mi|est)
scun|cheon
scun|ner
scup|per
scurfy (scur|fier,
  scur'fi|est)
scur'ril|ity
scur'ril|ous
scurry (as *n.*, *pl.*
  scur|ries; as *v.*,
  scur|ries,
  scur|ried,
  scur|ry|ing)
scur|vied
scur|vily
scurvy
scut|age
scu'tal
Scu|tari
scu|tate
scutch|eon
scutcher
scu'tel|la'tion
scu'tel|late
scu'tel|lum (*pl.*
  scu|tella)
scu'ti|form

scut|ter
scuttle (as *v.*,
 scut|tling)
scu'tum (*pl.*
 scuta)
Scylla and
 Cha'ryb|dis
scyphi|form
scyph|ose
scypho|zoan
scyphus (*pl.*
 scyphi)
scythe (as *v.*,
 scyth|ing)
Scythia
Scyth|ian
sea-bank
sea'bee
sea-bird
sea|board
sea-boat
sea-boot
sea-dog
sea|farer
sea|far'ing
sea-fish
sea|food
sea-girt
sea|go'ing
sea|gull
sea-horse
seal|ant
sea-legs
sealer
seal|ery (*pl.*
 sea|ler'ies)
sea-level
sea-lion
seal|skin
Sea'ly|ham
sea|man (*pl.*
 sea|men)
sea'man|like
sea|manly
sea'man|ship
seamer
seami|ness
seam|less
seam|stress
seamy (seam|ier,
 seami|est)
Seanad
se'ance
sea|plane
sea|port
sea|quake

sear (to scorch,
 withered) △ sere
searcher
search|less
search|light
search-party (*pl.*
 search-parties)
search-warrant
sea-room
sea-salt
sea|scape
sea-shanty (*pl.*
 sea-shanties)
sea-shore
sea|sick
sea|sick'ness
sea|side
sea'son
sea'son|able
sea'son|ably
sea'son|al
sea'son|ally
sea'son'er
sea'son|ing
sea'son|less
season-ticket
seat-belt
seat|ing
seat|less
Se|attle
sea-wall
sea|ward
sea|wards
sea-way
sea|weed
sea|whip
sea-wife
 (*pl.* sea-wives)
sea-wind
sea'wor'thi|ness
sea'wor'thy
sea-wrack
se'ba|ceous
se'bes|ten
se'bor|rhoea
se'bor|rhoeic
se'bum
sec'ant
se'ca|teurs
secco (*pl.* sec'cos)
se'cede
 (se|ced'ing)
se|ceder
se'ces|sion
se'ces|sional
se'ces'sion|ism

se'ces'sion|ist
se|clude
 (se|clud'ing)
se|clu|sion
se|clu'sion|ist
se|clus|ive
sec'ond *n.* & *a.*
se'cond *v.*
sec'ond|ar'ily
sec'ond|ari|ness
sec'ond|ary (*pl.*
 sec'ond|ar'ies)
Sec'ond|ary
 (*Geol.*)
se|conde (in
 fencing)
sec|onder
second-hand *a.* &
 adv.
sec|ondly
se'cond|ment
se|condo (*Mus.*, *pl.*
 se|condi)
se|crecy
se'cret
sec'ret|aire
sec'ret|arial
sec'ret|ariat
sec'ret|ary (*pl.*
 sec'ret|ar'ies)
secretary-bird
Secretary-
       General
sec'ret'ary|ship
se|crete
 (se|cret'ing)
se|cre'tion
se|cret|ive
se|cretor
se|cret|ory
sec'tar|ian
sec'tari'an|ism
sec'tari'an|ize
 (sec'tari'an|iz-
        ing)
sect|ary (*pl.*
 sect|ar'ies)
sec'tion
sec'tional
sec'tion'al|ism
sec'tion'al|ize
 (sec'tion'al|iz-
        ing)
sec'tion|ally
sec'tor
sec|toral

sec'tor|ial
secu|lar
secu'lar|ism
secu'lar|ist
secu'lar|ity
secu'lar|iza|tion
secu'lar|ize
 (secu'lar|iz|ing)
se'cund (*Biol.*)
Se'cun'dera|bad
se'cur|able
se'cure (as *v.*
 se'cur|ing)
se'cure|ment
se'cur|ity (*pl.*
 se'cur|it'ies)
se'dan
sedan-chair
sed'ate (as *v.*,
 sed|at'ing)
seda|tion
sed'at|ive
sed'ent|ar'ily
sed'ent|ari|ness
sed'ent|ary
Se'der
se'der|unt
se'dile (*pl.*
 se|dilia)
sedi|ment
sedi|ment|ary
sedi|menta|tion
se|di'tion
se|di'tious
se|duce
 (se|du'cing)
se|du'cer
se|du'cible
se|duc'tion
se|duct|ive
se|duct|ress
se|du|lity
sedu|lous
se|dum
see (saw, seen)
seed-bed
seed-cake
seed-corn
seeder
seed|ily
seedi|ness
seed|less
seed|ling
seeds|man (*pl.*
 seeds|men)

seedy (seed|ier,
  seedi|est)
see|ing
seek (sought)
seem|ing
seem|li|ness
seemly (seem|lier,
  seem|li|est)
seep|age
seer|sucker
see-saw
seethe (seeth|ing)
Se|feris
seg|ment
seg|mental
seg|ment|ary
seg|menta|tion
sego (*pl.* se|gos)
se|greg|able
se|greg|ate
  (se|greg|at|ing)
se|grega|tion
se|grega|tion|ist
se|greg|at|ive
segue (*Mus.*)
se|gui|dilla
sei|cent|ist
sei|cento
sei|cen|to|ist
seiche
Seid|litz
sei|gneur
sei|gneur|ial
sei|gnior|age
sei|gniory (*pl.*
  sei|gnior|ies)
seine (as *v.*,
  sein|ing)
Seine
seiner
seise (*Law*;
  seis|ing) △ seize
seisin
seis|mal
seis|mic
seis|mical
seis|mic|ally
seis|mo|gram
seis|mo|graph
seis|mo|grapher
seis|mo|graphic
seis|mo|
      graph|ical
seis|mo|graphy
seis|mo|lo|gical
seis|mo|lo|gist

seis|mo|logy
seis|mo|meter
seis|mo|met|ric
seis|mo|met|rical
seis|mo|metry
seis|mo|scope
seis|mo|scopic
seiz|able
seize (to grasp;
  seiz|ing) △ seise
seizin *use* seisin
seiz|ure
se|jant
se|lach|ian
se|la|dang
se|lah
sel|dom
se|lect
se|lectee
se|lec|tion
se|lect|ive
se|lect|iv|ity
se|lect|man (*pl.*
  se|lect|men)
se|lector
sel|en|ate
sel|enic
sel|eni|ous
sel|en|ite
sel|en|itic
sel|en|ium
sel|eno|cent|ric
sel|en|od|ont
sel|eno|grapher
sel|eno|graphic
sel|eno|graphy
sel|eno|lo|gist
sel|eno|logy
self (*pl.* selves but
  selfs in sense
  'self-coloured
  flower')
self-abuse
self-
    aggrandizement
self-appointed
self-assertive
self-assurance
self-assured
self-awareness
self-begotten
self-centred
self-confessed
self-confidence
self-confident
self-conscious

self-contained
self-contempt
self-control
self-controlled
self-critical
self-deception
self-defence
self-denial
self-discipline
self-disciplined
self-doubt
self-drive
self-educated
self-effacing
self-employed
self-esteem
self-evident
self-explanatory
self-fulfilling
self-fulfilment
self-heal
self-help
self-importance
self-important
self-imposed
self-induced
self-indulgence
self-indulgent
self-inflicted
self-interest
self|ish
self-knowledge
self|less
self-made
self-opinionated
self-perpetuating
self-pity
self-portrait
self-possessed
self-preservation
self-raising
self-respect
self-respecting
self-righteous
self-sacrifice
self-sacrificing
self|same
self-satisfaction
self-satisfied
self-service
self-styled
self-sufficiency
self-sufficient
self-taught
self-will
self-willed

Sel|juk
Sel|juk|ian
Sel|kirk
sell (sold)
sel|lo|tape *v.*
  (sel|lo|tap|ing)
Sel|lo|tape *n.*
  (*propr.*)
sell-out *n.*
selt|zer
sel|vage
se|man|tic
se|mant|ic|ally
se|man|ti|cist
se|mant|ics
sema|phore (as *v.*,
  sema|phor|ing)
sema|phoric
se|ma|si|olo|gical
se|ma|si|ology
se|matic
semb|lance
semée
sem|eme
se|men
se|mes|ter
semi
semi-basement
semi-bold
semi|breve
semi|circle
semi|cir|cu|lar
semi|co|lon
semi|con|duct|ing
semi|con|ductor
semi-conscious
semi|cyl|in|der
semi|cyl|in|drical
semi|demi|semi|
    qua|ver
semi-deponent
semi-detached
semi|dia|meter
semi-dome
semi-double
semi|final
semi|fin|al|ist
semi|fluid
semi-metal
sem|inal
sem|in|ally
semi|inar
sem|in|ar|ist
sem|in|ary (*pl.*
  sem|in|ar|ies)
sem|ini|fer|ous

se'mi|olo'gical
se'mi|ology
se'mi|otic
se'mi|ot|ical
se'mi|ot|ics
semi-permanent
semi-permeable
semi|pre'cious
semi|quaver
Sem'ite
Sem'itic
Sem'it|ism
Sem'it|ist
Sem'it|ize
 (Sem'it|iz|ing)
semi|tone
semi-trailer
semi|trop'ical
semi-uncial
semi|vowel
se'mo|lina
sem'pi|ter'nal
sem|plice
sem'pre
sempstress *use*
 seamstress
sen|arius (*pl.*
 sen|arii)
sen'ary
sen'ate
sen'ator
sen'at|orial
sen'at'or|ship
send (as *v.*, sent)
sendal
send-off *n.*
send-up *n.*
Se'neca
Se'ne|gal
Sen'egal|ese (*pl.*
 same)
sen'es|cence
sen'es|cent
sen'es|chal
sen'hor (*Port.* etc.,
 Mr)
sen|hora (*Port.*
 etc., Mrs)
sen'hor|inha
 (*Port.* etc., Miss)
sen'ile
sen'il|ity
se'nior
se'ni'or|ity
senna

sen'net
 (trumpet-call)
sen'nit (*Naut.*)
señor (*Sp., Mr; pl.*
 señ|ores)
señ'ora (*Sp.,* Mrs)
señ'or|ita (*Sp.,*
 Miss)
sens|ate
sen'sa'tion
sen'sa'tional
sen'sa'tion'al|ism
sen'sa'tion'al|ist
sen'sa'tion'al|ly
sense (as *v.,*
 sens|ing)
sense|less
sens|ibil'ity (*pl.*
 sens|ibil'it'ies)
sens|ible
sens|ibly
sens'it|ive
sens'it'iv|ity
sens'it|iza'tion
sens'it|ize
 (sens'it|iz|ing)
sens'it|izer
sens'ito|meter
sensor
sen'sor|ial
sen'sor|ium (*pl.*
 sen|soria)
sens|ory
sen|sual
sen'su'al|ism
sen'su'al|ist
sen'su|al'ity
sen'su'al|ize
 (sen'su'al|iz|ing)
sen'su|ally
sensum (*pl.* sensa)
sen|su'ous
sen|tence (as *v.,*
 sen|ten'cing)
sen'ten'tial
sen'ten|tious
sen'tience
sen'tiency
sen'tient
sen'ti|ment
sen'ti|mental
sen'ti|ment'al|ism
sen'ti|ment'al|ist
sen'ti|ment'al|ity

sen'ti|ment'al|ize
 (sen'ti|ment'al|iz|
 ing)
sen'ti|ment'ally
sen|tinel
sen'try (*pl.*
 sen|tries)
sentry-box
sentry-go
Se|nussi (*pl.* same)
Se'oul
sepal
sep'ar|ab'il|ity
sep'ar|able
sep'ar|ably
sep'ar|ate (as *v.,*
 sep'ar|at|ing)
sep'ara|tion
sep'ar|at|ism
sep'ar|at|ist
sep'ar|at|ive
sep'ar|ator
sep'ar|at|ory
Seph|ardi (*pl.*
 Seph|ardim)
Seph|ardic
se'pia
se'poy
sep|puku
sep'sis (*pl.*
 sep|ses)
septal
sept|ate
sep'ta|tion
sept|cen'ten'ary
 (as *n., pl.* sept|
 cen'ten'ar|ies)
Sep'tem|ber
sep'ten|arius (*pl.*
 sep'ten|arii)
sep'ten|ary (as *n.,*
 pl. sep'ten|ar|ies)
sep'ten|ate
sept|en|nial
sept|en|nium
sep'tet
sept|foil
sep'tic
sep'ti|caemia
sep'ti|caemic
sep'tic|ally
sep'ti|city
sep'ti|lat'eral
sep'til|lion
sep|timal
sep|time

sep'ti|val'ent
sep'tua|gen'arian
sep'tua|gen'ary
 (as *n., pl.* sep'tua|
 gen'ar|ies)
Sep'tua|ges'ima
Sep'tua|gint
sep'tum (*pl.*
 septa)
sep|tuple (as *v.,*
 sep'tup|ling)
sep'tup|let
se'pul|chral
se'pul|chrally
sep'ul'chre (as *v.,*
 sep'ul|chring)
sep'ul|ture
se'quel
se'quela (*pl.*
 se'que|lae)
se|quence
se|quent
se'quen|tial
se'quen'ti|al'ity
se'quen|tially
se|ques|ter
se'quest|rable
se'quest|ral
se'quest|rate
 (se'quest|rat|ing)
se'quest|ra'tion
se'quest|rator
se'quest|ro|tomy
 (*pl.* se'quest|ro|
 tom|ies)
se'quest|rum (*pl.*
 se|questra)
se|questra
se'quin
se'quinned
se|quoia
serac
se'ra|glio (*pl.*
 se'ra|glios)
se'rai
se'rang
se'rape
ser'aph (*pl.*
 ser|aphim)
ser|aphic
ser'aph'ic|ally
se'ras|kier
Ser|bia
Ser|bian
Serbo-Croat
Serbo-Croatian
Ser'bo|nian

sere (in gun; *Ecol.*)
△ sear
se|rein (fine rain)
ser|en|ade (as *v.*,
  ser|en|ad|ing)
ser|en|ata
se|ren|dip|it|ous
se|ren|dip|ity
se|rene (as *a.*,
 se|rener,
 se|renest)
se|ren|ity
Se|ren|ity (title;
 pl. Se|ren|it|ies)
serf|dom
ser|geant
sergeant-major
serial
seri|al|ism
seri|al|ist
seri|al|ity
seri|al|ize
 (seri|al|iz|ing)
seri|ally
seri|ate (as *v.*,
 seri|at|ing)
seri|atim
seri|ation
se|ri|ceous
seri|cul|tural
se|ri|cul|ture
seri|cul|tur|ist
se|ri|ema
series (*pl.* same)
serif
seri|graph
se|ri|grapher
se|ri|graphy
serin
ser|in|ette
se|ringa
serio-comic
serio-comically
ser|ious
ser|jeant (*Law*)
serjeant-at-arms
 (*pl.* serjeants-at-
  arms)
ser|mon
ser|mon|ize
 (ser|mon|iz|ing)
sero|lo|gical
sero|lo|gist
sero|logy
se|rosa
ser|os|ity

ser|ot|ine
sero|tonin
ser|ous
ser|pent
ser|pen|ti|form
ser|pent|ine (as *v.*,
 ser|pent|in|ing)
ser|pi|gin|ous
ser|pula (*pl.*
 ser|pu|lae)
serra (*pl.* ser|rae)
ser|ra|dilla
ser|ran
ser|rate (as *v.*,
 ser|rat|ing)
ser|ra|tion
ser|ried
ser|ru|late
ser|ru|la|tion
serum (*pl.* sera)
ser|val
ser|vant
serve (as *v.*,
 serv|ing)
server
serv|ery (*pl.*
 serv|er|ies)
Ser|vian
ser|vice (as *v.*,
 ser|vi|cing)
ser|vice|ab|il|ity
ser|vice|able
ser|vice|ably
ser|vice|man (*pl.*
 ser|vice|men)
ser|vice|wo|man
 (*pl.* ser|vice|
  wo|men)
ser|vi|ette
serv|ile
serv|il|ity
ser|ving
Serv|ite
ser|vitor
ser|vit|or|ship
ser|vit|ude
servo (*pl.* ser|vos)
ses|ame
ses|am|oid
ses|qui|
  cent|en|ary
 (as *n.*, *pl.* ses|qui|
  cent|en|ar|ies)
ses|qui|
  cent|en|nial
ses|qui|peda|lian

ses|qui|plic|ate
sess|ile
ses|sion
ses|sional
ses|terce
ses|ter|tium (*pl.*
 ses|ter|tia)
ses|ter|tius (*pl.*
 ses|ter|tii)
ses|tet
ses|tina
set (as *v.*, set,
 set|ting)
seta (*pl.* se|tae)
se|ta|ceous
set-back *n.*
se|ti|fer|ous
se|ti|ger|ous
seton
set|ose
sett *use* set
set|tee
set|ter
set|ter|wort
set|ting
settle (as *v.*,
 set|tling)
set|tle|ment
set|tler
set|tlor (*Law*)
set-to *n.* (*pl.*
 set-tos)
set-up *n.*
set|wall
Seurat
seven
sev|en|fold
sev|en|teen
sev|en|teenth
sev|enth
Seventh-day
 Ad|vent|ist
sev|en|ti|eth
sev|enty (as *n.*, *pl.*
 sev|en|ties)
sev|en|ty|fold
sever
sev|er|able
sev|eral
sev|er|ally
sev|er|alty
sev|er|ance
se|vere (se|verer,
 se|verest)
se|ver|ity (*pl.*
 se|ver|it|ies)

Sev|ern
sev|ery (*pl.*
 sev|er|ies)
Sev|ille
Sèvres
sew (sewn)
sew|age
se|wel|lel
sewer
sew|er|age
sewin
sew|ing
sexa|gen|arian
sexa|gen|ary (as
 n., *pl.*
 sexa|gen|ar|ies)
Sexa|ges|ima
sexa|ges|imal
sexa|ges|im|ally
sex|an|gu|lar
sex|cent|en|ary
 (as *n.*, *pl.* sex|
  cent|en|ar|ies)
sex|di|git|ate
sex|ennial
sex|foil
sex|ily
sexi|ness
sex|ism
sex|ist
sexi|syl|labic
sexi|syl|lable
sexi|va|lent
sex|less
sex|olo|gical
sex|olo|gist
sex|ology
sex|part|ite
sex|pot
sex|tain
sex|tant
sex|tet
sex|til|lion
sexto (*pl.* sex|tos)
sex|to|de|cimo (*pl.*
 sex|to|de|ci|mos)
sex|ton
sex|tuple (as *v.*,
 sex|tup|ling)
sex|tup|let
sexual
sexu|al|ist
sexu|al|ity
sexu|al|ize
 (sexu|al|iz|ing)
sexu|ally

sex|va|lent
sexy (sex|ier,
 sexi|est)
Sey|chelles
sforz|ando
sforz|ato
sfu|mato (in
 painting)
sgraf|fito (pl.
 sgraf|fiti)
shab|bily
shab|bi|ness
shabby
 (shab|bier,
 shab|bi|est)
shab|rack
Sha|bu|oth
shackle (as v.,
 shack|ling)
shad|dock
shade (as v.,
 shad|ing)
shaded
shade|less
sha|dily
sha|di|ness
sha|doof
shadow
shad|ow|graph
shad|ow|less
shad|owy
shady (sha|dier,
 sha|di|est)
Shaftes|bury
shaft|ing
shag (as v.,
 shagged,
 shag|ging)
shag|gily
shag|gi|ness
shaggy
 (shag|gier,
 shag|gi|est)
sha|green
shake (as v.,
 shook, shaken,
 shak|ing)
shake|able
shake|down n.
shake-out n.
shaker
Shake|speare
Shake|spear|ian
Shake|speari|ana
shake-up n.
sha|kily

sha|ki|ness
shako (pl. shakos)
shaky (sha|kier,
 sha|ki|est)
shale-oil
shall (should)
shal|loon
shal|lop
shal|lot
shal|low
 (shal|lower,
 shal|low|est)
sha|lom
shal|war
shaly (sha|lier,
 sha|li|est)
sham (as v.,
 shammed,
 sham|ming)
shaman
sham|an|ism
sham|an|istic
sham|at|eur
sham|at|eur|ism
shamble (as v.,
 sham|bling)
shambles
sham|bolic
shame (as v.,
 sham|ing)
shame|faced
shame|ful
shame|fully
shame|less
shammy (pl.
 sham|mies)
sham|poo
sham|rock
Shand|ean
shan|dry|dan
shandy (pl.
 shan|dies)
shan|dy|gaff
shang|hai v.
 (shang|haied)
Shang|hai
Shangri-La
Shan|non
shanny (pl.
 shan|nies)
shan|tung
shanty (pl.
 shan|ties)
shanty|man (pl.
 shanty|men)
shap|able

shape (as v.,
 shap|ing)
shape|less
shape|li|ness
shapely
 (shape|lier,
 shape|li|est)
share (as v.,
 shar|ing)
share|holder
share-out n.
shariah
shark-skin
sharpen
sharp|ener
sharper
sharp|ish
sharp|shooter
sharp-tongued
sharp-witted
Shasta (daisy)
Shas|tra
 (Hinduism)
shat|ter
shave (as v.,
 shav|ing)
shaven
shaver
Sha|vian
shav|ing
shchi (soup)
shea (tree)
shead|ing (in Isle
 of Man)
sheaf (pl.
 sheaves)
shear (as v., p.p.
 shorn but
 sheared of
 mechanical
 shears)
shear|bill
shear|ling
shear|tail
shear|water
sheath n.
sheathe v.
 (sheath|ing)
sheath|ing
sheave (as v.,
 sheav|ing)
she|been
shed (as v., shed,
 shed|ding)
shed|der
shed|ding

sheeny (as a.,
 sheen|ier,
 sheeni|est; as n.,
 pl. sheen|ies)
sheep (pl. same)
sheep-dog
sheep-fold
sheep|ish
sheep|like
sheep|meat
sheep-run
sheep|shank
sheep's-head
sheep|skin
sheer-legs
sheet|ing
Shef|field
sheikh
sheikh|dom
Sheila
shekel
She|ki|nah
Shel|donian
shel|drake (fem. &
 pl. shel|duck)
shelf (pl. shelves)
shelf-ful
 (pl. shelf-fuls)
shelf-mark
shel|lac (as v.,
 shel|lacked,
 shel|lack|ing)
shell|back
Shel|ley
shell|fish (pl.
 same)
shell-out n.
shell|proof
shell-shock
shelly
Shelta
shel|ter
shel|tie
shelve
shel|ving
she|mozzle
she|nan|igan
Sheol
shep|herd
shep|herd|ess
Shep|pey
Sher|aton
sher|bet
Sher|idan
she|rif (Muslim
 leader)

sher|iff (county
  officer)
sher'iff|alty (pl.
  sher'iff|al'ties)
Sher|lock Holmes
Sherpa
Sher'ring|ton
sherry (pl.
  sher|ries)
Shet|land
Shet|lander
shew|bread
Shiah
shib'bol|eth
shield|bug
shiel|ing
shif'tily
shif'ti|ness
shift|less
shifty (shif|tier,
  shif'ti|est)
shi|gella
shih-tzu
Shi'ite
shi'kar
shi|karee
shil'le||lagh
shil|ling
shil'lings|worth
shilly-shally
  (as v.,
  shilly-shallies,
  shilly-shallied,
  shilly-shallying)
shily use shyly
shim (as v.,
  shimmed,
  shim|ming)
shim|mer
shim|mery
shimmy (as n., pl.
  shim|mies; as v.,
  shim|mies,
  shim|mied,
  shim'my|ing)
shin (as v.,
  shinned,
  shin|ning)
shin-bone
shin|dig (festive
  gathering)
shindy (brawl,
  noise; pl.
  shin|dies)

shine (as v., in
  sense 'emit or
  reflect light'
shone, otherwise
shined, shin'ing)
shiner
shingle (as v.,
  shing|ling)
shingles
shingly
shin-guard
shi'ni|ness
shinny (shin|nies,
  shin|nied,
  shin'ny|ing)
shin-pad
Shinto
Shin'to|ism
Shin'to|ist
shinty (pl.
  shin|ties)
shiny (shi'nier,
  shi'ni|est)
ship (as v.,
  shipped,
  ship|ping)
ship|board
ship-broker
ship|builder
ship|build'ing
ship|lap
  (ship|lapped,
  ship'lap|ping)
ship|load
ship|mas'ter
ship|mate
ship|ment
ship|owner
ship|per
ship|ping
ship|shape
ship-way
ship|wreck
ship|wright
ship|yard
shi'ra|lee
shire-horse
Shir|ley (poppy)
shirr|ing
shirt-front
shirt|ily
shirti|ness
shirt|ing
shirt-sleeve
shirt-tail
shirt|waister

shirty (shir|tier,
  shir'ti|est)
shish ke'bab
shit (as v., shit,
  shit|ting)
Shiva use Siva
shiver
shiv|ery
shoaly
shocker
shock|ing
shock-proof
shod|dily
shod'di|ness
shoddy (as a.,
  shod|dier,
  shod'di|est)
shoe (as v., shod,
  shoe|ing)
shoe|black
shoe|horn
shoe-lace
shoe-leather
shoe|maker
shoe|mak'ing
shoe|shine
shoe-string
shoe-tree
sho'far (pl.
  sho|froth)
sho'gun
sho'gun|ate
Sho'lok|hov
shoot (as v., shot)
shooter
shoot|ing
shoot-out n.
shop (as v.,
  shopped,
  shop|ping)
shop-boy
shop-floor
shop-girl
shop|keeper
shop|lifter
shop|lift|ing
shop|man (pl.
  shop|men)
shop|per
shop|ping
shoppy
shop-soiled
shop|walker
shop-window
shop-worn
shoran

shore (as v.,
  shor|ing)
shore|ward
shore|wards
shore|weed
shor|ing
short|age
short|bread
short|cake
short-change v.
  (short-changing)
short-circuit v.
short|com'ing
shorten
short|fall
short|hand
short-handed
short|horn
short|ish
short-list v.
short-lived
shortly
short-sighted
short|stop
short-term a.
shorty (pl.
  short|ies)
Shos'ta|kov'ich
shot-firer
shot|gun
shot|proof
shot|ten
shoul|der
shoulder-bag
shoulder-blade
shoulder-pad
shoulder-strap
shove (as v.,
  shov|ing)
shove-halfpenny
shovel (as v.,
  shovelled,
  shov'el|ling)
shov'el|board
shov'el|ful (pl.
  shov'el|fuls)
shovel-head
shov'el|ler
show (as v., p.p.
  shown)
show|biz
show|boat
show-case
show-down n.
shower
shower-proof

showery
show|girl
show|ily
showi|ness
show|ing
show-jumper
show-jumping
show|man (*pl.*
 show|men)
show|man|ship
show-off *n.*
show-piece
show|room
showy (show|ier,
 showi|est)
shrap|nel
shred (as *v.*,
 shred¦ded,
 shred|ding)
shred|der
shrew|ish
Shrews|bury
shrieval
shriev|alty (*pl.*
 shriev|al¦ties)
shrilly
shrimper
shrine (as *v.*,
 shrin¦ing)
shrink (as *v.*,
 shrank, shrunk)
shrink|age
shrink-proof
shrink-wrap
 (shrink-
     wrapped,
 shrink-
     wrapping)
shrivel
 (shrivelled,
 shriv¦el|ling)
Shrop|shire
Shrove|tide
shrub|bery (*pl.*
 shrub|ber¦ies)
shrubby
 (shrub|bier,
 shrub¦bi|est)
shrug (as *v.*,
 shrugged,
 shrug|ging)
shrun|ken
shud|der
shuffle (as *v.*,
 shuff|ling)
shuffle-board

shufti
shun (shunned,
 shun|ning)
shut (shut,
 shut¦ting)
shut-down *n.*
shut-eye
shut-in *a.* & *n.*
shut-out *a.* & *n.*
shut|ter
shut¦ter|ing
shut¦ter|less
shuttle (as *v.*,
 shut¦tling)
shut¦tle|cock
shy (as *a.*, shyer,
 shy|est; as *v.*,
 shies, shied,
 shy|ing; as *n.*, *pl.*
 shies)
Shy|lock
shyly
shy|ness
shy|ster
sial (*Geol.*)
si¦al|agogue
si|amang
Si¦am|ese (as *n.*,
 pl. same)
Sib|el|ius
Si|ber¦ia
Si|ber¦ian
sib¦il|ance
sib¦il|ancy
sib¦il|ant
sib¦il|ate
 (sib¦il|at¦ing)
sib¦ila|tion
sib|ling
sib|ship
sibyl
sibyl|line
sic¦cat|ive
sice (six on dice)
△ syce
Si¦cil|ian
Si¦cily
sick-bay
sick-bed
sicken
sick|ish
sickle
sick-leave
sickle|bill
sickle-cell *a.*
sick¦li|ness

sick-list
sickly (sick|lier,
 sick¦li|est)
sick|ness
sick-pay
sick-room
side (as *v.*, sid¦ing)
side-arms
side|board
side|burns
side-car
sided
side|hill
side|kick
side|less
side|light
side|line
side|long
si¦der|eal
sid¦er|ite
side-road
sid¦ero|stat
side-saddle
side-show
side-slip (as *v.*,
 side-slipped,
 side-slipping)
sides|man (*pl.*
 sides|men)
side-step (as *v.*,
 side-stepped,
 side-stepping)
side-street
side-stroke
side-swipe (as *v.*,
 side-swiped,
 side-swiping)
side-track
side|walk
side|ward
side|wards
side|ways
side|wise
sid¦ing
sidle (sid¦ling)
Sid|ney
sie¦mens
Sien¦kie|wicz
si¦enna (pigment)
Si¦enna
si¦erra
Si¦erra Le¦one
Si¦erra Madre
Si¦erra Ne¦vada
si¦esta

sieve (as *v.*,
 siev|ing)
si¦faka
sifter
sighted
sight|less
sightli|ness
sightly (sight|lier,
 sight¦li|est)
sight-screen
sight|seeing
sight|seer
sight|worthy
sig¦il|late
sig¦lum (*pl.* sigla)
sigma
sig|mate
sig|moid
sig|nal (as *v.*,
 sig|nalled,
 sig¦nal|ling)
signal-box
sig|nal|ize
 (sig¦nal|iz¦ing)
sig|nal|ler
sig|nally
sig¦nal|man (*pl.*
 sig¦nal|men)
sig|nary (list of
 signs; *pl.*
 sig|nar¦ies)
sig¦nat|ory (as *n.*,
 pl. sig¦nat|or¦ies)
sig¦na|ture
sign|board
sig¦net
sig¦ni¦fic|ance
sig¦ni¦fic|ancy
sig¦ni¦fic|ant
sig¦nif¦ica|tion
sig¦ni¦fic¦at|ive
sig|nify
 (sig¦ni|fies,
 sig¦ni|fied,
 sig¦ni|fy¦ing)
sign-off *n.*
si¦gnor (*It.*, Mr; *pl.*
 si¦gnori)
si¦gnora (*It.*, Mrs)
si¦gnor|ina (*It.*,
 Miss)
si¦gnory (*pl.*
 si¦gnor|ies)
sign|post
sika
Sikh|ism

Sik'kim
sil'age (as v.,
  sila'ging)
si'lence (as v.,
  si'len'cing)
si'len'cer
si'lent
si'lenus (pl.
  si'leni)
si'lesia
sil'hou'ette (as v.,
  sil'hou'et'ted,
  sil'hou'et'ting)
sil'ica
sil'ic'ate
si'li'ceous
si'li'cic
si'li'ci'fer'ous
si'li'ci'fy
  (si'li'ci'fies,
  si'li'ci'fied,
  si'li'ci'fy'ing)
sil'icon (element)
sil'ic'one
  (polymer)
sil'ic'osis (pl.
  sil'ic'oses)
sil'ic'otic
sili'qua (pl.
  sili'quae)
sili'quose
sili'quous
silken
silk'ily
silki'ness
silk'worm
silky (sil'kier,
  sil'ki'est)
sil'ler
sil'lily
sil'li'man'ite
sil'li'ness
silly (as a., sil'lier,
  sil'li'est; as n., pl.
  sil'lies)
silo (pl. silos)
sil'ta'tion
silt'stone
silty (sil'tier,
  sil'ti'est)
Si'lur'ian
silva (pl. sil'vae)
sil'van
sil'ver
silver-fish
sil'veri'ness

silver|side
silver|smith
silver|ware
silver|weed
sil'very
sil'vi'cul'ture
sima
sim|ian
sim|ilar
sim'il'ar'ity (pl.
  sim'il'ar'it'ies)
sim'ile
si'mil'it'ude
Simla
sim'mer
sim'nel (cake)
Si'mon
si'mo'niac
si'mo'ni'acal
si'mo'ni'ac'ally
si'mony
sim'oom
sim'pat'ico
  (likeable)
sim'per
simple (sim'pler,
  sim'plest)
sim'ple'ton
sim'plex
sim'pli'city
sim'pli'fica'tion
sim'plify
  (sim'pli'fies,
  sim'pli'fied,
  sim'pli'fy'ing)
simp'lism
simp'listic
simply
si'mu'lac'rum (pl.
  si'mu'lacra)
simu'late
  (simu'lat'ing)
simu'la'tion
simu'lator
sim'ul'cast
sim'ul'tan'eity
sim'ul'tan'eous
sim'urg
sin (as v., sinned,
  sin'ning)
Si'nai
Si'na'itic
sin'an'thropus
sin'ap'ism

sin'cere
  (sin'cerer,
  sin'cerest)
sin'cer'ity (pl.
  sin'cer'it'ies)
sin'ci'put
sine'cure
si'ne'cur'ism
sine'cur'ist
sine die
sine qua non
sinew
sin'ew'less
sin'ewy
sin'fonia
sin'foni'etta
sin'ful
sin'fully
sing (sang, sung)
sing'able
Sin'ga'pore
singe (as v.,
  singe'ing)
singer
Singh
single (as v.,
  sing'ling)
sin'gle'stick
sing'let
sin'gle'ton
singly
sing'song
sin'gu'lar
sin'gu'lar'ity (pl.
  sin'gu'lar'it'ies)
sin'gu'lar'ize
  (sin'gu'lar'iz'ing)
Sin'hala
Sin'hal'ese (pl.
  same)
sin'is'ter
sin'is'tral
sin'is'tral'ity
sin'is'trally
sin'is'trorse
sink (as v., sank,
  sunk)
sink'able
sink'age
sinker
sink-hole
sink'ing
sin'less
sin'ner
Sinn Fein
Sinn Feiner

si'no'lo'gist
si'no'logue
si'no'logy
Si'no'mania
Si'no'phile
Si'no'phobe
Si'no'pho'bia
sin'ter
sinu'ate
sinu'os'ity (pl.
  sinu'os'it'ies)
sinu'ous
si'nus
si'nus'itis
si'nus'oid
si'nus'oidal
Sion *use* Zion
Siouan
Sioux (pl. same)
sip (as v., sipped,
  sip'ping)
si'phon
si'phon'age
si'phonal
si'phonet
si'phonic
si'phono'phore
siph'uncle
sip'pet
sir (as v., sirred,
  sir'ring)
sir'car
sir'dar
sire (as v., sir'ing)
siren
siren|ian
sir'gang
sir'loin
si'rocco (pl.
  si'roc'cos)
sirup *use* syrup
sisal
sis'kin
sis'soo
sissy (as n., pl.
  sis'sies)
sis'ter
sis'ter'hood
sister-in-law (pl.
  sisters-in-law)
sis'ter'li'ness
sis'terly
Sist'ine
sis'trum (pl.
  sis'tra)
Si'sy'phean

Si|sy|phus
sit (as v., sat,
 sit|ting)
sitar
sit|com
sit-down a.
site (as v., sit|ing)
sit|fast
sit-in n.
Sitka
si|to|pho|bia
sit|rep
sit|ter
sitter-in (pl.
 sitters-in)
sit|ting
sitting-room
situ|ate
 (situ|at|ing)
situ|ation
situ|ational
sit-upon n.
Sit|well
sitz-bath
Siva
Si|va|ism
Si|va|ite
six|ain
sixer
six|fold
six|pence
six|penny
six|teen
six|teenmo
six|teenth
sixthly
six|tieth
sixty (as n., pl.
 six|ties)
six|ty|fold
sixty-fourmo
sizar (assisted
 student)
siz|ar|ship
size (as v., siz|ing)
size|able
sizer
sizy
sizzle (as v.,
 sizz|ling)
sizz|ling
sjam|bok
skald (Scand. poet)
skaldic
Skara Brae

skate (as v.,
 skat|ing)
skate|board
skater
skean (dagger)
skean-dhu
ske|daddle (as v.,
 ske|dad|dling)
skein
skel|etal
skel|eton
skel|et|on|ize
 (skel|et|on|iz|ing)
sker|rick
skerry (pl.
 sker|ries)
sketch-book
sketch|ily
sketchi|ness
sketch-map
sketchy
 (sketch|ier,
 sketchi|est)
skew|back
skew|bald
skewer
skew-whiff
ski (as v., skis,
 ski'd, ski|ing)
ski-bob
skid (as v.,
 skid|ded,
 skid|ding)
skier (person using
 skis)
skiey use skyey
skiffle
ski-joring
ski-jump
skil|ful
skil|fully
ski-lift
skil|let
skilly
skim (as v.,
 skimmed,
 skim|ming)
skim|mer
skim|mia
skimp|ily
skimpi|ness
skimpy
 (skim|pier,
 skim|pi|est)

skin (as v.,
 skinned,
 skin|ning)
skin-deep
skin-diver
skin-diving
skin|flint
skin|ful (pl.
 skin|fuls)
skin|head
skin|less
skin|ner
skin|ni|ness
skinny (skin|nier,
 skin|ni|est)
skin-tight
skip (as v.,
 skipped,
 skip|ping)
skip|jack
skip|per
skip|pet
skir|mish
skir|ret
skirt|ing
ski-run
skit|ter
skit|tish
skittle (as v.,
 skit|tling)
skive (skiv|ing)
skiver
skivvy (pl.
 skiv|vies)
Skopje
skua
skul|dug|gery
skull-cap
sky (as n., pl.
 skies; as v., skies,
 skied, sky|ing)
sky-blue
sky-diver
sky-diving
Skye
skyer (in cricket)
skyey
sky-high
sky|jack
sky|lark
sky|light
sky|line
sky-rocket (as v.,
 sky-rocketed,
 sky-rocketing)
sky|sail

sky|scape
sky|scraper
sky|ward
sky|wards
sky|way
slab (as v.,
 slabbed,
 slab|bing)
slacken
slag (as v.,
 slagged,
 slag|ging)
slaggy (slag|gier,
 slag|gi|est)
slag-heap
slake (slak|ing)
sla|lom
slam (as v.,
 slammed,
 slam|ming)
slam|bang
slan|der
slan|der|ous
slang|ily
slangi|ness
slangy (slang|ier,
 slangi|est)
slant|ways
slant|wise
slap (as v.,
 slapped,
 slap|ping)
slap-bang
slap|dash
slap-happy
slap|stick
slap-up a.
slasher
slate (as v.,
 slat|ing)
slater
slat|tern
slat|ternly
slaty (sla|tier,
 sla|ti|est)
slaugh|ter
slaugh|ter|house
slaugh|ter|ous
slave (as v.,
 slav|ing)
slave-drive
 (slave-drove,
 slave-driven,
 slave-driving)
slave-driver
slaver

slavery
slave-trade
slavey
Slavic
slav|ish
Slav|ism
Sla|vo|nian
Slav|onic
Sla|vo|phile
Sla|vo|phobe
slay (slew, slain)
Slea|ford
sleaz|ily
sleazi|ness
sleazy (sleaz|ier,
 sleaz|iest)
sled (as v.,
 sled|ded,
 sled|ding)
sledge (as v.,
 sledging)
sledge-hammer
sleep (as v., slept)
sleeper
sleep|ily
sleepi|ness
sleep|less
sleep-walk
sleep-walker
sleepy (sleep|ier,
 sleepi|est)
sleepy|head
sleety (sleet|ier,
 sleeti|est)
sleeve|less
sleeve-note
sleigh
sleight
slen|der
 (slen|derer,
 slen|der|est)
slen|der|ize
 (slen|der|iz|ing)
slew
sley (weaver's
 reed)
slice (as v.,
 sli|cing)
slice|able
slicer
slicker
slid|able
slide (as v., slid,
 slid|ing)
slider
slide-rule

slide-valve
slide-way
slid|ing
slight|ish
Sligo
slily use slyly
slim (as v.,
 slimmed,
 slim|ming; as a.,
 slim|mer,
 slim|mest)
slime (as v.,
 slimed, slim|ing)
sli|mily
sli|mi|ness
slim|line
slim|mer
slim|mish
slimy (sli|mier,
 sli|mi|est)
sling (as v., slung)
slinger
slink (go
 stealthily; slunk)
slink|ily
slinki|ness
slink|weed
slinky (slin|kier,
 slin|ki|est)
slip (as v., slipped,
 slip|ping)
slip-knot
slip-on a.
slip|page
slip|per
slippered
slip|per|ily
slip|peri|ness
slip|per|wort
slip|pery
slippy (slip|pier,
 slip|pi|est)
slip-road
slip|shod
slip-stream
slip-up n.
slip|way
slit (as v., slit,
 slit|ting)
slither
slith|ery
sliver
slivo|vitz
slob|ber
slob|bery
sloe-gin

slog (as v.,
 slogged,
 slog|ging)
slo|gan
slog|ger
sloid
slop (as v.,
 slopped,
 slop|ping)
slope (as v.,
 slop|ing)
slope|wise
slop|pily
slop|pi|ness
sloppy (slop|pier,
 slop|pi|est)
sloshy (slosh|ier,
 sloshi|est)
slot (as v., slot|ted,
 slot|ting)
sloth
sloth|ful
sloth|fully
slot-machine
slouchy
 (slouch|ier,
 slouchi|est)
Slough
sloughy
 (slough|ier,
 sloughi|est)
Slo|vak
sloven
Slo|vene
Slo|venia
Slo|ven|ian
slov|en|li|ness
slov|enly
slov|enry
slow|coach
slow-worm
slub (as v.,
 slubbed,
 slub|bing)
sludgy (sludgier,
 sludgi|est)
slue use slew
slug (as v.,
 slugged,
 slug|ging)
slug|gard
slug|gish
sluice (as v.,
 sluicing)
sluice-gate
sluit (gully)

slum (as v.,
 slummed,
 slum|ming)
slum|ber
slum|berer
slum|ber|ous
slummy
 (slum|mier,
 slum|mi|est)
slur (as v.,
 slurred,
 slur|ring)
slurry
slushy (slush|ier,
 slushi|est)
slut|tish
sly (slyer, sly|est)
slyly
slype
smacker
smack|eroo
smal|lage
small|holder
small|hold|ing
small|ish
small-minded
small|pox
small|wares
smarmy
 (smar|mier,
 smar|mi|est)
smart alec
smarten
smart|ish
smart|weed
smarty (pl.
 smart|ies)
smasher
smash|ing
smash-up n.
smat|ter
smat|ter|ing
smeary
smegma
smeg|matic
smell (as v., smelt)
smell|able
smel|ler
smel|li|ness
smell-less
smelly (smel|lier,
 smel|li|est)
smelter
smelt|ery (pl.
 smelt|er|ies)
smidgen

smi'lax
smile (as v.,
 smil'ing)
smite (smote,
 smit'ten,
 smit'ing)
smith'er|eens
smith'ers
smith|ery (pl.
 smith'er|ies)
smithy (pl.
 smith'ies)
smock|ing
smock-mill
smoggy
 (smog|gier,
 smog'gi|est)
smok'able
smoke (as v.,
 smok'ing)
smoke-bomb
smoke|less
smoker
smoke-screen
smoke-stack
smo|kily
smo'ki|ness
smoko (pl.
 smokos)
smoky (smo|kier,'
 smo'ki|est)
smooth
smoothie
smooth|ish
smor'gas|bord
smorz|ando
smother
smoth|ery
smoul'der
smriti
smudge (as v.,
 smudging)
smudgy
 (smudg|ier,
 smudgi|est)
smug (smug|ger,
 smug|gest)
smuggle
 (smug|gling)
smug|gler
smut (as v.,
 smut'ted,
 smut|ting)
smut|tily
smut'ti|ness

smutty (smut|tier,
 smut'ti|est)
Smyrna
snack-bar
snaffle (as v.,
 snaff|ling)
snafu
snag (as v.,
 snagged,
 snag|ging)
snaggle-tooth (pl.
 snaggle-teeth)
snaggy
snake (as v.,
 snak|ing)
sna|kily
sna'ki|ness
snaky (sna|kier,
 sna'ki|est)
snap (as v.,
 snapped,
 snap|ping)
snap|dragon
snap|per
snap|pily
snap'pi|ness
snap|pish
snappy
 (snap|pier,
 snap'pi|est)
snap|shot
snare (as v.,
 snar'ing)
snarl-up n.
snarly
snatchy
snaz'zily
snaz'zi|ness
snazzy (snaz|zier,
 snaz'zi|est)
sneaker
sneak|ily
sneaki|ness
sneaky
 (sneak|ier,
 sneaki|est)
sneeze (as v.,
 sneez|ing)
sneeze|wort
sneezy
snib (as v.,
 snibbed,
 snib|bing)
snicker
sniff|ily
sniffi|ness

sniffle (as v.,
 sniff|ling)
sniffy (snif|fier,
 snif'fi|est)
snif|ter
snig|ger
sniggle
 (snig|gling)
snip (as v.,
 snipped,
 snip|ping)
snipe (as v.,
 snip|ing)
sniper
snip|pet
snip|pety
snip|ping
snivel (as v.,
 sniv'elled,
 sniv'el|ling)
snob|bery
snob|bish
snoek (barracouta)
snog (snogged,
 snog|ging)
snooker
snoopy
snoot|ily
snooti|ness
snooty (snoo|tier,
 snoo'ti|est)
snooze (as v.,
 snooz|ing)
snore (as v.,
 snor'ing)
snor|kel (as v.,
 snor'kelled,
 snor'kel|ling)
snorter
snot|tily
snot'ti|ness
snotty (snot|tier,
 snot'ti|est)
snouted
snouty
snow|ball
snow-boot
snow-bound
snow-cap
Snow|don
snow-drift
snow|drop
snow|fall
snow|flake
snow-goose (pl.
 snow-geese)

snow-line
snow|man (pl.
 snow|men)
snow-shoe
snow|storm
snow-white
snowy (snow|ier,
 snowi|est)
snub (as v.,
 snubbed,
 snub|bing)
snub|ber
snub-nosed
snuff-box
snuffer
snuffle (as v.,
 snuff|ling)
snuffy
snug (as a.,
 snug|ger,
 snug|gest)
snug|gery (pl.
 snug'ger|ies)
snuggle
 (snug|gling)
so (Mus.) use soh
soaker
so-and-so
 (pl. so-and-so's)
soap-box
soap|ily
soapi|ness
soap|stone
soap|suds
soapy (soap|ier,
 soapi|est)
So|ares
sob (as v., sobbed,
 sob|bing)
sober (soberer,
 sober|est)
sob'ri|ety
so'bri|quet
soc|age
so-called
soc|cer
so'ci|ab'il|ity
so'ci|able
so'ci|ably
so|cial
so'cial|ism
so'cial|ist
so'cial|istic
so'cial|ite
so'ci|al'ity
so'cial|iza|tion

so¦cial¦ize
 (so¦cial¦iz¦ing)
so¦ci¦ally
so¦ci¦etal
so¦ci¦ety (*pl.*
 so¦ci¦et¦ies)
So¦cin¦ian
socio-cultural
socio-economic
socio-linguistic
so¦ci¦olo¦gical
so¦ci¦olo¦gist
so¦ci¦ology
so¦ci¦omet¦ric
so¦ci¦omet¦rist
so¦ci¦ometry
socket (as *v.*,
 sock¦eted,
 sock¦et¦ing)
sock¦eye
socle
Soc¦rates
Soc¦ratic
sod (as *v.*,
 sod¦ded,
 sod¦ding)
soda
so¦dal¦ity (*pl.*
 so¦dal¦it¦ies)
soda-water
sod¦den
sodic
so¦dium
Sodom
sod¦om¦ite
sod¦om¦ize
 (sod¦om¦iz¦ing)
sod¦omy
Soe¦harto
so¦ever
sofa
sof¦fit
So¦fia
softa
soft¦ball
soften
softie
soft¦ish
soft-pedal *v.*
 (soft-pedalled,
 soft-pedalling)
soft-soap *v.*
soft¦ware
soft¦wood
sog¦gily
soggi¦ness

soggy (sog¦gier,
 sog¦gi¦est)
soh (*Mus.*)
Soho
soigné (*fem.*
 soignée)
soil¦less
soirée
so¦journ
so¦journer
sola (plant)
sol¦ace (as *v.*,
 sol¦acing)
so¦lan (gannet)
so¦lan¦der
solar
sol¦ar¦ism
sol¦ar¦ist
sol¦ar¦ium (*pl.*
 sol¦aria)
sol¦ar¦iza¦tion
sol¦ar¦ize
 (sol¦ar¦iz¦ing)
so¦la¦tium (*pl.*
 so¦la¦tia)
sola topi
sol¦dan¦ella
sol¦der
sol¦dier
soldier-like
sol¦dierly
sol¦dier¦ship
sol¦diery (*pl.*
 sol¦dier¦ies)
sole (as *v.*, sol¦ing)
sol¦ecism
sol¦ecist
sol¦ecistic
sol¦emn
so¦lem¦nity (*pl.*
 so¦lem¦nit¦ies)
sol¦em¦niza¦tion
sol¦em¦nize
 (sol¦em¦niz¦ing)
solen (mollusc)
solen¦oid
sol-fa
sol¦fa¦tara
sol¦feg¦gio (*pl.*
 sol¦feggi)
so¦li¦cit
 (so¦li¦cited,
 so¦li¦cit¦ing)
so¦li¦cita¦tion
so¦li¦citor

Solicitor-General
 (*pl.* Solicitors-
  General)
so¦li¦cit¦ous
so¦li¦cit¦ude
solid (as *a.*,
 sol¦ider,
 sol¦id¦est)
so¦lid¦ar¦ity
solid-drawn
so¦lidi¦fica¦tion
so¦lid¦ify
 (so¦lidi¦fies,
 so¦lidi¦fied,
 so¦lidi¦fy¦ing)
so¦lid¦ity
solid-state *a.*
so¦lid¦un¦gu¦late
sol¦idus (*pl.*
 sol¦idi)
so¦li¦fidian
so¦li¦fluc¦tion
So¦li¦hull
so¦li¦lo¦quist
so¦li¦lo¦quize
 (so¦li¦lo¦quizing)
so¦li¦lo¦quy (*pl.*
 so¦li¦lo¦quies)
soli¦ped
sol¦ips¦ism
sol¦ips¦ist
so¦lit¦aire
sol¦it¦ar¦ily
sol¦it¦ari¦ness
sol¦it¦ary (as *n.*, *pl.*
 sol¦it¦ar¦ies)
sol¦it¦ude
sol¦miz¦ate
 (sol¦miz¦at¦ing)
sol¦miza¦tion
solo (as *n.*, *pl.*
 so¦los)
so¦lo¦ist
Solo¦mon
So¦lon
So¦lo¦thurn
sol¦stice
sol¦sti¦tial
solu¦bil¦ity
solu¦bil¦iza¦tion
solu¦bil¦ize
 (solu¦bil¦iz¦ing)
sol¦uble
solus (*fem.* sola)
sol¦ute
so¦lu¦tion

So¦lu¦trean
solv¦able
solv¦ate
 (solv¦at¦ing)
sol¦va¦tion
solve (solv¦ing)
solv¦ency
solv¦ent
solver
Sol¦zhen¦it¦syn
soma
So¦mali
So¦ma¦lia
so¦matic
so¦ma¦to¦genic
so¦ma¦to¦logy
so¦ma¦to¦tonic
so¦ma¦to¦type
sombre
som¦brero (*pl.*
 som¦breros)
som¦brous
some¦body
some¦day
some¦how
some¦one
some¦place
som¦er¦sault
Som¦er¦set
some¦thing
some¦time *a.* &
 adv.
some¦times
some¦what
some¦when
some¦where
som¦ite
som¦itic
somn¦am¦bu¦lant
somn¦am¦bu¦lism
somn¦am¦bu¦list
som¦ni¦fer¦ous
som¦no¦lence
som¦no¦lency
som¦no¦lent
son¦ancy
son¦ant
sonar
son¦ata
son¦at¦ina
sonde
sone (unit)
son et lu¦mi¦ère
song¦bird
song¦book
song-cycle

song|ful
song|fully
song|ster
song|stress
song-thrush
sonic
son-in-law (pl.
  sons-in-law)
son'net (as v.,
  son'neted,
  son'net|ing)
son'net|eer
sonny
so'no|buoy
sono|meter
son'or|ity
son'or|ous
soon|ish
soot'er|kin
sooth (truth)
soothe (sooth|ing)
sooth|say
  (sooth|said,
  sooth|say'ing)
sooth|sayer
soot|ily
sooti|ness
sooty (soot|ier,
  sooti|est)
sop (as v., sopped,
  sop|ping)
soph|ism
soph|ist
soph|ister
soph|istic
soph|ist|ical
soph|ist|ic|ally
soph|ist|ic|ate (as
  v., soph'ist'ic|
            at'ing)
soph'ist|ic|ated
soph'ist|ica|tion
soph|istry (pl.
  soph'is|tries)
Soph|oc|les
sop'or'if'er|ous
sop'or|ific
sop|pily
sop'pi|ness
soppy (sop|pier,
  sop|pi|est)
sop'ra|nino (pl.
  sop'ra|ni'nos)
sop|ran|ist
sop|rano (as n.,
  pl. sop|ranos)

sora
sor'be|fa'cient
sor'bet
Sorb|ian
sorbo (pl. sor'bos)
sor|cerer
sor'cer|ess
sor|cery
sor'did
sor|dino (pl.
  sor|dini)
sor'dor
sore (sorer,
  sor'est)
sorel (deer)
  △ sorrel
Sor'en|sen
sor|ghum
so|rites (pl. same)
so'rit|ical
sor'op'tim|ist
sor|ori|cidal
sor|ori|cide
sor'or|ity (pl.
  sor'or|it'ies)
sor|osis (pl.
  sor|oses)
sorp|tion
sorra
sor'rel (herb)
  △ sorel
sor|rily
sor'ri|ness
sor'row
sor'row|ful
sor'row|fully
sorry (sor|rier,
  sor'ri|est)
sorter
sor'tie
sor'ti|lege
sor'ti|tion
sorus (pl. sori)
SOS
so-so
sos|ten'uto (as n.,
  pl. sos|ten'utos)
sot (as v., sot'ted,
  sot|ting)
so'teri|ology
So'thic
sot|tish
sotto voce
sou
sou|brette

soubriquet *use*
  sobriquet
sou|chong
soufflé
sou'fri'ère
sough
souk
soul
soul-destroying
soul|ful
soul|fully
soul|less
soul-searching
sound-box
sounder
sounding-board
sound-proof
sound-track
sound-wave
soup|çon
soup-kitchen
soup-spoon
soupy (soup|ier,
  soupi|est)
source (origin)
sour|puss
sou'sa|phone
souse (as v.,
  sous|ing)
sou|tache
sou|tane
souten|eur
souter
sou'ter'rain
South|amp'ton
south|bound
South|down
  (sheep)
south-east
south|easter
south-easterly (as
  n., pl.
  south-easterlies)
south-eastern
south-easterner
South|end (on
  Sea)
souther
south'er'li|ness
south|erly (as n.,
  pl. south'er|lies)
south|ern
south|erner
south'ern|most
south'ern|wood
south|ing

south|paw
South|port
south-south-east
south-south-west
south|ward
south|wards
south-west
south|wester
  (wind)
south-westerly
  (as n., pl. south-
          westerlies)
south-western
south-westerner
sou|venir
sou'wester (hat)
sov'er|eign
sov'er|eignty (pl.
  sov'er|eign|ties)
so'viet
so'vi'eto|lo'gist
sow (as v., p.p.
  sowed *or* sown)
sow|back
sow|bread
sower
Soweto
sow|thistle
soy (sauce)
soya (bean)
sozzled
spa (spring)
space (as v.,
  spa'cing)
space-bar
space|craft
space|man (pl.
  space|men)
space|ship
space|suit
spacial *use*
  spatial
spa|cious
spade (as v.,
  spad|ing)
spade|ful (pl.
  spade|fuls)
spade|work
spa|di'ceous
spa'dic|ose
spa|dille
spa'dix (pl.
  spa|dices)
spado (pl.
  spa|dos)
spa|ghetti

Spain
spall
spal|la'tion
spal|peen
Spam (*propr.*)
span (as *v.*,
  spanned,
  span|ning)
span|drel
spangle (as *v.*,
  spang|ling)
spangly
  (spang|lier,
  spang|li|est)
Span|iard
span|iel
Span|ish
spanker
spank|ing
span|ner
spar (as *n.*, pole,
  mineral, fight; as
  v., sparred,
  spar|ring)
spar|able
spa|raxis
spare (as *v.*,
  spar'ing; as *a.*,
  sparer, sparest)
spare-rib
sparge
  (spar|ging)
spar|ger
spar'ing
sparking-plug
sparkle (as *v.*,
  spark|ling)
spark|ler
spark-plug
spar|ling
spar|oid
spar|row
sparry
spars|ity
Sparta
Spar'ta|cist
Spar|tan
spasm
spas|modic
spas|mod'ic|ally
spas|tic
spas'tic|ally
spas|ti'city
spat (as *v.*,
  spatted,
  spat|ting)

spatch|cock
spate
spa'tha|ceous
spathe
spath'ic
spath|ose
spa|tial
spa'ti|al'ity
spa|tially
spat|ter
spat|ula
spatu|late
spavin
spavined
spawn
spay
speak (spoke,
  spoken)
speak|easy (*pl.*
  speak|easies)
speaker
spear|head
spear|mint
spear|wort
spec (speculation
  etc.)
spe'cial
spe'cial|ism
spe'cial|ist
spe'cial|istic
spe'ci|al'ity (*pl.*
  spe'ci|al'it|ies)
spe'cial|iza|tion
spe'cial|ize
  (spe'cial|iz|ing)
spe'cially
spe'cialty (*Law*;
  pl. spe'cial|ties)
spe'ci|ation
spe'cie
spe'ci|fi'able
spe|cific
spe'cif'ic|ally
spe'ci|fica|tion
spe'ci|fi'city
spe'cify
  (spe'ci|fies,
  spe'ci|fied,
  spe'ci|fy'ing)
spe'ci|men
spe'ci|olo'gical
spe'ci|ology
spe'ci|os'ity
spe'cious
speck (dot etc.)

speckle (as *v.*,
  speck|ling)
speck'tion|eer
specs (spectacles)
spec|tacle
spec|tacled
spec'tacu|lar
spec|tator
spec|tral
spec|trally
spectre
spec'tro|
  chem'istry
spec'tro|gram
spec'tro|graph
spec'tro|graphic
spec'tro|graphy
spec'tro|he'lio|
  graph
spec'tro|he'lio|
  scope
spec'tro|meter
spec'tro|met'ric
spec'tro|metry
spec'tro|pho'to|
  meter
spec'tro|scope
spec'tro|scopic
spec'tro|scop'ical
spec'tro|scop'ist
spec'tro|scopy
spec|trum (*pl.*
  spec|tra)
specu|lar
specu|late
  (specu|lat'ing)
specu|la'tion
specu|lat'ive
specu|lator
specu|lum (*pl.*
  spec|ula)
speech-day
speech|ful
speechi|fica'tion
speechi|fier
speech|ify
  (speechi|fies,
  speechi|fied,
  speechi|fy'ing)
speech|less
speed (as *v.*, sped
  but speeded in
  senses 'regulate
  speed of ' and
  'travel too fast')
speed|ball

speed|boat
speed|ily
speedi|ness
speedo (*pl.*
  speedos)
speedo|meter
speed|ster
speed-up *n.*
speed|way
speed|well
speedy
  (speed|ier,
  speedi|est)
speiss
spe'le|olo'gical
spe'le|olo'gist
spe'le|ology
spell (spelled *or*
  spelt)
spell|bind
  (spell|bound)
spell|binder
speller
spel|ter
spen|cer
Spen'cer|ian
spend (spent)
spender
spend|thrift
Spen|ser, E.
Spen'ser|ian
sperm
sper'ma|ceti
sperm|ary (*pl.*
  sperm|ar'ies)
sperm|atic
sperm|atid
sper'ma'to|blast
sper'ma'to|cyte
sper'ma'to|
  gen'esis
sper'ma'to|
  gon'ium
sper'ma'to|phore
sper'ma'to|phyte
sper'ma'to|zoid
sper'ma'to|zoon
  (*pl.*
  sper'ma'to|zoa)
spermi|cidal
spermi|cide
sper'mo|blast
sper'mo|cyte
sper'mo|gen'esis
sper'mo|gon'ium
sperm-oil

sper|mo|phore
sper|mo|phyte
sper|mo|zoid
sper|mo|zoon (*pl.*
sper|mo|zoa)
spew
Spey
sphag|num (*pl.*
sphagna)
sphal|er|ite
sphen|oid
sphen|oidal
sphere
spheric
spher|ical
spher|ic|ally
spher|oid
spher|oidal
spher|oidi|city
sphero|meter
spher|ular
spher|ule
spher|ul|ite
sphinc|ter
sphinc|teral
sphinc|teric
sphingid
sphinx
Sphinx (*Gr. myth.*)
sphra|gist|ics
sphyg|mo|gram
sphyg|mo|graph
sphyg|mo|ma|no|
          meter
spica
spic|ate
spic|ated
spice (as *v.*,
spi|cing)
spice|bush
spicery (*pl.*
spicer|ies)
spi|cily
spi|ci|ness
spick|nel
spicu|lar
spicu|late
spic|ule
spicy (spi|cier,
spi|ci|est)
spider
spider-man (*pl.*
spider-men)
spider|wort
spidery
spie|gel|eisen

spiel
spiff|ing
spiffy (spif|fier,
spif|fi|est)
spif|lic|ate
(spif|lic|at|ing)
spif|lica|tion
spig|nel
spigot
spike (as *v.*,
spik|ing)
spike|let
spike|nard
spi|kily
spi|ki|ness
spiky (spi|kier,
spi|ki|est)
spile (as *v.*, spiled,
spil|ing)
spill (spilled *or*
spilt)
spill|age
spil|li|kin
spill|way
spilth
spin (as *v.*, spun,
spin|ning)
spina bif|ida
spin|aceous
spin|ach
spinal
spindle (as *v.*,
spin|dling)
spindly
(spind|lier,
spind|li|est)
spin-drier
spin|drift
spin-dry
(spin-dries,
spin-dried,
spin-drying)
spine-chilling
spined
spinel
spine|less
spinet
spin|ifex
spi|ni|ness
spin|naker
spin|ner
spin|neret
spin|ney
spinning-jenny
(*pl.* spinning-
          jennies)

spinning-top
spinning-wheel
spin-off *n.*
spin|ose
spin|ous
Spin|oza
spin|ster
spin|thari|scope
spin|ule
spinu|lose
spinu|lous
spiny (spi|nier,
spi|ni|est)
spir|acle
spir|acu|lar
spir|acu|lum (*pl.*
spir|ac|ula)
spir|aea
spiral (as *v.*,
spir|alled,
spir|al|ling)
spir|ally
spir|ant
spire (as *v.*,
spir|ing)
spir|il|lum (*pl.*
spir|illa)
spirit (as *v.*,
spir|ited,
spir|it|ing)
spir|ited
spir|it|ism
spir|it|ist
spirit-lamp
spir|it|less
spirit-level
spir|itual
spir|itu|al|ism
spir|itu|al|ist
spir|itu|al|istic
spir|itu|al|ity (*pl.*
spir|itu|al|it|ies)
spir|itu|al|iza|tion
spir|itu|al|ize
(spir|itu|al|iz|ing)
spir|itu|ally
spi|ri|tuel
spir|itu|ous
spiri|valve
spir|ket|ing
spiro|chaete
spiro|graph
spiro|gyra
spiro|meter
spiry

spit (in sense 'eject
saliva' spat *or*
spit, spit|ting; in
sense 'pierce'
spit|ted,
spit|ting)
spitch|cock
spite (as *v.*,
spit|ing)
spite|ful
spite|fully
spit|fire
spittle
spit|toon
spitz (dog)
Spits|ber|gen
spiv
spiv|ish
spiv|very
splanch|nic
splanch|no|logy
splanch|no|tomy
(*pl.* splanch|no|
          tom|ies)
splash|back
splash-board
splash-down
splash|ily
splashy
(splash|ier,
splashi|est)
splat|ter
spleen|wort
spleeny
(spleen|ier,
spleeni|est)
splend|ent
splen|did
splen|di|fer|ous
splend|our
splen|ec|tomy (*pl.*
splen|ec|tom|ies)
splen|etic
splen|et|ic|ally
sple|nial
splenic
splen|itis
sple|nius (*pl.*
sple|nii)
splen|oid
spleno|logy
spleno|meg|aly
spleno|tomy (*pl.*
spleno|tom|ies)
splice (as *v.*,
spli|cing)

spline (as v.,
 splin'ing)
splin|ter
splin|tery
split (split,
 split|ting)
split-level
split|ter
splodge (as v.,
 splodging)
splodgy
 (splodgier,
 splodgi|est)
splotchy
 (splotch|ier,
 splotchi|est)
splurge (as v.,
 splur'ging)
splut|ter
splut|tery
Spode
spoil (as v., spoilt,
 except in sense
 'plunder', or
 spoiled)
spoil|age
spoiler
spoil-sport
spoke (as v.,
 spok|ing)
spoke-bone
spoke|shave
spokes|man (pl.
 spokes|men)
spokes|wo'man
 (pl.
 spokes|wo'men)
spoke|wise
spo'li|ation
spo'li|ator
spo'li|at'ory
spon|daic
spon|dee
spon'du|licks
spon'dyl|itis
sponge (as v.,
 spon'ging)
sponge-bag
sponge-cake
sponger
spon'gily
spon'gi|ness
spongy
 (spon'gier,
 spon'gi|est)
spon|sion

spon|son
spon|sor
spon'sor|ial
spon'sor|ship
spon'tan'eity
spon'tan'eous
spon|toon
spoofer
spook|ily
spooki|ness
spooky
 (spook|ier,
 spooki|est)
spoon|beak
spoon|bill
spoon'er|ism
spoon-feed
 (spoon-fed,
 spoon-feeding)
spoon|ful (pl.
 spoon|fuls)
spoon|ily
spooni|ness
spoony (as a.,
 spoon|ier,
 spooni|est; as n.,
 pl. spoon'ies)
spoor (track)
 △ spore
spor|adic
spor'ad'ic|ally
spor'an'gium (pl.
 spor'an'gia)
spore (Bot.)
 △ spoor
sporo|gen'esis
spo'ro|gen'ous
sporo|phyte
sporo|phytic
spor|ran (pouch)
sport|ily
spor'ti|ness
sport|ing
sport|ive
sports|man (pl.
 sports|men)
sports'man|like
sports'man|ship
sports|wo'man
 (pl.
 sports|wo'men)
sporty (spor|tier,
 spor'ti|est)
sporu|lar
spor|ule

spot (as v.,
 spot'ted,
 spot'ting)
spot|less
spot|light (as v.,
 spot|lighted or
 spot|lit)
spot-on
spot|ter
spot|tily
spot'ti|ness
spotty (spot|tier,
 spot'ti|est)
spouse
sprain
sprat (as v.,
 sprat'ted,
 sprat'ting)
sprawl
sprayer
sprayey
spray-gun
spread (as v.,
 spread)
spread-eagle v. &
 a. (as v.,
 spread-eagled,
 spread-eagling)
spreader
spree (as v.,
 speed)
sprig (as v.,
 sprigged,
 sprig|ging)
spriggy
 (sprig|gier,
 sprig'gi|est)
spright'li|ness
sprightly
 (spright|lier,
 spright'li|est)
sprig|tail
spring (as v.,
 sprang, sprung)
spring|board
spring|bok
spring-clean
springer
spring|ily
springi|ness
spring|tail
spring-tide (tide of
 greatest range)
spring|tide
 (springtime)
spring|time

springy
 (spring|ier,
 springi|est)
sprinkle (as v.,
 sprink|ling)
sprink|ler
sprink|ling
sprinter
sprit|sail
sprocket
spruce (as v.,
 spru'cing)
spruit
spry (spryer,
 spry|est)
spud (as v.,
 spud'ded,
 spud|ding)
spue use spew
spume (as v.,
 spum'ing)
spu|mous
spumy (spu|mier,
 spu'mi|est)
spunk|ily
spunki|ness
spunky
 (spun|kier,
 spun'ki|est)
spur (as v.,
 spurred,
 spur'ring)
spuri|ous
spur|rier
spurry (pl.
 spur|ries)
spurt
spur|wort
sput|nik
sput|ter
spu'tum (pl.
 sputa)
spy (as n., pl.
 spies; as v., spies,
 spied, spy'ing)
spy|glass
spy|hole
squab
squabble (as v.,
 squab|bling)
squab|bler
squabby
squacco (pl.
 squac'cos)
squad
squad|die

squad|ron
squail
squail-board
squalid
squal|id|ity
squall
squally
squal|oid
squalor
squama (*pl.*
  squa|mae)
squam|ose
squam|ous
squam|ule
squan|der
square (as *a.*,
  squarer,
  squarest; as *v.*
  squared,
  squar|ing)
squar|ish
squar|rose
squash
squashy
  (squash|ier,
  squashi|est)
squat (as *v.*,
  squat|ted,
  squat|ting; as *a.*,
  squat|ter,
  squat|test)
squat|ter
squaw
squawk
squeak
squeaker
squeak|ily
squeaki|ness
squeaky
  (squeak|ier,
  squeaki|est)
squeal
squealer
squeam|ish
squee|gee
squeez|able
squeeze (as *v.*,
  squeez|ing)
squelch
squib
squid (as *v.*,
  squid|ded,
  squid|ding)
squiffed

squiffy
  (squif|fier,
  squif|fi|est)
squiggle
squig|gly
squill
squinch
squint
squire (as *v.*,
  squir|ing)
squire|archy (*pl.*
  squire|ar|chies)
squir|een
squirm
squir|rel (as *v.*,
  squir|relled,
  squir|rel|ling)
squirt
squish
squishy
  (squish|ier,
  squishi|est)
squitch
Sri Lanka
stab (as *v.*,
  stabbed,
  stab|bing)
Stabat Mater
sta|bile
stability
sta|bil|iza|tion
sta|bil|ize
  (sta|bil|iz|ing)
sta|bil|izer
stable (as *a.*,
  stabler, stablest;
  as *v.*, sta|bling)
sta|ble|man (*pl.*
  sta|ble|men)
sta|bling
stably
stac|cato (as *n.*, *pl.*
  stac|ca|tos)
stacte
staddle
sta|dium (*pl.*
  sta|di|ums or Ant.
  stadia)
stadt|holder
Staël
staff (*pl.* staffs or
  Mus. staves)
staff|age
staff|ing
Staf|ford
Staf|ford|shire

stage (as *v.*,
  sta|ging)
stage-coach
stage|craft
stage-hand
stage-manage
  (stage-
       managing)
stage-manager
stager
stagey use stagy
stag|fla|tion
stag|ger
stag|ger|ing
stag-horn
stag|hound
sta|gily
sta|gi|ness
sta|ging
stag|nancy
stag|nant
stag|nate
  (stag|nat|ing)
stag|na|tion
stag|ni|col|ous
stagy (sta|gier,
  sta|gi|est)
stain|less
stair|case
stair|head
stair-rod
stair|way
staithe (wharf)
stake (post etc.;
  as *v.*, stak|ing)
stake-boat
stake|holder
Stak|han|ov|ite
sta|lac|tic
sta|lac|ti|form
sta|lac|tite
sta|lac|titic
Stalag
stal|ag|mite
stal|ag|mitic
stale (as *a.*, staler,
  stalest; as *v.*,
  stal|ing)
stale|mate (as *v.*,
  stale|mat|ing)
Sta|lin
Sta|lin|ism
Sta|lin|ist
stalk
stall|age
stal|lion

stal|wart
sta|men
stam|ina
stam|inal
stam|in|ate
sta|mi|ni|fer|ous
stam|mer
stam|pede (as *v.*,
  stam|ped|ing)
stamper
stanch (check
  flow) △ staunch
stan|chion
stand (as *v.*,
  stood)
stand|ard
stand|ard|iza|tion
stand|ard|ize
  (stand|ard|iz|ing)
stand-by (*pl.*
  stand-bys)
standee
stander
stand-in *n.*
stand-off *n.*
stand-offish
stand-pipe
stand|point
stand|still
stand-up *a.*
stan|hope
  (carriage)
stan|iel
Stan|ley
Stan|nar|ies
  (district))
stan|nary (*pl.*
  stan|nar|ies)
stan|nate
stan|nic
stan|nite
stan|nous
stanza
stan|za'd
stan|zaic
sta|pe|lia
stapes (*pl.* same)
sta|phylo|coc|cal
sta|phylo|coc|cus
  (*pl.* sta|phylo|
       coc|ci)
staple (as *v.*,
  stap|ling)
stapler

star (as v.,
 starred,
 star|ring)
star|board
starch
starch|ily
starchi|ness
starchy
 (star|chier,
 star|chi|est)
star|dom
star-dust
stare (as v.,
 star|ing)
star|fish
star-gazer
star-gazing
starkers
star|less
star|let
star|light
star|ling
star|lit
star|rily
star|ri|ness
starry (star|rier,
 star|ri|est)
starter
startle (as v.,
 start|ling)
star|va|tion
starve (as v.,
 starv|ing)
starve|ling
star|wort
stasis (pl. stases)
stat|able
statal
state (as v.,
 stat|ing)
State (political)
state|craft
statedly
state|hood
state|less
state|li|ness
stately (state|lier,
 state|li|est)
state|ment
Sta|ten (Island)
stater
state|room
states|man
 (pl.states|men)
states|man|like
states|manly

states|man|ship
static
stat|ical
stat|ic|ally
stat|ice
stat|ics
sta|tion
sta|tion|ary (not
 moving)
sta|tioner
sta|tion|ery (paper
 etc.)
station-master
station-wagon
stat|ism
stat|ist
stat|istic
stat|ist|ical
stat|ist|ic|ally
stat|isti|cian
stat|ist|ics
sta|tor (Electr.)
stato|scope
statu|ary (pl.
 statu|ar|ies)
statue
stat|ued
sta|tu|esque
sta|tu|ette
stat|ure
stat|ured
sta|tus (pl.
 sta|tuses)
sta|tus quo
stat|ut|able
stat|ute
stat|ut|or|ily
stat|ut|ory
staunch (loyal
 etc.) △ stanch
stave (as v.,
 staved or Naut.
 stove, stav|ing)
staves|acre
stay-bar
stayer
stay-rod
stay|sail
stead|fast
stead|ily
steadi|ness
stead|ing

steady (as a.,
 stead|ier,
 steadi|est; as v.,
 stead|ies,
 stead|ied,
 steady|ing)
steak (meat)
 △ stake
steak-house
steal (stole,
 stolen)
stealth|ily
stealthi|ness
stealthy
 (stealth|ier,
 stealthi|est)
steam|boat
steam-engine
steamer
steam|roller
steam|ship
steamy
 (steam|ier,
 steami|est)
steel|head
steeli|ness
steel|work
steely (steel|ier,
 steeli|est)
steel|yard
steen|bok
 (antelope)
steen|kirk
steepen
steep|ish
steeple
steeple|chase
steeple|chaser
steeple|chas|ing
steeple|jack
steer|age
steers|man (pl.
 steers|men)
steeve (as v.,
 steev|ing)
stein (beer-mug)
stein|bock (ibex)
stela (pl. stelae)
stele

stel|lar
stel|late
stel|lated
stel|li|form
stel|lu|lar
stem (as v.,
 stemmed,
 stem|ming)
stemma (pl.
 stem|mata)
stemple
Sten (gun)
sten|cil (as v.,
 sten|cilled,
 sten|cil|ling)
Stend|hal
ste|no|grapher
ste|no|graphic
ste|no|graphy
sten|osis (pl.
 sten|oses)
steno|type
steno|typ|ist
sten|ter
Sten|tor
sten|tor|ian
step (as v.,
 stepped,
 step|ping)
step|brother
step|child (pl.
 step|chil|dren)
step|daugh|ter
step|father
steph|an|otis
Ste|phen
Ste|phen|son, G.
step-ladder
step|mother
step-parent
steppe (grassy
 plain)
step|sis|ter
step|son
step|wise
ste|ra|dian
ster|cora|ceous
ster|coral
stere (unit)
ste|reo (pl.
 ste|reos)
ste|reo|bate
ste|reo|chem|istry
ste|reo|graph
ste|reo|graphy
stereo-isomer

ste¦reo¦metry
ste¦reo¦phonic
ste¦reo¦phon¦ic¦
   ally
ste¦reo¦phony
ste¦reo¦scope
ste¦reo¦scopic
ste¦reo¦scop¦ic¦
   ally
ste¦reo¦scopy
ste¦reo¦type (as v.,
  ste¦reo¦typ¦ing)
steric
ster¦ile
ster¦il¦ity
ster¦il¦iza¦tion
ster¦il¦ize
  (ster¦il¦iz¦ing)
ster¦il¦izer
ster¦let
ster¦ling
sternal
Sterne
stern¦most
stern¦ness
sternum (pl.
  stern¦ums)
ster¦nu¦tator
ster¦nu¦tat¦ory
stern¦ward
ster¦oid
ster¦oidal
sterol
ster¦tor¦ous
stet (as v., stet¦ted,
  stet¦ting)
stetho¦scope
stetho¦scopic
stetho¦scop¦ist
stetho¦scopy
stet¦son (hat)
steve¦dore
steven¦graph
Ste¦ven¦son, R. L.
stew¦ard
stew¦ard¦ess
sthenic
sti¦cho¦mythia
stick (as v., stuck)
sticker
stick¦ily
sticki¦ness
stick-in-the-mud
stick¦jaw
stickle¦back
stick¦ler

stick-up n.
sticky (stick¦ier,
  sticki¦est)
stiffen
stiff¦ener
stifle (sti¦fling)
stigma (pl.
  stig¦mas,
  stig¦mata of
  Christ)
stig¦matic
stig¦mat¦ic¦ally
stig¦mat¦ist
stig¦mat¦iza¦tion
stig¦mat¦ize
  (stig¦mat¦iz¦ing)
stil¦bene
stil¦boes¦trol
stil¦etto (pl.
  stil¦et¦tos)
still¦age
still¦born
stil¦li¦cide
still¦ness
still-room
stilly (f. still)
stil¦ted
Stil¦ton
stilus use stylus
stimu¦lant
stimu¦late
  (stimu¦lat¦ing)
stimu¦la¦tion
stimu¦lat¦ive
stimu¦lator
stimu¦lus (pl.
  stim¦uli)
stimy use stymie
sting (as v., stung)
sting¦aree
stinger
stin¦gily
stingi¦ness
sting-ray
stingy (stin¦gier,
  stin¦gi¦est)
stink (as v., stank
  or stunk, stunk)
stink¦ard
stinker
stink¦horn
stink¦pot
stink¦weed
stink¦wood
stint¦less
stipel

stipel¦late
sti¦pend
sti¦pen¦di¦ary
  (as n., pl.
  sti¦pen¦di¦ar¦ies)
sti¦pes (pl.
  stip¦ites)
sti¦pi¦form
stip¦it¦ate
sti¦piti¦form
stipple (as v.,
  stip¦pling)
stipu¦lar
stipu¦late (as v.,
  stipu¦lat¦ing)
stipu¦la¦tion
stipu¦lator
stip¦ule
stir (as v., stirred,
  stir¦ring)
Stir¦ling
stir¦pi¦cul¦ture
stirps (pl. stir¦pes)
stir¦rer
stir¦rup
stirrup-pump
stitch
stitch¦ery
stitch¦ing
stitch¦wort
stiver
stoa (portico; pl.
  stoas)
Stoa (Philos.)
stoch¦astic
stoch¦ast¦ic¦ally
stock¦ade (as v.,
  stock¦ad¦ing)
stock-breeder
stock¦broker
stock¦brok¦ing
stock-car
stock¦dove
stock¦fish
stock¦holder
Stock¦holm
stock¦ily
stocki¦ness
stock¦inet
stock¦ing
stock¦inged
stock¦ist
stock¦job¦ber
stock¦job¦bing
stock¦list

stock¦man (pl.
  stock¦men)
stock-market
stock¦pile (as v.,
  stock¦pil¦ing)
Stock¦port
stock-room
stock-still
stock-taking
Stock¦ton (on
  Tees)
stocky (stock¦ier,
  stocki¦est)
stock¦yard
stodgily
stodgi¦ness
stodgy (stodgier,
  stodgi¦est)
stoep (S. Afr.,
  veranda)
stoic
Stoic (Philos.)
sto¦ical
sto¦ic¦ally
stoi¦chi¦ometric
stoi¦chi¦ometry
sto¦icism
Sto¦icism (Philos.)
stoke (stok¦ing)
stoke¦hold
stoke¦hole
stoker
stokes (unit; pl.
  same)
stola (pl. sto¦lae)
stolid
stol¦id¦ity
sto¦lon
sto¦lon¦ate
sto¦loni¦fer¦ous
stoma
stom¦ach
sto¦mat¦itis
sto¦mato¦lo¦gical
sto¦mato¦lo¦gist
sto¦mato¦logy
stone (as v.,
  ston¦ing)
stone¦chat
stone¦crop
Stone¦haven
Stone¦henge
stone¦less
stone¦ma¦son
stone¦ma¦sonry
stone¦wall v.

stone|wall|ing
stone|ware
stone|weed
stone|work
stone|wort
sto|nily
sto|ni|ness
stonker
stony (sto|nier,
 sto|ni|est)
stony-broke
stooge (as v.,
 stoo|ging)
stool-ball
stool-pigeon
stop (as v.,
 stopped,
 stop|ping)
stop|cock
stop|gap
stop-go
stop-lamp
stop-light
stop|off n.
stop|over n.
stop|page
stop|per
stop|ping
stopple (as v.,
 stop|pling)
stop-press
stop-watch
stor|able
stor|age
storax
store (as v.,
 stor|ing)
store|house
store|keeper
store|man (pl.
 store|men)
store-room
storey (division of
 building)
stor|eyed
stori|ated
stori|ation
stor|ied
 (celebrated in
 legend)
stork's-bill
storm-cloud
storm|cone
storm|ily
stormi|ness
storm|proof

storm-trooper
storm-troops
stormy
 (stor|mier,
 stor|mi|est)
Stor|no|way
story (pl. stor|ies)
story-book
story-line
story-teller
stoup (flagon,
 basin)
stout-hearted
stout|ish
stove (as v.,
 stov|ing)
stow|age
stow|away n.
stra|bis|mal
stra|bis|mic
stra|bis|mus
straddle (as v.,
 strad|dling)
Stra|di|vari
Stra|di|varius
strafe (as v.,
 straf|ing)
straggle (as v.,
 strag|gling)
strag|gler
strag|gly
 (strag|glier,
 strag|gli|est)
straighten
straight|for|ward
strainer
straiten (to
 restrict)
strait-jacket
 (as v.,
 strait-jacketed,
 strait-jacketing)
strait-laced
stra|mo|nium
strange
 (stranger,
 strangest)
stranger
strangle
 (stran|gling)
strangle|hold
stran|gler
strangles
stran|gu|late
 (stran|gu|lat|ing)
stran|gu|la|tion

strang|uri|ous
strang|ury (pl.
 strang|ur|ies)
strap (as v.,
 strapped,
 strap|ping)
strap|hanger
strap|less
strap|pado (as n.,
 pl. strap|pa|dos)
strap|per
strap|ping
Stras|burg
stra|ta|gem
stratal
stra|tegic
stra|tegical
stra|tegic|ally
stra|tegics
strat|egist
strat|egy (pl.
 strat|egies)
Strath|clyde
strath|spey
 (dance)
stra|ticu|late
strati|fica|tion
strati|fica|tional
strat|ify
 (strati|fies,
 strati|fied,
 strati|fy|ing)
stra|ti|graphic
stra|ti|graph|ical
stra|ti|graphy
stra|to|cir|rus
stra|to|cracy (pl.
 stra|to|cra|cies)
strato-cruiser
stra|to|cu|mu|lus
stra|to|pause
stra|to|sphere
stra|to|spheric
stratum
 (pl. strata)
stratus (pl. strati)
Straus, Oskar
Strauss
Stra|vin|sky
straw|berry (pl.
 straw|ber|ries)
straw-board
straw-colour
strawy

streaky
 (streak|ier,
 streaki|est)
streamer
stream|line (as v.,
 stream|lin|ing)
street|car
street-walker
strengthen
strenu|ous
strep|to|coc|cal
strep|to|coc|cus
 (pl.
 strep|to|cocci)
strep|to|my|cin
Strepyan
stress|ful
stress|fully
stress|less
stretcher
stretchy
 (stretch|ier,
 stretchi|est)
stretto (as n., pl.
 stret|tos)
strew (p.p.
 strewn)
stria (pl. striae)
stri|ate (as v.,
 stri|at|ing)
stri|ation
stri|at|ure
stricken
strickle
stric|ture
stric|tured
stride (as v.,
 strode, strid|den,
 strid|ing)
stri|dency
stri|dent
stridu|lant
stridu|late
 (stridu|lat|ing)
stridu|la|tion
stri|gil
stri|gose
strik|able
strike (as v.,
 struck, strik|ing)
strike|bound
striker
strik|ing
striking-distance
striking-force
Strind|berg

string (as v.,
 strung)
strin|gency
strin|gendo
strin|gent
stringer
stringi|ness
stringy
 (string|ier,
 stringi|est)
strip (as v.,
 stripped,
 strip|ping)
strip|ling
strip|per
strip-tease
stripy (stri|pier,
 stri|pi|est)
strive (strove,
 striven,
 striv|ing)
stro|bila (pl.
 stro|bi|lae)
stro|bile
strob|ilus (pl.
 strob|ili)
stro|bo|scope
stro|bo|scopic
Strog'an|off
stroke (as v.,
 strok'ing)
stroller
stroma (pl.
 stro'mata)
stro|matic
Strom|boli
strong-arm a.
strong-box
strong|hold
strong|ish
strong-minded
strong-room
stron|tia
stron|tium
strop (as v.,
 stropped,
 strop|ping)
stroph|an'thin
strophe
strophic
stroppily
stroppiness
stroppy
 (strop|pier,
 strop'pi|est)
struc|tural

struc'tur'al|ism
struc'tur'al|ist
struc'tur'ally
struc'ture (as v.,
 struc|tured,
 struc'tur|ing)
struc'ture|less
stru|del
struggle (as v.,
 strug|gling)
strum (as v.,
 strummed,
 strum|ming)
struma (pl.
 stru'mae)
strum|ose
strum|ous
strut (as v.,
 strut'ted,
 strut|ting)
stru'thi|ous
strych|nic
strych|nine
strych'nin|ism
strych|nism
Stu'art
stub (as v.,
 stubbed,
 stub|bing)
stub'ble
stub|bly
stub|born
stubby (stub|bier,
 stub'bi|est)
stucco (as n., pl.
 stuc|coes; as v.,
 stuc|coes)
stud (as v.,
 stud'ded,
 stud|ding)
stud|ding
stu|dent
stu|dent|ship
stud-farm
stu'dio (pl.
 stu|dios)
stu'di|ous
study (as n., pl.
 stud|ies; as v.,
 stud|ies, studied,
 study|ing)
stuf|fily
stuf'fi|ness
stuff|ing

stuffy (stuf|fier,
 stuf'fi|est)
stul'ti|fica|tion
stul|tify
 (stul'ti|fies,
 stul'ti|fied,
 stul'ti|fy'ing)
stum (as v.,
 stummed,
 stum|ming)
stumble (as v.,
 stum|bling)
stumbling-block
stu'mer
stumper
stump|ily
stumpi|ness
stumpy
 (stum|pier,
 stum'pi|est)
stun (stunned,
 stun|ning)
stun|ner
stun|ning
stun|sail
stupa
stupe (as v.,
 stup'ing)
stu'pefa|cient
stu|pefac'tion
stu|pefact|ive
stu|pefier
stu|pefy
 (stu|pefies,
 stu|pefied,
 stu'pefy|ing)
stu|pen|dous
stu'pid (stu|pider,
 stu'pid|est)
stu|pid|ity
stu'por
stu'por|ous
stur|died
stur|dily
stur'di|ness
sturdy (as a.,
 stur|dier,
 stur'di|est; as n.,
 pl. stur|dies)
stur|geon
stut|ter
Stutt|gart
sty (as n., pl. sties;
 as v., sties, stied,
 sty'ing)
Stygian

style (as v.,
 styl'ing)
stylet
styl|ish
styl|ist
styl|istic
styl'ist'ic|ally
styl'ist|ics
styl|ite
styl|ize
 (styl|iz|ing)
stylo (pl. sty'los)
sty'lob|ate
sty'lo|graph
sty'lo|graphic
styl|oid
sty'lus (pl.
 styl|uses)
sty'mie (as v.,
 sty|mied,
 sty'mie|ing)
styp|tic
styrax
styr|ene
Styria
su'ab'il|ity
su'able
sua|sion
suas|ive
suav|ity
sub (as v., subbed,
 sub|bing)
sub|agency (pl.
 sub|agen'cies)
sub|agent
su|bah|dar
sub|al'pine
sub|al|tern
sub|aqua
sub|aquatic
sub'aque|ous
sub|arc'tic
sub|atomic
sub|category (pl.
 sub|categories)
sub|caudal
sub|class
sub|cla'vian
sub|clin'ical
sub|com'mit|tee
sub|con'ical
sub|con'scious
sub|con'tin'ent
sub|con|tract
sub|con'tractor

sub|con'trary (as
  n., pl.
  sub|con'trar'ies)
sub|cord'ate
sub|crit'ical
sub|cul'tural
sub|cul'ture
sub|cu'ta'ne|ous
sub|cu'ticu'lar
sub|deacon
sub|di'ac'on|ate
sub|div|ide
  (sub|div'id'ing)
sub|di'vi'sion
sub|dom'in'ant
sub|du|able
sub|dual
sub|due
  (sub|dued,
  sub|du'ing)
sub-edit
  (sub-edited,
  sub-editing)
sub-editor
sub-editorial
su'ber|eous
su|beric
su'ber|ose
sub|fam'ily (pl.
  sub|fam'il'ies)
sub|floor
sub|form
sub|fusc
sub|genus (pl.
  sub|gen'era)
sub|gla'cial
sub|group
sub|head'ing
sub|hu'man
sub|ja'cent
sub|ject
sub|jec'tion
sub|ject|ive
sub|ject'iv|ism
sub|ject'iv|ist
sub|ject'iv'ity
sub|join
sub|joint
sub ju'dice
sub|jug'able
sub|jug|ate
  (sub|jug'at'ing)
sub|juga'tion
sub|jug|ator
sub|junct|ive
sub|king'dom

sub|lap'sarian
sub|lease (as v.,
  sub|leas'ing)
sub|let (sub'let,
  sub'let|ting)
sub-lieutenant
sub'lim|ate (as v.,
  sub|lim|at'ing)
sub|lima|tion
sub|lime (as a.,
  sub|limer,
  sub|limest; as v.,
  sub|lim'ing)
sub|lim'inal
sub'lim|ity (pl.
  sub|lim'it|ies)
sub'lin|gual
sub|lit'toral
sub|lun'ary
sub-machine-gun
sub-man
  (pl. sub-men)
sub'mar|ine
sub'mar|iner
sub|max'il'lary
sub|me'di'ant
sub|men'tal
sub|merge
  (sub|mer'ging)
sub|mer'gence
sub|mers|ible
sub|mer'sion
sub|mic'ro|scopic
sub|mini'ature
sub'mis|sion
sub'mis|sive
sub'mit
  (sub|mit'ted,
  sub|mit'ting)
sub|mul'tiple
sub|nor'mal
sub|nor'mal|ity
sub|nuc'lear
sub|ocu'lar
sub|or'bital
sub|or'der
sub|or'dinal
sub|or'din|ate (as
  v., sub'or'din|
      at'ing)
sub|or'dina|tion
sub|or'din'at|ive
sub|orn
sub|orna'tion
sub|ox'ide

sub|phy'lum (pl.
  sub|phyla)
sub-plot
sub|poena (as v.,
  sub|poenaed)
sub|prior
sub|re'gion
sub|re'gional
sub|rep'tion
sub|roga'tion
sub|rout'ine
sub|scribe
  (sub|scrib'ing)
sub|scriber
sub|script
sub|scrip'tion
sub|sec'tion
sub|sel'lium (pl.
  sub|sel'lia)
sub|sequence
sub|sequent
sub|serve
  (sub|ser|ving)
sub|ser'vi|ence
sub|ser'vi|ency
sub|ser'vi|ent
sub|set
sub|shrub
sub|side
  (sub|sid'ing)
sub|sid|ence
sub|si'di|ar'ily
sub|si'di|ary (as
  n., pl.
  sub|si'di|ar'ies)
sub|sid|iza'tion
sub|sid|ize
  (sub|sid|iz'ing)
sub|sidy (pl.
  sub'sid|ies)
sub|sist
sub|sist|ence
sub|soil
sub|sonic
sub|son'ic|ally
sub|spe'cies
sub|spe'cific
sub|stance
sub|stand'ard
sub|stan'tial
sub|stan'tial|ism
sub|stan'tial|ist
sub|stan'ti|al'ity
sub|stan'tially

sub|stan'ti|ate
  (sub'stan'ti|
      ating)
sub|stan'ti|ation
sub|stant|ival
sub|stant'iv'ally
sub|stant|ive
sub|sta'tion
sub|stitu|ent
sub|sti'tut|able
sub|sti|tute (as v.,
  sub|sti'tut'ing)
sub|sti'tu'tion
sub|sti'tu'tional
sub|sti'tu'tion|ary
sub|sti'tut|ive
sub|strate
sub|stratum (pl.
  sub|strata)
sub|struc'tural
sub|struc'ture
sub|sume
  (sub|sum'ing)
sub|sump'tion
sub|ten'ancy (pl.
  sub|ten'an'cies)
sub|ten'ant
sub|tend
sub|ter|fuge
sub|ter'minal
sub|ter'ra'nean
sub|til'iza'tion
sub|til|ize
  (sub'til|iz'ing)
sub|title (as v.,
  sub|tit'ling)
subtle (subt'ler,
  subt'lest)
sub'tlety (pl.
  sub'tle|ties)
subtly
sub|tonic
sub|to'pia
sub|to'pian
sub|to'tal
sub|tract
sub|trac|tion
sub|tract|ive
sub|tra'hend
sub|trop'ical
subu|late
sub|urb
sub|urban
sub|urb'an|ite
sub|urb'an|iza|
      tion

sub|urb|an|ize
  (sub|urb|an|iz|
         ing)
Sub|urbia
sub|ven|tion
sub|ver|sion
sub|vers|ive
sub|vert
sub|way
sub|zero
suc|ced|an|eous
suc|ced|an|eum
  (pl. suc|ced|anea)
suc|ceed
suc|cen|tor
suc|cess
suc|cess|ful
suc|cess|fully
suc|ces|sion
suc|ces|sional
suc|cess|ive
suc|cessor
suc|cin|ate
suc|cinct
suc|cinic
suc|cory (pl.
  suc|cor|ies)
Suc|coth
suc|cour
suc|cuba (pl.
  suc|cu|bae)
suc|cu|bus (pl.
  suc|cubi)
suc|cu|lence
suc|cu|lent
suc|cumb
suc|cursal
such|like
sucker
suck|ing
suckle (suckled,
  suck|ling)
suck|ling
suc|rose
suc|tion
suc|tor|ial
suc|tor|ian
Su|dan
Su|dan|ese (as n.,
  pl. same)
su|dar|ium (pl.
  su|daria)
su|dat|orium (pl.
  su|dat|oria)
su|dat|ory (as n.,
  pl. su|dat|or|ies)

sud|den
su|dori|fer|ous
su|dor|ific
Sudra
sudsy (sud|sier,
  sud|si|est)
sue (sued, su|ing)
suede
suet
su|ety
Suez
suf|fer
suf|fer|able
suf|fer|ance
suf|fice (suf|ficed,
  suf|fi|cing)
suf|fi|ciency (pl.
  suf|fi|cien|cies)
suf|fi|cient
suf|fix
suf|fixa|tion
suf|foc|ate
  (suf|foc|at|ing)
suf|foca|tion
Suf|folk
suf|fragan
suf|frage
suf|fra|gette
suf|fra|gist
suf|fuse
  (suf|fus|ing)
suf|fu|sion
Sufi
Sufic
Suf|ism
sugar
sugar-daddy (pl.
  sugar-daddies)
sug|ari|ness
sugar-loaf (pl.
  sugar-loaves)
sug|ary
sug|gest
sug|gest|ib|il|ity
sug|gest|ible
sug|ges|tion
sug|gest|ive
sui|cidal
sui|cid|ally
sui|cide (as v.,
  sui|cid|ing)
sui gen|eris
su|il|line
suit (set of clothes)
  △ suite
suit|able

suit|ab|il|ity
suit|ably
suit|case
suite (set of
  furniture or
  rooms) △ suit
suit|ing
suitor
su|ki|yaki
sul|cate
sul|cus (pl. sulci)
sulk|ily
sulki|ness
sulky (sul|kier,
  sul|ki|est)
Sulla
sul|lage
sul|len
sully (sul|lies,
  sul|lied,
  sul|ly|ing)
sulpha (class of
  drugs)
sulph|am|ate
sulph|amic
sulph|an|il|am|ide
sulph|ate
sulph|ide
sulph|ite
sul|phon|am|ide
sulph|on|ate
sulph|ona|tion
sulph|one
sulph|onic
sul|phur
sul|phur|ate
  (sul|phur|at|ing)
sul|phura|tion
sul|phur|ator
sul|phur|eous
sul|phur|et|ted
sul|phuric
sul|phur|iza|tion
sul|phur|ize
  (sul|phur|iz|ing)
sul|phur|ous
sul|phury
sul|tan
sul|tana
sul|tan|ate
sul|trily
sul|tri|ness
sul|try (sul|trier,
  sul|tri|est)

sum (as v.,
  summed,
  sum|ming)
su|mac
Su|ma|tra
Su|mer
Su|mer|ian
summa (pl.
  sum|mae)
sum|mar|ily
sum|mar|ist
sum|mar|ize
  (sum|mar|iz|ing)
sum|mary (as n.,
  pl. sum|mar|ies)
sum|ma|tion
sum|ma|tional
sum|mer
summer-house
sum|merly
summersault use
  somersault
summer time
  (time)
summer-time
  (season)
sum|mery
summing-up (pl.
  summings-up)
sum|mit
sum|mitry
sum|mon
sum|moner
sum|mons
sum|mum bonum
sumo (pl. su|mos)
sump|tu|ary
sump|tu|os|ity
sump|tu|ous
sun (as v., sunned,
  sun|ning)
sun|bathe
  (sun|bath|ing)
sun|beam
sun-blind
sun|burn
sun|burned
sun|burnt
sun|burst
Sunda
sun|dae
Sun|dan|ese
  (Java)
Sun|day
sun-deck
sun|der

Sun|der|land
sun|dew
sun|dial
sun|down
sun|downer
sun-dress
sun-dried
sun|dries|man (*pl.*
  sun|dries|men)
sun|dry (as *n.*,
  pl. sun|dries)
sun|fast
sun|fish
sun|flower
sun-glasses
sun-god
sun-hat
sunken
sun-lamp
sun|light
sun|lit
sunn (fibre)
Sunna
Sunni
sun|nily
sun|ni|ness
Sunn|ite
sunny (sun|nier,
  sun|ni|est)
sun|rise
sun-roof
sun|set
sun|shade
sun|shine
sun|shiny
sun|spot
sun|stroke
sun-suit
sun-tan (as *v.*,
  sun-tanned,
  sun-tanning)
sun-trap
sun-up
Sun Yat-sen
sup (as *v.*, supped,
  sup|ping)
su|per
su|per|able
su|per|abound
su|per|abund|
        ance
su|per|abund|ant
su|per|add
su|per|ad|di|tion
su|per|al|tar
su|per|an|nu|able

su|per|an|nu|ate
su|per|an|nu|ated
su|per|an|nu|
        ation
su|per|aqueous
su|perb
su|per|cal|en|der
su|per|cargo (*pl.*
  su|per|car|goes)
su|per|ce|les|tial
su|per|charge
  (su|per|
      char|ging)
su|per|char|ger
su|per|cili|ary
su|per|cili|ous
su|per|class
su|per|co|lum|nar
su|per|
  con|duct|iv|ity
su|per|cool
su|per|crit|ical
super-ego (*pl.*
  super-egos)
su|per|el|eva|tion
su|per|em|in|ence
su|per|em|in|ent
su|per|eroga|tion
su|per|erog|at|ory
su|per|fam|ily (*pl.*
  su|per|fam|il|ies)
su|per|fat|ted
su|per|fe|cunda|
        tion
su|per|feta|tion
su|per|fi|cial
su|per|fi|ci|al|ity
  (*pl.* su|per|fi|ci|
      al|it|ies)
su|per|fi|cially
su|per|fi|cies (*pl.*
  same)
su|per|fine
su|per|flu|ity (*pl.*
  su|per|flu|it|ies)
su|per|flu|ous
su|per|gi|ant
su|per|heat
su|per|heater
su|per|het|ero|
        dyne
su|per|hu|man
su|per|hu|meral
su|per|im|pose
  (su|per|im|
      pos|ing)

su|per|im|posi|
        tion
su|per|
  in|cum|bent
su|per|in|duce
  (su|per|
      in|du|cing)
su|per|in|tend
su|per|in|tend|
        ence
su|per|in|tend|
        ency
su|per|in|tend|ent
su|per|ior
Su|perior, Lake
su|peri|or|ess
su|peri|or|ity (*pl.*
  su|peri|or|it|ies)
su|per|ja|cent
su|per|lat|ive
su|per|lun|ary
su|per|man (*pl.*
  su|per|men)
su|per|mar|ket
su|per|mun|dane
su|per|nacu|lar
su|per|nacu|lum
su|per|nal
su|per|nat|ant
su|per|nat|ural
su|per|nat|ur|al|
        ism
su|per|nat|ur|al|
        ist
su|per|nat|ur|ally
su|per|nova (*pl.*
  su|per|no|vae)
su|per|
      nu|mer|ary
  (as *n.*, *pl.* su|per|
    nu|mer|ar|ies)
su|per|or|der
su|per|or|dinal
su|per|or|din|ate
su|per|
      phos|phate
su|per|phys|ical
su|per|pose
  (su|per|pos|ing)
su|per|posi|tion
su|per|power
su|per|scribe
  (su|per|scrib|ing)
su|per|script
su|per|scrip|tion

su|per|sede
  (su|per|sed|ing)
su|per|sedence
su|per|sed|ure
su|per|ses|sion
su|per|sonic
su|per|son|ic|ally
su|per|star
su|per|sti|tion
su|per|sti|tious
su|per|store
su|per|stratum
  (*pl.* su|per|strata)
su|per|struc|tural
su|per|struc|ture
su|per|tanker
su|per|tax
su|per|tem|poral
su|per|ter|rene
su|per|tonic
su|per|vene
  (su|per|ven|ing)
su|per|ven|tion
su|per|vise
  (su|per|vising)
su|per|vi|sion
su|per|visor
su|per|vis|ory
su|pin|ate
  (su|pin|at|ing)
su|pina|tion
su|pin|ator
su|pine
sup|per
sup|plant
supple (as *a.*,
  sup|pler,
  sup|plest; as *v.*,
  sup|pling)
sup|plely
sup|ple|ment
sup|ple|mental
sup|ple|ment|ally
sup|ple|ment|ary
  (as *n.*, *pl.* sup|ple|
    ment|ar|ies)
sup|ple|menta|
        tion
sup|ple|tion
sup|plet|ive
sup|pli|ant
sup|plic|ant
sup|plic|ate
  (sup|plic|at|ing)
sup|plica|tion
sup|pli|cat|ory

sup|plier
sup|ply (as n., pl.
 sup|plies; as v.,
 sup|plies,
 sup|plied,
 sup|ply|ing)
sup|port
sup|port|able
sup|port|ably
sup|porter
sup|port|ive
sup|port|less
sup|pos|able
sup|pose
 (sup|pos|ing)
sup|posi|tion
sup|posi|tional
sup|posi|tious
 (hypothetical)
sup|posi|ti|tious
 (spurious)
sup|pos|it|ory (pl.
 sup|pos|it|or|ies)
sup|press
sup|press|ible
sup|pres|sion
sup|press|ive
sup|pressor
sup|pur|ate
 (sup|pur|at|ing)
sup|pura|tion
sup|pur|at|ive
sup|ra|lap|sarian
sup|ra|max|il|lary
su|pra|mund|ane
su|pra|na|tional
su|pra|or|bital
sup|ra|renal
su|pra|seg|mental
su|prem|acist
su|prem|acy
su|preme
suprême (in
 cooking)
su|premo (pl.
 su|premos)
sura (in Koran)
surah (fabric)
sural
surat
sur|charge (as v.,
 sur|char|ging)
sur|cingle
sur|coat
sur|cu|lose

sure (surer,
 surest)
sure-footed
surely
surety (pl.
 sure|ties)
sur|face (as v.,
 sur|fa|cing)
sur|fact|ant
surf-bird
surf|board
sur|feit
surfer
sur|fi|cial
sur|fi|cially
surf-riding
surfy (surf|ier,
 surfi|est)
surge (as v.,
 sur|ging)
sur|geon
sur|gery (pl.
 sur|ger|ies)
sur|gical
sur|gic|ally
sur|ic|ate
Sur|inam
sur|lily
sur|li|ness
surly (sur|lier,
 sur|li|est)
sur|mise (as v.,
 sur|mis|ing)
sur|mount
sur|mount|able
sur|mul|let
sur|name (as v.,
 sur|nam|ing)
sur|pass
sur|pass|ing
sur|plice
sur|pliced
sur|plus
sur|plus|age
sur|prise (as v.,
 sur|pris|ing)
surra
sur|real
sur|real|ism
sur|real|ist
sur|real|istic
sur|real|ist|ic|ally
sur|re|but|ter
sur|re|join|der
sur|ren|der
sur|rep|ti|tious

sur|rey (carriage)
Sur|rey (county)
sur|rog|ate
sur|round
sur|round|ings
sur|tax
sur|tout
sur|veil|lance
sur|vey
sur|veyor
sur|vival
sur|vive
 (sur|viv|ing)
sur|vivor
sus (as v., susses,
 sussed, suss|ing)
Su|san
Su|sanna
sus|cept|ib|il|ity
 (pl. sus|cept|ib|il|
 it|ies)
sus|cept|ible
sus|cept|ibly
sus|cept|ive
su|shi
sus|lik
sus|pect
sus|pend
sus|pender
sus|pense
sus|pense|ful
sus|pens|ible
sus|pen|sion
sus|pens|ive
sus|pens|ory
sus|pi|cion
sus|pi|cious
sus|pira|tion
sus|pire
 (sus|pired,
 sus|pir|ing)
suss use sus
Sus|sex
sus|tain
sus|tain|able
sus|tain|ment
sus|ten|ance
sus|tenta|tion
su|sur|ra|tion
su|sur|rus
sut|ler
Sutra
sut|tee
su|tural
su|ture (as v.,
 su|tur|ing)

Suva
Su|wan|nee
 (River)
su|zer|ain
su|zer|ainty
swab (as v.,
 swabbed,
 swab|bing)
swaddle
 (swad|dling)
swaddy (pl.
 swad|dies)
Swa|deshi
swag (as v.,
 swagged,
 swag|ging)
swage (as v.,
 swa|ging)
swag|ger
swag|gie
swag|man (pl.
 swag|men)
Swa|hili
swal|low
swallow-dive (as
 v., swallow-
 diving)
swami
Swam|mer|dam
swampy
 (swamp|ier,
 swampi|est)
swan (as v.,
 swanned,
 swan|ning)
swanky
 (swank|ier,
 swanki|est)
swan|like
swan|nery (pl.
 swan|ner|ies)
swans|down
Swan|sea
swan-song
swan-upping
swap (as v.,
 swapped,
 swap|ping)
swa|raj
swa|raj|ist
sward (grass)
swar|ded
swar|thily
swar|thi|ness

swarthy
(swar'thier,
swar'thi|est)
swash'buck|ler
swash'buck|ling
swas|tika
swat (hit sharply;
swat'ted,
swat|ting)
△ swot
swathe (as *v*.,
swath'ing)
swat|ter
Swa'zi|land
swear (as *v*.,
swore, sworn)
swearer
swear-word
sweater
sweatily
sweati|ness
sweat-shirt
sweaty
(sweat|ier,
sweati|est)
swede (turnip)
Swede (native of
Sweden)
Swe'den
Swe'den|borg
Swed'ish
sweep (as *v*.,
swept)
sweep|back
sweeper
sweep|ing
sweep|stake
sweet|bread
sweeten
sweet'ener
sweet'en|ing
sweet|heart
sweetie
sweetie-pie
sweet|ing
sweet|ish
sweet|meal
sweet|meat
sweet-shop
sweet-william
swell (as *v*., *p.p*.
swol|len *or*
swelled)
swell|ing
swel|ter

swerve (as *v*.,
swer|ving)
swift|let
swig (as *v*.,
swigged,
swig|ging)
swim (as *v*., swam,
swum,
swim|ming)
swim|mer
swim|meret
swim|mingly
swim-suit
Swin|burne
swindle (as *v*.,
swind|ling)
swind|ler
Swin|don
swine (*pl*. same)
swine-herd
swin|ery (*pl*.
swiner|ies)
swing (as *v*.,
swung)
swing-boat
swing-door
swinge|ing
swinger
swing|ing
swingle (as *v*.,
swin|gling)
swin'gle|tree
swin'ish
swipe (as *v*.,
swip'ing)
swipple
swirly (swir|lier,
swir'li|est)
swishy (swish'ier,
swishi|est)
switch|back
switch-blade
switch|board
switch-over *n*.
swither
Swit'zer|land
swivel (as *v*.,
swiv'elled,
swiv'el|ling)
swizz
swizzle
swizzle-stick
swob *use* swab
swol|len
swop *use* swap
sword (weapon)

sword-dance
sworded
sword|fish
sword-play
swords|man (*pl*.
swords|men)
swot (study hard
etc.; as *v*.,
swot'ted,
swot|ting)
△ swat
sy'bar|ite
sy'bar|itic
sy'bar'it|ical
sy'bar'it|ism
sybil *use* sibyl
sy'ca|more
syce (*Anglo-Ind*.
groom) △ sice
sy'co|nium (*pl*.
sy'co|nia)
sy'co|phancy
sy'co|phant
sy'co|phantic
sy'co|phant|
ic'ally
syc|osis (*pl*.
syc|oses)
Syd'en|ham
Syd|ney
sy'en|ite
sy'en|itic
syl|lab|ary (*pl*.
syl'lab|ar|ies)
syl|labic
syl'lab|ic'ally
syl'lab|ica|tion
syl|labi|city
syl|labi|fica|tion
syl'lab|ize
(syl'lab|iz|ing)
syl|lable (as *v*.,
syl'lab|ling)
syl'la|bub
syl|labus
syl|lep|sis (*pl*.
syl|lep|ses)
syl|lep'tic
syl|lo'gism
syl|lo'gistic
syl|lo'gize
(syl|lo'giz|ing)
sylph
sylph|like
sylvan *use* silvan
sym|biont

sym'bi|osis (*pl*.
sym'bi'oses)
sym'bi'otic
sym'bi'ot'ic|ally
sym|bol (as *v*.,
sym|bolled,
sym|bol|ling)
sym|bolic
sym|bol|ical
sym|bol'ic|ally
sym|bol|ics
sym|bol|ism
sym|bol|ist
sym|bol|iza|tion
sym|bol|ize
(sym'bol|iz|ing)
sym'bol|ogy
sym|bolo|logy
sym|met'ric
sym|met'rical
sym|met'ric|ally
sym|met'rize
(sym'met'riz|ing)
sym|met'ro|
pho'bia
sym|metry (*pl*.
sym'met|ries)
sym|path|ec'tomy
(*pl*. sym'path|
ec'tom|ies)
sym|path|etic
sym|path|et|
ic'ally
sym|path|ize
(sym'path|iz|ing)
sym|path|izer
sym|pathy (*pl*.
sym'path|ies)
sym|pet'al|ous
sym|phonic
sym|phon'ic|ally
sym|pho'ni|ous
sym|phon|ist
sym|phony (*pl*.
sym|phon|ies)
sym|phyl'lous
sym|physial
sym|physis (*pl*.
sym|physes)
sym|po'dial
sym|po|di|ally
sym|po|dium (*pl*.
sym|po|dia)
sym|po'siac
sym|po'sial
sym|po'si|arch

sym|po|si|ast
sym|po|sium (*pl.*
 sym|po|sia)
symp|tom
symp|to|matic
symp|to|mat|ic|
 ally
symp|to|mato|
 logy
syn|aer|esis (*pl.*
 syn|aer|eses)
syn|aes|thesia
syn|aes|thetic
syn|agogal
syn|ago|gical
syn|agogue
syn|al|lag|matic
syn|an|ther|ous
syn|an|thous
syn|apse
syn|apsis (*pl.*
 synapses)
syn|aptic
syn|arth|rosis (*pl.*
 syn|arth|roses)
sync
syn|carp
syn|chon|drosis
 (*pl.* syn|chon|
        droses)
synchro-
       cyclotron
syn|chro|mesh
syn|chronic
syn|chron|ic|ally
syn|chron|ism
syn|chron|iza|
       tion
syn|chron|ize
 (syn|chron|iz|
        ing)
syn|chron|ous

syn|chrony (*pl.*
 syn|chron|ies)
syn|chro|tron
syn|clinal
syn|cline
syn|copal
syn|co|pate
 (syn|co|pat|ing)
syn|co|pa|tion
syn|cope
syn|cretic
syn|cret|ism
syn|cret|ist
syn|cret|istic
syn|cret|ize
 (syn|cret|iz|ing)
syn|cyt|ial
syn|cyt|ium (*pl.*
 syn|cytia)
syn|dac|tyl
syn|dac|tyl|ism
syn|dac|tyl|ous
syn|dac|tyly
syn|desis (*pl.*
 syn|deses)
syn|des|mosis (*pl.*
 syn|des|moses)
syn|detic
syn|dic
syn|dic|al|ism
syn|dic|al|ist
syn|dic|ate (as *v.*,
 syn|dic|at|ing)
syn|dica|tion
syn|drome
syn|dromic
syn|ec|doche
syn|eco|logy
syn|er|getic
syn|er|gic
syn|er|gism
syn|er|gistic

syn|ergy
syn|gamy
syn|gen|esis
syn|gnath|ous
syn|iz|esis (*pl.*
 syn|iz|eses)
synod
syn|odal
syn|odic
syn|od|ical
syn|oec|ious
syn|onym
syn|onymic
syn|onym|ity
syn|onym|ous
syn|onymy (*pl.*
 syn|ony|mies)
syn|op|sis (*pl.*
 syn|op|ses)
syn|op|tic
syn|op|tical
syn|op|tic|ally
syn|opt|ist
syn|ost|osis
syn|ovia
syn|ovial
syn|ov|itis
syn|tactic
syn|tact|ical
syn|tact|ic|ally
syn|tagma
syn|tag|matic
syn|tag|mic
syn|tax
syn|thesis (*pl.*
 syn|theses)
syn|thes|ist
syn|thes|ize
 (syn|thes|iz|ing)
syn|thes|izer
syn|thetic
syn|thet|ical

syn|thet|ic|ally
syph|ilis
syph|il|itic
syph|il|ize
 (syph|il|iz|ing)
syph|il|oid
syphon *use*
 siphon
Sy|ra|cuse
syren *use* siren
Syria
Syriac
Syrian
syr|inga
syr|inge (as *v.*,
 syr|inge|ing)
syr|in|geal
syr|inx
Syro-Phoenician
syrup
syr|upy
sys|sar|cosis (*pl.*
 sys|sar|coses)
sys|taltic
sys|tem
sys|tem|atic
sys|tem|at|ic|ally
sys|tem|at|ics
sys|tem|at|ism
sys|tem|at|ist
sys|tem|at|ize
 (sys|tem|at|iz|
              ing)
sys|temic
sys|tem|ic|ally
sys|tole
sys|tolic
syzygy (*pl.*
 syzy|gies)

tab 259 **tamarack**

T

tab (as *v.*, tabbed,
 tab|bing)
tab|ard
tab|aret
ta|basco (pepper;
 pl. ta|bas|cos)
Ta|basco (sauce;
 propr.)
tabby (*pl.*
 tab|bies)
tab|er|nacle
ta|bes
ta|betic
tab|inet
tabla
tab|la|ture
table (as *v.*,
 ta|bling)
tab|leau (*pl.*
 tab|leaux)
table d'hôte (*pl.*
 tables d'hôte)
ta|ble|land
ta|ble|spoon
ta|ble|spoon|ful
 (*pl.* ta|ble|spoon|
 fuls)
tab|let
table|ware
tab|lier
ta|bling
tab|loid
ta|boo
ta|bor
tab|ouret
tabu|lar
tab|ula rasa (*pl.*
 tabu|lae rasae)
tabu|late
 (tabu|lat|ing)
tabu|la|tion
tabu|lator
taca|ma|hac
tac-au-tac
ta|cet
tach|ism
tach|is|to|scope
tach|is|to|scopic
tacho (*pl.* tachos)

tacho|graph
ta|cho|meter
ta|chy|car|dia
ta|chy|grapher
ta|chy|graphic
ta|chy|graph|ical
ta|chy|graphy (*pl.*
 ta|chy|graphies)
ta|chy|meter
ta|chy|metry
ta|cit
Ta|cit|ean
ta|cit|urn
ta|cit|urn|ity
Ta|citus
tack|ily
tacki|ness
tackle (as *v.*,
 tack|ling)
tacky (tack|ier,
 tacki|est)
taco (*pl.* ta|cos)
tact|ful
tact|fully
tac|tic
tac|tical
tac|tic|ally
tac|ti|cian
tac|tics
tact|ile
tac|til|ity
tact|less
tac|tual
Ta|djik|is|tan
tad|pole
tae|nia (*pl.*
 tae|niae)
tae|ni|oid
taf|feta
taff|rail
Taffy (*pl.* Taf|fies)
tafia
tag (as *v.*, tagged,
 tag|ging)
Ta|ga|log
ta|getes
ta|glia|telle
Ta|gus
Ta|hiti

Ta|hi|tian
tah|sil
tah|sil|dar
taiga
tail|back
tail-bay
tail-board
tail|coat
tail-end
tail|ing
tail|less
tailor
tail|or|ess
tailor-made
tail|piece
tail|pipe
tail|plane
tail|stock
taint|less
tai|pan
Tai|pei
Tai|wan
Taj Ma|hal
tak|able
tak|ahe
take (as *v.*, took,
 taken, tak|ing)
take-away *n.* & *a.*
take-home *a.*
take-off *n.*
take-over *n.*
taker
takin
tak|ing
tala
tal|apoin
tal|bot
talc (as *v.*,
 talcked,
 talck|ing)
talcky
talc|ose
talc|ous
tal|cum
tale|bearer
tale|bear|ing
tal|ent
tal|en|ted
tal|ent|less

talent-scout
ta|les (*Law*)
ta|les|man (juror,
 pl. ta|les|men)
tale|tel|ler
Ta|lia|co|tian
tali|pes
tali|pot
tal|is|man (*pl.*
 tal|is|mans)
tal|is|manic
talk|athon
talk|at|ive
talk|fest
talkie
talk|ing
talking-to (*pl.*
 talking-tos)
tall|age
tall|boy
Talleyrand-
            Périgord
Tal|lis
tall|ish
tall|lith
tal|low
tal|lowy
tally (as *n.*, *pl.*
 tal|lies; as *v.*,
 tal|lies, tal|lied,
 tal|ly|ing)
tally-ho (as *n.*, *pl.*
 tally-hos)
tal|ly|man (*pl.*
 tal|ly|men)
tally-sheet
Tal|mud
Tal|mudic
talon
taloned
ta|lus (ankle, *pl.*
 tali)
ta|lus (slope of wall
 etc., *pl.* ta|luses)
ta|male
ta|man|dua
tam|an|oir
tam|ar|ack

tam|arin
(marmoset)
tam'ar|ind (fruit,
tree)
tam'ar|isk
tam|bour
tam|boura
tam|bourin
(drum)
tam'bour|ine
(jingling
instrument)
tame (as a., tamer,
tamest; as v.,
tam'ing)
tame|ab'il|ity
tame|able
tamer
Tamil
Ta'mil|ian
Tamil Nadu
tammy (pl.
tam|mies)
tam-o'-shanter
tam'pan
tam'per
tamper-proof
tamp|ing
tam|pion (stopper)
tam'pon (Med.)
tam'pon|ade
tam'pon|age
tam-tam
tan (as v., tanned,
tan|ning)
tan|ager
Tan|agra
tan'dem
tan'door
tan'doori
Tan|gan'yika,
Lake
tan|gelo (pl.
tan|gelos)
tan|gency (pl.
tan|gen|cies)
tan|gent
tan'gen|tial
tan'gen|tially
tan'ger|ine
(orange)
Tan'ger|ine (of
Tangier)
tan|ghin
tan|gib|il'ity
tan|gible

tan|gibly
Tan|gier
tangi|ness
tangle (as v.,
tan|gling)
tangly (tan|glier,
tan'gli|est)
tango (as n., pl.
tan'gos)
tan|gram
tangy (tang|ier,
tangi|est)
tan|ist
tan|istry
tanka
tank|age
tank|ard
tanker
tank|ful (pl.
tank|fuls)
tan|nable
tan|nage
tan|nate
tan'ner
tan'nery (pl.
tan'ner|ies)
Tann|häuser
tan'nic
tan'nin
Tan'noy (propr.)
tansy (pl. tan|sies)
tan|talic
tan'talite
tan'tal|iza'tion
tan'tal|ize
(tan'tal|iz|ing)
tan'talum
tan'talus
tan'ta|mount
tan'tra
tan|tric
tan|trism
tan|trist
tan|trum
Tan|za'nia
Taoi|seach
Tao'ism
Tao'ist
tap (as v., tapped,
tap|ping)
tapa
tap-dance (as v.,
tap-dancing)
tap-dancer
tape (as v.,
tap'ing)

tape-measure
taper
tape-record
tap'es|tried
tap'es|try
(pl.tap'es|tries)
tape|worm
ta'pi|oca
ta'pir
ta'pir|oid
tapis (on the)
ta'pote|ment
tap'pet
tap|room
tap|ster
tapu
tar (as v., tarred,
tar|ring)
tara|diddle
tara|kihi
ta'ran|tella
(dance)
tar'ant|ism
(dancing mania)
ta'ran|tula
(spider)
ta'rax|acum
tar|boosh
Tar|den'ois|ian
tar'di|grade
tard|ily
tar'di|ness
tardy (tar|dier,
tar'di|est)
tare (as v., tar'ing)
tar'get (as v.,
tar'geted,
tar'get|ing)
Tar|gum
Tar|gum|ist
tar'iff
tar|latan
tar'mac v.
(tar|macked,
tar'mack|ing)
Tar'mac n.
(propr.)
tar|nish
taro (plant; pl.
taros)
tarot (game)
tar'pan
tar|paulin
Tar|peian
tar'pon
tar'ra|gon

Tar'ra|gona
tarry a. (tar|rier,
tar'ri|est)
tarry v. (tar|ries,
tar|ried,
tar'ry|ing)
tarsal
tar'sia (intarsia)
tar|sier (animal)
tar'sus (pl. tarsi)
tar|tan
tar'tar (deposit,
sauce)
Tar'tar (people
etc.)
Tar'tar|ean (of
Tartarus)
Tar'tar|ian
tar|taric
tar'tar|ize
(tar'tar|iz|ing)
Tar|tarus (Gr.
Myth.)
Tar|tary (in Asia)
tart|let
tart|rate
Tar|tuffe
Tar'tuf|fian
Tar'tuff|ism
tarty (tar|tier,
tar'ti|est)
Tar'zan
task|mas'ter
task|mis'tress
Tas|ma'nia
Tas|ma'nian
tas'sel
tas'selled
tas'sie
Tasso
taste (as v.,
tast|ing)
taste|able
taste-bud
taste|ful
taste|fully
taste|less
taster
tas'tily
tas'ti|ness
tasty (tas'tier,
tas'ti|est)
tat (as v., tat'ted,
tat|ting)
ta-ta
ta'tami

tater
ta|tou (armadillo)
tat|ter
tat|ter|de|ma|lion
tattered
Tat|ter|sall
tat|tery
tat|tily
tat|ti|ness
tat|ting
tattle (as v.,
 tat|tling)
tat|tler
tat|too
tat|too|ist
tatty (as n., pl.
 tat|ties; as a.,
 tat|tier, tat|ti|est)
tau (Gr. letter)
Taun|ton
Taur|ean
taur|ine
Taurus
tauten
tau|to|chrone
tau|tog
tau|to|lo|gical
tau|to|lo|gic|ally
tau|to|lo|gist
tau|to|lo|gize
 (tau|to|lo|giz|ing)
tau|to|log|ous
tau|to|logy (pl.
 tau|to|lo|gies)
tau|to|mer
tau|to|meric
tau|to|mer|ism
tau|to|phony (pl.
 tau|to|phon|ies)
tav|ern
taw|drily
taw|dri|ness
taw|dry
 (taw|drier,
 taw|dri|est)
taw|ni|ness
tawny
taws
tax|ab|il|ity
tax|able
taxa|tion
taxi (as n., pl.
 taxis; as v., taxis,
 taxied, taxi|ing)
taxi-cab
taxi|dermal
taxi|dermic

taxi|derm|ist
taxi|dermy
taxi-man
 (pl. taxi-men)
taxi|meter
taxis
tax|man (pl.
 tax|men)
taxon (pl. taxa)
taxo|nomic
taxo|nom|ical
taxo|nom|ic|ally
tax|on|om|ist
tax|onomy
tax|payer
Tay|side
tazza
T-bone
Tchai|kov|sky
te (Mus.)
tea-bag
tea-break
tea|cake
teach (taught)
teacher
tea-chest
teach-in
teach|ing
tea-cloth
tea-cosy
 (pl. tea-cosies)
teacup
tea|cup|ful (pl.
 tea|cup|fuls)
teal (duck; pl.
 same)
tea-lady
 (pl. tea-ladies)
tea-leaf
 (pl. tea-leaves)
team|ster
tea-party
 (pl. tea-parties)
tea-planter
tea|pot
tea|poy
tear (as v., tore,
 torn)
tear|away
tear-drop
tear|ful
tear|fully
tear-gas
tear|ing
tear-jerker
tea-room

teary (tear|ier,
 teari|est)
tease (as v.,
 teas|ing)
tea|sel
teaser
tea-set
tea-shop
tea|spoon
tea|spoon|ful (pl.
 tea|spoon|fuls)
tea-time
tea-tray
Tech
tech|ne|tium
tech|nic
tech|nical
tech|nic|al|ity (pl.
 tech|nic|al|it|ies)
tech|nic|ally
tech|ni|cian
tech|ni|cist
Tech|ni|color
Tech|ni|colored
tech|nique
tech|no|cracy (pl.
 tech|no|cra|cies)
tech|no|crat
tech|no|cratic
tech|no|lo|gical
tech|no|lo|gic|ally
tech|no|lo|gist
tech|no|logy (pl.
 tech|no|lo|gies)
tec|tonic
tec|ton|ic|ally
tec|ton|ics
tec|tor|ial
tec|trix (pl.
 tec|trices)
ted (v., ted|ded,
 ted|ding)
ted|der
teddy (bear; pl.
 ted|dies)
Te Deum
te|di|ous
te|dium
tee (as v., teed)
teen|age
teen|aged
teen|ager
teensy
teensy-weensy
teeny (teen|ier,
 teeni|est)

teeny-bopper
teeny-weeny
Tees|side
tee|ter
teethe v.
 (teeth|ing)
tee|to|tal
tee|to|tal|ism
tee|to|tal|ler
tee|tot|ally
tee|totum
Te|gu|ci|galpa
tegu|lar
tegu|ment
tegu|mental
tegu|ment|ary
Teh|ran
tek|nonym|ous
tek|nonymy
tek|tite
tel|aes|thesia
tel|aes|thetic
tel|amon (pl.
 tel|amones)
Tel Aviv
tele|cam|era
tele|cast
tele|cine
tele|com|mu|ni|
 ca|tion
tel|edu
tele|film
tele|genic
tele|gonic
tele|gony
tele|gram
tele|graph
tele|grapher
tele|graph|ese
tele|graphic
tele|graph|ic|ally
tele|graph|ist
tele|graphy
tele|kin|esis (pl.
 tele|kin|eses)
Te|le|mann
tele|mark
tele|meter
tele|metry
tele|olo|gic
tele|olo|gical
tele|olo|gic|ally
tele|olo|gism
tele|olo|gist
tele|ology
tele|ost

tele|path
tele|pathic
tele|path|ic|ally
tele|path|ist
tele|path|ize
 (tele|path|iz|ing)
tele|pathy
tele|phone (as v.,
 tele|phon|ing)
tele|phonic
tele|phon|ic|ally
tele|phon|ist
tele|phony
tele|photo
tele|pho|to|
        graphic
tele|pho|to|
        graphy
tele|port
tele|porta|tion
tele|printer
tele|prompter
tele|re|cord
tel|ergy
tele|scope (as v.,
 tele|scop|ing)
tele|scopic
tele|scop|ic|ally
Tele|type (propr.)
tele|type|writer
tele|view
tele|viewer
tele|vise
 (tele|vis|ing)
tele|vi|sion
tele|visor
tele|visual
telex
tell (as v., told)
teller
tell|ing
tell-tale
tel'lur|ate
tel'lur|ian
tel'luric
tel'lur|ide
tel'lur|ite
tel'lur|ium
tel'lur|ous
telly (pl. tel|lies)
tel|pher
tel|pher|age
tel|son
Tel'ugu
tem'er|ari|ous
te'mer|ity

tem|per
tem|pera
tem|pera|ment
tem|pera|mental
tem|pera|
        ment|ally
tem|per|ance
tem|per|ate
tem|per'at|ive
tem|per'at|ure
tempered
tem|per|some
tem|pest
tem|pes'tu|ous
Temp|lar
tem|plate
temple
tempo (pl.
 tem'pos)
tem|poral
tem'por'al|ity (pl.
 tem'por'al|it|ies)
tem'por|ally
tem'por|ar|ily
tem'por|ari|ness
tem'por|ary
 (as n., pl.
 tem'por|ar|ies)
tem'por|iza|tion
tem'por|ize
 (tem'por|iz|ing)
temp'ta|tion
tempter
tempt|ing
temp|tress
tem|pura
ten|ab'il|ity
ten|able
ten|ace
ten|acious
ten|acity
ten'acu|lum (pl.
 ten|acula)
ten|ancy (pl.
 ten|an|cies)
ten|ant
ten|ant|able
ten|antry
tench (pl. same)
tend|ency (pl.
 tend|en|cies)
ten'den|tious
tender (one who
 tends)

ten'der a.
 (ten|derer,
 ten'der|est)
ten'der|foot
ten'der|ize
 (ten'der|iz|ing)
ten'der|loin
ten'din|itis
ten'din|ous
ten|don
ten|dril
Ten'eb'rae n. pl.
tene|ment
tene|mental
tene'ment|ary
Ten'er|ife
ten'es|mus
tenet
ten|fold
tenné
ten'ner
Ten'nes|see
ten|nis
tenno (pl. ten'nos)
Ten'ny|son
Ten'ny|son|ian
tenon
ten|oner
tenor
teno|tomy (pl.
 teno|tom|ies)
ten|pins
ten|rec
tense (as a.,
 tenser, tensest;
 as v., tens|ing)
tense|less
tens|ile
tens'il|ity
ten'si|meter
ten|sion
ten|sional
tens|ity
ten'son
ten'sor
tent|acle
tent|acled
ten'ta'cu|lar
ten'ta'cu|late
tent'at|ive
tenter
ten'ter|hook
tenuis (pl. tenues)
tenu|ity
tenu|ous
ten|ure

ten|urial
ten|uto
teo|calli
te|pee
tepid
tep'id|ity
te|quila
te'rai
ter|aph (pl.
 ter|aphim)
te'ra'to|genic
te'ra'to|geny
te'ra'to|lo'gical
te'ra'to|lo'gist
te'ra'to|logy (pl.
 te'ra'to|lo'gies)
te'ra|toma
ter|bium
terce (Eccl.)
ter|cel
ter'cen'ten|ary (as
 n., pl. ter|
 cen'ten|ar|ies)
ter'cent|en|nial
ter|cet
ter|eb|ene
ter|eb|inth
ter|eb|inth|ine
ter|ebra (pl.
 ter'eb|rae)
ter|eb|rant
ter|edo (pl.
 ter|edos)
Ter|ence
Ter|esa
ter|ete
ter|gal
ter'gi'ver|sate
 (ter'gi'ver|
        sat|ing)
ter'gi'ver|sa'tion
ter'gi'ver|sator
ter'mag|ant
 (woman)
Ter'mag|ant
 (deity)
ter|min|able
ter|minal
ter|min|ally
ter|min|ate
 (ter|min|at|ing)
ter|mina|tion
ter|mina|tional
ter|min|ator
ter|miner
ter|min|ism

ter|min|ist
ter|mino|lo|gical
ter|mino|lo|gic|
     ally
ter|mino|lo|gist
ter|mino|logy (*pl.*
 ter|mino|lo|gies)
ter|minus (*pl.*
 ter|mini)
ter|mit|arium
ter|mit|ary (*pl.*
 ter|mit|ar|ies)
ter|mite
termly
ter|mor
tern|ary
tern|ate
terne-plate
te|ro|tech|no|logy
terp|ene
Terp|si|chore
Terp|si|chor|ean
terra alba
 (mineral)
ter|race (as *v.*,
 ter|ra|cing)
ter|ra|cotta
ter|rain
ter|ra|mare
ter|ra|pin
Terra|pin
 (building; *propr.*)
ter|raque|ous
ter|rar|ium (*pl.*
 ter|raria)
ter|razzo (*pl.*
 ter|raz|zos)
ter|rene
terre|plein
ter|rest|ri|al
ter|rest|ri|ally
ter|ret
terre-verte
ter|rible
ter|ribly
ter|ri|col|ous
ter|rier
ter|rific
ter|rif|ic|ally
ter|rify
 (ter|ri|fies,
 ter|ri|fied,
 ter|ri|fy|ing)
ter|ri|gen|ous
ter|rine
ter|rit|or|ial

ter|rit|ori|al|ism
ter|rit|ori|ally
ter|rit|ory (*pl.*
 ter|rit|or|ies)
ter|ror
ter|ror|ism
ter|ror|ist
ter|ror|istic
ter|ror|iza|tion
ter|ror|ize
 (ter|ror|iz|ing)
terry (*pl.* ter|ries)
ter|tian
ter|tiary (as *n.*, *pl.*
 ter|tiar|ies)
Ter|tiary (*Geol.*,
 Eccl.; *pl.*
 Ter|tiar|ies)
ter|va|lent
Tery|lene (*propr.*)
terz|etto (*pl.*
 terz|et|tos)
tesla (unit)
Tesla (coil)
tes|sel|late
 (tes|sel|lat|ing)
tes|sel|la|tion
tes|sera (*pl.*
 tes|serae)
tes|seral
tes|sit|ura
testa (*pl.* testae)
test|ab|il|ity
test|able
tes|ta|ceous
test|acy (*pl.*
 test|acies)
testa|ment
testa|ment|ary
test|ate
test|ator
test|at|rix
test-drive (as *v.*,
 test-drove,
 test-driven,
 test-driving)
testee
tester
test|icle
tes|ticu|lar
tes|ticu|late
test|ify (testi|fies,
 testi|fied,
 testi|fy|ing)
test|ily
tes|ti|mo|nial

testi|mony (*pl.*
 testi|mon|ies)
testi|ness
testis (*pl.* testes)
tes|to|ster|one
test-tube
tes|tu|dinal
tes|tudo (*pl.*
 tes|tu|dos)
testy (test|ier,
 testi|est)
te|tanic
te|tan|ic|ally
tet|an|ize
 (tet|an|iz|ing)
tet|an|oid
tet|anus
tet|any
tetch|ily
tetchi|ness
tetchy (tetch|ier,
 tetchi|est)
tête-à-tête
tether
tet|ra|chord
tet|ra|cyc|lic
tet|ra|cyc|lin
tet|rad
tet|ra|dac|tyl
tet|ra|dac|tyl|ous
tet|ra|ethyl
tet|ra|gon
tet|ra|gonal
tet|ra|gon|ally
tet|ra|gram
Tet|ra|
    gram|maton
tet|ra|gyn|ous
tet|ra|hed|ral
tet|ra|hed|ron (*pl.*
 tet|ra|hedra)
tet|ra|logy (*pl.*
 tet|ra|lo|gies)
tet|ra|mer|ous
tet|ra|meter
tet|ra|morph
tetr|and|rous
tet|ra|ploid
tet|ra|pod
tet|ra|pod|ous
tet|ra|pter|ous
tet|rarch
tet|rarch|ate
tetr|arch|ical
tetr|archy (*pl.*
 tetr|ar|chies)

tet|ra|stich
tet|ra|style
tet|ra|syl|labic
tet|ra|syl|lable
tetr|atomic
tet|ra|va|lent
tetr|ode
tetr|ox|ide
Teuton
Teut|onic
Texan
Texas
text|book
tex|tile
tex|tual
tex|tu|al|ism
tex|tu|al|ist
tex|tu|ally
tex|tural
tex|ture (as *v.*,
 tex|tur|ing)
Thack|eray
Thai
Thai|land
thal|amus (*pl.*
 thal|ami)
tha|las|sic
thaler
tha|lid|om|ide
thal|lic
thal|lium
thal|lo|gen
thal|loid
thal|lo|phyte
thal|lous
thal|lus (*pl.* thalli)
thal|weg
Thames
than|age
tha|nato|logy
thane
thane|dom
thane|ship
thank|ful
thank|fully
thank|less
thanks|giv|ing
thank-you *n.*
thar (goat)
that (*pl.* those)
that|cher
That|cher
thau|ma|trope
thau|mat|urge
thau|mat|ur|gic
thau|mat|ur|gical

thau|mat|ur|gist
thau|mat|urgy
the|andric
the|an|thropic
the|archy (*pl.*
 the|ar|chies)
theatre
theatre-goer
the|at|ric
the|at|rical
the|at|ric|al|ism
the|at|ric|al|ity
Theban
theca (*pl.* thecae)
theine
their (*possessive a.*)
△ there, they're
the|ism
the|ist
the|istic
the|ist|ical
them|atic
them|at|ic|ally
them|selves
thenar
thence|forth
thence|for|ward
theo|bro|mine
theo|cent|ric
theo|cracy
 (divine govt., *pl.*
 theo|cra|cies)
theo|crasy (divine
 union etc.)
theo|crat
Theo|critus
theo|di|cean
theo|dicy (*pl.*
 theo|di|cies)
theo|dol|ite
the|od|ol|itic
Theo|dor|akis
theo|gony (*pl.*
 theo|gon|ies)
theo|lo|gian
theo|lo|gical
theo|lo|gic|ally
theo|lo|gist
theo|lo|gize
 (theo|lo|giz|ing)
theo|logy
theo|machy (*pl.*
 theo|mach|ies)
theo|mania
theo|phany (*pl.*
 theo|phan|ies)
theo|phoric
Theo|phras|tus

theo|phyl|line
theo|pneust
the|orbo (*pl.*
 the|or|bos)
the|orem
the|or|em|atic
the|or|etic
the|or|et|ical
the|or|et|ic|ally
the|or|eti|cian
the|or|ist
the|or|ize
 (the|or|iz|ing)
the|ory (*pl.*
 the|or|ies)
theo|soph
theo|sopher
theo|sophic
theo|soph|ical
theo|soph|ist
theo|soph|ize
 (theo|soph|iz|ing)
theo|sophy (*pl.*
 theo|soph|ies)
thera|peutic
thera|peut|ical
thera|peut|ic|ally
thera|peut|ist
ther|ap|ist
ther|apy (*pl.*
 ther|ap|ies)
Thera|vada
there (as in *over*
 there) △ their,
 they're
there|about
there|abouts
there|af|ter
thereby
there|fore
therein
thereof
thereto
there|to|fore
there|upon
theri|an|thropic
therio|morphic
ther|mae *n. pl.*
ther|mal
ther|mally
thermic
ther|mi|dor
ther|mion
ther|mi|onic
ther|mis|tor
therm|ite
ther|mo|
      chem|istry
ther|mo|couple

ther|mo|dyn|amic
ther|mo|
       dyn|amics
ther|mo|elec|tric
ther|mo|
    el|ec|tri|city
ther|mo|gen|esis
ther|mo|gram
ther|mo|graph
ther|mo|la|bile
ther|mo|lu|min|
        es|cent
ther|mo|lysis
ther|mo|lytic
ther|mo|meter
ther|mo|met|ric
ther|mo|met|rical
ther|mo|met|ric|
          ally
ther|mo|metry
ther|mo|nuc|lear
ther|mo|phile
ther|mo|pile
ther|mo|plas|tic
Ther|mo|pylae
Ther|mos (*propr.*)
ther|mo|set|ting
ther|mo|sphere
ther|mo|stable
ther|mo|stat
ther|mo|static
ther|mo|stat|ic|
          ally
ther|mo|tactic
ther|mo|taxic
ther|mo|taxis
ther|mo|tropic
ther|mo|trop|ism
the|saurus (*pl.*
 the|sauri)
thesis (*pl.* theses)
Thes|pian
Thes|sa|lon|ika
theta
the|ur|gic
the|ur|gical
the|ur|gist
the|urgy
they're (= *they*
 are) △ their,
 there
thi|am|ine
thicken
thick|ener
thick|en|ing
thicket
thick|head
thick|ish
thick|ness

thick|set
thief (*pl.* thieves)
thieve (thiev|ing)
thiev|ery
thiev|ish
thigh-bone
thiller
thimble
thim|ble|ful (*pl.*
 thim|ble|fuls)
Thimbu
thin (as *v.*,
 thinned,
 thin|ning; as *a.*,
 thin|ner,
 thin|nest)
thing|amy (*pl.*
 thing|am|ies)
thingy (*pl.*
 thing|ies)
think (as *v.*,
 thought)
think|able
thinker
think|ing
think-tank
thin|ner
thin|nish
thio-acid
thio-sulphate
thio|urea
thirs|tily
thirs|ti|ness
thirsty (thirs|tier,
 thirs|ti|est)
thir|teen
thir|teenth
thir|ti|eth
thirty (*pl.*
 thir|ties)
thirty|fold
thirty-two-mo (*pl.*
 thirty-two-mos)
this (*pl.* these)
thistle
thistle|down
thistly
thixo|tro|pic
thixo|tropy
thole-pin
tholos (*pl.* tholoi)
Thomas (*pl.*
 Thom|ases)
Thom|ism
Thom|ist
Thom|istic

Thom|ist|ical
thor|acic
thorax (pl.
 thor|aces)
thoria
thor|ium
thorn|back
thorn|bill
thorn|tail
thorny (thor|nier,
 thor|ni|est)
thor|ough
thor|ough|bred
thor|ough|fare
thor|ough|go|ing
thor|ough|wax
thought|ful
thought|fully
thought|less
thou|sand
thou|sand|fold
thou|sandth
thral|dom
thrash (beat etc.)
 △ thresh
thrasher (bird)
thra|son|ical
thra|son|ic|ally
thread|bare
thread|fish
thread|worm
thready
 (thread|ier,
 threadi|est)
threaten
three-
 dimensional
three|fold
three|pence
three|penny
three-ply
three-point
three-quarter
three-quarters
three|some
three-wheeler
threm|mato|logy
thren|ode
thren|odial
thren|odic
thren|od|ist
thren|ody (pl.
 thren|od|ies)
thresh (beat out
 corn) △ thrash
thresher (shark)

thresh|old
thrift|ily
thrif|ti|ness
thrift|less
thrifty (thrif|tier,
 thrif|ti|est)
thriller
thrive (throve or
 thrived, thriven
 or thrived,
 thriv|ing)
throat|ily
throati|ness
throaty
 (throat|ier,
 throati|est)
throb (as v.,
 throbbed,
 throb|bing)
throe (pang)
throm|bin
throm|bo|cyte
throm|bose
 (throm|bos|ing)
throm|bosis (pl.
 throm|boses)
throm|botic
throm|bus (pl.
 thrombi)
throne (as v.,
 thron|ing)
throstle
throstle-frame
throttle (as v.,
 throt|tling)
through
through|out
through|put
through|way
throw (as v.,
 threw, thrown)
throw-away a. &
 n.
throw-back n.
throw-in n.
throw-off n.
throw-out n.
throw|ster
thrum (as v.,
 thrummed,
 thrum|ming)
thrummy
 (thrum|mi|er,
 thrum|mi|est)
thrust (as v.,
 thrust)

thruster
Thu|cyd|ides
thud (as v.,
 thudded,
 thud|ding)
thug (gen.)
Thug (hist.)
thug|gery
thuja
thu|lium
thumb-nail
thumb|screw
thumper
thump|ing
thun|der
thun|der|bolt
thun|der|clap
thunder-cloud
thun|der|ing
thun|der|ous
thun|der|storm
thun|der|struck
thun|dery
Thur|gau
thur|ible
thuri|fer
thuri|fer|ous
thuri|fica|tion
Thurs|day
thwart-ship a.
thwart-ships adv.
thy|la|cine
thym|ine
thymol
thymus (pl.
 thymi)
thymy
thyr|oid
thyr|ox|ine
thyr|sus (pl.
 thyrsi)
ti (Mus.) use te
ti|ara
Ti|ber
Ti|ber|ius
Ti|bet
Ti|betan
tibia (pl. ti|biae)
ti|bial
ti|bio|tar|sus (pl.
 ti|bio|tarsi)
Tib|ul|lus
tic (twitch)
tice
Ti|cino

tick (click, mark,
 etc.)
ticker-tape
ticket (as v.,
 tick|eted,
 tick|et|ing)
tickety-boo
tickle (as v.,
 tick|ling)
tick|ler
tick|lish
tickly (tick|lier,
 tick|li|est)
tick-tack
tick-tock
tidal
tid|ally
tid|dler
tiddly (tid|dlier,
 tid|dli|est)
tiddly-wink
tide (as v., tid|ing)
tide-mark
tide|way
ti|dily
ti|di|ness
tid|ings pl.
tidy (as v., ti|dies,
 ti|died, ti|dy|ing;
 as a., ti|dier,
 ti|di|est)
tie (as v., tied,
 ty|ing)
tie-bar
tie-break
tie-breaker
Tien Shan
tie-pin
tier (row)
tiered
tif|fany (pl.
 tif|fan|ies)
tif|fin
ti|ger
ti|ger|ish
tiger-lily (pl.
 tiger-lilies)
tiger's-eye
Tighna|bruaich
tight
tighten
tight|rope
tight|wad
ti|gon
tig|ress
tiki

tilde
tile (as *v.*, til¦ing)
tiler
til¦ing
till¦age
til¦ler
tim¦bale (dish)
tim¦ber
timber-line
timbre
Tim¦buc¦too
 (*allus.*)
Tim¦buktu (place)
time (as *v.*,
 tim¦ing)
time¦keeper
time¦keep¦ing
time¦less
time-limit
time¦li¦ness
timely (time¦lier,
 time¦li¦est)
tim¦eous
time¦piece
timer
time-scale
time-sheet
time-signal
time-switch
time¦table (as *v.*,
 time¦tab¦ling)
time-worn
timid
tim¦id¦ity
ti¦mo¦cracy (*pl.*
 ti¦mo¦cra¦cies)
ti¦mo¦cratic
tim¦or¦ous
tim¦othy (grass)
Tim¦othy
tim¦pani *n. pl.*
tim¦pan¦ist
tin (as *v.*, tinned,
 tin¦ning)
tinc¦tor¦ial
tinc¦ture (as *v.*,
 tinc¦tur¦ing)
tin¦dal
tin¦der
tinder-box
tinea
tinge (as *v.*,
 tinge¦ing)
tingle (as *v.*,
 tin¦gling)

tin¦gly (tin¦glier,
 tin¦gli¦est)
ti¦nily
ti¦ni¦ness
tin¦ker
tinkle (as *v.*,
 tink¦ling)
tin¦ner
tin¦nily
tin¦ni¦ness
tin¦nitus
tinny (tin¦nier,
 tin¦ni¦est)
tin-opener
tin-pan (alley)
tin-plate *v.*
 (tin-plating)
tin¦sel (as *v.*,
 tin¦selled,
 tin¦sel¦ling)
tin¦tin¦nab¦ular
tin¦tin¦nab¦ulary
tin¦tin¦nabu¦
 la¦tion
tin¦tin¦nab¦ulous
tin¦tin¦nab¦ulum
 (*pl.*
 tin¦tin¦nab¦ula)
Tin¦tor¦etto
tin¦ware
tiny (ti¦nier,
 ti¦ni¦est)
tip (as *v.*, tipped,
 tip¦ping)
tip-off *n.*
tip¦per
Tip¦per¦ary
tip¦pet
tipple (as *v.*,
 tip¦pling)
tip¦pler
tippy (tip¦pier,
 tip¦pi¦est)
tip¦sily
tip¦si¦ness
tip¦staff (*pl.*
 tip¦staffs *or*
 tip¦staves)
tip¦ster
tipsy (tip¦sier,
 tipsi¦est)
tipsy-cake
tip¦toe (as *v.*,
 tip¦toed,
 tip¦toe¦ing)
tip¦top

tip-up *a.*
tir¦ade
ti¦rail¦leur
Ti¦ranë
tire (exhaust;
 tir¦ing) △ tyre
tire¦less
tire¦some
tir¦ing
tiro (*pl.* tir¦os)
tis¦sue
Ti¦tan
ti¦tan¦ate
ti¦tanic
ti¦tan¦ic¦ally
ti¦ta¦nium
tit¦bit
tithe (as *v.*,
 tith¦ing)
Ti¦tian
tit¦il¦late
 (tit¦il¦lat¦ing)
tit¦il¦la¦tion
tit¦iv¦ate
 (tit¦iv¦at¦ing)
tit¦iva¦tion
tit¦lark
title (as *v.*, ti¦tling)
title-deed
title-page
tit¦mouse (*pl.*
 tit¦mice)
Tito
ti¦trate (ti¦trating)
ti¦tra¦tion
titre
tit¦ter
tittle
tittle-tattle (as *v.*,
 tittle-tattling)
tit¦tup
 (tit¦tup¦ing)
tit¦tuppy
ti¦tu¦ba¦tion
titu¦lar
Ti¦tus
 An¦dron¦icus
Ti¦voli
tizzy (*pl.* tiz¦zies)
T-joint
T-junction
tmesis (*pl.* tmeses)
toad¦flax
toad¦ish
toad¦stone
toad¦stool

toady (as *n.*, *pl.*
 toad¦ies; as *v.*,
 toad¦ies,
 toad¦ied,
 toady¦ing)
toaster
to¦bacco (*pl.*
 to¦bac¦cos)
to¦bac¦con¦ist
To¦bago
to¦bog¦gan
toby (jug)
toc¦cata
Toch¦ar¦ian
tocher
to¦coph¦erol
Tocque¦ville
toc¦sin
to¦day
toddle (tod¦dling)
tod¦dler
toddy (*pl.*
 tod¦dies)
to-do (*pl.* to-dos)
toe (as *v.*, toed,
 toe¦ing)
toe-cap
toe-nail
tof¦fee
tog (as *v.*, togged,
 tog¦ging)
toga
to¦gether
tog¦gery
toggle (as *v.*,
 tog¦gling)
Togo
To¦go¦lese (*pl.*
 same)
toile
toiler
toi¦let
toi¦letry (*pl.*
 toi¦let¦ries)
toil¦some
To¦kay
token
Tokyo
To¦ledo
tol¦er¦able
tol¦er¦ably
tol¦er¦ance
tol¦er¦ant
tol¦er¦ate
 (tol¦er¦at¦ing)
tol¦era¦tion

To|lima
toll-bridge
toll-gate
Tol|stoy
Tol|tec
Tol|tecan
tolu|ene
toluic
toluol
toma|hawk
to|mal|ley
to|mato (*pl.*
 to|ma|toes)
tom|bac
tom|bola
tom|boy
tomb|stone
tom-cat
to|ment|ose
to|ment|ous
to|mentum (*pl.*
 to|menta)
tom|fool|ery (*pl.*
 tom|fool|er|ies)
tommy (*pl.*
 tom|mies)
tommy-gun
tommy-rot
to|mo|graph
to|mo|graphic
to|mo|graphy
to|mor'row
tom|tit
tom-tom (as *v.*,
 tom-tommed,
 tom-tomming)
ton (2,000 or
 2,240lb.)
tonal
ton|al|ity
ton|ally
tondo (*pl.* tondi)
tone (as *v.*,
 ton|ing)
tone-deaf
tone|less
toneme
tonemic
tonga
Tonga
tong|kang
tongue (as *v.*,
 tongued,
 tonguing)
tongue-tied
tonic

ton|ic|ally
toni|city
to|night
ton|ish
tonka (bean)
ton|nage
tonne (1000 kg.)
ton|neau
to|no|meter
ton|sil
ton|sil|lar
ton|sil|lec|tomy
 (*pl.* ton|sil|
  lec|tom|ies)
ton|sil|litis
ton|sor|ial
ton|sure (as *v.*,
 ton|sur|ing)
ton|tine
ton-up
tool-box
tooth (*pl.* teeth)
tooth|ache
tooth|brush
tooth-comb
tooth|ily
toothi|ness
tooth|less
tooth|paste
tooth|pick
tooth-powder
tooth|wort
toothy (tooth|ier,
 toothi|est)
tootle (toot|ling)
tootsy (*pl.*
 toot|sies)
top (as *v.*, topped,
 top|ping)
to|paz
to|pazo|lite
top-boot
top|coat
topee *use* topi
top|gal'lant
top-heavy
Tophet
to|phus (*pl.* tophi)
topi
to|pi|arian
to|pi|ar|ist
to|pi|ary
topic
top|ical
top|ic|al|ity
top|ic|ally

top|knot
top|less
top|mast
top|most
top-notch *a.*
to|po|grapher
to|po|graphic
to|po|graph|ical
to|po|graph|ic|
  ally
to|po|graphy
to|po|lo|gical
to|po|lo|gic|ally
to|po|lo|gist
to|po|logy
top|onym
top|onymic
top|onymy
topos (*pl.* topoi)
top'per
top|ping
topple (top|pling)
top|sail
top-shell
top|side
top|soil
topsy-turvy
toque
to|quilla
tor (hill) △ torr
Torah
Tor'bay
tor|chère
torch|light
torch|lit
tor|chon (lace)
tor|eador
tor|ero (*pl.*
 tor|eros)
tor|eutic
tor|eut|ics
toric
tor|ment
tor|mentil
tor|mentor
tor|nadic
tor|nado (*pl.*
 tor|na|does)
tor|oid
tor|oidal
tor|oid|ally
To|ronto
tor|ose

tor|pedo (as *n.*, *pl.*
 tor|pedoes; as *v.*,
 tor|pedoes,
 tor|pedoed,
 tor|pedo|ing)
tor|pefy
 (tor|pefies,
 tor|pefied,
 tor|pefy|ing)
tor'pid
tor|pid|ity
tor|por
tor|por|ific
tor|quate
torque
torr (unit; *pl.*
 same) △ tor
tor|re|fac|tion
tor|refy
 (tor|re|fies,
 tor|re|fied,
 tor|re|fy|ing)
tor|rent
tor|ren|tial
tor|ren|tially
Tor|ri'cel|lian
tor|rid
tor|rid|ity
tor|sion
tor|sional
torso (*pl.* tor'sos)
tort (*Law*)
torte (pastry; *pl.*
 tor'ten *or* tor'tes)
tort|feasor
tor'ti|col'lis
tor|tilla
tor|tious
tor|toise
tor|toise|shell
tor|trix
tor|tu|os'ity
tor|tu|ous
tor|ture (as *v.*,
 tor'tur|ing)
tor|turer
tor|tur|ous
tor|ula (*pl.*
 toru|lae)
torus (*pl.* tori)
Tory (*pl.* Tor|ies)
Tory|ism
Tosca
toss-up *n.*
tot (as *v.*, totted,
 tot|ting)

to|tal (as v.,
 to|talled,
 tot'al|ling)
to'tal'it|arian
to'tal'it|ari'an|ism
to'tal|ity
to'tal|iza|tion
to'tal|iz'ator
to'tal|ize
 (to'tal|iz|ing)
to'tal|izer
tot|ally
tote (tot'ing)
to'tem
to|temic
to'tem|istic
tot'ter
tot'tery
tou'can
touch|down
tou'ché
touch|ily
touchi|ness
touch-line
touch-paper
touch|stone
touch-type
 (touch-typing)
touch-typist
touch|wood
touchy (touch|ier,
 touchi|est)
toughen
toughie
tough|ish
Tou|louse
Toulouse-Lautrec
tou'pee
tour|aco (pl.
 tour|acos)
Tou|raine
tour|ism
tour|ist
tour|istic
tour|isty
tour|ma|line
tour|na|ment
tour|ne|dos (beef;
 pl. same)
tour|ney
tour|ni|quet
tousle (tous|ling)
to'var|ish
to|ward
to|wards

towel (as v.,
 tow'elled,
 tow'el|ling)
tower
towery
townee
town|scape
Towns|end
towns|folk
town|ship
towns|man (pl.
 towns|men)
towns|people
towns|wo'man
 (pl.
 towns|wo'men)
town|ward
town|wards
tow-path
tow-rope
tox|aemia
tox|aemic
toxic
tox'ic|ally
tox|icity (pl.
 tox'icit|ies)
tox'ico|lo'gical
tox'ico|lo'gist
tox'ico|logy
tox'ico|mania
toxin
toxo|phil'ite
toxo|phily
toy-box
tra'be|ate
tra'be|ation
tra'bec|ula (pl.
 tra'becu|lae)
tra'becu|lar
tra'becu|late
tra'cas|serie
trace (as v.,
 tra'cing)
trace|able
tracer
tracer|ied
tracery (pl.
 tracer|ies)
tra|chea (pl.
 tra|cheae)
trach|eal
trach|eate
tra'che|otomy (pl.
 tra'che|otom|ies)
trach|oma
trach|omat|ous

trach'yte
trach'ytic
track|age
tracker
track|way
tract
tract|ab'il|ity
tract|able
tract|ably
Tract|arian
Tract|ari'an|ism
tract|ate
trac|tion
trac|tional
tract|ive
trac|tor
trad|able
trade (as v.,
 trad|ing)
trade-in n.
trade mark
trade-off n.
trader
tra'des|can'tia
trades|man (pl.
 trades|men)
trades|people
trade-unionism
trade-unionist
tra'di|tion
tra'di|tional
tra'di|tion'al|ism
tra'di|tion'al|ist
tra'di|tion|ally
tra'di|tion|ary
tra'di|tion|ist
trad|itor (pl.
 trad|it'ors or
 trad|it|ores)
tra|duce
 (tra'du'cing)
tra'duce|ment
tra|ducer
tra'du'cian
tra'du'ci'an|ism
tra'du'ci'an|ist
tra|duc'tion
traf|fic (as v.,
 traf|ficked,
 traf'fick|ing)
traf'fic|ator
traf|ficker
traffic-light
trag|ac'anth
tra|gedian
tra'gedi|enne

tra'gedy (pl.
 tra'ged|ies)
tra'gic
tra'gical
tra'gic|ally
tra'gi|com'edy (pl.
 tra'gi|com'ed|ies)
tra'gi|comic
tra'gi|com'ic|ally
trago|pan
trailer
trainee
trainer
train-oil
train-spotter
traipse
 (traip|sing)
trait
traitor
trait'or|ous
trait|ress
tra'ject|ory (pl.
 tra'ject|or|ies)
Tra'lee
tram|car
tram|lines
tram|mel (as v.,
 tram|melled,
 tram'mel|ling)
tra|mon'tana
tra|mont|ane
trample
 (tramp|ling)
tram'po|line
 (as v.,
 tram'po|lin'ing)
tram'po|lin'ist
tram|way
trance
tranche
tranny (pl.
 tran|nies)
tran|quil
tran|quil|lity
tran|quil|liza|tion
tran|quil|lize
 (tran|quil|liz|ing)
tran|quil|lizer
tran|quilly
trans|act
trans|ac'tion
trans|actor
trans|al'pine
trans|at'lantic
trans|ceiver
tran|scend

tran|scend|ence
tran|scend|ency
  (*pl.* tran|scend|
    en|cies)
tran|scend|ent
tran|scend|ental
tran|scend|ent|al|
    ism
tran|scend|ent|
    ally
trans|
    con|tin|ental
tran|scribe
  (tran|scrib|ing)
tran|scriber
tran|script
tran|scrip|tion
tran|scrip|tional
tran|script|ive
trans|ducer
tran|sect
tran|sec|tion
tran|sept
tran|septal
trans|fer (as *v.*,
  trans|ferred,
  trans|fer|ring)
trans|fer|ab|il|ity
trans|fer|able
trans|feree
trans|fer|ence
trans|fer|rer
trans|fer|rin
trans|fig|ura|tion
Trans|fig|ura|tion
  (festival)
trans|fig|ure
  (trans|fig|ur|ing)
trans|fin|ite
trans|fix
trans|fix|ion
trans|form
trans|form|able
trans|forma|tion
trans|forma|
    tional
trans|form|at|ive
trans|former
trans|fuse
  (trans|fus|ing)
trans|fu|sion
trans|gress
trans|gres|sion
trans|gres|sional
trans|gress|ive
trans|gres|sor

tran|ship
  (tran|shipped,
  tran|ship|ping)
tran|ship|ment
trans|hum|ance
tran|si|ence
tran|si|ency
tran|si|ent
trans|il|lu|min|ate
  (trans|
    il|lu|minating)
trans|il|lu|mina|
    tion
trans|ire
tran|sistor
tran|sist|or|iza|
    tion
tran|sist|or|ize
  (tran|sist|or|iz|
    ing)
transit (as *v.*,
  trans|ited,
  trans|it|ing)
trans|ition
trans|itional
trans|ition|ary
trans|it|ive
trans|it|iv|ity
trans|it|or|ily
trans|it|ori|ness
trans|it|ory
trans|lat|able
trans|late
  (trans|lat|ing)
trans|la|tion
trans|la|tional
trans|lator
trans|lit|er|ate
  (trans|lit|er|
    at|ing)
trans|lit|era|tion
trans|lit|er|ator
trans|lo|ca|tion
trans|lu|cence
trans|lu|cency
trans|lu|cent
trans|lun|ary
trans|mar|ine
trans|mi|grant
trans|mi|grate
  (trans|
    mi|grat|ing)
trans|mi|gra|tion
trans|mi|grator
trans|mi|grat|ory
trans|miss|ible

trans|mis|sion
trans|miss|ive
trans|mit
  (trans|mit|ted,
  trans|mit|ting)
trans|mit|table
trans|mit|tal
trans|mit|ter
trans|mog|ri|fica|
    tion
trans|mog|rify
  (trans|mog|ri|
    fies,
  trans|mog|ri|
    fied,
  trans|mog|ri|
    fy|ing)
trans|mont|ane
trans|mut|ab|il|
    ity
trans|mut|able
trans|mu|ta|tion
trans|mut|at|ive
trans|mute
  (trans|mut|ing)
trans|muter
trans|na|tional
trans|oceanic
tran|som
tran|sonic
trans|pa|cific
trans|pad|ane
trans|par|ency
  (*pl.* trans|par|
    en|cies)
trans|par|ent
trans|pierce
  (trans|pier|cing)
tran|spir|able
tran|spira|tion
tran|spir|at|ory
tran|spire
  (tran|spir|ing)
trans|plant
trans|plant|able
trans|planta|tion
trans|pon|der
trans|pont|ine
trans|port
trans|port|ab|il|
    ity
trans|portable
trans|porta|tion
trans|porter
trans|pos|able
trans|posal

trans|pose
  (trans|pos|ing)
trans|poser
trans|posi|tion
trans|posi|tional
trans|pos|it|ive
trans|sexual
trans|sexu|al|ism
trans-Siberian
tran|sub|stan|ti|
    ate
  (tran|sub|stan|ti|
    at|ing)
tran|sub|stan|ti|
    ation
tran|suda|tion
tran|sud|at|ory
tran|sude
  (tran|sud|ing)
trans|ur|anic
Trans|vaal
trans|versal
trans|vers|al|ity
trans|vers|ally
trans|verse
trans|vest
trans|vest|ism
trans|vest|ist
trans|vest|ite
Tran|syl|va|nia
tran|ter
trap (as *v.*,
  trapped,
  trap|ping)
trap|door
tra|peze
tra|pez|ium (*pl.*
  tra|pezia *or*
  tra|pezi|ums)
trap|ezoid
trap|ez|oidal
trap|pean
trap|per
Trap|pist
Trap|pist|ine
trash|ery
trashi|ness
trashy (trash|ier,
  trashi|est)
trass
trat|toria
trauma (*pl.*
  trau|mas)
trau|matic
trau|mat|ic|ally
trau|mat|ism

trav|ail
travel (as v.,
 trav|elled,
 trav|el|ling)
trav|el|ler
trav|elogue
tra|vers|able
tra|versal
tra|verse
 (tra|vers|ing)
trav|er|tine
trav|esty (n., pl.
 trav|es|ties; as v.,
 trav|es|ties,
 trav|es|tied,
 trav|es|ty|ing)
Tra|viata
tra|vois (pl. same)
trawler
trawl-net
tray|ful (pl.
 tray|fuls)
treach|er|ous
treach|ery (pl.
 treach|er|ies)
treacle
treacly
tread (as v., trod,
 trod|den)
treadle (as v.,
 tread|ling)
tread|mill
tread-wheel
treason
treas|on|able
treas|on|ably
treas|ure (as v.,
 treas|ur|ing)
treas|urer
treas|ury (pl.
 treas|ur|ies)
treat|able
treat|ise
treat|ment
treaty (pl.
 treat|ies)
treble (as v.,
 treb|ling)
trebly
trebu|chet
tre|cent|ist
tre|cento
tree (as v., treed,
 tree|ing)
tree-house
treen

tree-top
trefa
tre|foil
tre|hala
trek (as v.,
 trekked,
 trek|king)
trek|ker
trel|lis (as v.,
 trel|lis|ing)
trellis-work
trem|at|ode
tremble (as v.,
 trem|bling)
trem|bler
trem|bly
 (trem|blier,
 trem|bli|est)
tre|mend|ous
trem|olo (pl.
 trem|olos)
tremor
tremu|lous
trench|ancy
trench|ant
trench|er|man (pl.
 trench|er|men)
trend|ily
trendi|ness
trend-setter
trendy (as n., pl.
 trend|ies; as a.,
 trend|ier,
 trendi|est)
trental
Trentino-Alto
 Adige
tre|pan (as v.,
 tre|panned,
 tre|pan|ning)
tre|pana|tion
tre|pang
tre|phina|tion
tre|phine (as v.,
 tre|phin|ing)
trep|ida|tion
tres|pass
tres|passer
trestle
Tret'ya|kov
 (Gallery)
Trevi
Tre'vith|ick
Trev'or
tri|able
tri|acet|ate

tri|acid
triad
tri|adelph|ous
tri|adic
tri|age
tri|and|rous
tri|angle
tri|an|gu|lar
tri|an|gu|lar|ity
tri|an|gu|late
 (tri|an|gu|lat|ing)
tri|an|gu|la|tion
tri|an|te|lope
Trias
Tri|as|sic
tri|atomic
tri|axial
trib|ade
trib|ad|ism
tribal
tri|bal|ism
tri|bal|ist
tri|bal|istic
tri|bally
tri|basic
tribes|man (pl.
 tribes|men)
trib|let
tri|bo|elec'tri'city
tri|bo|logy
tri|bo|
 lu'min'es'cence
tri|bo|meter
tri|brach
tri|brachic
tri|bu|la'tion
tri|bu'nal
tribu|nate
trib|une
tri|bu'ni|cial
tri|bu'ni|cian
tri|bu'ni|tial
trib'u|tary (as n.,
 pl. trib'u|tar'ies)
trib|ute
tri'car
trice (as v.,
 tri'cing)
tri|cent'en'ary
 (pl. tri|
 cent'en'ar'ies)
tri'ceps
tri'chi|asis
tri'china (pl.
 tri'chi|nae)
trich'in|osis

trich'in|ous
tri|chlor'ide
tricho|gen'ous
tricho|lo'gical
tricho|lo'gist
tricho|logy
trich|ome
tricho|monad
tricho|moni'asis
tricho|pathic
tricho|pathy
tri|chord
tri'cho|tomic
tri'cho|tom|ize
 (tri'cho'tom|iz|
        ing)
tri'cho'tom|ous
tri'cho|tomy (pl.
 tri'cho|tom'ies)
tri|chroic
tri|chro'ism
tri|chro'matic
tri|chro'mat|ism
trick'ery (pl.
 trick'er'ies)
trick'ily
tricki|ness
trick|ish
trickle (as v.,
 trick|ling)
trickly
trick'sily
tricksi|ness
trick|ster
tricksy
tricky (trick|ier,
 tricki|est)
tri|clinic
tri|clin'ium (pl.
 tri|clinia)
tri|col'our
tri|col'oured
tri|corn
tricot
tri|
 coty'le|don'ous
tri|crotic
tri|cuspid
tri|cycle (as v.,
 tri'cyc|ling)
tri'cyc|list
tri|dac'tyl
tri|dac'tyl|ous
tri|dent
tri|dent'ate
Tri|dent'ine

tri|di'git|ate
tri|di'men|sional
tri|duum
tri'dy|mite
tri|en'nial
tri|en'ni|ally
tri|en'nium (*pl.*
  tri|en'ni|ums)
trier (one who
  tries)
tri'er|archy (*pl.*
  tri'er|arch'ies)
tri|fa'cial
trif|fid (fictional
  plant)
tri'fid (three-lobed)
trifle (as *v.*,
  tri|fling)
tri|fler
tri|focal
tri|fo'li|ate
tri|for|ium (*pl.*
  tri|foria)
tri|form
tri|furc'ate (as *v.*,
  tri|furc'at|ing)
tri'gam|ist
tri'gam|ous
tri'gamy (*pl.*
  tri'gam|ies)
tri|gem'inal
tri|gem'inus (*pl.*
  tri|gem'ini)
trig'ger
tri'glyph
tri'glyphic
tri'glyph|ical
tri'gon
tri'gonal
tri'gon|ally
tri'gon|eutic
tri'go'no|met'ric
tri'go'no|
        met'rical
tri'go'no|metry
tri|gram
tri|graph
tri'gyn|ous
tri|hed'ral
tri|hed'ron (*pl.*
  tri|hedra *or*
  tri|hed'rons)
tri|hyd'ric
trike (as *v.*,
  trik'ing)
tri|la'bi|ate

tri|lam'|nar
tri|lat'eral
trilby (*pl.*
  tril|bies)
tri|lemma
tri|lin'ear
tri|lin'gual
tri|lit'eral
tri|lith
tri|lithic
tri|lithon
trill'ing
tril|lion
tril|lionth
tri|lob'ate
tri|lob'ite
tri|locu'lar
tri|logy (*pl.*
  tri|lo'gies)
trim (as *a.*,
  trim'mer,
  trim'mest; as *v.*,
  trimmed,
  trim'ming)
tri|maran
trimer
tri|meric
tri|mer'ous
tri|mes'ter
tri|mest'ral
tri|meter
tri|met'ric
tri|met'rical
trim|mer
trim|ming
tri|morphic
tri|morph|ism
tri|morph'ous
tri'nal
Trini|dad
Trin|it'ar|ian
Trin'it'ari|an|ism
tri|nit'ro|tolu|ene
tri|nit'ro|toluol
trin|ity (*pl.*
  trin|it'ies)
Trin|ity (*Theol.*)
trin|ket
trin|ketry
tri|no'mial
tri|no'mi|al|ism
trio (*pl.* tri'os)
tri'ode
tri|oeci'ous
tri'olet
tri'ox'ide

trip (as *v.*,
  tripped,
  trip'ping)
tri|part'ite
tri|par'ti'tion
tri|pet'al'ous
tri|phibi|ous
triph|thong
triph|thongal
tri|phyl'lous
tri|pin'nate
tri|plane
triple (as *v.*,
  trip|ling)
trip|let
trip|lex
trip|lic|ate (as *v.*,
  trip'lic|at|ing)
trip'lica|tion
tri|pli'city
trip|loid
trip|loidy
triply
tri|pod
tri|podal
Tri|poli
tri|pos
trip|per
trip|tych
tri|ptyque
Tri|pura
trip-wire
tri|quetra (*pl.*
  tri|quet'rae)
tri'quet'ral
tri'quet'rous
tri|reme
Tris|agion
tri|sect
tri|sec'tion
tri|sector
tri|shaw
tri|skelion
tris|mus
Tris|tan und
  Is|olde
tri|stich'ous
tri|stig'matic
tri|styl'ous
tri|sul'cate
tri|syl'labic
tri|syl'lable
trit|ag'on|ist
trite (triter,
  tritest)
tri|tern'ate

tri|the'ism
tri|the'ist
tri'ti|ate
  (tri'ti|at'ing)
tri'ti|ation
tri'tium
tri'ton (newt,
  nucleus)
Tri'ton (*Gr. Myth.*)
tri'tone
trit'ur|able
trit'ur'ate
  (trit'ur|at'ing)
trit'ura|tion
trit'ur'ator
tri|umph
tri|umphal
tri|umph|ally
tri|umph|ant
tri|um|vir
tri|um|viral
tri|um'vir|ate
tri|une
tri|un'ity (*pl.*
  tri|un'it'ies)
tri|valent
trivet
trivia
triv'ial
tri'vi|al'ity (*pl.*
  tri'vi|al'it|ies)
trivi'al|iza|tion
trivi'al|ize
  (trivi'al|iz|ing)
trivi'ally
triv|ium
tro'car
tro|chaic
tro|chal
tro|chan'ter
troche (lozenge
  etc.)
tro|chee (in metre)
troch|ilus
troch|lea (*pl.*
  troch|leae)
troch|lear
troch|oid
troch|oidal
tro|chus
trod *see* tread
trodden *see* tread
trog'lo|dyte
trog'lo|dytic
trog'lo'dyt|ism
tro'gon

troika
troil|ism
Tro|ilus and
  Cres|sida
Tro|jan
troll (dwarf etc.)
trol|ley
trol|ley|bus
trol|lop
Trol|lope
trom|bone
trom|bon|ist
trom|mel
tro|mo|meter
tro|mo|met|ric
trompe
troop (mil. unit,
  crowd) △ troupe
trooper
troop-ship
tro|pae|olum
trope
trophic
tro|phied
tropho|blast
tropho|neur|osis
  (*pl.* tropho|
       neur|oses)
trophy (*pl.*
  tro|phies)
tropic
trop|ical
trop|ic|ally
trop|ics
trop|ism
tro|po|lo|gical
tro|po|logy (*pl.*
  tro|po|lo|gies)
tro|po|pause
tro|po|sphere
tro|po|spheric
troppo
trot (as *v.*,
  trot|ted,
  trot|ting)
Trot
troth
Trot|sky
Trot|sky|ism
Trot|sky|ist
Trot|sky|ite
trot|ter
tro|tyl
trou|ba|dour
trouble (as *v.*,
  troub|ling)

trouble-maker
trouble-shooter
trouble|some
trough
trounce
  (troun|cing)
troupe (actors etc.)
  △ troop
trouper
trouser
trouser-suit
trous|seau (*pl.*
  trous|seaus)
trout (*pl.* same)
trouv|ère (poet)
Tro|va|tore
trover
Trow|bridge
trowel (as *v.*,
  trow|elled,
  trow|el|ling)
tru|ancy
tru|ant
truce
tru|cial
truck|age
trucker
truckle
  (truck|ling)
truck|ler
truc|ulence
truc|ulency
truc|ulent
trudge (trudging)
trudgen
true (as *a.*, truer,
  tru|est; as *v.*,
  trued, tru|ing)
truffle
tru|ism
truly
Tru|man
tru|meau (*pl.*
  tru|meaux)
trump|ery (*pl.*
  trump|er|ies)
trum|pet (as *v.*,
  trum|peted,
  trum|pet|ing)
trum|peter
truncal
trun|cate (as *v.*,
  trun|cat|ing)
trun|ca|tion
trun|cheon

trundle (as *v.*,
  trun|dling)
trunk-call
trunk|ful (*pl.*
  trunk|fuls)
trunk-line
trunk-road
trun|nion
Truro
trustee
trust|ee|ship
trust|ful
trust|fully
trust|ily
trusti|ness
trust|wor|thily
trust|wor|thi|ness
trust|worthy
trusty (trus|tier,
  trus|ti|est)
truth
truth|ful
truth|fully
try (as *v.*, tries,
  tried, try|ing)
try-on *n.*
try-out *n.*
tryp|ano|some
tryp|ano|so|mi|
             asis
tryp|sin
tryp|tic
try-sail
tryst
tsar
tsar|ev|ich
tsar|ina
tsar|ism
tsar|ist
tsetse
T-shirt
T-square
tsu|nami
Tswana
tua|tara
tub (as *v.*, tubbed,
  tub|bing)
tuba
tu|bal
tubby (tub|bier,
  tub|bi|est)
tub|by|ish
tube (as *v.*,
  tub|ing)
tubec|tomy (*pl.*
  tubec|tom|ies)

tube|less
tuber
tubercle
tuber|cu|lar
tuber|cu|late
tuber|cu|la|tion
tuber|cu|lin
tuber|cu|losis
tuber|cu|lous
tuber|ose
tuber|os|ity
tuber|ous
tub|ful (*pl.*
  tub|fuls)
tu|bi|col|ous
tu|bi|corn
tu|bi|form
tu|bi|lin|gual
tub|ing
tu|bu|lar
tu|bule
tu|bu|lous
tuck-box
tucker
tuck-shop
Tu|dor
Tu|dor|esque
Tues|day
tufa
tu|fa|ceous
tuff (rock)
tuf|fa|ceous
tuf|fet
tug (as *v.*, tugged,
  tug|ging)
tug|boat
Tuil|er|ies
tu|ition
tu|itional
tu|ition|ary
tu|lar|aemia
tu|lar|aemic
tul|chan
tu|lip
Tul|la|more
tulle (net)
tul|war
tumble (as *v.*,
  tum|bling)
tum|ble|down
tumble-drier
tum|bler
tum|bler|ful (*pl.*
  tum|bler|fuls)
tum|ble|weed
tum|brel

tu'me|fa'cient
tu'me|fac'tion
tumefy
 (tu'me|fies,
 tu'me|fied,
 tu'me|fy'ing)
tu'mes|cence
tu'mes|cent
tu'mid
tu'mid|ity
tummy (pl.
 tum|mies)
tu'mor|ous
tu'mour
tum'tum (cart)
tu'mu|lar
tu'mult
tu'mul'tu|ary
tu'mul'tu|ous
tu'mu|lus (pl.
 tu'muli)
tun (as v., tunned,
 tun|ning)
tuna-fish
tun|dish
tun|dra
tune (as v.,
 tun'ing)
tune|able
tune|ful
tune|fully
tuner
tung|state
tung|sten
tung|stic
tu'nic
tu'nica (pl.
 tu|nicae)
tu'nic|ate
tu'nicle
Tunis
Tu|nisia
Tu'nis|ian
tun'nel (as v.,
 tun|nelled,
 tun'nel|ling)
tun'nel|ler
tunny (pl.
 tun|nies)
tup (as v., tupped,
 tup|ping)
tup|pence
tup|penny
tuque
Tur|anian
tur'ban

turbaned
turb|ary
tur'bel|larian
tur'bid
tur'bid|ity
tur|binal
tur'bin|ate
tur'bina|tion
tur|bine
tur'bit (pigeon)
turbo-charger
tur'bo|fan
turbo-jet
turbo-prop
tur'bot (fish)
tur'bu|lence
tur'bu|lent
Tur'co|phile
Tur'co|phobe
turd|oid
tur|een
turf (as n., pl.
 turves or turfs)
turfy
Tur|genev
tur'gid
tur'gid|es'cence
tur'gid|es'cent
tur'gid|ity
tur|gor
Turin
tur'ion
Turk
tur'key
Tur'key
Turki (lang.
 group)
Turkic
Turk|ish
Turk'is|tan
Turk|men'is|tan
Tur'ko|man (pl.
 Tur'ko|mans)
tur|meric
tur|moil
turn-cap
turn|coat
Turner
turn|ery (pl.
 turn|er'ies)
tur'nip
tur|nipy
turn|key
turn-off n.
turn-on n.
turn|over

turn|pike
turn-round n.
turn|stile
turn|stone
turn|table
turn-up n.
tur'pen|tine (as v.,
 tur'pen|tin'ing)
tur|peth
tur'pi|tude
turps
tur|quoise
tur'ret
tur|reted
turtle
turtle-dove
turtle-neck
turtle-shell
Tus'can
Tus'cany
tusker
tusky
tus'ser
tuss|ive
tussle (as v.,
 tuss|ling)
tus|sock
tus|socky
tut (as v., tut'ted,
 tut'ting)
tu'tel|age
tu|telar
tu'tel|ary
tu|tenag
tu'tor
tu'tor|age
tu'tor|ess
tu'tor|ial
tu'tori|ally
tut'san
tutti
tut'ti|frutti
tut-tut (tut-tutted,
 tut-tutting)
tutty
tutu
Tu'valu
tu-whit, tu-whoo
 (owl's cry)
tux'edo (pl.
 tux|edos)
tuy'ère
twaddle (as v.,
 twad|dling)
twad|dly

twangle
 (twan|gling)
tweak
twee (tweer,
 tweest)
tweed
tweedle
twee'dle|dee
twee'dle|dum
tweedy
tweeny (pl.
 tween|ies)
tweet
tweeter
tweezer
twelfth
twelve
twelve|fold
twelve|month
twen|ties
twen'ti|eth
twenty
twen'ty|fold
twerp
twicer
twiddle (as v.,
 twid|dling)
twid|dler
twid|dly
twig (as v.,
 twigged,
 twig|ging)
twiggy
twi|light
twi'lit
twill (fabric)
twin (as v.,
 twinned,
 twin|ning)
twine (as v.,
 twin'ing)
twinge
twink
twinkle (as v.,
 twink|ling)
twink|ler
twinkly
twirl
twirly
twist
twist|able
twister
twisty (twis'tier,
 twis'ti|est)

twit (as *v.*,
 twit|ted,
 twit|ting)
twitch
twitch-grass
twitch|ily
twitchi|ness
twitchy
 (twitch|ier,
 twitchi|est)
twite (linnet)
twit|ter
two-dimensional
two-edged
two-faced
two|fold
two|pence
two|penny
two|some
two-step
two-time (two-
 timing)
two-timer
tych|ism
tych|ist
Ty|cho|nian
Ty|chonic

ty|coon
tyke
ty|lo|pod
ty|lo|pod|ous
tym|pan
tym|panic
tym|pan|ites
tym|pan|itic
tym|pan|itis
tym|panum (ear-
 drum;
 pl. tym|pana)
Tyne and Wear
Tyne|mouth
type (as *v.*,
 typ|ing)
type-cast (as *v.*,
 type-cast,
 type-casting)
type|face
type|script
type|set|ter
type|set|ting
type|write
 (type|wrote,
 type|writ|ten,
 type|writ|ing)

type|writer
typh|litic
typh|litis
typh|oid
typh|oidal
ty|phonic
ty|phoon
typh|ous *a.*
typhus *n.*
typ|ical
typ|ic|al|ity
typ|ic|ally
typi|fica|tion
typi|fier
typ|ify (typi|fies,
 typi|fied,
 typi|fy|ing)
typ|ing
typ|ist
typo (*pl.* ty|pos)
ty|po|grapher
ty|po|graphic
ty|po|graph|ical
ty|po|graph|ic|
 ally
ty|po|graphy (*pl.*
 ty|po|graph|ies)

ty|po|lo|gical
ty|po|lo|gist
ty|po|logy
ty|po|nym
tyr|an|nical
tyr|an|nic|ally
tyr|an|ni|cidal
tyr|an|ni|cide
tyr|an|nize
 (tyr|an|niz|ing)
tyr|an|no|saur
tyr|an|nous
tyr|anny (*pl.*
 tyr|an|nies)
tyr|ant
tyre (of wheel)
 △ tire
Tyr|ian
Ty|rol
Ty|ro|lean
Ty|ro|lese
Ty|rone
Tyr|rhene
Tyr|rhen|ian
tzar *use* tsar
tzi|gane

U

ubi|ety (*pl.*
  ubi|et|ies)
ubi|quit|arian
ubi|quit|ous
ubi|quity
udal
ud|al|ler
ud|al|man (*pl.*
  ud|al|men)
ud|der
udo|meter
Uf|fizi
ufo (*pl.* ufos)
Uganda
ugli (fruit)
ug|lify (ug|li|fies,
  ug|li|fied,
  ug|li|fy|ing)
ug|lily
ug|li|ness
ugly (ug|lier,
  ug|li|est)
Ug|rian
Ug|ric
Ui|gur
Uit|lander
ukase
ukiyo-e (Jap. art)
Ukraine
Ukrain|ian
uku|lele
Ulan Bator
ul|cer
ul|cer|able
ul|cer|ate
  (ul|cer|a|ting)
ul|cera|tion
ul|cer|at|ive
ul|cer|ous
ul|ema
uli|gin|ose
uli|gin|ous
ull|age
Ulls|wa|ter
ulna (*pl.* ul|nae)
ul|nar
ulo|trichan
ulo|trich|ous
ul|ster (coat)

Ul|ster
Ul|ster|man (*pl.*
  Ul|ster|men)
Ul|ster|wo|man
  (*pl.*
  Ul|ster|wo|men)
ul|ter|ior
ul|tima
ul|ti|mate
ul|ti|matum (*pl.*
  ul|ti|mat|ums)
ul|timo
ul|ti|mo|gen|it|ure
ul|tra
ul|tra|cen|tri|fuge
ultra-high
ul|tra|ism
ultra|ist
ul|tra|mar|ine
ul|tra|mic|ro|
         scope
ul|tra|mont|ane
ul|tra|mont|an|
         ism
ul|tra|mont|an|ist
ul|tra|mun|dane
ul|tra|sonic
ul|tra|son|ic|ally
ul|tra|son|ics
ul|tra|sound
ul|tra|struc|ture
ul|tra|vi|olet
ultra vires
ulu|lant
ulu|late
  (ulu|lat|ing)
ulu|la|tion
Ulys|ses
um|bel
um|bel|lar
um|bel|late
um|bel|li|fer
um|bel|li|fer|ous
um|bel|lule
um|ber
um|bil|ical
um|bil|ic|ate
um|bil|icus
umbles

umbo (*pl.* um|bos)
um|bonal
um|bon|ate
um|bra (*pl.*
  um|brae)
um|brage
um|bra|geous
um|bral
um|brella
um|brel|laed
um|brette
Um|bria
Um|brian
um|bri|fer|ous
um|iak
um|laut
um|pir|age
um|pire (as *v.*,
  um|pir|ing)
ump|teen
ump|teenth
umpty
un|abashed
un|abated
un|able
un|abridged
un|ab|sorbed
un|ac|cen|ted
un|ac|ceptable
un|ac|com|mod|
        at|ing
un|ac|com|pan|
        ied
un|
  ac|com|plished
un|ac|count|able
un|ac|count|ably
un|ac|coun|ted
un|ac|cus|tomed
un|ac|know|
      ledged
un|ac|quain|ted
un|ad|mit|ted
un|adop|ted
un|adorned
un|adul|ter|ated
un|ad|ven|tur|ous
un|ad|vis|able
un|ad|vised

un|ad|visedly
un|af|fected
un|af|fili|ated
un|afraid
un|aided
un|ali|en|able
un|al|loyed
un|al|ter|able
un|al|ter|ably
un|altered
un|al|ter|ing
un|am|bigu|ous
un|am|bi|tious
un|amen|able
un|amended
un-American
un|ami|able
un|amused
un|amus|ing
un|ana|lys|able
un|ana|lysed
un|an|im|ity
un|an|im|ous
un|an|nounced
un|an|swer|able
un|answered
un|apos|tolic
un|ap|par|ent
un|ap|peal|able
un|ap|peal|ing
un|ap|peas|able
un|ap|peased
un|ap|pet|iz|ing
un|ap|pre|ci|ated
un|ap|pre|ci|
      at|ive
un|ap|proach|
      able
un|ap|pro|pri|
      ated
un|ap|proved
un|apt
un|ar|gu|able
un|armed
un|ar|tistic
un|ar|tist|ic|ally
un|as|cer|tain|
      able

un|as|cer|tain|
         ably
un|as|cer|tained
un|ashamed
un|asked
un|as|sail|able
un|as|sail|ably
un|as|sis|ted
un|as|sum|ing
un|at|tached
un|at|tain|able
un|at|ten|ded
un|at|tes|ted
un|at|tract|ive
unau (sloth)
un|au|thentic
un|au|thent|ic|
         ated
un|au|thor|ized
un|avail|able
un|avail|ing
un|avoid|able
un|avoid|ably
un|avowed
un|aware
un|awares
un|backed
un|bal|anced
un|bap|tized
un|bar
 (un|barred,
 un|bar|ring)
un|bear|able
un|bear|ably
un|beat|able
un|beat|ably
un|beaten
un|be|com|ing
un|be|fit|ting
un|be|friended
un|be|got|ten
un|be|known
un|be|liev|able
un|be|liev|ably
un|be|liever
un|be|liev|ing
un|bend (un|bent)
un|biased
un|bib|lical
un|bid|dable
un|bid|den
un|bind
 (un|bound)
un|blem|ished
un|blest
un|block

un|blush|ing
un|bolt
un|born
un|bosom
un|bound
un|boun|ded
un|break|able
un|break|ably
un|brib|able
un|bridle
un|bridled
un-British
un|broken
un|broth|erly
un|brushed
un|buckle
 (un|buck|ling)
un|build
 (un|built)
un|bur|den
un|bur|ied
un|busi|ness|like
un|but|ton
un|cage
 (un|ca|ging)
uncalled-for
un|can|did
un|can|nily
un|can|ni|ness
un|canny
 (un|can|ni|er,
 un|can|ni|est)
un|cap
 (un|capped,
 un|cap|ping)
uncared-for
un|car|ing
un|case
 (un|cas|ing)
un|caused
un|ceas|ing
un|cen|sored
un|ce|re|mo|ni|
         ous
un|cer|tain
un|cer|tainty (pl.
 un|cer|tain|ties)
un|cer|ti|fic|ated
un|cer|ti|fied
un|chain
un|chal|lenge|
         able
un|chal|lenged
un|change|ab|il|
         ity
un|change|able

un|changed
un|chan|ging
un|char|ac|ter|
         istic
un|char|ac|ter|
         ist|ic|ally
un|char|it|able
un|char|it|ably
un|charted
un|chartered
un|checked
un|chiv|al|rous
un|chris|tian
un|cial
un|ci|form
un|cin|ate
un|cir|cum|cised
un|civil
un|civ|il|ized
un|civ|illy
un|claimed
un|clasp
un|clas|si|fied
uncle
un|clean
un|cleanly
un|clean|ness
un|clear
un|clench
un|clip
 (un|clipped,
 un|clip|ping)
un|clog
 (un|clogged,
 un|clog|ging)
un|close
un|clothe
un|clothed
un|clouded
un|cluttered
unco (pl. un|cos)
un|coil
un|col|oured
un|comely
un|com|fort|able
un|com|fort|ably
un|com|mer|cial
un|com|mit|ted
un|com|mon
un|
 com|mu|nic|at|
         ive
un|com|pan|
         ion|able
un|com|plain|ing
un|com|pleted

un|com|plic|ated
un|com|pli|ment|
         ary
un|com|prom|
         ising
un|con|cealed
un|con|cern
un|con|cerned
un|con|di|tional
un|con|di|tion|
         ally
un|con|di|tioned
un|con|fined
un|con|firmed
un|con|form|able
un|con|form|ity
un|con|genial
un|con|geni|ally
un|con|nected
un|con|quer|able
un|conquered
un|con|scion|able
un|con|scion|ably
un|con|scious
un|con|sidered
un|con|sti|tu|
         tional
un|con|sti|tu|tion|
         ally
un|con|strained
un|con|straint
un|con|sumed
un|con|tain|able
un|con|tam|in|
         ated
un|con|tested
un|con|trol|lable
un|con|trol|lably
un|con|trolled
un|con|tro|
         ver|sial
un|con|tro|
         ver|ted
un|con|tro|
         vert|ible
un|con|ven|tional
un|con|ven|tion|
         ally
un|con|victed
un|con|vinced
un|con|vin|cing
un|cooked
un|co|op|er|at|ive
un|co|or|din|ated
un|cork
un|cor|rec|ted

un|cor|rob|or|
　　　　　ated
un|cor|rup|ted
un|count|able
un|count|ably
un|coun|ted
un|couple
　(un|coup|ling)
un|couth
un|cov|en|an|ted
un|cover
un|crit|ical
un|crit|ic|ally
un|cross
un|crowned
un|crush|able
unc|tion
unc|tu|ous
un|cul|tiv|ated
un|cul|tured
un|cured
un|curl
un|cur|tailed
un|cur|tained
un|customed
un|cut
un|dam|aged
un|dated
un|daun|ted
un|de|ceive
　(un|de|ceiv|ing)
un|de|cided
un|de|ci|pher|
　　　　　able
un|declared
un|defeated
un|defen|ded
un|defiled
un|defined
un|delivered
un|demand|ing
un|demo|cratic
un|demo|crat|ic|
　　　　　ally
un|demon|strat|
　　　　　ive
un|deni|able
un|deni|ably
un|der
un|der|achieve
　(un|der|
　　　achiev|ing)
un|der|achiever
un|der|act
under-age
un|der|arm

un|der|belly (pl.
　un|der|bel|lies)
un|der|bid (as v.,
　un|der|bid,
　un|der|bid|ding)
un|der|body (pl.
　un|der|bod|ies)
un|der|bred
un|der|car|riage
un|der|charge
　(un|der|
　　　　　char|ging)
un|der|clay
un|der|cliff
un|der|clothes
un|der|cloth|ing
un|der|coat
un|der|cook
un|der|cover
un|der|croft
un|der|cur|rent
un|der|cut
　(un|der|cut,
　un|der|cut|ting)
un|der|developed
un|der|do
　(un|der|did,
　un|der|done,
　un|der|do|ing)
un|der|dog
un|der|done
un|der|dress
un|der|em|phasis
un|der|em|phas|
　　　　　ize
　(un|der|
　　em|phas|iz|ing)
un|der|em|ployed
un|der|em|ploy|
　　　　　ment
un|der|es|tim|ate
　(as v., un|der|
　　es|tim|ating)
un|der|es|tima|
　　　　　tion
un|der|ex|pose
　(un|der|
　　　ex|pos|ing)
un|der|ex|pos|ure
un|der|feed
　(un|der|fed)
un|der|felt
un|der|floor
un|der|flow
un|der|foot
un|der|gar|ment

un|der|gird
un|der|glaze
un|der|go
　(un|der|went,
　un|der|gone)
un|der|gradu|ate
un|der|ground
un|der|growth
un|der|hand
un|der|han|ded
un|der|hung
un|der|lay (as v.,
　un|der|laid)
un|der|lie
　(un|der|lay,
　un|der|lain,
　un|der|ly|ing)
un|der|line (as v.,
　un|der|lin|ing)
un|der|linen
un|der|ling
un|der|manned
un|der|
　　　　men|tioned
un|der|mine
　(un|der|min|ing)
un|der|most
un|der|neath
un|der|
　　　　nour|ished
un|der|pants
under-part
un|der|pass
un|der|pay
　(un|der|paid)
un|der|pin
　(un|der|pinned,
　un|der|pin|ning)
un|der|play
un|der|plot
un|der|
　　　　priv|ileged
un|der|pro|duc|
　　　　　tion
un|der|proof
un|der|prop
　(un|der|propped,
　un|der|
　　　　prop|ping)
un|der|quote
　(un|der|quot|ing)
un|der|rate
　(un|der|rat|ing)
un|der|ripe
un|der|score
　(un|der|scor|ing)

un|der|sea
un|der|seal
under-secretary
　(pl. under-
　　　secretaries)
un|der|sell
　(un|der|sold)
un|der|set (as v.,
　un|der|set,
　un|der|set|ting)
under-sexed
un|der|shirt
un|der|shoot
　(un|der|shot)
under-side
un|der|signed
un|der|sized
un|der|skirt
un|der|slung
un|der|spend
　(un|der|spent)
un|der|staffed
un|der|stand
　(un|der|stood,
　un|der|stand|
　　　　　ing)
un|der|stand|able
un|der|stand|ably
un|der|state
　(un|der|stat|ing)
un|der|state|ment
un|der|steer
un|der|strap|per
un|der|study (as
　n., pl.
　un|der|stud|ies;
　as v.,
　un|der|stud|ies,
　un|der|stud|ied,
　un|der|study|
　　　　　ing)
under-surface
un|der|take
　(un|der|took,
　un|der|taken,
　undertaking)
un|der|taker
un|der|tak|ing
un|der|things
un|der|tint
un|der|tone
un|der|tow
un|der|valu|ation
un|der|value
　(un|der|val|ued,
　un|der|valu|ing)

un|der|wa|ter
un|der|wear
un|der|weight
un|der|wing
un|der|wood
un|der|world
un|der|write
 (un|der|wrote,
 un|der|writ|ten,
 un|der|writ|ing)
un|der|writer
un|des|cen|ded
un|deserved
un|deserv|ing
un|designed
un|desir|ab|il|ity
un|desir|able
un|desir|ably
un|desired
un|desir|ous
un|detec|ted
un|deter|mined
un|deterred
un|developed
un|devi|ating
un|dia|gnosed
und|ies
un|dif|fer|en|ti|
            ated
un|di|ges|ted
un|dig|ni|fied
un|di|luted
un|di|min|ished
un|dimmed
un|dine
un|dip|lo|matic
un|dip|lo|mat|ic|
            ally
un|dis|cip|lined
un|dis|closed
un|dis|cov|er|able
un|dis|covered
un|dis|crim|in|
          at|ing
un|dis|guised
un|dis|mayed
un|dis|puted
un|dis|solved
un|
  dis|tin|guished
un|dis|trib|uted
un|dis|turbed
un|di|vided
un|di|vulged

undo (un|does,
 un|did, un|done,
 un|do|ing)
un|do|mes|tic
           ated
un|done
un|doubted
un|dreamed
un|dreamt
un|dress
un|drink|able
un|due
un|du|lant
un|du|late (as v.,
 un|du|lat|ing)
un|du|la|tion
un|du|lat|ory
un|duly
un|du|ti|ful
un|du|ti|fully
un|dy|ing
un|earned
un|earth
un|earth|li|ness
un|earthly
un|ease
un|eas|ily
un|easi|ness
un|easy
 (un|eas|ier,
 un|easi|est)
un|eat|able
un|eaten
un|eco|nomic
un|eco|nom|ical
un|eco|nom|ic|
          ally
un|edifying
un|ed|ited
un|edu|cated
un|em|bar|rassed
un|emo|tional
un|emo|tion|ally
un|em|phatic
un|em|phat|ic|
          ally
un|em|ploy|able
un|em|ployed
un|em|ploy|ment
un|emp|tied
un|en|cumbered
un|end|ing
un|en|dowed
un|en|dur|able
un|en|dur|ably
un-English

un|en|joy|able
un|en|lightened
un|en|ter|pris|ing
un|en|thu|si|astic
un|en|thu|si|ast|
           ic|ally
un|en|vi|able
un|equable
un|equal
un|equalled
un|equally
un|equi|vocal
un|equi|voc|ally
un|err|ing
un|es|cor|ted
un|es|sen|tial
un|es|tab|lished
un|eth|ical
un|eth|ic|ally
un|even
un|even|ness
un|event|ful
un|event|fully
un|ex|act|ing
un|ex|am|ined
un|ex|cav|ated
un|ex|cep|tion|
            able
un|ex|cep|tion|
            ably
un|ex|cep|tional
un|ex|cit|ing
un|ex|clus|ive
un|ex|ecuted
un|ex|hausted
un|ex|pec|ted
un|ex|pi|ated
un|ex|plain|able
un|ex|plain|ably
un|ex|plained
un|ex|plored
un|ex|posed
un|ex|pressed
un|ex|pur|gated
un|fad|ing
un|fail|ing
un|fair
un|faith|ful
un|faith|fully
un|fal|ter|ing
un|fa|mil|iar
un|fa|mi|li|ar|ity
un|fash|ion|able
un|fash|ion|ably
un|fa|shioned
un|fasten

un|fathered
un|fath|om|able
un|fathomed
un|fa|vour|able
un|fa|vour|ably
un|fed
un|feel|ing
un|feigned
un|fem|in|ine
un|fenced
un|fer|men|ted
un|fer|til|ized
un|fettered
un|fi|lial
un|filled
un|filtered
un|fin|ished
un|fit
un|fit|ted
un|fit|ting
un|fix
un|flag|ging
un|flap|pab|il|ity
un|flap|pable
un|flap|pably
un|flat|ter|ing
un|fla|voured
un|fledged
un|flinch|ing
un|flustered
un|focused
un|fold
un|forced
un|fore|see|able
un|fore|seen
un|for|get|table
un|for|get|tably
un|for|giv|able
un|for|giv|ably
un|for|given
un|for|giv|ing
un|for|got|ten
un|formed
un|for|mu|lated
un|forth|com|ing
un|for|ti|fied
un|for|tu|nate
un|foun|ded
un|freeze
 (un|froze,
 un|frozen,
 un|freez|ing)
un|fre|quen|ted
un|friend|li|ness

un|friendly
 (un|friend|lier,
 un|friend|li|est)
un|frock
un|fruit|ful
un|ful|filled
un|funny
un|furl
un|fur|nished
un|gain|li|ness
un|gainly
un|gal|lant
un|gen|er|ous
un|genial
un|gentle
un|gen|tle|manly
unget-at-able
un|gil|ded
un|glazed
un|god|li|ness
un|godly
un|gov|ern|able
un|grace|ful
un|grace|fully
un|gra|cious
un|gram|mat|ical
un|gram|mat|ic|
 ally
un|grate|ful
un|grate|fully
un|grudging
un|gual
un|guarded
un|guent
un|gui|cu|late
un|guis (pl.
 un|gues)
un|gula (pl.
 un|gu|lae)
un|gu|late
un|gum
 (un|gummed,
 un|gum|ming)
un|hal|lowed
un|hampered
un|hand
un|hand|some
un|hang
 (un|hung)
un|hap|pily
un|hap|pi|ness
un|happy
 (un|hap|pier,
 un|hap|pi|est)
un|har|bour
un|harmed

un|har|ncss
un|health|ily
un|healthi|ness
un|healthy
 (un|health|ier,
 un|healthi|est)
un|heard
unheard-of
un|heeded
un|heed|ful
un|heed|ing
un|help|ful
un|help|fully
un|her|al|ded
un|he|roic
un|he|ro|ic|ally
un|hes|it|at|ing
un|hid|den
un|hinge
 (un|hin|ging)
un|his|toric
un|his|tor|ical
un|hitch
un|ho|li|ness
un|holy
 (un|ho|lier,
 un|ho|li|est)
un|hon|oured
un|hook
un|hoped
un|hope|ful
un|horse
 (un|hors|ing)
un|house
 (un|hous|ing)
un|hur|ried
un|hur|ry|ing
un|hurt
un|hy|gienic
un|hy|gien|ic|ally
Uniat
uni|ax|ial
uni|cam|eral
uni|cel|lu|lar
uni|col|oured
uni|corn
uni|cuspid
uni|cycle
un|idea'd
un|ideal
un|iden|ti|fied
uni|di|men|sional
un|idio|matic
uni|dir|ec|tional
uni|fi|able
uni|fica|tion

uni|fier
uni|form
uni|form|it|arian
uni|form|ity (pl.
 uni|form|it|ies)
unify (uni|fies,
 uni|fied,
 uni|fy|ing)
uni|lat|eral
uni|lat|er|ally
uni|lin|gual
uni|lit|eral
un|il|lu|min|ated
uni|locu|lar
un|ima|gin|able
un|ima|gin|ably
un|ima|gin|at|ive
un|ima|gined
un|im|paired
un|im|par|ted
un|im|pas|sioned
un|im|peach|able
un|im|peded
un|im|port|ance
un|im|port|ant
un|im|pos|ing
un|im|pressed
un|im|pres|sion|
 able
un|im|press|ive
un|im|proved
un|im|pugned
un|in|dexed
un|in|fec|ted
un|in|flec|ted
un|in|flu|enced
un|in|formed
un|in|hab|it|able
un|in|hab|ited
un|in|hib|ited
un|ini|ti|ated
un|injured
un|in|spired
un|in|spir|ing
un|in|struc|ted
un|in|sur|able
un|in|sured
un|in|tel|li|gent
un|in|tel|li|gible
un|in|tel|li|gibly
un|in|ten|ded
un|in|ten|tional
un|in|ten|tion|ally
un|in|ter|ested
un|in|ter|est|ing
un|in|ter|rup|ted

uni|nuc|le|ate
un|in|vent|ive
un|in|ves|ti|gated
un|in|vited
un|in|vit|ing
un|in|volved
union
uni|on|ism
uni|on|ist
uni|on|istic
uni|on|iza|tion
uni|on|ize
 (uni|on|iz|ing)
uni|par|ous
uni|part|ite
uni|ped
uni|per|sonal
uni|pla|nar
uni|pod
uni|po|lar
unique
uni|serial
uni|sex
uni|sexual
uni|sexu|al|ity
uni|sexu|ally
uni|son
un|is|sued
unit
unit|arian
Unit|ari|an|ism
unit|ary
unite (unit|ing)
unit|ive
unity (pl. unit|ies)
uni|va|lent
uni|valve
uni|ver|sal
uni|ver|sal|ism
uni|ver|sal|ist
uni|ver|sal|istic
uni|ver|sal|ity
uni|ver|sal|ize
 (uni|ver|sal|iz|
 ing)
uni|ver|sally
uni|verse
uni|ver|sity (pl.
 uni|ver|sit|ies)
uni|vo|cal
un|jaun|diced
un|join
un|joint
un|just
un|jus|ti|fi|able
un|jus|ti|fi|ably

un|kempt
un|kind
un|kissed
un|knit
 (un|knit|ted,
 un|knit|ting)
un|knot
 (un|knot|ted,
 un|knot|ting)
un|know|able
un|know|ing
un|known
un|la|belled
un|lace
 (un|la|cing)
un|laden
un|la|dy|like
un|la|men|ted
un|latch
un|law|ful
un|law|fully
un|leaded
un|learn
 (un|learned *or*
 un|learnt)
un|leash
un|leavened
un|less
un|li|censed
un|like
un|like|li|hood
un|like|li|ness
un|likely
 (un|like|lier,
 un|like|li|est)
un|lim|ited
un|lined
un|li|quid|ated
un|lis|ted
un|lit
unlived-in
un|load
un|lock
un|looked
un|loose
 (un|loos|ing)
un|loosen
un|lov|able
un|loved
un|love|li|ness
un|lovely
un|lov|ing
un|luck|ily
un|lucki|ness

un|lucky
 (un|luck|ier,
 un|lucki|est)
un|maid|enly
un|make
 (un|made,
 un|mak|ing)
un|man
 (un|manned,
 un|man|ning)
un|man|age|able
un|man|age|ably
un|manly
un|man|ner|li|
        ness
un|man|nerly
un|marked
un|mar|ket|able
un|mar|riage|able
un|mar|ried
un|mas|cu|line
un|mask
un|match|able
un|matched
un|mean|ing
un|meant
un|meas|ur|able
un|meas|ured
un|melo|di|ous
un|mel|ted
un|mem|or|able
un|mem|or|ably
un|men|tion|able
un|men|tion|ably
un|mer|chant|
         able
un|mer|ci|ful
un|mer|ci|fully
un|mer|ited
un|met|alled
un|meth|od|ical
un|met|rical
un|mil|it|ary
un|mind|ful
un|mis|tak|able
un|mis|tak|ably
un|mit|ig|ated
un|mixed
un|modi|fied
un|modu|lated
un|mo|les|ted
un|moral
un|moth|erly
un|mo|tiv|ated
un|moun|ted
un|mourned

un|moved
un|muffle
 (un|muf|fling)
un|mu|sical
un|mu|sic|ally
un|mu|til|ated
un|muzzle
 (un|muzz|ling)
un|name|able
un|named
un|na|tional
un|nat|ural
un|nat|ur|ally
un|nav|ig|able
un|ne|ces|sar|ily
un|ne|ces|sary
un|neigh|bourly
un|nerve
 (un|nerv|ing)
un|no|ticed
un|numbered
un|ob|jec|tion|
           able
un|ob|jec|tion|
           ably
un|ob|scured
un|ob|serv|ant
un|ob|served
un|ob|struc|ted
un|ob|tain|able
un|ob|tain|ably
un|ob|trus|ive
un|oc|cu|pied
un|of|fend|ing
un|of|fi|cial
un|of|fi|cially
un|oiled
un|opened
un|op|posed
un|or|gan|ized
un|ori|ginal
un|ori|gin|al|ity
un|ori|gin|ally
un|or|na|men|ted
un|or|tho|dox
un|os|ten|ta|tious
un|owned
un|ox|id|ized
un|pack
un|paged
un|paid
un|painted
un|paired
un|pal|at|able
un|pal|at|ably
un|par|alleled

un|par|don|able
un|par|don|ably
un|par|lia|ment|
            ary
un|pat|en|ted
un|pat|ri|otic
un|pat|terned
un|paved
un|peace|ful
un|peeled
un|peg
 (un|pegged,
 un|peg|ging)
un|per|ceived
un|per|cept|ive
un|per|formed
un|per|suaded
un|per|suas|ive
un|per|turbed
un|phi|lo|sophic
un|phi|lo|
        soph|ical
un|phi|lo|soph|ic|
            ally
un|pick
un|pin
 (un|pinned,
 un|pin|ning)
un|pit|ied
un|pi|ty|ing
un|placed
un|planned
un|planted
un|plastered
un|play|able
un|play|ably
un|pleas|ant
un|pleas|ing
un|pledged
un|ploughed
un|plucked
un|plug
 (un|plugged,
 un|plug|ging)
un|plumbed
un|po|etic
un|po|et|ical
un|po|et|ic|ally
un|pointed
un|pol|ished
un|po|lit|ical
un|polled
un|pol|luted
un|popu|lar
un|popu|lar|ity
un|pos|sessed

un|posted
un|prac|tical
un|prac|tised
un|pre|ced|en|ted
un|pre|dict|ab|il|
    ity
un|pre|dict|able
un|pre|dict|ably
un|pre|ju|diced
un|pre|med|it|
    ated
un|pre|pared
un|pre|pos|sess|
    ing
un|pre|sent|able
un|pre|sum|ing
un|pre|sump|tu|
    ous
un|pre|tend|ing
un|pre|ten|tious
un|pre|vent|able
un|priced
un|primed
un|prin|cipled
un|print|able
un|prin|ted
un|privi|leged
un|pro|cur|able
un|pro|duct|ive
un|pro|fes|sional
un|pro|fes|sion|
    ally
unp|rof|it|able
un|prof|it|ably
un|pro|gress|ive
un|prom|is|ing
un|promp|ted
un|pro|nounce|
    able
un|proph|etic
un|pro|pi|tious
un|pros|per|ous
un|pro|tec|ted
un|prov|able
un|proved
un|proven
un|pro|vided
un|pro|voked
un|pub|lished
un|punc|tual
un|punc|tu|al|ity
un|punc|tu|ally
un|punc|tu|ated
un|pun|ish|able
un|pun|ished
un|puri|fied

un|put|down|able
un|quali|fied
un|quench|able
un|quenched
un|ques|tion|able
un|ques|tion|ably
un|ques|tioned
un|ques|tion|ing
un|quiet
un|quot|able
un|ransomed
un|rati|fied
un|ravel
  (un|rav|elled,
  un|rav|el|ling)
un|reach|able
un|read
un|read|able
un|readi|ness
un|ready
un|real
un|real|istic
un|real|ist|ic|ally
un|real|ity
un|real|iz|able
un|real|ized
un|reas|on|able
un|reas|on|ably
un|reas|on|ing
un|re|cept|ive
un|re|cip|roc|ated
un|reckoned
un|re|claimed
un|re|cog|niz|able
un|rec|og|niz|ably
un|re|cog|nized
un|re|con|ciled
un|re|cor|ded
un|re|covered
un|rec|ti|fied
un|re|deemed
un|re|dressed
un|reel
un|re|fined
un|re|flected
un|re|formed
un|re|futed
un|re|gar|ded
un|re|gen|er|ate
un|re|gistered
un|re|gret|ted
un|regu|lated
un|re|hearsed
un|rein
un|re|lated
un|re|laxed

un|re|lent|ing
un|re|li|ab|il|ity
un|re|li|able
un|re|li|ably
un|re|lieved
un|re|mark|able
un|re|mark|ably
un|re|membered
un|re|mit|ting
un|re|mu|ner|at|
    ive
un|re|nounced
un|re|pealed
un|re|peat|able
un|re|pent|ant
un|re|por|ted
un|rep|res|ent|at|
    ive
un|rep|res|en|ted
un|re|proved
un|re|quited
un|re|served
un|res|ist|ing
un|re|solved
un|re|spons|ive
un|rest
un|rest|ful
un|res|tored
un|res|trained
un|res|tric|ted
un|re|turned
un|re|vealed
un|re|vised
un|re|war|ded
un|re|ward|ing
un|rhyth|mical
un|rhyth|mic|ally
un|rid|able
un|rid|den
un|riddle
un|right|eous
un|rip (un|ripped,
  un|rip|ping)
un|ripe
un|ripened
un|risen
un|ri|valled
un|roll
un|ro|man|tic
un|ro|man|tic|ally
un|roof
un|root
un|rope
  (un|rop|ing)
un|royal
un|ruffled

un|ru|li|ness
un|ruly
  (un|ru|lier,
  un|ru|li|est)
un|saddle
  (un|sad|dling)
un|safe
un|said
un|sal|ar|ied
un|sale|able
un|salted
un|sanc|ti|fied
un|sanc|tioned
un|san|it|ary
un|sapped
un|sat|is|fact|or|
    ily
un|sat|is|fact|ory
un|sat|is|fied
un|sat|is|fy|ing
un|sat|ur|ated
un|sa|voury
un|say (un|said)
un|scal|able
un|scarred
un|scathed
un|scen|ted
un|sched|uled
un|schol|arly
un|schooled
un|sci|en|tific
un|sci|en|tif|ic|
    ally
un|scramble
  (un|scram|bling)
un|scratched
un|screw
un|scrip|ted
un|scru|pu|lous
un|seal
un|sea|son|able
un|sea|son|ably
un|seasoned
un|seat
un|sea|wor|thi|
    ness
un|sea|worthy
un|sec|on|ded
un|se|cured
un|seeded
un|see|ing
un|seem|li|ness
un|seemly
  (un|seem|lier,
  un|seem|li|est)
un|seen

un|seg|reg|ated
un|se|lec|ted
un|self|con|scious
un|self|ish
        ated
un|sen|sa|tional
un|sent
un|sen|ti|mental
un|sen|ti|ment|
        ally
un|sep|ar|ated
un|ser|vice|able
un|settle
(un|set|tling)
un|sex
un|shackle
(un|shack|ling)
un|shaded
un|shake|able
un|shaken
un|shared
un|sharpened
        like
un|shaven
un|sheathe
un|shed
un|shell
un|sheltered
un|ship
(un|shipped,
 un|ship|ping)
un|shock|able
un|shod
un|shrink|able
un|sighted
un|sight|li|ness
un|sightly
(un|sight|li|er,
 un|sight|li|est)
un|signed
un|sink|able
un|sized
un|skil|ful
un|skilled
un|skimmed
un|sling
(un|slung)
un|smil|ing
un|smoked
un|snarl
un|so|ci|able
un|so|ci|ably
un|so|cial
un|so|cially
un|soiled
un|sold
un|sol|dierly
un|so|li|cited

un|solv|able
un|solved
un|soph|ist|ic|
        ated
un|sor|ted
un|sought
un|sound
un|spar|ing
un|speak|able
un|speak|ably
un|spe|ci|fied
un|spec|tacu|lar
un|spent
un|spilled
un|spilt
un|spoiled
un|spoilt
un|spoken
un|sport|ing
un|sports|man|
        like
un|spot|ted
un|stable
un|stained
un|stamped
un|starched
un|stated
un|states|man|
        like
un|stat|ut|able
un|stat|ut|ably
un|stead|fast
un|stead|ily
un|steadi|ness
un|steady
un|ster|il|ized
un|stick
(un|stuck)
un|stifled
un|stimu|lated
un|stin|ted
un|stint|ing
un|stirred
un|stitch
un|stock|inged
un|stop
(un|stopped,
 un|stop|ping)
un|stop|pable
un|stop|pably
un|stop|per
un|strained
un|strap
(un|strapped,
 un|strap|ping)
un|strati|fied

un|streamed
un|strengthened
un|stressed
un|string
 (un|strung)
un|struc|tured
un|stud|ied
un|stuffed
un|stuffy
un|sub|dued
un|sub|jug|ated
un|sub|scribed
un|sub|sid|ized
un|sub|stan|tial
un|sub|stan|ti|
        ated
un|suc|cess
un|suc|cess|ful
un|suc|cess|fully
un|sugared
un|sug|gest|ive
un|suit|ab|il|ity
un|suit|able
un|suit|ably
un|suited
un|sul|lied
un|sung
un|sup|plied
un|sup|port|able
un|sup|pressed
un|sure
un|sur|mount|
        able
un|sur|pass|able
un|sur|passed
un|sur|veyed
un|sus|cept|ible
un|sus|pec|ted
un|sus|pect|ing
un|sus|pi|cious
un|sus|tain|able
un|sus|tained
un|swal|lowed
un|sweetened
un|swept
un|swerv|ing
un|sym|met|rical
un|sym|path|etic
un|sym|path|et|ic|
        ally
un|sys|tem|atic
un|sys|tem|at|ic|
        ally
un|tack
un|tain|ted
un|taken

un|tal|en|ted
un|tame|able
un|tamed
un|tangle
 (un|tan|gling)
un|tapped
un|tar|nished
un|tasted
un|taught
un|taxed
un|teach
 (un|taught)
un|teach|able
un|tech|nical
un|tempered
un|temp|ted
un|ten|able
un|ten|an|ted
un|ten|ded
Un|ter|walden
un|tes|ted
un|tether
un|thanked
un|thank|ful
un|thank|fully
un|thatched
un|thickened
un|think|able
un|think|ing *a.*
un|thought|ful
unthought-of
un|thread
un|threatened
un|threshed
un|thrifty
un|throne
 (un|thron|ing)
un|ti|dily
un|ti|di|ness
un|tidy
 (un|ti|dier,
 un|ti|di|est)
un|tie (un|tied,
 un|ty|ing)
un|til
un|timely
un|tinged
un|tir|ing
un|titled
unto
un|told
un|touch|able
un|touched
un|to|ward
un|trace|able
un|traced

un|trained
un|tram'melled
un|trans|lat'able
un|trans|port|
          able
un|trav'elled
un|treat'able
un|treated
un|tried
un|trod'den
un|troubled
un|true
un|truly
un|trust'worthy
un|truth
un|truth'ful
un|truth'fully
un|tuned
un|tune'ful
un|tune'fully
un|turned
un|tutored
un|twine
 (un|twin'ing)
un|twist
un'used
un|usual
un|usu'ally
un|ut'ter|able
un|ut'ter|ably
un|uttered
un|vac'cin|ated
un|val'ued
un|van'quished
un|var'ied
un|var'nished
un|vary'ing
un'veil
un|ven'til|ated
un|veri'fi|able
un|veri'fied
un|versed
un|vis'ited
un|vi'ti|ated
un|voiced
un|wakened
un|wanted
un|war'ily
un|war'like
un|warmed
un|war'rant|able
un|war'rant|ably
un|war'ran'ted
un'wary
 (un|war'ier,
 un|wari|est)

un|washed
un|watched
un|watered
un|waver|ing
un|weakened
un|weaned
un|wear'ied
un|weary
un|weary'ing
un|wed
un|wed'ded
un|weeded
un|weighed
un|wel'come
un|wel'comed
un|well
un|wept
un|whipped
un|whitened
un|whole'some
un|wiel'dily
un|wiel'di|ness
un|wieldy
un|will'ing
un'wind
 (un|wound)
un|wink'ing
un|wiped
un|wired
un|wis'dom
un'wise
un|wished
un|withered
un|wit'nessed
un|wit'ting
un|wo'manly
un|wonted
un|wooded
un|work'able
un|worked
un|work'man|like
un|world'li|ness
un|worldly
un'worn
un|wor'ried
un|wor'shipped
un|wor'thily
un|wor'thi|ness
un'worthy
 (un|wor'thi|er,
 un|wor'thi|est)
un|wounded
un|woven
un'wrap
 (un|wrapped,
 un|wrap|ping)

un|wrinkled
un|writ'able
un|writ'ten
un|wrought
un|wrung
un|yield'ing
un'yoke
 (un|yok'ing)
un'zip (un|zipped,
 un'zip|ping)
up (as v., upped,
 up|ping)
Upan|ishad
upas (tree)
up'beat
up|braid
up|bring|ing
up|build
 (up|built)
up|cast (up|cast)
up-country
up'date
 (up|dat'ing)
up-end
up|field
up|fold
up|grade
 (up|grad'ing)
up|growth
up|heaval
up|hill
up|hold (up'held)
up'hol|ster
up'hol|sterer
up'hol|stery
uph'roe
up|keep
up|land
up|lift
up'ly'ing
up|most
upon
up'per
upper-class
upper-cut
up'per|most
up'pish
up'pity
Upp|sala
up|raise
 (up|rais|ing)
up|right
up|rise (up'rose,
 up|risen,
 up|ris|ing)
up|ris'ing n.

up'roar
up'roari|ous
up|root
up|rush
up'set (as v.,
 up'set,
 up'set|ting)
up'shot
upside-down
up'si|lon
up|stage (as v.,
 up|sta'ging)
up|stair
up|stairs
up|stand|ing
up|start
up|stream
up-stroke
up|surge
up|swept
up|swing
upsy-daisy
up'take
up|throw
up|thrust
up|tight
up|til'ted
up|town
up'turn
up'ward
up'wards
up|warp
up'wind
ur'acil
ur|aemia
ur|aemic
ur'aeus
Ural-Altaic
Urals
ur'anic
ur'an|ism
ur|anium
ur|ano|graphy
ur|ano|metry
ur'an|ous
ur'ate
urban
ur'bane
urb|an|ism
urb|an|ist
urb|an|ite
ur|ban|ity
urb|an|iza|tion
urb|an|ize
 (urb|an|iz|ing)
ur'ce|ol|ate

ur|chin
Urdu
urea
ureter
ureteral
uret|eric
ureter|itis
uretero|tomy (*pl.*
 uretero|tom|ies)
ur|eth|ane
ur|ethra (*pl.*
 ur|eth|rae)
ur|eth|ral
ur|eth|ritis
ur|eth|ro|tomy
 (*pl.* ur|eth|ro|
  tom|ies)
urge (as *v.*,
 ur|ging)
ur|gency
ur|gent
uric
urim
ur|inal
ur|in|alysis (*pl.*
 ur|in|alyses)

ur|in|ary
ur|in|ate
 (ur|in|at|ing)
ur|ina|tion
ur|ine
ur|in|ous
uro|chord
uro|dele
uro|gen|ital
uro|logy
uro|pygium
urs|ine
ur|tic|aria
ur|tic|ate
 (ur|tic|at|ing)
ur|tica|tion
Uru|guay
us|able
us|age
us|ance
use (as *v.*, us|ing)
use|ful
use|fully
use|less
user
usher

ush|er|ette
us|que|baugh
usual
usu|ally
usu|cap|tion
usu|fruct
usu|fruc|tu|ary
 (*pl.* usu|fruc|tu|
  ar|ies)
us|urer
us|uri|ous
usurp
usurpa|tion
usurper
us|ury
Utah
uten|sil
uter|ine
uter|it|is
uterus (*pl.* uteri)
ut|ile
util|it|arian
util|it|ari|an|ism
util|ity (*pl.*
 util|it|ies)
util|iz|able

util|iza|tion
util|ize
 (util|iz|ing)
ut|most
Uto|pia
Uto|pian
uto|pi|an|ism
Ut|recht
ut|ricle
ut|ricu|lar
Ut|rillo
Ut|tar Pra|desh
ut|ter
ut|ter|ance
ut|terly
ut|ter|most
U-turn
uvula (*pl.* uvu|lae)
uxori|cidal
uxori|cide
uxori|ous
Uz|bek
Uz|bek|is|tan

V

va|cancy (*pl.*
 va|can|cies)
va|cant
va|cat|able
va|cate
 (va|cat|ing)
va|ca|tion
vac|cinal
vac|cin|ate
 (vac|cin|at|ing)
vac|cina|tion
vac|cin|ator
vac|cine
vac|cinia
va|cil|late
 (va|cil|lat|ing)
va|cil|la|tion
va|cu|ity
va|cu|olar
va|cu|ola|tion
va|cu|ole
va|cu|ous
va|cuum (*pl.*
 va|cu|ums *or*
 techn. vacua)
vade-mecum
Va|duz
vaga|bond
vagal
va|gari|ous
vag|ary (*pl.*
 vag|ar|ies)
va|gina
va|ginal
va|gin|is|mus
va|gin|itis
vag|rancy
vag|rant
vague (vaguer,
 vaguest)
vaguish
vagus (*pl.* vagi)
vain (conceited)
 △ vane, vein
vain|glori|ous
vain|glory
vain|ness
Vaisya
Val|ais

val|ance (short
 curtain)
va|le|dic|tion
va|le|dict|orian
va|le|dict|ory
vale (valley)
 △ veil
val|ence (*Chem.*)
Va|len|cia
Va|len|ci|ennes
valency (*pl.*
 valen|cies)
val|en|tine
val|er|ate
va|lerian
va|leric
valet (as *v.*,
 val|eted,
 val|et|ing)
va|le|tu|din|arian
va|le|tu|din|ary
val|gus
Val|halla
vali|ant
valid
val|id|ate
 (val|id|at|ing)
val|ida|tion
va|lid|ity
va|lise
Val|kyrie
val|lec|ula (*pl.*
 val|lec|ulae)
val|lec|ular
val|lec|ulate
Valle d'Aosta
Val|letta
val|ley
val|lum
va|lo|nia
val|or|iza|tion
val|or|ize
 (val|or|iz|ing)
val|or|ous
val|our
valse
valu|able
valu|ably
valu|ation

valu|ator
value (as *v.*,
 val|ued,
 valu|ing)
value|less
valuer
va|luta
valv|ate
valve
valved
valv|ular
valv|ule
valv|ulitis
vam|brace
va|moose
 (va|moos|ing)
vam|pire
vam|piric
vam|pir|ism
vam|plate
van|ad|ate
va|nadic
va|na|dium
van|ad|ous
Van Allen (belt)
Van|cou|ver
van|dal (*gen.*)
Van|dal (*hist.*)
Van|dalic
van|dal|ism
van|dal|ize
 (van|dal|iz|ing)
Van Dyck
vane
 (weathercock)
 △ vain, vein
vaned
va|nessa
 (butterfly)
Va|nessa
Van Eyck
Van Gogh
van|guard
va|nilla
va|nil|lin
van|ish
Van|it|ory (*propr.*)
van|ity (*pl.*
 van|it|ies)

van|quish
vant|age
Van 't Hoff
Va|nu|atu
vapid
va|pid|ity
va|por|ific
va|pori|form
va|pori|meter
va|por|iz|able
va|por|iza|tion
va|por|ize
 (va|por|iz|ing)
va|por|izer
va|por|ous
va|pour
va|pourer
va|poury
va|quero (*pl.*
 va|queros)
var|actor
Va|ran|gian
varec
vari|ab|il|ity (*pl.*
 vari|ab|il|it|ies)
vari|able
vari|ably
vari|ance
vari|ant
vari|ate
vari|ation
vari|ational
va|ri|cella
vari|co|cele
vari|col|oured
var|ic|ose
var|ic|os|ity
varie|gate
 (varie|gat|ing)
varie|ga|tion
vari|etal
vari|et|ist
vari|ety (*pl.*
 vari|et|ies)
vari|form
va|ri|ola
va|ri|olar
vari|ole
vari|ol|ite

vari|ol|itic
vari|ol|oid
vari|ol|ous
vario|meter
vari|orum
vari|ous
va'ris|tor
varix (*pl.* var|ices)
var|let
var|letry
var|mint
varna
var|nish
var|sity (*pl.*
 var|sit|ies)
var'so'vi|ana
var'so'vi|enne
varus
varve
varved
vary (var|ies,
 var|ied,
 vary|ing)
vas (*pl.* vasa)
vasal
vas|cu|lar
vas|cu'lar|ity
vas|cu'lar|ize
 (vas|cu'lar|iz|ing)
vas|cu|lum (*pl.*
 vas|cula)
vas de|fer|ens (*pl.*
 vasa
 de|fer|en|tia)
vas|ec'tom|ize
 (vas|ec'tom|iz|
  ing)
vas|ec'tomy (*pl.*
 vas|ec'tom|ies)
vase|ful (*pl.*
 vase|fuls)
vas|el|ine (*v.*
 vas|el|in|ing)
Vas|el|ine (*propr.*)
va'si|form
vaso-active
vaso-motor
va'so|pres'sin
vas|sal
vas'sal|age
vast
vas'ti|tude
vat (as *v.*, vat|ted,
 vat|ting)
vat|ful (*pl.*
 vat|fuls)

vatic
Vat|ican
va'ti|cinal
va'ti|cin|ate
 (va'tic|in|at|ing)
va'ti|cina|tion
va'ti|cin|ator
va'ti|cin|at'ory
Vaud
vaude|ville
vaude'vil|lian
Vaud|ois (*pl.*
 same)
Vaughan
 Wil|liams
vault
vaul|ted
vaunt
vav'as|ory (*pl.*
 vav'as|or|ies)
vav'as|our
Va'vilov
vec|tor
vec|torial
Veda (Hinduism,
 pl. same)
Ve|danta
Ve|dantic
Ve|dant|ist
Vedda
 (aboriginal)
ved|ette
Vedic
veer
Vega Car|pio
ve|gan
ve'get|able
ve|getal
ve'get|arian
ve'get|ari'an|ism
ve'get|ate
 (ve'get|at|ing)
ve|geta|tion
ve'get|at|ive
ve'he|mence
ve'he|ment
vehicle
vehicu|lar
vehm|ge'richt
veil (covering)
 △ vale
veil|less
vein (blood-vessel
 etc.) △ vain, vane
vein|let
vein|stone

veiny (vein|ier,
 veini|est)
ve'la|men (*pl.*
 ve'la|mina)
ve'lar
Ve'láz|quez
veld
veld|schoen
ve|leta
vel'le|ity (*pl.*
 vel'le'it|ies)
vel|lum
 (parchment etc.)
 △ velum
ve'lo'ci|meter
ve'lo'ci|pede
ve'lo|city (*pl.*
 ve'lo'cit|ies)
ve|lour
ve|louté
ve|lum
 (membrane; *pl.*
 vela) △ vellum
ve'lu'tin|ous
vel'vet
vel'vet|een
vel|vety
vena cava (*pl.*
 ve'nae cavae)
ve|nal
ve'nal|ity
ve|nally
vena|tion
vena|tional
ven|dace
vendee
vender
ven|detta
vend|ible
vendor
ven|eer
ve'ne|punc'ture
ven'er|ab'il|ity
ven'er|able
ven'er|ably
ven'er|ate
 (ven'er|at|ing)
ven'era|tion
ven'er|ator
ve'ner|eal
ve'ner|eally
ve'nere'olo'gical
ve'nere'olo'gist
ve'nere'ology
ven|ery
ve'ne|sec'tion

Ve|ne|tian
Ven|eto
Ven|ez'uela
ven|geance
venge|ful
venge|fully
ve|nial
ve'ni|al|ity
ve'ni|ally
Ven|ice
ven|ison
Ven|ite
Venn (diagram)
venom
venomed
ven'om|ous
ven|ose
ven|os|ity
ven|ous
vent|age
vent-hole
ven'ti|duct
ven'ti|fact
ventil
vent'il|ate
 (vent'il|at|ing)
vent'ila|tion
vent'il|at'ive
vent'il|ator
vent|ral
vent|rally
vent|ricle
vent'ric|ose
vent'ri|cu|lar
vent'ri|lo'quial
vent'ri|lo'quism
vent'ri|lo'quist
vent'ri|lo'quistic
vent'ri|lo'quize
 (vent'ri|lo'quiz|
  ing)
vent'ri|lo'quous
vent'ri|lo'quy
ven|ture (as *v.*,
 ven'tur|ing)
ven|turer
ven'ture|some
ven|turi
venue
ven|ule
Venus
Ven|usian (of
 planet)
ve'ra|cious
ve'ra|city
ver|anda

ver|at|rine
verbal
verb|al|ism'
verb|al|ist
verb|ali|stic
verb|al|iza|tion
verb|al|ize
 (verb|al|iz|ing)
verb|ally
ver|ba|tim
ver|bena
ver|bi|age
verb|ose
verb|os|ity
ver|bo|ten
verd|ancy
verd|ant
verd-antique
ver|derer
Verdi
ver|dict
ver|di|gris
ver|di|ter
ver|dure
ver|dured
ver|dur|ous
verge (as v.,
 ver|ging)
ver|ger
ver|glas
ve|ri|dical
ve|ri|dic|ally
ve|ri|est
veri|fi|able
veri|fi|ably
ve|ri|fica|tion
veri|fier
verify (veri|fies,
 veri|fied,
 veri|fy|ing)
ver|ily
ve|ri|sim|ilar
ve|ri|si|mil|it|ude
ver|ism
ver|ismo (pl.
 ver|is|mos)
ver|ist
ver|it|able
ver|it|ably
ver|ity
ver|juice
Ver|laine
Ver|meer
ver|meil
ver|mian
ver|mi|celli

ver|mi|cide
ver|mi|cu|lar
ver|mi|cu|late
ver|mi|cu|la|tion
ver|mi|cu|lite
ver|mi|form
ver|mi|fuge
ver|mil|ion
ver|min
ver|min|ate
 (ver|min|at|ing)
ver|mina|tion
ver|min|ous
ver|mi|vor|ous
Ver|mont
ver|mouth
ver|na|cu|lar
ver|nal
ver|nal|iza|tion
ver|nal|ize
 (ver|nal|iz|ing)
ver|nally
ver|na|tion
Verner's law
vern|icle
ver|nier (scale)
Ver|nier (man)
ver|onal
ver|on|ica (plant)
Ver|on|ica
ver|ruca (pl.
 ver|ru|cae)
ver|ru|cose
ver|ru|cous
Ver|sailles
ver|sant
ver|sat|ile
ver|sat|il|ity
verse (as v.,
 vers|ing)
ver|set
vers|icle
ver|si|col|oured
ver|si|cu|lar
ver|si|fica|tion
ver|si|fier
ver|sify
 (ver|si|fies,
 ver|si|fied,
 ver|si|fy|ing)
ver|sin
ver|sine
ver|sion
verso (pl. ver|sos)
ver|sus

ver|tebra (pl.
 ver|teb|rae)
ver|teb|ral
ver|teb|rally
ver|teb|rate
ver|teb|ra|tion
ver|tex (pl.
 ver|ti|ces)
ver|tical
ver|tic|al|ity
ver|tic|ally
ver|ti|cil
ver|ti|cil|late
ver|ti|gin|ous
ver|tigo (pl.
 ver|ti|gos)
ver|vain
verve
ver|vet
very
Very (light)
Ve|sa|lius
ve|sica
ves|ical a.
ves|ic|ant
ves|ic|ate
 (ves|ic|at|ing)
ves|ica|tion
ves|ic|at|ory
ves|icle n.
ve|si|cu|lar
ve|si|cu|late
ve|si|cu|la|tion
ves|per
ves|per|tine
ves|pi|ary (pl.
 ves|pi|ar|ies)
vesp|ine
ves|sel
vesta
ves|tal
ves|ti|ary (as n.,
 pl. ves|ti|ar|ies)
ves|ti|bu|lar
ves|ti|bule
vest|ige
ves|ti|gial
ves|ti|ture
vest|ment
vest|ral
vestry (pl.
 vest|ries)
vest|ry|man (pl.
 vest|ry|men)
ves|ture
Ve|su|vius

vet (as v., vet|ted,
 vet|ting)
vetch
vetch|ling
vetchy
vet|eran
ve|ter|in|arian
vet|er|in|ary
 (as n., pl.
 vet|er|in|ar|ies)
vet|iver
veto (as n., pl.
 ve|toes; as v.,
 ve|toes, ve|toed,
 ve|to|ing)
vexa|tion
vexa|tious
vexed
vex|il|lo|logy
vex|il|lum (pl.
 vex|illa)
via
vi|ab|il|ity
vi|able
vi|ably
via|duct
vial (phial) △ vile
vi|al|ful (pl.
 vi|al|fuls)
vi|and
vi|at|icum (pl.
 vi|at|ica)
vibes
vi|bracu|lar
vi|bracu|lum (pl.
 vi|brac|ula)
vi|brancy
vi|brant
vi|bra|phone
vi|bra|phon|ist
vi|brate
 (vi|brat|ing)
vi|brat|ile
vi|bra|tion
vi|bra|tional
vi|brat|ive
vi|brato (pl.
 vi|bra|tos)
vi|brator
vi|brat|ory
vi|bris|sae
vi|burnum
vicar
vic|ar|age
vi|car|ial
vi|cari|ate

vi¦cari¦ous
vice (as *v.*, viced,
 vi¦cing)
vice-admiral
vice-chairman
 (*pl.*
 vice-chairmen)
vice-chancellor
vice-consul
vice¦ger¦ency (*pl.*
 vice¦ger¦en¦cies)
vice¦ger¦ent
vice¦like
vicen¦nial
vice-president
vice¦regal
vice¦reine
vice¦roy
vice¦royal
vice¦roy¦alty
vi¦ces¦imal
vice versa
Vichy (water)
vichy¦ssoise
vi¦cin¦age
vi¦cinal
vi¦cin¦ity (*pl.*
 vi¦cin¦it¦ies)
vi¦cious
vi¦cis¦si¦tude
vi¦cis¦si¦tu¦din¦
 ous
vic¦tim
vic¦tim¦iza¦tion
vic¦tim¦ize
 (vic¦tim¦iz¦ing)
vic¦tor
Vic¦toria
Vic¦tor¦ian
Vic¦tori¦ana
vic¦tori¦ous
vic¦tory (*pl.*
 vic¦tor¦ies)
vic¦tress
victual (as *v.*,
 victualled,
 victual¦ling)
victual¦ler
victual¦less
vi¦cuña
vide (see)
vi¦de¦licet
video (*pl.* vid¦eos)
video¦phone
video¦tape (as *v.*,
 video¦tap¦ing)

vi¦di¦mus
vie (vied, vy¦ing)
vi¦elle
Vi¦enna
Vi¦en¦nese
Vien¦tiane
Viet¦nam
Vi¦et¦nam¦ese
view
view¦able
viewer
view¦finder
view¦point
vi¦ges¦imal
vi¦ges¦im¦ally
vi¦gil
vi¦gil¦ance
vi¦gil¦ant
vi¦gil¦ante
vign¦er¦on
vign¦ette (as *v.*,
 vign¦et¦ting)
vign¦et¦ter
vign¦et¦tist
vig¦or¦ous
vig¦our
vi¦hara
Vi¦king
vi¦la¦yet
vi¦li¦fica¦tion
vili¦fier
vil¦ify (vili¦fies,
 vili¦fied,
 vili¦fy¦ing)
villa
vil¦lage
vil¦la¦ger
vil¦lain
vil¦lain¦ess
vil¦lain¦ous
vil¦lainy (*pl.*
 vil¦lain¦ies)
Villa-Lobos
vil¦lan¦elle
vil¦leg¦gia¦tura
vil¦lein (serf)
vil¦lein¦age
vil¦li¦form
Vil¦lon
vil¦lose
vil¦los¦ity
vil¦lous
vil¦lus (*pl.* villi)
vi¦min¦eous
vina
vi¦na¦ceous

vi¦nai¦grette
vin¦cible
vin¦cu¦lum (*pl.*
 vin¦cula)
vin¦dic¦able
vin¦dic¦ate
 (vin¦dic¦at¦ing)
vin¦dica¦tion
vin¦dic¦at¦ive
vin¦dic¦ator
vin¦dic¦at¦ory
vin¦dict¦ive
vin¦egar
vin¦eg¦ar¦ish
vin¦eg¦ary
vinery (*pl.*
 viner¦ies)
vine¦yard
vingt-et-un
vini¦cul¦ture
vi¦ni¦fica¦tion
vin or¦din¦aire
vin¦os¦ity
vin¦ous
Vin¦son (Massif)
vin¦tage
vin¦ta¦ger
vint¦ner
viny (vin¦ier,
 vini¦est)
vi¦nyl
viol
vi¦ola
vi¦ol¦able
vi¦ola¦ceous
vi¦ola da gamba
vi¦ola d'amore
vi¦ol¦ate
 (vi¦ol¦at¦ing)
vi¦ola¦tion
vi¦ol¦ator
vi¦ol¦ence
vi¦ol¦ent
vi¦olet
vi¦olin
vi¦ol¦in¦ist
vi¦ol¦ist
vi¦ol¦on¦cel¦list
vi¦ol¦on¦cello (*pl.*
 vi¦ol¦on¦cel¦los)
vi¦ol¦one
vi¦per
vi¦peri¦form
vi¦per¦ine
vi¦per¦ish
vi¦per¦ous

vi¦rago (*pl.*
 vi¦ra¦gos)
viral
vir¦elay
vire¦ment
vi¦reo (*pl.* vi¦reos)
vir¦es¦cence
vir¦es¦cent
vir¦gate
Vir¦gil
Vir¦gil¦ian
vir¦gin
Vir¦gin (Islands)
vir¦ginal
vir¦gin¦ally
Vir¦ginia
Vir¦gin¦ian
vir¦gin¦ity
Virgo (*pl.* Vir¦gos)
Vir¦goan
virgo in¦tacta
vir¦gule
vi¦ri¦des¦cence
vi¦ri¦des¦cent
vi¦ri¦dian
vi¦ri¦dity
vir¦ile
vir¦il¦ism
vir¦il¦ity
viro¦lo¦gical
viro¦logist
viro¦logy
virtu (love of fine
 arts)
vir¦tual
vir¦tu¦al¦ity
vir¦tu¦ally
vir¦tue
vir¦tu¦osic
vir¦tu¦os¦ity
vir¦tu¦oso (*pl.*
 vir¦tu¦osi)
vir¦tu¦ous
viru¦lence
viru¦lent
virus
visa (as *v.*,
 vi¦saed)
vis¦age
vis¦aged
vis-à-vis
vis¦cacha
vis¦cera
vis¦ceral
vis¦cero¦tonic
vis¦cid

vis¦cid¦ity
vis¦co¦meter
vis¦cose
vis¦cosi¦meter
vis¦cos¦ity (*pl.*
 vis¦cos¦it¦ies)
vis¦count
vis¦countcy (*pl.*
 vis¦count¦cies)
vis¦count¦ess
vis¦county (*pl.*
 vis¦coun¦ties)
vis¦cous (sticky)
Vishnu
Vish¦nu¦ism
Vish'nu¦ite
vis¦ib¦il¦ity
vis¦ible
vis¦ibly
Visi¦goth
vi¦sion
vi¦sional
vi¦sion¦ari¦ness
vi¦sion¦ary (*pl.*
 vi¦sion¦ar¦ies)
vi¦sion¦ist
visit (as *v.*,
 vis¦ited,
 vis¦it¦ing)
vis¦it¦able
vis¦it¦ant
vis¦ita¦tion
vis¦it¦at¦orial
vis¦itor
vis¦it¦orial
visor
vi¦sored
vista
vis¦taed
Vis¦tula
visual
visu¦al¦ity
visu¦al¦iza¦tion
visu¦al¦ize
 (visu¦al¦iz¦ing)
visu¦ally
vi¦tal
vi¦tal¦ism
vi¦tal¦ist
vi¦tal¦istic
vi¦tal¦ity
vi¦tal¦iza¦tion
vi¦tal¦ize
 (vi¦tal¦iz¦ing)
vi¦tally
vit¦amin

vit¦am¦in¦ize
 (vit¦am¦in¦iz¦ing)
vi¦tel¦lary
vi¦tel¦lin
vi¦tel¦line
vi¦tel¦lus (*pl.*
 vi¦telli)
viti¦ate
 (viti¦at¦ing)
viti¦ation
viti¦ator
viti¦cul¦ture
Vi¦toria (in Spain
 & Brazil)
vit¦re¦ous
vit¦res¦cence
vit¦res¦cent
vit¦ri¦fac¦tion
vit¦ri¦fi¦able
vit¦ri¦fica¦tion
vit¦ri¦form
vit¦rify (vit¦ri¦fies,
 vit¦ri¦fied,
 vit¦ri¦fy¦ing)
vit¦riol
vit¦ri¦olic
vit¦ri¦ol¦ize
 (vit¦ri¦ol¦iz¦ing)
Vi¦tru¦vian
vitta (*pl.* vit¦tae)
vi¦tu¦per¦ate
 (vi¦tu¦per¦at¦ing)
vi¦tu¦pera¦tion
vi¦tu¦per¦at¦ive
vi¦tu¦per¦ator
viva (viva voce; as
 v., vi¦vaed)
viva ('long live')
vi¦vace
vi¦va¦cious
vi¦va¦city
viv¦ar¦ium (*pl.*
 viv¦aria)
vivat
viva voce *n.*
viva-voce *v.*
 (viva-voced,
 viva-voceing)
vi¦vax
vi¦ver¦rine
vivid
vivi¦fica¦tion
viv¦ify (vivi¦fies,
 vivi¦fied,
 vivi¦fy¦ing)
vi¦vi¦par¦ity

vi¦vi¦par¦ous
vi¦vi¦sect
vi¦vi¦sec¦tion
vi¦vi¦sec¦tional
vi¦vi¦sec¦tion¦ist
vivi¦sector
vixen
viz¦ier
viz¦ier¦ate
viz¦ier¦ial
viz'sla (dog)
Vlach
voc¦able
vo¦cabu¦lary (*pl.*
 vo¦cabu¦lar¦ies)
vocal
vo¦calic
vo¦cal¦ism
vo¦cal¦ist
vo¦cal¦ity
vo¦cal¦iza¦tion
vo¦cal¦ize
 (vo¦cal¦iz¦ing)
vo¦cally
vo¦ca¦tion
vo¦ca¦tional
vo¦ca¦tion¦ally
voc¦at¦ive
vo¦ci¦fer¦ance
vo¦ci¦fer¦ant
vo¦ci¦fer¦ate
 (vo¦ci¦fer¦at¦ing)
vo¦ci¦fera¦tion
vo¦ci¦fer¦ator
vo¦ci¦fer¦ous
vodka
vogue
voguish
voice (as *v.*,
 voicing)
voice-over *n.*
void¦able
void¦ance
voile
vo¦lant
vo¦lar
vol¦at¦ile
vol¦at¦il¦ity
vo¦lat¦il¦iza¦tion
vo¦lat¦il¦ize
 (vo¦lat¦il¦iz¦ing)
vol-au-vent
vol¦canic
vol¦can¦ic¦ally
vol¦cani¦city

vol¦cano (*pl.*
 vol¦ca¦noes)
volet
Volga
vol¦it¦ant
vo¦li¦tion
vo¦li¦tional
vol¦it¦ive
völ¦ker¦
 wan¦der¦ung
vol¦ley
volley-ball
vol¦plane (as *v.*,
 vol¦plan¦ing)
volt (*Electr.*)
Volta
volt¦age
vol¦taic
Vol¦taire
vol¦ta¦meter
volte (in fencing)
volte-face
volt¦meter
vo¦lu¦bil¦ity
vol¦uble
vol¦ubly
vol¦ume
vol¦umed
vo¦lu¦met¦ric
vo¦lu¦met¦ric¦ally
vo¦lu¦min¦os¦ity
vo¦lu¦min¦ous
vol¦un¦tar¦ily
vol¦un¦tari¦ness
vol¦un¦tar¦ism
vol¦un¦tar¦ist
vol¦un¦tary (as *n.*,
 pl. vol¦un¦tar¦ies)
vo¦lun¦teer
vo¦lup¦tu¦ary
vo¦lup¦tu¦ous
vo¦lute
vo¦luted
vo¦lu¦tion
volva
vo¦mer
vomit (as *v.*,
 vom¦ited,
 vom¦it¦ing)
vo¦mit¦orium (*pl.*
 vo¦mit¦oria)
vom¦it¦ory (*pl.*
 vom¦it¦or¦ies)
voo¦doo
voo¦doo¦ism
voo¦doo¦ist

vo¦ra|cious
vo¦ra|city
Vor|arl¦berg
vor¦tex (*pl.*
  vor|texes or *sci.*
  vor|tices)
vor¦tical
vor¦ti|cella
vor¦ti|cism
vor¦ti|cist
vor¦ti|city
vor¦tic|ose
vor¦ticu|lar
vot¦able
vo¦tar|ess
vo¦tar|ist
vo¦tary (*pl.*
  vo¦tar|ies)
vote (as *v.*,
  vot¦ing)

voter
vo¦tive
vouch
voucher
vouch|safe
  (vouch|saf¦ing)
vous|soir
vowel
vow¦el|ize
  (vow¦el|iz|ing)
vow¦elled
vow¦el|less
vox pop|uli
voy¦age (as *v.*,
  voy|aging)
voy¦age|able
voy|ager
voy¦eur
voy¦eur|ism

vraic
Vul¦can
Vul¦can|ist
vul¦can|ite
vul¦can|iz|able
vul¦can|iza|tion
vul¦can|ize
  (vul¦can|iz|ing)
vul¦can|izer
vul¦cano|lo¦gical
vul¦cano|lo¦gist
vul¦cano|logy
vul¦gar
vul¦gar|ian
vul¦gar|ism
vul¦gar|ity (*pl.*
  vul¦gar|it¦ies)
vul¦gar|iza|tion

vul¦gar|ize
  (vul¦gar|iz|ing)
vul|gate (*gen.*)
Vul|gate (Bible)
vul¦ner|ab¦il|ity
vul¦ner|able
vul¦ner|ably
vul¦ner|ary (*pl.*
  vul¦ner|ar¦ies)
vulp|ine
vul|ture
vul¦tur|ine
vul¦tur|ish
vul¦tur|ous
vulva
vul¦var
vulv|itis
Vyrnwy, Lake

W

wacke (rock)
wacky (wack|ier,
 wacki|est)
wad (as v.,
 wad|ded,
 wad|ding)
wad|able
wad|ding
waddle (as v.,
 wad|dling)
waddy
wade (wad|ing)
wader
wadi
wafer
wafery
waffle (as v.,
 waff|ling)
wag (as v.,
 wagged,
 wag|ging)
wage (as v.,
 wa|ging)
wager
wag|gery (pl.
 wag|ger|ies)
wag|gish
waggle (as v.,
 wag|gling)
wag|gly
Wag|ner
Wag|ner|ian
wagon
wag|oner
wag|on|ette
wag|on|ful (pl.
 wag|on|fuls)
wagon-lit (pl.
 wagons-lits)
wag|tail
Wa|habi
waif
wains|cot
wains|coted
wains|cot|ing
wain|wright
waist|band
waist|coat
waisted

waist|line
waiter
wait|ress
waive (forgo,
 waiv|ing)
waiver
wake (as v., woke,
 woken, wak|ing)
Wake|field
wake|ful
wake|fully
waken
Wal|ach
Wa|lach|ian
Wal|den|ses
Wal|den|sian
Wales
walk|able
walk|about
walker
walkie-talkie
walk-on a.
walk-over n.
walk|way
wal|laby (pl.
 wal|la|bies)
Wal|lace
wal|lah
wal|la|roo (pl.
 wal|la|roos)
Wal|la|sey
Wal|len|stein
wal|let
wall-eye
wall-eyed
wall|flower
Wal|loon
wal|lop (as v.,
 wal|loped,
 wal|lop|ing)
wal|low
wall|pa|per
wal|nut
Wal|pole
Wal|pur|gis
wal|rus
Wal|sall
waltz
waltzer

wam|pum
wan|der
wan|derer
wan|der|lust
wan|deroo (pl.
 wan|der|oos)
wan|doo (pl.
 wan|doos)
wane (as v.,
 wan|ing)
waney
wangle (as v.,
 wan|gling)
Wan|kel (engine)
wan|ness
want|ing
wan|ton
wan|ton|ness
wap|en|take
wap|iti
war (as v.,
 warred,
 war|ring)
warble (as v.,
 warb|ling)
warb|ler
war-cry
 (pl. war-cries)
war-dance
war|den
warder
ward|ress
ward|robe
ward|room
ware|house (as v.,
 ware|hous|ing)
ware|house|man
 (pl. ware|house|
 men)
war|fare
war-game
war|head
war-horse
war|ily
wari|ness
war|like
war|lock
war-lord
warmer

warm-hearted
warm|ish
war|mon|ger
warmth
warm-up n.
warn|ing
war-paint
war-path
war|rant
war|rant|able
war|rantee
war|ranter (gen.)
war|rantor (Law)
war|ranty (pl.
 war|rant|ies)
war|ren
war|rener
War|ring|ton
war|rior
War|saw
war|ship
wart-hog
war|time
warty (wart|ier,
 warti|est)
War|wick
War|wick|shire
wary (war|ier,
 wari|est)
wash|able
wash-basin
wash|board
wash-day
washer
wash|er|man (pl.
 wash|er|men)
wash|er|wo|man
 (pl. wash|er|
 wo|men)
wash|ery (pl.
 wash|er|ies)
wash-house
wash|ily
washi|ness
wash|ing
Wash|ing|ton
wash|land
wash-out n.
wash-room

wash-stand
washy (wash|ier,
  washi|est)
wasp|ish
was|sail
was|sailer
was'sail|ing
Was'ser|mann
  (test)
wast|able
wast'age
waste (as v.,
  wast'ing)
waste|ful
waste|fully
waste|land
waste-paper
waste-pipe
waster
wast'rel
watch-dog
watcher
watch|ful
watch|fully
watch|maker
watch|man (pl.
  watch|men)
watch-night
watch|word
wa'ter
water-bed
water-boatman
  (pl. water-
  boatmen)
water-borne
water-bottle
water-closet
water-colour
wa'ter|course
wa'ter|cress
wa'terer
wa'ter|fall
Wa'ter|ford
water-fowl
wa'ter|front
water-gate
water-hen
water-hole
water-ice
wa'teri|ness
water-line
wa'ter|logged
Wa'ter|loo (pl.
  Wa'ter|loos)
wa'ter|man (pl.
  wa'ter|men)

wa'ter|mark
water-mill
wa'ter|proof
water-rat
wa'ter|shed
wa'ter|side
water-ski
  (water-ski'd,
  water-skiing)
wa'ter|spout
water-table
wa'ter|tight
wa'ter|way
water-wings
wa'ter|works
wa'tery
Wat'son
wat|so'nia
watt (unit)
watt|age
wattle (wat|tling)
watt|meter
wave (as v.,
  wav'ing)
wave|band
wave-form
wave|guide
wave|length
wave|let
waver (falter)
wa'vily
wa'vi|ness
wavy (wa'vier,
  wa'vi|est)
wax|berry (pl.
  wax|ber'ries)
wax|bill
wax|cloth
waxen
wax|ily
waxi|ness
wax-paper
wax|wing
wax|work
waxy (wax|ier,
  waxi|est)
way-bill
way|bread
way|farer
way|far'ing
way|lay
  (way|laid,
  way'lay|ing)
way-out a.
way|side
way|ward

weaken
weak|ish
weak'li|ness
weak|ling
weakly
  (weak|lier,
  weak'li|est)
weak|ness
weald
wealden
wealth
wealthi|ness
wealthy
  (wealth|ier,
  wealthi|est)
wean|ling
weapon
weap|onry (pl.
  weap'on|ries)
wear (as v., wore,
  worn)
wear|able
wearer
weari|less
wear|ily
weari|ness
weari|some
weary (wear|ier,
  weari|est)
weasel (as v.,
  weaseled,
  weas'el|ing)
weas|elly
weather
weather-beaten
weather-board
weath'er|cock
weath'er|man (pl.
  weath'er|men)
weath'er|most
weath'er|proof
weave (as v.,
  wove, woven,
  weav|ing)
weaver
web (as v.,
  webbed
  web|bing)
webby
weber (unit)
Weber (name)
web-footed
wed (wed|ded,
  wed'ded or wed,
  wed|ding)
wed|ding

wedge (as v.,
  wedging)
Wedg'wood
  (propr.)
wed|lock
Wed'nes|day
weed-killer
weedy (weed|ier,
  weedi|est)
wee (weer, weest)
week|day
week|end
week|ender
weekly (as n., pl.
  week|lies)
weeny (ween|ier,
  weeni|est)
weep (as v., wept)
weepie n.
weepy a.
  (weep|ier,
  weepi|est)
weever (fish)
wee'vil
wee|vily
We|gener
Wehr|macht
weigh
weigh|able
weigh|bridge
weight
weight|ily
weighti|ness
weight|less
weight-lifter
weight-watcher
weighty
  (weight|ier,
  weighti|est)
Weill
Wei'mar|aner
weir (dam)
weird
weirdo (pl.
  weirdos)
Weis|mann
Weis'mann|ism
wel|come (as v.,
  wel'com|ing)
welder
wel|fare
well-being
well-head
well|lies
wel'ling|ton (boot)
Wel'ling|ton

well|nigh
well-off
well-wisher
welsh (default)
Welsh (of Wales)
welsher
Welsh|man (pl.
 Welsh|men)
Welsh|pool
Welsh|wo;man
 (pl.
 Welsh|wo;men)
*Welt|an;schau|
 ung*
wel;ter
wel;ter|weight
wench
Wendic
Wend|ish
Wendy
Wens;ley|dale
wen;tle|trap
were|wolf (pl.
 were|wolves)
Wes;ley
west|about
west|bound
West Brom|wich
west;er|ing
west;er|ly (as n., pl.
 west;er|lies)
west|ern
west|erner
west;ern|ize
 (west;ern|iz|ing)
west;ern|most
west|ing
West|meath
West|min;ster
West;pha;lia
west|ward
west|wards
wet (as v., wet;ted,
 wet|ting)
wether (ram)
wet|lands
wet-nurse (as v.,
 wet-nursing)
wet|table
wet;tish
Wex|ford
whack
whacker
whack|ing
whacko

whale (as v.,
 whal;ing)
whale|bone
whaler
wham (as v.,
 whammed,
 wham|ming)
whang
whangee
wharf (as n., pl.
 wharves)
wharf|age
wharf|inger
what|ever
what|so;ever
wheat
wheat|ear
wheaten
wheat|meal
Wheat|stone
 (bridge)
wheedle (as v.,
 wheed|ling)
wheed|ler
wheel|bar;row
wheel|chair
wheeler
wheel|ies
wheel|less
wheel|wright
wheeze (as v.,
 wheez|ing)
wheez;ily
wheezi|ness
wheezy
 (wheez;ier,
 wheezi;est)
whelk
whelp
whence
when|ever
when|so;ever
where|abouts
where|af;ter
whereas
whereby
where|fore
wherein
whereof
where|so;ever
where|upon
wher|ever
where|withal
wherry (pl.
 wher|ries)

wher;ry|man (pl.
 wher;ry|men)
whet (as v.,
 whet;ted,
 whet|ting)
whether
whet|stone
whey
which|ever
whiff
whiffle (as v.,
 whiff|ling)
Whig
Whig|gery
Whig|gish
Whig|gism
while (as v.,
 whil;ing)
whilst
whim
whim|brel
whim|per
whim|sical
whim;sic|al;ity
 (pl. whim;sic|al|
  it;ies)
whim;sic|ally
whimsy (pl.
 whim|sies)
whin|chat
whine (as v.,
 whin;ing)
whinge
 (whin;ging)
whinny (as v.,
 whin|nies,
 whin|nied,
 whin;ny|ing)
whin|sill
whin|stone
whiny (whi|nier,
 whi;ni|est)
whip (as v.,
 whipped,
 whip|ping)
whip|cord
whip|lash
whip|per
whipper-in (pl.
 whippers-in)
whipper-snapper
whip|pet
whip;pi|ness
whip;poor|will

whippy
 (whip|pier,
 whip;pi|est)
whip-saw
whip|ster
whip|stock
whirl
whir;li|gig
whirl|pool
whirl|wind
whir;ly|bird
whirr
whisk
whis|ker (hair)
whiskered
whis|kery
whis|key (Ir. &
 US)
whisky (Scotch, pl.
 whis|kies)
whis|per
whist
whistle (as v.,
 whist|ling)
whist|ler
white (as a.,
 whiter, whitest;
 as v., whit;ing)
white|bait
white|beam
white|cap
White|chapel
white-eye
White|hall
whiten
whitener
whiten|ing
white-out n.
white|thorn
white-throat
white|wash
white|wood
whither
whith;er|so;ever
whith;er|ward
whit|ing
whit;ish
whit|leather
whit|low
Whit;man
Whit|sun
Whit;sun|tide
whittle
 (whit;tling)
Whit|worth
 (thread)

whity
whiz (as v.,
  whizzed,
  whizz|ing)
whiz-bang
whiz-kid
whizzer
whoa
who|dunit
who|ever
whole
whole-hearted
whole|meal
whole|sale (as v.,
  whole|sal|ing)
whole|saler
whole|some
wholly
whom|ever
whom|so'ever
whoop
whoo|pee
whop (whopped,
  whop|ping)
whop|per
whore (prostitute)
whore-house
whorl
whorled
whor'tle|berry
  (pl. whor'tle|
        ber'ries)
whose
whose|so'ever
who|so'ever
Wich|ita
wicked
  (wick|eder,
  wick'ed|est)
wicker
wick'er|work
wicket
wick|iup
Wick|low
wide (wider,
  widest)
wide|awake
wide-eyed
widen
wide-ranging
wide|spread
widgeon
widget
wid|ish
widow
wid|ower

width
width|ways
width|wise
Wie'land
wield
Wiener (schnitzel)
wife (pl. wives)
wig (as v., wigged,
  wig|ging)
Wigan
wiggle (as v.,
  wig|gling)
wiggly (wig|gl'ier,
  wig'gli|est)
Wig|town
wig'wam
Wil'ber|force
wilco
wild|cat
wil'de|beest
wil'der|ness
wild|fire
wild|fowl
wild-goose chase
wild|ing
wild|life
wile (as v., wil'ing)
wil'ful
wil|fully
wi'lily
wi'li|ness
wil'let
Wil|liam
wil'lies
will|ing
will-o'-the-wisp
wil'low
willowy
will-power
willy-nilly
Wilton
Wilt|shire
wily (wi'lier,
  wi'li|est)
Wimble'don
wimple (as v.,
  wimp|ling)
Wimpy (propr.)
Wims|hurst
  (machine)
win (as v., won,
  win|ning)
wince (as v.,
  win'cing)
win'cey
win'cey|ette

winch
Win|ches'ter
wind (to coil etc.;
  wound)
wind|age
wind|bag
wind-break
wind|breaker
wind-cheater
winder
Win'der|mere
wind|fall
Wind|hoek
wind|ily
windi|ness
wind-jammer
wind|lass
win|dle|straw
wind|mill
win'dow
window-box
win'dowed
window-ledge
window-pane
window-sill
wind|pipe
wind|screen
wind|shield
wind-sock
Wind|sor
wind-swept
wind-tunnel
wind-up n.
wind|ward
windy (win|dier,
  win'di|est)
wine (as v., wined,
  win'ing)
wine|bottle
wine-cellar
wine|glass
wine-grower
wine-growing
wine|press
winery (pl.
  winer'ies)
wine-taster
winger
wing-nut
wing-span
wing-tip
winker
winkle (as v.,
  wink|ling)
win'ner
win|ning

Win'ni|peg
win'now
win|nower
wino (pl. winos)
win|some
win'ter
win'ter|green
win'ter|ize
  (win'ter|iz|ing)
winter-time
wint'ri|ness
wintry (wint|rier,
  wint'ri|est)
winy (f. wine)
wipe (as v.,
  wip|ing)
wipe-out n.
wiper
wire (as v.,
  wir'ing)
wire|less
wir'ily
wiri|ness
wir|ing
wiry (wir|ier,
  wiri|est)
Wis|con|sin
wis'dom
wise (as a., wiser,
  wisest; as v.,
  wis|ing)
wise|acre
wise|crack
wis'ent
wish|bone
wish|ful
wish|fully
wish-wash
wishy-washy
wispy (wis|pier,
  wis'pi|est)
wis|taria
wist|ful
wist|fully
witch|craft
witch-doctor
witch|ery (as pl.
  witch|er'ies)
witch|etty (pl.
  witch'et|ties)
witch-hunt
wit'ena|ge'mot
withal
with|draw
  (with|drew,
  with|drawn)

with|drawal
withe
wither
with|er|shins
with|hold
 (with|held)
within
with|out
with|stand
 (with|stood)
withy (*pl.*
 with|ies)
wit|less
wit|loof
wit|ness
wit|ter
Witt|gen|stein
wit|ti|cism
wit|tily
wit|ti|ness
wit|ting
witty (wit|tier,
 wit|ti|est)
wiz|ard
wiz|ardry (*pl.*
 wiz|ard|ries)
wiz|ened
wobble (as *v.*,
 wob|bling)
wob|bler
wob|bli|ness
wob|bly
 (wob|blier,
 wob|bli|est)
wodge
woe|be|gone
woe|ful
woe|fully
woggle
wolf (as *n.*, *pl.*
 wolves)
Wolf, H.
 (composer)
wolf-cub
Wolfe, J. (general)
wolf|hound
wolf|ish
wolf-pack
wolf|ram
wolf|ram|ite
wolfs|bane
wolf|skin
wolf-whistle
 (wolf-whistling)
Wol|las|ton
Wol|sey

Wol|ver|hamp|ton
wol|ver|ine
wo|man (*pl.*
 wo|men)
wo|man|hood
wo|man|ish
wo|man|ize
 (wo|man|iz|ing)
wo|man|izer
wo|man|kind
wo|man|li|ness
womb
wom|bat
wo|men|folk
won|der
won|der|ful
won|der|fully
won|der|land
won|der|ment
won|drous
wonky (won|kier,
 won|ki|est)
wont (what is
 customary)
won't (= *will not*)
wood|bind
wood|bine
wood|chuck
wood|cock
wood|craft
wood|cut
wood|cut|ter
wooden
wood|en|ness
woodi|ness
wood|land
wood-louse (*pl.*
 wood-lice)
wood|man (*pl.*
 wood|men)
wood|pecker
wood|pie
wood|pile
wood|ruff
wood|rush
wood-shed
woods|man (*pl.*
 woods|men)
wood|wind
wood|work
wood|worm
woody (wood|ier,
 woodi|est)
wooer
woofer
Woolf, V.

wool|len
wool|li|ness
woolly (as *n.*, *pl.*
 wool|lies; as *a.*,
 wool|lier,
 wool|li|est)
Wool|sack (House
 of Lords)
wool-skin
woo|mera
wooz|ily
woozi|ness
woozy (woo|zier,
 woo|zi|est)
wop (as *v.*,
 wopped,
 wop|ping)
Worces|ter
word|age
word-blind
word-deaf
word|ily
wordi|ness
word-perfect
word|smith
Words|worth
wordy (word|ier,
 wordi|est)
work|ab|il|ity
work|able
work|ably
work|aday
work|aholic
work-basket
work-bench
work-camp
work|day
worker
work-force
work-horse
work|house
work-in *n.*
work-load
work|man (*pl.*
 work|men)
work|man|like
work|mate
work-out *n.*
work|piece
work-room
work|sheet
work|shop
work-shy
work-table
world
world|li|ness

world|ling
worldly
 (world|lier,
 world|li|est)
worldly-wise
world-view
world-weary
world-wide
worm-cast
worm|eaten
wormer
worm-hole
worm|wood
wormy
 (wor|mier,
 wor|mi|est)
wor|rier
wor|ri|ment
wor|ri|some
worry (as *v.*,
 wor|ries,
 wor|ried,
 wor|ry|ing; as *n.*,
 pl. wor|ries)
worse
worsen
wor|ship (as *v.*,
 wor|shipped,
 wor|ship|ping)
wor|ship|ful
wor|ship|fully
wor|ship|per
worst
wors|ted
worth
wor|thily
wor|thi|ness
worth|less
worth|while
worthy (as *a.*,
 wor|thier,
 wor|thi|est; as *n.*,
 pl. wor|thies)
wotcher
would
would-be
wouldn't
Woulfe (bottle)
wound|wort
wrack
wraith
Wran|gell
wrangle (as *v.*,
 wran|gling)
wran|gler

wrap (as *v.*,
 wrapped,
 wrap|ping)
wrap|around
 a. & *n.*
wrap|page
wrap|per
wrasse (fish)
wrath
wrath|ful
wrath|fully
wreak
wreath
wreathe
 (wreath|ing)
wreck
wreck|age
wrecker
wren
Wren (service-
    woman)

wrench
wrest
wrestle (as *v.*,
 wrest|ling)
wrest|ler
wretch (wretched
 person) △ retch
wretched
wriggle (as *v.*,
 wrig|gling)
wrig|gly
 (wrig|glier,
 wrig|gli|est)
wring (wrung)
wrinkle (as *v.*,
 wrink|ling)
wrinkly
 (wrink|lier,
 wrink|li|est)
wrist
wrist|band

wrist|let
wrist-watch
writ
writ|able
write (wrote,
 writ|ten,
 writ|ing)
write-off *n.*
writer
write-up *n.*
writhe (as *v.*,
 writh|ing)
wrong|doer
wrong|do|ing
wrong-footed
wrong|ful
wrong|fully
wroth
wry (wryer,
 wry|est)

wry|bill
wry|mouth
wry|neck
Wu|han
wun|der|kind
Würt|tem|berg
wy|an|dotte
wych-elm
Wych|er|ley
wych-hazel
Wyc|lif
 (theologian)
Wyc|liffe (College,
 Hall)
Wye
Wyke|ham|ist
Wy|om|ing
wy|vern

X

xanth|ate
xanthic
Xan|thippe
xanth|oma (*pl.*
 xanth|omas *or*
 xanth|omata)
xan¦tho|phyll
xe¦bec
Xen|akis
xe¦no|gamy
xeno|lith

xenon
xeno|phobe
xe¦no|pho¦bia
xe¦no|pho¦bic
Xen|ophon
xer|an¦themum
xero|graph
xero|graphic
xero|graphy
xero|phile
xero|phil¦ous

xero|phyte
xerox *v.*
Xerox *n.* (*propr.*)
Xerxes
Xhosa
xi (Gr. letter)
xiph|oid
Xmas
xo¦anon (*pl.*
 xo¦ana)
X-ray

xy¦lem
xy¦lene
xy¦lo|carp
xy¦lo|carp¦ous
xy¦lo|graph
xy¦lo|graphy
xy¦lon|ite
xy¦lo|phag¦ous
xy¦lo|phone
xy¦lo¦phon|ist
xyst¦us (*pl.* xysti)

Y

yacht
yacht-club
yachts|man (*pl.*
 yachts|men)
yaffle
ya¦hoo (*pl.*
 ya¦hoos)
Yah¦veh
Yah|vist
yak (ox)
Yale (lock; *propr.*)
yam¦mer
Yang|tze
Yan¦kee
Ya|oundé
yap (as *v.*,
 yapped,
 yap|ping)
yapp
 (bookbinding)
yap¦per
yard|age
yard-arm
yard|stick
Yaren
Yar|mouth
yar|mulka
yar¦row
yash|mak
yata|ghan
year-book
year|ling
year-long
yearn
yeast
yeasti|ness

yeasty (yeast|ier,
 yeasti|est)
Yeats
yel¦low
yellow-belly (*pl.*
 yellow-bellies)
yellow-bill
yel¦low|ham|mer
yel¦low|ish
yel|lowy
yelper
Yemen
yen (Jap. mon.
 unit; *pl.* same)
yen (longing; as *v.*,
 yenned,
 yen|ning)
Ye¦ni|sei
yeo|man (*pl.*
 yeo|men)
yeo|manry (*pl.*
 yeo¦man|ries)
Yeo¦vil
yerba maté
yes (as *n.*, *pl.*
 yeses)
yes-man (*pl.*
 yes-men)
yes¦ter|day
yester-eve
yes¦ter|morn
yes¦ter|night
yester-year
yeti
Yev¦tu|shenko
yew-tree
Ygg|drasil

Yid|dish
Yid|disher
yield
yin (*Chin. Philos.*)
yip|pee
ylang-ylang
yobbo (*pl.*
 yob¦bos)
yo¦del (as *v.*,
 yo|delled,
 yo¦del|ling)
yo¦del|ler
yoga
yogh
yog|hurt
yogi
yo¦gic
yoicks
yoke (harness; as
 v., yok¦ing)
yokel
Yo¦ko|hama
yolk (of egg)
yolked
yolk-sac
yolky
Yom Kippur
yon¦der
yoni
yoo-hoo
 (*pl.* yoo-hoos)
yorker
York|ist
York|shire
York¦shire|man
 (*pl.* York¦shire|
 men)

York¦shire|
 wo¦man
 (*pl.* York¦shire|
 wo¦men)
Yor¦uba
young
young|ish
young|ster
your
you're (= *you are*)
yours
your|self (*pl.*
 your|selves)
youth
youth|ful
youth|fully
Yo-Yo (*propr.*; *pl.*
 Yo-Yos)
Ypres
yt¦ter|bium
yt|trium
yuan (*pl.* same)
Yu|ca|tán
yucca
Yu¦go|slav
Yu¦go|sla¦via
Yu¦go|sla¦vian
Yu¦kon
yule
yule-log
yule-tide
yummy
 (yum|mier,
 yum¦mi|est)
yum-yum

Z

za¦ba¦gli¦one
zaf¦fre
Zaïre
Zam¦bezi
Zam¦bia
zany (as *n.*, *pl.*
  za¦nies; as *a.*,
  za¦nier, za¦ni¦est)
Zanzi¦bar
zap (zapped,
  zap¦ping)
za¦pa¦te¦ado (*pl.*
  za¦pa¦te¦ados)
Za¦ra¦thus¦tra
za¦riba
Zau¦ber¦flöte
zealot (*gen.*)
Zealot (*hist.*)
zeal¦otry
zeal¦ous
zebra
zeb¦rine
zebu (ox)
zedo¦ary
Zee¦land
Zee¦man (effect)
zein
Zeit¦geist
ze¦min¦dar
ze¦nana
Zend
Zend-Avesta
Zener (*Cards*)
zen¦ith
zen¦ithal
ze¦ol¦ite
zephyr

Zep¦pelin
zero (as *n.*, *pl.*
  zeros)
zer¦oth
zest¦ful
zesty (zes¦ti¦er,
  zes¦ti¦est)
zeta (Gr. letter)
ze¦tetic
zeugma
zeug¦matic
Zeus
zibet
zig¦gurat
zig¦zag (as *v.*,
  zig¦zagged,
  zig¦zag¦ging)
zil¦lah
Zim¦babwe
zinc (as *v.*, zinced,
  zinc¦ing)
zin¦cic
zinco (as *n.*, *pl.*
  zin¦cos)
zin¦co¦graph
zin¦co¦graphy
zin¦co¦type
zincy
Zin¦garo (*pl.*
  Zin¦gari)
zingy (zing¦ier,
  zingi¦est)
zin¦nia
Zion
Zi¦on¦ism
Zi¦on¦ist

zip (as *v.*, zipped,
  zip¦ping)
zip-bag
Zip code (*US*)
zip¦per
zippy (zip¦pier,
  zip¦pi¦est)
zir¦con
zir¦co¦nium
zither
zith¦er¦ist
zloty (*pl.* zlotys *or*
  same)
zo¦diac
zo¦di¦acal
zo¦etrope
zoic
Zola
Zöllner's lines
zombie
zonal
zon¦ary
zon¦ate
zonda
zone (as *v.*,
  zon¦ing)
zo¦ogeo¦graphy
zo¦ography
zo¦oid
zo¦oidal
zo¦olatry
zo¦olo¦gical
zo¦olo¦gist
zo¦ology
zo¦omancy
zo¦omorphic
zo¦omorph¦ism

zo¦ophyte
zo¦ophytic
zo¦oplank¦ton
zo¦ospore
zo¦otomy
zori (Jap. sandal)
zoril (animal)
Zo¦ro¦as¦trian
zou¦ave
zuc¦chetto (*pl.*
  zuc¦chet¦tos)
zuc¦chini (*pl.* same
  or zuc¦chi¦nis)
zug¦zwang
Zulu
Zur¦ich
zwie¦back
Zwingli
Zwing¦lian
zwit¦ter¦ion
zy¦gal
zygo-dactyl
zy¦go¦dac¦tyl¦ous
zy¦goma (*pl.*
  zy¦go¦mata)
zy¦go¦matic
zy¦go¦morphic
zy¦go¦morph¦ous
zy¦gosis (*pl.*
  zy¦goses)
zy¦go¦spore
zy¦gote
zy¦mase
zy¦mosis (*pl.*
  zy¦moses)
zy¦motic
zy¦murgy

OXFORD

MORE OXFORD PAPERBACKS

Details of a selection of other Oxford Paperbacks follow. A complete list of Oxford Paperbacks, including The World's Classics, Twentieth-Century Classics, OPUS, Past Masters, Oxford Authors, Oxford Shakespeare, and Oxford Paperback Reference, is available in the UK from the General Publicity Department, Oxford University Press (RS), Walton Street, Oxford, OX2 6DP.

In the USA, complete lists are available from the Paperbacks Marketing Manager, Oxford University Press, 200 Madison Avenue, New York, NY 10016.

Oxford Paperbacks are available from all good bookshops. In case of difficulty, customers in the UK can order direct from Oxford University Press Bookshop, 116 High Street, Oxford, Freepost, OX1 4BR, enclosing full payment. Please add 10 per cent of the published price for postage and packing.

OPUS

*General Editors: Christopher Butler,
Robert Evans, Alan Ryan*

OPUS is a series of accessible introductions to a wide range of studies in the sciences and humanities.

METROPOLIS

Emrys Jones

Past civilizations have always expressed themselves in great cities, immense in size, wealth, and in their contribution to human progress. We are still enthralled by ancient cities like Babylon, Rome, and Constantinople. Today, giant cities abound, but some are pre-eminent. As always, they represent the greatest achievements of different cultures. But increasingly, they have also been drawn into a world economic system as communications have improved.

Metropolis explores the idea of a class of supercities in the past and in the present, and in the western and developing worlds. It analyses the characteristics they share as well as those that make them unique; the effect of technology on their form and function; and the problems that come with size—congestion, poverty and inequality, squalor—that are sobering contrasts to the inherent glamour and attraction of great cities throughout time.

Also available in OPUS:

MEDICINE IN OXFORD PAPERBACKS

Oxford Paperbacks offers an increasing list of medical studies and reference books of interest to the specialist and general reader alike, including The Facts series, authoritative and practical guides to a wide range of common diseases and conditions.

CONCISE MEDICAL DICTIONARY
Third Edition

Written without the use of unnecessary technical jargon, this illustrated medical dictionary will be welcomed as a home reference, as well as an indispensible aid for all those working in the medical profession.

Nearly 10,000 important terms and concepts are explained, including all the major medical and surgical specialities, such as gynaecology and obstetrics, paediatrics, dermatology, neurology, cardiology, and tropical medicine. This third edition contains much new material on pre-natal diagnosis, infertility treatment, nuclear medicine, community health, and immunology. Terms relating to advances in molecular biology and genetic engineering have been added, and recently developed drugs in clinical use are included. A feature of the dictionary is its unusually full coverage of the fields of community health, psychology, and psychiatry.

Each entry contains a straightforward definition, followed by a more detailed description, while an extensive crossreference system provides the reader with a comprehensive view of a particular subject.

Also in Oxford Paperbacks:

Drugs and Medicine   Roderick Cawson and Roy Spector
Travellers' Health: How to Stay Healthy Abroad 2/e
Richard Dawood
I'm a Health Freak Too!
Aidan Macfarlane and Ann McPherson
Problem Drinking   Nick Heather and Ian Robertson

OXFORD REFERENCE

Oxford is famous for its superb range of dictionaries and reference books. The Oxford Reference series offers the most up-to-date and comprehensive paperbacks at the most competitive prices, across a broad spectrum of subjects.

THE CONCISE OXFORD COMPANION TO ENGLISH LITERATURE

Edited by Margaret Drabble and Jenny Stringer

Based on the immensely popular fifth edition of the *Oxford Companion to English Literature* this is an indispensable, compact guide to the central matter of English literature.

There are more than 5,000 entries on the lives and works of authors, poets, playwrights, essayists, philosophers, and historians; plot summaries of novels and plays; literary movements; fictional characters; legends; theatres; periodicals; and much more.

The book's sharpened focus on the English literature of the British Isles makes it especially convenient to use, but there is still generous coverage of the literature of other countries and of other disciplines which have influenced or been influenced by English literature.

From reviews of *The Oxford Companion to English Literature Fifth Edition*:

'a book which one turns to with constant pleasure . . . a book with much style and little prejudice' Iain Gilchrist, *TLS*

'it is quite difficult to imagine, in this genre, a more useful publication' Frank Kermode, *London Review of Books*

'incarnates a living sense of tradition . . . sensitive not to fashion merely but to the spirit of the age' Christopher Ricks, *Sunday Times*

Also available in Oxford Reference:

The Concise Oxford Dictionary of Art and Artists
edited by Ian Chilvers
A Concise Oxford Dictionary of Mathematics
Christopher Clapham
The Oxford Spelling Dictionary   compiled by R. E. Allen
A Concise Dictionary of Law   edited by Elizabeth A. Martin